About the Authors

KEVIN FINUCANE, solicitor, is a director of Coyle Hamilton Ltd. and is legal advisor to its Employee Benefits and Investment Division. He is chairman of the Association of Pension Lawyers in Ireland and has lectured widely on pensions law.

BRIAN BUGGY, solicitor, is an associate in the Commercial Department of Matheson Ormsby Prentice. He has specialised for many years in pensions law and is a member of the Legislation and Parliamentary Committee of the Association of Pension Lawyers in Ireland. He has lectured extensively both to the Law Society and the APLI.

Irish Pensions Law and Practice

Kevin Finucane
Brian Buggy

Oak Tree Press
Dublin

Oak Tree Press
Merrion Building
Lower Merrion Street
Dublin 2, Ireland

A catalogue record of this book is
available from the British Library.

ISBN 1-86076-030-9 paperback
ISBN 1-86076-036-8 hardback

Printed in Ireland by Colour Books Ltd.

Contents

FOREWORD

As the authors of this book point out, there has been a Pension Law in Ireland since the days of the Brehon Law. In more modern times, the prospect of a pension and, for persons in the private sector, membership of an occupational pension scheme, have become among the most attractive features of employment. However, until the passing of the Pensions Act, 1990, the legislature in this country had strenuously avoided any mention of pension rights other than in relation to public sector schemes. Private sector employers operated pension schemes over which almost the only legal controls were the limitations imposed by the Finance Acts in order to obtain tax relief, and the Trustee Acts dating from the last century. As a result, very large sums of money were frequently under the control of employers, although theoretically held in trust for their employees to secure their pensions. Needless to say, this led to abuses, particularly where the employer ran into serious financial problems.

Those abuses, several of which were highly publicised, and the changing and more transient nature of employment, were the principal factors leading to the setting up of the National Pensions Board in 1986 by the then Minister for Social Welfare. The National Pensions Board made five reports in all, the first of which contained recommendations which were to a very large part included in the Pensions Act, 1990.

The Act, and the various amendments to it, and regulations made under it, have provided a modern and sophisticated scheme of checks and balances to regulate occupational pension schemes. Indeed, as a result, we in Ireland have one of the most protected and regulated pension industries in the world. It has also, by its very nature, created a labyrinth of detailed procedures and rights which has to be negotiated by all connected with pensions, be they employers, employees, trustees, accountants, lawyers or actuaries. At the same time, public sector schemes, and in particular those dealing with semi-State or former semi-State companies, are suffering from serious complications caused by increased privatisation of such bodies.

Into all this apparent chaos now comes order with the publication of this book by joint authors who have practical experience of advising on and operating pension schemes. It provides a fund — if I may be excused the pun — of information covering every aspect of Pensions Law, very clearly set out with useful introductions to each chapter setting out the history of each subject. It is, therefore, much more than a quick reference book — indeed, the authors have taken upon themselves not only the task of setting out the law as it is, but also the much more difficult task of explaining why the various provisions exist. Apart from making this difficult area of the law easier to understand, this also makes the book very readable. It is only when one looks at the chapter headings that one realises just how many aspects of life, both private and commercial, are affected by pension problems from marital breakdowns to the merging and reconstruction of companies.

I expect this book to be on the desk, rather than on the bookshelves, of everyone concerned with the administration of or advising on pension funds, as it will be a daily practical guide for them. I can only commend the authors on filling the information gap which opened with the passing of the 1990 Act.

The Hon. Mr Justice Brian McCracken

PREFACE

The legal framework regulating pensions provision in Ireland is one of the most advanced in Europe. With the implementation of the Pensions Act, 1990 and the many regulations issued pursuant to that Act it has also become an extremely complex area of Irish law. The law continues to develop apace. The Family Law Act, 1995 came into force on 1 August 1996. This Act is dealt with in Chapter 15. Draft regulations to accompany the Act are awaited. The Pensions (Amendment) Act, 1996 came into force on 2 July 1996. This is principally a technical piece of legislation which effects numerous amendments to the original Pensions Act, 1990. Appropriate reference to the 1996 Act is made throughout the work. The Family Law (Divorce) Bill, 1996 was published on 17 June 1996 and was passed by the Dáil on 25 September 1996. It is currently before the Seanad. The Employment Equality Bill, 1996 was published on 1 July 1996. The new Equality Bill excludes pension rights and a Pensions (Equality) Bill is proposed to fill the gap. At the time of writing this bill has not yet been drafted.

Writing the first legal text book in any particular area presents its own difficulties. We have attempted to deal with all of those matters which would be of concern to persons involved with or interested in the law and practice relating to pensions. In contrast with the highly developed statutory regime, there is little Irish case law relating to pension schemes and, of those authorities that exist, the greater number are unreported judgements. Extensive reference is therefore made to Superior Court decisions of England and Commonwealth jurisdictions including Australia and New Zealand. As these are common law jurisdictions they have well developed principles of equity and trusts and the decisions of those courts may be considered to be of persuasive authority. In the absence of appropriate Irish authorities they will at least assist in consideration of the many problems which can arise in relation to pension schemes.

Whilst we are of course solely responsible for the contents of this book we would like to express our thanks to all those who assisted in the preparation of this work. In particular, we wish to thank Clive Slattery of the Retirement Benefits District of the Revenue Commissioners for his observations on Chapters 6 & 7 and Conor McGinn of the Department of Finance and Damian Smyth of the Department of the Environment in relation to Chapter 8. We are grateful to the Controller, Stationery Office, Dublin for permission to reproduce the Pensions Act, 1990 in consolidated form.

We also acknowledge the assistance of Roderick Buckley of A&L Goodbody, Judge John Cooke of the European Court of First Instance, Raymonde Kelly and Paul Kenny of Irish Pensions Trust Limited and Ultan Stephenson of McCann Fitzgerald all of whom read drafts of parts of or the entire of the book at various stages and who provided comments and suggestions. We are also grateful to Mr. Justice Brian McCracken for kindly contributing the foreword.

Each of us also acknowledge the assistance provided by our colleagues. In the Employee Benefits Division of Coyle Hamilton: Kieran Kelly, Managing Director, Malcolm Henson, Deputy Managing Director, Joe Byrne, Group Actuary/Director, Eric Ware, Pensions Manager, Ken McKenna, Director and Brian Mulcair, Actuarial Department. In Matheson Ormsby Prentice: Stuart Margetson, litigation partner, William Prentice, banking & commercial partner, Rod Ensor, insolvency partner, Pauline O'Donovan, commercial partner, Ciaran Desmond, tax associate, Denis Cagney, EU law department, Siobhan Heaney, information officer, George Brady and Karen Gibbons, commercial department.

Thanks also to Bernie O'Connell and Helen O'Connell who typed earlier drafts of the manuscript and to Pat Earley who was indispensable in finalising large parts of the text.

Brian Buggy especially thanks Gerardine for her endless patience and encouragement during this project.

Kevin Finucane particularly thanks Cathy for her support and invaluable comments.

Whilst we have taken every care to ensure that we have stated Irish law as it relates to pensions as at 1 October 1996, it can happen in a work of this size that inaccuracies may occur. We will be grateful for any observations in this regard from readers.

Kevin Finucane & Brian Buggy
October 1996

TABLE OF CASES

Note: References are to paragraph number

TABLE OF STATUTES

Note: References are to paragraph number

1. Constitutions of the Irish Free State and of Ireland

2. Acts

3. Statutory Instruments

4. Rules of Court

5. European Union Legislation

6. European and International Conventions

7. United Kingdom Legislation

Abbreviations

AVC	Additional Voluntary Contribution
CPI	Consumer Price Index
Disclosure Regulations	Occupational Pension Schemes (Disclosure of Information) Regulations, 1991
Finance Act	Finance Act, 1972
FLA	Family Law Act, 1995
Funding Standard Regulations	Occupational Pension Schemes (Funding Standard) Regulations, 1993
IAPF	Irish Association of Pension Funds
life office	life assurance company
Pensions Act	Pensions Act, 1990
PLR	Pensions Law Reports
practice notes	practice notes of the Revenue Commissioners
Preservation Regulations	Occupational Pension Schemes (Preservation of Benefits) Regulations, 1992
PRSI	Pay Related Social Insurance
RAC	Retirement Annuity Contract
Revenue	Revenue Commissioners
Special Calculations Regulations	Occupational Pension Schemes (Preservation of Benefits) (Special Calculations) Regulations, 1993

1

Provision of Pensions

INTRODUCTION

1.1 A pension is an income payable on retirement or on death and is usually payable for life. A pension scheme is an arrangement to facilitate the payment of a pension. Pension schemes may also provide lump sum benefits on retirement and on death. These benefits are not strictly pensions as there is no income involved. For convenience, however, the term "pension scheme" is used in this work to include arrangements that provide lump sum benefits.

1.2 There are three categories of pension scheme which are considered in this work. The first is an occupational pension scheme. This is a pension scheme established by an employer for employees and which is either approved by the Revenue Commissioners under Chapter II of Part I of the Finance Act, 1972,[1] or is a scheme established by statute or otherwise financed by the State. The latter will be referred to in this work as public sector schemes. Private sector occupational pension schemes and funded public sector schemes are established under trust so that the assets of each scheme are legally separate from those of the employer. "Occupational pension scheme" is defined in the principal legislation governing pension schemes in Ireland, the Pensions Act, 1990. The Pensions Act only applies to occupational pension schemes, as so defined,[2] and its definition is examined below.[3] There is no legal requirement in Ireland for an employer to establish a pension scheme for its employees.

1.3 The second category of pension scheme is a pension policy taken out by a self-employed person or a person who is not included in an

---

1 As subsequently amended, in particular by the Finance Act, 1974.

2 Except with regard to equal treatment under Part VII of the Act which has a somewhat wider application.

3 See para. 1.37.

employer sponsored pension scheme. Such schemes are set up under a policy of assurance effected with a life office and approved by the Revenue Commissioners.[4] They are referred to as self-employed arrangements (or often, "retirement annuity contracts" or "RACs") and are governed by provisions of the Income Tax Act, 1967, under which certain tax reliefs are available to the individual. Self-employed and occupational pension arrangements are, however, mutually exclusive. A person cannot, under tax law, be included in both at the same time in relation to the same employment nor is it permissible to transfer benefits from one régime to the other. Self-employed arrangements are not subject to the Pensions Act.[5]

1.4 The third category is an arrangement by an employer for one or more employees which is not approved by the Revenue Commissioners under the Finance Act. These are referred to as unapproved arrangements and are uncommon in Ireland. Unapproved arrangements are not governed by the requirements of the Pensions Act, unlike occupational pension schemes.

1.5 A broad examination of pensions would not be complete without a consideration of social welfare pensions. Ireland has a two-tiered approach to the provision of pensions or retirement benefits. First, there is a State social welfare retirement pension which promises a basic level of pension and, secondly, there are the occupational pension schemes and self-employed arrangements which supplement the State pension. The State pension is a flat-rate pension, which means that the same amount is paid to a high earner as to someone on a low income. Ireland operates a social insurance system, one of the objectives of which is to finance the State social welfare pension (Pay Related Social Insurance, or PRSI) and almost all employed persons are covered by the system. There is also a means-tested retirement pension for those who have paid insufficient or no insurance contributions. Pensions can also be paid to widowed spouses and orphans in certain circumstances.

1.6 As the State pension is fixed at a modest level, it is not surprising that the private sector and indeed the State itself have seen the

---

4 There are also approved group self-employed arrangements established under trust — see para. 6.70.

5 Except with regard to equal treatment under Part VII. See Chapter 16.

need to supplement the State pension by establishing occupational pension schemes. Individuals have also met this need by effecting self-employed arrangements. Before the State social welfare pension system was implemented, pension schemes (or superannuation schemes as they were then called) were established, from the eighteenth century onwards, for certain persons employed in the public service. It is from these earlier superannuation schemes that the modern public sector and private sector occupational pension schemes evolved.

1.7 Those taking out a self-employed arrangement can, subject to Revenue requirements, decide how much to contribute and can vary contributions in the future in accordance with their requirements. In contrast, promising pensions to employees represents a substantial financial commitment by the sponsoring employer, whether it be the State or a private firm. For example, if a man retires today at age 65 and is to be granted a pension for life of £15,000, it would take approximately £135,000 to secure with a life assurance company (life office) the payment of that pension for life.[6] An employee's pension is now regarded as a form of deferred remuneration, which builds up in value with each year of service completed. If an employer waits until retirement and then pays the pension out of resources available at that point, it may experience cash-flow problems — indeed, the employer may simply be unable to meet the cost. This is one of the reasons why employers usually set aside moneys in advance to meet the future cost of pensions as opposed to waiting until the pension has to be paid. This method of financing is referred to as "advance funding", which should be distinguished from a "pay-as-you-go" approach. The latter involves no advance funding and is the financing method adopted by the State. Most public sector schemes are financed on a pay-as-you-go basis.

1.8 For the purposes of funding in advance, the employer can set aside money in its accounts to meet future costs. This is known as a book reserve and is the way in which pensions are funded in some EU countries.[7] As the fund is still in the company's control, there must often be concern as to the security of the fund from the employee's

---

6 This assumes that it will take £9 of cash to secure £1 of pension. This is a rough rate of exchange.

7 Notably Germany and Austria.

perspective, particularly were the employer to go into liquidation. There are few if any schemes which operate a book reserve in Ireland. There would be a stronger sense of security if the fund were to be held by a third party for the benefit of the persons on whose behalf the fund has been established. The most effective way of setting up an arrangement of this kind, where a third party holds the assets subject to conditions and for certain specific purposes, is by establishing a trust. It is for this reason that the Revenue Commissioners give certain tax reliefs to schemes established under trust and this is also why private occupational pension schemes are almost without exception regulated by trust law.

1.9 There are approximately £16.3 billion in assets currently under the management of Irish occupational pension schemes. The current pensions environment is heavily regulated. Members of pension schemes can enforce their entitlement to pension benefits under statute[8] and the general law.[9] A pensions industry has developed around the management and administration of pension schemes. There are lawyers, actuaries, employee benefits consultants, insurance brokers, auditors, investment managers and life offices that specialise in pensions matters. All this is relatively recent. Pension provision was somewhat simpler prior to this century.

HISTORY OF PENSIONS

1.10 The earliest regulation of pensions can be found in the brehon laws. The brehon laws imposed a legal responsibility on the kin group to take care of its members who were aged, blind, deaf, sick or insane. The kin group comprised the descendants through the male line of the same great-grandfather. Pension provision was therefore a matter of family obligation.[10] The brehon law gradually fell into disuse and, by the 1600s, was largely displaced by English feudal law. Pensions nonetheless developed on an ex-gratia basis. Employers made provision on retirement for certain employees as a reward for service.

---

8 The Pensions Act, 1990.

9 The law of trusts.

10 See Kelly F. (1988): *A Guide to Early Irish Law*, Dublin: Dublin Institute for Advanced Studies, pp. 93 & 271. The requirement of maintenance is contained in a fragmentary legal text "Do brethaib gaire" ("on judgments of maintenance").

1.11 The first pension schemes in the modern sense were established in the public sector. The first such scheme was a fund established for customs and excise officers by treasury warrant in 1712. This was extended to include other civil servants during the course of the eighteenth century. The Superannuation Act, 1834 extended the scheme further and made it non-contributory. The significance of this legislation is that the benefits provided under it formed the basis of the limits on retirement and death benefits which the Revenue Commissioners subsequently imposed in this century as a condition of Revenue approval. Pensions were calculated on the basis of service completed at retirement and salary at or near retirement. Prior to the 1834 Act, pension benefits were granted up to a maximum of 100 per cent of the employee's salary after 50 years of service, with proportionately smaller benefits for shorter service. The 1834 Act introduced a cap on pension benefits of 2/3rds of salary after 45 years of service. In no case could benefits exceed this limit.[11] The 1834 Act stipulated that, save in exceptional circumstances, retirement age was no later than 65. Today, 65 is still the normal retirement age for most pension schemes. The schedule to the Act listed the Registrar of Deeds and the Board of Charitable Donations and Bequests amongst the Irish officers of the Crown to be included for superannuation. The Act also gave a power to add more persons by warrant.[12]

1.12 The first taxation legislation which provided for Revenue approval was the Income Tax Act, 1918, which was quickly followed by the Finance Act, 1921. The tax régime that followed nurtured the growth of private occupational pension schemes, which, because of Revenue requirements, were largely established under trust. Surprisingly, aside from tax Acts and legislation affecting trustees, there was no statutory regulation of pension schemes until the introduction of the Pensions Act, 1990. Section 32 of the Income Tax Act, 1918 gave income tax relief in respect of the payment of premiums for life assurance on the taxpayer or his wife. The relief could not exceed 7 per cent of the capital sum insured nor could it exceed one-sixth of his total chargeable income. The Finance Act, 1921[13] exempted from income tax any

---

11 s.10. A form of three-year averaging of final salary was also included (s.12). The 2/3rds limit is also one of the main benefit limits imposed by the Revenue Commissioners as a condition of their approval of pension schemes.

12 s.14.

13 Coincidentally, also s.32.

approved superannuation fund and provided that employer and employee contributions to the fund were deductible for income tax purposes.[14] To be approved by the Revenue, the fund had to be established under irrevocable trusts with respect to a trade or undertaking in the United Kingdom[15] by persons residing there.[16] The employer was required to contribute to the fund. Subsequent legislation modified the tax régime and consolidating legislation was incorporated in the Income Tax Act, 1967, which is still the legislation affecting self-employed arrangements. Occupational pension schemes are now approvable under the Finance Act, 1972.

STATE SOCIAL WELFARE PENSIONS

1.13 The first statutory system of welfare was the Poor Law system. This applied in England from 1597 but was only introduced in Ireland by the Poor Law Relief (Ireland) Act, 1838. The Poor Law assistance was particularly mean and was consequently unpopular.[17] The social welfare system as we know it today, and in particular that part of it which provides pensions, gradually developed from 1838 primarily as a result of legislation in the early part of this century.

1.14 The first means-tested social welfare retirement pension was provided in 1908. This was a non-contributory old age pension payable from age 70. The concept of a social insurance scheme was introduced by the National Insurance Act, 1911, which established compulsory insurance in the UK and Ireland for certain categories of employee. Contributions were paid by employees and employers, and benefits were provided by the State. These included unemployment, maternity and sickness benefits, but not retirement pensions.[18] There followed a widow's and orphan's insurance-based pension scheme in 1935, as well

---

14 s.32(1).

15 This legislation was passed the year before the establishment of Saorstát Éireann.

16 s.32(3) sets out the main requirements.

17 Poor Law later became "home assistance". Home assistance was finally replaced by supplementary welfare allowance under the Social Welfare (Supplementary Welfare Allowance) Act, 1975.

18 Not all benefits provided in Great Britain were applied to Ireland. Medical benefit was not extended. See Cousins, M. (1995): *The Irish Social Welfare System Law and Social Policy*, Dublin: Round Hall Press: p. 14.

as a means-tested one. A contributory old age pension was introduced in 1961,[19] payable from age 70, and an insurance-based retirement pension was introduced in 1970, payable from age 65.[20] The retirement age for the contributory old age pension was reduced to age 66 in 1977.

1.15 As mentioned in the introduction, the Irish social welfare system provides a flat-rate social welfare pension. The main legislation governing social welfare benefits in Ireland is now contained in the Social Welfare (Consolidation) Act, 1993.[21] As its name indicates, the Act consolidates previous legislation on social welfare. Social welfare pensions are provided on the basis of either social insurance or social assistance. Social insurance involves the principle that individuals should insure themselves during their working careers to provide for their retirement (as well as other benefits such as disablement and unemployment benefits). The term "insurance" is used in a wide sense to connote the pooling of risk in order to meet the liability to provide retirement benefits. Insurance contributions in the form of Pay Related Social Insurance (PRSI) are paid to the State, and the State undertakes to pay a retirement pension. Social assistance, on the other hand, involves the payment of an allowance to an individual where there have been no, or insufficient, insurance contributions. Social assistance is granted on a means-tested basis, whereas social insurance benefits are payable regardless of financial circumstances, once the conditions for payment are met.

1.16 There are still two insurance-based retirement pensions: the contributory old age pension payable from age 66[22] and the retirement pension payable from age 65.[23] There is also an old age non-contributory pension. The old age non-contributory pension is only payable on satisfying a means test. In addition, the pensioner must have attained age 66 and be living in the State. The non-contributory pension is lower than the contributory pensions.

---

[19] Social Welfare (Amendment) Act, 1960.

[20] Social Welfare Act, 1970.

[21] See Clarke, R. (1995): *Annotated Guide to Social Welfare Law*, London: Sweet & Maxwell, for a detailed review of the legislation.

[22] Now provided under s.83 of the Social Welfare (Consolidation) Act, 1993.

[23] Now provided under s.88 of the 1993 Act.

1.17 Different qualifying conditions apply to the two insurance-based contributory pensions, as well as there being a later retirement age for the old age pension. Both pensions are "flat-rate" pensions, which means that the amount of pension does not vary in amount according to levels of salary. A Green Paper on a national income related pension scheme was published in Ireland in 1976, and this recommended pay related retirement pensions, but no legislation was introduced and so the flat-rate basis of social welfare pensions remains in Ireland.[24]

1.18 By way of contrast, the basis upon which employees pay contributions to the insurance scheme was changed from a flat-rate to a pay related basis with the introduction of PRSI.[25] PRSI now extends to almost all employees[26] and also, as far as the contributory old age pension and the widow's and orphan's contributory pensions are concerned, to most self-employed persons.[27]

1.19 The principal conditions that must be satisfied in order to obtain the retirement pension and the old age contributory pension are set out in Figure 1.1, as are the main differences between the two benefits. Although there are differences between the benefits from the minimum rate upwards, the amount of pension is the same at the maximum rate. Also, only one pension can be paid — it is not permissible to receive both.

1.20 In addition to the retirement and contributory old age pensions, there are also survivors' contributory pensions,[28] contributory orphans'

---

24 The issue was revisited by the National Pensions Board who, for reasons of cost and because of the ratio of contributors to pensioners, expressed reservations as to whether an earnings-related pension would be sustainable in the long term — Final Report of the National Pensions Board 1993 (Pl. 9979) para. 16.15.

25 PRSI was introduced, partially, in 1974 but a full changeover was not made until 1979.

26 s.9 of the 1993 Act — but there are certain limited exceptions contained in Part II of the First Schedule to the Act.

27 s.17 of the 1993 Act subject to the exceptions contained in Part III of the First Schedule.

28 s.100 of the 1993 Act.

FIGURE 1.1: STATE SOCIAL WELFARE CONTRIBUTORY PENSION — BROAD SUMMARY OF CONDITIONS

Feature	*Retirement Pension*	*Contributory Old Age Pension*
Payable from	Age 65	Age 66
Must have retired from employment?	Yes, from age 65 until age 66. From age 66, no[29]	No
Includes Self-employed?	No	Yes[30]
For how long must insurance contributions have been paid?	At least since prior to age 55 with at least 156 contributions paid	At least since prior to age 56 or 57 (depending on date of birth) with at least 156 contributions paid
What yearly average of insurance contributions must have been paid or credited to get the maximum rate of pension?	48 weeks' yearly average from 5 April 1979 (or later date of starting insurable employment) to the end of the tax year before pension age[31]	Same
What yearly average of insurance contributions must have been paid or credited to get the minimum rate of pension?	24 weeks' yearly average from 1953[32] (or later date of starting insurable employment) to the end of the tax year before 65.	20 weeks' yearly average from 1953[33] (or later date of starting insurable employment) to the end of the tax year before 65
Is the minimum rate the same for the retirement pension and the old age pension?	No	No
Is a survivor's pension[34] payable on the death of the insured person?	Yes	Yes

29 But a person who is a Class J PRSI contributor can work part-time and draw the retirement pension.

30 Self-employed must be paying Class S PRSI to be eligible.

31 If this condition is not satisfied, the Department of Social Welfare will recalculate from 1953.

32 The significance of 1953 is that if a person left insurable employment before 1953 and re-entered after 5 January 1953 (if male) or 6 July 1953 (if female) the yearly average is calculated from the date of re-entering insurable employment. The earlier insurable employment is ignored for working out the average unless it otherwise works to the person's advantage to count it.

33 See previous note.

34 Formerly known as a widow's pension, but since 28 October 1994 it is applicable to both widows and widowers.

allowances[35] and invalidity pensions.[36] The survivor's contributory pension used to be known as the widow's contributory pension but was extended to widowers with effect from 28 October 1994.[37] The survivor's pension is payable on the death of the survivor's husband or wife but only where the survivor is not cohabiting with someone else. Subject to those conditions, it is payable automatically where the deceased spouse was receiving the retirement pension or contributory old age pension with an entitlement to an increase for the survivor. It can also be payable where no retirement pension was being paid to the deceased spouse, but in this case certain PRSI conditions must be met. An orphan's contributory allowance is payable when both parents are dead or in certain circumstances where only one parent has died.[38] In all cases, one of the parents must have at least 26 weeks' PRSI. Orphans' pensions are payable until age 18 (or 21 if in full-time education by day at a recognised school or college).[39] Invalidity pension is payable in circumstances of serious incapacity. The person must be permanently incapable of work and must satisfy PRSI conditions.[40] Invalidity pension is not available to the self-employed paying Class S PRSI contributions.

1.21 Having discussed the nature of State social welfare pensions, it is appropriate now to look at the cost to the State of providing these pensions. It is estimated that the cost of social welfare pensions[41] will rise from £1,196 million (for the financial year 1990) to £2,423 million in 2035. That is an increase of over 100 per cent in 45 years.[42] The increase over the period is not uniform with the increase over the final

---

35 s.106.

36 s.95.

37 By s.11 of the Social Welfare Act, 1994. The non-contributory equivalent pension (the widow's non-contributory pension) is still only payable to widows.

38 For example, where one parent is unknown or has refused or failed to provide for the child.

39 There is also a non-contributory (means-tested) orphan's pension.

40 A total of 260 weeks' PRSI with at least 48 paid or credited in the last tax year before the claim.

41 Comprising both social insurance and social assistance pensions.

42 Final Report of the National Pensions Board: *Developing the National Pension System* (Pl. 9979) p.37.

25 years (2011–2035) being more than double that over the previous 20 years. Figure 1.2 represents this in graph form. The Final Report of the National Pensions Board published in 1993 addressed issues relating to the future development of the national pensions system. The report explains this phenomenal jump in cost by reference to factors such as the ageing population, effects of emigration and the

FIGURE 1.2: THE COST OF PROVIDING SOCIAL WELFARE PENSIONS

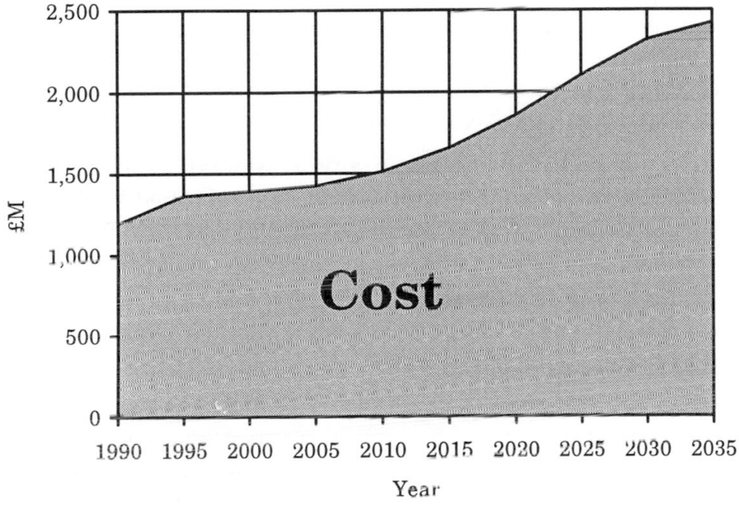

Source: Figures derived from Final Report of the National Pensions Board.

maturing of the social insurance pension schemes.[43] Figure 1.3 illustrates in graph form the National Pensions Board's population projections to 2036.[44] It can be seen that whilst total population is expected to decrease, so also, after 2011, is the working population (those between ages 16 and 65), and a steady decrease is expected in the numbers of children (ages 0–15). By contrast, it is projected that the number of those aged over 65 will increase by approximately 64 per cent in the 40 years from 1996 to 2036. In 1991, there were nearly 5.4 persons at working ages (as opposed to those actually employed) for every one person over age 65. This is expected to drop to 3 persons

43 *Ibid.* p.38.

44 The figures are derived from a table of information on p.39 of the Report.

of working age for every one person over age 65 in 2036. Since the cost of social welfare is funded on a pay-as-you-go basis from the working population, this has serious implications for the State, as there will be a proportionately lower working population from which to deduct social insurance contributions, and yet a greater retired population who will be an immediate liability for pension payments. The National Pensions Board concludes:

> The Board notes that demographic patterns indicate a considerable increase in the proportion of elderly people in the population over the first half of the next century. . . . At the same time the ratio of persons in the economically active age group to those over age 65 is projected to fall. . . . This would result, in the absence of any change, in an increasing burden of the cost of pensions falling on future generations of PRSI contributors and taxpayers.
>
> This is an important factor in any consideration of the development of future pension arrangements and raises serious questions about the capacity of the present financing arrangements to meet these emerging costs.[45]

FIGURE 1.3: PROJECTIONS OF TOTAL POPULATION

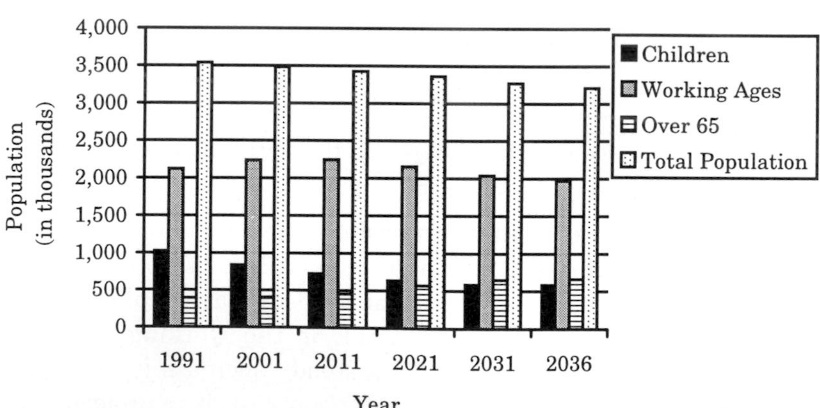

1.22 This problem is not peculiar to Ireland. Other countries in the EU are facing into a similar problem of an ageing population. It is of comfort, however, to note that in Ireland there is a significant participation of employees in occupational pension schemes. The most recent

45 *Ibid.* p.47.

statistics from the Pensions Board[46] indicate that there are approximately 484,880 persons (other than pensioners and former employees) included in occupational pension schemes.[47] It is not surprising therefore that the National Pensions Board recommends that:

> [T]he coverage of occupational pension schemes and personal pension arrangements on a voluntary basis should continue to be encouraged, in particular the existing tax treatment should be maintained.[48]

In the following sections, occupational pension schemes and self-employed arrangements are examined in greater detail, as is the legislation which regulates them.

OCCUPATIONAL PENSION SCHEMES

Public Sector Schemes

1.23 According to figures quoted by the National Pensions Board, public sector schemes account for approximately 270,000 employees.[49] Common features of public sector schemes are that they are established either by or under statute and are normally regulated by similar rules. Public sector schemes are found in both the public sector itself and in state-sponsored bodies. The public sector would include the civil service and central and local government services, such as the Gardaí, defence forces and health services. State-sponsored bodies would include Aer Lingus, ESB, Telecom and An Post. Public sector schemes are considered in more detail in Chapter 8.

1.24 Many public sector schemes are unfunded, which means that pensions are paid out of current resources. Some, however, notably

---

46 The Pensions Board Annual Report 1995, p.16. This is the total number of persons included in schemes registered with the Pensions Board. As all schemes must register, it is fairly accurate. There is, however, a certain element of double counting in Pensions Board statistics as a member of two pension schemes will be counted twice. The total number of persons included will therefore be less than the figure quoted. These figures also exclude death-benefit-only schemes and AVC schemes.

47 There are no comprehensive statistics on pension-scheme membership — see generally Hughes, G. (1984): *Private Pensions in OECD Countries*, OECD, Chapter 1.

48 Final Report of the National Pensions Board (Pl. 9979) 1993 p.202.

49 *Ibid.* p.51.

certain commercial state-sponsored bodies, have established funds that build up reserves to meet pension liabilities. Whether they are funded or unfunded, they are all occupational pension schemes under the Pensions Act and are accordingly subject to the Act. However, the unfunded schemes are generally exempted from the funding requirements of Part IV of the Act (because they are unfunded) and the preservation of leaving service benefits under Part III (because public sector schemes have their own preservation requirements). The funded schemes are generally not exempted from these requirements. By way of contrast, all public sector schemes must meet the disclosure of information requirements of Part V and the equality principle under Part VII.

1.25 Another distinguishing characteristic of unfunded public sector schemes is that they do not need to be approved by the Revenue under the Finance Act, 1972. Approval is unnecessary because appropriate tax reliefs are granted automatically under section 17 of the Act.[50] However, funded public sector schemes are in a different position. Funded schemes are operated on the basis that contributions from the state body and the employees are invested in a fund. The investments will yield an income and capital gain return. Section 17, whilst giving tax reliefs to these schemes, does not exempt the fund from income and capital gains tax. To secure exemption from tax on the fund's investments, the State body must obtain exempt approval from the Revenue in the same way as a private occupational pension scheme. This involves establishing the scheme under irrevocable trusts, which means that all funded public sector schemes are governed by trust law.

Private Sector Pension Schemes

1.26 The development of pension schemes in the private sector has been facilitated by certain tax reliefs accorded to schemes approved by the Revenue Commissioners. The basis of relief is that tax is deferred until retirement. Contributions to the pension scheme by the employer and its employees are fully relieved against tax, and the investment return on the pension fund is exempt from income and capital gains taxes. Pensions in payment are, however, subject to income tax in the same way as salary.[51]

---

[50] See para. 6.74 et seq.

[51] See para. 6.9.

1.27 Private occupational pension schemes are almost invariably established under trusts. This means that trustees are appointed by the sponsoring employer to manage the scheme and hold the assets of the scheme (the "trust fund") in accordance with regulations and rules contained in written trust documents. The trustees may be individuals appointed by the employer, trustees appointed on behalf of the members, independent trustees, corporate trustees or, indeed, the sponsoring employer itself. Even where the sponsoring employer holds the fund on trust, those assets are separate from the employer's business and cannot be taken, for example, by a liquidator for the benefit of creditors on a liquidation. The trust documents are most likely to consist of a formal trust deed and rules governing the scheme, but a deed is not strictly necessary. What is essential is that there be clear evidence of an intention to create a trust.[52]

1.28 It is a condition for the granting of Revenue approval that the scheme be established under irrevocable trusts. This means that the employer cannot subsequently revoke the trust it has already established and apply the fund to a different purpose or to its own use. The Revenue will, however, allow the employer to wind up the scheme at a future date, subject to specific requirements. The reason for stipulating irrevocable trusts from a Revenue perspective is that tax relief is granted in order to support and encourage retirement benefit provision in the private sector, and so it should not be possible to divert pension scheme moneys to a different use at a subsequent date. The moneys must be used for bona fide retirement or death benefit provision.

1.29 It is possible to structure a scheme in order to permit more than one employer to participate in it. There are two principal circumstances where this may arise. First, employers in a corporate group (for example, companies with a common parent) may wish to participate in one scheme for employees of the group, rather than establish a number of separately constituted schemes. Secondly, employers in a particular industry sector, who are otherwise unconnected with each other, can establish a scheme applicable to employees employed within that industry. The latter schemes are known as "industry-wide schemes".[53] Under the framework of exempt approval regulated by the Revenue

---

[52] See generally Chapter 3 on the trust documents that constitute pension schemes, and Chapter 4 on trustees.

[53] The most prominent example is the Construction Industry Federation scheme.

Commissioners, there are specific requirements that must be met before a scheme covering a group of employers can be established.[54]

1.30 This work is primarily concerned with approved pension schemes. Sometimes (albeit rarely) an employer establishes an unapproved pension scheme for one or more of its employees. This may be done unwittingly, where the employer promises a pension without establishing an approved scheme. The employer may for instance agree in the contract of employment to provide a pension but neglect to set up an approved scheme. This is an issue that must be considered carefully when drafting the employment contract.[55] Alternatively, the employer may choose to set up an unapproved arrangement.[56]

SELF-EMPLOYED ARRANGEMENTS

1.31 Not all working people are included in occupational pension schemes. There is another form of pension arrangement which is available — a self-employed arrangement. This is somewhat of a misnomer as self-employed arrangements are not just intended for the self-employed. Anyone who is not included in an occupational pension scheme can contribute to a self-employed arrangement.[57]

1.32 As with private occupational pension schemes, there are certain tax reliefs attaching to self-employed arrangements.[58] Contributions are invested in a policy issued by a life office, and the fund at retirement can be used to provide pension and other benefits at that point, subject to certain conditions imposed by the Revenue Commissioners.[59]

PENSIONS LEGISLATION

1.33 Having identified some of the principal features of occupational pension schemes and self-employed arrangements, it is relevant, at

---

54 See para. 6.22 et seq.

55 See Chapter 5.

56 On the tax consequences, see para. 6.84 et seq.

57 Self-employed arrangements are sometimes referred to as personal pensions, but this tends to confuse these arrangements with UK personal pension schemes which are wholly different arrangements.

58 Granted pursuant to s.235 of the Income Tax Act, 1967.

59 See para. 6.59 et seq.

this point, to examine the legislation which regulates these arrangements.

The Pensions Act

1.34 The Pensions Act, 1990 was enacted on 24 July 1990. Its preamble describes it to be

> An Act to regulate occupational pension schemes and to provide for equal treatment of men and women under occupational benefit schemes, for those purposes to provide for the establishment of a body (to be know as An Bord Pinsean — The Pensions Board) to supervise such schemes and their operation, to define the functions of that body and to provide for connected matters.

There are nine parts to the Act. Different parts of the Act came into force on different dates. The preliminary and general provisions (Part I) and the provisions relating to the Pensions Board (Part II) came into force on 21 December 1990. The substantive provisions dealing with preservation, funding and disclosure (Parts III, IV and V) were brought into force on 1 January 1991, but other provisions were deferred until later, notably the equal treatment provisions of Part VII (1 January 1993) and the introduction of member trustee representation pursuant to section 62 (21 December 1993).[60] Part VIII, dealing with compulsory and voluntary reporting to the Board, and Part IX, providing for court orders regarding arrears of contributions and revesting of trust property, were inserted by the Pensions (Amendment) Act, 1996 and came into force on 2 July 1996.

1.35 The Pensions Act has been amended by five Acts of the Oireachtas.[61] In addition, there have been 20 regulations and orders made under the Act, including three complete replacements of earlier regulations.[62] Two significant trends can be deduced from this. The first is that the regulation of pensions is a complex matter and it has proved difficult to establish a fully satisfactory regulatory régime from the outset. For example, one set of regulations made under the Act is the member trustee regulations. The first regulations were made in July 1993, only to be revoked and replaced by new regulations

---

60 See Appendix III for a complete list of dates and cross-references to the appropriate statutory instruments.

61 The Social Welfare Acts, 1991, 1992 and 1993 and the Social Welfare (No. 2) Act, 1993 and the Pensions (Amendment) Act, 1996.

62 The regulations and orders are listed in Appendix III.

in December 1993, some five months later![63] A similar fate befell the Disclosure Regulations.[64] The second trend is that pensions regulation is likely to become more complex in the future. Two new Parts were inserted in the Pensions Act by the Pensions (Amendment) Act, 1996, and the regulations made under the Act have added considerable complexity to the original legislation. For example, there are the Occupational Pension Schemes (Preservation of Benefits) (Special Calculations) Regulations, 1993, which govern transfers of an employee's benefits from one scheme to another of the same employer,[65] and the member trustee regulations mentioned earlier.

1.36 To be fair to the Pensions Board and the Minister for Social Welfare, these regulations are prepared with significant input from representatives of the various bodies involved in the pensions industry, who meet in committees and sub-committees established and overseen by the Board. The complexity is therefore contributed to by the pensions industry. The Pensions Board takes its role very seriously and has issued guidance notes on aspects of the Act, in order to enhance communication and understanding.[66] It has also issued useful explanatory leaflets aimed at trustees with little or no knowledge of pensions matters.[67]

1.37 Part I of the Pensions Act contains most of the definitions used in the Act, including the key definition of "occupational pension

---

63 The Occupational Pension Schemes (Member Participation in the Selection of Persons for Appointment as Trustees) Regulations, 1993 (SI No 216 of 1993) and the Occupational Pension Schemes (Member Participation in the Selection of Persons for Appointment as Trustees) (No.2) Regulations, 1993 (SI No 399 of 1993).

64 The Occupational Pension Schemes (Disclosure of Information) Regulations, 1990 (SI No 332 of 1990) were replaced by the Occupational Pension Schemes (Disclosure of Information) Regulations, 1991 (SI No 215 of 1991).

65 The regulations are considered at para. 12.69 et seq.

66 To date, guidance notes have been issued on preservation of benefits (Part III of the Act), equality (Part VII), disclosure of information (Part V), the member trustee regulations (Part VI — s.62) and whistle blowing (Part VII).

67 "So You're a Pension Scheme Trustee?", "Is my pension secure?", "What do you know about your pension scheme?", "What happens to my pension if I leave?, "Selecting Member Trustees", "The Pensions Board". All brochures are available from the Pensions Board.

scheme", which is abbreviated to "scheme" in the definitions section.[68] The Pensions Act applies to all occupational pension schemes. Part VII, however, applies to a wider category of schemes referred to as "occupational benefit schemes". Subject to that qualification, if a pension scheme is not an "occupational pension scheme", it is not subject to the requirements of the Act. There are three conditions that must be satisfied before a scheme falls within the definition and consequently becomes subject to the terms of the Act. The first is that it must be a scheme or arrangement comprised in one or more instruments or agreements. It must therefore be in writing. Oral arrangements are not regulated by the Act. Secondly, it must provide or be capable of providing certain benefits to employees in the State. The benefits are either benefits payable at normal, late or early retirement or leaving service or are benefits for a spouse or dependant or others, payable on death. Schemes that provide benefits payable exclusively to persons in another country are not governed by the Act. Thirdly, the scheme must satisfy one of the following conditions:

1. It has been approved by the Revenue under Chapter II of Part I of the Finance Act, 1972. This effectively means schemes approved under section 15 or exempt approved schemes under section 16 of the Finance Act.[69]
2. The application for Revenue approval is under consideration. This covers schemes where the formal approval application is pending with the Revenue. More significantly, it includes schemes that have received interim Revenue approval on the basis of an interim deed but have not yet submitted for full exempt approval.[70]
3. The scheme is a statutory scheme to which section 17 of the Finance Act applies. This comprises schemes established by or under any enactment.[71]
4. The benefits under the scheme are paid in whole or in part out of moneys provided from the Central Fund or moneys provided by the Oireachtas. This will include the vast majority of public sector

---

68 s.2.

69 See para. 6.6 et seq.

70 See para. 6.15 et seq.

71 See para. 6.74 et seq.

schemes. Most of those schemes will also be statutory schemes covered by section 17 of the Finance Act, but some public sector schemes (for example, the civil service non-established scheme)[72] have not yet been put on a statutory footing.

5. The scheme has been approved by the Revenue for the purpose of one or more of the following: section 32 of the Finance Act, 1921, section 34 of the Finance Act, 1958 or sections 222 or 229 of the Income Tax Act, 1967. These provisions refer to schemes that are approved under the old code of Revenue approval as opposed to the new code.[73]

1.38 The preamble to the Pensions Act states one of the purposes of the Act as being "to provide for the equal treatment of men and women under occupational benefit schemes". The Act seeks to achieve this under Part VII, which applies not to occupational pension schemes but to occupational benefit schemes. The latter includes the former but has a far wider application. For example, in addition to including pension schemes, the definition includes schemes or arrangements relating to sickness or invalidity (such as permanent health insurance) and schemes or arrangements relating to accidents, injuries or diseases arising out of employment. This would include personal accident insurance. It also extends, subject to certain conditions, to self-employed persons. Part VII is actually the implementation into Irish law of EU equality directives and is considered in detail in Chapter 16.

Family Law Act, 1995

1.39 The Family Law Act, 1995 facilitates the adjustment of pension scheme benefits in circumstances where a judicial separation order is granted or a foreign divorce or separation is recognised in this jurisdiction. The Family Law Act is not restricted to occupational pension schemes as defined by the Pensions Act but applies to every type of pension arrangement. Application can be made by a spouse to the Court for a pension adjustment order, which is an order earmarking part of the pension scheme member's benefits for payment to the spouse. There is also provision for an order to be granted on behalf of a dependent child. Having obtained a pension adjustment order,

---

72 See para. 8.23.

73 See para. 6.4.

the spouse can subsequently have the earmarked pension split in her favour. The effect of splitting the pension is that the spouse receives a pension wholly independent of the pension scheme member. The Family Law Act is analysed fully in Chapter 15.

Trustee Act, 1893

1.40 As most pension schemes are established under trust, the significance of trust law is apparent. Although there is a substantial body of case law governing trusts and trustees, the only legislation (aside from the Pensions Act) that affects trusts is the Trustee Act, 1893.[74] The main features of the Trustee Act that are of relevance to pension schemes are the provisions that concern the appointment and removal of trustees, the protection of trustees from liability in certain circumstances and the permitting of investment in certain authorised securities.[75]

Finance Act, 1972

1.41 Chapter II of Part I of the Finance Act, 1972, together with the Practice Notes published by the Retirement Benefits District of the Revenue Commissioners form the basis upon which the Retirement Benefits District grants exempt approval to occupational pension schemes. Whilst the Pensions Act has gained considerable prominence in the pensions industry since its enactment in 1990, the significance of the Finance Act and the role of the Retirement Benefits District cannot be overestimated. The history of private occupational pensions has shown that their development has been facilitated by the tax treatment of exempt approved schemes.

1.42 The main reliefs granted to exempt approved schemes under the Finance Act are:

1. Tax relief on member contributions
2. Tax relief on employer contributions
3. Income and capital gains tax exemption on the investment return on the trust fund

---

74 There is one subsequent Act extending the investments which are authorised under the 1893 Act — see para. 4.43.

75 See Chapter 4.

4. Up to 1.5 times final remuneration, which can be taken as a tax-free lump sum on retirement.

All pensions are ultimately subject to income tax when they commence to be paid.[76]

1.43 All schemes established by or under Statute, that is public sector schemes, are automatically granted the first two reliefs without the need for exempt approval from the Retirement Benefits District. Accordingly, most exempt approved schemes are private sector schemes. There are, however, some notable exceptions. Any public sector scheme that is funded must seek exempt approval in order to gain advantage of the third relief set out above. Public sector schemes financed on the pay-as-you-go basis do not need to do so, as the third relief is irrelevant to them.

Income Tax Act, 1967

1.44 Similar comments as to the significance of the Revenue's role can be made with regard to self-employed arrangements. The approval and regulation of self-employed arrangements is governed by the Income Tax Act, 1967, primarily section 235. The following are the main reliefs available to a person who effects a self-employed arrangement:

1. Tax relief on contributions to the arrangement
2. Income and capital gains tax exemption on the investment return on the contributions
3. Tax-free cash on retirement of one-quarter of the value of the fund.

As with exempt approved schemes, the pension is ultimately subject to income tax.[77]

---

76 The approval process and the taxation position are considered in depth in Chapter 6.

77 Self-employed arrangements are considered at para. 6.59 et seq.

REGULATORY BODIES

1.45 Having reviewed the legislation affecting pension arrangements, it will be appreciated that the legislation can conveniently be divided into two categories: tax legislation (the Finance Act, 1972 and the Income Tax Act, 1967) and pensions legislation (the Pensions Act, 1990, the Family Law Act, 1995 and, to the extent that pension schemes are established under trust, the Trustee Act, 1893). The Revenue Commissioners are responsible for regulating the tax treatment of pension arrangements. The Pensions Board is charged with regulating occupational pension schemes and the operation of the Pensions Act. The role of each of these regulatory bodies will now be discussed.

The Revenue Commissioners

1.46 A favourable tax environment for pensions was introduced by the Income Tax Act, 1918 and the Finance Act, 1921. The former Act granted tax relief on employee contributions to deferred annuity contracts issued by life offices, but the relief was deferred until retirement. The latter legislation granted immediate relief on contributions, provided that the annuity contract was approved by the Revenue Commissioners. This approval process was the forerunner of modern Revenue approval of pension schemes. The tax régime was improved further in the Finance Act, 1958, whereby life offices were exempted from tax in respect of income earned on contributions to approved policies. Also, self-employed persons or certain persons in employment were given the opportunity to make contributions to approved policies. The self-employed arrangements were subsequently consolidated in the Income Tax Act, 1967, and the self-employed policies became known as section 235 policies.[78] Following a legislative change in the UK to revise and consolidate the tax treatment and approval of pension schemes,[79] a similar approach was taken in Ireland in the Finance Act, 1972. This legislation, with some subsequent amendments, still governs the approval of occupational pension schemes in Ireland. Self-employed arrangements are still regulated under the Income Tax Act, 1967.

1.47 The Revenue Commissioners have a role, to some extent, in all the categories of pension schemes referred to earlier. The contributory

---

[78] After the section in the Income Tax Act, 1967 which governs such policies.

[79] Finance Act, 1970.

state pension is subject to income tax, unless a pensioner's allowances and reliefs eliminate the liability to tax. Statutory schemes are afforded tax reliefs under the Finance Act, 1972.[80] But it is in the area of private occupational pension schemes and self-employed arrangements that the Revenue's role is particularly significant. Private occupational pension schemes are almost always exempt approved schemes under Chapter II of Part I of the Finance Act or are waiting to receive exempt approval. To obtain exempt approval, these schemes must be established under irrevocable trust. The Retirement Benefits District is the section of the Revenue that regulates approved schemes and grants, refuses or withdraws approval.[81] Self-employed arrangements are also Revenue approved arrangements under the control of the Retirement Benefits District. In self-employed arrangements, pension and death benefits are provided under insurance policies issued in accordance with the requirements of section 235 of the Income Tax Act, 1967.[82]

1.48 Exempt approved occupational pension schemes are only permitted, under the terms of the approval, to provide benefits on retirement or death within certain limits imposed by the Revenue. One such limit (although there are exceptions to it) is that an exempt approved scheme can promise a pension of up to 1/60th of final remuneration for each year of company service.[83] It is no coincidence that many pension schemes promise a pension calculated in this manner, and it can therefore be seen that Revenue limits have a direct impact on the way in which pension schemes are designed.

The Pensions Board

1.49 The Pensions Board, which was established by the Pensions Act, 1990, was the result of recommendations made by the National Pensions Board in 1987 in its First Report.[84] The National Pensions Board was established in 1986 by the Minister for Social Welfare to submit proposals on the regulation of occupational pension schemes, including requirements concerning standards of administration, funding, transferability of benefits and disclosure of information. The result was their

---

80 s.17 — see para. 6.74 et seq.

81 This is considered in detail in Chapter 6.

82 See para. 6.59 et seq.

83 See para. 7.5 for a definition of final remuneration.

84 First Report of the National Pensions Board (Pl. 4776) 29 January 1987.

First Report, which became the blueprint for the Pensions Act.[85] In particular, the First Report recommended the establishment of a national pensions board to monitor and supervise the operation of the proposed Pensions Act.

1.50 The legislature dropped the word "National" and instead called the new regulator the Pensions Board. The Pensions Board is officially known as "An Bord Pinsean — The Pensions Board".[86] It is a body corporate established by the Pensions Act[87] as of 21 December 1990.[88] The First Schedule to the Act sets out the membership of the Board and the procedures that apply to it. The Board consists of a chairman and 14 ordinary members, all of whom are appointed by the Minister for Social Welfare.[89] The Minister has complete discretion with regard to the appointment of three of the ordinary members, but the remaining 11 must be chosen from various interest groups,[90] including representatives of the professions involved in pensions (lawyers, actuaries, accountants), of the employers and trade unions and of occupational pension schemes. The current make-up of the Board's ordinary members is set out in Figure 1.1.

1.51 The term of office of the chairman is five years and there is no facility for re-appointment.[91] The term of office for ordinary members

---

85 The National Pensions Board had other terms of reference as well, which resulted in subsequent reports: the Report on the Extension of Social Insurance to the Self-Employed (Pl. 5411), the Report on the Tax Treatment of Occupational Pension Schemes (Pl. 5475), the Report on Equal Treatment for Men and Women in Occupational Pension Schemes (Pl. 6606) and Developing the National Pension System — the Final Report of the National Pensions Board (Pl. 9979).

86 s.9(1)

87 para. 1 of the First Schedule and s.9(1)

88 Pensions Act, 1990 (Part II) (Establishment Day) Order, 1990 as enabled by s.8.

89 para. 2 of the First Schedule as amended by s.40 of the Pensions (Amendment) Act, 1996.

90 Listed in para. 8(1).

91 A new chairman can be appointed within the five years when the previous chairman had resigned, died, was removed or became disqualified — para. 5A as inserted by s.40(b) of the Pensions (Amendment) Act, 1996.

is such period not exceeding five years as the Minister determines.[92] The term of office of the first ordinary members of the Board has, in fact, been five years. There is provision for re-appointment, appointment of new members, where the term of office is not renewed and for

FIGURE 1.4: CURRENT REPRESENTATION ON THE PENSIONS BOARD

*Nominated by**	*No. of Members*
Minister for Social Welfare	1
Minister for Finance	1
Minister for Social Welfare (appointed directly)*	3
Association of Pension Lawyers in Ireland	1
Society of Actuaries in Ireland	1
Irish Business and Employers Confederation**	2
Irish Congress of Trade Unions**	2
Irish Insurance Federation	1
Consultative Committee of Accountancy Bodies in Ireland	1
Irish Association of Pension Funds	1
Total	14

* Three persons can be appointed directly by the Minister for Social Welfare without being representatives of a particular body or of the Minister. In addition the Minister must appoint one person as his representative.

** One of each must also be a trustee of an occupational pension scheme.

resignation and removal of members.[93] Each member including the chairman has one vote at meetings[94] and the quorum for meetings is five.[95] On an equality of votes, the chairman has a casting vote. A chief executive has been appointed in accordance with the requirements of section 15 to manage and control the administration and business of the Board. The chief executive may not be a member of the Board.[96] In order to assist and advise the Board, committees may be established

92 para. 10(2).

93 paras. 11–15.

94 para. 22.

95 para. 19.

96 s.15(3).

and may consist of non-Board members as well as Board members.[97] In the year 1995 there were five committees and various sub-committees which met a total of 62 times in the year.[98] The Board may, in addition, employ staff, of whom there are currently 16[99] (excluding the Chief Executive), and may retain advisers and consultants.[100] Without the consent of the Board, Board members, staff, advisers, consultants and committee members are forbidden to disclose, on penalty of a fine not exceeding £1,500, any information obtained by them while performing, or having performed, their duties.[101]

1.52 The functions of the Board are set out in section 10 of the Pensions Act. The following is a summary of those functions:

1. Monitor and supervise the operation of the Act.
2. Monitor and supervise pensions developments.
3. Advise the Minister for Social Welfare on the Board's functions and pensions matters.
4. Issue guidelines on the duties and responsibilities of trustees and generally on the operation of the Act.[102]
5. Issue codes of practice on specific aspects of trustee responsibilities.
6. Encourage training for trustees.
7. Advise the Minister on standards for trustees and their implementation.
8. Publish an annual report and such other reports as it considers necessary.
9. Perform such tasks as the Minister may from time to time request.

---

97 s.14.

98 The Pensions Board Annual Report 1995.

99 *Ibid.*

100 s.12.

101 s.24 as amended by s.7 and s.43 of the Pensions (Amendment) Act, 1996.

102 The facility to issue general guidelines was introduced by s.5 of the Pensions (Amendment) Act, 1996.

The Board is also given such powers as are necessary or incidental to the performance of these functions.[103] The last item (9.) gives the Minister for Social Welfare considerable latitude to expand the role of the Board. Finally, the Minister, with the consent of the Minister for Finance, may confer additional functions on the Board, but these must be connected with the above functions.[104]

1.53 Perhaps the most important function of the Board is monitoring and supervising the operation of the Pensions Act. One of the ways the Board does this is by undertaking an inspection or investigation into the state and conduct of a scheme. The Board may either carry out the investigation itself or may authorise in writing any person it considers necessary to do so.[105] The publication of any report by the Board arising from an investigation will enjoy absolute privilege.[106] There are three circumstances which might prompt the Board to initiate an investigation:

1. A complaint received in respect of the scheme (for example, from a member)
2. The failure by the trustees to furnish information to the Board as is prescribed by the Act (for example, failing to submit an actuarial funding certificate)
3. A spot-check audit of a scheme.

Investigations have certainly arisen with regard to the first two situations. The Pensions Board has recently commenced spot-check audits to ensure compliance with the disclosure of information requirements of the Pension Act.[107]

1.54 In carrying out an investigation into the state and conduct of a scheme, the Board will require certain information from the trustees. The Board may seek the information from the trustees voluntarily or,

---

[103] s.10(2).

[104] s.11(1).

[105] s.18(1) as amended by s.6(1)(a) of the Pensions (Amendment) Act, 1996.

[106] s.18(9) as inserted by s.6(1)(d) of the Pensions (Amendment) Act, 1996.

[107] This was forewarned in the Fourth Annual Report of the Pensions Board (1994), p.26.

alternatively, may invoke the provisions of section 18 of the Act. Section 18(2) empowers the Board as follows:

> The Board or an authorised person may, in relation to a scheme, require the *employer* concerned or the *trustees* of the scheme to furnish it within such reasonable period as may be specified with such information *and explanations* and such books of account and other documents in relation to the scheme as may be specified.[108]

1.55 This is usually referred to as a "section 18 notice". The notice can be given to the employer or the trustees or both. There is no requirement that the notice be in writing — the information and explanations required could be specified orally. However, it can be expected that section 18 notices will be in writing and it would be reasonable for an employer or trustee to insist on this in order to identify and record precisely what is sought. There is no limit stated in the section as to the documents that the Board can require to be furnished, other than that they relate to the scheme. What is more, the Board can require explanations to be given, presumably answers to questions raised by the Board or the authorised person. This somewhat extensively drafted section must be subject to the overriding right of the trustees and employer to legal professional privilege and, in the case of explanations, to the constitutional protection against self-incrimination, particularly if the investigation is a prelude to, or is in the course of, a prosecution under the Act.

1.56 It may be wondered why the Act permits the appointment of an authorised person to inspect or investigate on behalf of the Board. The reason is to be found in section 18(3),[109] which enables an authorised person to carry out an inspection on the premises of the employer, the trustees or an agent, and to carry out an examination or inquiry. A summary of the investigator's powers is as follows:

1. Enter the premises of any employer, trustee *or agent*;[110] a warrant from the District Court is required where a private dwelling is concerned.[111]

---

[108] Emphasis added.

[109] As amended by s.6(1)(b) of the Pensions (Amendment) Act, 1996.

[110] Emphasis added.

[111] s.18(4A) as inserted by s.6(1)(c) of the Pensions (Amendment) Act, 1996.

2. Where the investigator considers it necessary, choose to be accompanied by a member of the Garda Síochána.[112]
3. On being refused access, apply to the District Court for a warrant.[113]
4. Make an examination or inquiry[114] to determine compliance with the Pensions Act.[115]
5. Inspect and take copies of records relating to the scheme.[116]
6. Remove and retain books of account and other documents and records in relation to the scheme for a reasonable period for their further examination or for legal proceedings.[117]
7. Require any person to give reasonable assistance regarding data equipment (computers, for example) provided that the person has charge of or is concerned with its operation.[118]

Authorised persons must produce their certificate of appointment (or a copy) on request by an affected person.

1.57 This power to enter premises or undertake an examination or inquiry is entirely independent of section 18(2). In other words, no notice is required, provided that entry is sought at a reasonable time, such as normal business hours. What is more significant, however, is that section 18(3) extends to *agents* as well as the trustees and the employer. "Agents" is defined to include (not comprise) "the actuaries, auditors and other accountants and the financial and other advisers to the scheme".[119] This is a wide and open-ended definition which could also include the solicitors who are customarily instructed by the trustees or the employer in connection with the scheme; insurance

---

[112] s.18(4C) as also so inserted.

[113] s.18(4B) and (4D) as also so inserted.

[114] There is no entitlement to examine under oath.

[115] s.18(3A) as inserted by s.6(1)(b) of the Pensions (Amendment) Act, 1996.

[116] *Ibid.*

[117] *Ibid.*

[118] *Ibid.*

[119] s.18(6).

brokers; pensions consultants; life offices; and administration managers.

1.58 It would seem that agents are only required to provide information or answer queries where an authorised person has been appointed to enter premises or carry out an examination under subsection (3). A simple request for information under section 18(2) does not appear to apply to agents. However, in a piece of ambiguous drafting, section 18(4) extends the duty to produce or provide information to "any person being an officer or employee of the employer or a trustee or agent".[120] It is unclear whether this sub-section is qualifying section 18(2), section 18(3) or both. It is suggested that the most logical interpretation is that, to the extent that it refers to officers or employees of the employer or a trustee, it qualifies section 18(2), and to the extent that it refers to those people and to employees or officers of any *agent*, it qualifies section 18(3), which is the sub-section that refers to agents.

1.59 Wilful obstruction of an authorised person is an offence punishable on summary conviction by a fine not exceeding £1,500 and/or a term of imprisonment of up to one year or on conviction on indictment to a fine not exceeding £10,000 and/or a term of imprisonment of up to two years. So too is a refusal without reasonable excuse to produce to the authorised person information, documents, material or explanations sought or a refusal, without reasonable cause, to answer any question put by the authorised person concerning the affairs of the scheme.[121]

1.60 Given the serious consequences of a breach of section 18, it would be prudent for the trustees, employer or agent (as the case may be) to take (at least) the following measures if the Board exercises its powers under section 18:

1. Obtain a copy of the authorised person's certificate of appointment.
2. Ensure that all enquiries and questions are recorded in writing.
3. Respond in writing with such answers and explanations as are sought.

---

[120] This includes a former officer, employee or agent — s.18(7).

[121] s.18(5) as amended by s.43 of the Pensions (Amendment) Act, 1996.

4. Identify and list all documents sought by the Board or inspected by the authorised officer.
5. Remove from the Board's access all information that is protected by legal professional privilege.
6. In the case of entry and inspection, seek to restrict access to business hours and ensure that a solicitor is present to advise.

1.61 Another way in which the Board can obtain information about a scheme is through the Revenue Commissioners. All approved schemes under Chapter II of Part I of the Finance Act, 1972 are required to furnish the Retirement Benefits District of the Revenue with trust documentation such as the trust deeds and rules. Explanatory booklets and announcements issued to members must also be filed. The Retirement Benefits District retains copies of these documents and the Pensions Board is entitled under section 4 of the Pensions Act to any information held by the Revenue for the purposes of Chapter II of Part I of the Finance Act relating to occupational pension schemes within the meaning of the Pensions Act. It is understood that the Board does avail itself of this facility from time to time. This entitlement to information can operate in reverse as well. The Revenue can seek any information held by the Board for the purposes of the Pensions Act.

1.62 The Board is required under Parts III to VII of the Act to determine certain issues specified in the Act on application in writing by any one of the following:[122] the trustees, an employer, a member or prospective member or such other persons as are prescribed by the Minister for Social Welfare. The Minister has prescribed an authorised trade union representing a member or members and any agent,[123] in addition to the above.[124] Some powers to determine issues are specific to a particular Part of the Act, others apply to each Part. The issues common to each Part are the following:

---

[122] As specified in s.38(3).

[123] The definition of "agent" is considered at para. 1.57.

[124] Occupational Pension Schemes (Preservation of Benefits) Regulations, 1992, Art.10.

1. Whether any provision of the applicable Part of the Act (including the appropriate schedule, if any) and any regulations made thereunder conflicts with any rule of the scheme[125]
2. Whether it is a defined benefit or a defined contribution scheme.

Rather than providing for one general power of determination of these issues, each substantive Part contains its own provision requiring the issue to be determined by the Board with reference to that Part of the Act.[126] There are also issues which are specific to Parts III and VII. Figure 1.5 lists these specific issues as well as the general ones. An appeal to the High Court on a point of law is permitted to be made by either the person who made the initial application or any other person who would have been permitted to do so.[127]

FIGURE 1.5: SPECIFIC ISSUES TO BE DETERMINED BY THE BOARD

Issue	*Part of Act applicable*	*Section empowering Board to make determination*
Whether a scheme is a defined benefit scheme or a defined contribution scheme for the purposes of this Part.	Parts III, IV, V, VI and VII	ss 38(2)(b), 53(2)(b), 58(2)(b), 64(A)(2)(b), 75(1)(a) respectively.
Whether the provisions of a Part (including any regulations issued and any applicable Schedule) conflicts with any rule of a scheme.	Parts III, IV, V and VI	ss. 38(2)(a), 53(2)(a), 58(2)(a), 64(A)(2)(a) respectively.
Whether a member's service in relevant employment may be treated as terminated for the purposes of this Part.	Part III	s.38(2)(c)
Whether any rule of a scheme, which is also an occupational benefit scheme[128] for the purposes of this Part, complies with the principle of equal treatment and whether and to what extent any such rule is rendered null and void by section 71[129]	Part VII	s.75(1)(b) & (c)

---

[125] In the case of sex discrimination under Part VII, the question is whether the rule conflicts with the principle of equal treatment rather than the entire of Part VII. However, any non-compliance with Part VII is a non-compliance with the principle of equal treatment and so, in effect, the determination is whether the rule conflicts with Part VII.

[126] In relation to Parts III, IV, V, VI and VII of the Pensions Act, ss.38(2), 53(2), 58(2), 64(A)(2) and 75(1) respectively.

[127] In relation to Parts III, IV, V, VI and VII of the Pensions Act, ss.38(4), 53(3), 58(3), 64(A)(3) and 75(3) respectively.

[128] This term is used exclusively in Part VII of the Act — see Chapter 16.

[129] The compulsory levelling up provision of Part VII — see para. 16.35 et seq.

PROFESSIONS AND BODIES

1.63 There are several professions and bodies associated with the field of pensions. These are set out below:

1.64 ***Lawyers***: It is hardly surprising that lawyers (solicitors and barristers) have an important role in the area of pensions given that nearly all private occupational pension schemes and many public sector schemes are established under trust and consequently governed by trust law. Furthermore, schemes are usually regulated by complex trust documentation which requires the involvement of lawyers. Pensions law is, however, not just a branch of trust law, but an area of law in its own right. Its distinctiveness is reinforced by the complex framework of pensions regulation in Ireland, both under the Finance Act, 1972 and the Pensions Act, 1990. In recognition of this, a group of lawyers specialising in pensions law formed the Association of Pension Lawyers in Ireland on 17 May 1990.[130] The Association was subsequently incorporated on 28 May 1996. The APLI nominates one member to the Pensions Board.

1.65 ***Employee Benefits Consultants***: These are also known as pensions consultants and they are firms which specialise in the provision of pensions consultancy services to employers and trustees. Some also act as professional trustees. In addition to consultancy, they may also provide actuarial, administration, scheme management and documentation services, such as scheme rules and explanatory booklets for scheme members. Those firms that provide pensions management services will normally include personnel who are members of the Irish Institute of Pensions Managers or the Pensions Management Institute (the UK equivalent body to which the IIPM is affiliated). Employee Benefits Consultants are usually also insurance brokers and would usually be members of the Irish Brokers Association (the IBA).

1.66 ***Brokers***: Insurance brokers are independent intermediaries who have agencies (that is, they can place insurance business) with five or more insurers. Most brokers are members of the Irish Brokers Association (IBA). Whilst most employee benefits consultants are also independent intermediaries, the reverse is not the case. Few intermediaries have the resources and skills to provide employee benefits consultancy.

---

130 Coincidentally the date of the *Barber* judgment on equal treatment.

1.67 ***Life Offices***: Life assurance companies are authorised to undertake life assurance business in Ireland either under the European Communities (Life Assurance) Regulations, 1984 or under the European Communities (Life Assurance) Framework Regulations, 1994. The latter regulations implement the Third Life Directive and permit life offices authorised in another EU member state to carry on business in Ireland. Pensions have traditionally been effected through life office policies of assurance such as endowment or with-profit policies, although most life offices now usually provide unit-linked investment products. Self-employed arrangements can only be provided through a life office policy,[131] and most small (and some larger) occupational pension schemes are still arranged in this way. Many larger schemes are, however, invested with investment managers such as subsidiaries of licensed banks. The insurance of death benefits under a pension scheme may only be effected with life offices.[132] The body which represents the Irish-established life offices and foreign life offices that have branches in Ireland is the Irish Insurance Federation. The IIF currently nominates one person as a member of the Pensions Board.

1.68 ***Investment Managers***: Life offices historically provided (and still provide) all services to pension scheme trustees, including administration, actuarial work, documentation, insurance and investment. This "packaged" approach does not suit all schemes and many trustees and employers now seek to unbundle the package by giving the administration and actuarial work (for example) to employee benefit consultants and giving the investment management functions to another institution. The term "investment manager" is here used to describe an institution that is providing solely investment management services to the scheme. The investment manager, in this context, can be a life office providing only investment services, or can be an investment bank, a unit trust, a stockbroker or other specialist fund manager. The representative body applicable to investment managers is the Irish Association of Investment Managers (the IAIM).

1.69 ***Actuaries***: The role of the actuary extends to most aspects of the operation of pension schemes. They advise primarily on the funding and solvency of schemes. Their role was given statutory rec-

---

[131] Except for certain group schemes — see para. 6.70 et seq.

[132] This is as a consequence of the regulation of life assurance business — see Chapter 11.

ognition in the Pensions Act in that the trustees of defined benefit schemes are required to file an actuarial funding certificate with the Pensions Board which sets out the solvency position of the scheme and must also have periodic actuarial valuations prepared by the actuary. The funding certificate is signed by the actuary, who takes individual responsibility for it. To be qualified to prepare funding certificates and valuations, actuaries must be either Fellows of the Institute of Actuaries or Fellows of the Faculty of Actuaries.[133] The overall representative body of actuaries in Ireland is the Society of Actuaries, which currently nominates a representative to the Pensions Board.[134]

1.70 ***Auditors***: Auditors are involved with pensions as auditors both of companies and of pension schemes. When auditing the accounts of a company, auditors must take into account the cost of providing pension and death benefits in accordance with specific standards.[135] Accountants will also audit pension scheme accounts in certain circumstances, to comply with either Revenue requirements[136] or those of the Pensions Act.[137] In auditing pension scheme accounts they must again have regard to specified standards.[138] They are also permitted to prepare an alternative annual report in certain circumstances under the Pensions Act.[139] The Consultancy Committee of Accountancy Bodies in Ireland currently nominates one person to the Pensions Board.

WHISTLE BLOWING AND RESTORATION OF RESOURCES

1.71 As can be seen from the previous section, there are potentially many professional advisers who can have an involvement in the operation of a pension scheme. If there are any concerns about the security of scheme assets, professional advisers may spot the early warning signs. In order to ensure that advisers heed those signs and

---

[133] Subject to certain exceptions, see para. 9.6.

[134] For more information on actuaries, see Chapter 9.

[135] SSAP 24 — see Chapter 13.

[136] In connection with small self-administered schemes — see para. 6.77 et seq.

[137] See para. 13.12 et seq.

[138] SORP 1 — see Chapter 13.

[139] para. 13.46 et seq.

notify the appropriate authorities, a new part (Part VIII) was inserted into the Pensions Act by the Pensions (Amendment) Act, 1996, providing for compulsory reporting to the Pensions Board of misappropriation of the resources of an occupational pension scheme.

1.72 This "whistle-blowing" obligation is imposed on any "relevant person", which is defined[140] to comprise the auditor, actuary or trustee of the scheme, any insurance intermediary[141] in relation to the scheme, any investment business firm[142] that has advised on the scheme or received payment in relation to investment of the scheme's resources, any person who has been instructed to prepare or who has prepared an annual report of the scheme, or any person appointed by the trustees to carry out any of their duties under section 59 of the Act.

1.73 This is a wide definition which should include all professional advisers, with the notable exception of lawyers who are acting in an advisory capacity in the conduct of legal proceedings. The duties under section 59 are to ensure that contributions are received, to invest the fund, to pay the benefits, to keep proper records, to wind up the scheme in accordance with the Act and scheme rules where required. A lawyer who undertakes any of these duties falls within the definition, although it would be unusual for a lawyer to do so. However, barristers and solicitors are given a specific defence for failure to blow the whistle where, in the ordinary scope of their professional engagement, they are assisting or advising in the preparation of legal proceedings.[143]

1.74 The obligation to report occurs if:

> a person has reasonable cause to believe that a material misappropriation or fraudulent conversion of the scheme resources has

---

140 By s.82.

141 Within the meaning of s.2 of the Insurance Act, 1989.

142 Within the meaning of s.2 of the Investment Intermediaries Act, 1995.

143 s.83(6).

occurred, is occurring or is to be attempted[144] in relation to a scheme to which he is a relevant person.[145]

There is no obligation to report where the relevant person formed the belief as a result of information obtained prior to 2 July 1996.[146] Failure to comply with this requirement or knowingly or wilfully making an incorrect report is an offence which, on summary conviction, could result in a fine not exceeding £1,500, or in imprisonment for a term not exceeding one year, or both, or, on conviction on indictment, could result in a fine not exceeding £10,000, or imprisonment for up to two years, or both.[147] It is a defence for the accused person to show that the failure to report was attributable to another relevant person failing to do so and that the accused took such reasonable steps as were open to them to secure compliance by the other person.[148]

1.75 In addition to a compulsory reporting requirement, there is also a voluntary reporting procedure.[149] Any person (whether a relevant person or not) can make a report to the Pensions Board, whether in writing or otherwise, on any matter concerning the state and conduct of the scheme, whether or not a compulsory report is required. The person is protected from being sued by the client or by any other person because no duty to which the person may be subject shall be regarded as contravened and no liability or action will lie against the person in any court. For both these protections to apply, the report must be made in good faith.

1.76 To complement the whistle-blowing provisions of Part VIII, the Pensions (Amendment) Act, 1996 has given a power to the High Court, on the application of the Pensions Board, to restore any resources of a scheme that have been wrongfully paid or transferred to any person.[150] The Court must be satisfied that the wrongful payment or transfer is likely to jeopardise the rights and interests of the mem-

---

144 The Bill as originally drafted referred to "being contemplated".

145 s.83(1).

146 The date the Pensions (Amendment) Act, 1996 was passed — s.83(2).

147 s.83(3) and (4).

148 s.83(5).

149 In s.84.

150 s.39 inserting a new s.88 into the Pensions Act.

bers under the scheme. The Court may order such person, and any other person who was knowingly concerned, to take such steps as the Court may direct in order to restore the resources of the scheme to the level that they would have been if the wrongful payment or transfer had not been made. Arguably, this would require not only a restoration of resources actually transferred, but also the compensation of the scheme for the loss of any investment return that would otherwise have accrued to the scheme had the wrongful payment or transfer not been made. The scope of the provision is, however, as yet uncertain.

1.77 A misuse or misappropriation of the resources of a scheme may not yet have occurred, but the Pensions Board may suspect that it may occur in the future. To prevent such wrongdoing from arising, the High Court may (again on the application of the Pensions Board) grant an injunction against a person where the Court is satisfied that there is a reasonable likelihood that the person will commit any act that constitutes a misuse or misappropriation of any of the resources of the scheme. The Court must be satisfied, however, that the misuse or misappropriation is likely to jeopardise the rights and interests under the scheme of the members of the scheme.[151] Also, where the state and conduct of a scheme are being investigated by or on behalf of the Board, the Court can grant an injunction prohibiting any person from disposing of, selling, pledging, charging or otherwise dealing with any scheme resources, provided that the Court is satisfied that the order is desirable to ensure that the rights and interests under the scheme of the members are not jeopardised pending the outcome of the investigation.[152]

---

[151] s.90(1) of the Pensions Act as inserted by s.39 of the Pensions (Amendment) Act, 1996.

[152] s.90(3).

2

Occupational Pension Scheme Design

INTRODUCTION

2.1 Almost all private occupational pension schemes are exempt approved schemes. Once established, they will be governed by the terms of a trust and will have trustees appointed. Many public sector occupational pension schemes are established under trust as well. When an employer decides to establish a pension scheme, one of the first issues will be what benefits it wishes to provide under the scheme. This issue is generally a matter for the employer alone, although unions or other employee representatives may, in practice, be consulted. The trustees of the scheme will usually only be appointed once the scheme design has been determined. Their role is to administer the scheme in accordance with that design. The benefits are usually set out in a set of rules appended or scheduled to a trust deed.[1]

2.2 Before committing itself to setting up a pension scheme, an employer may decide in the first instance to effect life insurance cover to provide a defined death in service benefit for employees (usually expressed as a multiple of salary). A scheme of this kind is generally referred to as a group life scheme. The intention would be to introduce pension benefits at a future date. However, an employer may set up a group life scheme as the only employee benefit that it intends to provide. Assuming that a pension scheme is to be established, the employer will usually employ benefit consultants to advise on the most appropriate options. The most fundamental decision in scheme design is whether the scheme is to be defined benefit or defined contribution.

DEFINED BENEFIT AND DEFINED CONTRIBUTION SCHEMES

2.3 Defined benefit schemes and defined contribution schemes are the only two categories of pension scheme as far as the Pensions Act is concerned. It is essential to know which category a scheme falls into, in that, as can be seen from Figure 2.1, there are far more onerous

---

[1] See generally Chapter 3.

FIGURE 2.1: COMPARISON OF TRUSTEE DUTIES UNDER THE PENSIONS ACT

Pensions Act Requirement	*Cross Ref.*	*Applicable to* *Defined Benefit Scheme*	*Defined Contribution Scheme*
Fees due to the Board	s.25	Yes	Yes
Duty to register scheme	s.60	Yes	Yes
Provision of preserved benefits	ss.28, 29, 30 and 31	Yes	Yes
Non-entitlement to a refund of contributions in respect of service after 31 December 1990	s.32	Yes	Yes
Revaluation of preserved benefit	s.33	Yes	No
Member with preserved benefit entitled to a transfer payment	s.34	Yes	Yes
Bar on forfeiture of, or lien on, preserved benefit in certain circumstances	s.36	Yes	Yes
Production of an actuarial funding certificate	s.42	Yes	No
Requirement to meet the actuarial funding standard	ss.42 & 45	Yes	No
Specified statutory priorities on a winding up	s.48	Yes	No*
Actuarial valuation	s.56(1) & Regs.	Yes	No**
Provision for the Board to direct a reduction in benefits in specified circumstances	s. 50	Yes	No
Disclosure of basic information about the scheme	s. 54 & Regs.	Yes	Yes
Obligation to prepare audited accounts	s. 56(1) & Regs.	Yes	No
Disclosure of actuarial valuation report	s.56(2) & Regs.	Yes	No
Disclosure of audited accounts and auditor's report	s.56(2) & Regs.	Yes	Yes (if prepared)
Full annual report	s.55(1) & Regs.	Yes	No
Abbreviated annual report instead of full annual report	s.55(1) & Regs.	Yes (subject to size)	Yes
Appointment of Member Trustees	s.62 and Member Trustee Regs.	Yes	Yes
Compliance with equal treatment	s.66	Yes	Yes

* Priorities for defined contribution schemes are set out in the formal documents.

** Defined contribution schemes which are small self-administered may be required by the Revenue to prepare actuarial valuations.[2]

"Regs" refers to the Occupational Pension Schemes (Disclosure of Information) Regulations, 1991.

---

2 See para. 6.82.

obligations imposed on the trustees of a defined benefit scheme than on those of a defined contribution scheme. The cost of administering the former is consequently greater than that of administering the latter and this is an important factor in determining the sponsoring employer's choice of design.

2.4 Most commonly, a defined benefit scheme is a scheme that provides a pension at retirement calculated by reference to service completed to and salary at or near retirement. A typical example is a pension of 1/60th of pensionable salary for each year of service. In a defined contribution scheme, the pension will amount to whatever can be purchased from the member's individual retirement account. The retirement account is the value of employer and employee's contributions paid into the scheme and any investment return on those contributions. For example, a member's account at retirement at age 65 may amount to £90,000. This sum may be sufficient to purchase a pension by way of annuity of £10,000 per annum for life.[3]

2.5 There are, however, more precise definitions in section 2 of the Pensions Act. A defined benefit scheme is defined as a scheme that is not a defined contribution scheme. One must therefore examine the definition of defined contribution scheme to determine what is a defined benefit scheme. The Pensions Act defines such a scheme as follows:

> "defined contribution scheme" means, subject to section 27, a scheme which, under its rules, provides long service benefit, *the rate or amount of which is in total directly determined by the amount of the contributions paid by or in respect of the member*[4] and includes a scheme the contributions under which are used, directly or indirectly, to provide —
>
> (a) benefits, other than long service benefit, and
>
> (b) long service benefit the rate or amount of which is in total directly determined by the part of the contributions aforesaid that is used for the provision of the long service benefit.

---

3 This is by way of illustration assuming £9 of cash will purchase £1 of pension annuity.

4 Emphasis added.

2.6 This is a complex definition that is worth analysing in detail, particularly as a defined benefit scheme is whatever a defined contribution scheme is not. The following are the conditions that must be complied with in order for a scheme to be a defined contribution scheme:

1. The arrangement in question is a "*scheme*", which is defined to be an "*occupational pension scheme*".[5] This includes schemes approved by the Revenue under the Finance Act, 1972 and statutory schemes.[6]
2. The scheme must promise, under its rules, benefits payable on retirement ("*long service benefit*").[7]
3. The retirement benefits must be directly determined by contributions paid by the members and/or by contributions paid by the sponsoring employer in respect of the members.[8]
4. The scheme may include death benefits payable otherwise than after retirement[9] ("*benefits, other than long service benefit*"), as well as retirement benefits. This is the effect of paragraphs (a) and (b) of the definition.
5. However, the scheme may not provide such death benefits to the exclusion of retirement benefits. This is the effect of the "*and*" between paragraphs (a) and (b). A scheme that provides death in service benefits only is a defined benefit scheme.

The most important condition is no. 3. The essence of a defined contribution scheme is that the employer, and usually the scheme member, make a pre-determined series of payments into the scheme (hence "defined contribution"). The payments are usually expressed as a percentage of salary. These are invested up to retirement and the pension at retirement is whatever the member's fund at that point can buy. The pension is determined directly by the contributions and the

---

5 s.2.

6 The definition of occupational pension scheme is considered earlier — para. 1.37.

7 "Long service benefit" is a defined term in s.2.

8 The definition refers to "member" in the singular, but it must be taken to include all members of the scheme.

9 This will usually be death in service benefits in relation to which see Chapter 11.

investment return on those contributions. Examples of defined contribution and defined benefit schemes are set out in Examples 2.1 and 2.2.

2.7 A defined benefit scheme must also be an occupational pension scheme as it is defined as a *scheme* other than a defined contribution scheme, and "scheme" means "occupational pension scheme". A defined benefit scheme may also promise retirement benefits, or "long service benefits" as they are defined in the Act. If the scheme provides retirement benefits which are not directly determined by contributions made by the member and/or employer, the scheme is a defined benefit scheme. Rather than being directly determined by contributions, defined benefit schemes are usually linked to a person's salary at or near retirement and their period of service in the company or whilst in the scheme. Occasionally, the benefits under such schemes are calculated by reference to a person's service linked to a monetary amount or very rarely may be a pre-determined fixed amount.

Example 2.1

The following is an example of how a defined contribution scheme operates:

> *United Widgets has established its Widgets Pension Scheme. The employer (United Widgets) agrees to pay 5 per cent per annum of each member's salary into the scheme, provided that each member matches that contribution of 5 per cent out of their own pay. The total of 10 per cent of salary is paid into the fund on a monthly basis and each member's contribution is identified as being attributable to the member (and not to any other member) as is the employer's contribution paid in respect of the member. The fund builds up over time with investment return and all the subsequent contributions paid in monthly. At a member's retirement, the value of the fund attributable to that member is determined and a pension is secured with that amount of money.*
>
> *Michael Pidgeon is a member of the United Widgets scheme. He joined the scheme in 1976 and is retiring at age 65 in 1996. When he retires he is told that his total fund at that point is worth £140,000. This will provide a pension of approximately £15,500 for life when the cash is used to purchase an annuity.*[10]

---

10 Annuity rates change from time to time and so this is only an illustration. On annuities — see para. 10.82 et seq.

Example 2.2

The following is an example of how a defined benefit scheme operates:

Acme Manufacturing promises the following pension at normal retirement (age 65) to its employees — 1/60th of the employee's final salary for each completed year of service in the company's employment. Final salary is the average salary of an employee in the last three years before retirement.

In return the employee must pay 5 per cent of salary each year to help the employer meet the cost of providing this benefit.

Tom Thumb is an employee who retired at age 65 having completed 20 years of service. His last three years' salaries were £23,000, £21,000 and £19,000, which means that his final averaged salary is £21,000. He is entitled to 1/60th of £21,000 for each year of service (i.e. 20 years) and so his pension is 20 x 1/60 x £21,000 = £7,000.

2.8 There are some schemes (very few) that promise partly defined benefits and partly defined contribution benefits. These are known as "hybrid schemes". The liability to provide defined benefits in a scheme may form only a very small part of the overall liabilities of the scheme, the balance being defined contribution benefits. For example, one member may be promised a benefit of 2/3rds of final salary at retirement (defined benefit) and the remaining 99 members may receive pensions based solely on the value at retirement of a defined contribution of (say) 5 per cent of salary by each member and 5 per cent by the employer. Nonetheless, such a hybrid scheme is a defined benefit scheme because not all of the benefits are directly determinable by contributions made by or in respect of all of the members. Thus, the scheme must satisfy the funding standard requirements of Part IV of the Act.

2.9 An exception is, however, made under section 27(2) with respect to the calculation of preserved benefits[11] for early leavers from the pension scheme. It states that where part of the retirement benefits under a defined benefit scheme are, in fact, calculated on a defined contribution basis, the part calculated on that basis will be treated as a defined contribution scheme, and the remainder will continue to be treated as a defined benefit scheme. A reference in Part III and the

---

[11] On preservation of benefits see para. 2.34 and 2.40 and Chapter 12 below.

Second Schedule[12] to a defined contribution scheme is to be construed as including reference to that part of a hybrid scheme that is deemed to be such. Similar considerations apply to the part of a hybrid that is deemed to be a defined benefit scheme.[13] This special treatment for hybrid schemes has no wider effect than in connection with preservation.

2.10 All public sector and semi-state schemes are established as defined benefit schemes.[14] Most new private sector schemes tend to be defined contribution schemes. Employers are attracted to defined contribution schemes because of lower compliance costs and an identifiable limit on annual funding expenses. Nonetheless, some new defined benefit schemes are still being established.

2.11 There are additional costs and more onerous regulations associated with establishing and administering a defined benefit scheme than with establishing and administering a defined contribution scheme. This has discouraged some employers who would otherwise have wished to establish defined benefit schemes. Employers setting up schemes for the first time are unfettered in their decisions. Employers with existing defined benefit schemes must act with caution. A switch from defined benefit to defined contribution could constitute a breach of the employment contract and could even amount to constructive dismissal of an employee.[15]

2.12 A possible alternative for an employer is to establish a defined contribution scheme in which the employer indicates, but does not promise, that it will fund the scheme at a rate determined by an actuary in order to provide target but unguaranteed benefits, such as a pension of 2/3rds of final salary or 1/60th of final salary for each year of service. The objective is to establish a defined benefit arrangement but without the promise or guarantee. These schemes are referred to as target benefit schemes. The true target benefit scheme must make it very clear that the illustrated final benefits at retirement are not guaranteed but are based solely on the pension that can be secured

---

12 Which calculates preserved benefits.

13 s.27(3)

14 See generally Chapter 8.

15 These issues are considered further in Chapter 5.

by the then value of member and employer contributions. Otherwise the scheme will, in fact, be a defined benefit scheme.

2.13 In considering the design of a pension scheme it is tempting to focus solely on the intended benefits. There are, however, certain preliminary issues that must be addressed.

ELIGIBILITY AND CONTRIBUTIONS

2.14 The first question is to determine who is to be eligible to join the scheme. The employer may intend to open the scheme to a specific category of employee but may, unwittingly, in the documents that govern the scheme permit entry to a wider category. Eligibility conditions must be examined with extreme care.[16] One of the considerations in connection with eligibility is whether or not employees are required to join the scheme. A compulsory entry scheme (that is, a scheme that employees are required to join) reflects the terms of the employment contract. If employees are required under the terms of their employment to join the scheme, the scheme rules will reflect this fact. A difficulty may, however, arise for the trustees of the scheme where the employee is required to contribute to the scheme and refuses to sign an authorisation permitting deductions to be made from salary.

2.15 The employees may or may not be required to contribute to the scheme — that is, the scheme may be contributory or non-contributory. Non-contributory schemes are less common than contributory schemes and are rare in the case of defined contribution schemes. However, many contributory schemes have a non-contributory category, usually for senior management.

SOCIAL WELFARE INTEGRATION OR CO-ORDINATION

2.16 Another fundamental decision is whether social welfare retirement benefits are to be taken into account in determining the overall benefit structure. A scheme that takes into account social welfare entitlements is said to be "integrated" or "co-ordinated" with State benefits. The employer decides the level of overall retirement benefit

---

[16] See para. 3.29 et seq. and (in connection with sex discrimination) paras. 16.30 and 16.50 et seq.

(including social welfare pension) that is to be promised to employees — see Figure 2.2. The social welfare pension provides part of that benefit and the pension scheme meets the balance. Example 2.3 illustrates how this can work in a defined benefit scheme.

FIGURE 2.2: INTEGRATION WITH STATE SOCIAL WELFARE RETIREMENT PENSION

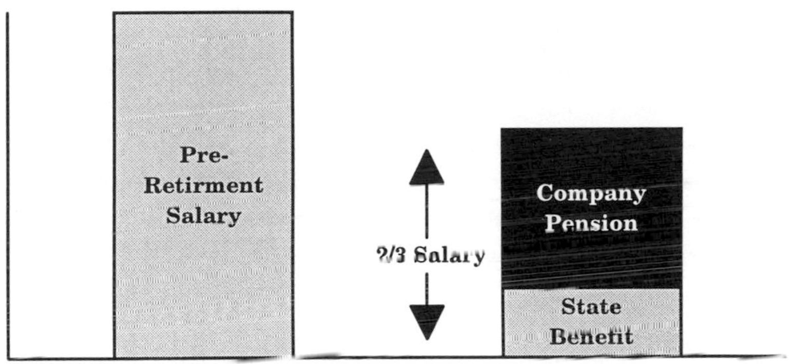

This illustration shows how the company pension and the state social welfare pension are added together to work out the target pension — in this case 2/3rds of salary. The company pension is less than 2/3rds, the state pension making up the difference. It is important to note that the higher the pre-retirement salary, the less significant is the deduction of the state social welfare pension.

Example 2.3

The most common method of off-setting or integrating the State retirement pension is to incorporate the social welfare off-set in the salary definition used to calculate pension and (usually) the member's contribution rate. This special definition of salary is normally called "pensionable salary". The typical objective is that the pension after 40 years will be 2/3rds of final salary less the State pension. This might be done by stating pensionable salary to be salary less 1.5 times the single person's State retirement pension. The following is an example:

Pension at normal retirement = *2/3rds of pensionable salary*

Pensionable Salary	=	*Salary minus 1.5 times single persons's State retirement pension.*
Single person's State retirement pension	=	*£4,000 (illustration only)*
Salary	=	*£18,000*
Pensionable Salary	=	*£18,000 – £6,000 (i.e. £4,000 x 1.5)*
	=	*£12,000*
Total pension income is as follows.		
2/3rds of pensionable salary	=	*£8,000*
State retirement pension	=	*£4,000*
Total pension	=	*£12,000*

The most common off-set is 1.5 times the State pension. Other off-sets might be 1 x State Pension or 2 x State pension. Obviously, the higher the off-set, the lower the ultimate company pension, but also the lower the member's contribution into the scheme.

BENEFIT DESIGN — DEFINED BENEFIT SCHEMES

2.17 There are many possible benefit structures for defined benefit schemes and it is important to be aware of the various options when reviewing a scheme's benefits, particularly having regard to its formal rules. Set out below are the principal types of benefits that tend to be included in defined benefit schemes. Few schemes would promise all these benefits, but all would include at least some of them in the scheme rules.

Retirement Benefits

2.18 The vast majority of defined benefit schemes (unless they are group life only schemes)[17] provide retirement benefits calculated by reference to salary at or near to retirement and to service completed to retirement.[18] As a sharp increase in salary at retirement could

---

17 That is, which only provide benefits on death in service.

18 Some schemes (usually quite old schemes) promise benefits of a set amount of money per year of service and so these schemes are not linked to salary at all — for example, £100 of pension for each year of company service. Other schemes (these would be even rarer) promise a set pension irrespective of service completed. Nonetheless, in both cases, as they guarantee a particular benefit at retirement, they are regarded as defined benefit schemes.

make a significant difference in pension, many schemes require salary (for the purposes of calculating retirement benefits) to be averaged over a period of years — for example, over the last three years to retirement. In addition, most private occupational pension schemes (and some public sector schemes) are integrated with State social welfare retirement pensions, and so the final salary is reduced to take account of the fact that the State retirement pension is payable in addition to the scheme pension.[19] The final salary to be used for the purpose of calculating pension (whether it be averaged or not, or integrated or not) is typically referred to as "Final Pensionable Salary". The service to be taken into account for calculating pension (usually called "Pensionable Service") is likely to be either service since the date of joining the company or service since becoming a member of the pension scheme.[20] There is often a gap between joining the company and joining the scheme because, for example, the employee must satisfy an age or service requirement to be eligible to join the scheme. Where this is so, the latter period of service will produce a lower pension benefit than the former.

2.19 Determining what salary and service to take into account is not in itself sufficient to calculate the pension. An accrual rate is also required. The accrual rate determines what fraction of salary (final pensionable salary) is promised as a retirement pension for each year of service (pensionable service). The pension may be said to be "earned" through service — the greater the service, the higher the pension. The most prevalent accrual rate in private occupational pension schemes is 1/60th of final pensionable salary for each year of pensionable service, with the intention that after 40 years of service the pension will be 40/60ths (or 2/3rds) of final pensionable salary. The maximum permissible pension for Revenue approved schemes is 2/3rds of final remuneration, and so pension scheme accrual rates are structured with this in mind.[21] Public sector schemes offer an accrual rate of 1/80th of final pensionable salary for each year of pensionable

---

19 See para. 2.16 above.

20 By this is meant service since becoming a member for retirement benefits. Most schemes will include employees for death in service lump sum benefits immediately on entering service, but will not include them for retirement benefits until they have satisfied eligibility conditions — for example, attaining age 25 or completing 12 months' service.

21 On Revenue limits see generally Chapter 7.

service.[22] After 40 years this would amount to 40/80ths (or half) of final pensionable salary.

2.20 It can be seen that the higher the denominator in the fraction (60, 80), the lower the overall pension. Also, the less service a member completes to normal retirement, the lower the pension. Schemes providing a better accrual rate than n/60ths are uncommon, except in certain senior management schemes. In such schemes an accrual rate of, for example, 1/45th of final pensionable salary for each year of pensionable service might be provided. The effect of a better accrual rate is that the member can earn the same pension over a shorter period than a member who is promised a pension based on a lower accrual rate. For example, the employee who is promised an n/60ths pension will only receive a pension of 2/3rds of final pensionable salary after 40 years (i.e. 40/60 = 2/3). In contrast, the employee who is given an n/45ths pension will reach the 2/3rds level after only 30 years (i.e. 30/45 = 2/3). Given the current trend towards changing jobs more frequently, it is increasingly less likely that an employee will stay in one job for as much as 40 years, and so the advantages of a better accrual rate are obvious. An even better pension promise is to be given a pension of 2/3rds of final pensionable salary irrespective of years of service completed.[23] Such a pension promise is unlikely to be seen anywhere other than at senior management level.

2.21 Defined benefit schemes promise a pension at retirement and usually provide a facility for early and late retirement. The State social welfare retirement pension is payable from age 65 and it is no coincidence that the same age is generally chosen as the normal retirement date for occupational pension schemes. However, the sponsoring employer can select an earlier or a later date as being normal retirement, but in the case of a Revenue approved scheme, the earliest permissible date is generally age 60 and the latest is age 70.[24] Early and late retirement options are often subject to employer consent.

---

22 They also give a cash gratuity which makes them as favourable overall as a 1/60th scheme.

23 This will nonetheless be subject to overall Revenue limits, usually requiring a minimum of ten years of service to be completed before 2/3rds can be granted. See para. 7.13.

24 But there are exceptions — see para. 7.9 et seq.

2.22 To determine what is early and what is late, it is necessary to identify precisely what is the "normal pensionable age" or "normal retirement date", as it is often called. "Normal pensionable age" is defined in the Pensions Act[25] and may be summarised to be the earliest age at which a member has an unqualified right to receive an immediate retirement benefit under the scheme rules, or age 60, if later. In some cases, there may be compulsory retirement prior to age 60, in which case this earlier age will be the normal pensionable age. For example, normal retirement for pilots is age 55. The member may have a right to retire at a given age (for example, age 60) but this may not be a genuine normal pensionable age. If the member can opt to retire at that age but benefits are penalised by an actuarial factor exceeding 0.25 per cent for each complete month by which the member's age at retirement falls short of a later age (for example, age 65), the later age rather than the earlier age will be regarded as normal pensionable age.[26]

2.23 Having decided upon the method of calculating pensions, the employer must then decide for how long a pension will be paid and whether it will be increased to give a measure of protection against inflation. On the former question, the employer has, in a sense, no choice. The Revenue require that pensions must be payable for life.[27] But the employer can provide a guarantee that the pension will be paid for at least a minimum period so that if the member dies before the period expires, the pension will continue to be paid for the balance of the period.[28] The most common guaranteed period is five years, but the Revenue will permit anything up to a 10 year guarantee.[29] As for pension increases, some schemes guarantee pension increases to pensioners, but this can be expensive for a scheme to fund and an alternative is for the employer to grant discretionary increases from time to time, but to reserve the right to discontinue the increases at any time. There is as yet no legislative requirement to increase pensions.[30]

---

25 s.2(1).

26 s.2(1) definition of "early retirement rule" inserted by s.42(b) of the Social Welfare Act, 1993 and amended by s.2(b) of the Pensions (Amendment) Act, 1996.

27 With the exception of certain dependants' pensions — see para. 2.26 below.

28 The guarantee originates from annuity contracts issued by life offices.

29 See para. 7.46 and 7.47.

30 Unlike in the UK where limited price indexation has been introduced in respect of pensions.

Commutation

2.24 Private occupational pension schemes almost always give members the right, within limits imposed by the Revenue,[31] to exchange part of their pension for a tax-free lump sum. This is referred to as "commutation". The usual cash entitlement is 3/80ths of final pensionable salary for each year of service. After 40 years, this would amount to 120/80ths, or 1.5 times final pensionable salary. If a member exercises the option to exchange pension for cash, the pension is reduced actuarially. Public sector and semi-state schemes established in accordance with the model rules do not provide for a commutation option. Instead, they provide a separate tax-free gratuity of up to 1.5 times final pensionable salary after 40 years service. In effect, public sector schemes deem the commutation option to be exercised, and automatically reduce members' pensions, which is why the accrual rate for public sector pension is n/80ths rather than n/60ths.

Death in Retirement Pensions

2.25 The pension being paid to a pensioner ceases on the pensioner's death, except where it has been guaranteed for a period of years, in which case it will continue to be paid until the expiry of the guarantee (or will be converted into a lump sum equivalent and paid in that form). Unless the pension scheme provides additional benefits on the death of a member in retirement, all benefits will cease at that point. This would potentially cause serious hardship to a widowed spouse who would have no income from the pension scheme and would have to rely upon the State survivor's contributory pension or the widow's non-contributory pension. Accordingly, most defined benefit schemes provide an additional benefit in these circumstances, referred to as a spouse's death in retirement pension.[32] This is generally expressed as a percentage of the member's pension — for example, 50 % of the member's pension. The assumption is made that the widowed spouse needs less income than the member and spouse needed before the member's death, and consequently the spouse's pension will be lower

---

[31] Up to 1.5 times final remuneration after 20 years. A sliding scale applies for lesser periods. See generally para. 7.14 et seq.

[32] Older schemes may refer to this as a widow's pension but discrimination against widowers is now no longer permitted — see Chapter 16.

than the member's former pension.[33] A scheme is not restricted to providing a spouse's pension. The Revenue will permit a pension to be paid to any dependant of the member.[34] Accordingly, some schemes provide a dependant's pension, with discretion for the trustees as to which dependant or combination of dependants should receive the pension. An alternative approach, and one that recognises the problems of marital breakdown, is to provide a spouse's pension but include a discretion on the part of the trustees to pay the spouse's pension to another dependant in circumstances of separation.[35]

2.26 Some schemes specifically address the issue of pensions for children. A scheme may promise children's pensions on the death of the member, in addition to, and paid concurrently with, a spouse's pension. Children in this case means minor children (under 18) or those over 18 but under a specified age (usually 21) and, in the latter case, in receipt of full-time education or vocational training. Pensions cease when the child ceases to fall within this age limit. Again, the children's pensions are usually expressed as a percentage of the member's pension or of the spouse's pension. For example, the scheme may pay 25 per cent of the member's pension equally to all children. Another common method is to provide 10 per cent of the member's pension for the first child and 5 per cent each for the next three children (in order of succession). Children's pensions will usually be paid to the surviving parent or other guardian.

2.27 A further issue arises on the death of a spouse who was receiving a spouse's death in retirement pension. If the spouse's pension ceases when the spouse dies, what benefits do the children receive? There may be children's pensions already in payment and these will continue to be paid. Sometimes the scheme rules will state that the children's pensions are doubled if the spouse dies. Other schemes, particularly those that do not promise children's pensions, nonetheless may make provision for the children by way of an orphan's pension. An orphan's pension arises on the death of the spouse and involves the continued payment of the spouse's pension for the benefit

---

33 The Revenue, in any event, restricts any one dependant's pension to 2/3rds of the member's maximum pension in connection with exempt approved schemes — see para. 7.39.

34 See para. 7.38.

35 This issue is considered in more detail in Chapter 15.

of the children, as if the spouse had never died.[36] Payment continues until the dependence of the children is deemed under the provisions of the scheme to have ceased.

2.28 As with the member's pension, a spouse's pension, dependant's pension or children's pension can be increased either on a discretionary basis or as a matter of right under the rules.

Death in Service Benefits

2.29 There are two types of death in service benefit that can be provided under a defined benefit scheme. One is a lump sum benefit and the other a dependant's pension. The lump sum benefit will be a multiple of the member's salary before death, or a part of the fund, or a combination of both. The multiple of salary is almost always a death benefit, which is insured with a life office.[37] This might, for example, be a benefit of three times salary or six times salary. The part of the fund that can be paid out on death could be one of the following:

1. A refund of contributions paid by the member (if any) without interest
2. A refund of the member's contributions (if any) with a specified rate of interest
3. The actuarial value of the member's benefit at death.

The payment from the fund may be in addition to the insured lump sum or may be the only benefit payable. Schemes typically offer a lump sum plus a refund of contributions without interest — for example, three times salary plus a refund of contributions. If the scheme is non-contributory, there can be no refund of member contributions as none were paid in the first place.

2.30 The lump sum benefit is generally paid out under a discretionary trust, although in some schemes the trustees have no discretion but

---

[36] A variant is to pay the spouse's pension to the children where the spouse has predeceased the member and the member subsequently dies. In such a case, there is no spouse living on the death of the member and so, but for this feature, no further pension would be paid to the children.

[37] See para. 11.6 et seq. If a scheme is sufficiently large it may be able to bear the risk of a death claim without insuring it.

must pay it to the deceased member's estate, or perhaps the spouse. If the trustees are given a discretion, they are usually empowered to pay the lump sum to one or more of a wide class of beneficiaries, including the spouse, children, dependants and other relatives. The member may also be given the opportunity of completing a letter of wishes or nomination form, indicating who should receive the benefit on the member's death. The nomination form is almost always expressed to be non-binding on the trustees. This means that the trustees can override the member's wishes if they believe that circumstances merit it. In very rare cases a member may die leaving no relative or dependant of any description. To avoid a situation where the trustees would be obliged to pay a benefit to the State as bona vacantia (under the Succession Act, 1965) the rules of the scheme may provide that no benefit will become payable in such a case.

2.31 The maximum benefit that the Revenue will permit to be paid in lump sum form under an exempt approved scheme is four times final remuneration[38] plus a refund of contributions with interest.[39] If a scheme promises a greater lump sum (for example, six times final remuneration) the balance above four times must be used to provide pensions (rather than a lump sum) for dependants of the member, such as a spouse or children.

2.32 A scheme may also provide a spouse's or dependant's pension on death in service of the member, and possibly children's pensions. As with the lump sum benefit, these pensions are normally insured with a life office, so that, on death, the pension is met by the insurance policy rather than the pension fund. Similar comments apply to death in service pensions as they do to the death in retirement pensions already described above, but there is one key difference. Spouses' (or other dependants') and children's pensions payable on death in retirement are calculated by reference to a member's pension that has already commenced to be paid. On death in service, the member has died before retirement — that is before starting to receive the pension. Accordingly, death in service pensions are usually calculated as a percentage of the expected pension the member would have received at retirement had the member lived that long, but assuming that the salary stayed the same as it was at death. Therefore, instead of having

---

38 See para. 7.36.

39 See para. 7.37.

a spouse's pension of (say) 50 per cent of the member's pension, the death in service equivalent is 50 per cent of the pension the member would have received at retirement.[40]

2.33 An important factor with all insured death benefits is that the death benefit promised under the rules is capable of being insured by a life office at a reasonable rate. If the rules promise a benefit but insurance either cannot be obtained or can only be effected at a prohibitive premium, the trustees of the scheme may be forced to take on the risk without insurance. Careful drafting is therefore required in the rules with regard to these benefits.

Leaving Service Benefits

2.34 The two principal benefits that can be provided on leaving service are a refund of member contributions and a deferred pension. The refund is self-explanatory but obviously only applies where the scheme is contributory. Refunds are currently taxed at 25 per cent.[41] A deferred pension is a pension promised at a future date — that is, the pension is deferred until actual retirement. It is deferred because the member is leaving service without receiving an immediate pension. The Pensions Act has had a profound effect on the benefits that must be provided in the event of a member leaving service before retirement and not receiving an early-retirement pension. Before the Act, schemes were under no obligation to provide any benefits when a member left service. If it was a contributory scheme, the member would receive either a refund of member contributions or a deferred pension secured by those contributions. If the member left service because of redundancy, a more generous pension might be payable, but that differed from scheme to scheme.

2.35 The Pensions Act made four major changes to this leaving service régime.[42] First, members can now choose to take a refund of contributions only in certain limited circumstances. The reason for this is to promote bona fide retirement provision. Secondly, a minimum deferred pension must be payable regardless of what the scheme rules provide. Thirdly, the minimum deferred pension must

---

40 Spouse's death in service pensions are considered further at para. 11.10 et seq.

41 See para. 7.52 et seq.

42 These are all considered in detail in Chapter 12.

be revalued (increased) during the period from leaving service until normal retirement to give a measure of protection against inflation. Finally, the Act introduced an entitlement of members to transfer their benefits to the scheme of a new employer or to a buy-out bond, thus providing for portability of pensions.

BENEFIT DESIGN — DEFINED CONTRIBUTION SCHEMES

2.36 The design of benefits under a defined contribution scheme is somewhat simpler than a defined benefit scheme in that it is primarily based upon member choice. The sophisticated benefits payable under defined benefit schemes are nonetheless still relevant to a defined contribution scheme in that, within limits, the member can choose the types of benefit that could be provided under a defined benefit scheme.

Retirement and Death in Retirement Benefits

2.37 Defined contribution schemes, unlike defined benefit schemes, do not guarantee the level of pension a member will receive on retirement. On the contrary, the member's pension is determined solely by the contributions paid into the scheme by the employer, in respect of the member, and by the member (assuming that the member contributes) and by the investment return on those contributions over the period of investment to retirement. At retirement, the member is usually given a choice of benefits which can be secured with the value of the fund. This will include a pension for the member as well as pensions for the spouse, children and other dependants on the member's death, and provision for increases on all or any of these pensions. The value of the member's fund may be sufficient to provide only some of these benefits. The benefits that can be bought with the fund are similar to those described above with regard to defined benefit schemes, but the level of benefit is not guaranteed.

Commutation

2.38 Commutation rights under a defined contribution scheme are similar to those under a defined benefit scheme. Cash payments are paid out first and the balance (if any) is used to secure pension benefits.

Death in Service Benefits

2.39 As with defined benefit schemes, there are two possible death in service benefits: a lump sum and a spouse's pension. The possibilities with regard to the lump sum benefit are similar to defined benefit schemes in that an insured multiple of salary can be provided, or a part or the whole of the fund attributable to the member will be paid, or a combination of both. The spouse's pension is calculated on a different basis. In a defined contribution scheme it is not possible to calculate in advance the member's expected pension because there is no formula linked to salary and service that can be employed. Accordingly, spouses' pensions are normally calculated on the basis of a fraction or percentage of a member's salary — for example, 4/9ths of salary.

Leaving Service Benefits

2.40 As with a defined benefit scheme, the benefits on leaving service under a defined contribution scheme will be a deferred pension or a refund of contributions, or possibly a combination of both. The Pensions Act has had a similar impact on defined contribution schemes, although it is easier to administer the Pensions Act compliance requirements in defined contribution schemes. It is important to note, however, that there is no revaluation requirement for deferred pensions. It is unnecessary as the member's fund receives the benefit of any investment return between leaving service and retirement which should, in itself, give a measure of protection against inflation.

3

TRUST CONSTITUTION

INTRODUCTION

3.1 The benefit design of an occupational pension scheme can be a complex matter, as can be seen from the previous chapter. It is desirable that the benefit structure be clearly set out in detailed and unambiguous formal rules. In order to communicate the benefit details to employees an explanatory booklet or announcement is essential. This chapter considers the essential terms that need to be included in the formal scheme documents. It also examines the legal issues that arise concerning pension scheme explanatory literature. The chapter also considers how the provisions of the trust deed may be amended, and circumstances in which schemes are established by interim trust deed. Pension schemes are established in an employment context and so the impact of the employment contract is also explored. First, however, it is proposed to look at the various ways in which an occupational pension scheme can be established.

FORMAL ESTABLISHMENT

3.2 The vast majority of occupational pension schemes in Ireland are established under trust and in written form. A pension arrangement does not, however, have to be in written form nor constituted under a trust. There are a number of reasons why an employer would wish to establish the pension arrangement under trust:

1. In a trust the pension assets are legally separate from those of the employer — this gives greater security to members. The pension assets do not form part of the employer's assets.

2. The employer, the members and other beneficiaries have independent rights of action against the trustees of the scheme.

3. A pension scheme established under trust enjoys specific tax benefits if it is exempt approved by the Revenue Commissioners.[1]

An occupational pension scheme can be established in any of the following ways:

1. Trust Deed and Rules
2. Declaration of Trust and Rules
3. Letter of Exchange and Rules
4. Contract of Employment.

3.3 Multi-member occupational pension schemes are most frequently established by trust deed. A pension arrangement established for a single employee may be effected by means of a declaration of trust or a simple letter of exchange to which rules are attached. The latter method is often adopted by life offices to establish single-member schemes. In each case, provided that the documentation complies with Revenue requirements, such arrangements will qualify for exempt approval. It is unusual for pension arrangements to be established solely by way of a contract of employment. Such an arrangement would not be capable of receiving Revenue exempt approval as it is not established under trust. Further, a pension arrangement is intended to operate over a long period of time and must allow for changing circumstances. For example, an employee may be unmarried when he joins a scheme and in the course of employment he may marry and have children. He may leave employment. The contract of employment lacks flexibility and is not the appropriate vehicle within which to draft pension arrangements. It is recognised, however, that pension arrangements are a part of the contractual arrangements between an employer and its employees.[2]

3.4 In practice, the formal documentation of a pension scheme which is established under trust usually consists of a trust deed and rules. The reason for the division between trust deed and rules appears to originate in the practice of life offices in establishing pension schemes. A very simple form of trust document was used and to this was scheduled a detailed set of rules. The rules dealt with the actual benefit structure and set out detailed provisions with respect to these

---

1 As to the Revenue requirements for exempt approval, see Chapter 6.

2 See para. 3.58 below and also Chapter 5.

benefits. This division between trust deed and rules has been retained as a matter of practice. However, there is no legal requirement to divide the formal provisions of the pension scheme in this manner.

CONTENTS OF TRUST DEED

3.5 It is neither possible nor practical to attempt to list exhaustively the contents of a declaration of trust or trust deed. There are, however, certain provisions which must be contained in the trust deed, the absence of which will leave the pension arrangement seriously flawed. Further, the Revenue require certain matters to be included in the Trust Deed if it is to qualify for exempt approval.[3] It is important that all of the provisions of the pension scheme established under trust are set out clearly and precisely in the formal documentation. Under trust law three things are required to establish a trust:

1. Certainty of words
2. Certainty of subject matter
3. Certainty of objects.

The absence of any of the above may cause a trust to fail for lack of certainty.[4] "Certainty of words" requires that the words used to create a trust are imperative — there must be a clear intention to create a trust. "Certainty of subject matter" means that the subject matter of the trust must be defined clearly — in a pension scheme trust this would refer to the fund and the benefits to be paid. "Certainty of objects" requires that the beneficiaries of the trust must be ascertainable.[5] If the rules of a pension scheme are so uncertain that the purpose for which the scheme is established is unclear, such a scheme may fail for lack of certainty. In practice, pension schemes are established by written documentation which will state clearly the principal

---

3 See the Revenue Practice Notes.

4 It is quite possible that in such circumstances, it could be argued that even though the trust itself has failed, the members have rights as against the employer under their contract of employment. See para. 3.58 below and Chapter 5. If the scheme is contributory, a resulting trust may arise in favour of the members with respect to their contributions.

5 A detailed discussion of the technical requirements to establish a trust is outside the scope of this work; see Delany, H. (1996): *Equity and the Law of Trusts in Ireland,* Dublin: Round Hall Sweet & Maxwell.

purpose for which they are established, so this should not present difficulties. Set out in the following paragraphs are those matters that either must or should be dealt with in the formal trust documentation. It may happen that the pension scheme is established by interim trust deed to be followed by a definitive trust deed and rules which will set out in detail the precise terms of the trust and the structure of the pension scheme. The issue of establishment of a pension scheme by interim deed is discussed later.[6] In the following paragraphs, particular reference is made to those provisions that should be included if an interim trust deed is used.

Parties

3.6 The trust document will need to state the parties to the arrangement. These will be the employer establishing the scheme and the trustees. It was common in the case of small schemes for the employer to appoint itself as sole trustee. Whilst the assets will be legally separate if the employer is trustee, this does not afford the members the same level of security as where there are separate trustees.

Establishment and Purpose

3.7 The trust document must state in clear language that an irrevocable trust is established, and the purpose for which it is established. The main purpose will be to provide relevant benefits in accordance with the provisions of the Finance Act, 1972 (as amended) being payable to or in respect of employees of the employer.[7] If an interim deed is adopted for establishment of the scheme, it may be advisable to include in the relevant clause reference to benefits being in accordance with the announcement or explanatory booklet issued to members.[8] The reason for this is that the interim deed itself will contain little or no detail with respect to

---

6 See para. 3.39.

7 The relevant clause will usually also provide that benefits may be paid in respect of employees of any associated employer within the meaning of the trust documentation and as permitted by Revenue practice. See para. 6.6.

8 In the UK it is a frequent practice to append to the Interim Trust Deed the announcement leaflet issued by the employer.

the benefits. Therefore the trustees should be able to refer to the announcement for guidance.[9]

Appointment and Removal of Trustees

3.8 The trust document must provide for the appointment of the first and subsequent trustees.[10] The clause dealing with trustees should state clearly that the first trustees are appointed, and make provision for removal of such trustees and resignation of trustees by notice. Provisions allowing trustees to resign may be implied into the trust deed depending on its construction.[11] It is recommended, however, that a specific right to resign on notice be included. The deed should also provide for vesting of the trust property in the trustees.

Duties and Responsibilities of Trustees

3.9 Details of the duties and responsibilities of the trustees should be set out in the formal trust documentation. In the absence of these provisions, trust law will impose specific duties and responsibilities on the trustees.[12] Although not a legal requirement, it is, however, good practice to include them in the trust deed. The relevant provisions, whether contained in an interim trust deed or a definitive trust deed, should require the trustees to collect and safeguard the assets constituting the fund of the scheme. The deed should give powers to the trustees to invest those assets and for that purpose to appoint an investment manager or managers, to appoint custodians of the fund, to appoint other advisors, and to permit the trustees to rely on such advice as may be received. The trust documentation will need to differentiate between those powers of the trustees that are mandatory and those that are discretionary. The documentation should also identify those decisions that require the consent of the employer, such as augmentation of benefits or disposal of surplus.[13]

---

9 See para. 3.48.

10 Regarding appointment and removal of trustees generally, see Chapter 4.

11 See *Davis* v. *Richards & Wallington Industries Limited* [1990] 1 WLR 1511. It had been thought, prior to this case, that in the absence of a clause allowing a trustee to resign, an application to Court under the Trustee Acts (UK) would be necessary.

12 Regarding duties and responsibilities of trustees imposed by trust law, see para. 4.27 et seq.

13 The duties and responsibilities of trustees and the balance of power between trustees and the employer are discussed in detail in Chapter 4.

Powers of Amendment

3.10 It is important that the trust document should contain a specific power allowing the provisions of the trust deed and rules to be amended. No matter how comprehensive are the trust deed and rules, all the circumstances in which the pension scheme will operate cannot be foreseen at the time of drafting. Further, by its very nature, a pension arrangement must be flexible and capable of change. Specific powers of amendment are therefore required.[14] It is established that, in the absence of an express power of amendment, neither the employer nor the trustees will have power to amend the provisions of the scheme.[15] The clause providing for amendment should state that amendments may be made with retrospective effect. In the absence of such provision, it is arguable that amendments may only be made prospectively.

3.11 ***Power of Amendment may operate retrospectively***. It is clear that, whether or not a retrospective amendment may be made to the provisions of a pension scheme trust is dependent upon the true construction of the power of amendment in the trust document. An interesting discussion on this point is to be found in the Australian case *Gra-ham Australia Pty Ltd* v. *Perpetual Trustees Ltd.*[16] That case did not concern a pension scheme trust but a unit trust in which the Plaintiff held investments. The defendant was the trustee. The trust deed provided that the unit holders could redeem units by requesting the manager to repurchase all or any of their units. The price paid for a unit was calculated on the value of the unit as at the date at least seven days before the request was made rather than the current

---

14 For an example of the difficulties created by an inadequate amendment clause see the case of *Re Alfred Herbert, Limited Pension and Life Assurance Scheme's Trust* [1960] 1 WLR 271.

15 *Re Miller* [1897] 1 IR 290 and *Re Johnson's Settlement* [1944] IR 529 both of which cases concerned private trusts, one being of money and the other of property. A more recent case covering a pension scheme is *Re Reevie and Montreal Trust Co. of Canada* (1984) 46 OR(2d)667. That part of the judgment in *Re Reevie* relating to powers of amendment has been approved by the Supreme Court of Canada in the case *Air Products Canada* v. *Schmidt* [1995] PLR 75. Under trust law, a trust may be terminated with the consent of all the beneficiaries entitled to the trust property (the rule in *Saunders* v. *Vautier* (1841) Cr & Ph 240). However, in all but the smallest pension schemes this would present practical difficulties.

16 [1992] PLR 193

value of the unit. The fall in world equities on Black Monday in October 1987 resulted in a significant fall in the value of the investments in the fund. A large number of unit holders requested the manager of the fund to repurchase the units held by them. Because of the valuation provisions in the trust document, if the manager had complied with the request, the interests of those unit holders remaining in the fund would have been significantly prejudiced. The manager proposed an amendment to the trust deed relating to the manner in which units were valued. The trustee, concerned that the amendment might adversely affect the unit holders, required that the amendment be approved by an ordinary resolution of the unit holders in accordance with the amendment clause in the trust deed. The appropriate ordinary resolution was duly passed. The unit holders who had previously served notice on the manager requesting the purchase of their units objected to the amendment and it fell to the court to determine, among other things, whether the exercise of the power of amendment in the trust deed was correct. At the first hearing, the Judge declared that the deed executed in accordance with the resolution was valid and binding on all unit holders. The plaintiff appealed to the Supreme Court of Western Australia. In dismissing the appeal, Malcolm C.J. stated:

> In my opinion, Kennedy J was clearly correct both in his conclusion and the reasons for it. As a matter of construction, the provisions of the trust deed gave to the requisite majority of the unit holders the power to amend the trust deed, subject to the execution of an amending deed in the manner followed in relation to the second supplemental deed. Power extended to enable amendments to be made to enable the vested or accrued rights of a unit holder to be defeated by an amendment duly made, even where the amendment only applied to a unit holder because the unit holder remains such by reason of a breach of contract by the Manager.[17]

3.12 ***Power of Amendment — Pension Fund closed or in wind-up.*** Powers of alteration were also considered in the case of *Re Edward Jones Benevolent Fund.*[18] That case concerned a non-contributory pension fund constituted by a deed and rules. The

---

[17] The breach of contract referred to is the fact that the manager had not complied with the request for repurchase of the units.

[18] (Unreported, UK High Court, 8 March 1985). See transcript of judgement reproduced in Inglis-Jones, N. (1989): *The Law of Occupational Pension Schemes*, London: Sweet & Maxwell.

Court determined that powers of alteration in a pension trust deed, on their construction, continued to be effective following closure of the fund. Pursuant to the rules of the scheme, the sponsoring employer gave notice in writing terminating its liability to pay contributions. On the effective date of such notice the fund was carried on as a closed fund[19] pursuant to the Rules. The court found it necessary to determine, among other things, whether the power of alteration and amendment in the rules survived closure of the fund. In determining that it did so survive, the Court stated:

> I can see no reason why the power to alter — limited, as it is, by certain safeguards — should cease to exist merely because the company has determined its contributions and the Trustees have decided . . . to continue the fund on a closed basis. The proviso to rule 27 explains what is meant by continuing the fund on a closed basis. It means that no further benefits will accrue after the date of the termination of contributions and that liability to provide benefits to pensioners and other former members of the fund existing at the date of termination is preserved in and retained by the fund. . . . The proviso has the effect of stopping the clock but it does not have the effect of excluding powers to augment benefits, and there is no reason why it should have the effect of excluding powers to augment benefits and there is no reason why it should have the effect of excluding powers of alteration. Indeed, as it appears to me, it is in just the circumstances that the fund is being operated as a closed fund that powers of augmentation and alteration are most likely to be required.

3.13 In *Re Edward Jones* reference was made to the case of *Goodblatt and Ors* v. *John and Ors*[20] in which case the Court had to deal with a pension scheme which was in the course of winding up. The Court in *Goodblatt* took the view, based on the terms of the scheme before it, that the powers, trusts and provisions including the power of alteration of the rules, had come to an end at the commencement of winding up. Again the decision was arrived at on the basis of construction of the provisions of the trust deed. The decision in *Re Edward Jones* appears quite sensible in the context of a scheme which, although

---

19 A closed fund is one that is no longer open to new members. The membership is "closed". Existing members may still make contributions to the fund if the rules permit.

20 (Unreported, High Court, 22 May 1973, Foster, J.).

closed, was to continue for the benefit of the then existing members. The position of a scheme that is in winding-up is more difficult.[21]

3.14 ***Limitations on Power of Amendment.*** The power of amendment in the formal trust document is often limited to prevent any amendment that would prejudice Revenue approval of the scheme. Often there is also a restriction which prevents amendments that may prejudice benefits that have already accrued to members of the scheme (without their express consent). This is a very restrictive amendment power and the practical difficulties of obtaining member consent render it unlikely that any benefit reduction could be effected.

3.15 It is advisable to include in the amendment power, in the case of a defined benefit scheme, a provision that the trustees shall have the power to make such amendments, including amendments that would reduce benefits accrued to members, as the Pensions Board may direct in the context of a funding proposal.[22] However, in the absence of such a provision, a direction issued by the Pensions Board to the trustees would nonetheless be effective notwithstanding any restriction in the trust or rules.[23]

3.16 It is not certain whether a power of amendment in a trust deed may itself be amended. The accepted view appears to be that it may not be amended in the absence of very clear language in the trust deed permitting such amendment. There is, however, no direct case on this point, rather the matter rests on general trust principles.[24]

3.17 The Courts in England and certain Commonwealth jurisdictions have shown themselves willing to impose restrictions on the exercise by an employer of the power of amendment. This has happened in circumstances where it appeared that the purported exercise

---

21 See para. 17.22 and also *Jones* v. *Williams* [1989] PLR 17, *Thrells Ltd (1974) Pension Scheme (In Liquidation)* v. *Lomas* [1992] PLR 234.

22 The issues of funding of pension schemes and requirements imposed on trustees by the Pensions Act are considered in Chapter 9. On funding proposals see para. 9.51 et seq.

23 Pursuant to s.53 of the Pensions Act.

24 See "British Pension Lawyer" (No. 51, July 1993 at p.1 et seq.).

of the power by the employer was for a purpose other than that for which the power was granted.[25]

Agreement to Execute the Definitive Deed

3.18 If an interim trust deed is used to establish a pension scheme, it should contain a specific undertaking on the part of the employer and the trustees to execute a definitive trust deed within a specified period of time, usually 24 months. Such a clause is a requirement of the Revenue Commissioners. It is, in any event, logical, as a definitive deed is required in order that the scheme will be properly documented. Such an undertaking may be actionable by the trustees or the members in the event that it is breached by the employer.[26]

Trustee Exclusion of Liability and Indemnity

3.19 The formal trust documentation will usually contain provisions, firstly, excluding liability of the trustees except in limited circumstances and, secondly, setting out specific indemnities in favour of the trustees.[27] The terms of such provisions may vary considerably. Some deeds contain clauses excluding all liability except such as results from fraud. Others may have more limited exclusion clauses. The indemnity clauses will also vary.

Investment

3.20 The Trust Deed should provide the trustees with full investment powers with respect to the funds of the pension scheme. These powers should be drafted as widely as possible. In the absence of such

---

[25] See *British Coal Corporation* v. *British Coal Staff Superannuation Scheme Trustees Ltd* [1993] PLR 303; and see also *Re Vauxhall Motor Pension Fund* [1989] 1 PLR 31, *Lock* v. *Westpac Banking Corporation* [1991] PLR 167, *Imperial Group Pension Trust Limited* v. *Imperial Tobacco Limited* [1991] 1 WLR 589, *U.E.B. Industries Limited* v. *W.S. Brabant* [1991] PLR 109, and the more recent cases of *Lloyds Bank Pension Trust Corporation Limited* v. *Lloyds Bank plc* [1996] PLR 263 and *Hillsdown Holdings plc* v. *The Pensions Ombudsman* (*Financial Times Weekend* 13/14 July 1996), both of which cases concerned trustee powers of amendment and restrictions on exercise of same; see also para. 5.26 et seq.

[26] See *Davis* v. *Richards & Wallington Industries Limited* [1990] 1WLR 1511 discussed at para. 3.43.

[27] See the discussion of this matter at para. 4.88 et seq.

provision, the power of the trustees to invest will be restricted by statute.[28]

Delegation by Trustees

3.21 There should be specific provisions allowing the trustees to delegate certain of their duties to third parties. Examples are the duty to invest the assets of the fund, the duty to maintain records of the scheme, its administration, and the entitlements of individual members. The office of a trustee is a personal one. In the absence of specific powers of delegation, the trustees would not have power to delegate and any purported delegation would be a breach of trust.[29] It should be noted that trustees remain responsible for the acts of their delegates.

Augmentation

3.22 The deed should provide that any benefits payable under the scheme may be augmented subject to Revenue limits not being exceeded. Augmentation refers to an increase in benefits beyond the strict entitlement under the trust deed. Such power of augmentation may be exercisable at the discretion of the trustees with the consent of the principal employer or by the principal employer with the agreement of the trustees and subject to any additional contributions being made by the employer to the fund. Sometimes the power of augmentation is conferred on either the trustees or the employer alone.

Trustee Procedures

3.23 It is important that the formal trust documentation sets out the manner in which trustees may conduct their business. This is not a legal requirement, but is good practice. Provision should be made for meetings, conduct of such meetings, including quorum and voting at meetings. It is usual that trustees of a pension scheme may have "interests" in the scheme as beneficiaries (if they are members) or they may be members of management. Trade union officials and professional trustees may also have "interests" in the scheme. The formal trust documentation should contain a provision allowing the trustees

---

28 See para. 4.42 and Chapter 10 on Investment.

29 *Re O'Flanagan & Ryans Contract* [1905] 1 IR 280.

to participate in meetings and join in making decisions notwithstanding a conflict of interest.[30]

Associated Employers

3.24 A facility should be included to allow an associated employer to participate in the pension arrangement. This is a useful provision particularly where there is a group of companies associated with the sponsoring employer. This will usually involve the associated employer entering into a deed of adherence to which the principal employer and the trustees are also parties. Under this deed the adhering company covenants to observe the terms of the trust documentation. Such adherence will be subject to the approval requirements of the Revenue Commissioners.[31]

Winding up

3.25 The trust documentation should provide for the circumstances in which the pension scheme may be wound up. If the pension arrangement is established, initially, by means of an interim trust deed, it is important that the interim deed contain winding-up provisions. In the absence of such provisions and if the principal employer went into liquidation, the trustees would be faced with a difficult situation and it might prove necessary to make application to the High Court for directions as to how the scheme should be wound-up.[32] The trust documentation should also provide for a situation where any associated employer discontinues participation in the scheme. This is often referred to as "partial winding up".

Distribution on Winding-up

3.26 The trust documentation should also set out how the assets of the pension scheme will be distributed by the trustees when the scheme is wound up. The Pensions Act contains specific provisions in relation to the winding-up of defined benefit schemes but not defined contribution schemes.[33] If a scheme is being wound up and only an interim deed has been executed, and the principal employer is not

---

[30] See detailed discussion on trustees' conflicts of interest at para. 4.29 et seq.

[31] See para. 6.22 et seq.

[32] See Chapter 17 for a detailed discussion of winding-up.

[33] s.48 Pensions Act.

itself in liquidation, the Revenue Commissioners will require that a definitive deed is executed prior to completion of the winding-up.

Perpetuity Period

3.27 Pension scheme trusts, in common with other trusts, were subject to the rule against perpetuities.[34] For this reason, all trust deeds establishing pension schemes included a perpetuity period.[35] However, the Pensions Act now excludes approved pension schemes (and schemes capable of receiving such approval) from the application of the rule.[36]

THE RULES

3.28 There is no absolute position as to the matters to be included in the rules rather than in the definitive deed. To an extent, this is a matter to be decided by the employer and the trustees. However, it is usual that the deed will deal with the administration of the trust, and the rules set out the specific provisions in relation to the pension scheme as they affect the members. The rules will usually provide for the matters set out in the following paragraphs.

Eligibility

3.29 The rules should state clearly who is eligible to join the pension scheme. Some schemes cross-refer in the definitive documents to the explanatory booklet in relation to eligibility requirements. This is undesirable as it blurs the distinction between the formal scheme documentation and the explanatory literature issued to

---

[34] In *Re Thomas Meadows & Co. Ltd.* [1970] 3 WLR 524.

[35] The modern rule against perpetuities prescribes limits on a donor's or grantor's power to postpone the "vesting" of the ownership of their property in the future. The rule requires that any future interest in property, whether real or personal, must vest within the perpetuity period. The perpetuity period has been settled by the courts as a life or lives in being plus a further period of 21 years. The rule applies to any kind of property, whether real or personal, legal or equitable. Modern occupational pension schemes, which make provision for payment of benefits in many different circumstances and upon contingencies that may never happen, could, but for the exemption in the Pensions Act, fall foul of the rule against perpetuities.

[36] s.61A as inserted in the Pensions Act by s.25 of the Pensions (Amendment) Act, 1996.

members by the employer. The formal documentation is intended to be binding, the explanatory literature is for assistance in comprehension but is not intended to be binding. It is quite usual that not all employees of an employer will be eligible to join the scheme. The employer may want to restrict entry to the scheme and will do so by introducing eligibility conditions in the formal rules and the booklet. There are many different types of eligibility conditions that can be imposed. For example, there may be a minimum period of service which must be completed prior to a person becoming eligible. It is also usual to provide maximum and minimum ages at which a person may join. An employer may establish a scheme for a particular group of employees only — for example, office employees but not works employees.

3.30 The rules should also provide a discretion to the employer to determine that other employees, not falling within the strict eligibility requirements, may also be admitted to the scheme. It is inevitable that there will be some individual cases where it is appropriate for a person to be allowed to join the scheme although they do not fall within the eligibility requirements. Some schemes provide that employees will only be eligible to join at the discretion of the employer. Schemes may also provide that employees may be eligible to join for certain benefits only — for instance, death in service benefits.

3.31 Under Irish law, an employer may require that its employees, if they meet the eligibility requirements of a pension scheme, join the scheme.[37] In many schemes membership is only open to full-time employees. The exclusion of part-time employees is a practice that requires careful consideration.[38]

Contributions

3.32 Schemes may be contributory or non-contributory. That is, the members of the scheme may or may not be required to contribute a percentage of their earnings towards provision of the pension bene-

---

[37] This requirement is not permitted under English law pursuant to s.160 Pension Schemes Act, 1993. Furthermore, under English law a member is entitled at any time to opt out of a pension arrangement whilst still remaining an employee. The ability of the Irish employer to require scheme membership will, of course, depend on the employment contract between the employer and its employee.

[38] See para. 16.50 et seq.

fits. If the scheme is contributory, it is important that the member on joining the scheme authorises the employer to make payroll deductions in respect of member contributions; otherwise, such deductions would be contrary to the Payment of Wages Act, 1991.[39] The appropriate authority is usually included in the membership application form which will be appended to the booklet and will be completed and signed by the member on joining the scheme. The rules will also make provision for payment of contributions by the employer. It is a Revenue requirement for exempt approval that a minimum proportion of the cost of benefits under an occupational pension scheme be paid for by the employer.[40]

Benefits

3.33 The rules should set out clearly the benefits that will be payable to members and will reflect the benefit design that the sponsoring employer has chosen to implement. The benefits that can be provided under occupational pension schemes are considered elsewhere.[41]

Leaving Service

3.34 The rules should contain provision in relation to members who leave service for reasons other than retirement. They should state what benefits are payable to a member on leaving service. Prior to enactment of the Pensions Act these provisions varied greatly. Some schemes provided no benefit at all, some a refund of member contributions only (and without interest), others granted a deferred benefit payable at retirement, being the pension accrued to the date of leaving service. Since the enactment of the Pensions Act, all pension schemes must provide a minimum preserved benefit.[42]

Transfer Provisions

3.35 Before enactment of the Pensions Act, entitlement to transfers of accrued benefits between schemes varied considerably. Many pen-

---

39 s.5(1)(c) Payment of Wages Act, 1991.

40 At present, the requirement is that the employer must contribute not less than 1/60th of the cost of providing benefits. See para. 6.37.

41 See Chapter 2.

42 See Chapter 12 generally for a full discussion of the preservation requirements of the Pensions Act.

sion schemes did not allow members a right to transfer at all. Schemes might also require either the consent of the trustees or the employer for a transfer. The concept of the "portable pension" now has legislative support in the preservation provisions of Part III of the Pensions Act.[43]

Payment

3.36 The rules will contain provision for payment of pensions. Pensions are paid in much the same way as salary or wages, usually on a monthly basis and subject to deduction of income tax on the PAYE basis. The trustees will usually delegate the task of paying pensions to the employer, a life office or a professional pensions administrator. The trust deed must authorise the trustees to use a paying agent.

General

3.37 Included among the general provisions of the Rules will be clauses dealing with:

1. *Liens on benefits* — where an employee is dismissed or voluntarily leaves employment to avoid dismissal the benefit payable under the pension scheme may be stated to be fixed with a lien in favour of the employer in respect of any moneys due by the member to the employer.[44]
2. *Unclaimed benefits* — for administrative reasons, the rules will usually provide that any instalment of a pension which remains unclaimed for in excess of a stated period (such as 12 months) may be forfeited.

---

[43] The issue of transfers on leaving service is dealt with at para. 12.57 et seq.

[44] With respect to liens on benefits, forfeiture of unclaimed instalments of pension and prohibition of assignment, the reader should note the provisions of s.36 of the Pensions Act which disapply any such lien or forfeiture provisions in favour of the employer so far as they might affect a preserved benefit under the Pensions Act except only in cases of bankruptcy, assignment or charges. In this context, the recent case of *Lovett* v. *The Minister for Education, Ireland and the Attorney General* (Unreported, High Court, 11 July 1996, Kelly, J.) is worthy of note. That case concerned a statutory scheme established pursuant to the Teachers Superannuation Act, 1928. A purported forfeiture of pension was held by the Court to be *ultra vires* the powers of the Minister under the legislation. See para. 8.71. See also para. 12.86 et seq.

3. *Prohibitions on assignment and bankruptcy* — trust law treats pension rights as an asset of the member like any other asset. As such, they would be capable of being charged as security or assigned to a third party. However, because the purpose of the pension arrangement is to provide for the retirement of the member and because the Revenue prohibit any assignment or charging of pension benefits, the pension scheme rules (or trust documents) invariably contain provisions prohibiting members from charging or assigning their benefits under the scheme, and preventing their benefits from being taken by a creditor if they are adjudicated as bankrupt. The Pensions Act now specifically permits trustees of pension schemes to apply scheme provisions which forfeit pension benefits in cases of bankruptcy, purported assignment or charges.[45]

Definitions

3.38 It is important that terms used in the deed and rules are clearly and precisely defined. Absence of clarity and precision may lead to the provisions being vague and incapable of enforcement if not void for uncertainty.[46] There are many terms used in pension scheme rules which will require careful definition. Typically, there will be definitions relating to:

1. "Employer" and "Associated Employer" — the definition will specify a principal employer, who will be the main sponsoring employer, and the rules will usually make provision for associated employers which may by deed of adherence participate in the pension arrangement.

2. "Eligible Employee" or "Qualifying Employee" — this definition will set out those employees of the employer who are considered to be employees for the purposes of the pension scheme. The definition is important and will operate together with the rules relating to eligibility referred to above.[47]

3. "Normal Pension Date" or "Normal Retirement Date" — the Revenue require that schemes specify a date at which the normal pension benefit will become payable. This is usually age 65 to corre-

---

45 s.36(2) as inserted in the Pensions Act by s.13 of the Pensions (Amendment) Act, 1996. See para. 12.86 et seq.

46 See para. 3.5 above.

47 See para. 3.31.

spond with the State pension. Scheme rules can also give discretion to the employer, to alter normal retirement to any other date between age 60 and age 70. Historically, pension ages for males and females tended to be the same in Irish pension schemes. This was not so in the UK where state pension ages were different. Following the decision of the European Court of Justice in *Barber* v. *Guardian Royal Exchange Assurance*,[48] pension ages for males and females must be the same in respect of service after 17 May 1990. This is also required by Part VII of the Pensions Act.[49]

4. "Salary", "Pensionable Salary" or "Pensionable Remuneration" — one of these terms is usually defined for the purpose of determining the member's contribution to the scheme. Contribution is generally expressed as a rate per cent of pensionable salary or pensionable remuneration. Pensionable Salary/Remuneration may be restricted to basic pay only or may also be defined to include other elements of remuneration such as bonus, shift allowance and commission.

5. "Pensionable Salary" or "Pensionable Remuneration" are usually also defined for the purpose of determining the member's benefit (often in conjunction with definitions of "Final Pensionable Salary" or "Final Pensionable Remuneration" — as to which, see below). Many pension schemes are integrated with State pension benefits. This means that the pension provided by a pension scheme takes into account and is designed to supplement the State pension. In drafting the rules of such a scheme this "integration" is most usually effected in the definition of "pensionable salary".[50]

6. "Final Pensionable Salary" or "Final Pensionable Remuneration" is a term included in defined benefit schemes for the purposes of calculating pension benefits.[51]

---

48 [1990] 2 CMLR 513

49 For a detailed discussion on equality requirements and pension schemes see Chapter 16.

50 See para. 2.16.

51 See para. 2.18.

INTERIM DEEDS

3.39 An interim trust deed may be used where it is desired to establish the pension arrangement without delay. The employer will wish to commence the scheme in this manner if:

1. There are time constraints on the employer relating to establishment of the pension scheme; or
2. The precise basis of the pension scheme in terms of benefits to be provided is not fully decided by the employer prior to the time that the employer wishes to admit employees to the scheme.

3.40 Generally, the Revenue Commissioners discourage the use of interim deeds to establish defined contribution schemes but accept that it is desirable in establishing a defined benefit scheme. The specific advantages obtained by setting up the scheme with an interim deed is that member contributions will be eligible for tax relief, and transfer payments from other schemes to the new scheme will be permitted. Investment return on the fund of the pension scheme will not, however, be exempt from taxation until the definitive documentation is put in place.[52]

3.41 In the past, pension arrangements were frequently established under trust by means of a simple form of interim trust deed. Such trust deeds were often not more than two or three pages, establishing the pension arrangement in merest outline, specifying the principal purpose of the scheme, appointing the first trustees, providing for removal and appointment of other trustees and containing an undertaking to execute a definitive deed and rules within a stated period of time. On receipt of properly executed interim trust documentation and an explanatory booklet or announcement which had been actually issued to employees, interim approval of the scheme would be granted by the Revenue Commissioners. In many cases, no definitive deed and rules were subsequently put in place. This practice was recognised as dangerous. Interim trust deeds have become more detailed documents and to some extent the distinction between an interim trust deed and a definitive trust deed has become blurred. In many cases it will be possible to put a definitive form of trust deed in place at the outset, particularly in the case of defined contribution schemes. However, the rules of a defined benefit scheme are more complex.

---

[52] See paras. 6.15 et seq.

Their drafting is usually a joint task between the employer, the employer's consultants and the employer's legal advisors.

3.42 It can happen in practice that, although a pension scheme has been established by interim trust deed, no definitive trust documentation is in fact executed. In the 1980s there were many such pension schemes in Ireland. Following enactment of the Pensions Act, there has been an impetus to put in place definitive documentation. There are still, however, schemes without formal documentation. In the absence of definitive trust documentation difficulties may arise in a situation where the principal employer ceases to trade and the pension scheme falls to be wound up. The interim deed may be silent as regards the procedures to be adopted and the priorities to be applied on a winding-up. There may also be difficulties in determining the precise benefits to which members are entitled in the absence of definitive documentation. However, it is sometimes the case that the terms of the definitive trust documentation, including in particular any rules relating to winding up, may be agreed by the employer and the trustees but not formally adopted in the manner required by the interim deed.

3.43 In such circumstances, the trustees of the scheme will have to determine whether the scheme falls to be wound up under the provisions of the interim deed alone or whether account should be taken of the draft definitive deed and rules, if such exist. This matter was considered in the English case of *Davis* v. *Richards & Wallington Industries Limited.*[53] In that case, the Court held that draft rules which had not been formally adopted were nevertheless effective and binding on the employers and trustees concerned. In the facts of the case, the Court was able to apply the principle that "equity looks on that as done which ought to be done."[54] The facts were that a pension scheme for a group of companies was established by interim deed in 1975. This scheme was contributory. The deed provided that the principal employer, the various group companies and the trustees would execute a definitive trust deed and rules within 24 months of the date of the interim deed. In September 1981, the definitive deed which had been prepared by an insurance company (which held the funds of the

53 [1990] 1 WLR 1511.

54 The Court referred to Snell, E. (1982): *Principles of Equity*, London: Sweet & Maxwell: 28th edition: p.41.

scheme) and the trustees' pension consultant, was submitted to the companies for execution. In July 1982 the companies that were then in financial difficulties terminated the scheme. The scheme was in surplus. In August 1982 the definitive deed and a further amending deed were executed by the principal employer and two of the three trustees. The third trustee resigned by letter indicating that he was no longer willing to act as a trustee and his name was removed from the deed. The rules appended to the definitive deed dealt with the consequence of termination of the scheme by directing the trustees as to the application of the assets of the fund to provide for the pensions and other benefits promised by the scheme. They empowered the trustees to increase pension benefits out of the surplus, if any, of the fund, and authorised the trustees to repay any balance of the surplus to the employers who had contributed to the scheme. The Court had to determine whether the definitive deed and rules, having only been executed by the principal employer and two of the trustees, were binding.

3.44 The Court held that, notwithstanding the fact that the requirements of the interim deed had not been complied with, the rules were, nevertheless, effective, stating:

> Once the rules have been duly made and approved, the undertaking by Industries and by each of the associated companies and by the trustees to execute the deed came into effect. This obligation was an absolute one and, once the twenty-four months from 24 April 1975 had expired, and once the rules had been approved, it was one, in my judgment, which could have been specifically enforced. Industries and the associated companies were not volunteers against whom specific enforcement could not be ordered. They were employers who had offered and who were offering to their respective employees a pension scheme to be regulated under rules which they had contracted to bring into effect. The employees had an interest in the rules being brought into effect. The trustees had been appointed administrators of the pension scheme for the purposes of Chapter II of Part II of the Finance Act, 1970. As such they had responsibilities to the employee members of the scheme. So, in my judgment, once the rules had been approved and once the 24 months had expired, the undertaking to execute the deed would have been specifically enforceable at the suit of the trustees. It is a well known maxim of equity that "equity looks on that as done which ought to be done.". . . So, in my opinion, the obligation to execute the definitive deed could have been enforced also by the beneficiaries, the employees. . . . Want of execution by these companies [the associated companies] does not, in my judgment, detract from

the efficacy of the rules. Equity looks on that as done which ought to be done.

3.45 Where the definitive deed is put in place some time after establishment of the interim deed, the question may arise as to whether the definitive document applies retrospectively.

RETROSPECTIVE EFFECT OF DEFINITIVE DEED

3.46 In the English case of *Re Imperial Foods Limited Pension Scheme,* the Court had to consider whether an indemnity clause contained in a definitive deed could apply with respect to alleged breaches of trust committed before the date of adoption of the definitive deed. The interim trust deed establishing the relevant pension scheme did not contain any indemnity clause and the clause in the definitive deed did not express itself, on its face, to act retrospectively. No authorities were cited to the court on the matter. The Court held that the definitive trust deed, and therefore the indemnity clause, operated from the commencement of the scheme and not from the date of adoption of the definitive trust deed. It stated:[55]

> But, on principle, I think that it must be that the definitive trust deed governs the situation from the commencement. There are a number of occasions in law in which a fund is held on trust, but at the particular point there is no final definitive trust deed. At that stage the trusts have not been finally defined, particularly, one may say in relation to administrative matters. . . . For example, funds are collected for the purpose of establishing a particular charity. Obviously the funds are from the moment of their collection held on trust, but the people who are collecting may not know how much they are going to get in, whether it is worthwhile starting off with a trust deed or not. When they have got in enough, then the law says that the persons who collect the fund are given implied authority effectively to declare those trusts by a deed: see *Attorney General* v. *Matheson* [1907] 2 Ch. 383. It would be quite absurd to think that the moneys collected were not throughout their lives governed by the terms of that trust deed. . . . What, after all, is the purpose of an interim trust deed and pension scheme? It is not by its very nature clearly to define fully the trust upon which the fund is to be held but

---

55 The following quotation is taken from a transcript of the Judgement given by Walton J. on 27 January 1986. This matter is not covered in the report of the *Imperial Food* Case in [1986] 1 WLR 717. The transcript appears in Inglis-Jones, N. (1989): *Law of Occupational Pension Schemes*, London: Sweet & Maxwell.

> to get the fund started. The analogy with the situation in *Attorney General* v. *Matheson* appears to me to be very close. Of course the machinery for the drafting of the final trust deed is quite different, and it may very well be that in both cases a person who had contributed to the fund in question would be in a position to object to some provision which was never contemplated, but which was put or attempted to be put into the final trust deed. For example, provision for a different charity, or in our particular case, for the payment of pensions to totally different classes of person. That situation can be met when it arises. But in a case where it does not, it appears to me that the obvious intention of all parties, from start to finish is that the pension fund should throughout be held upon the same trusts and that those trusts should be the trusts as defined in the definitive trust deed. After all, is it not definitive and intended to be definitive of the trust? If not, why is it so called?

3.47 The reasoning of Walton J., set out above, appears persuasive. There are, however, situations in which it is difficult to see how or why such reasoning should apply. For example, it is quite common to find in definitive trust documentation a provision granting the employer a lien over benefits payable to a member in the event that such member owes moneys to the employer or has been found guilty of some fraud against the employer.[56] Such provisions are, however, rarely contained in an interim trust deed. It is arguable that it would be inequitable for a Court to allow such provision to be enforced with retrospective effect. As with other questions which may arise relating to the trust deed and rules of a pension scheme, the correct interpretation of any provision may well depend on a consideration of the entire of the trust deed and rules and the employment context in which such documentation operates.

ANNOUNCEMENTS AND BOOKLETS

3.48 In order to obtain Revenue approval it is necessary for the employer to issue an announcement or explanatory booklet summarising the benefits provided under the scheme to its employees.[57] In practice, the Revenue Commissioners will accept an announcement letter which sets out the principal terms of the scheme. It is not always possible for all provisions to be included at an early stage. It is very important that there are no discrepancies between the formal trust

---

[56] Although these provisions are now usually modified to take account of the overriding preservation requirements imposed by the Pensions Act.

[57] See s.15(2)(b) Finance Act, 1972, see paras. 6.19 et seq.

documentation and the announcements or explanatory booklets. Announcements and explanatory booklets should always defer to the formal documentation and contain a clause to the effect that they are subject to the trust deed and rules. The purposes of the announcement and the explanatory booklet are:

1. To set out concisely and in readily understandable language the objectives and the principal benefits under the pension arrangement
2. To comply with the requirements of the Revenue Commissioners regarding approval of schemes
3. To comply with the requirements of the Occupational Pension Schemes (Disclosure of Information) Regulations, 1991.[58]

3.49 Regulatory requirements with respect to the announcement or booklet are considered later.[59]

3.50 Announcements are also used to notify members of changes in the pension scheme. Difficulties may arise where a change is notified to members in an announcement but a formal amendment of the pension scheme is not made.[60]

Conflict Between Booklets, Announcements and the Trust Deed

3.51 If there are discrepancies between the explanatory booklet or an announcement and the formal trust documentation, it is not always clear which will prevail or whether the employee has an independent contractual right against the employer to enforce the terms of the booklet.[61] As mentioned above, the explanatory booklet should contain a term providing that the formal trust documentation will prevail. This is recommended because the formal trust documentation is intended to contain all of the detail with respect to the establishment and operation of the pension arrangement, whereas the explanatory booklet is only intended to contain an explanation in lay terms of the pension arrangement.

---

58 SI No 215 of 1991. See Chapter 13 for a detailed discussion of these Regulations.

59 See paras. 6.19 et seq. and Chapter 13.

60 See para. 3.51 et seq. below for a detailed discussion on this point.

61 Regard should also be had to the amendment clause in the trust deed. This may provide that amendments may be effected by means of an announcement.

3.52 The explanatory booklet should contain a statement that the booklet is no more than an explanation of the principal features of the pension scheme and that it cannot override the actual provisions of the formal trust documentation. The note should further state that individual members may obtain copies of the formal trust documentation as it applies to them. The booklet should also include the name of the person to whom members may address any queries regarding the pension scheme as it applies to them. If these statements are made in the booklet, it should be more difficult to establish a contractual claim where there is a discrepancy between the booklet and the formal trust documentation. It would be argued by the employer that the booklet did not constitute a contract. *Irish Pensions Trust Limited* v. *The First National Bank of Chicago* [62] provides an example of the effectiveness of exclusion language. The case concerned allocation of a surplus in a pension fund arising on the winding up of a scheme. Much of the case concerned interpretation of the winding-up rule in the pension deed. In this regard, part of the plaintiff's claim was that a sentence in the explanatory booklet for the scheme constituted a contractual promise which the employer was estopped from breaching. The sentence in the booklet read as follows:

> If the pension plan should be terminated, the money in the trust must be used to provide benefits to the plan participants.

The Court, however, held that the sentence did not constitute an estoppel. As a separate issue, the Court also held, dismissing a further contention of the plaintiffs, that the sentence was not admissible as an aid to construction of the trust deed. It stated:

> It seems to me that that case cannot be made on the existing evidence. There is no evidence to show that this was a statement upon which any particular employee or employees relied. However, most of all it seems to me that that particular sentence, whilst undoubtedly significant in the context of the present case and which, understandably, appeals to the individual employees with whom one can have sympathy, one must look at that one sentence in the light of a document of some ten pages which is dealing with matters of very considerable interest — extensions of the scheme, complex references to rights and benefits, examples and demonstrations. To take that one sentence alone is to take it very un-

---

[62] (Unreported, High Court, 15 February 1989, Murphy J.).

fairly out of context, particularly when the immediately preceding paragraph expressly provides:

> "This summary describes the highlights of the Dublin Branch Benefits Program. Each Plan herein described is subject to the terms and conditions of the formal documentation which govern the obligations and benefits provided under the various plans."

Any reasonable person realises that this is a complex matter, as the argument over the last 24 hours has demonstrated. If one wants to consider matters of detail and the precise rights of parties, one would have to refer to the underlying documentation and perhaps get legal assistance in relation to it. It seems to me, therefore, that this memorandum is not admissible to aid construction and that it does not operate and has not been shown to operate as an estoppel against the Bank. In these circumstances it seems to me that the Bank are entitled to the surplus and that they are not estopped from claiming that right.[63]

3.53 An example of the explanatory booklet prevailing over the formal trust documentation is the English case of *Icarus (Hertford) Limited* v. *Driscoll.*[64] In that case the Court held that, on the facts of the case, an estoppel did arise. The Plaintiff company (which was in liquidation) had established a pension scheme under trust. The scheme was an insured scheme and the deed provided that full provision would be contained in a group life policy. The policy was issued later. Subsequently, the accrual rate for pensions for all employees was reduced and the scheme was made non-contributory. Announcements of the changes were made to all members, and revised booklets were issued to members. No formal documentation of the changes appears to have been made, nor was any endorsement of the policy prepared. It appeared from the evidence that both the Plaintiff and the life office acted upon the basis that the policy had been amended to incorporate the changes. Upon liquidation there was a surplus in the Plaintiff's pension scheme. Depending on which accrual rate applied this surplus would vary by as much as five times. The clause dealing with amendment provided that amendments should be in writing with the consent of the life office and could not adversely affect members without their written consent.

---

63 For a further example of the effectiveness of exclusion language in a scheme booklet see *Dorrell* v. *May & Baker Limited* [1991] PLR 31.

64 [1990] PLR 1

3.54 The Court held that the parties to the pension scheme (meaning the employer, the life office and the members), having conducted themselves on the basis that the scheme had been amended, could not now go back on that. It stated:

> I have come to the conclusion that the parties to the scheme are estopped from contending that the scheme provides for any rate other than 1/270th of the final pensionable salary. *In Amalgamated Investment & Property Co. Ltd (In Liquidation)* v. *Texas Commerce International Bank Limited* [1982] 1QB84, Lord Denning referred to the principles which are to be applied in what is often called estoppel by convention. He said at page 122:
>
> > "The doctrine of estoppel is one of the most flexible and useful in the armoury of the law. It has become overloaded with cases. That is why I have not gone through them all in this judgment. It has evolved during the last 150 years in a sequence of separate developments: proprietary estoppel, estoppel by representation of fact, estoppel by acquiescence and promissory estoppel. At the same time it has been sought to be limited by a series of maxims: estoppel is only a rule of evidence, estoppel cannot give rise to a cause of action, estoppel cannot do away with the need for consideration and so forth. All these can now be seen to merge into one general principle shorn of limitation. When the parties to a transaction proceed on the basis of an underlying assumption — either of fact or law — whether due to misrepresentation or mistake makes no difference — on which they have conducted the dealings between them — neither of them will be allowed to go back on that assumption when it would be unfair or unjust to allow him to do so. If one of them does seek to go back on it the Courts will give the others such remedy as the equity of the case demands."
>
> All the parties to the scheme, namely the Plaintiff, the [life office] and the members, have since 1978 proceeded on the basis that the rate of accrual was 1/270th and they cannot now go back on it. Further, I believe that it would not be unjust or unfair to hold them to that. In fact it would be odd for me to decide that the rate was 1/60th or 1/80th when all the parties had accepted and worked on the basis that it was 1/270th."[65]

---

[65] See also *Mettoy Pension Trustees Ltd.* v. *Evans* [1990] 1 WLR 1587, where there was an inconsistency between the booklet and the deed, though in that case the parties agreed that the booklet prevailed and the Court did not therefore have to determine the matter; also *Boccia* v. *Bata Industries Limited* (Unreported, Ontario High Court, 12 June 1989).

3.55 In practice, changes to the benefit structure of a pension scheme are often notified to members by way of an announcement, and formal amendment of the trust documentation follows in due course. Such an announcement is issued by or on behalf of the employer and would usually be binding on the employer as a matter of contract. The trustees of the pension scheme would, arguably, not be bound by the announcement unless they had joined in the announcement or had issued it. The formal trust documentation will contain provisions for amendment of the documentation and, until these are complied with, the change in benefit structure would not be binding upon the trustees. It is important therefore that the employer should ensure before issuing an announcement that the changes proposed are permitted by the formal trust documentation.

3.56 If the trustees themselves are not party to the notification, announcement or other document issued to the members, and have not acquiesced in the issuing of it, it is difficult to see how they can be joined in any action by a member where, subsequently, the benefits offered to such member under the formal rules are different from those in the announcement or booklet. The English Court of Appeal found in *Re Duke of Norfolk's Settlement Trusts*[66] that a trust document does not constitute a contractual relationship between the trustees and the beneficiaries. In the absence of appropriate wording, however, an announcement or explanatory booklet can constitute a contractual relationship between the employer and the members.

3.57 Another area in which difficulties can arise and which relates to information is where information regarding entitlements on retirement is furnished to a member approaching retirement age. If an error is made in furnishing such information, this may amount to a negligent mis-statement. Failure by an employer to inform its employees of the rights and entitlements under a pension scheme may also amount to a breach of contract. In *Scally* v. *Southern Health and Social Services Board*[67] the English House of Lords held that the plaintiff's employer was in breach of contract in failing to inform the plaintiff that he could purchase added years of pension entitlement provided that such

---

[66] [1982] 1 Ch. 61.

[67] [1991] 4 All ER 563.

right was exercised within a 12-month period.[68] However, a recent English case, *Hamar* v. *The Pensions Ombudsman*,[69] has held that trustees are not under an obligation to explain the benefits payable under a pension scheme or to inform members of the manner in which benefits may be claimed.

THE PENSION TRUST AND THE CONTRACT OF EMPLOYMENT

3.58 It is important to consider the interaction between the pension scheme documentation and the contract of employment. It may be said that an employee's pension rights arise under both the contract of employment and the terms of the pension scheme documentation. In other words, the pension rights are partly derived from contract law and partly from trust law. There have been many cases on this question in the UK.[70] In the context of the examination of the formal trust documentation, it is, however, important to bear in mind that anything said about pension entitlements in the contract of employment can have an effect on the interpretation of the formal pension scheme trust documentation. Whilst strictly, pension rights are set out in a pension trust and are therefore equitable in nature, they arise in the context of the contract of employment. It is therefore frequently argued that the rights can be characterised as contractual. In *Kerr* v. *British Leyland (Staff) Trustees Limited*[71] Fox L.J., referring to the trusts of a pension scheme, said:

> Now this is not a case of a trust where the beneficiaries are simply volunteers. The beneficiaries here are not volunteers. Rights derive from contractual and commercial origins. They have purchased their rights as part of their terms of employment.[72]

3.59 Another case on the point is *Mihlenstedt* v. *Barclays Bank International Limited.*[73] In *Mihlenstedt*, Nourse, L.J., referring to a rule

---

[68] See para. 5.17 where this case is considered; see also *AC Brown* v. *Royal Veterinary College* [1989] PLR 43.

[69] [1996] PLR 1.

[70] This question is examined in Chapter 5.

[71] (Unreported, UK Court of Appeal, 26 March 1986).

[72] Note also *McMenamin* v. *Ireland* [1994] 2 ILRM 368 per Geoghegan J. at p. 378.

[73] [1989] PLR 91 and see also *Parry* v. *Cleaver* [1970] AC 1.

relating to an ill-health pension scheme that enabled the bank "at its discretion after consulting his medical advisor . . . [to] vary or suspend any such pension", said:

> If therefore the matter had rested on the trust deed and the rules alone I would have held that the Bank was under no obligation in regard to the Plaintiff's application for an ill-health pension. But it was a term of her contract of employment with the Bank that she should be entitled to membership of the pension scheme and to the benefits thereunder. From that it must follow, as a matter of necessary implication, that the bank became contractually bound, so far as it lay within its power, to procure for the plaintiff the benefits to which she was entitled under the scheme.

3.60 The formal trust documentation will usually contain a provision allowing for its amendment. It is also common for such documentation to provide that the employer may cease to make contributions to the scheme by appropriate notice. Effectively, this will mean that the pension arrangements are subject to amendment and to termination. Any reference to pension arrangements in the contract of employment should be couched in language that will give effect to the provisions of the formal pension documentation allowing for amendment or termination. In the absence of such language, the intent of the provisions of the formal trust documentation may be frustrated.

3.61 Contracts of employment are often drafted so that the only "pension right" of an employee conferred by the contract of employment is a right to be a member of the employer's pension scheme upon the terms and subject to the conditions of the trust deed and rules governing the pension scheme (this will include, of course, the right of the employer by notice to terminate its liability to make contributions to the pension scheme). If the provisions relating to pension in the contract of employment are drafted in this manner, the "pension promise" in the pension scheme is not a legal liability of the employer. Employees will have a right to be members of the scheme (if they are in fact eligible under the provisions of the scheme itself) but their only claim for pension is a claim against the trustees of the pension scheme to the extent of the assets available under the trust. It is unusual for the employer to give a contractual guarantee that a particular amount of pension will be payable in the event that the assets of the pension scheme are not sufficient.[74]

3.62 Members of the senior management of companies may have pension arrangements which are made directly through a service agreement. These are, effectively, unfunded pension arrangements.[75] Such a pension promise is a direct liability of the employer. It is also possible for an employer in the contract of employment to promise a form of pension and to fulfil this promise through a pension scheme.

THE PENSION TRUST — INTERACTION WITH LEGISLATION

3.63 There are several pieces of legislation which affect occupational pension schemes. Some, under their terms, override the formal trust documentation. Others do not. For instance, certain of the requirements of the Revenue Commissioners, as set out in the Finance Act 1972,[76] do not override the formal pension scheme documentation. Much of the Pensions Act[77] has overriding effect. Where legislative provisions such as those in the Pensions Act have overriding effect, it is not essential that reference to them be included in the formal documents. In drafting the formal trust documentation, provisions should be included to take account of legislation, which, although binding on trustees, nevertheless does not override the formal documentation. If this is not done, compliance by the trustees with such legislation might, in certain circumstances, amount to a breach of trust by the trustees as they are bound by the terms of the formal trust documents. Failure to comply with the legislative provisions may attract criminal sanction and endanger the approval of the scheme by the Revenue.

---

74 Article 9 and Schedule C para. 14 of the Disclosure Regulations requires the trustees of a pension scheme to inform members (and others) in writing as to whether, in fact, the employer has made any such guarantee.

75 See para. 5.6 and paras. 6.84 et seq.

76 Principally Chapter II Part I Finance Act 1972 (as amended and added to by subsequent legislation).

77 Part III (Preservation of Benefits)(by s.37(1)), Part IV (Funding Standard)(by s.53(1)), Part V (Disclosure of Information in Relation to Schemes)(By s.58(1)), Part VI (Trustees of Schemes)(by s.64A(1)), Part VII (Equal Treatment for Men and Women)(by s.66)

3.64 The extent to which legislative provisions are stated in the trust deed and rules will depend on the employer's intentions in preparing the documentation. It may be felt desirable that the formal documents constituting the pension scheme should be entirely comprehensive and self-contained to the greatest extent possible. If such is the object of the employer, detailed reference to the provisions of the Pensions Act and detailed reference to Revenue limits on benefits will be included in the documentation. A disadvantage of the incorporation of statutory provisions into the formal documentation is that the legislation and regulations may subsequently be amended. The documentation will then require amendment if it is to be helpful rather than misleading.

REVIEW OF SCHEME DOCUMENTATION

3.65 As noted above,[78] in practice, benefit changes and other alterations in pension scheme structure are usually introduced to members by announcements. Formal documentation usually follows some months (or longer) in arrears. Changes may also be introduced by legislation. For instance, the provisions of section 48 of the Pensions Act[79] have overriding effect and operate notwithstanding the provisions of the formal documentation.[80] There is no legal obligation on the employer or the trustees to update the formal documentation to incorporate these changes.[81] Best practice would, however, suggest that the formal documentation be reviewed at regular intervals and, if necessary, updated. The UK Goode Committee in its report on Pension Law Reform recommended that the formal trust documentation be reviewed and consolidated at least every five years.[82]

---

78 See para. 3.55

79 s.48 sets out the priorities of payment in winding up of a defined benefit scheme.

80 s.53 Pensions Act

81 Neither the Pensions Act nor the Finance Act, 1972 contain provisions imposing such an obligation.

82 Report of the Pension Law Review Committee at para. 4.12.20. The Goode Committee considered that such a consolidation would assist members (who have a right to and may wish to consult the scheme documentation), lay trustees (who must administer the Scheme and apply the

3.66 Under Irish law, (both under trust law and the provisions of the Disclosure Regulations[83]) members of pension schemes have rights to inspect and to obtain copies of the formal trust documentation including any documents which amend or supplement such documentation. If the formal documentation is contained in a definitive deed and a number of amending deeds, the documentation may (for practical purposes) be incomprehensible to a lay person. There may be an argument to be made for statutory intervention to compel regular reviews and consolidation of documentation if it should appear that the intention of Part V of the Pensions Act, and the Disclosure Regulations is being frustrated.

---

deed and rules) and the scheme actuaries (who must advise and act on the basis of the formal documentation). The UK Government White Paper on Pension Law Reform considered the recommendation of the Goode Committee regarding regular review of scheme documentation. The White Paper considered that this was a matter for best practice rather than legislation. No provision requiring regular consolidation has been included in the UK Pensions Act, 1995.

83 SI No 215 of 1991.

4

TRUSTEES

INTRODUCTION

4.1 The trust concept has evolved in English and Irish common law over hundreds of years. General trust law has developed principally by reference to family trusts. The pension scheme trust is a relatively modern concept. There are significant differences between a pension scheme trust and a traditional family trust.[1] In a pension scheme trust the beneficiaries are employees and their dependants. The pension scheme will be a part of the employment arrangements between the employer and its employees. The benefits provided to employees under the pension scheme are not gifts from the employer — they are a reward for service. Also, in many pension schemes the members contribute toward the cost of the benefits.[2] A further difference is that many pension schemes promise a specific benefit and the employer has a liability to make up the cost of such benefit if the fund is insufficient. In such a pension scheme the employer has a continuing liability to meet the cost of providing the benefit.[3]

4.2 The role of the trustee in a pension scheme established under trust is of vital importance. The trustee must ensure that the terms of the pension scheme trust are carried out, that the assets of the pension scheme are secure and are properly invested, that its members and other beneficiaries are dealt with in accordance with the terms of

---

1 See Chapter 5 for a detailed discussion of the position of the occupational pension scheme in the employment relationship. See also Moffat, G. "Pension Funds: A Fragmentation of Trust Law?" 56 MLR 471.

2 See Chapter 2.

3 This type of pension scheme is called a defined benefit scheme. See Chapter 2 for a full discussion of the various types of occupational pension scheme.

the trust and that the benefits promised by the pension scheme are paid. The First Report of the National Pensions Board, the Maxwell affair[4] in England and the subsequent report of the Pension Law Review Committee[5] all highlight the importance of the trustee in relation to the proper operation of a pension scheme. The rest of this chapter will consider how trustees are appointed and removed, the nature of their duties and powers, trustees' liabilities and protection of trustees.

4.3 It should be noted that under the Pensions Act the term "trustees of a pension scheme" has an extended meaning.[6] Where a pension scheme is not established under trust, then, for the purposes of the Pensions Act, the term refers to the administrator of the scheme.[7]

APPOINTMENT AND REMOVAL OF TRUSTEES

4.4 Any individual may be appointed a trustee.[8] A body corporate may also be a trustee.[9] The first trustees of an occupational pension

---

4 The Maxwell affair refers to the wholesale misappropriation of the assets of two pension funds, namely those of Maxwell Communications Corporation and Mirror Group Newspapers.

5 The Pension Law Review Committee was established in June 1992 by the Secretary of State for Social Security of the United Kingdom. The Committee was established as a direct result of the public outcry which followed the Maxwell affair. The Committee furnished its report (which is in two volumes) to the Secretary of State for Social Security in September 1993. Many of their recommendations have now been introduced into UK law by the UK Pensions Act, 1995.

6 s.2(1).

7 Except for the purpose of s.59 (General Duties of Trustees of Pension Schemes), s.62 (Selection of Member Trustees), s.63 (Appointment and Removal of Trustees by Court) s.63A (Suspension) and s.64 (Appointment and Removal of Trustees by Pensions Board).

8 There is nothing in Irish law to prevent a minor from being appointed a trustee. s.20 of the UK Law of Property Act, 1925 renders void the appointment of a minor as a trustee. There is no Irish equivalent legislation. However, given that the role of trustee is an active one, it is sensible that appointments of minors should not be made. It should also be noted that the regulations which provide for selection of member trustees (SI No 399 of 1993) require that a person nominated for appointment as a member trustee must be aged 18 years or more.

scheme will be appointed by the employer at the time of establishment of the pension scheme. Such trustees may be:

1. The sponsoring company (employer) itself
2. Named individuals — (whether directors of the employer, other members of management, employees, pensioners or others)
3. A trustee company (established by the employer for the purpose)
4. A professional trustee company or individual
5. A combination of the above.

4.5 There is no legal reason why members of management or of the scheme may not be appointed trustees.[10] The formal trust documentation will contain provisions for appointment and removal of trustees. Where a pension scheme is established by a non-Irish corporation or by the wholly-owned subsidiary of such a corporation, some trustees may be non-resident. There is no legal prohibition on such appointments. There is, however, an issue with regard to approval of such schemes by the Revenue and this is discussed later.[11]

Corporate Trustees

4.6 Sometimes, for reasons of administrative convenience, a corporate trustee is appointed as the sole trustee of the pension scheme. The advantages of using a corporate trustee are that there is continuity as to ownership of the assets of the pension scheme, and appointment and removal of the officers of a corporate trustee is a relatively simple matter. Once the corporate trustee is appointed, and for so long as it remains trustee, no further deed of appointment or removal is required — all that is subsequently required is a change of directorship. If a corporate trustee is used, it will be necessary to comply with the various requirements of the Companies Acts, 1963–1990, including public disclosure requirements. If a corporate trustee is to

---

9 Provided that its Memorandum of Association does not prohibit it from acting in a trust capacity. See *Re Munster & Leinster Bank Ltd* [1907] IR 237.

10 But see the remarks below with regard to conflicts of duty and interest at para. 4.29 et seq.

11 See para. 6.28 et seq.

act as sole trustee, the formal trust documentation must permit it. It should also be noted that if a member trustee election is initiated pursuant to the Member Trustee Regulations,[12] it will not be possible to retain a sole corporate trustee. If a corporate trustee is to be used, then, as a matter of practice, care should be taken to ensure that the principal objects set out in the Memorandum of Association of the body corporate empower that body corporate to act as a pension scheme trustee.

4.7 The directors of a trustee company stand in a fiduciary position in relation to the trust. This means that their actions and the manner in which they exercise their powers are open to scrutiny by the Court. In the English case of *Re French Protestant Hospital,*[13] it was held that the directors of a corporate trustee were in a fiduciary position in relation to the trust and, therefore, they were not entitled to receive payment for their services, and could not introduce a by-law which enabled them to make a profit out of their trust. Danckwerts J. stated:

> It is said by Mr Warren for the applicants, who are the Governor and Directors, that it is the Corporation which is the trustee of the property of the charity in question and that the Governor and Directors are not trustees. It seems to me that in a case of this kind, the Court is bound to look at the real situation which exists in fact. It is obvious that the Corporation is completely controlled under the provisions of the Charter by the Governor, Deputy Governor and Directors and that those are the persons who in fact control the corporation and decide what shall be done. It is plain that those persons are as much in a fiduciary position as trustees in regard to any acts which are done with respect to the Corporation and its property. Therefore it seems to me plain that they are, to all intents and purposes, bound by the rules which affect trustees.[14]

---

12 The Occupational Pension Schemes (Member Participation in the Selection of Persons for Appointment as Trustees)(No.2) Regulations, 1993 (SI No 399 of 1993). "Member trustee election" here refers to a "standard arrangement" under the Regulations. An "alternative arrangement" under the Regulations would permit retention of a corporate trustee. Generally, with regard to Member Trustees see Chapter 14.

13 [1951] Ch. 567.

14 See also the case of *Abbey Malvern Wells Limited* v. *The Ministry of Local Government and Planning* [1951] Ch. 728 and *Australian Securities Commission* v. *AS Nominees Limited* [1996] PLR 298.

4.8 It is not clearly settled in either English or Irish case law as to whether a director of a corporate trustee can avoid personal liability where the trustee company itself is found to be in breach of trust. The prudent advice is that such directors should carry out their responsibilities as if they were appointed trustees in their personal capacity.[15]

4.9 A valid trust may be established with only one trustee. However, if it is proposed to appoint individual trustees, it is recommended, for practical reasons, that not less than three individuals be so appointed. If an individual trustee should die, resign or become unavailable for some other reason, the remaining trustees will be able to continue to conduct the operation of the pension scheme. There is also no upper limit on the number of trustees imposed by Irish law.

Appointment and Removal Generally

4.10 Generally there are three ways in which trustees can be appointed or removed — that is, under the terms of the trust instrument, under the Trustee Act, 1893 or under the Pensions Act. The power of appointment and removal of trustees of a pension scheme is usually vested in the employer. The formal trust documentation will provide that the employer may by a deed or instrument in writing appoint and remove the trustees. A new trustee must consent to act as trustee and will therefore be a party to the deed of appointment. As a matter of practice, it is unusual for the formal trust document to require that a trustee, who is retiring or being removed, be joined as a party to the deed of appointment or removal. But it is preferable that a trustee who is retiring or being removed, and is available, be joined as a party to the deed. If the assets of the pension scheme are actually held or registered in the names of the individual trustees, the provisions of section 12 of the Trustee Act, 1893 will be of assistance. Under the Trustee Act, 1893, if a new trustee is appointed in place of a retiring trustee and the deed of appointment contains a declaration by the appointor vesting the trust property in the new and existing trustees, that appointment will operate so as to vest the assets of the trust.[16] The retiring trustee does not have to be joined in

---

15 Also with respect to liability of directors of a trust company under the Pensions Act, see para. 4.86.

16 s.12 Trustee Act, 1893. It should be noted that pursuant to s.12(3) the vesting provisions of s.12(1) do not apply to any legal estate or interest in

the deed of appointment. However, if a trustee is being removed but is not being replaced by a new trustee, the vesting provisions in section 12(1) of the Trustee Act, 1893 will not apply. In such case, it is necessary for the retiring trustee to join in the deed in order to be divested of the trust assets.[17] The Court has an inherent jurisdiction to remove a trustee if this appears to be in the interests of the beneficiaries.[18]

4.11 It is not usual for trustees to be required to consent to the appointment of a new trustee or the removal of an existing trustee. Such provisions can create difficulties. The power of appointment and removal of trustees is a power that is usually exercisable by the employer entirely at its own discretion (with or without notice).[19]

4.12 It is common for the deed removing a trustee to contain a specific discharge in favour of the retiring trustee. It is desirable for trustees to obtain a discharge, as it releases them from any future liability in relation to the pension trust. The question sometimes arises as to whether on replacement of a number of individual trustees (being the first trustees) by a corporate trustee (a replacement sometimes effected for reasons of administrative convenience), the individual trustees can be validly discharged from their trusts. If the removal is effected pursuant to the power provided by section 10 of the Trustee Act, 1893, the trustees being removed will not be discharged from their trusts because of the provisions of section 10(2)(c). However a

---

copyhold or customary land, land conveyed by way of mortgage to secure money subject to the trust and to stocks or shares or other property which is only transferable in books kept by a company or other body, or only transferable in a manner directed by statute. Legal interests in copyhold land do not arise (this was an old form of property interest) and customary land refers to land held in commonage.

17 s.12(2) and there must be at least two remaining trustees.

18 *Arnott* v. *Arnott* (1924) 58 ILTR 145 at 147; see also *Pollock* v. *Ennis* [1921] I IR 181.

19 This power is fettered in the case of trustees appointed pursuant to the Occupational Pension Schemes (Member Participation in the Selection of Persons for Appointment as Trustees) Regulations, 1993. See para. 14.3 below.

properly drafted trust deed will modify section 10(2)(c) and this should not in practice be a problem.[20]

Appointment of Trustees by the Pensions Board

4.13 In practice, situations may arise where the normal procedure for appointment of a trustee, by the employer, cannot operate. This may happen where the employer has ceased business or gone into liquidation. It can also happen that the existing trustees of a pension scheme may be unwilling or unable to act. In such circumstances, the interests of the pension scheme members could be prejudiced. It is important that the members should be able to take action to have trustees appointed. The first report of the National Pensions Board highlighted the unsatisfactory nature of the remedies available at that time to members (being a petition to the Court). The Pensions Act provides a means whereby members may apply to the Pensions Board to have trustees appointed.

4.14 Section 64 of the Pensions Act[21] states that where, in relation to a pension scheme, there are no trustees or the trustees cannot be found, the Pensions Board may, if it considers it necessary to do so, by order under the seal of the Pensions Board:

1. Appoint a new trustee or new trustees of the scheme in substitution, where appropriate, for any existing trustee or trustees
2. Vest the assets of the scheme in the persons appointed trustees of the scheme by such order, where necessary subject to transfer in the books of any bank, corporation or company.

4.15 Section 64 also provides for publication by the Board of an order appointing trustees, the powers of trustees so appointed, a right of appeal by persons having an interest in any such order or proposed order, the appointment of a body corporate as sole trustee, the transfer of any land, registered under the Registration of Title Act, 1964

---

20 s.10(2)(c) Trustee Act, 1893 provides that, except where the trust was established with one trustee, a trustee cannot be discharged under s.10 unless there are at least two remaining trustees; however s.10(5) of the Act provides that: "This Section applies only if and as far as a contrary intention is not expressed in the instrument, if any, creating the trust, and shall have effect subject to the terms of that instrument and to any provisions therein contained."

21 As amended by s.28 Pensions (Amendment) Act, 1996.

and which land is affected by an order made by the Pensions Board, and the transfer of any assets registered in the books of any bank, corporation or company and which assets are affected by an order made by the Pensions Board under section 64.

Appointment of Trustees by the Court

4.16 The Pensions Board may make application to the High Court on petition for an order:

1. For the removal of a trustee of a scheme and the appointment of a new trustee
2. That the trustee so removed shall not act as a trustee of a scheme for such period as the Court may order.[22]

The Pensions Act provides for matters such as the powers, authorities and discretions of any trustee appointed by order of the Court;[23] the power of the Court to include in any order, provision for vesting of property;[24] the making of payments from the resources of the scheme;[25] and the transfer of any land registered under the Registration of Title Act, 1964, which land is affected by an order of the Court.[26] Any such order will not operate as a discharge to the trustee who is removed to any greater extent than could an appointment of a new trustee under the power of appointment contained in the relevant trust document.[27]

4.17 Section 25 of the Trustee Act, 1893 provides that the High Court may, whenever it is expedient to appoint a new trustee or new trustees and it is found inexpedient, difficult or impracticable to do so without the assistance of the Court, make an Order for the appointment of a new trustee or new trustees either in substitution for or in addition to any existing trustee or trustees, or where there is no exist-

---

22 s.63(1) as amended by s.49 Social Welfare Act, 1993.

23 s.63(4).

24 s.63(5).

25 s.63(5).

26 s.63(7).

27 s.63(6).

ing trustee. This section was used in the case of *Re Castle Brand Ltd*[28] to appoint new trustees where the existing trustees of the pension scheme had resigned. In that case, the employer was in liquidation and the formal trust documentation consisted only of an interim trust deed which did not make provision for appointment of trustees. Section 36 of the Trustee Act, 1893 provides that such order may be made on the application of any person beneficially interested in the subject matter of the trust, or on the application of any person duly appointed as trustee.[30] The Trustee Act, 1893 also makes provision for vesting orders consequent upon such order of appointment.

Appointment of Trustees Pursuant to Section 10 of the Trustee Act, 1893

4.18 Section 10 of the Trustee Act, 1893 provides, in limited circumstances, for the appointment of a trustee either by the employer or the surviving or continuing trustees or trustee. Under that section, where a trustee is dead, desires to be discharged from their trust, refuses or is unfit to act, or is incapable of acting, the person or persons nominated for the purpose of appointing new trustees by the trust instrument, if any, or if there is no such person or no such person able and willing to act, then the surviving or continuing trustees or trustee for the time being or the personal representatives of such persons, may, by writing, appoint another person or other persons to be a trustee or trustees in the place of the trustee who is dead, retiring or unwilling to act. The section applies only if and to the extent that a contrary intention is not expressed in the trust instrument and has effect subject to the terms of the trust instrument.[30]

4.19 It can happen in practice that a trustee may be unwilling or, through some disability be unable to act. Clearly this presents difficulties. In such a case, it is important that the employer or the trustees are able to make a new appointment in place of such a trustee. If the formal trust documentation is inadequate, the Trustee Act, 1893 provides a mechanism whereby this difficulty may be overcome.

---

28 (Unreported, High Court, 23 March 1985, Hamilton J.).

29 The procedure is set down in the Rules of the Superior Courts 1986, Order 3, and the Rules of the Circuit Court 1950, Rule 48.

30 s.10(5) Trustee Act, 1893.

Suspension of Trustees under Pensions Act

4.20 Under section 63A of the Pensions Act,[31] the High Court has power on application by the Pensions Board to suspend a trustee. This application may be made by the Board in the circumstances set out in section 63A(1). These include circumstances in which the scheme is under investigation by the Board, where proceedings have been instituted against the trustee for an offence involving fraud or dishonesty, or where the trustee is in the course of being adjudicated bankrupt.

Appointment and Removal — A Fiduciary Power

4.21 The question arises as to whether the power of the employer to appoint and remove a trustee is or is not subject to fiduciary constraints as to its exercise. This is of practical importance in the context of pension schemes. For instance, on the winding up of a solvent pension scheme, trustees often have discretion as to the disposal of any surplus. An employer might seek to influence the outcome of the trustees' deliberations. It might do this either by attempting to remove trustees which it did not favour, or by appointing additional trustees sympathetic to its interests. Until recently, it appeared well settled by a line of English cases that the power conferred on a settlor to appoint a trustee of a trust is one subject to fiduciary constraints and, therefore, one subject to review by the Courts.

4.22 The starting point in these authorities is the decision of Kay J. in *Re Skeats' Settlement.*[32] The case involved a marriage settlement where a husband and wife (who were not trustees) were given power to appoint "any other person or persons to be a trustee or trustees . . .". The husband and wife purported to exercise that power by appointing new trustees, one of whom was the husband himself. It was held that the appointment was invalid. Kay J. came to his decision on two grounds. First, that the power to appoint trustees is a fiduciary power which could not be exercised for the benefit of the donee and must be exercised in the best interests of the beneficiaries. In the circumstances of the case, the appointment by the donee of himself was not in the best interests of the beneficiaries. The second ground for the decision was that the express power in the settlement was "to appoint any *other* person" and this precluded the appoint-

---

31 As inserted by s.27 of the Pensions (Amendment) Act, 1996.

32 (1889) 42 Ch.D 522.

ment of one of the donees of the power himself. With regard to the general ground for the decision that the power is a fiduciary power, Kay J. stated:

> The ordinary power of appointing new trustees, under a settlement such as this, of course imposes upon the person who has the power of appointment the duty of selecting honest and good persons who can be trusted with the very difficult, onerous and often delicate duties which trustees have to perform. He is bound to select to the best of his ability the best people he can find for the purpose. Is that power of selection a fiduciary power or not? I will try it in this way, which I offered as a test in the course of the argument. Suppose, as happens not infrequently, the trustees, under the terms of the Deed of Trust are entitled to remuneration by way of annual salary or payment. Could a person who has a power of appointment put the office of trustee up for sale and sell it to the best bidder? It is clear that would be entirely improper. Could he take any remuneration for making the appointment? In my opinion, certainly not. Why not? The answer is that he cannot exercise the power for his own benefit. Why not again? The answer is inevitable. Because it is a power which involves a duty of a fiduciary nature: and I therefore come to the conclusion, independently of any authority, that the power is a fiduciary power.

Re Skeats' Settlement (which was a decision at first instance) was approved by the Court of Appeal in *Re Shortridge.*[33] In that case, Lindley L.J. said:

> Again, the judgment of Lord Justice Kay, then Mr Justice Kay, in *Re Skeats' Settlement* is a clear decision that a power to appoint new trustees is a fiduciary power.

4.23 Whilst the decision in *Re Skeats' Settlement* has not been judicially challenged, it should be noted that the case concerned a private settlement, as did *Re Shortridge*, rather than a pension scheme trust. In the case of *Mettoy Pension Trustees Limited* v. *Evans,*[34] Warner J., in reviewing the nature of powers conferred on employers and trustees under pension scheme documentation, mentioned, albeit only in passing:

---

[33] [1895] 1 Ch. 278.

[34] [1990] WLR 1587.

> The power to appoint new trustees (*which is of course fiduciary*[35]) is given by the Deed to the employer as is a power to require a trustee to retire.

The case of *Re Skeats' Settlement* was not referred to in the judgment.

4.24 The question has been posed elsewhere[36] as to whether the principle enunciated in *Re Skeats' Settlement* applies to pension scheme trusts. In *Cowan* v. *Scargill*[37] Sir Robert Megarry VC held that the general law of trusts will apply to pension scheme trusts. Warner J. in *Mettoy* v. *Evans* stated that there are no special rules of construction for pension scheme trusts. However, in *Imperial Group Pension Trust Limited* v. *Imperial Tobacco Limited*[38] Browne-Wilkinson VC stated that "pension scheme trusts are of a quite different nature to traditional trusts". In the absence of any authority to the contrary, it is suggested that the Irish Courts would be influenced by the UK authorities that the power to appoint a trustee of a pension scheme is a fiduciary power and the exercise of such power is therefore open to challenge in the Courts.[39]

Member Trustees

4.25 The first report of the National Pensions Board recommended that members of funded schemes with more than 50 members should have a legal right to require the employer to hold an election for member trustees.[40] This recommendation was carried forward in section 62 sub-section (1) of the Pensions Act, which states:

> The Minister shall provide by regulations in respect of schemes having not less than a specified number of members, that the members of any such scheme may select, or approve of the selection by the employer concerned, of a person or a specified number

---

35 Emphasis added.

36 See *British Pension Lawyer* (March 1991 Article by David Pollard) and Inglis-Jones, N. (1989): *Law of Occupational Pension Schemes,* London: Sweet & Maxwell: p. 406.

37 [1985] 1 Ch. 270.

38 [1991] 1 WLR 589.

39 The question arose again in the English courts in *Simpson Curtis Pension Trustees* v. *Readson Limited* [1994] PLR 289. *Skeats Settlement* was not referred to in the case. However, in *Simpson Curtis* there was no dispute between the parties as to the appropriateness of the nominated trustee.

40 First Report of the National Pensions Board (Pl. 4776), Chapter 2 para. 35

of persons who shall be appointed to be a trustee or trustees of the scheme (or who shall be retained as such trustee or trustees, as the case may be).[41]

On 27 July 1993, the Minister for Social Welfare made regulations entitled the Occupational Pension Schemes (Member Participation in the Selection of Persons for Appointment as Trustees) Regulations, 1993. Having been found deficient in a number of respects, these Regulations were entirely replaced by further regulations entitled Occupational Pension Schemes (Member Participation in the Selection of Persons for Appointment as Trustees) (No. 2) Regulations, 1993[42] made by the Minister on 21 December 1993 and which came into force on 1 January 1994. These Regulations now provide for the selection by members of pension schemes of trustees. This subject is considered in detail later.[43]

Small Self-Administered Schemes

4.26 The Revenue Commissioners have certain special requirements in the case of what are called "small self-administered schemes".[44] A scheme is generally regarded as small self-administered where it has fewer than 12 members, the fund of which is not fully administered and insured by a life office.[45]

For such a scheme to be exempt approved it must have a "pensioneer trustee" — that is, an individual or body widely involved with occupational pension schemes and their approval, and who is prepared to undertake to the Revenue Commissioners that no termination of the scheme will be consented to otherwise than in accordance with the approved terms of the winding-up rule. Where a body corporate is proposed as trustee of such a scheme, the Revenue Commissioners require that the directors, or a majority of them, should be acceptable as pensioneer trustees in their own right.[46] The object of these re-

---

41 s.62(1) as substituted by s.15 of the Social Welfare (No.2) Act, 1993.

42 SI No 399 of 1993.

43 See Chapter 14.

44 See Revenue Practice Notes.

45 In certain circumstances larger schemes are deemed to be small self administered. See para. 6.78.

46 There is no public register of such pensioneer trustees. However, the Retirement Benefits District does maintain a list for internal use.

quirements is to inhibit the operation of such a scheme for tax avoidance purposes.[47]

DUTIES OF TRUSTEES

4.27 It can be seen from the previous section that there are various ways in which a person can be appointed as trustee of a pension scheme. Once appointed, the trustee assumes onerous duties and is usually given wide-ranging discretionary powers. Although it is not a legal requirement, in practice the principal powers and duties of pension scheme trustees are usually set out in the trust documentation. Most of the duties of pension scheme trustees arise out of equitable principles and not the Trustee Acts or the Pensions Act.

4.28 The first report of the National Pensions Board concluded that no attempt should be made to list exhaustively the duties of pension scheme trustees in legislation, but that the general duties of trustees should be outlined. The Pensions Act broadly codifies some of the principal duties of trustees established under the common law. The Pensions Act provides that "without prejudice to the duties of trustees generally and in addition to complying with the other requirements of the Pensions Act", the duties of pension scheme trustees shall include:

- To ensure, in so far as is reasonable, that the contributions payable by the employer and the members of the scheme, where appropriate, are received
- To provide for the proper investment of the resources of the scheme in accordance with the rules of the scheme
- To make arrangements, where appropriate, for the payment of the benefits as provided for under the Rules of the Scheme as they become due
- To ensure that proper membership and financial records are kept
- If the scheme is wound up, to apply the resources of the scheme in discharging its liabilities without undue delay in accordance with the rules of the scheme and, in the case of defined benefit schemes, in accordance with the provisions of section 48 of the Pensions Act
- To register the pension scheme with the Pensions Board.[48]

---

47 Generally see para. 6.77 et seq.

Before examining the specific duties of trustees in detail it is appropriate to explore the possible conflicts of interest that a trustee may have.

Conflict of Duty and Interest

4.29 It is a general principle of trust law, which is equally applicable to the trustees of a pension scheme, that trustees must not put themselves in a position where their own interest and their duty as trustees conflict.[49] Trustees, for instance, cannot buy trust property or use information gained as a trustee to their own commercial advantage. With respect to use of information, modern trust documentation will contain strict confidentiality provisions imposing a duty of confidentiality on trustees. This is important and desirable. Given the nature of the trustee's role with respect to the pension scheme, trustees will be privy to confidential and sensitive information. Such information might touch on the personal circumstances of an employee member or the financial circumstances of the employer. The information is received by trustees in that capacity and must be kept confidential and only used for the purposes of the trust.[50]

4.30 Clearly situations can arise where a trustee will have a conflict of interest. For instance, in a situation of a winding up of a pension scheme which has member trustees, and the trustees have discretion with respect to augmentation of benefits, it may be possible for a decision of the trustees to benefit one part of the membership of the scheme over another. A director of the employer, who is also a trustee, might be in a conflict situation if a proposal were put to the trus-

---

48 s.59 and s.60 of the Pensions Act as amended by the Social Welfare Acts, 1991 and 1992.

49 See the very interesting discussion on this point in Noble, R. "The Exercise of Trustees' Discretion under a Pension Scheme" 1992 JBL 261 at p.266.

50 The duty of confidentiality will be owed by the trustee to those parties furnishing information and to those persons to whom the information relates. Thus it is owed principally to the employer and the members. The Courts will assist a plaintiff who proves that a person has made improper use of confidential information without the plaintiff's consent. See *Saltman Engineering Co. Ltd.* v. *Campbell Engineering Co. Ltd* [1948] 65 RPC 203, *House of Spring Gardens Ltd. and Ors* v. *Point Blank Limited and Ors* [1984] IR 611.

tees to advance a loan from the fund to the employer in a situation where the employer was in some financial difficulty.

4.31 It is not entirely clear whether a trustee in such position can act or should apply to Court for directions. If on application to Court, by an aggrieved beneficiary for instance, a decision of the trustees in such circumstances were held to be in breach of trust, the decisions of the trustees would be invalid. Properly drafted trust documentation should contain a provision allowing trustees to act notwithstanding a conflict of interest.

4.32 The UK case of *Manning* v. *Drexel Burnham Lambert Holdings Limited (In Liquidation)*[51] is of interest. In that case the four plaintiffs were trustees of the pension scheme. The sponsoring employer was in insolvent liquidation. The plaintiffs were also beneficiaries. They found themselves in the position where they had a discretion as to the application of a surplus in the fund of the pension scheme and, being advised that they had a conflict of interest, application was made to Court requesting that the Court should exercise the discretion on behalf of the trustees. The formal trust documentation did not contain any provision allowing trustees to act notwithstanding a conflict of interest.

4.33 The Court had to decide, first, whether the trustees were entitled to apply to the Court for directions in a situation where they had a conflict of interest. Lindsay J., having reviewed what he referred to as the general rule of equity as enunciated in a line of cases,[52] held that the general rule was as set down by Sankey J. in *Regal (Hastings) Limited* v. *Gulliver*: "that no-one who has duties of a fiduciary nature to perform is allowed to enter into engagements in which he has or can have a personal interest conflicting with the interests of those whom he is bound to protect". Lindsay J. held that this rule did not apply with such force as to deny the Court even the jurisdiction to

---

51 [1994] PLR 75.

52 Lindsay J referred to *Aberdeen Railway Company* v. *Blakie Brothers* (1854) 1 Macq. 461 and 471; *Regal (Hastings) Limited* v. *Gulliver* [1967] 2 AC 134; *Phipps* v. *Boardman* [1967] 2 AC 46; *Bray* v. *Ford* [1896] AC 44; *Re William Makin and Son Limited* [1992] PLR 177; *British Coal Corporation* v. *British Coal Staff Superannuation Scheme Trustees Limited* [1993] PLR 303.

give directions where directions are sought by trustees who are in a position of conflict.

4.34 In the *Manning* case, Lindsay J. proceeded to give the directions sought. It is unfortunate that the court did not directly address the question as to whether a specific provision in the trust documentation allowing trustees to act notwithstanding a conflict of interest would be effective. In the case of *Bray* v. *Ford*, Lord Herschell (at p. 51) said:

> It is an inflexible rule of a Court of Equity that a person in a fiduciary position, such as the respondent's, is not, *unless otherwise expressly provided*[53], entitled to make a profit; he is not allowed to put himself in a position where his interest and duty conflict.

Lindsay J. in *Manning* referring to *Bray* v. *Ford* said:

> I have heard no argument and I do not attempt to rule on the subject, identified by Vinelott J.[54] as difficult, of whether the general rule can be overcome by express provision in the trust deed, although I do note that in *Bray* v. *Ford*, Lord Herschell, on a closely related point, included the words "unless otherwise expressly provided". But even if the difficulties can be so overcome, there will be trust deeds which do not have such a provision and there will also be trust deeds which cannot be amended to include it.

Lindsay J. also referred to the report of the Goode Committee which had recommended that schemes should provide, in stated circumstances, for member elected trustees. Lindsay J. proceeded to recommend that when the English legislature was determining the extent to which it would enact the recommendations of the Goode Committee that it consider the creation of a clear exception to the so-called "General Rule of Equity".

4.35 It is clear from the passage quoted above that the Court in *Manning* had some doubt as to whether express language in the trust documentation was of itself sufficient to allow trustees to act in a conflict-of-interest situation. It is suggested that the apparent doubt expressed by the Court is not of such importance. In any trust, including a pension scheme trust, a conflict between duty and interest may

---

53 Emphasis added.

54 In *Re William Makin and Son Limited.*

arise. The law has always recognised this and allows for such conflicts to exist. For example, there is no doubt but that a charging clause in a pension scheme trust which allows professional trustees to charge for their services will be enforced by the Courts. The judgment of Lord Herschell in *Bray* v. *Ford* was followed by Danckwerts J. in *Re the French Protestant Hospital*[55] Danckwerts J., having quoted from the judgment in *Bray* v. *Ford*, stated:

> Lord Herschell clearly recognised that in some cases it may not be improper to have a provision, sometimes described as a charging clause, which enables the trustees to be paid; and clauses are often inserted in wills and settlements which do enable trustees to be paid for their services.

4.36 Furthermore, the legislature in enacting the provisions of section 62 of the Pensions Act has recognised that conflicts of interest may arise. The law provides that members of a pension scheme, and therefore beneficiaries, may be appointed as trustees. Clearly, the view of the legislature is that the benefits that may flow from such rights will outweigh the difficulties that may be created. There has not yet been a reported case in Ireland or England in which it has been necessary for the Court to decide whether trustees may rely upon a provision in trust documentation that they may act notwithstanding a conflict of interest. It is submitted that an Irish Court would enforce such a provision. In the absence of legislation or a clear decision of the Irish Courts on the point, it is advisable that trustees ensure that the formal trust documentation contain a properly drafted provision allowing trustees to act notwithstanding a conflict of interest. If trustees find themselves with a conflict of interest and the formal trust documentation does not assist, it is arguable that they cannot then amend the trust documentation to correct the omission. They may have to apply to Court for directions.

4.37 The trustees of a pension scheme must be allowed to carry out their duties free from outside pressure. Such pressures might be imposed by senior management on a director who is a trustee, by fellow employees on an employee who is a trustee, or by a trade union on an official appointed as a trustee. A trustee who is in a position of being unable to act free from such pressures may be obliged to make application to Court for directions or, in an extreme situation, to resign. It would be prudent for a trustee in such a situation to seek independ-

---

[55] [1951] 1 Ch. 567

ent legal advice. An example of the importance of a trustee obtaining such advice is to be found in the US case of *Donovan (Secretary of the United States Department of Labor)* v. *Bierwirth*.[56] In that case, which concerned a hostile takeover of the Grumman Corporation, the trustees were advised by the legal officer of the Grumman Corporation itself. In the circumstances of the case, that legal officer could hardly have been expected to furnish independent advice and the trustees' actions received considerable criticism from the Court. If a trustee in exercising a power or discretion under a trust does so for an improper motive, that will constitute a fraud on the power, and will, on application to the Court, be set aside.[57]

4.38 Another situation in which trustees can commonly find themselves with a conflict of duty and interest is where a receiver or liquidator of a company becomes trustee of the Company's pension scheme. An example is to be found in the UK case *Thrells Limited (1974) Pension Scheme (in Liquidation)* v. *Peter Lomas*.[58]

4.39 The conflicts identified above arise from a trustee's duties and interests being potentially divergent. Assuming that a trustee can overcome the conflict issue, there will be a number of statutory and common law duties which must be discharged. These are considered in the following paragraphs.

Specific Duties

4.40 ***To Ensure that Contributions are Paid:*** Under common law a trustee has a duty to get in the trust property. In the context of a pension scheme, the trustee must ensure (so far as is possible) the collection of the contributions both from the employer and from the members (if appropriate) that are necessary to maintain the scheme. The contributions include those to provide for retirement and also death benefits. Unless there is a provision in the pension scheme documentation to the contrary, this duty may extend to an obligation on the trustee to issue legal proceedings where necessary to collect in

---

56 US Court of Appeals; Second Circuit, 680 F.2d 263 (1982)

57 See for example *Duke of Portland* v. *Topham* (1864) 11 H.L.C. 32

58 [1992] PLR 233. This case and the issue of conflict of interest in the case of receiverships and liquidations is considered in Chapter 17 at 17.52.

the trust property.[59] This duty is restated in section 59(a) of the Pensions Act which provides that trustees of schemes shall:

> . . . ensure, in so far as is reasonable, that the contributions payable by the employer and the members of the scheme, where appropriate, are received.

The obligations of the Employer to pay contributions (in appropriate schemes) and the recovery of contributions where the employer is insolvent are discussed elsewhere.[60]

4.41 ***To Safeguard the Assets:*** A trustee has a duty to safeguard the contributions constituting the fund of the pension scheme. This is one of the most important duties of the trustee. It has always been so in the law of trusts[61] and is identified again by the First Report of the National Pensions Board[62] and in England by the Report of the Pension Law Review Committee.[63] The issues of safeguarding and custody of trust assets are discussed later.[64]

4.42 ***To Invest the Assets:*** A trustee has a duty to invest the fund of the scheme for the benefit of the members.[65] The trust documentation will normally set out precise and wide powers of investment. It is important that the powers of investment of the trustees be dealt with in the trust documentation, as in the absence of such provision the forms of investment open to pension scheme trustees under the Trustee Acts are quite restrictive.

4.43 Section 1 of the Trustee Act, 1893, as substituted by section 1 of the Trustee (Authorised Investments) Act, 1958, provides that trus-

---

59 See *Re Tucker* (1894) 1 Ch. 724, *Re Brogden* (1886) 38 Ch.D at p. 546.

60 See Chapters 5 and 17.

61 See *MacNamara* v. *Carey* (1867) I.R. Eq. 9

62 Whilst not so stated in the Report, it is a theme running through the recommendations made in the Report in relation to collection of contributions, disclosure of information and the funding standard for defined benefit schemes.

63 See their Report. Volume 1 Chapter 4.10. With regard to the safeguarding of pension scheme assets see also Chapter 10.

64 See Chapter 10.

65 See s.59(b) Pensions Act. The subject of investment of pension assets is discussed in Chapter 10.

tees may invest in certain stated authorised investments, and section 2 of the 1958 Act further empowers the Minister for Finance to vary the list of authorised investments by addition, alteration or deletion. The list of authorised investments is currently:

1. Irish government securities
2. Securities guaranteed as to capital and interest by the Minister for Finance
3. British government securities
4. Real securities in Ireland
5. Securities and mortgages of certain local authorities and similar bodies
6. Bank of Ireland stock
7. Certain loan stock of the Bank of Ireland and Allied Irish Banks plc
8. Securities of the ESB, ACC and Bord na Móna
9. Debentures or debenture stock of public quoted industrial and commercial companies registered in Ireland provided that the total of such debentures and stock does not exceed the paid-up share capital and that a dividend of at least 5 per cent has been paid on the ordinary shares in each of the preceding 5 years
10. Interest-bearing deposit accounts in specified banks, and credit institutions, including ACC and ICC and the major building societies.[66]

It will be noted that absent from the above list are ordinary shares in publicly quoted companies and any of the more modern forms of investment such as unit trusts.[67]

4.44 It is not enough for a trustee to exercise only the degree of care that a person would exercise if they were investing their own money.

---

[66] This list of authorised investments is as set out in the 1958 Act as amended by orders of the Minister for Finance being Statutory Instrument numbers 285/1967, 241/1969, 377/1974, 344/1977, 407/1979, 58/1983, 366/1983, 224/1985, 372/1986, 327/1990 and 756/1992.

[67] s.4 of the Trustee Act 1893 provides that: "The preceding sections shall apply . . . and the powers conferred thereby shall be *in addition to* the powers conferred by the instrument, if any, creating the trust."

The reality in a pension scheme trust is that moneys or other assets are vested in the trustees for the purposes of benefiting other persons — the members and their dependants. The duty of care required was stated by Lindley L.J. in *Re Whiteley. Whiteley* v. *Learoyd*[68] as follows:

> The duty of the Trustee is not to take such care only as a prudent man would take if he had only himself to consider; the duty rather is to take such care as an ordinary prudent man would take if he were minded to make an investment for the benefit of other people for whom he felt morally bound to provide.

4.45 Given the complexity and sophistication of potential investments, it is most usual for the trustees to appoint an investment manager or managers to whom the duty of investment and management is delegated.[69] The selection and appointment of an investment manager is a matter that may be left entirely to the trustees by the trust documentation, or it may be a matter for the joint decision of the employer and the trustees, or it may be entirely a decision for the employer. The appointment of an investment manager does not, however, absolve the trustees from their duty of care with respect to the security and investment of the pension scheme assets. Notwithstanding that the employer, as an interested party, may well be involved in the selection process, the trustees remain ultimately responsible for the investment. It is prudent that trustees should carry out periodic reviews of investment performance, and at least annually.[70]

4.46 ***To Be Familiar with Trust Documentation:*** A trustee has a duty to be familiar with the terms and provisions of the trust documentation, to be aware of the rules governing the operation of the pension scheme and the law as it affects the operation of the trust. The beneficiaries of the pension scheme will rely on the trustees to carry out the objects of the pension scheme trust in accordance with its terms. It is evident that the trustee must therefore be familiar with the terms of the trust and of the obligations imposed by the

---

68 (1886) Vol. 33 Ch.D. 347 at 355, see also *Stacey* v. *Branch* [1995] 2 ILRM 136.

69 Note that the trustees must have power under the trust deed to delegate: see para. 4.64 and para. 10.65 et seq.

70 *Nestlé* v. *National Westminster Bank plc* [1994] 1 All ER 118. This was also recommended by the Pensions Law Review Committee in the UK for inclusion in legislation as a duty of trustees. The recommendation was not followed in the subsequent UK Pensions Act, 1995.

Pensions Act. In practice, this means that a new trustee should obtain a copy of all the formal trust documentation (the Interim Trust Deed, the Definitive Trust Deed and any amending Deeds and resolutions of the employer company if the scheme has been established by resolution), copies of any announcements issued to employees and copies of any explanatory booklets. Announcements of changes in benefits issued by the employer to members may have effect notwithstanding that formal trust documentation may not have been put in place.[71] The trustees may also have been required to sign undertakings to the Revenue Commissioners with respect to conduct of the scheme and payment of benefits. New trustees should obtain copies and be familiar with such undertakings. The trustees are entitled to get into their possession the documentation constituting the trust, and the Courts will enforce this right.[72] The importance of being familiar with the trust documentation may be seen in *Nestlé* v. *National Westminster Bank*. In that case, one of the grounds of claim for breach of trust was that the trustee (the Bank) had failed to appreciate its powers of investment contained under a will. The Court of Appeal (Dillon L.J.) stated:

> It was the duty of the Bank to acquaint itself with the scope of its powers under the will.

4.47 ***To Act in Accordance with the Provisions of the Pension Scheme Trust:*** A trustee must carry out the pension scheme trust in accordance with its terms. This means just what it says. If some action is required under the pension scheme — for instance, the payment of the benefit — then the trustee must see that this is done. Equally, if some action is not permitted by the trust, then no matter how worthwhile it may be, it is not permissible for the trustees to take such action. The failure to take action required by the trust and the taking of action not authorised by the trust documentation may amount to a breach of trust.

4.48 ***To Act with Care and in the Best Interests of the Beneficiaries:*** Trustees, in their conduct of the administration of a pension scheme, must act with ordinary prudence. The standard of care re-

---

71 *Mettoy Pension Trustees Limited* v. *Evans* [1991] 2 All ER 513.

72 *Tiger* v. *Barclays Bank plc* [1952] 1 All ER 85

quired of a trustee was stated by Lindley L.J. in *Re Whiteley. Whiteley* v. *Learoyd* refered to earlier.[73]

4.49 A trustee has a duty to act, at all times, in the best interests of the beneficiaries of the pension scheme. This duty is owed to all beneficiaries, whether they be active members, deferred pensioners, contingent beneficiaries or pensioners. A trustee cannot prefer one class of beneficiary above another.[74] This is not to say that the trustee cannot make a decision the effect of which is to confer a greater benefit on one class of beneficiary (for instance, on a winding-up). What is meant is that in reaching a decision, the trustee must give equal consideration to the interests of all beneficiaries. Clearly this can lead to difficulties.[75]

4.50 The duty of a trustee to act in the best interests of all beneficiaries is often considered in the context of the trustee's power of investment. There have been several cases in which trustees have been sued for breach of trust, it being alleged that the trustees in exercising their powers of investment were preferring one class of beneficiary above another.[76]

4.51 ***To Notify Members:*** A trustee has a duty to inform members in relation to the investments of the pension fund and of the trustees' dealings with the pension fund.[77] There is authority in the UK that trustees are not obliged to explain the benefits payable or the means of qualifying for such benefits under pension schemes.[78] The Pensions Act, Part V, and the Occupational Pension Schemes (Disclosure of Information) Regulations, 1991 also impose obligations on trustees with respect to disclosure of information to members and other bene-

---

73 See para. 4.44.

74 This will include sex equality — See Chapter 16.

75 See for instance *Manning* v. *Drexel Burnham Lambert Holdings (In Liquidation).*

76 Examples are *Nestlé* v. *National Westminster Bank, Withers* v. *Teachers Retirement System of the City of New York* (1978) 477 F.Sup. 1248

77 *Chaine-Nickson* v. *Bank of Ireland* [1976] IR 393.

78 *Hamar* v. *The Pensions Ombudsman* [1996] PLR 1. Whilst trustees may not be obliged to explain the benefits payable under the scheme, the employer may have such obligation, see *Scally* v. *Southern Health and Social Services Board* [1991] 4 All ER 563 and see para. 5.17

ficiaries.[79] It is clear from general trust law that a beneficiary has a right to see and inspect trust documents, and to require information with regard to the trust property and the administration of the trust by the trustees. In *Low* v. *Bouverie*[80] it was held that any person who has an interest in the trust property may demand information whether the interest is vested or contingent.[81]

4.52 ***To Take Advice:*** A Trustee (other than a professional trustee) is not expected to have expert knowledge as to all those matters which will affect the operation of a pension scheme. It is clear, however, that trustees have a duty to seek and obtain appropriate advice before taking decisions on matters where they do not have expert knowledge. In *Nestlé* v. *National Westminster Bank*, Dillon L.J. stated:

> It is understandable that the Bank had doubts, as to its powers to invest in ordinary shares. It is inexcusable that the Bank took no step at any time to obtain legal advice as to the scope of its power to invest in ordinary shares.[82]

4.53 ***To Ensure that Benefits are Paid:*** A trustee has a duty to ensure that the members and other beneficiaries of the pension scheme receive the benefits to which they are entitled, when they are entitled to receive them.[83] An example of a difficult area that may require the exercise of a discretion by the trustee is the payment of a lump sum benefit on the death in service of a member.

4.54 ***To Comply with Revenue Requirements:*** A trustee has a duty to ensure that the conditions laid down by the Revenue Commissioners

---

79 See Chapter 13.

80 [1891] 3 Ch. 82

81 See also *Re Tillot* [1892] 1 Ch. 86 — if a trustee fails to furnish information requested, the beneficiary has a right to apply to Court and the trustee will be fixed with the costs of such application; *Re Skinner* [1904] 2 Ch. 785; *Re Lindsay* [1904] 2 Ch. 785. s.3(1)(k)(ii) of the Terms of the Employment Act, 1994 requires that employers furnish employees with details of terms and conditions relating to pensions and pension schemes. s.5(1) of the same Act requires any change in such terms or conditions to be notified by the employer to the employee within one month of the change. This notification can be made in the form of a booklet. These disclosure provisions are addressed to employers, not trustees.

82 At p.123. However, the Bank was not ultimately found to be in breach of trust.

83 See s.59(c) Pensions Act.

in granting exempt approval to the scheme are observed. If Revenue approval is lost, both the members and the employer will suffer. They will suffer through the loss of tax relief on contributions and the loss of tax exemptions on investment gains. The trustee has a responsibility to ensure, so far as is possible, that this does not happen.[84]

4.55 ***To Keep Records:*** A trustee has a duty to be responsible for the day-to-day administration of the pension scheme, for keeping accounts and records,[85] and for the provision of information to beneficiaries as required.[86] This is usually delegated to either benefits consultants or life offices or may, possibly, be handled by a pensions department of the sponsoring employer.

4.56 ***Not to Profit from Trust:*** A trustee must not, unless authorised, make any profit from the trust. Trustees of pension schemes will often be members, and therefore beneficiaries, of the pension scheme. Trustees may also be professional advisers to the pension scheme, such as solicitors. A pension scheme may also have professional trustees. It is necessary for the trust documentation to contain provisions expressly authorising trustees who may be beneficiaries of the pension scheme to receive benefits, and trustees who may be professional advisors to be paid for their services.[87]

4.57 ***To Ensure Adequate Funding:*** The trustee of a defined benefit scheme has a duty to ensure that the pension scheme is adequately funded to meet the future liabilities of the pension scheme to pay benefits. The trustees of a defined benefit scheme are required[88] to cause actuarial funding certificates and valuations to be prepared by an actuary from time to time and within time periods specified by

---

84 As to Revenue requirements generally see Chapter 6. On withdrawal of approval see para. 6.30 et seq.

85 *Crawford* v. *Crawford* (1867) LR 1 Eq. 436

86 *Moore* v. *McGlynn* [1894] 1 IR. 74 and see s.59(d) and Part V of the Pensions Act.

87 It should be noted that where the formal trust documentation does not make provision for trustees to be paid for their services those trustees may not amend the trust documentation to include such provision — *Re The French Protestant Hospital* [1951] 1 Ch. 567. See also the consideration above of trustees' conflicts of duty and interest at paras. 4.29 to 4.39.

88 s.42 of the Pensions Act.

the Pensions Act. Where the actuarial funding certificate does not meet the funding standard set out in the Pensions Act, the trustees are required to submit a funding proposal to the Pensions Board. It should be noted that compliance by the trustees with the funding standard set out in the Pensions Act will not necessarily satisfy their general duty to ensure that the scheme is adequately funded. This subject is discussed in detail later.[89]

The Pensions Act

4.58 The Pensions Act imposes certain specific duties on trustees of schemes, which are in addition to those noted above:

1. To furnish information to the Pensions Board or an authorised person in connection with any investigation or inspection of a scheme[90]
2. To register the Scheme with the Pensions Board[91] and to pay registration fees due to the Pensions Board[92]
3. To comply with the preservation requirements set out in Part III of the Pensions Act, including the transfer from a scheme of a preserved benefit[93] and the receipt into a scheme of a preserved benefit[94]
4. In the case of defined benefit schemes:

---

89 See Chapter 9.

90 s.18 as amended by s.6 Pensions (Amendment) Act, 1996.

91 s.60. With respect to registration, more detailed provisions have been made by the Minister for Social Welfare by the Occupational Pension Schemes (Registration) Regulations, 1991 (SI No 325 of 1991). Trustees should have regard to these Regulations.

92 s. 25. Registration fees are prescribed by Regulation made by the Minister for Social Welfare. Fees are currently laid down in the Occupational Pension Schemes (Fees) Regulations, 1991 (SI No 372 of 1991) and the Occupational Pension Schemes (Fees) (Amendment) Regulations, 1992 (SI No 367 of 1992).

93 s.34(4).

94 s.34(6).

- To cause preparation of an actuarial funding certificate[95] and to submit it to the Pensions Board[96]
- To prepare a funding proposal (in a situation where an actuarial funding certificate does not meet the requirements of Part IV of the Pensions Act)[97]
- To comply with a direction issued by the Pensions Board[98] by:
  - (i) Notification to members
  - (ii) Reduction of benefits and causing a further funding certificate to be prepared[99]

5. To disclose certain specified information to members, prospective members, spouses, trade union representatives and others[100]
6. To prepare an annual report concerning the operation of the scheme[101]
7. To have the accounts of the scheme audited and an actuarial valuation prepared.[102] It should be noted that there are differing requirements for defined benefit and defined contribution schemes and schemes of different sizes[103]
8. To ensure that the provisions of the scheme comply with the principle of equal treatment contained in Part VII of the Pensions Act[104]
9. To report a material misappropriation or fraudulent conversion of the scheme's resources to the Pensions Board.[105]

---

95 s.42(2).

96 s.42(1).

97 s.50(1).

98 s.50(1).

99 s.50(3).

100 s.54(1).

101 s.55(1).

102 s.56(1).

103 See the Disclosure Regulations and Chapter 13

104 s.71(2), 72(3) and 73(2). The duty at 8. is also specifically imposed on the employer.

Inquiry by Trustee

4.59 In view of the extensive duties imposed on trustees, it is prudent for a new trustee to make inquiries as to the establishment of the scheme. In particular, such a person should satisfy themselves:

1. As to the constitution of the scheme (that it is properly documented)
2. As to the solvency of the scheme (if a defined benefit scheme)
3. As to the scheme's tax status with the Revenue Commissioners (that it is exempt approved)
4. If the scheme is funded, that the fund of the scheme is secure and an investment manager or life office has been appointed
5. That all contributions due to date have been received and invested
6. That the general requirements of the Pensions Act including registration, preservation and disclosure requirements have been complied with by the existing trustees
7. That there are no claims against the trustees, whether actual or pending, in particular that there are no claims with respect to sex discrimination.

POWERS OF TRUSTEES

4.60 In order to carry out their duties, trustees of a pension scheme are normally given extensive powers under the trust documentation. These powers can be divided, broadly, between powers that must be exercised by the trustee and powers that are discretionary. Powers that must be exercised by the trustee may still have a discretionary element. For example, trustees have a duty to invest the assets of the pension scheme and for this purpose will be given power under the trust documentation to do so. The choice of investments or, if appropriate, the choice of investment manager, is often a matter for the discretion of the trustees. It is usual for discretionary powers of trustees conferred under trust documentation to be restricted in some way. For instance, a discretionary power to augment benefits may require the consent of the employer. Examples of powers conferred on trustees by the trust documentation are:

---

[105] s.83 Pensions Act, as inserted by s.38 of the Pensions (Amendment) Act, 1996. See para. 1.71 et seq.

1. To amend the trust deed and rules — this power is usually subject to the consent of the employer. It may be more usual for the power to amend the trust deed and rules to be given to the employer subject to the consent of the trustees. Trustees cannot amend the formal trust documentation so as to divest themselves of their powers.[106]
2. To effect investment, including power to appoint an investment manager (often subject to the agreement of the employer)
3. To augment benefits (usually subject to consent or agreement of the employer)
4. To delegate certain functions, such as payment of benefits, to third parties
5. To choose the recipient for death in service lump sum benefits (where appropriate).

Discretionary Powers

4.61 Many powers given to trustees under scheme documentation are discretionary. It is desirable that this should be so as all possible situations that may arise in the life of a scheme cannot be envisaged and provided for in advance in the scheme documentation. Equally, situations can arise which are not entirely clear-cut and which require the exercise of judgment. Examples of such situations might include:

1. Increases in pensions in payment (or deferment) on a winding-up of the scheme
2. Payment of dependants' pensions where a member dies leaving a legal spouse and a "common law" spouse[107]
3. Death in service lump sum benefits
4. Early retirement on grounds other than ill-health.[108]

Well-drafted trust documentation will provide trustees with discretionary powers enabling them to take or refrain from taking action in situations such as those set out above.

---

[106] See para. 3.21.

[107] See Chapter 15.

[108] This is more usually a matter for the employer's decision.

4.62 The exercise by trustees of discretionary powers is a difficult area and one that has been the subject of much litigation in the United Kingdom.[109] Claims tend to originate from potential beneficiaries, employers and liquidators. Clearly, a trustee cannot prevent some other party from instituting proceedings, and the Courts have an inherent jurisdiction to deal with questions arising from the construction of pension scheme trust documents. The circumstances in which the Courts will intervene and review the exercise by a trustee of a power are discussed below.[110]

4.63 Where trustees exercise a discretion under a pension scheme, they are not required to disclose to scheme beneficiaries the reasons for such decision. In *Wilson and Another* v. *The Law Debenture Trust Corporation plc*,[111] the trustee (Law Debenture Trust Corporation) had, following the sale of a business, made a transfer to a new pension scheme of part of a pension fund. The Plaintiffs, being beneficiaries and transferring employees, were unhappy with the transfer amount and sought disclosure of documents to reveal the trustees' reasons for exercising their discretion. The trustees (the Defendants) relied on the decision in *Re Londonderrys Settlement*[112] that trustees were not obliged to disclose the reasons for their decisions. The Plaintiffs argued that the principle enunciated in that case was not appropriate to the modern sophisticated pension scheme trust. The Court, holding for the Defendants, held that it was wrong in principle to suggest that the trustees of a pension scheme were under a more onerous obligation to account to their beneficiaries than they could have appreciated on taking up their appointment. That would be the effect if such a long-established trust-law principle were to be overturned in the manner suggested by the Plaintiffs. The Court said that any such amendment to trust law as it applies to pension schemes would be a matter for legislation.

---

[109] See Nobles, R.L. "The Exercise of Trustees' Discretion under a Pension Scheme" 1992 JBL 261.

[110] See para. 4.66 et seq.

[111] [1994] PLR 141.

[112] [1965] Ch. 918.

Delegation of Powers

4.64 Many of the powers conferred on trustees to allow them to carry out their duties are in practice delegated by the trustees. For example, the power to invest the fund of the scheme is one which, in many schemes, would be delegated to an investment manager or a life office. Payment of benefits is a matter often delegated by trustees to the employer or a life office. The administration of the pension scheme is also a matter which is increasingly being delegated by pension trustees. It is not possible for trustees to delegate their powers to a third party unless this is specifically authorised by the formal trust documentation. Historically, trustees were chosen because the person appointing them had confidence and trust in them. Because of this essentially personal character of the office, the law did not allow for delegation of functions by a trustee.[113] However, such delegation is permitted if the formal trust documentation so allows.

4.65 Such delegates might be an investment manager (in investing funds) or stockbroker (in buying or selling securities) or a solicitor (in dealing in the property of the fund). It is important that the appointment or delegation is authorised by the trust documentation and that there is no other default on the part of the trustee. For instance, if the trustee failed to supervise the delegate or agent properly, the trustee could be held liable. In practice, trustees should regularly review the delegation of their powers. They should be satisfied that where powers are delegated there are proper controls in place.

Review by Court

4.66 Pension scheme documentation confers numerous powers on trustees. Some powers are stated to be exercisable by trustees alone, some types of power are exercisable by the trustees with the consent of the employer, some powers are stated to be exercisable at the discretion of the trustees, and others are conferred on the employer to be exercised either at its discretion or with the consent of the trustees. Reported cases, particularly in England, reveal problems that have arisen where the employer or the trustees have exercised powers, for instance, in deciding whether a scheme is to continue, where schemes are to be merged, whether a surplus is to be applied in enhancing benefits or by way of repayment to the employer, or in determining

---

113 *Re O'Flanagan's and Ryan's Contract* [1905] 1 IR 280

the amount of bulk transfer payments.[114] It is important to consider the circumstances in which the Court will review the exercise of a power by the trustees. This has been considered by the Irish High Court in *Crowe Engineering Limited* v. *Lynch and Ors*[115] and by the English Court of Appeal in the case of *Re Hastings-Bass Deceased.*[116]

4.67 *Crowe Engineering Limited* v. *Lynch and Ors* concerned an application by the trustees of a pension scheme for directions as to the disposition of a lump sum death benefit. Carroll J. stated that the Court would only interfere with the exercise of a discretion by the trustees if it were mala fide or ultra vires their powers under the trust documentation. In *Re Hastings-Bass Deceased*, Buckley L.J. in the course of his judgment stated:

> to sum up the preceding observations in our judgment where by the terms of the trust a trustee is given the discretion as to some matter which he acts in good faith, the Court should not interfere with his action notwithstanding that it does not have the full effect which he intended, unless (1) what he has achieved is unauthorised by the power conferred upon him; or (2) it is clear that he would not have acted as he did (a) had he not taken into account considerations which he should not have taken into account or (b) had he not failed to take into account considerations which he ought to have taken into account.

4.68 It is clear that the Courts will interfere with the exercise of a power by a trustee under any one of the following circumstances:

1. Where such trustee acts in bad faith
2. Where such trustee acts outside the authority conferred by the trust documentation
3. If it can be shown that the trustee would not have acted in that way if he had either taken into account some fact which was overlooked or if he had not taken into account some fact which in the circumstances he had taken into consideration.

---

114 See *Stannard* v. *Fisons Pension Trust Limited* [1991] PLR 225; *Re Courage Group's Pension Scheme* [1987] 1 WLR 495; *Re Imperial Foods Limited Pension Scheme* [1986] 1 WLR 717.

115 (Unreported, High Court, 24 July 1991, Carroll J.).

116 [1975] Ch. 25.

4.69 In circumstances where trustees are conferred with a power by the trust documentation and are under a fiduciary duty to consider whether or in what way they should exercise their power, the Courts will not normally compel its exercise. The Courts will intervene on the basis set out in *Crowe Engineering Limited* v. *Lynch and Ors* and *Re Hastings-Bass Deceased*. Where, however, a trustee is conferred with a trust power — that is, a power which the trustee is obliged to exercise, but in respect of which the trustee has a discretion as to how the power may be exercised — the Court will intervene if the trustee fails to exercise the power.[117]

4.70 Recent English cases reveal a new development as to the basis on which the Courts are prepared to intervene to review the exercise of a power, whether by trustees or an employer. These cases show a development away from traditional trust principles and towards an analysis of an occupation pension scheme, partly in terms of traditional trust-law concepts and partly in terms of modern employment law.[118] There is as yet no Irish reported case dealing with this subject.

TRUSTEE MEETINGS

4.71 In discharging their duties and exercising their powers, the trustees will usually meet together. Trustees should hold regular meetings, set out agendas for such meetings and keep minutes. The frequency of such meetings will depend on the size of the pension scheme and its maturity. A new scheme may require more frequent meetings than a well-established scheme. Trustees should certainly hold meetings not less than once in every year.[119] There are no specific legal obligations with respect to the business conducted at trustee meetings. However, the matters set out in the following paragraphs should, as a matter of good practice, be covered in an annual meeting of the trustees.

---

[117] See in *Re Gulbenkian's Settlements* [1970] AC 508, cited with approval by Warner J. in *Mettoy Pension Trustees Limited* v. *Evans* [1991] 2 All ER 513 and by Vinelott in *Re William Makin and Son Ltd* [1992] PLR 177.

[118] See paras. 5.27, 5.33 et seq.; also *Imperial Group Pension Trust Limited* v. *Imperial Tobacco Limited*, *Mettoy Pension Trustees Limited* v. *Evans*, *Re William Makin and Son Ltd*.

[119] This is not a legal requirement in Ireland or in the UK. The Goode Committee Report recommended the introduction of a statutory requirement that trustee meetings be not less frequent than annual.

Contributions

4.72 The trustees should confirm that all contributions due to the scheme from the employer and from the members (as appropriate) have been received to date and invested.

Payment of Benefits

4.73 The trustees should review payments of benefits and, in particular, any death claims and make decisions (if appropriate) on the disposal of lump sum death benefits and any other claims arising on death of a member. In practice, payment of benefits may be a matter that has been delegated to a pensions committee or, more typically, may be handled by the employer direct with benefit consultants, a life office or an investment manager.

Investment

4.74 The investment performance of the pension scheme fund should be reviewed and, in particular, the trustees should consider investment strategy and review the performance and suitability of the investment manager. It is desirable that, at least annually, a representative of the investment manager should attend and present a report to the trustees.

Assets

4.75 The identity and location of the assets representing the fund of the pension scheme should be confirmed. The assets should be in the names of either the trustees or the trustees' authorised nominee.

Funding (Defined Benefit Schemes)

4.76 The latest actuarial report and advice should be reviewed by the trustees with a view to determining:

1. Adequacy of scheme funding
2. Whether the funding position needs to be reviewed
3. The date of the next actuarial valuation.

It may be appropriate for the scheme's actuary to attend the meeting to assist and answer questions arising under this item of business.

Membership Records

4.77 The trustees should confirm that membership records are properly kept and that they are in order. It may be appropriate for the administration manager and benefit consultant to attend.

Accounts

4.78 Confirmation should be obtained that the latest scheme accounts are in order and, if appropriate, have been audited.[120]

Disclosure of Information

4.79 The trustees should confirm that the requirements of the Disclosure Regulations have been satisfied and, in particular, that:

1. All written queries or requests for information received by the trustees have been properly dealt with and written responses issued
2. The annual report for the relevant year has been prepared and issued within the time required
3. Explanatory booklets issued to members are up to date and reflect the current benefit structure.

4.80 Minutes should be kept of trustee meetings. It is usual only to record the actual decisions made. As a matter of prudence, the reasons for the decisions should not be recorded[121] because minutes of trustee meetings, in general, form evidence of the matters to which they refer, which can be relied on in civil proceedings.

4.81 Under trust law, trustees are required to act unanimously in relation to the exercise of any powers unless the trust document itself provides otherwise.[122] Modern pension scheme documentation will usually contain detailed provisions relating to the conduct of business

---

[120] For the requirement to audit the accounts, see Chapter 13 and the Occupational Pension Schemes (Disclosure of Information) Regulations, 1991 (SI No 215 of 1991). The Disclosure Regulations require schemes of a certain size to have audited accounts. Of course, if the trust deed itself requires the trustees to have the accounts of the scheme audited then they must be audited irrespective of the requirements of the Regulations.

[121] As to the disclosure of deliberations of trustees see *Re Londonderrys Settlement* [1965] Ch. 918; *Wilson and Another* v. *The Law Debenture Trust Corporation* PLC [1994] PLR 141 and para. 4.63.

[122] *Luke* v. *South Kensington Hotel Co. Ltd.* (1879) 11 Ch.D. 121

by trustees, will provide that trustee decisions may be made by a majority and that such decisions will bind the minority. The Courts will enforce such provisions.[123]

LIABILITIES OF TRUSTEES

Breach of Trust

4.82 The biggest risk or liability for a pension scheme trustee is that of personal liability. This can arise where a beneficiary of the trust brings an action against the trustees for breach of trust. An action for breach of trust may be brought against a trustee:

1. Because of the trustee's own wrongful act
2. For negligence
3. For improper exercise of a power (fraud on power)
4. As a result of any of 1., 2. or 3. having been done by a co-trustee.

4.83 Trustees will be in breach of trust if they fail to do something which they are required to do under the terms of the trust, or if they do something that they are not empowered to do. A fraud on a power refers to the exercise of a power properly given to a trustee, but for a purpose other than that for which it was given. It is clear that the duties of trustees are onerous and are strictly reviewed by the Courts. If a trustee is adjudged to be in breach of trust and there is a shortfall in the assets of the pension fund, the trustee will be obliged to make good the difference from his or her own assets. The intentions of the trustee are not relevant. A trustee may act with the best of intentions but if a breach of trust is committed, the trustee will still be liable. This could happen, for instance, where trustees pay a lump sum death benefit to a person who does not fall within the class of beneficiaries set out in the trust documentation. Whilst the action may have been taken for compassionate reasons, it would nevertheless be in breach of trust. A breach of trust may also expose the trustees to claims by third parties, such as banks, in relation to dealings with the pension scheme.[124]

---

[123] In *Re Butlins Settlement Trusts* [1976] Ch. 251.

[124] See para. 4.100 below.

4.84 Subject to the terms of the trust documents, personal liability does not end when a trustee retires or is removed. That trustee will still be responsible for and retain liability in respect of his or her actions or inactions whilst a trustee.[125] A liability of a deceased trustee will become a liability of that trustee's estate.

4.85 Court decisions have established that a higher standard of care is required of professional trustees than lay trustees.[126] Professional trustees will need to take care to manage properly any conflicts between their role as trustees and their interest as professionals receiving remuneration (usually from the employer) for acting as trustees. A professional trustee may also provide benefit-consultancy services to the employer, and this will also require management of the conflict of interest.

4.86 Where the trustee of a pension scheme is a body corporate, it would be prudent for the directors of that body corporate to regard themselves as in the same position and to have the same potential liability as individual trustees.[127] Trustees can also incur criminal liabilities under the Pensions Act for breaches of that Act. The penalties on conviction can be considerable — on summary conviction, a fine not exceeding £1,500 or imprisonment for a term not exceeding one year (or both), and, on conviction on indictment, to a fine not exceeding £10,000 or imprisonment for a term not exceeding two years (or both).[128] Where a corporate body is a trustee of a pension scheme, the Pensions Act may impose joint liability on the trustee company and any director, secretary, manager or other officer of such body

---

125 s.43 of the Statute of Limitations, 1957 provides that the limitation on an action for breach of trust is six years. This was considered in *Murphy* v. *AIB* [1994] 2 ILRM 220. s.44 of that Statute states that there shall be no limitation period in the case of an action alleging fraud.

126 See the report of the Scarman Committee, the Powers and Duties of Trustees (Law Com. No.23 (1982) para. 2.15: "Professional trustees, such as banks, are under a special duty to display expertise in every aspect of their administration of the trust." Referred to in *Nestlé* v. *National Westminster Bank*. See also *Bartlett* v. *Barclays Bank Trust Co. Ltd.* [1980] 1 Ch. 515, and *Re Waterman's Will Trusts* [1952] 2 All ER 1054.

127 See para. 4.7 above.

128 s.3(3) Pensions Act as amended by s.43 of the Pensions (Amendment) Act, 1996.

corporate.[129] The Pensions Act also imposes continuing fines in the case of continuing offences.[130] Having considered the possible liabilities of trustees, it is appropriate to look at the ways in which these liabilities can be reduced or eliminated.

Advice

4.87 Trustees should be mindful to carry out carefully the duties imposed on them. Where appropriate, they should take advice from professionals — benefit consultants, actuaries, solicitors, investment managers, accountants.[131] It is reasonable for a trustee to obtain advice from a competent professional, and action in accordance with such advice will be difficult to challenge. Many pension scheme deeds include a specific power for the trustees to obtain and rely on professional advice and exonerate the trustees from liability for loss resulting from reliance on such advice. If trustees, having taken advice, are still unclear as to a course of action, or if they consider themselves unable to act because of a conflict of interest, they can make application to the High Court by Special Summons for directions.[132]

Exoneration Clauses

4.88 Formal trust documents may contain a clause excusing the trustees from a duty which would otherwise arise under law. For example, the trust deed may excuse the trustee from any liability which might otherwise accrue to them in the case of the trust fund being invested badly, and consequently decreasing in value. Such exoneration clauses would be subject to the limitation that they would not

---

129 s.3(4) Pensions Act.

130 s.3A Pensions Act as inserted by s.44 Pensions (Amendment) Act, 1996.

131 In practice, and depending on the nature of the action or decision which the Trustees are considering, it may not be appropriate for them to take advice from an "in-house" legal officer of the employer and they should seek independent legal advice. See *Donovan (Secretary of the United States Department of Labour)* v. *Bierwirth* (US Court of Appeals, 1982) which case is considered at para. 4.37.

132 The procedure is set out in the Rules of the Superior Courts 1986, Order 3 rules 1 and 2. But note the remarks of Carroll J. in *Crowe Engineering Limited* (Unreported, High Court, 24 July 1991) as to the limits on the Court's power to give directions or guidance to trustees or to exercise a discretion for trustees in certain circumstances.

excuse loss resulting from wilful default or fraud and in the case of a professional trustee negligence.

Indemnity

4.89 ***Under Trust Law:*** Under trust law a trustee is entitled to indemnity out of the trust property with respect to all expenses and costs properly incurred in the furtherance of benefiting the trust.[133] Having regard to all the circumstances of the case, a trustee will not be entitled to such indemnity if at the same time the trustee is in breach of trust and is obliged to make restitution to the trust fund. In practice, one claim would be set off against the other and only the balance paid.

4.90 ***Under the Trustee Act, 1893:*** Section 24 of the Trustee Act, 1893 provides a limited indemnity for trustees as follows:

> A trustee shall, without prejudice to the provisions of the instrument, if any, creating the trust, be chargeable only for money and securities actually received by him notwithstanding his signing any receipt for the sake of conformity, and shall be answerable and accountable only for his own acts, receipts, neglects or defaults and not for those of any other trustee, nor for any banker, broker, or other person with whom any trust moneys or securities may be deposited nor for the insufficiency or deficiency of any securities nor for any other loss, unless the same happens through his own wilful default; and may reimburse himself or pay or discharge out of the trust premises, all expenses incurred in or about the execution of his trusts or powers.

4.91 On first examination, the terms of section 24 might appear quite wide. However, this is not so. section 24 was substantially reenacted in England as section 30 of the Trustee Act, 1925. Two cases will illustrate the limited interpretation that the English Courts placed on section 24.[134] In *Re Windsor Steam Coal Company (1901) Ltd.,*[135] it was held that the exemption from liability does not apply where a trustee (even though as a result of an honest mistake) misapplied trust funds by paying them to the wrong person. In *Re Vick-*

---

133 *Re Grimthorpe* [1958] Ch. 615.

134 That is on s.30 Trustee Act, 1925.

135 [1929] 1 Ch. 151 at 166.

ery, Vickery v. *Stephens,*[136] the Court held that the words "nor for any other loss, unless the same happens through his own wilful default" did not mean that a trustee is never liable for breach of trust unless the breach is occasioned by the trustee's own wilful default. The Court limited the words to certain specific losses. These were losses occasioned by the trustee's signing receipts for the sake of conformity or by reason of the wrongful act or default of another trustee or of an agent with whom trust money or securities have been deposited or for the insufficiency or deficiency of securities or some other analogous loss.

4.92 ***Under Trust Documentation:*** Section 24 of the Trustee Act, 1893 provides that it is without prejudice to the provisions of the trust instrument, by implication permitting the trust instrument to confer a wider indemnity.[137] Properly drafted trust documentation will normally contain a provision indemnifying the trustee in certain circumstances from a breach of trust. In practice, the indemnity provisions will vary in trust documentation. Some are quite wide (so far as exemption of the trustee is concerned) and cover all personal liability except where the trustee is guilty of a fraudulent action. Another form of indemnity clause (less common) will not give exemption where the trustee is guilty of negligence. It is, however, usual to exclude negligence from the indemnity in the case of a professional trustee. Such trustees are paid for their services and should not therefore escape liability for negligence. A new trustee should check carefully the indemnity clause in the trust documentation. The indemnity is usually given by the employer.[138]

4.93 It is now common to find in trust documentation a form of indemnity which provides that the employer shall indemnify the trustee and, to the extent that the employer fails to do so, the trustee shall be indemnified out of the fund. In the case of a breach of trust which causes actual loss to the fund, there is an argument to be made

---

136 [1931] 1 Ch. 572.

137 s.30 of the English Trustee Act, 1925 does not contain similar language giving rise to the possible interpretation of s.30 as being exhaustive — see Matthews, P. (1989): "The Efficacy of Trustee Exemption Clauses in English Law", *The Conveyancer*, Jan/Feb. p.42.

138 As to whether the formal trust documentation can be amended retrospectively to include an indemnity provision, see para. 3.46 et seq.

that, failing indemnity from the employer, a trustee should not be indemnified out of the fund, as this is clearly to the detriment of the members and will cause them loss through no fault of their own.

4.94 It should be remembered that the indemnity clause will operate so as to protect the trustee from personal loss — the trustee will be indemnified by the employer. If a breach of trust (resulting in a loss to the fund) is alleged, the trustee will nevertheless be a defendant in legal proceedings. In the event that judgment is entered against the trustee, the trustee will have to make good the loss to the fund. The trustee will, in turn, have a claim against the employer under the indemnity clause for reimbursement. The trustee will also incur legal expenses in defending the action. These costs should also be recoverable under the indemnity provisions from the employer. If, however, the action has arisen out of the employer's insolvency the trustee may be in a very difficult position.

4.95 If it is proposed that a corporate trustee be appointed as a trustee of a pension scheme, whether alone or with other trustees, care should be taken to ensure that the indemnity provisions are sufficiently wide to cover the directors of the corporate trustee. A provision may be included in the formal trust deed to the effect that provisions of the deed relating to individual trustees shall apply to the board of directors of any body corporate appointed as trustee.

Insurance

4.96 It is possible for trustees to obtain insurance cover. This is usually purchased by the employer. There are two types of insurance cover — namely, liability insurance (or trustee liability insurance as it is often referred to) and fidelity insurance. Liability insurance is structured as a personal liability insurance policy which seeks to protect trustees against losses that they may incur resulting from legal claims being made against them. Such a policy may also provide for reimbursement to the employer and/or the scheme where the trustee is indemnified either by the employer or out of the assets of the scheme. Fidelity insurance provides indemnity against loss suffered by the pension scheme through dishonest or fraudulent acts of a trustee, employer or certain other third parties (including investment managers, advisors).

4.97 Liability insurance, therefore, is a direct insurance cover for the employer and the trustee and an indirect cover for the pension scheme fund itself. Fidelity insurance is a direct insurance cover for the pension scheme fund and an indirect insurance cover for the trustee. An advantage of liability insurance over an indemnity in the trust documentation is that the former should make good a loss to the fund (whilst giving cover to the trustees). The Goode Committee, in the course of its report, considered the matter of insurance for trustees and whether such should be made compulsory. It concluded that this was unnecessary.[139]

4.98 Insurance cover may be arranged by the employer and premiums paid by the employer. The employer will have an insurable interest in the scheme and will usually be a named insured under the policy. If the premium is to be paid as an expense out of the fund, the trust documentation would need to provide for this. The extent of cover under such policies will vary. They may exclude acts and omissions that are knowingly and intentionally committed. Whilst purporting to give insurance cover against breach of trust, in reality such policies may limit cover to losses resulting from trustees' carelessness only. The language would require to be checked carefully and the exclusions examined. The liability insurance should cover not only the liability of a trustee to make good any deficit in the fund, but also legal costs and expenses in defending any action (whether or not such defence is successful).

4.99 Apart from limitations presented by the terms of liability insurance policies, there are some other difficulties. Section 200 of the Companies Act, 1963 restricts the extent to which a company may, by contract, indemnify a director or other officer against liability. The section renders void any such arrangements except in limited circumstances. The effect of this section may be to render void liability insurance effected by a pension trustee company to cover directors of that company or directors who are themselves trustees. A further difficulty is that liability insurance is written on a "claims-made" basis. This means that the policy must be in force at the time the claim is made. If the policy is in force, a past trustee will be covered in respect of a claim arising from actions taken whilst he or she was a trustee. However, if the policy has lapsed for any reason, none of the trustees will have cover. If there has been an adverse claims experience, cover may become too expensive and unobtainable. Except in the case of the

---

139 See the report of the Pension Law Review Committee Vol. 1 paras. 4.5.62 to 4.5.64

winding-up of a pension scheme, it is not at present possible to purchase run-off cover. The purchase by an employer of liability insurance covering employee trustees may be a taxable benefit-in-kind. It does not appear that the Irish Revenue Commissioners have sought to tax this as a benefit-in-kind.

TRUSTEES AND THIRD PARTIES

Liabilities to Third Parties

4.100 As already noted, a trustee who incurs costs and expenses in the proper conduct of the business of the trust, is entitled to indemnity out of the trust assets. A third party, such as a bank which deals with trustees on behalf of a pension scheme and advances moneys to the trustees for the purposes of the trust has no direct contractual right against the trust fund but would have a right to be subrogated to the trustees' right of indemnity.[140] Where, however, the trustees are in breach of trust, their right of indemnity may be curtailed or non-existent, and in such case the third-party creditor would have no right of subrogation.[141] The indemnity clauses in modern pension scheme trusts are, however, often very wide and may cover breaches of trust other than those resulting from a trustee's wilful default or fraud. Whilst there is no Irish case on the point, English and Scottish case law would appear to indicate that a trustee cannot be indemnified under the trust instrument for breach of trust which is the result of the trustee's own fraud or gross negligence.[142]

4.101 Apart from the above claim by subrogation against the fund, a third-party creditor which has advanced moneys to a pension fund on the basis of a transaction which subsequently transpires to be in excess of the trustees' powers and void may have a right to restitution of mon-

---

[140] See *Moore* v. *McGlynn* [1894] 1 IR 74, *Strickland* v. *Symons* (1884) 26 Ch.D. 245, *Re Grimthorpe* [1958] Ch. 615.

[141] In *Re Oxley* [1914] I Ch. 604.

[142] See Matthews above. Matthews refers to the English case of *Pass* v. *Dundas* (1880) 43 L.T. 665 and the Scottish cases of *Rae* v. *Meek* (1889) 14 App. Cas 558 and *Clarke* v. *Clarkes Trustees* 1925 S.C. 693. Matthews' conclusion on this point has been criticised by the Jersey Court of Appeal in *Midland Bank Trustee (Jersey) Limited* v. *Federated Pension Services Limited* [1996] PLR 179.

eys which have been paid through the equitable doctrine of tracing. A right to trace will, of course, only be of benefit if the fund is solvent.[143]

Attachment of Pensions

4.102 At law, a third party which is owed money by a pensioner may, having obtained a court judgment against that person, seek to recover those moneys by attachment of the pension. This can be done by application to Court to be appointed receiver by way of equitable execution over the pension.[144] The order may be made on an ex parte application. The making of the order would be notified to the trustees of the pension scheme and the pensioner. The Court has power on application by the judgment debtor or any other person affected to vary or discharge the order. The provisions of the Pensions Act prohibiting forfeiture of preserved benefits are not relevant in this case as they only apply to forfeiture clauses in pension scheme deeds.

4.103 The Revenue Commissioners have powers of attachment under the Finance Act, 1988. It is unclear whether these could extend to attachment of pensions. The legislation specifically excludes wages or salaries but is silent as to pensions.[145]

[143] See *Shanahan's Stamp Auctions Ltd* v. *Farrelly* [1962] IR 386, and generally: Delany, H. (1996): *Equity and the Law of Trusts in Ireland*, Dublin: Round Hall Sweet & Maxwell. See also para. 10.34.

[144] Circuit Court Rules, 1950, Order 38; Superior Court Rules, 1986 Order 45 Rule 9.

[145] s.73 Finance Act, 1988.

5

THE EMPLOYMENT RELATIONSHIP AND PENSIONS

INTRODUCTION

5.1 Occupational pension schemes are established and administered in the context of an employment relationship. Because of the tax benefits afforded to exempt approved occupational pension schemes,[1] many employers will provide pension arrangements through the means of an exempt approved scheme.[2] This will require that the scheme is set up under irrevocable trusts. The employer promises to arrange such a pension, the employee expects to receive a pension, and the actual pension benefit is provided by a third party — namely, the trustees of the pension scheme. The pension arrangement therefore involves three parties from the outset.

5.2 Under the traditional trust, the settlor (the person creating the trust) transferred property to trustees to be administered for beneficiaries as the objects of the settlor's bounty. Those beneficiaries were the objects of the settlor's generosity but did nothing legally to earn that bounty. It has been remarked in a number of cases that pension scheme trusts are quite different from the traditional family trust.[3] The members are employees, they work for the employer who has established the scheme. The scheme is usually presented to new members as a valuable benefit and part of the payment by the employer for their work. The employees who are beneficiaries under the scheme cannot be described as mere volunteers. It is more correct to say that their rights have commercial and contractual origins. They earn the benefits payable under the scheme (even in a non-

---

[1] See Chapter 6.

[2] Although unfunded statutory schemes will not be established under trust, see Chapter 8 generally regarding public sector schemes.

[3] For example, *Imperial Group Pension Trust Ltd* v. *Imperial Tobacco Ltd* [1991] 1 WLR 589 per Browne-Wilkinson V.-C. at 597.

contributory scheme) by their labour,[4] and those benefits may be regarded as a form of deferred remuneration.[5]

5.3 For this reason, among others, some have argued, both academically[6] and in the Courts, that the old decisions of the chancery Courts may not apply to pension- scheme trusts. The Courts in England[7] and in certain commonwealth jurisdictions[8] have, however, been reluctant to accept this proposition entirely. In these decisions, the Courts have been unwilling to allow an employer to effect amendments to a pension scheme, which were perceived to affect members' rights prejudicially. Whilst accepting the principles set out above as to the different nature of pension scheme trusts, the Courts nevertheless arrived at their decisions in the traditional manner by construction of the trust documentation. There has not yet been any reported Irish case in which these issues have been considered.

5.4 This chapter considers the nature of these pension rights, the extent to which employment law and contract law may apply, the role of the employer, the variation of pension rights, and particular issues including termination of employment and termination of the pension scheme, pension rights in the context of dismissals and compensation claims, other documentation such as booklets and announcements and pension rights in insolvencies.

---

4 See *Mihlenstedt* v. *Barclays Bank International* [1989] PLR 91.

5 *McMenamin* v. *Ireland* [1994] 2 ILRM 368 per Geoghegan J. At 378 (note that this case concerned a statutory scheme and not one established under trust); see also *Cowan and Ors* v. *Charlesworth and Ors* [1989] PLR 79 per Vinelott J. at 87.

6 See Moffat, G. (1993): "Pension Funds: A Fragmentation of Trust Law?" 56 MLR 471.

7 See, for example, Warner J. in *Mettoy Pension Trustees Ltd* v. *Evans* [1991] 2 All ER 513 at p. 537: "There are no special rules governing the construction of pension scheme documents."

8 See the decision of the New Zealand Court of Appeal in *UEB Industries Limited* v. *W.S. Brabant* [1991] PLR 109 in which Cooke P. stated at p.111: "But in any event these considerations of the merits are of little importance [referring to his earlier consideration of the scheme operating in an employment context]. What must be decisive are the terms of the trusts constituted by the particular scheme."

PENSIONS AND THE EMPLOYMENT CONTRACT

5.5 As already stated, pensions are established in the context of an employment relationship. An employer may document the pension arrangements that it makes for its employees in a number of ways. The following paragraphs examine the different methods that the employer can adopt, the use of explanatory booklets and announcements, disclosure obligations and tax issues.

Direct Contractual Promise

5.6 An employer can make a direct contractual promise to an employee with respect to pensions. The right to a pension and the details of benefits are documented in the contract of employment made between the employer and the employee. From the point of view of an employee, this has the benefit that it is a direct contractual right owed by the employer to the employee. Any variation in the pension promise would require the consent of the employee.[9] However, it has a number of disadvantages. Such a pension arrangement would not be capable of approval by the Revenue Commissioners as an exempt approved pension scheme, and therefore would not entitle the employer, or the employee, to the taxation reliefs and exemptions afforded to exempt approved occupational pension schemes.[10] As an unapproved retirement benefit scheme there would also be adverse tax consequences for the employee.[11] Further, the employee has no guarantee that the pension will be paid in the event of the insolvency of the employer.

5.7 It is possible for the employer to be contractually bound to pay a pension without so intending. In *Turner and Others* v. *Hospitals*

---

9 Under contract law, subject to the terms of the contract itself, an employment contract cannot be varied by one party without the consent of the other. The pension scheme trust will, if properly drafted, provide that it may be amended by the employer with the consent of the trustees (or vice versa). If the terms of the pension scheme have become part of the contract of employment, any such amendment may, as a matter of employment law, require the consent of the employee members. It would be possible to include language in the employment contract allowing amendment at the discretion of the employer. Exercise of this power by the employer would be subject to the principle that such amendment would not constitute a constructive dismissal of the employee.

10 See Chapter 6.

11 See paras. 6.84 et seq.

Trust (1940) Ltd. (in voluntary liquidation),[12] a case which arose on the winding-up of the Hospital Sweeps, the High Court had to determine whether a portion of a pension payable to certain ex-employees was an ex-gratia pension or whether it arose on foot of a contractual obligation owed by the employer to its employees. On the basis of the documentation[13] put before the Court by the defendants, the Court found that the plaintiffs were entirely reasonable in understanding those documents as conferring on them a contractual right to the benefits in question. The Court stated:

> I do not think that the plaintiffs could have been expected to have understood the implications of these memoranda without very careful explanation. Having heard the evidence of [named plaintiffs] . . . I have no hesitation in concluding that the plaintiff employees . . . never understood and that the defendant by its servants and agents could not reasonably have taken them to have understood that any part of the pension was ex gratia, in the sense that it could be discontinued at any time without any obligation to compensate. The expression "ex gratia" is not used in either of the memoranda relied on but even if it had been I think that it would have required personal explanation.[14]

5.8 It is apparent from this case that if the employer does not intend to be contractually bound (other than in accordance with the terms of the formal trust documentation), it must use clear and unambiguous language in communications with employees.[15] An example of the potential difficulties that can arise where there is a difference between the terms of contract and the pension deed may be seen in *Desmond Doyle* v. *Paul Burke-Kennedy and Others.*[16] The case concerned a dispute between two partners in an architects' practice as to the date agreed for retirement. The respondents claimed that age 60 was agreed and relied, inter alia, on the normal retirement date specified

---

12 [1994] ELR 35.

13 The defence relied in particular on two memoranda circulated to employees during their employment. The report of the case unfortunately does not quote the memoranda.

14 *Ibid.* per Geoghegan J. at p.37.

15 See para. 5.12 et seq. below regarding explanatory booklets; see also *Irish Pensions Trust Limited* v. *First National Bank of Chicago* (Unreported, High Court, 15 February 1989, Murphy J.).

16 (Unreported, High Court, 22 March 1991, Lardner J.).

in the pension deed and the explanatory booklet. On the evidence, the Court determined that there was no agreement between the partners that they must retire at age 60.

Right to Membership of a Pension Scheme

5.9 Rather than establish a direct contractual pension right, the employer can promise the employees, under the terms of the contract of employment, that they will be entitled to membership under the employer's pension scheme. This scheme is set up separately under trust[17] as an exempt approved occupational pension scheme. From the point of view of the employer, this may entail a contractual obligation that there will always be a pension scheme in some form. The precise extent of the obligation will depend on the terms used in the contract. If the contract refers to membership of the employer's pension scheme (as that scheme may be amended from time to time), this may permit the employer to vary the pension rights of employees prospectively.

Right to Membership Subject to Terms

5.10 The employer may contract with the employee in the contract of employment that the employee will, if eligible, be offered membership of the pension scheme established by the employer and that the employee's rights and entitlements will be in accordance with the terms of that pension scheme as those terms may be varied from time to time. This form of pension promise differs from that discussed in the previous paragraph because here the employer does not make a contractual promise that the employee will be a member of the pension scheme. The formal terms of the pension scheme, which are made between the employer and the trustees of the pension scheme, would include a right for the employer to terminate its liability to make contributions to the scheme and would also include a right for the employer, with the consent of the trustees, to amend the terms of the pension scheme. It is arguable that a pension promise in this form confers on the employee rights to pension benefit as they accrue only and does not confer prospective rights. If the reference to amendment of the pension scheme is omitted from the contract, it might be argued that an employee has a contractual right to the pension benefits as they stood at the time the employee joined the scheme.

---

[17] As to State-sector schemes which are not set up under trust, see Chapter 8.

Membership as a Condition of Employment

5.11 The employer may require the employee as a condition of employment to join the employer's pension scheme.[18] This would appear to make the terms of the pension scheme part of the contract of employment. However, those terms would usually include the right of the employer to terminate its obligation to pay contributions to the scheme at a future date.

Booklets/Announcements

5.12 In order to obtain Revenue approval for a pension scheme, an employer is required to issue an announcement or explanatory booklet to its members, setting out the main features of the scheme.[19] A booklet or announcement is also required to comply with the Pensions Act Disclosure Regulations.[20] It is important that there are no material inconsistencies between the pension information set out in the booklet and the formal trust documentation. The explanatory booklet should also contain a clause to the effect that the booklet is intended only as a guide to the principal terms of the scheme and that it cannot override the provisions of the formal trust documentation. The booklet should also contain a statement that any member may obtain a copy of the formal trust documentation and the name and address of the person from whom it may be obtained and to whom any queries regarding the scheme may be addressed.[21] If these statements are made in the booklet, it should be more difficult to establish a contractual claim in the event of a discrepancy between the booklet and the formal documentation. In the absence of such excluding language, it may happen that the booklet or announcement may prevail over the trust deed.

---

18 This requirement is sometimes imposed in pension arrangements in Ireland. In new schemes it ensures that there are sufficient members at the outset to make the scheme viable. It may also help avoid the difficulty with which an employer could otherwise be faced if an employee who has not made proper pension provision requests membership of the scheme in later years. Compulsory membership is not permitted under UK law. s.160 Pension Schemes Act, 1993 (previously s.15 Social Security Act, 1986).

19 See para. 6.19.

20 See Chapter 13.

21 This would usually be the personnel manager, human resources manager or financial controller.

5.13 *Irish Pensions Trust Limited* v. *The First National Bank of Chicago* provides an example of the effectiveness of exclusion language in booklets.[22] In that case, the exclusion was effective and the formal trust documents prevailed.

5.14 An example of the booklet prevailing over the deed is found in the UK case *Icarus (Hertford) Limited* v. *Driscoll*,[23] which case arose on the liquidation of the plaintiff company. The company had established a defined benefit scheme through a life office. At one point, the accrual rate under the scheme was reduced and the scheme made non-contributory. This change was notified to all employees but no amendment was made to the formal documentation. In the circumstances, the Court held that the parties to the scheme (meaning the employer, the life office and the members) were estopped from contending that the scheme had not been amended.[24]

5.15 In practice, changes in benefit structure of a pension scheme are often notified to members by way of an announcement, the formal documentation being subsequently amended. The announcement is issued on behalf of the employer and would usually bind the employer as a matter of contract. Unless it is joined in by the trustees (which would be unusual), it will not bind the trustees. It may be argued, however, that as the trustees are required by the Pensions Act[25] to announce such changes in the benefit entitlements, the announcement is also issued on their behalf and with their acquiescence and is binding on them. Failing such acquiescence, and in the absence of confirmatory conduct, it would be necessary for the amendment procedure set out in the formal documents to be followed in order to bind the trustees.

Disclosure of Information

5.16 The disclosure obligations in relation to pension schemes that exist under the present law are examined later.[26] Obligations are imposed on employers under Revenue approval requirements to fur-

---

22 This case has been discussed in detail at para. 3.52. See also the English case *Dorrell* v. *May & Baker Limited* [1991] PLR 31.

23 [1990] PLR 1.

24 See para. 3.53 et seq.

25 Under Part V of the Pensions Act and the Disclosure Regulations made thereunder; see Chapter 13.

26 See Chapter 13.

nish notifications to members and under the Terms of Employment (Information) Act, 1994 employers are obliged to notify the terms of the pension arrangements to employees. The Pensions Act and the Occupational Pension Schemes (Disclosure of Information) Regulations, 1991[27] impose obligations on trustees of pension schemes to furnish information to members. The Regulations oblige the employer to comply with requests for information from the trustees to enable them to meet their obligations under the Act and the Regulations. These matters are dealt with elsewhere.[28]

5.17 Dependent upon the terms of the contract of employment and the pension scheme, an employer may have a positive obligation to inform a member of a scheme of benefits and any action necessary on the part of the employee to enjoy those benefits. In *Scally* v. *Southern Health and Social Services Board*,[29] the plaintiffs were medical doctors employed by health and social-service boards in Northern Ireland. Their contracts of employment incorporated regulations, from time to time in force, governing superannuation. An amendment was made in the regulations allowing members to buy added years of service provided that action was taken within a stated period following the change. The plaintiffs, being unaware of the change, did nothing. Subsequently, the plaintiffs brought action against the health boards claiming, inter alia, breach of an implied term of the contract of employment. At the trial, the plaintiffs were unsuccessful but they succeeded on appeal. The UK Court of Appeal held that in the circumstances a term could be implied into the plaintiffs' contracts obliging the health boards to notify the plaintiffs of their entitlements. The health boards were found to be in breach of this implied term and were liable to the plaintiffs. The Court stated:

> The problem is a novel one which could not arise in the classical contractual situation in which all the contractual terms, having been agreed between the parties, must, ex hypothesi, have been known to both parties. But in the modern world it is increasingly common for individuals to enter into contracts, particularly contracts of employment, on complex terms which have been settled in the course of negotiations between representative bodies or organisations and

---

27 SI No 215 of 1991.

28 Chapter 13.

29 [1991] 4 All ER 563.

> many details of which the individual employee cannot be expected to know unless they are drawn to his attention.[30]

5.18 If an employer furnishes incorrect information to an employee regarding pension entitlements, on the basis of which information an employee retires and is subsequently refused re-employment (on discovery of the mistake), the employer may be liable for constructive dismissal. In the UK case of *Brown* v. *The Royal Veterinary College*,[31] an employee was given early-retirement figures which were one-third higher than they should have been. On the basis of the information, the employee took early retirement. He subsequently discovered the error and applied for his old job back — which was refused. The Tribunal found that this amounted to a constructive and unfair dismissal.

Tax Issues

5.19 The taxation issues relating to the establishment and administration of pension schemes are discussed fully later.[32] The tax exemptions and reliefs afforded by the legislation to approved occupational pension schemes are such as to make it attractive for employers to establish pension arrangements that meet the Revenue requirements necessary to qualify for exempt approval. In the case of exempt approved pension schemes, the contributions of the employer and the members are fully allowable for tax purposes.[33] Employee contributions are usually deducted by the employer from gross pay and therefore are free of PRSI deduction as well.[34] The investment roll-up on the fund of the scheme is exempt from Income Tax and Capital Gains Tax. When benefits come to be paid out of the scheme, these are taxed under the PAYE system.

5.20 Contributions by an employer on behalf of an employee to an unapproved pension scheme are taxable on the employee as a benefit in kind. The taxation treatment of unapproved arrangements is considered later.[35]

---

30 *Ibid.* per Lord Bridge at p.569.

31 [1989] PLR 43 (UK Industrial Tribunal).

32 See Chapter 6.

33 See paras. 6.37 and 6.41.

34 See para. 6.39.

35 See paras. 6.84 et seq.

THE EMPLOYER

5.21 The employer establishes the pension scheme and it is therefore appropriate to consider its role in relation to the pension scheme. In this context, this section will also consider how associated employers may join the scheme, how the employer may vary the terms of the scheme or terminate it, and issues arising on a reorganisation or takeover of the employer.

The Role of the Employer

5.22 An employer has a direct interest in the structure and the success of the scheme. The pension scheme will be an important part of the benefit package which is offered to employees by the employer. Any failure of the scheme to deliver the expected or promised benefit may result in a direct cost to the employer.

5.23 If it is intended that the scheme will be capable of being exempt approved by the Revenue Commissioners, then it will be established under irrevocable trusts and the employer will be required to contribute not less than one-sixth of the cost of the benefits.[36] The role of the employer will differ depending upon whether the scheme is a defined benefit scheme or a defined contribution scheme.[37] The employer's role in a defined benefit scheme is more involved as the employer is usually obliged to meet the balance of the cost of benefits. In either type of scheme, the power to appoint the investment manager is usually vested in the trustees, but often subject to the consent of the employer. Investment performance will be of great importance to the employer in a defined benefit scheme as it has an obligation to meet the benefits promised. In defined contribution schemes it is now becoming more common to find provision allowing members some input as to the choice of investment.[38]

5.24 The employer will retain the power to appoint and remove the trustees.[39] In many smaller schemes, the employer may also act as

---

36 See para. 6.41.

37 As to the meaning of defined benefit and defined contribution schemes, see para. 2.3.

38 In a scheme which invests in unitised funds this may amount to a choice as to the type of funds in which the individual member's retirement account may be invested.

39 See para. 4.21 for a more detailed discussion of the role of the employer in the appointment and removal of the trustees.

trustee. This would not now be regarded as good practice, particularly in light of the legislative provision that has been made for appointment of trustees by members,[40] and it is becoming less common except in the case of quite small schemes. Power to amend the terms of the scheme, if given to the trustees, should be exerciseable only with the consent of the employer. Power to admit employees to membership on a discretionary basis will be vested in the employer, or in the trustees with the consent of the employer. Any power of the trustees to augment benefits on retirement of an individual member will usually require the consent of the employer. A trustee power to augment benefits on the wind-up of a scheme may also require employer consent. These powers and reservations reflect the role of the employer, both as employer and as sponsor of the pension scheme.

Associated Employers

5.25 Where there is a group organisation, it is often convenient to operate a single scheme for all the companies in the group.[41] The Revenue commissioners permit companies to participate in a group scheme provided that the companies are sufficiently associated. For associated companies to participate in the same scheme, it is necessary for the trust deed to permit such participation. The usual requirement is that the company which is to participate should enter into a deed of adherence or participation with the principal employer and the trustees, under which the adhering company is admitted to the scheme and agrees to perform its obligations under the trust documentation.[42]

Variation in Pension Rights

5.26 It has already been noted that pension arrangements are required to be flexible because of their long-term nature. They must be capable of alteration and, if necessary, termination. The employer's ability to vary pension rights will depend on the manner in which the pension promise is documented. Pension rights are most commonly put in place by a trust deed and rules which are summarised in the

---

40 The Occupational Pension Schemes (Member Participation in The Selection of Persons for Appointment as Trustees)(No.2) Regulations, 1993. These Regulations are dealt with in Chapter 14.

41 See para. 18.57 et seq. for a further discussion regarding group reorganisations and pensions.

42 See para. 3.24 and 6.22.

explanatory literature issued to members.[43] The trust documentation will provide that it may be amended or varied, whether by the trustees with the consent of the employer, or vice versa, or by the employer or the trustees alone.[44] The trust deed will also reserve the right of the employer to discontinue contributions to the scheme. From an employment law viewpoint, it is not sufficient that these rights be reserved only in the formal trust documentation. The reality is that most employees will never read the trust deed and rules and this is usually known by the employer. It is very important, from the point of view of protection of the employer, that these rights of amendment and termination should be brought clearly to the attention of employees in their terms and conditions of employment or the employment contract.[45] To do otherwise is to risk a claim for breach of contract or constructive dismissal in the event that the employer seeks to introduce amendments or to discontinue the scheme without employee consent.[46]

5.27 In exercising its powers under the formal documents of the pension scheme, the employer may be under an implied duty not to damage the relationship of trust and confidence between itself and its employees. This principle has been identified by the English Courts in employment cases and was applied by the English High Court to pensions in *Imperial Group Pension Trust Limited* v. *Imperial Tobacco Limited* where it was stated:

> [T]he employers will not, without reasonable and proper cause, conduct themselves in a manner calculated or likely to destroy or

---

43 That is, the announcement letter, explanatory booklet or employee benefits booklet issued to employees.

44 See para. 3.10.

45 Whether written contracts of employment exist will depend on the employer. Good practice would dictate that all employees should have written contracts or a set of standard terms and conditions of employment may apply. s.3 of the Terms of Employment (Information) Act, 1994 requires employers to furnish employees with a statement of their terms and conditions of employment not later than two months after commencement of employment.

46 See *Turner and Others* v. *Hospitals Trust* (1940) Ltd. (in voluntary liquidation) above.

> seriously damage the relationship of confidence and trust between employer and employee.[47]

This case concerned a pension scheme trust. The question before the Court was whether there was any constraint on the manner in which an employer might exercise a right to give or withhold consent to a proposed amendment. The Court held that the duty of good faith set out above applies. This requires that the employer must give due consideration to the interests of the employees and not just to its own interests. Having given such consideration, however, the employer is not constrained from acting in self interest. The *Imperial Tobacco* case has been referred to with approval in Commonwealth jurisdictions.[48] The case was referred to by the English High Court in a subsequent case *British Coal Corporation* v. *British Coal Staff Superannuation Scheme Trustees Limited*,[49] which concerned a proposal by the employer to amend the terms of the company pension scheme. The effect of the amendment would be to prevent payment of part of a surplus in the fund to the members. Referring to the earlier *Imperial Tobacco* case the Court stated:

> What he [the employer] cannot do is to set limits to the benefits provided for members or pensioners for a collateral purpose without regard to their legitimate expectations.[50]

The *Imperial Tobacco* case has not been judicially considered in any reported Irish case. One practical difficulty which arises is that the extent of this duty is difficult to establish with respect to pension schemes.

5.28 The Occupational Pension Schemes (Disclosure of Information) Regulations, 1991[51] require that any material alteration in the provisions of a pension scheme be notified to the members of the scheme within six months of the date of the alteration.[52] If the provisions of

---

47 [1991] 1 WLR 589 at p.597.

48 *UEB Industries Limited* v. *Brabant* [1991] PLR 109 (New Zealand) and *Air Products Canada* v. *Schmidt* [1995] PLR 75 (Canada).

49 [1993] PLR 303.

50 *Ibid.* per Vinelott J. at para. 64.

51 SI No 215 of 1991.

52 *Ibid.* at Article 9(4).

the pension scheme are part of the contract of employment, then any variation in those provisions must, under the Terms of Employment (Information) Act, 1994[53] be notified to the employees concerned within one month of the date the change takes effect.

Reconstructions and Takeovers

5.29 The pensions aspects of reconstructions and takeovers are examined in detail later.[54]

5.30 In the event that a company is sold, any existing contracts of employment remain in place. Any pension scheme established for employees will usually continue as before.[55] In the case of the sale by a company of a division or business as a going concern, the provisions of the European Communities (Safeguarding of Employees' Rights on Transfer of Undertakings) Regulations, 1980[56] will apply. Broadly, these require that, on completion of the sale, the rights and obligations of the employer arising from contracts of employment existing at the time of completion are transferred to the purchaser of the division or business. The Regulations contain particular requirements with respect to pensions which are discussed later.[57] In order for the Regulations to apply, an employment relationship must exist at the date of transfer.[58] If there is no employment relationship, then there is no transfer of rights and obligations to the transferee (the purchaser).[59] The question of whether or not an employment relationship exists at the date of the transfer is complex, and a detailed review of this area is outside the scope of this work.[60]

---

53 s.5(1) of that Act.

54 See Chapter 18.

55 As to the concerns of vendors and purchasers of companies with regard to pension matters, see paras. 18.4 et seq. It may be that the company being sold has participated in a group scheme. In such case, the company will have to secede from that scheme and this may involve a partial winding-up of the scheme.

56 SI No 306 of 1980.

57 See para. 18.14 et seq.

58 Article 3 of the Regulations.

59 See *Ryan* v. *Braids Ltd.* [1995] ELR 81.

60 Regard should be had to the English House of Lords decision in *Litster* v. *Forth Dry Dock Engineering Co.* [1990] 1 AC 546, to s.15 of the Unfair

5.31 Frequently in business and share sales, for reasons of commercial confidentiality, very little news of an impending sale is allowed to be made public. Employees and their representatives (if any) often, therefore, hear of a takeover or sale only shortly before completion if not afterwards. The reasons for such confidentiality are readily understandable in a commercial context. Care should, however, be taken by employers and their advisors where possible to communicate in good time with employees prior to a takeover or sale to assure employees as to future arrangements.[61]

5.32 In the case of senior employees, a share sale or business sale may trigger "golden-parachute" clauses in their contracts of employment. Such provisions are not uncommon in the case of senior management, particularly of publicly quoted companies. Such clauses will provide that in the case of a sale, for example, upon completion, the relevant employee will be entitled to an amount equal to a multiple of salary. Such clauses may also make provision in relation to pensions. From the point of view of the purchaser of a business, it is important to ensure that there is adequate funding for any additional pension entitlements.

Discretions

5.33 As already noted,[62] the formal trust documentation will usually reserve certain matters to the discretion of the employer. These would include discretion:

1. To admit as members employees who are not eligible under the rules
2. To augment benefits coming into payment
3. To grant increases in pensions in payment or deferment
4. To augment benefits payable on a wind-up.

In any case where these powers are truly at the discretion of the employer, the formal documentation should state this clearly. Further,

---

Dismissals (Amendment) Act, 1993 and the recent EAT decision on that section in *Brett v. Niall Collins Ltd. (In Receivership)* [1995] ELR 69.

61 In the context of business sales, such communication is required by Regulation 7 of the Transfer of Undertakings Regulations. There is no such requirement in the case of share sales.

62 Above at para. 5.24 and at Chapter 3.

any explanatory booklets or announcements to members should also make this clear. These powers may also be given to trustees to exercise at their discretion, although usually with the consent of the employer. The question of trustees' discretions has been examined above.[63]

5.34 It may be said that, in the absence of very clear terms to the contrary, which are brought to the attention of employees in a comprehensible manner, the regular exercise of a discretion by an employer will create at least an obligation on the part of the employer to give bona fide consideration to the interests of the employees when faced with a decision such as augmentation of benefits on a wind-up or increase of pensions in payment. Coupled with the development in the area of pensions law of the principle of an implied term of confidence and good faith as between the employer and its employees (which is considered above), the Courts, in the UK at least, are making inroads into the traditional concept that the interpretation of the terms of the trust deed alone will always determine matters in any dispute regarding pension entitlements.

5.35 Where an employer has regularly exercised a discretion to augment benefits, the question arises as to whether this can amount to a contractual right of members to the grant of such benefits in the future. In purchase and sale transactions where a pension scheme is involved, the purchaser's advisors, in trying to ascertain the extent of the purchaser's future obligations to the scheme members, will inquire as to the practice of granting pension increases. The question may also be considered relevant in assessing an appropriate transfer value if there is to be a bulk transfer.[64] It is submitted, however, that the continued exercise of a discretion by an employer does not of itself amount to a contractual right. It may create an expectation among members of a scheme that benefits will be augmented in the future, but that expectation, however morally correct it may be, does not necessarily create an enforceable right.

5.36 Where the trust deed confers a discretionary power on the employer this power may be subject to fiduciary constraints. The issue has received some consideration in the context of the winding-up of

---

63 See para. 4.61 et seq.

64 For a detailed discussion of the pension issues involved in purchase and sale transactions, see Chapter 18.

pension schemes. In *Mettoy Pension Trustees Limited* v. *Evans,*[65] an English case, the Court had to consider a discretionary power to augment benefits on a wind-up. The employer company was the subject of both a receivership and a liquidation order,[66] whilst the company pension scheme was in surplus. The Court found that the discretionary power to augment benefits was a fiduciary power. In the circumstances, it could not be exercised by the employer as it was in liquidation and the directors therefore no longer had any powers.[67] Nor could it be exercised by either the receiver or the liquidator as their duties to debenture holders and general creditors respectively meant that they had a conflict of interest. It fell to the Court to direct the trustees as to how the surplus in the fund might be distributed on the winding-up. In this context, the right of the members to be considered for augmentation of benefit had to be taken account of:

> In my opinion it is not correct to say that the rights of the beneficiaries under the scheme are satisfied when they have received their mandatory benefits and that anything more lies in the bounty of the employer. I think the beneficiaries have a right to be considered for discretionary benefits.[68]

5.37 *Mihlenstedt* v. *Barclays Bank International Limited*[69] is also of interest. In that case, the English Court of Appeal had to consider the right of an employee to receive an ill-health pension. It was a term of the plaintiff's contract of employment that she be entitled to membership of a non-contributory pension scheme set up by the bank. The rules of the scheme provided that an ill-health pension would be payable if the bank so determined. The bank contended that it had the power, exerciseable for its own benefit, to grant or withhold the pension. It was further argued on behalf of the bank that it was not under any enforceable obligation to consider a case put to it for ill-health pension, nor if it should improperly consider a case could it be

---

65 [1991] 2 All ER 513.

66 In corporate insolvencies it is not uncommon for a receiver to be appointed to a company and for a liquidator to also be appointed. Their roles are quite different. See also paras. 17.46 et seq.

67 Under company law, the powers of the directors of a company cease on the appointment of a liquidator — see para. 17.51.

68 *Mettoy* per Warner J at p.550.

69 [1989] PLR 91.

under an obligation to reconsider the case. The Court did not accept these arguments, stating:

> It is unnecessary to consider what might be the position under the law of trusts if the trust deed stood alone, and the plaintiff's rights were to be found only within the four corners of the trust deed and rules. It is unnecessary, because this is a case in which the plaintiff's status as a member springs from her contract of employment with the Bank. The Bank holds out this pension scheme to its staff as a valuable part of the staff's overall remuneration package. That being so, when one finds that under the rules of the pension scheme certain functions are entrusted to the Bank, it is, in my view, necessarily implicit in the contract of employment that the Bank agrees with the employee that it will duly discharge those functions in good faith. In particular, if a member of the Bank staff will become entitled to payment of an ill-health pension if the Bank is of the relevant opinion concerning the state of health of the employee, it is an implied term of the contract that the Bank will properly consider a genuine claim by an employee that her health qualifies her for an ill-health pension.[70]

PENSION RIGHTS ON TERMINATION

5.38 In an employment relationship, termination of employment (other than resulting from retirement at normal pension date) or of a pension scheme may happen and the entitlements of employees and the possible consequences are now examined.

Termination of Employment

5.39 Termination of employment may occur for a variety of reasons. It may be that the employee leaves service voluntarily, by way of enforced or voluntary redundancy, as the result of a dismissal, or employment may be terminated because of early retirement or death. The trust documentation should make provision for and stipulate what benefits a member is entitled to on leaving service for any reason and what benefits arise on death. Employees who leave service to take up other employment should, under the terms of the trust deed, be entitled to a deferred benefit or a refund of their contributions or a combination of these. The pension rights of a member on leaving

---

70 *Ibid.* per Nicholls LJ at p.104. In fact, the plaintiff lost her appeal, the Court finding on the evidence that the Bank had given the matter proper and careful consideration. See also *Doyle* v. *Manchester Evening News Limited* [1989] PLR 47.

service are dealt with later.[71] The pension rights of and in respect of a member whose employment is terminated by way of dismissal, injury or death are examined below.

Termination of Pension Scheme

5.40 Termination of a pension scheme can arise in a number of situations:

1. To allow for changes in circumstances the employer will normally reserve the right to discontinue contributions and to terminate the scheme.
2. The terms of the scheme may also require the scheme to be terminated at the end of a stated period to avoid the application of the rule against perpetuities.[72]
3. Provision must also be made in the formal trust documentation for termination of the scheme in the event of bankruptcy, liquidation or receivership of the employer.[73]

5.41 The formal trust documentation should contain detailed provision dealing with the manner in which the scheme is to be dealt with on winding-up. If the scheme is established by an interim trust deed,[74] it is good practice to ensure that such deed contain a proper winding-up provision. In the absence of such provisions, and if the scheme falls to be wound up prior to definitive documentation being put in place, the trustees can find themselves in difficulty in determining the proper manner in which to deal with the fund. The Revenue Commissioners, whilst requiring that a scheme should provide for circumstances in which it may be terminated, do not have any particular requirements as to the priority of payments on winding-up. The Revenue do require that benefits be secured by transfer pay-

---

71 See Chapter 12.

72 See para. 3.27. This will be subject to application of s.61A of the Pensions Act (as inserted by s.25 of the Pensions (Amendment) Act, 1996) which disapplies the rule against perpetuities in the case of approved pension schemes.

73 The insolvency of the employer may mean that the scheme is also insolvent. Alternatively, the scheme may be quite solvent. These various circumstances are dealt with in Chapter 17.

74 See para. 3.39 regarding the circumstances in which a scheme would be established by interim deed.

ments to other approved schemes or by the purchase of deferred non-assignable annuity contracts or other suitable policies; they further require that the scheme should provide for the payment of any ultimate surplus to the employer.[75] In the case only of defined benefit schemes, the Pensions Act now prescribes an order of priority for payment of benefits on a winding-up.[76] This order of priorities is not, however, exhaustive, being limited to certain benefits.

Unfair Dismissal/Wrongful Dismissal

5.42 Where an employee, who is also a pension scheme member, is successful in proving unfair dismissal or wrongful dismissal,[77] the question of the correct measure of compensation for lost pension rights will arise.

5.43 ***Unfair Dismissal:*** The principal form of redress available under the Unfair Dismissals Act, 1977 to an employee who is found to have been unfairly dismissed is payment of compensation in respect of any financial loss suffered by the claimant.[78] Financial loss in relation to the dismissal of an employee includes any actual loss and any estimated prospective loss in relation to superannuation.[79] The assessment of lost pension rights is now one of the major heads of claim in unfair dismissal claims. It may be necessary to obtain actuarial advice regarding the estimate of loss and for an actuary to present evidence to the Employment Appeals Tribunal. The Tribunal must assess the actual loss incurred by the claimant between the date of dismissal and the date of the hearing. The Tribunal will then have to make an assessment as to the future loss that the claimant will suffer. The value of any pension benefit enjoyed by the claimant will be taken into account in assessing weekly remuneration. The assess-

---

75 Revenue Practice Notes.

76 s.48 of the Pensions Act.

77 A claim for unfair dismissal is statutory being brought under the provisions of the Unfair Dismissals Acts, 1977–1993 and proceedings will usually be commenced in the Employment Appeals Tribunal. A claim for wrongful dismissal is brought under the common law and proceedings are in the Courts.

78 s.7(1) of the 1977 Act.

79 s.7(3) of the 1977 Act.

ment of the value of lost future entitlements is more complex.[80] The Tribunal will usually assess the value over the period until the claimant gains, or is likely to gain, alternative comparable employment. The Tribunal will also take account of the possibility that the claimant might have left employment in circumstances in which no benefit would be payable.[81] The total compensation award that the Tribunal may make is limited to a maximum of 104 weeks' remuneration.[82] Irrespective of the behaviour of the employer, the Tribunal does not have any jurisdiction to award exemplary damages. It may also happen that the Tribunal will find the claimant to be in part responsible for the dismissal, and in such case the Tribunal may proportionately reduce the award otherwise payable.[83]

5.44 Alternatively, the Tribunal is empowered under the Unfair Dismissals Act, 1977 to order that an employee who has been unfairly dismissed, be re-instated.[84] The effect of such an award is that the employee must be treated as if no dismissal had ever taken place. This means that all benefits enjoyed prior to dismissal are restored, including pension benefits. An award of re-engagement — a further alternative that the Tribunal may order[85] — does not have the same effect. Such re-engagement may be in a different position and on such terms and conditions as the Tribunal may deem fit, usually ignoring the period between the date of dismissal and the date of the award.

5.45 If an employee is found to have been unfairly dismissed, and as a result becomes entitled to an early-retirement pension, this will be taken into account in assessing the compensation due to the employee with respect to financial loss for the period from the date of dismissal to the date of the hearing.

---

80 An example of the assessment of pension loss by the EAT may be found in *Legett* v. *Barry's Tea Limited* [UD 207/89]

81 See for example *Bunyan* v. *United Dominions Trust (Ireland) Limited* [UD 66/1980], *Kavanagh* v. *Carrick-on-Suir UDC* [UD 505/1982].

82 s.7(1)(c) of the 1977 Act as amended by s.6 of the Unfair Dismissals (Amendment) Act, 1993.

83 s.7(2) of the 1977 Act.

84 s.7(1)(a) of the 1977 Act.

85 s.7(1)(b) of the 1977 Act.

5.46 ***Wrongful Dismissal:*** In wrongful dismissal cases, the claim is brought under contract law. The claim is founded on breach of contract and, therefore, the correct measure of damages for pension loss should be the additional pension rights which would have accrued from the date of dismissal up to the time when the employment contract could have been lawfully terminated. For example, if an employee who is wrongfully dismissed was employed under a contract which allowed the employer to terminate by three months' notice, the employee should be compensated for the pension rights lost by that early termination. If the scheme is a defined benefit scheme, the lost benefit will be that which would have accrued by an additional three months' service. In the case of a defined contribution scheme, the benefit lost will be the additional three months' contributions and the investment return on those contributions over the same period.

5.47 Where there is a claim for loss of earnings, pension benefits which may become payable to a plaintiff as a result of the dismissal should not be taken into account in assessing the damages — that is, such benefits should not reduce the amount of damages otherwise payable by the defendant by way of compensation. This was held to be the case in *Hopkins* v. *Norcross*.[86] In that case, the plaintiff, on the termination of his employment, became entitled to an immediate pension. The plaintiff sought compensation for loss of earnings caused by the wrongful termination of his contract. His employer in defence, among other things, claimed that the amount received by the plaintiff in pension benefit over the period from the date of dismissal up to the date when the contract would have terminated under its terms should be deducted from any award for loss of earnings. The Court held that no such deduction should be made and that the provision of a pension was akin to insurance arrangements put in place by a person to provide compensation for themselves in the case of accident.

5.48 Some pension deeds contain clauses to the effect that nothing in the deed or rules of the relevant scheme shall prevent the employer from dismissing an employee nor shall anything in the deed or rules be used to add to a claim for loss in any proceedings arising out of or in connection with a dismissal. Whether a provision like this will be effective will depend on the extent to which the provision forms part

---

[86] [1992] PLR 109.

of the contract of employment. For example, if the pension rights of an employee who has been wrongfully dismissed are found to be contractual rights, but the exclusion clause in the deed is not found to be part of the contract (perhaps because it was not sufficiently brought to the attention of the employee), then the exclusion clause will be of no effect. Exclusion clauses have been considered in an employment context by the English High Court in *Micklefield* v. *SAC Technology Limited*.[87] It would appear from that case that an exclusion clause will be effective provided that it forms an express part of the contract of employment. The case concerned a share option scheme under which the plaintiff had been granted an option. It was a term of the scheme that no option could be exercised after employment ceased for any reason whatsoever. The plaintiff was employed under a contract which provided for termination by either party on six months' notice. The plaintiff had been granted an option under the scheme. On 3 February 1988, the plaintiff gave notice of his intention to exercise the option. On 11 February, the employer terminated his employment and gave him six months' salary in lieu of notice. The company refused to allow the plaintiff to exercise the option. The plaintiff brought the action claiming that the employer had wrongfully repudiated the option agreement by wrongfully dismissing him and in so doing disqualifying him from exercising the option. The Court, in holding against the plaintiff, stated that damages for loss of an option could not be claimed by an employee who was wrongfully dismissed before the date for exercise of the option if the option scheme expressly stated that the option lapsed on termination of employment and that the option holder was not entitled to any compensation for loss of the option if the option holder ceased to be employed by the company for any reason whatsoever. This case concerned a senior employee who was a member of management. It is doubtful whether an Irish Court would give effect to an exclusion clause of this type in a pension scheme deed where an employee had been wrongfully or unfairly dismissed in the absence of clear evidence that the exclusion clause had been brought to the attention of the employee and explained to him. To date, such a clause has not been tested in any reported Irish case where a pension benefit was at issue.

---

87 [1991] 1 All ER 275.

Compensation Claims for Injury and Death

5.49 Compensation claims for injury or death may be brought against employers or third parties. The principles applied by the Courts as regards damages awards and allowance for pension benefits have been the same. In assessing damages due by defendants, Courts have disallowed attempts by defendants to have entitlements to pension rights or accelerated payment of pensions taken into account in assessing compensation for loss of earnings by the plaintiff. The usual argument of the employer has been that the head of claim is loss of earnings and, whereas future earnings have been lost, there is a substitute salary/wage in the form of an early-retirement pension which has now become available. It is argued that this early-retirement pension should be taken into account in assessing the amount of the compensation. The argument of the plaintiff, which has been accepted by the Courts, has been that the pension arrangements are something which the employer and employee have established. Employees may contribute money or may be taken to contribute by their work for the employer. For those benefits to be taken into account in assessing a loss-of-earnings claim would be to allow the wrongdoer to benefit from its wrong.[88]

5.50 However, where a person is in receipt of a pension under a statutory scheme and the relevant statute permits review of the amount of pension in the light of a compensation award, the pension may be subject to reduction in view of the compensation received.[89] This issue has been the subject of a number of superior Court decisions in the context of army pensions. In *Breen* v. *The Minister for*

---

88 See *Murphy* v. *Cronin* [1966] IR 699 which concerned a claim for compensation by a widow and the issue of reduction of damages under s.50 of the Civil Liability Act, 1961 in respect of a refund of contributions received by the widow from a scheme of which her deceased husband had been a member. This has also been the decision of the English House of Lords in *Parry* v. *Cleaver* [1970] AC 1 and also in *Smoker* v. *London Fire Authority* [1991] 2AC 502. See also the remarks of McKenzie J. in *O'Loughlin* v. *Teeling* [1988] ILRM 617 at 619, which case concerned the deduction of social welfare disability benefit from a damages award. The remarks of the Judge echo the majority in *Parry* v. *Cleaver*.

89 *The State (Thornhill)* v. *The Minister for Defence*[1986] IR 1, *Breen* v. *The Minister for Defence* [1988] IR 242, *O'Loughlin* v. *The Minister for the Public Service* [1985] IR 631, *O'Looney* v. *The Minister for the Public Service* [1986] IR 543.

Defence,[90] the High Court held that the Ministry was correct in discontinuing a "wound pension" payable to the plaintiff under the Army Pensions Act, 1923, following a compensation award the actuarial value of which exceeded the value of the pension on an annual basis. The Court held that this was expressly permitted by the legislation (as amended).[91] The plaintiff successfully appealed to the Supreme Court,[92] which held that the High Court judge had failed to apply properly the decision of the Supreme Court in *The State(Thornhill)* v. *The Minister for Defence*.[93] In that case, the Supreme Court held that the Minister, under the Army Pensions Act, 1923, was obliged to adopt fair procedures in his review of pensions. Further, the Minister was not obliged to abate a pension because the actuarial value on an annual basis of a compensation award exceeded that of the pension. Rather, the Court stated that all the circumstances of the case should be considered.

Employee Protection on Insolvency

5.51 The insolvency of an employer will usually constitute a winding up event for the purposes of any occupational pension scheme established by that employer. The insolvency may mean that as a practical matter the continuation of the pension scheme is not possible as the employer is no longer making contributions.[94] The rules of the scheme will set out how the fund is to be dealt with on the winding-up, and this matter is discussed in detail later.[95]

5.52 On liquidation or receivership of an insolvent employer which had established a pension scheme, often the employer will have failed to make contributions to the pension scheme on its own behalf and may also have failed to pay over contributions deducted from employees' pay. The Protection of Employees (Employers' Insolvency) Act, 1984 provides that the Minister, on application, shall make a payment out of

---

90 [1988] IR 242.

91 By s.13 of the Army Pensions Act, 1923.

92 (Unreported, Supreme Court, 20 July 1990).

93 [1986] IR 1.

94 Apart from the inability to meet Revenue requirements, a defined benefit scheme might not be able to continue to meet the funding standard set down in Part IV of the Pensions Act.

95 See Chapter 17.

the Social Insurance Fund[96] in respect of unpaid relevant contributions.[97] Relevant contributions are defined as contributions falling to be paid by the employer in accordance with an occupational pension scheme, either on its own account or in respect of employees.[98] The total sum payable in respect of employer contributions is the lesser of:

1. The amount payable by the employer in the 12 months preceding the insolvency[99]
2. The amount certified by an actuary as being necessary to meet the liabilities of the scheme to the employees on the dissolution.[100]

The total sum payable in respect of employee contributions is such sums as were deducted from employees' pay in the 12 months preceding the date on which the employer became insolvent.[101]

5.53 Any unpaid pension contributions are a preferential debt in a liquidation or receivership.[102] This means that in any liquidation or receivership these amounts, together with any other preferential debts, must be paid in priority to all unsecured debts of the company and also any debts due to holders of floating charges. Debts secured by a fixed charge have priority over these preferential debts.[103] Liquidators' fees and expenses, examiners' fees and certified creditors in an examinership also have priority over preferential debts.[104] Where

---

96 This fund was originally established by s.26 of the Redundancy Payments Act, 1967 for the purpose of providing a fund out of which certain payments prescribed by that Act, such as weekly redundancy payments and rebates to employers, might be made. The title of the fund was changed to its present title by s.39(1) of the Social Welfare Act, 1991.

97 s.7(1) of the 1984 Act.

98 s.7(2) of the 1984 Act.

99 "Insolvency" is defined exhaustively (for the purposes of the 1984 Act only) in s.1(3) of the Act.

100 s.7(3) of the 1984 Act.

101 s.7(4) of the 1984 Act.

102 s.285 (liquidations) and s.98 (receiverships) Companies Act, 1963 (both as amended by the Companies (Amendment) Act, 1982).

103 s.285 and s.98 Companies Act, 1963.

104 As to examinerships and pensions, see paras. 17.55 et seq.

there is an insufficiency of assets to meet all of the preferential debts of a company, those debts are abated on a pro rata basis.[105] Where a payment is made out of the Insolvency Fund in respect of unpaid pension contributions, the Minister is subrogated to the rights of the members as a preferential creditor in the liquidation or receivership.[106]

5.54 The 1984 Act requires the Minister to make a payment from the Insolvency Fund with respect to contributions due to an "occupational pension scheme." In *Re Cavan Rubber Ltd. (In Liquidation),*[107] the Employment Appeals Tribunal had to consider what this expression meant. In that case, which concerned pension arrangements made by the employer company for its employees, the formal trust documentation had not been executed, rules had not been adopted and the Revenue Commissioners had not given approval to the scheme. A booklet explaining the scheme had been issued to members, a fund had been established with a life office, and contributions had been deducted from employees' pay. The EAT held that the arrangement was clearly a " scheme " for the provision of pension benefits and that it had been established by an employer for its employees. It therefore constituted an "occupational pension scheme" for the purposes of the 1984 Act. It should be noted that the pension arrangement in the *Cavan Rubber* case would not be an occupational pension scheme within the meaning of the Pensions Act as it was not approved or being considered for approval by the Revenue Commissioners.[108]

5.55 If the employer is an individual person and is adjudicated bankrupt pursuant to the Bankruptcy Act, 1988, that Act provides preferential status for any payments due by the bankrupt pursuant to any pension scheme, whether in respect of contributions due by the bankrupt or by employees and deducted by the bankrupt from their wages or salary.[109]

---

105 s.285(7)(a) Companies Act, 1963.

106 s.10(3) of the 1984 Act.

107 [1992] ELR 79.

108 As required by s.2(1) of the Pensions Act.

109 s.81(1)(f) Bankruptcy Act, 1988.

5.56 Under the Pensions Act,[110] the Pensions Board may seek an order from the Court directing payment by an employer to a scheme of unpaid contributions (whether employer or employee). In the case of pension scheme insolvencies, this provision may be of benefit to scheme members. However, in many such cases the employer will also be insolvent. Generally, the provision effectively allows the Pension Board to take on the function of the trustees in collecting contributions. However, whereas the trustees must act in the interests of the members, there is no specific duty on the Pensions Board to do so. Pension scheme members may have no redress if action of the Pensions Board under the new provisions proves to be contrary to their interests (for instance, by leading to a winding-up of the scheme or even the employer). It is, at this stage, unclear in what circumstances the Pensions Board might seek an order under the Pensions Act. The criteria that the Court may apply in deciding to grant an order are also unknown.

---

110 s.87 as inserted in that Act by s.39 of the Pensions (Amendment) Act, 1996.

6

REVENUE APPROVAL

INTRODUCTION

6.1 The tax treatment of occupational pension schemes which provide retirement and death benefits for persons in employment is regulated under the Finance Act, 1972 ("the Finance Act"). These are referred to in the Finance Act as retirement benefits schemes. The approval of pension arrangements for persons in non-pensionable employment, such as the self-employed, is governed by the provisions of sections 235–238 of the Income Tax Act, 1967.

6.2 The basic philosophy behind the tax treatment of approved pension arrangements is that employers, employees and the self-employed should be encouraged to make provision for retirement by deferring payment of tax, but that certain limits should be imposed on benefits. In an approved retirement benefits scheme, specific limits on pensions and other benefits are set, which, in effect, limit the amount that can be contributed to the scheme. In a self-employed arrangement, there are no direct limits on benefits, but benefits are indirectly restricted in that contributions cannot exceed 15 per cent of earnings each year, rising to 20 per cent from age 55.[1] Generally, contributions to an approved arrangement are fully tax-relieved up to certain limits and the income and gain from any fund established under the scheme are tax exempt, but the benefits are taxed when the pension commences to be paid. Taxation is therefore deferred until payment. In theory, the arrangement is tax neutral. In practice, tax neutrality is distorted by reason of the fact that a part of the pension can be exchanged for a tax-free cash sum. Also, in the case of an approved retirement benefits scheme, a refund of employee contributions may be permissible. The refund is taxed at only 25 per cent, whereas the em-

---

[1] See para. 6.68.

ployee may have obtained full tax relief at the marginal rate when paying the contributions into the scheme.

6.3 The legislation governing the taxation of pension schemes dates back to the Income Tax Act, 1918 and the Finance Act, 1921. The same legislation applied in the United Kingdom, and so the provision of pensions and the overall design of pension schemes were very similar in the UK and Ireland until UK legislation diverged in the 1970s. The tax framework for both Ireland and the UK was, in turn, modelled on the statutory pension provisions for civil service employees. The civil service schemes traditionally provided pensions calculated on the basis of a fraction of salary for each year of service — in other words, pension was earned by service: the longer the service, the greater the pension. Revenue approved self-employed arrangements are of more recent origin. An approval procedure was introduced in the Finance Act, 1958.[2]

6.4 The Finance Act codifies earlier legislation on the tax treatment and approval procedures for retirement benefits schemes, but with some modifications. This was a welcome development at the time as, previously, practitioners had had to establish more than one scheme to achieve an overall benefit package for employees. The Act also made certain modifications to the tax code. A distinction is drawn between schemes approved prior to 6 April 1972 (referred to as "Old Code" schemes)[3] and schemes approved under the Finance Act since that date (referred to as "New Code" schemes). Certain transitional provisions apply in relation to Old Code Schemes but those transitional provisions ceased to have effect on 6 April 1980. The transitional provisions and the law relating to Old Code schemes are not considered in this work.

6.5 Self-employed arrangements are examined later, but the main focus of this chapter is the occupational pension scheme. Special considerations apply to schemes established by or under statute and these are also considered later.[4] The beneficial tax consequences of pension scheme approval are such that unapproved pension arrangements are rare. Issues relating to unapproved schemes are, however, also dis-

---

2 s.40.

3 Under s.32 of the Finance Act, 1921, s.34 of the Finance Act, 1958 or ss.222 or 229 of the Income Tax Act, 1967.

4 At para. 6.74 et seq.

cussed towards the end of the chapter.[5] First, it is proposed to examine occupational pension schemes approved under the Finance Act.

EXEMPT APPROVED SCHEMES

6.6 The approval provisions of the Finance Act are concerned with "retirement benefits schemes" for employees. A retirement benefits scheme is defined by the Finance Act as a scheme for the provision of benefits consisting of or including relevant benefits, but does not include any scheme under the Social Welfare Acts providing such benefits.[6] "Relevant benefits" means

> any pension, lump sum, gratuity or other like benefit given or to be given on retirement or on death, or in anticipation of retirement, or, in connection with past service, after retirement or death, or to be given on or in anticipation of or in connection with any change in the nature of the service of the employee in question, except that it does not include any benefit which is to be afforded solely by reason of the death or disability of a person resulting from an accident arising out of or in the course of his office or employment and for no other reason.[7]

Approval is at the discretion of the Revenue Commissioners ("the Revenue"),[8] although practice notes have been issued, which set out the basis upon which discretionary approval is implemented by them. There is an alternative approval procedure in which the Revenue have no discretion to refuse approval, but the benefits that can be provided on this basis are limited and the procedure is rarely, if ever, used.[9]

6.7 Schemes can be approved under section 15 of the Finance Act on satisfying certain conditions and can also be exempt approved under section 16. To be exempt approved under section 16, a scheme must

---

5 At para. 6.84 et seq.

6 s.14.

7 s.13(1).

8 s.15(4).

9 This mandatory approval procedure is examined at para. 6.90 et seq.

be established under irrevocable trusts.[10] These schemes are called "exempt approved schemes". Schemes approved under section 15 do not have to be so established and are referred to merely as approved schemes. The tax treatment of ordinary approved schemes is less favourable than exempt approved schemes, in that there is no tax relief for employee contributions and the pension fund itself is taxed. Hence, practically all private sector pension schemes are established under irrevocable trusts and are exempt approved under section 16. Accordingly, reference in this work to an approved scheme can be taken to mean a scheme established under irrevocable trusts — that is, an exempt approved scheme, unless the context indicates otherwise.

6.8 An irrevocable trust in the context of a pension scheme is a trust that is incapable of being revoked by the employer. To ensure that there is no revocation, the Revenue will insist that the scheme is expressed to be held under irrevocable trusts and that the provisions governing the scheme forbid the refund of moneys to the employer otherwise than in specified circumstances. In addition, the governing documentation must state that the main purpose of the scheme is the provision of relevant benefits to employees. In practical terms, this means that the employer cannot fund in advance to provide benefits for employees and then at a later stage decide to take a return of the fund. The employer will normally, however, reserve the right to wind up the scheme, in which eventuality the employer must take a return of any surplus that has not been distributed to members.

6.9 The tax treatment of a scheme established under irrevocable trusts is as follows:

1. The income and gain derived from investments of the scheme are exempt from income tax and capital gains tax.[11] However, foreign securities may be subject to withholding tax at source.[12]

---

10 There is also discretion in s.16(1)(b) for the Revenue to grant exempt approval to schemes which are not established under irrevocable trusts having regard to "any special circumstances".

11 s.16(2) Finance Act and s.21 Capital Gains Tax Act, 1975. In this regard, financial futures and traded options which are dealt in or quoted on any futures exchange or stock exchange (whether or not situated in the State) are deemed to be investments — Finance Act, 1988 s.30.

2. The employer's ordinary annual contributions are deductible for tax purposes as an expense in the year they are paid.[13]
3. The employer's contribution will not be assessed as income of the employee.
4. The employee's ordinary annual contributions (if any) will be allowed as a deduction for income tax under Schedule E in the tax year when the contributions are paid.[14]
5. The legal and other expenses incurred by the employer on the establishment or alteration of the scheme will be allowable for tax relief purposes.
6. Pensions in payment are chargeable to income tax in the hands of the recipient.[15]

6.10 One of the main requirements of the Revenue Commissioners in granting or withholding exempt approval is that certain limitations on benefits be observed. The limits are set out in the practice notes and limit each of the benefits listed below. These benefit limits are considered further in Chapter 7, but the following is a summary of them:

1. **Member's Own Pension:** This is up to 2/3rds of final remuneration[16] at normal retirement, or a lower proportion if the member has completed less than ten years' company service at that date.
2. **Lump Sum on Retirement:** The amount that can be taken in cash form in lieu of pension at normal retirement is a maximum of 1.5 times final remuneration, or a lower proportion if the member has completed less than 20 years' company service.
3. **Lump Sum on Death before Retirement:** The total payable on death before retirement in lump sum form is limited to four times

---

12 Except in the case of the UK, the tax may be recovered only in limited circumstances and the cost of recovery may outweigh the advantage in so doing.

13 s.16(4). Special contributions are treated differently — see para. 6.42.

14 s.16(5)(a). Special contributions are again treated differently — see para. 6.38

15 s.20 Finance Act, 1972.

16 The meaning of "final remuneration" is considered at para. 7.5 et seq.

annual remuneration, plus a repayment of the member's contributions to the scheme (with reasonable interest).

4. **Dependants' Pension on the Member's Death:** Dependants' pensions are limited in total to the maximum pension that the member is permitted to receive — any one dependant's pension is limited to 2/3rds of such total.

5. **Pension Increases:** Increases in the maximum approvable pension can be guaranteed up to the rate of increase in the Consumer Price Index from the date of retirement. Alternatively, a flat rate of up to 3 per cent per annum can be guaranteed.

APPROVAL PROCEDURE

6.11 Having identified the type of scheme that can be submitted for approval, it is necessary to examine the approval procedure itself. The responsibility for approval and monitoring of Revenue requirements in connection with pension schemes rests with the Retirement Benefits District of the Revenue Commissioners.

Procedure

6.12 The procedure for approval of a retirement benefits scheme under Part I Chapter II of the Finance Act is set out in the First Schedule First Part to that Act. An application must be made in writing to the Retirement Benefits District of the Revenue Commissioners (quoting the Retirement Benefits District reference number, if the employer has established any schemes in the past). The application must be supported by the following:

1. A copy of the instrument or other document constituting the scheme — a deed, company board resolution or letter of exchange[17]
2. A copy of the rules of the scheme[18]
3. Except where the application is made on setting-up of the scheme, a copy of the accounts of the scheme for the last year for which such accounts have been made
4. Such other information (including actuarial reports) as the Revenue considers relevant.[19]

---

17 See Chapter 3.

18 But see para. 6.15 et seq.

6.13 Application should be made before the end of the first year of assessment for which approval is required,[20] but in practice a period of grace of up to three months after the relevant 5 April will be allowed for any such application to be made.[21] Confirmation of approval will be sent by the Retirement Benefits District to the applicant and approval will date from the date of the deed or other instrument establishing the scheme. If application is not made within the period specified or the period of grace, the scheme is technically an unapproved arrangement and must in any event be notified to the Revenue within three months of its first coming into operation.[22]

6.14 In practice, the Revenue require more information on application for approval. A list of the requirements is set out in the practice notes. In addition to including a copy of the instrument establishing the scheme and the rules of the scheme, the application should normally include the following information:

1. A copy of each announcement made to employees about the scheme — all employees who have a right to be members of the scheme must be given written particulars of all essential features of the scheme that concern them[23]
2. A copy of any actuarial report or advice received by the administrator or the employer in connection with the scheme
3. The tax districts and district Revenue references of each participating employer and the employees
4. Information about the method of funding adopted and particulars of special contributions paid by each participating employer
5. Where the new scheme supersedes any previous scheme, copies of any waiver forms signed by employees in connection with any transfer of benefits to the new scheme
6. Particulars of any other schemes under which any of the employers participate and under which their employees may benefit

---

19 First Schedule Part I para. 1.

20 *Ibid.*

21 Practice notes.

22 First Schedule Part I para. 3.

23 s.15(2)(b).

7. Where a group scheme is established (more than one participating employer), information about the relationship or degree of association between the participating employers together with any deeds of adherence[24]
8. The number of initial entrants
9. Where benefits are secured by an insurance policy, a certificate that the policy is or will be in standard form appropriate to the scheme and acceptable to the Revenue as satisfying section 50(4) of the Corporation Tax Act, 1976
10. Whether there are any 20% Directors.[25]

Interim Approval

6.15 It is recognised that a newly established scheme may take many months to be "bedded down", and the benefit provisions may need to be modified during this period. In addition, the full provisions of schemes tend to be quite complex and it is accepted that it may take some time for the full terms to be reduced to writing. With this in mind, the Revenue have agreed on an interim procedure for approval of retirement benefits schemes. The Revenue will normally accept that a scheme is effectively established by an interim deed or declaration creating an irrevocable trust and setting out the main purposes of the scheme. The interim deed must be followed by a definitive deed, and a covenant must be included in the interim deed by the employer, and normally by the trustees, that the definitive deed and rules of the scheme will be executed within two years of the establishment of the scheme. The application on an interim basis must be made within the same time limits as those where full documentation is submitted and the same period of grace of three months also applies.[26]

6.16 In response to the interim application, the Revenue will confirm in writing receipt of the documents and will furnish a Retirement Benefits District reference number for the scheme. From a tax perspective, immediate relief on a provisional basis is allowed in respect of contributions made by employees, but the Revenue insist that the principal features of the scheme are communicated in writing to every

---

[24] See para. 6.24.

[25] On which, see para. 6.79 below.

[26] Practice notes.

member before this relief is granted. Life offices may treat the premiums from an interim approved scheme as pension business.[27] However, where pensions contributions are made to an investment manager other than a life office, these may not be invested in an exempt fund until full exempt approval is obtained.

6.17 For one-person arrangements, the Revenue will normally grant full exempt approval retrospectively from the date of commencement of the scheme without the requirement for an interim procedure at all, providing there is no undue delay.[28]

6.18 Where approval has been obtained on an interim basis, full exempt approval will be granted subsequently, on furnishing the Revenue with the rules of the scheme or definitive deed and rules as appropriate. The normal exempt approval letter will then be issued and exempt approval will be granted with effect from the date of the interim deed or declaration of trust.

Disclosure of Information

6.19 The practice notes list the details required to be given to employees under section 15(2)(b) of the Finance Act before approval is granted. To a large extent, these requirements have, for practical purposes, been superseded by the disclosure regulations under the Pensions Act[29] but, nonetheless, the disclosure requirements under the Finance Act are independent and distinct from Pensions Act requirements. The following details must be given to employees who are members or who have a right to be members of an exempt approved scheme:

1. The basis on which pensions payable at normal retirement age are to be calculated
2. The rights under the scheme of an employee who retires early or withdraws from service

---

27 *Ibid.*

28 *Ibid.*

29 See generally Chapter 13.

3. The benefits payable on death in service and any spouses'[30] and dependants' pensions payable on death after retirement
4. Commutation rights or any separate rights to lump sum benefit
5. The rate at which an employee is required to contribute.

Employees are entitled only to information relating to their own benefits. This is significant where there are several categories in a scheme. Employees need only be furnished with information relating to their own category of benefit.[31]

6.20 The Revenue may by notice require additional information from the administrator of the scheme and from every employer who pays contributions.[32] A formal notice must be responded to within 30 days from the date of the notice, but in practice the Revenue will normally seek the information informally. However, if an administrator or employer fails to respond to an informal request, a formal notice can be expected. Failure to comply with a notice carries a liability to penalty under section 500 of the Income Tax Act, 1967.[33] The Revenue may require any of the following by notice:

1. Particulars of the contributions paid under the scheme
2. Particulars of returns of contributions, commutation or other lump sum payments, or any other payments made to an employer
3. Copies of the accounts of the scheme and such other information and particulars (including actuarial reports) as the Revenue consider relevant.[34]

---

30 The Finance Act refers to "widow" but not "widower" in many places. This must be interpreted to include "widower" — Interpretation Act, 1937 s.11(b). Reference in this text will from here onwards be to "spouse" rather than widow or widower.

31 Practice notes.

32 First Schedule Part I para. 2.

33 As amended by s.4(5) of the Finance (Miscellaneous Provisions) Act, 1968.

34 The Revenue used to issue regular notices on items (1.) and (2.) until the 1980s.

Scheme Changes

6.21 In addition to the initial application for approval, where changes have been made to the scheme, those changes must be notified to the Revenue. The changes may be effected by a deed of variation, amending rules, a board resolution or a supplementary letter of exchange.[35] If approval of a scheme change is not obtained from the Revenue, the original approval will cease.[36] It is therefore essential that amending documents are sent to the Revenue and that their approval is sought to all changes.

Group Schemes

6.22 Many schemes involve the participation of only one employer. Some, however, involve a number of employers, each of which participates in one scheme. The scheme may provide a common benefit basis for all employees in the group or may offer different benefit structures for each employer's employees.

6.23 For the Revenue to approve of the participation of more than one employer in a group scheme, normally there must be a sufficiently close association between the employers. For example if one employer is a wholly owned subsidiary of another or if both are subsidiaries of a common parent, the Revenue will permit the participation of both employers in a group scheme. Approval must be sought in each case and evidence of the degree of association must be given. The Revenue will allow participation provided that there is at least a 50 per cent shareholding by one of the other, directly or indirectly. Alternatively, even if there is no direct relationship there may be enough links between the employers to put a case to the Revenue that there is a sufficient degree of association between the employers by reason of community of interest. There may for example be common management or interdependent operations.

6.24 In addition, each employer must be bound by the rules of the scheme. This is usually achieved by way of a deed of adherence, whereby the new employer adheres to the scheme and undertakes to observe the duties and obligations of an employer under the pension scheme. Each employer may separately contribute in respect of its

---

35 Depending upon the provisions for variation in the formal documentation — see Chapter 3.

36 s.15(6).

own employees or, alternatively, one employer in a group, usually referred to as the "principal employer", can pay contributions in respect of the group. The rules must provide for withdrawal of an employer where the grounds for admitting the employer to the group scheme in the first place no longer obtain.

6.25 The main exception to the requirement of a shareholding connection or community of interest is industry schemes. It is possible to establish schemes with more than one employer where the only connection is a trade, industry or professional association. The best known industry-wide scheme in Ireland is probably the Construction Industry Federation scheme. It is important to ensure that the provisions of such a scheme set out in precise terms how the fund is split on an employer ceasing to participate and what sanctions are available to the other employers if one of them fails to pay contributions.

Administrator

6.26 The Finance Act secures compliance with the provisions of Part I Chapter II by imposing certain obligations and liabilities upon the administrator, who is defined as the person or persons having the management of the scheme.[37] It is a requirement of approval that an administrator who is resident in the State be appointed.[38] Although schemes are usually administered by professionals, such as life offices and benefit consultants, the persons normally designated as the administrator are the trustees of the scheme, if (as is normal) the scheme is established by trust. The administrator may therefore be the employer, where the employer is trustee, or, for example, individual trustees. More than one person can constitute the administrator.

6.27 The responsibilities of the administrator are considered below and in the next chapter as they arise under each appropriate subject. As a general point, if the administrator defaults, cannot be traced or dies, the employer becomes liable instead for any tax due and must discharge the duties of the administrator.[39] In this context, "employer" includes any factor, agent, receiver, branch or manager of the

---

37 s.13(1).

38 s.15(2)(c).

39 First Schedule Part 1 para. 4(1).

employer in the State.[40] Even if the scheme is subsequently terminated or approval is withdrawn, the liability of the administrator and the employer continues. Liability also continues in circumstances where a person's appointment as administrator is terminated.[41]

Residence of Trust

6.28 Revenue practice since November 1994 requires that, in order for a scheme to receive approval, the trust must be resident in Ireland. Residence will be determined by establishing the place of effective management of the trust. If all the trustees are resident abroad, the scheme will not be approved. It is possible, however, to have both Irish resident and non-resident trustees, provided that the Irish resident trustees have control and supervision of the scheme's administration. Generally, the Revenue require that a majority of the trustees must be resident in the state.

6.29 It is understood that for schemes with foreign trustees established prior to November 1994, the Revenue may permit the existing trusteeship structure to remain provided that there is an Irish resident administrator. The reason for requiring an Irish resident administrator is that the Revenue cannot enforce fiscal obligations in other jurisdictions.[42]

WITHDRAWAL OF APPROVAL

6.30 The Revenue have discretion under section 15(5) of the Finance Act to withdraw approval if, in their opinion, the facts concerning any scheme or its administration cease to warrant the continuance of its approval. Notice must be issued to the administrator of the scheme, specifying the date of withdrawal and the reasons. Unlike the equivalent notice under section 235(5) of the Income Tax Act, 1967 for self-employed schemes, section 15(5) does not specify that the date of withdrawal may pre-date the date of the notice. It could be argued, therefore, that the omission of those words in section 15(5) means that the withdrawal of approval cannot pre-date the notice of withdrawal. Nonetheless, the practice notes state that the date of withdrawal will normally be that of the event which triggered withdrawal

---

40 *Ibid.* para. 4(3).

41 *Ibid.* para. 4(2).

42 *Buchanan* v. *McVey* [1954] IR 89.

of approval, which in some cases could be the beginning of the tax year or even the date of commencement of the scheme.[43]

6.31 There are many reasons why the Revenue may withdraw approval. A scheme may be administered in such a way that Revenue limits are exceeded in regard to benefits, or the scheme is substantially over-funded, or there might, for example, be a persistent failure to furnish such information as the Revenue Commissioners have sought. The consequences of withdrawal of approval are quite serious. Contributions paid by the employer in respect of the employee after the date of withdrawal of approval would become taxable in the hands of the employee under section 18 of the Finance Act and employee contributions would cease to enjoy relief for income tax purposes. Tax will be chargeable under sections 21 and 22 on any payments made out of the fund on which relief has been given under section 16. Payments subject to the tax charge would comprise refunds of employee contributions, commutation of pension for triviality or serious ill-health[44] or lump sum benefits exceeding those authorised by the scheme rules as were in force prior to the effective date from which approval was lost. However, if payments are not authorised by the scheme rules, liability will arise under Part VI of the First Schedule. Repayments to an employer are taxable under section 23 as income chargeable to tax under Case IV of Schedule D or as a receipt of the employer's trade or profession.

OVERSEAS EMPLOYERS AND EMPLOYEES

6.32 Some schemes approved under the Finance Act include employees resident abroad. Special conditions apply in this case, which are examined later in this section. Schemes may also be sponsored by overseas employers and the requirements that must be met for approval purposes are now considered.

Non-resident Employers

6.33 Employers who are not resident for tax purposes in Ireland can establish a scheme that is approvable in the State if it relates wholly to persons employed in the State. If the scheme relates to employees in the State and employees in another jurisdiction, the Revenue will

---

43 Practice notes.

44 See para. 7.20.

regard the part of the scheme applicable to employees in this jurisdiction as being a separate scheme from that relating to employees in the foreign jurisdiction, and the Irish part of the scheme will be approvable.[45] In this regard, the Revenue rely on section 14(3) of the Finance Act, which empowers them to treat a retirement benefits scheme relating to two or more different classes of employee as being two or more separate retirement benefits schemes. However, since the revision of the Ireland/UK Double Taxation Agreement, reciprocal approval between Ireland and the UK is, in practice, unlikely to be granted in respect of schemes seeking approval on or after 6 April 1994.[46]

Non-resident Employees

6.34 Where Irish employees are not assessable to Irish tax on their remuneration or are only assessable on the remittance basis, the scheme does not need to conform to Revenue limits in this jurisdiction but may be so approved if required. However, an employee who is only on leave of absence or secondment from an Irish employer can be deemed to remain a member of the Irish scheme in certain circumstances.[47]

6.35 Employee contributions may be either continued or suspended during temporary absence, based on remuneration at the point when temporary absence commenced.[48] Remuneration can be increased in line with salaries for that grade of employee, provided that the scheme rules permit. Contributions can be continued even if no salary is paid.

EMPLOYER AND EMPLOYEE CONTRIBUTIONS

6.36 So far, the approval procedures under the Finance Act for retirement benefits schemes have been examined. Approved schemes are financed by contributions made by the sponsoring employer and (if applicable) the employees. The tax treatment of employer and

---

45 Practice notes.

46 Because Revenue requirements have markedly diverged between the two jurisdictions since the 1970s — see Protocol to the Ireland/UK Double Taxation Agreement replacing Article 17.

47 See para. 6.56 et seq. below.

48 Practice notes.

employee contributions both on being paid into a scheme and on being refunded is the subject of this and the following section.

Employee Contributions

6.37 Employee contributions to an exempt approved scheme, subject to certain conditions, are tax relieved — that is, they are allowed to be deducted as an expense in determining the employee's income tax liability.[49] The aggregate amount of contributions[50] allowed to be deducted in any year cannot exceed 15 per cent of the employee's remuneration from the employer for the year of employment in respect of which the contributions are made.[51] An employee may contribute in excess of 15 per cent, but only contributions up to the 15 per cent limit are relieved, although there is a limit to the maximum employee contribution an employee can make, in that contributions cannot be so high that the employee's prospective benefits are likely to exceed overall benefit limits.[52] Furthermore, the employer must contribute at least one-sixth of the total aggregate contributions of employer and employee — the "one-sixth rule".[53] A high contribution rate from the employee could result in the employer's fraction of total contributions falling short of one-sixth.

6.38 The Finance Act and the practice notes distinguish between ordinary annual contributions and contributions which are not ordinary annual contributions.[54] The latter are generally referred to as special contributions. Ordinary annual contributions can be set off against income tax in the year in which they are paid.[55] Special contributions can be apportioned among such years as the Revenue direct.[56] The practice notes amplify the meaning of ordinary annual con-

---

[49] s.16(5) Finance Act.

[50] Including additional voluntary contributions and any special contributions.

[51] s.16(5)(c).

[52] On which, see the summary at para. 6.10 above and Chapter 7.

[53] See para. 6.41.

[54] s.16(5)(b).

[55] s.16(5)(a).

[56] s.16(5)(b).

tribution. It is regarded as an amount payable each year until normal retirement date (or during the maximum period taken into account in computing pension) and is a fixed amount each year, or fixed by reference to a stated basis — for example, 5 per cent of salary in each year. With regard to tax relief on special contributions, the Revenue will grant relief in the year of payment up to the maximum limit of 15 per cent and will then spread forward the relief to subsequent tax years. If spreading forward is not practical, relief will be spread backwards up to a maximum period of 10 years.[57]

6.39 Employees can seek tax relief from the Revenue on an individual basis for contributions paid. Employers automatically calculate PAYE deductions by reference to net pay — that is, pay after deducting ordinary annual contributions — referred to as the "net pay arrangement". In this way, employees are not required to seek relief individually. As well as being administratively simpler, the net pay arrangement has the advantage of securing relief not only against income but also, incidentally, against Pay Related Social Insurance and Income and Youth Levies as well. Relief against PRSI and levies is not available on an individual basis. Special contributions cannot be included in the net pay arrangement, and so no relief against PRSI or levies is available in respect of special contributions.

6.40 Some schemes offer a facility to employees to improve their benefits by paying additional voluntary contributions ("AVCs"). Alternatively, employers sometimes establish a separate AVC scheme under irrevocable trusts. Whichever approach is adopted, AVCs must be aggregated with ordinary annual contributions and special contributions so that the maximum total on which tax relief can be obtained is limited to 15 per cent of remuneration. In addition, AVCs must be added to all other contributions to determine whether the one-sixth rule is satisfied. As with ordinary annual contributions, AVCs can be paid under the net pay arrangement provided that they also satisfy the ordinary annual contribution test. AVCs falling into the special contribution category must be treated for tax purposes as

---

57 Stipulated by s.498 of the Income Tax Act, 1967 as amended by s.4(5) of the Finance (Miscellaneous Provisions) Act 1968.

special contributions. Payment of AVCs must be monitored to ensure that overall prospective benefit limits are not exceeded.[58]

Employer Contributions

6.41 The employer must contribute to an approved or exempt approved scheme.[59] For defined contribution schemes, the employer must contribute at least annually, but will typically contribute at similar intervals to the employee — for example, monthly or weekly. With defined benefit schemes, the timing of contributions is largely a matter for the employer.[60] As with employee contributions, the main restrictions are the one-sixth rule[61] and the requirement that overall Revenue benefit limits on retirement are not likely to be exceeded. The one-sixth rule applies to all schemes of the employer — for example, contributions to an AVC scheme, a main scheme and a separate top-up scheme for (say) executives must all be aggregated to determine if the one-sixth rule is satisfied. Defined contribution schemes must satisfy the rule on a year-by-year basis. Defined benefit schemes will satisfy the rule if at normal retirement the employer will have contributed at least one-sixth of total contributions over the period of membership of the scheme to retirement.[62]

6.42 Section 16(4) of the Finance Act states that any sum paid by way of contribution to the scheme shall, for the purposes of Case I or Case II of Schedule D, be allowed to be deducted as an expense incurred in the year in which it is paid. The amount deductible is confined to contributions paid in respect of employees of a trade or undertaking assessable on the employer to Irish tax. As with employee contributions, section 16(4) and the practice notes distinguish between an employer's ordinary annual contributions and special contributions. A special contribution is treated as being an expense either incurred in the year in which it is paid or spread over such period as the Revenue determine. Relief in the year of payment is usually obtained where the special contribution does not exceed the ordinary annual contribution for that year. Otherwise, it will be spread forward. The period

---

58 On benefit limits see Chapter 7.

59 Other than an AVC scheme.

60 See Chapter 9 on the issue of funding a defined benefit scheme.

61 See para. 6.37.

62 Practice notes.

of spread is obtained by dividing the special contribution by the ordinary contribution with a maximum of five years. For example, if the ordinary contribution for the year is £30,000 and the special contribution is £90,000 the period of spread is 90,000 ÷ 30,000 = 3 years.

TAXATION OF REFUNDS

6.43 The main objective of a pension scheme is to provide benefits on retirement or death in service or both. In these circumstances, moneys are paid out of the scheme, but there are other circumstances in which moneys can be refunded to an employer or employee.

Refunds to the Employer

6.44 A refund of moneys from a scheme to an employer can arise only where the scheme is in surplus. Much has been written regarding what constitutes a surplus, and the topic is considered elsewhere.[63] A refund includes a payment of money, but a payment to the employer by way of a transfer of assets (for example, shares) or other transfer of assets for money's worth is also included in the concept of refund. The Revenue stipulate in the practice notes that they will only permit a refund in three situations:

1. On a winding-up of the scheme
2. Where the proceeds of an insurance policy must be used to provide benefits for an individual employee and the surrender value of the policy exceeds the value of benefits to the employee
3. Where a surplus in the fund cannot be reduced otherwise than by refund and the Revenue issue a declaration requiring a refund to be made.

6.45 The first situation is relatively straightforward from a Revenue point of view. Once the winding-up of the scheme has occurred and the fund has been applied in accordance with the terms of the trust to provide deferred or immediate benefits for members and/or other beneficiaries, any surplus can be paid to the employer and will be taxed in accordance with section 23 of the Finance Act.

---

[63] See Chapter 17 regarding surplus on a winding-up and Chapter 18 regarding a surplus in the context of a corporate acquisition.

6.46 The second situation arises in cases where the scheme is individually funded — that is, where each member's benefits are individually allocated: there is no element of pooled funding among members.[64] If an employee leaves service and the value of the fund allocated to that employee exceeds the value of benefits to be paid, the rules of the scheme must provide that the excess be paid over to the employer.

6.47 The third situation is where the scheme remains in existence but the Revenue regard it as being overfunded. The Revenue have no objection to a reasonable reserve in the ongoing funding of a scheme. But where assets exceed 110 per cent of liabilities the Revenue are most likely to require action to reduce the surplus. Action can take the form of the employer either taking a contribution holiday (that is, ceasing to pay contributions for a period of time) or improving the benefits under the scheme within Revenue limits. In neither of these cases does the employer take a refund. However, where the Revenue take the view that a surplus will be retained in the scheme without reasonable prospect of being significantly reduced by contribution holiday or benefit improvement, a refund may be required. This might arise as a consequence of a redundancy programme, as a significant contraction in the workforce could result in a substantial surplus arising in the fund. A refund could only be made where the rules of the scheme permit.

6.48 The tax treatment of refunds to the employer is dealt with in section 23 of the Finance Act. If the scheme relates to a trade or profession carried on by the employer (the vast majority of private occupational schemes), the refund is treated for income tax purposes as a receipt of that trade or profession receivable when the payment falls due (as opposed to when it is actually paid) or on the last day on which the trade or profession is carried on, if earlier. If the scheme does not relate to a trade or profession, the refund is taxable under Schedule D Case IV, but is no tax is charged to the extent that it relates to contributions paid in by the employer where such contributions failed to attract tax relief at date of payment into the scheme.

---

64 On pooled funding, see Chapter 9.

Refunds to Employees

6.49 An employee may be given the option on leaving service to take a refund of employee contributions. Under s.21 of the Finance Act[65] the refund is taxed at 25 per cent. Tax is payable by the administrator of the scheme under Schedule D Case IV. Refunds of employee contributions are discussed elsewhere.[66]

TRANSFERS TO OTHER SCHEMES

6.50 The taxation of employee contribution refunds referred to in the previous paragraph arises on the employee leaving service. There are other options open to employees on leaving service. The Pensions Act provides that employees who satisfy certain criteria are entitled to have their benefits transferred to the scheme of a new employer. The Revenue Commissioners have always recognised the possibility of a transfer in these circumstances and have prescribed certain requirements before a transfer can be effected. The Revenue requirements concerning these transfers (commonly known as "transfer payments") are now examined.

6.51 Subject to certain exceptions,[67] a transfer payment can be received by a pension scheme provided that both ceding scheme and receiving scheme are approved schemes or have been approved on an interim basis[68] or are statutory schemes.[69] The transfer may be effected by either a transmission of assets from the ceding scheme to the receiving scheme, or the assignment of an assurance policy from the trustees of one scheme to the other.[70] The ceding scheme will certify the part of the transfer payment that relates to the employee's

---

65 As amended by s.6(b) of the Finance Act, 1992.

66 para. 7.52 et seq.

67 See para. 6.54.

68 See para. 6.15 et seq.

69 Statutory schemes are examined at para. 6.74 et seq. below.

70 In the public sector transfer network, it is possible that no transfer of assets will take place — see para. 8.48 et seq.

contributions and also that part which relates to contributions paid after 1 January 1991.[71]

6.52 The receiving scheme will provide additional benefits to the transferring employee.[72] The trustees of the receiving scheme may invest the transfer payment with the intention that at retirement the value of the transfer payment, together with investment return, will be used to purchase additional benefits for the employee. Alternatively, where the scheme is a defined benefit scheme, the transfer payment can be converted into additional years and months of service counting for retirement benefits under the receiving scheme. For example, a receiving scheme provides a pension of 1/60th of salary for each year of service in the company. The trustees, on taking actuarial advice, may determine that a transfer payment of (say) £40,000 is equivalent to granting the transferring employee an additional three years of company service or 3/60ths of salary. Either method of providing additional benefits will be acceptable to the Revenue.

6.53 In almost all cases, the benefits of a transferring employee must be transferred in total. Furthermore, where the employee's benefits are provided under more than one scheme of the employer, all benefits must be transferred.[73] Only part of the benefits may be left in the ceding scheme (with the balance being transferred to the receiving scheme) where the benefits remaining relate to spouses' and/or dependants' pensions. In these circumstances, benefits relating to the employee alone are transferred to the receiving scheme.

6.54 Transfer payments cannot be made from an approved or exempt approved scheme to an unapprovable scheme (a scheme which gives rise to a tax liability under section 18 of the Finance Act).[74] Transfers can be made to schemes established in another country ("overseas schemes") — that is, schemes or parts of schemes that

---

71 To ensure compliance with the preservation requirements of the Pensions Act — see Chapter 12.

72 s.34(6) of the Pensions Act requires it in the case of preserved benefits — on preservation see Chapter 12. In the case of non-preserved benefits, scheme rules usually stipulate that credit is to be given for transfer payments.

73 Practice notes.

74 See para. 6.84 et seq.

cater for employees abroad, who are not liable to Irish income tax. The practice in relation to such schemes has been revised considerably in recent years. A transfer will be permitted in the following circumstances:

1. The employee requests the transfer.
2. The rules of the ceding scheme permit such a transfer.
3. The overseas scheme is willing to accept the transfer.
4. The overseas scheme is established under trust in the country to which the employee is relocating and has received appropriate approved status in that country.
5. The receiving scheme must normally be an existing group scheme of the receiving employer in which the employee has been included for retirement benefits.
6. A transfer to a country other than the country of the overseas scheme or to an off-shore trust is not permitted.
7. The maximum amount that can be commuted under the ceding scheme must be notified to the receiving scheme. The receiving scheme must undertake that no greater amount of cash can be commuted than the maximum so notified and must further undertake to obtain an equivalent undertaking from any subsequent scheme to which the employee's benefits are transferred.
8. Formal application must be made to the Revenue in all cases except under reciprocal arrangements with the United Kingdom or where an employee moves to a public office or institution within the European Union — for example, the European Commission.

6.55 Where a transfer payment is made to the receiving scheme, additional benefits will be provided under that scheme. The receiving scheme may provide the employee with the maximum benefits that would normally be appropriate to that employee's service with the new employer plus the additional benefits which the transfer payment can purchase if invested in the receiving scheme. Total benefit may not, however, exceed 2/3rds of final remuneration under the receiving scheme (taking into account all retained benefits).[75]

---

[75] Retained benefits are considered at para. 7.61 et seq.

TEMPORARY ABSENCE/SECONDMENT

6.56 An employee who is on leave of absence or secondment from an employer (whether remaining in the State or going abroad) can be deemed to remain a member of the employer's scheme provided that there is an expectation of a return to active pensionable employment. Where the period of absence is less than five years no submission to the Revenue is required. Where it exceeds five years, Revenue approval will be required but will normally be granted on condition that the employee is not included in any other occupational pension scheme and there is a clear expectation of return.

6.57 Where there is no secondment but the employee is sent abroad to another company within a group and the employer still has control over that employee, the employee can remain a member of the scheme. In the latter case, however, the matter should be referred to the Retirement Benefits District. Secondment to a Government department can be of unlimited duration.

6.58 Employee contributions may continue to be made during absence but income tax relief is allowable only against the income (if any) from the employment to which the scheme relates. If the employee is working abroad, relief will be granted on income remitted to Ireland from the same source of pensionable employment. Any overseas employer must reimburse the Irish employer for the employer contributions under the scheme unless the Revenue agree otherwise.

SELF-EMPLOYED ARRANGEMENTS

6.59 Whilst the primary focus of this chapter has been the tax treatment of occupational pension schemes, it is now appropriate to examine self-employed arrangements. It should be noted at the outset that the term "self-employed arrangement" is a little misleading. This type of arrangement may, in certain circumstances, be availed of by persons in employment as well as by self-employed people.

6.60 Self-employed arrangements are approvable by the Revenue and can attract similar tax reliefs as approved schemes under the Finance Act. Approval is under either section 235 or section 235A of the Income Tax Act, 1967 ("the Income Tax Act"). Unlike the case of approved schemes, the person effecting the arrangement can only invest in an insurance policy such as a with-profit or unit-linked policy — it is not permissible to invest directly in assets such as equities or gilts,[76] (unless a trust scheme is involved).[77] Tax relief is given on premiums paid by the individual to the insurer (qualifying premiums) and the income and gain from the underlying investments of the policy are exempt from corporation tax in the hands of the insurer.[78]

6.61 The approval procedure is straightforward. The insurer submits a standard form policy to the Revenue, the terms of which comply with the requirements of section 235 or 235A of the Income Tax Act, as applicable. If the Revenue approve the terms of the policy, it can be classified as an approved policy for issue to individuals seeking to effect self-employed arrangements. When a policy is effected, the insurer issues a retirement annuity certificate (RAC). The individual can claim the appropriate tax reliefs on submission of the RAC to the local Inspector of Taxes.

Persons who May Effect a Self-Employed Arrangement

6.62 Those who can effect a self-employed arrangement must fit into one of the following categories:

1. Self-employed
2. Salaried employee whose earnings are non-pensionable
3. Anyone who has more than one source of earnings and one of those sources is non-pensionable.

In each case, individuals must be chargeable to tax in respect of relevant earnings from any trade, profession, office or employment carried on or held by them, or would but for an insufficiency of profits or gains be so chargeable to tax.[79] The insurer will normally seek a declaration to this effect.

6.63 Relevant earnings consist of income of the individual chargeable to tax in the year of assessment in which tax relief on qualifying premiums is sought, being:

---

[76] On investment generally, see Chapter 10.

[77] See para. 6.70 et seq.

[78] Corporation Taxes Act, 1976 ss.41 and 50(4).

[79] s.235(1).

1. Income from an office or employment other than a pensionable office or employment
2. Income from property that is attached to or forms part of the emoluments of an office or employment of profit held by the individual
3. Income chargeable under Schedule D, which is immediately derived from the individual's trade or profession
4. Earned income.[80]

Individuals who are included in a sponsored superannuation scheme, other than a scheme under which the individual is only entitled to a lump sum death benefit before 70, are in pensionable employment. Earnings relating to that pensionable employment cannot be included as relevant earnings.[81] "Sponsored superannuation scheme" is a somewhat convoluted definition but it basically comprises approved schemes and statutory schemes under the Finance Act.[82] A member of an unapproved scheme may therefore effect a self-employed arrangement. Also, an employee in pensionable employment may have earnings relating to a non-pensionable office, employment or trade. That individual can effect a self-employed arrangement in respect of those earnings, as they are treated as relevant earnings under section 235. For example, an employee who is included in an employer's pension scheme and receives director's fees from another company may effect a self-employed arrangement in respect of that office and that income.

Approval Conditions

6.64 Section 235 of the Income Tax Act sets out the requirements for approval of annuity contracts that secure as their main benefit a life annuity for the individual to commence payment at any date between age 60 and 70. Section 235A[83] permits individuals to obtain life assur-

---

80 s.235(7) Relevant earnings is expressed to exclude remuneration from an investment company of which the individual is a proprietary director or proprietary employee. "Proprietary director" and "proprietary employee" are defined in s.13 of the Finance Act but these definitions were subsequently repealed but not in relation to s.235(7) — Schedule I Part III para. 4 of the Finance Act, 1972 as amended by s.64(2) of the Finance Act, 1974.

81 s.235(8).

82 s.235(9).

83 Inserted by s.66 of the Finance Act, 1974.

ance cover on their death or to provide for an annuity directly for their spouse. It can be seen therefore that policies approved under section 235 provide pension benefits, whereas section 235A policies provide death benefits. To achieve a comprehensive arrangement, an individual may take out both section 235 and section 235A policies. In respect of both section 235 and 235A, the policies must be issued by persons lawfully carrying on in the State the business of granting annuities on human life.

6.65 The approval conditions applicable to section 235 policies are set out in section 235(2). The Revenue may, at its discretion, vary the strict conditions of section 235(2) in accordance with section 235(3). The conditions that must be satisfied under section 235(2) are:

1. The only benefit that can be paid during the individual's lifetime is an annuity payable to the individual.
2. No more than one-quarter of the value of the annuity can be exchanged for a cash lump sum (i.e. commuted).[84]
3. The annuity can only commence to be payable between the ages of 60 and 70. It should be noted that there is no concept of early retirement with these arrangements (in contrast to approved schemes under the Finance Act) except on grounds of ill-health. Nor is payment linked to retirement. For example, an individual can elect to receive payment under the annuity whilst still in business or employment. Although a specific date must be selected from the outset, the individual can have a change of mind at any time subsequently.
4. The only other benefit that can be paid is an annuity to the spouse on the death of an individual. If no annuity becomes payable on death, a return of premiums may be paid with reasonable interest or life office's bonuses. This is payable to the personal representative.
5. The annuity to the spouse cannot be greater than that paid to the individual.
6. Annuities must be payable for the life of the annuitant.
7. The policy must not be capable of assignment, surrender or (except in case of 2. above) commutation.[85]

---

84 Inserted by s.65(b) Finance Act, 1974.

85 Inserted by s.65(b) Finance Act, 1974.

6.66 The Revenue may approve a self employed arrangement on a discretionary basis which provides for one or more of the following:

1. An annuity can be paid to a dependant instead of the spouse.
2. Ill-health early retirement is permissible where individuals are permanently incapable through infirmity of mind or body from carrying on their own occupation or any similar occupation for which they are trained or fitted. This is quite a restrictive condition.
3. Retirement may be permissible before age 60 (but not earlier than age 50) if this is customary in the individual's occupation — similarly with retirement after age 70 (but not later than 80).
4. An annuity can be guaranteed up to 10 years notwithstanding earlier death[86] and can be expressed to terminate on marriage or remarriage or other circumstances.
5. A guaranteed pension can be assignable by will, or in certain circumstances by the personal representative.

6.67 One significant drawback of section 235 policies is that the only death benefit payable prior to "retirement" is a return of premiums plus reasonable interest/bonuses. In contrast, approved schemes under the Finance Act can promise death in service pensions and a lump sum. Consequently, section 235 was amended by section 66 of the Finance Act, 1974, which inserted a new section 235A. Section 235A permits the approval of policies issued for the purposes of providing insured death benefits. In practice, only lump sum death benefits are provided under section 235A policies. For that reason, it is not proposed to detail the requirements relating to annuities under section 235A.[87] However, in theory, certain annuities can also be provided. The conditions relating to lump sum insured benefits are straightforward. A policy can be approved provided that the sole benefit secured by the policy is a lump sum on death of the individual before age 70, or a later age if it is customary in the individual's occupation to retire later. The lump sum must be payable to the individual's personal representative.[88]

---

86 See para. 7.46 et seq. on guaranteed pensions.

87 The conditions are set out in s.235A(2).

88 s.235A(1)(b)

Relief on Qualifying Premiums

6.68 Relief on qualifying premiums is granted pursuant to section 236 of the Income Tax Act. Qualifying premiums will be deducted from or set off against an individual's relevant earnings in the year of assessment in which the premium is paid.[89] The amount that can be deducted (in aggregate for all section 235 and 235A policies) is 15 per cent of net relevant earnings rising to 20 per cent for persons aged 55 or over during the year of assessment,[90] of which no more than 5 per cent can relate to section 235A policies.[91]

6.69 Net relevant earnings is defined in section 236(4) as relevant earnings less certain payments and deductions. Husbands and wives are treated separately for this purpose — that is, their incomes are not aggregated.[92] Broadly, net relevant earnings are relevant earnings less such deductions as capital allowances, losses and allowable mortgage-interest relief.[93] Deductions must be set off against non-relevant earnings before they can be set off against relevant earnings.[94]

Trust Schemes

6.70 Most self-employed arrangements are set up under individual contracts with an insurer. The one exception is a scheme for a group of individuals established under trust. Examples of trust schemes are those operated by the Bar Council for barristers, the Institute of Chartered Accountants in Ireland for chartered accountants and the Law Society for solicitors. Trust schemes are exempt from income tax and capital gains tax.[95]

6.71 A trust scheme can be approved by the Revenue under sections 235(4) and 235A(5). The following conditions must be satisfied:

---

89 s.236(1).

90 s.236(1A) as inserted by s.4(1)(a) of the Finance Act, 1978 and substituted by s.13 of the Finance Act, 1996.

91 s.236(1B) as also inserted by s.4(1)(a) of the Finance Act, 1978.

92 s.235(6).

93 A full description is set out in ss.236(4)–(7). See Judge, N. (1995-96): *Irish Income Tax,* Dublin: Butterworths: para. 16.208.

94 s.236(6).

95 s.235(4) and s.235A(5) and Capital Gains Tax Act, 1975 s.21.

1. The scheme must be established under irrevocable trusts by a body of persons comprising or representing individuals engaged in or connected with a particular occupation (or group of occupations).
2. It is established for the benefit of such individuals for the purpose of providing them with retirement annuities, either with or without benefits for their families or dependants.
3. It is established under the law of and administered in the State.

6.72 Trust schemes can provide for retirement annuities under section 235 or insured death benefits under section 235A, but normally they provide both. Two possible advantages over individual arrangements are as follows: first, trust schemes can invest in unit trusts or directly in securities such as equities and government stock, whereas individuals are confined to investing with an insurance company. Secondly, a trust scheme may be in a position to secure better insurance rates for death benefits than an individual. Trust schemes may also invest in approved policies with an insurer, in which case a group policy will be issued in the names of the trustees of the scheme.[96]

OTHER SCHEMES

6.73 This chapter has focused on the two principal Revenue approved régimes: exempt approved schemes and self-employed arrangements. Pension schemes for proprietary directors, known as small self-administered schemes, are a category of exempt approved scheme with special conditions attaching to them. These conditions will be explored in this section. There is no obligation on an employer to establish an approved scheme, and so unapproved arrangements arise occasionally. These will be discussed shortly as will mandatory approved schemes which are not subject to the discretionary approval process. First, it is proposed to examine statutory schemes which enjoy specific tax reliefs under the Finance Act.

---

96 The scheme must ultimately secure a pension by purchasing an annuity with the proceeds of the invested fund.

Statutory Schemes

6.74 A statutory scheme is a retirement benefits scheme[97] established by or under any enactment. For example, the civil service superannuation scheme is established under the Superannuation and Pensions Act, 1963, and the local government scheme under the Local Government (Superannuation) Act, 1980. Statutory schemes are not approved, as such, under the Finance Act, but enjoy certain tax exemptions and are liable to tax in specified instances. A distinction is drawn in the Finance Act between statutory schemes and statutory schemes established under a public statute — that is, between all statutory schemes, on the one hand, and statutory schemes other than schemes established under private statute, on the other.

6.75 Statutory schemes established by public statute are subject to the following conditions in respect of employee contributions:[98]

1. Ordinary annual contributions from any officer or employee are deductible as an expense incurred in the year in which contributions are paid, in assessing tax under Schedule E.
2. A special contribution (that is, a contribution that is not an ordinary annual contribution) can, as the Revenue think proper, either be treated as an ordinary annual contribution or spread forward or backwards into other tax years for the purposes of granting relief.
3. The aggregate amount of contributions allowed to be deducted in any year is limited to 15 per cent of remuneration for that year.

A member of a statutory scheme (whether established by public statute or not) is not liable to tax as a benefit in kind in respect of contributions paid into the scheme by the employer. In this regard, statutory schemes enjoy the reliefs granted under section 19 of the Finance Act.[99] The administrator of a statutory scheme established under public statute has the same liability to account for tax on refunds of employee contributions as does the administrator of an approved

---

97 See para. 6.6.

98 s.17 Finance Act.

99 See para. 6.85.

scheme.[100] A similar liability arises in connection with accounting for tax on certain commutation payments.[101]

6.76 Whilst a statutory scheme is not an approved scheme under section 15 of the Finance Act, it may obtain approval from the Revenue in the same way as any private occupational scheme. If exempt approval is obtained, the scheme can commence to fund in advance for the benefits promised under the scheme and enjoy the same exemptions from income and capital gains tax as are enjoyed by exempt approved schemes. Conversely, a statutory scheme that does not enjoy exempt approved status cannot in practice be a funded scheme, but will operate on a pay-as-you-go basis.[102]

Small Self-Administered Schemes

6.77 In 1979, the Revenue introduced special requirements for certain small schemes which included directors. These small schemes are known as "small self-administered schemes". There are approximately 400 of these schemes in existence.[103] The purpose of the special requirements is to ensure that these schemes are bona fide established for the sole purpose of providing relevant benefits, as required by the Finance Act[104] and, having regard to the identity of interests between the employer, the beneficiaries and the trustees. Revenue practice was substantially revised with effect from 8 January 1996 by circular from the Retirement Benefits District.

6.78 A small self-administered scheme is a scheme with fewer than 12 members which is "self-administered". A self-administered scheme is any scheme which is not fully administered and insured by a life office. A self-administered scheme with 12 or more members is also regarded as small where any one of the following conditions applies:

---

100 s.21 and see para. 7.52.

101 s 22 and see para. 7.21.

102 On pay-as-you-go, see para. 9.19.

103 Slattery, C. (1996): "Small Self-Administered Schemes", paper delivered to the IAPF Southern Branch, 9 May.

104 s.15(2)(a).

1. The scheme is operated primarily for a few 20% Directors but some relatively low-paid employees with entitlement to insignificant benefits are included to bring membership to 12 or more.
2. Most or all of the members are 20% Directors.
3. Sixty-five per cent or more of the assets of the scheme relate to 20% Directors, their spouses or dependants.

It may not be necessary to regard a scheme with fewer than 12 members as small, where all are at arm's length from each other, from the employer and from the trustees. This is a matter for Revenue discretion in each case.

6.79 A 20% Director is one who is or becomes the beneficial owner of shares that carry more than 20 per cent of the voting rights in the company providing the benefits or in a company which controls that company. The voting rights of shares owned by the director's spouse and minor children are aggregated for this purpose, as are the voting rights relating to any shares held by the trustees of any settlement to which the director or spouse has transferred assets. Directors who cease to be such will still be regarded as 20% Directors if, within three years of normal retirement or earlier retirement or leaving service, they were 20% Directors.[105]

6.80 There are principally four restrictions imposed upon small self-administered schemes: the requirement to appoint a pensioneer trustee, the forbidding of certain investments, special reporting requirements to the Retirement Benefits District, and benefit restrictions. A pensioneer trustee is an individual or body widely involved with occupational pension schemes and their approval, who is prepared to give an undertaking to the Revenue not to consent to any termination of a scheme of which the individual or body is trustee, otherwise than in accordance with the terms of the winding-up rule approved by the Revenue. Where a corporate body wishes to act as pensioneer trustee, the directors, or a majority of them, should be acceptable as pension-

---

[105] This definition originally contained in a circular dated January 1977 replaced the definitions of "proprietary director" and "proprietary employee" which applied to "old code" schemes. These old code definitions were repealed by s.64(1) of the Finance Act, 1974.

eer trustees in their own right.[106] The pensioneer trustee must ensure that the contributions paid into the scheme, the nature of the scheme investments and the level of benefits paid out all comply with Revenue requirements. The pensioneer trustee must also ensure that all information required to be submitted to the Revenue, such as actuarial reports and accounts, is so submitted.

6.81 The following investments are not permitted in small self-administered schemes:

1. Loans to members of the scheme or any other individual having a contingent interest under the scheme (for example, a relative)
2. Acquisition of the employer's property or other fixed assets
3. Acquisition of shares or debentures in the employer
4. Loans secured or unsecured to the employer[107]
5. Pride-in-possession articles such as works of art, jewellery, vintage cars and yachts
6. Holiday homes
7. Acquisition of property as an investment unless it can be shown that all of the following conditions apply:
    - The vendor is at arm's length.
    - There is no borrowing.
    - The property will be let and eventually sold on an arms-length basis.
    - Scheme investments match scheme liabilities (in particular, there are sufficient liquid assets to ensure that annuities can be purchased).

---

[106] Some additional requirements on a pensioneer trustee are under consideration by the Revenue: a more comprehensive undertaking, the necessity for an appropriate professional qualification and annual returns of all schemes of which it is pensioneer trustee. Slattery, C. (1996): "Small Self-Administered Schemes", paper delivered to the IAPF Southern Branch, 9 May.

[107] An exception might be made regarding a very short-term loan at commercial rate where its absence might result in company failure.

Reference to the employer company includes any associated company or any subsidiary or associated company of a subsidiary. The last restriction (7. above) came into effect in September 1990 in relation to small self-administered schemes. However, in relation to schemes that are deemed to be small on the basis of the 65 per cent of assets test,[108] the investment restriction at 7. applies only to investments made after 1 January 1996.

6.82 The Revenue require that an actuarial report be submitted to it at intervals of no greater than three years, whether the small self-administered scheme is a defined benefit scheme or a defined contribution scheme. Annual accounts will also be required.

6.83 Certain benefit restrictions are imposed on small self-administered schemes. Pensions must be secured by an annuity. The purchase can be deferred for up to five years from retirement provided that the scheme incorporates a five-year guarantee, at least.[109] This enables the trustees to choose a financially opportune time, having regard to prevailing annuity rates, to purchase the annuity. Benefits payable on death in service must be insured from the outset in so far as they exceed the value from year to year of the member's interest in the fund. Full commutation of pension on grounds of serious ill-health[110] will only be permitted on application to the Revenue with supporting medical reports. Early retirement will only be permitted where the 20% Director severs all connections with the employer, including the disposal of the director's shareholding. Finally, the benefits of 20% Directors (whether under a small self-administered scheme or not) are subject to special restrictions, which are examined in the following chapter.[111]

Unapproved Arrangements

6.84 It is quite open to an employer to establish for one or more employees a pension arrangement that is not approved under the Finance Act. The consequences from a tax point of view of establishing

---

108 See para. 6.78 above.

109 On five-year guarantees, see para. 7.46.

110 On which, see para. 7.21.

111 At para. 7.65 et seq.

an unapproved arrangement are set out in section 18 of the Finance Act. The employee is charged to tax under Schedule E in respect of payments made by the employer to provide relevant benefits to the employee or to the employee's spouse, dependants, children or personal representatives.[112] Similarly, there is a charge to tax under Schedule E where the employer has promised the benefit in advance by securing it with a third party (for example, a life office), but has not fully secured the benefit in advance.[113] The cost of providing the benefit will be worked out either as an annual sum or as a single sum. If treated as a single sum, the charge will arise when the employee acquires the right to the benefit or an increase in the benefit.[114]

6.85 Employees who are not assessable to income tax on the emoluments of their employment or who are assessable on those emoluments, but only on the remittance basis, are not subject to a tax charge under section 18(1). If no payment of benefit is ultimately made and an event has occurred precluding such payment being made, an employee can apply to the Revenue for a repayment of tax paid. If a part but not the whole of the benefit is paid, the employee can apply for such relief as the Revenue deems just and reasonable. All applications must be made within six years of the occurrence of the event.[115]

6.86 Any investment return, whether income or capital gain, is taxable in the hands of the employer. As with approved pension schemes, the pension is subject to income tax when finally received by the employee in retirement.

6.87 Contributions by the employee are not tax deductible, but contributions paid by the employer are, in practice, tax deductible, in that usually they are wholly and exclusively incurred for the benefit of the trade and are not of a capital nature. There are no limits on what benefits the employer can provide under an unapproved arrangement and this is of particular significance in cases where an employer wishes to provide retirement benefits in excess of limits imposed by the Revenue Commissioners under approved schemes. This

---

[112] s.18(1) and s.18(5).

[113] s.18(2).

[114] s.18(3).

[115] s.19(3).

might arise, for example, where the employer in the contract of employment has promised retirement benefits to the employee in excess of what the Revenue will approve.

6.88 The employer is obliged to notify its Inspector of Taxes of the existence of such an arrangement within three months of the date when the scheme first came into operation.[116] The employer may also be required to furnish further information about the employees to which the arrangement relates or information about other schemes of the employer, if the Revenue serves a notice to that effect.[117] The administrator of the arrangement may also be required by the Revenue to furnish such particulars as the Revenue requires.[118]

6.89 Unapproved arrangements may be set up under trust, or by agreement with a particular employee or under a contract of employment. The arrangement can be either funded or unfunded.

Mandatory Approved Schemes

6.90 A mandatory approved scheme is a scheme which complies with certain criteria specified in section 15(2) and (3) of the Finance Act. Once these criteria have been met, the Revenue Commissioners are obliged to grant the scheme approved status — they have no discretion whatsoever.

6.91 The general conditions which must be satisfied before a scheme is granted mandatory approval are as follows:

1. The scheme is bona fide established for the sole purpose of providing relevant benefits in respect of service as an employee, being benefits payable to, or to the spouse, children or dependants or personal representatives of, the employee.
2. The scheme is recognised by the employer and employees to whom it relates, and all employees who are, or have a right to be, members of the scheme have been given written particulars of all essential features of the scheme which concern them.

---

116 First Schedule Part I para. 3(2).

117 *Ibid.*

118 *Ibid.* para. 3(3).

3. There is a person resident in the State who will be responsible for the discharge of all duties imposed on the administrator of the scheme.[119]
4. The employer is a contributor to the scheme.
5. The scheme is established in connection with some trade or undertaking carried on in the State by a person resident in the State.
6. No amount can be paid, whether during the subsistence of the scheme or later, by way of repayment of an employee's contributions under the scheme.

6.92 There are specific conditions regarding benefits as follows:

1. Pension benefit must not exceed 1/60th of final remuneration for each year of service (maximum 40 years) on retirement at normal retirement date.
2. Normal retirement must be not earlier than 60 and not later than 70.[120]
3. The maximum pension payable to a spouse on death prior to retirement is 2/3rds of the pension that could have been payable to the employee had the latter retired at normal retirement date with no change in final remuneration.
4. Any lump sum payable on death before retirement shall not exceed four times the employee's final remuneration.
5. Any benefit for a spouse on death after retirement shall not exceed 2/3rds of the pension payable to the employee.
6. Any pensions for children or dependants of an employee who dies before retirement or who dies after retirement shall not exceed in aggregate one-half of the pension payable in 3. or 5. above, whichever is applicable.
7. No pension can be surrendered, commuted for a cash sum or assigned except in the case of commutation to a lump sum not ex-

---

[119] See para. 6.26 et seq.

[120] Retirement for women could be as early as age 55 prior to 6 April 1992. This different treatment for women was removed by s.6(a) of the Finance Act, 1992.

ceeding 3/80ths of final remuneration for each year of service up to a maximum of 40 years.

8. No other benefits are payable under the scheme.

6.93 Mandatory approved schemes are rarely, if ever, found in practice, except in the case of *Hancock* annuities,[121] as the benefits that can be provided are quite restrictive. For example, under a discretionary exempt approved scheme the employee can receive a pension of 2/3rds of final remuneration after 10 years of service, whereas under the mandatory approved scheme, 2/3rds can only be provided after 40 years. Also, there is no entitlement to a refund of employee contributions under a mandatory scheme.

OTHER TAXATION ISSUES

Value Added Tax

6.94 Value Added Tax ("VAT") is an important taxation issue which arises in connection with some pension schemes. The vast bulk of small pension schemes (typically under 50 members) are administered by life offices through an insured arrangement where the charges for administering the scheme are built into the premiums payable and consequently there are no VAT issues.[122] Many larger schemes are handled on a fee basis, where there will be administration, accountancy, legal and, for defined benefit schemes, actuarial fees. The management of a pension scheme is normally regarded by the Revenue as a taxable activity and VAT is chargeable.

6.95 Where consultancy services are given to the sponsoring employer in, for example, the establishment of the scheme, an employer can obtain a VAT input credit provided that the invoices have been made out to the employer. In addition, fees relating to the maintenance of the pension scheme are also considered to be part of the employer's

---

[121] That is, the outright purchase of an annuity at the time of or after the member's retirement or for a widowed spouse or dependant. The outright purchase of a deferred annuity on leaving service is also possible. It takes its name from the case of *Hancock* v. *General Reversionary and Investment Company Limited* 7 TC 358, in which a lump sum was used to purchase a pension for the company secretary. It is understood that there are about three such arrangements submitted to the Retirement Benefits District each year.

[122] See para. 10.13 et seq.

taxable business where the invoices are made out to the employer and the scheme provides that the costs of administering the scheme are to be met by the employer rather than the scheme. If the scheme's provisions state that the costs are to be borne by the scheme, VAT is not recoverable as the invoices will be made out to the trustees of the scheme who will usually not be registered for VAT.[123] No deduction can be taken for VAT on expenses incurred in connection with the buying and selling of shares, such as investment advice and brokerage fees.

6.96 In some cases, the employer will incur expenditure on behalf of the scheme and be reimbursed by the trustees. In such a case, the employer will be able to claim any VAT credited in connection with the expenditure but must account for VAT on any amounts received by way of reimbursement. The reimbursement could take the form of either a direct payment by the trustees to the employer or an offset against the employer's contributions to the scheme.

Capital Acquisitions Tax

6.97 Another relevant taxation issue concerns capital acquisitions tax. Where the trustees of a pension scheme pay out a death benefit either by way of lump sum or pension to a beneficiary under the scheme on the death of a member, the payment is deemed to be an inheritance from the member.[124] The trustees have a secondary liability to the Revenue for any capital acquisitions tax payable.[125] Unless the payment is to the spouse of the member (in which case the inheritance is exempt from capital acquisitions tax), the safest course for the trustees to take is to reserve the maximum capital acquisitions tax liability until they receive a certificate of discharge from the beneficiary.[126] As for benefits payable directly to the member, the Act specifically excludes such payments from being regarded as a gift or

---

[123] Unless perhaps a professional trustee is involved.

[124] s.56(4) Capital Acquisitions Tax Act, 1976. Pensions are capitalised for the purpose of CAT calculation — s.5(2)(b), see Bohan, B. (1995): *Capital Acquisitions Tax*, Dublin: Butterworths: para. 5.23.

[125] s.35(2).

[126] The certificate of discharge is obtained pursuant to s.48 of the Capital Acquisitions Tax Act, 1976 from the Capital Taxes Branch of the Revenue Commissioners.

inheritance.[127] However, in the case of the payment of a retirement benefit to an employee where the scheme is not approved under the Income Tax Acts, the Revenue may decide that the payment is excessive if the employee is a relative of the employer, or if the employer is a private company and the employee is deemed to have control of that company.[128] The consequence of such a decision is that capital acquisitions tax is chargeable.

Probate Tax

6.98 Lump-sum benefits under approved schemes are often payable on death to the legal personal representative (effectively to the estate of the deceased). Lump-sum benefits under section 235A policies are always payable to the legal personal representative. Probate tax is imposed on the estates of individuals who die on or after 18 June 1993.[129] Certain types of property are exempt from the tax,[130] including property arising from a sponsored superannuation scheme, a trust scheme or part of a trust scheme approved under section 235 or 235A,[131] a section 235 or 235A individual arrangement[132] or a statutory scheme.[133] It can be seen, therefore that benefits from all approved arrangements under the Finance Act and under Chapter III of Part XII of the Income Tax Act are exempted from probate tax. If the death benefit is not payable to the deceased's estate, no probate tax is payable. Typically in approved schemes, the trustees are given a discretion to pay the death benefit directly to any one or more of a class of beneficiaries, and there is no obligation to pay the benefit to the estate.

Deposit Interest Retention Tax

6.99 Exempt approved schemes and self-employed arrangements are exempt from deposit interest retention tax in respect of deposits

---

127 s.56(1).

128 "Private company" and "control" have special meanings contained in s.16(2).

129 Part VI Finance Act, 1993.

130 *Ibid.* s.112.

131 See para. 6.59 et seq.

132 *Ibid.*

133 See para. 6.74 et seq.

made on or after 1 January 1993. The exemption is granted to any "pension scheme" which is defined to be either of the following:

1. An exempt approved scheme within the meaning of s.16 of the Finance Act
2. A retirement annuity or a trust scheme to which s.235 or 235A of the Income Tax Act applies.[134]

Deposit interest retention tax is applicable to any "relevant deposit". A pension scheme, as so defined, is excluded from the definition of "relevant deposit" provided that the scheme beneficially owns the interest.[135]

6.100 In order to obtain exemption, a declaration must be made in the prescribed form. It must state that the interest on deposit in respect of which the declaration is made is beneficially owned by the pension scheme and the declaration must be made and signed by the person to whom the interest is payable. The declaration must also contain a certificate that the declaration and information contained in it are true and correct. The certificate must be signed by the administrator, in the case of an exempt approved scheme, the life office in the case of a self-employed arrangement or the trustees where the self-employed arrangement is established under trust. The declaration must contain the name and address of the pension scheme, the tax reference number of the scheme and such other information as the Revenue may reasonably require.[136]

---

[134] s.31 Finance Act, 1986, definition inserted by s.22(1)(a)(ii) of the Finance Act, 1992.

[135] s.31, definition as substituted by Finance (No 2) Act, 1992 s.3(a)(ii)(II).

[136] s.37B as inserted by s.22(1)(c) of the Finance Act, 1992 and amended by s.3(c) of the Finance (No 2) Act, 1992.

FIGURE 6.1: COMPARISON OF BENEFIT LIMITS

Benefit	Exempt Approved Scheme (Discretionary Basis)	Exempt Approved Scheme (Mandatory Basis)	Self-Employed Arrangement
Retirement Pension	2/3rds of Final Remuneration (where at least 10 years of service)	1/60th of Final Remuneration for each year of service (maximum 40 years)	No limit. Benefits are limited by reference to maximum contributions
Tax-Free Cash on Retirement	1.5 times Final Remuneration (where at least 20 years of service)	3/80ths of Final Remuneration for each year of service (maximum — 40 years)	25 per cent of value of Fund
Death-in-Service Lump-Sum Benefits	4 times Final Remuneration plus a refund of employee contributions with interest	4 times Final Remuneration	Cover obtained by premiums paid. Maximum premiums are 5 per cent of Net Relevant Earnings
Death-in-Service Dependant's Pension (Maximum of any one pension)	2/3rds of Member's pension expectation assuming no change in Final Remuneration	Same. Payment is confined to the Spouse	Cover obtained by premiums paid. Maximum premiums are 5 per cent of Net Relevant Earnings
Death-in-Retirement Dependant's Pension (Maximum of any one pension)	2/3rds of Member's pension (ignoring commutation)	Same. Payment is confined to the Spouse	Annuity can be paid to spouse or other dependant. Limited by reference to overall contributions permitted
Refunds of Member Contribution	Yes. Taxed at 25 per cent.	No.	No.
Maximum Member Contribution Subject to Tax Relief	15 per cent of Remuneration	15 per cent of Remuneration	15 per cent of Net Relevant Earnings rising to 20 per cent from age 55
Final Remuneration	Last year's earnings or average of any consecutive three ending not earlier than 10 years before retirement, if greater	Average of the last three years, only	Not applicable
Normal Retirement	Between ages 60 and 70	Between ages 60 and 70	Between ages 60 and 70
Early Retirement	From age 50 or earlier, if ill-health	Only on ill-health grounds (from any age)	On ill-health grounds only (from any age)
Pension Increases	Up to 3 per cent, or the Consumer Price Index, of maximum approvable pension	None	Yes. Limited only by reference to overall maximum contributions permissible

7

Benefit Limits for Exempt Approved Schemes

INTRODUCTION

7.1 The tax treatment of pension schemes was considered in the previous chapter.[1] The vast majority of private occupational pension schemes and many public sector schemes are either exempt approved by the Revenue Commissioners ("the Revenue") under section 16 of the Finance Act, 1972 or are awaiting formal approval.[2] Whether or not the Revenue grant exempt approval is a matter for their discretion.[3] However, the Revenue, in their Practice Notes (now called the Revenue Pensions Manual), have laid down detailed criteria as to how their discretion will be exercised. In particular, the maximum benefits that can be provided under an exempt approved scheme are set out in detail.

7.2 The purpose of this chapter is to summarise the principal benefit limits imposed by the Revenue in the Practice Notes with regard to the exempt approval of occupational pension schemes. Approved schemes are not obliged to provide benefits at the level of these limits. They can, and usually do, promise lower or more restricted benefits in practice. The purpose of the Revenue limits is to prevent a scheme from offering benefits in excess of those limits.

7.3 Defined benefit schemes normally promise benefits based on a fraction of salary for each year of service, and therefore there is similarity between that method of calculation and the way in which

---

1 Chapter 6.

2 On the interim status of schemes awaiting formal exempt approval, see para. 6.15.

3 It is possible to obtain approval on a mandatory basis (that is, where the Revenue has no discretion) — see para. 6.90 et seq.

Revenue limits operate — Revenue limits are calculated by reference to a fraction of salary at or near retirement and years of service. On the other hand, defined contribution schemes do not promise benefits calculated by reference to a fraction of salary. A defined contribution scheme involves the investment of specified employer and employee contributions. The contributions, with investment return, over the period of membership to retirement are then applied to provide whatever benefits can be bought with that fund at retirement. There is no promise of (say) a pension of 2/3rds of salary. Nevertheless defined contribution schemes are obliged to stay within the Revenue limits, and in such schemes, where a significantly high level of contribution is maintained, periodic actuarial reviews must be undertaken to ensure that the benefits estimated to be obtainable at retirement will not exceed Revenue limits.

7.4 A broad outline of the key limits is set out in Figure 7.1 Many are expressed in terms of fractions. For example the pension payable to an employee on retirement cannot exceed 2/3rds of the employee's "Final Remuneration". Final remuneration is therefore the starting point in an examination of these limits.[4]

FINAL REMUNERATION

7.5 "Final Remuneration" comprises total pay of an employee in respect of employment except where pay includes fluctuating elements such as bonus or commission. To bring some stability into the definition, the fluctuating elements of pay must be averaged over the preceding three years. For most employees, either the last year of pay or the rate of basic pay at retirement can be selected, plus averaged fluctuating elements of pay. But, if salary was higher in former years, either of the following calculations can be selected instead:

1. The average of the total emoluments for any three or more consecutive years, ending not earlier than 10 years before retirement (in this regard, previous years' pay can be indexed upwards, known as "dynamisation", to reflect cost of living increases)
2. Pay in any one of the five years prior to retirement (similarly indexed or dynamised).

---

[4] Final Remuneration is defined in the practice notes.

No averaging of fluctuating elements of pay is required where 1. is selected.

FIGURE 7.1: KEY REVENUE LIMITS

Pension: Up to 2/3rds of final remuneration at normal retirement or a lower proportion if the member has completed less than 10 years' company service at that date.

Lump-Sum Commutation: The amount which can be taken tax-free in cash form in lieu of pension at Normal Pension Date (commutation) is a maximum of 1.5 times final remuneration, or a lower proportion, if the member has completed less than 20 years' company service.

Total Payable in Lump-Sum Form on Death Before Retirement: The total payable on death before retirement in lump sum form is limited to four times annual remuneration, plus a repayment of the value of member's contributions to the scheme with reasonable interest.

Dependants' Pensions on Member's Death: Dependants' pensions are limited in aggregate to the maximum pension that the member is permitted by the Revenue to receive (that is, 2/3rds of final remuneration) — any one dependant's pension is limited to 4/9ths of final remuneration (that is, 2/3rds of 2/3rds).

Pension Increases in Retirement: Increases in any year in the maximum approvable pension can be guaranteed up to the rate of increase in the Consumer Price Index from the date of retirement. Alternatively, a flat rate of up to 3 per cent per annum can be guaranteed.

7.6 In addition, benefits in kind can be taken into account, such as a company car. This is not regarded as a fluctuating element of pay, and therefore the taxable benefit in kind in any one year can be taken into account as part of pay in that year.

Example 7.1

Julius Caesar retires on 31 December 2004 and has the following remuneration in the five years prior to retirement:

Year 2004	*£21,000*
(This is also his rate of pay at retirement)	
Year 2003	*£20,000*
Year 2002	*£19,500*
Year 2001	*£19,000*
Year 2000	*£18,500*

Julius has no fluctuating elements of pay. His salary in the years before year 2000 is lower than in the subsequent years to retirement. The most favourable calculation of final remuneration is to take the rate of salary at retirement which is his salary in the year 2004 — that is, £21,000. Three year averaging will at most produce a figure of £20,167.

However, for the purposes of calculating final remuneration, remuneration for earlier years can be adjusted by cost-of-living increases measured by the consumer price index (CPI). For simplicity, let us assume that CPI over the previous five years has been a constant 4 per cent per annum. The adjusted remuneration for the five year period would be as follows:

Year 2004	*£21,000*
Year 2003	*£20,800*
Year 2002	*£21,091*
Year 2001	*£21,372*
Year 2000	*£21,642*

The average of years 2000, 2001 and 2002 produces a final remuneration of £21,368, which is greater than his rate of salary at retirement (i.e. £21,000), but the adjusted year 2000 figure of £21,642 is higher still. The higher figure will therefore be chosen. In all subsequent examples, for the sake of simplicity, inflation adjustments are not made in calculating final remuneration.

7.7 20% Directors[5] cannot choose pay in any single year in the last five years before retirement. They are restricted to the average of any three consecutive years ending not earlier than ten years before retirement. The logic behind this is that 20% Directors have a fair degree of control in the company and may be able to manipulate salaries close to retirement to engineer a pension beyond what would normally be expected. Averaging is intended to restrict the effect of salary manipulation.

7.8 In exceptional cases of promotion or where special increases in pay have been awarded, the Revenue may require three year averaging of salary even where the employee is not a 20% Director.

RETIREMENT DATES

7.9 It can be seen from the previous section that final remuneration is calculated by reference to remuneration at or near to retirement. Revenue practice refines the meaning of retirement by introducing the concept of "normal retirement". Schemes are required to include a normal retirement date so that benefits can be calculated by reference to retirement at that date. Most schemes provide a normal retirement age of 65 for both men and women but in some schemes,[6] normal retirement may be as early as age 60.[7]

7.10 The Revenue Commissioners accept a normal retirement age of between 60 and 70, but in exceptional cases will accept a retirement age earlier than age 60 if the particular occupation is one in which employees traditionally retire at an earlier date. Pilots may have a normal retirement age of age 55, and it can be expected, for example, that a jockey could persuade the Revenue Commissioners to a normal retirement date of age 50.

---

5 On which, see para. 6.79 and para. 7.65 below.

6 For example, executive or senior management schemes or many public sector schemes.

7 Before being equalised at age 60, the revenue permitted women to have a normal retirement age of 55 — that is, earlier than men. Women who had age 55 as normal retirement age could retain it notwithstanding the subsequent equalisation to age 60. However, benefits must now be equalised pursuant to Part VII of the Pensions Act — see Chapter 16.

7.11 Once normal retirement date has been established, an employee who retires before or after that date will be regarded as having taken early or late retirement as the case may be. The significance of this is that Revenue limits differ for early and late retirement. The following sections explore these limits in the context of normal retirement, late retirement and early retirement.

BENEFITS AT NORMAL RETIREMENT DATE

Pension

7.12 Without exception, a pension scheme can promise a pension at normal retirement date of 1/60th of final remuneration for each year of service up to a maximum of 40 years. After 40 years, the pension will be 40/60ths of final remuneration — that is, 2/3rds of final remuneration, which is the overall maximum permissible.

7.13 A scheme can promise a pension benefit greater than 1/60th of final remuneration for each year of service — as much as 2/3rds of final remuneration once the employee has completed 10 years of service to normal retirement date. If less than 10 years are completed, the maximum benefits are calculated in accordance with the following scale which is colloquially referred to as the "uplifted N/60ths scale".

TABLE 7.1: UPLIFTED N/60THS SCALE

Years of Service to Normal Retirement Age	Maximum Pension as a Fraction of Final remuneration
1–5	1/60th for each year
6	8/60ths
7	16/60ths
8	24/60ths
9	32/60ths
10 or more	40/60ths

Fractions of a year can be interpolated into the scale from year 6 onwards.

Example 7.2

Octavian is a member of the Centurion Pension Scheme. His normal retirement date is age 65 and he retires at 65 having completed 20 years of service. His final remuneration is £21,000. His pension scheme provides him with a pension of 2/3rds of final remuneration — that is, £14,000 per annum. Since he has completed at least 10 years of service, the pen-

sion promise is within Revenue limits. His colleague Marcus is also retiring at age 65. His final remuneration is £25,000 and his pension entitlement under the scheme is 2/3rds of final remuneration. However, he has only completed eight years of service and so, on the uplifted scale, he is only entitled to 24/60ths of £25,000 = £10,000 per annum.

Exchanging Pension for Cash (Commutation)

7.14 The vast majority of private sector pension schemes give employees the option of exchanging part of their pension for a cash lump sum. The rate of exchange will either be specified in the rules of the scheme or in explanatory literature or will be determined from time to time by the trustees on actuarial advice. Public sector schemes do not have a commutation facility but instead provide a gratuity on retirement, which is separate from the pension.[8]

7.15 A uniform basis of exchanging pension for cash should apply to all scheme members, subject to different ages and sex and to all schemes with a substantially common membership. There are three rates of exchange from pension to cash that are permitted:

1. Each £9 of cash reduces the residual pension by £1 per annum.
2. The exchange rate will be calculated in accordance with specially designed tables which must change if any of the assumptions upon which they are based is varied.
3. The exchange rate will be individually calculated by a qualified actuary.

The range of commutation factors permitted by the Revenue at age 65 is between 9.0 and 9.8. For commutation at lower ages, the maximum range can be increased by a factor of 0.02 per month. For later ages the range must be decreased by the same factor per month. If pensions are subject to increases in payment, the commutation factors can be enhanced but this requires certification by the actuary.

7.16 The cash lump sum obtained from commutation is tax-free in the employee's hands and so it is a valuable benefit. It is one of the few examples in the field of pensions where the tax treatment of pensions is not tax-neutral.

---

8 On which, see paras. 8.13 and 8.30.

7.17 It is not surprising therefore that the Revenue imposes certain limits on the right to exchange pension for cash. As with the limits for pension, there is a basic scale entitlement which will be granted as of right by the Revenue Commissioners. This scale entitlement is 3/80ths of final remuneration for each year of service subject to a maximum of 40 years. After 40 years the entitlement will be 120/80ths of final remuneration, which simplifies out at 1.5 times final remuneration.

7.18 Schemes can provide a cash benefit of greater than this scale benefit in a similar way to the calculation of pension limits. When the employee has completed at least 20 years of service the maximum of 1.5 times final remuneration can be given as cash. Where less than 20 years' service has been completed, the maximum cash entitlement is set out in Table 7.2.

TABLE 7.2: THE UPLIFTED 3N/80THS SCALE

Years of Service	80ths of Final Remuneration
1–8	3 (for each year of service)
9	30
10	36
11	42
12	48
13	54
14	63
15	72
16	81
17	90
18	99
19	108
20 or more	120

Fractions of a year can be interpolated into the scale

Example 7.3

Octavian in his Centurion Scheme (see Example 7.2) is entitled to exchange part of his pension for an immediate cash sum on retirement. The maximum cash sum allowed by the scheme permitted to be given 1.5 times final remuneration. In Octavian's case, his cash entitlement is 1.5 x £21,000 = £31,500. This is in accordance with Revenue limits, as Octavian has completed 20 years' service and is permitted to be given 1.5 times final remuneration on the uplifted 3N/80ths scale. However, his colleague Marcus has only completed eight years' service and so his maximum cash entitlement is 24/80ths of 25,000 (3/80 x 8 x £25,000) = £7,500.

7.19 As with the calculation of pension benefits, a lump sum benefit on the uplifted 3N/80ths scale cannot, when aggregated at retirement with any other lump sum retirement benefit received or receivable, exceed 120/80ths of final remuneration.

7.20 There are two grounds upon which the Revenue Commissioners will permit the entire pension to be exchanged for cash. The first is where the value of the pension in aggregation with the pension under any other scheme of the same employer does not exceed £260 per annum. This is a practical exception to the general rule designed to avoid having to pay out pensions of a trivial nature. The second is where a person is in circumstances of serious ill-health. In cases where expectation of life is unquestionably very short by contrast with life expectation of a normal healthy person at that age (i.e. terminal illness), a scheme may provide for full commutation of pension. Adequate medical evidence should be obtained in all cases.

7.21 Where full commutation is made on the grounds of triviality or serious ill-health, part of the lump sum may be chargeable to tax on the administrator of the pension scheme under section 22 of the Finance Act, 1972.[9] Tax is charged at the rate of 10 per cent on the amount (if any) by which the lump sum exceeds the maximum lump sum that could be obtained from the scheme other than in circumstances of ill-health. If the maximum is subject to trustee consent, it is assumed for the purposes of section 22 that the trustees have exercised their consent.

7.22 For schemes that provide a gratuity of 3N/80ths of final remuneration separately from the pension — public sector schemes, for example — and the pension itself is commuted for a lump sum, the whole of the commuted pension will be chargeable to tax under section 22.

---

9 The administrator is the person or persons having the management of the scheme — see para. 6.26.

RETIREMENT AFTER NORMAL RETIREMENT DATE

7.23 The practice notes permit three different options for an employee who remains in service after normal retirement date:

1. The employee draws pension immediately at normal retirement date and, if desired, exchanges part (or possibly the whole) of the pension for a lump sum.
2. The employee defers drawing pension but immediately exercises the option to commute (i.e. exchanges for cash) part of the pension for a lump sum.
3. The employee defers all benefits until the later date of retirement.

Where an employee selects option 1. and takes all benefits immediately on retirement, the Revenue limits at normal retirement apply.

7.24 Where the commutation option is exercised immediately on normal retirement, either the whole or a part of the pension will be exchanged for cash. If the whole pension is commuted, Revenue limits on normal retirement apply. However, if only part of the pension is commuted and the remaining pension is deferred in accordance with option 2., Revenue limits on normal retirement also apply even though the pension is deferred to a later date. However, the deferred pension can be increased actuarially to reflect later commencement.

Example 7.4

Grace O'Malley is aged 65 and has reached the normal retirement age in the Pirates Superannuation Scheme. She has been in service for 25 years and is entitled under the rules of the Pirates Superannuation Scheme to a pension of 2/3rds of her final remuneration. Her final remuneration is £21,000 and so her pension is £14,000 per annum. The scheme allows her to commute pension up to 1.5 times her final remuneration — that is, £31,500. She decides to take her tax-free cash immediately and defer retirement until she is aged 70. This will leave her with a residual pension of roughly £10,500 per annum on a typical exchange rate from pension to cash (£9 of cash reduces pension by £1).[10] This is calculated as follows: £31,500 (cash) ÷ 9 (factor) = £3,500; £14,000 (pension) – £3,500 = £10,500. The residual pension of

---

10 Pension income can be converted to an immediate cash sum and vice versa by applying appropriate actuarial factors. One commonly accepted conversion factor is the 9:1 ratio referred to in the text — see para. 7.15.

£10,500 can be increased until she retires at age 70 by reference to increases in the consumer price index (CPI). If we assume that CPI runs at an annual rate of 4 per cent from 65 to 70, the residual pension will be increased to £12,775 at age 70.

7.25 The third situation is a little more complex. Where all benefits are deferred until later date of retirement, the greater of the following alternatives can be selected:

1. The employee's maximum benefits are calculated as if the later date of retirement is normal retirement date. If the employee has completed at least 10 years of service at that point, the maximum limit is 2/3rds of final remuneration. The uplifted N/60ths scale applies where completed service is less than 10 years. An employee who has already completed 40 years by normal retirement will already be entitled to a maximum limit of 2/3rds of Final Remuneration. In this case, for every year of service after normal retirement date an additional 1/60th of final remuneration can be added, up to a maximum of 5/60ths.
2. As an alternative, the maximum benefit calculated at normal retirement date can be increased actuarially to reflect the fact that the employee retires at a later date and may take account of the yield on the scheme's investments over that later period.

7.26 Similarly, if the employee commutes part or all of the pension for a lump sum on late retirement, the alternatives are as follows:

1. The employee's maximum benefits are calculated as if the later date of retirement is normal retirement date. If the employee has completed at least 20 years of service at that point, the maximum limit is 120/80ths of Final Remuneration. The uplifted 3N/80ths scale applies where completed service is less than 20 years. An employee who has already completed 40 years by normal retirement date will already be entitled to a maximum limit of 120/80ths of Final Remuneration. In this case, the maximum lump sum is calculated at normal retirement date and then for each year after normal retirement a fraction of 3/80ths of final remuneration can be added, up to a maximum of 5 years.
2. As an alternative, the maximum lump sum can be calculated at normal retirement date and then increased until later date of retirement in accordance with an interest rate commensurate with the

yield on the scheme's investments or, where the scheme is operated under an insurance contract, at a reasonable rate of increase.

RETIREMENT BEFORE NORMAL RETIREMENT DATE

7.27 Employees who retire before reaching Normal Retirement Date may take an early pension or lump sum provided that either

1. They have reached age 50, or
2. Irrespective of age, they are retiring because of incapacity.

If retiring because of incapacity an employee's maximum pension can be greater than if retiring on age grounds. Incapacitated employees can be given a pension calculated as if they had remained in service until their normal retirement. However, Final Remuneration must be calculated by reference to their actual date of retirement.

7.28 Incapacity in this context must be relatively serious. It amounts to physical or mental deterioration which is bad enough to prevent the individual from following their normal occupation or which very seriously impairs their earning capacity.

7.29 The position is a little more complex where the employee retires merely on age grounds. In such a case it is still necessary to work out what the maximum pension would have been had the employee remained in service until normal retirement date. Once that figure has been obtained, the maximum pension is then reduced in the proportion that the number of years of actual service bears to the number of years of potential service to normal retirement date. The following formula is used in the practice notes to describe this:

$$\frac{N}{NS} x\, P$$

Where:

N	=	Number of years of actual service
NS	=	Number of years of actual service completed, together with potential service to normal retirement date
P	=	Maximum pension approvable had the employee served until normal retirement date.

As an alternative, maximum benefits can be calculated on the basis of 1/60th of Final Remuneration for each year of actual service, if this produces a greater maximum than the above formula.

Example 7.5

Tom Thumb is a member of the Digit Benefit Scheme. His scheme promises him a pension of 2/3rds of his final remuneration at his normal retirement date of age 65. Having obtained his employer's consent, he is taking early retirement at age 55. He has been employed by Digit for the past 10 years — since he was 45. He has final remuneration of £30,000 at age 55. His maximum early retirement pension on the N/NS x P formula is as follows:

N = 10 (years 45 to 55)
NS = 20 (years 45 to 65)
P = 2/3 x final remuneration = 2/3 x £30,000 = £20,000

$$\frac{10}{20} \times £20{,}000 = £10{,}000 \text{ per annum}$$

As an alternative, the maximum could be calculated as 1/60th of final remuneration for each year of actual service — that is, 10/60 x £30,000 = £5,000. But, as the result of the first method is greater, the Revenue maximum will be £10,000.

7.30 Retained benefits[11] must be taken into account where the aggregate of the employee's past and potential service (NS in the above) is less than 40.

7.31 There is one further proviso. If an employee's actual service at early retirement is less than 10 years, the pension must be calculated by reference to the maximum pension approvable at normal retirement date for that number of years service applying the uplifted N/60ths scale, or if lower, 2/3rds of final remuneration less retained benefits.[12] For example if the actual number of years of service to early retirement is six years, the pension cannot exceed 8/60ths of final remuneration on the uplifted scale.

7.32 Where part or all of the pension is exchanged for a cash sum, the maximum lump sum is calculated in a similar way. In cases of incapacity, an employee can receive a lump sum benefit of the same amount as could have been received had the employee remained in service until normal retirement date. Obviously, final remuneration is again calculated by reference to the date of early retirement.

---

[11] See para. 7.61 et seq.

[12] On retained benefits, see para. 7.61 et seq.

7.33 On early retirement by reason of age, either of the following formulas can be used, whichever is the greater:

$$\frac{3}{80} \times \text{Final Remuneration} \times \text{Service Completed}$$

or

$$\frac{N}{NS} \times LS$$

Where:

N = Number of years of actual service
NS = Number of years of actual and potential service to normal retirement date
LS = Maximum lump sum receivable had the employee retired at normal retirement date.

In calculating LS the uplifted 3N/80ths scale may be used.[13]

7.34 If the employee's actual service is less than 20 years, the lump sum cannot exceed the maximum approvable at normal retirement date for the same service in accordance with the 3N/80ths uplifted scale.[14]

BENEFITS ON DEATH IN SERVICE

7.35 The limits set out in the previous sections assume that the employee does not die before retirement. There are different limits which apply on death in service. Most pension schemes provide some form of benefit on the death of an employee in service, as distinct from the death of a pensioner or former employee. The death in service benefits that can be provided under an exempt approved scheme are:

1. A cash lump sum benefit
2. A pension or pensions payable to a spouse and/or other dependants (such as children).

---

13 See para. 7.18.

14 See para. 7.18.

7.36 The maximum lump sum payable on death in service is four times the deceased employee's final remuneration,[15] which can be calculated as the annual rate of remuneration payable at date of death. Some schemes provide that the lump sum is payable directly to the legal personal representative of the deceased employee, but other schemes establish a discretionary trust, whereby the trustees are given discretion to pay the lump sum benefit in such proportions as they determine to one or more of a specified class of beneficiaries.[16] The Revenue place no restrictions on who can receive the benefit. The trustees can (if the rules of the scheme permit) also convert the lump sum into a pension by buying an annuity with the cash. The lump sum must be paid out within two years of date of death, or, if it has not been paid out at that point, it should be transferred to a separate account outside the scheme.

7.37 In addition to the four times salary maximum, a refund of employee's own contributions (if any) can be paid in lump sum form, either with or without interest.

7.38 As well as providing lump sum benefits, some schemes provide spouses' and/or other dependants' pensions on the death of an employee in service. An important distinction to bear in mind at this point is that the death in service lump sum benefit can be paid to anyone in accordance with the rules of the scheme. Pensions, on the other hand, must be paid to "dependants", which is defined in the practice notes as:

1. The lawful spouse
2. A child under 18, or over 18 but in receipt of full-time educational or vocational training
3. Any person who is wholly or substantially dependent financially on the employee or was so dependent at the time of the employee's death.

Thus, in the case of the death in service lump sum benefit, if the trustees choose to pay the lump sum in pension form rather than as a

---

[15] Or £5,000 if greater than four times final remuneration, which is unlikely, in practice.

[16] See also para. 2.30.

lump sum, they are then constrained to pay the resultant pension to a dependant.

7.39 A separate spouse's pension, or indeed a dependant's pension, can be paid up to a maximum of 2/3rds of the maximum pension that the employee could have received at normal retirement date — that is, taking into account potential future service to retirement as well as past service of the employee. In making this calculation, no potential change in final remuneration can be taken into account. The maximum pension in this case will also include any lump sum payable at retirement. The lump sum will be converted into a pension equivalent in order to work out the maximum pension.

7.40 In addition, if pensions are to be payable to more than one dependant, the aggregate of all pensions payable cannot exceed the maximum pension that the employee could have received at normal retirement date (again assuming no change in final remuneration). No one pension can exceed the 2/3rds maximum mentioned in the preceding paragraph. This allows for a mix of spouse's and children's pensions if required, and indeed can include dependants other than children. For example, the spouse's pension could be 50 per cent of the member's prospective pension, and a further 50 per cent could be used to provide children's pensions. If the spouse's pension is 2/3rds (the maximum permitted), the children's pensions would be limited to one-third.

7.41 In the context of the provision of a spouse's pension, a practical problem that may arise is where a foreign divorce has been obtained or there has been a nullity decree.[17] In cases of nullity, the former spouse, was never a spouse and, unless the spouse is financially dependent, no pension can be paid to that former spouse. Similarly in the case of a foreign divorce, if the foreign divorce is recognised in Ireland, the former spouse is no longer a spouse, and again financial dependency must be established. Dependency may, for example, take the form of continuing maintenance payments. If the foreign divorce is not recognised in this jurisdiction, the spouse is still a spouse and the pension can be paid.[18]

---

[17] This is considered in Chapter 15.

[18] But a pension adjustment order may alter the position — see Chapter 15.

7.42 Spouses' pensions may continue for life or may cease on remarriage. A spouse's pension may also continue to be paid, on the spouse's death, to any surviving children. This is known as an "orphan's pension". Children's pensions must cease when the child attains age 18 or ceases to be in full-time educational or vocational training, if later. Pensions payable to other dependants are required to continue for life.

BENEFITS ON DEATH IN RETIREMENT

7.43 Many pension schemes provide a pension to a pensioner's spouse on the pensioner's death. Sometimes the pension is referred to as a dependant's pension rather than a spouse's pension. As with death in service spouses' or dependants' pensions, there is a limit on similar pensions payable on death in retirement.

7.44 The maximum pension that can be paid to the spouse, or other dependant, in an exempt approved scheme is 2/3rds of the maximum pension that could have been approved for the employee. This is so even where the employee's own pension is less than the maximum. If there is more than one dependant's pension, the maximum that can be paid to any one dependant is 2/3rds of the employee's maximum pension. The total of all dependants' pensions cannot exceed the maximum pension approvable for the employee. For example, a scheme may provide a 2/3rds pension for the employee's spouse, but if there are to be separate children's pensions, the maximum that can be shared between the children is a further one-third.

Example 7.6

Diarmuid who is a member of the Fianna Pension and Death Benefit Scheme has just died at the age of 72. He was receiving a pension of £24,000 per annum before he died. This was the maximum pension allowable under Revenue limits. On his death, the scheme provides a pension to his widow, Gráinne, and a pension to his only child Diarmuid junior who is aged 19 and is in university. The maximum permissible widow's pension is 2/3rds of the maximum approvable pension for Diarmuid senior — that is, 2/3rds of £24,000 = £16,000 per annum. The maximum pension for Diarmuid junior is one-third of £24,000 = £8,000 per annum. The widow's pension is payable for life, but the child's pension can only be paid until Diarmuid junior ceases to be in full-time education or vocational training.

7.45 In calculating the employee's maximum pension, regard can be had to any deferred pension granted by a former employer, provided that the former employer's scheme did not itself grant a spouse's pension. This only applies where a spouse's pension is being provided under the second scheme.

7.46 A further benefit typically provided under pension schemes is a guarantee attaching to the member's pension.[19] The normal guarantee period is five years, but the Revenue will permit a guarantee for up to 10 years. Take the example of a five-year guarantee. Were a pensioner to die after year 2, the balance of three years could either be paid as a lump sum or continue to be paid as pension for the remaining three years. Payment can be made to the spouse, other dependants, the legal personal representative or a nominated beneficiary. Payment will be determined in accordance with the rules of the scheme. The lump sum option is only available in schemes which provide a guarantee of no more than five years and which have a normal retirement date earlier than age 70. If the guarantee is for a longer period, or retirement is later than age 70, the balance of the guaranteed pension can only be paid in pension form.

7.47 A scheme may provide a guaranteed pension and a spouse's or dependant's pension. The spouse's or dependant's pension can be either overlapping or non-overlapping. The term "overlapping" means that the spouse's or dependant's pension comes into payment immediately on death of the pensioner even though the pensioner's pension is payable to the end of the guarantee period. The spouse receives two pensions until the guarantee expires. A "non-overlapping pension" is the reverse. The spouse's or dependant's pension does not commence to be paid until the end of the guarantee period. Only a non-overlapping pension can be provided where the guaranteed period is greater than five years.

7.48 As with death in service pensions, an orphan's pension can be paid on the death of the spouse or other dependant. Spouses', de-

---

[19] Note that the member's pension can be guaranteed but not any spouse's pension.

pendants' and children's pensions are payable for the same periods as death in service pensions.[20]

7.49 Employees can opt to exchange part of their pension for a separate dependant's pension or to increase a dependant's pension already payable under the scheme rules on their death. This is normally referred to as an optional dependant's pension and is an option that the vast majority of pension schemes permit. The dependant's pension is payable on death of the employee. The only limit that the Revenue impose is that the optional dependant's pension cannot exceed in amount the reduced pension that the employee retains. For the purpose of this calculation, employees can take into account any lump sum payable to them by way of commutation or any separate lump sum gratuity.

WITHDRAWAL FROM SERVICE

7.50 The death of an employee cuts short their service with their employer and their membership of the employer's pension scheme. The other events that terminate service are voluntary withdrawal, redundancy or dismissal. Withdrawal from service is probably one of the more complex issues faced by the administrator of a pension scheme as, not only do provisions of the Pensions Act apply,[21] but limits are also imposed by the Revenue Commissioners on benefits.

7.51 As a preliminary point, it should be determined whether the employee is taking early retirement or merely leaving service. The circumstances under which an employee can take an immediate early retirement benefit have been considered earlier,[22] but in all other cases of leaving service before normal retirement date, immediate benefits cannot (in broad terms) be given. Instead, benefits are deferred until normal retirement date or such earlier date as is permissible under the early-retirement rules. Hence these benefits are referred to as "deferred pensions".

7.52 There is one exception to the rule that an employee who leaves service cannot receive an immediate benefit. This is the right under

---

20 See para. 7.42.

21 See Chapter 12.

22 At para. 7.27 et seq.

certain circumstances to take a refund of employee contributions, which, under section 21 of the Finance Act, 1972[23] are taxed at 25 per cent. Tax is payable by the administrator of the scheme under Schedule D Case IV. The refund can be either without interest or with interest at a reasonable rate. With certain insurance policies, the payment will be the surrender value of the policy which may include investment return.

7.53 Where employees opt to take a refund of all their contributions, no other benefits can be granted under the pension scheme. In cases where an employee is entitled to a preserved benefit under the Pensions Act,[24] the right to receive a refund of contributions is restricted. Only contributions paid prior to 1 January 1991 can be refunded. The Revenue will permit a refund of pre-1991 contributions to be paid notwithstanding that the employee has a deferred pension in respect of service after the 1 January 1991. The Revenue refer to the provision of a partial refund of contributions and a deferred pension as "mixed benefits".

7.54 The Revenue will permit mixed benefits in other instances. If part of an employee's benefits relates to a transfer of benefits from the scheme of a former employer and the former scheme was non-contributory or the conditions of transfer prohibited the employee from receiving a refund of contributions from the transfer payment relating to the former scheme, the Revenue will permit a deferred pension to be granted in respect of that transfer and allow a refund of contributions in the second scheme. Also, where a transfer has been received from a former employer's scheme, the new scheme could obtain a substantial windfall by reason of a total refund of employee contributions. To protect the member's transfer payment from the former scheme, the Revenue will permit a refund of the contributions in the second scheme only.

7.55 If a contributory scheme subsequently becomes a non-contributory scheme, the Revenue will allow a refund of contributions up to the date that the scheme changed to being non-contributory. A deferred pension can then be granted based on the non-contributory element of the benefit.

---

23 As amended by s.6(b) of the Finance Act, 1992.

24 See Chapter 12.

7.56 An employee who has taken a refund of contributions on leaving service may subsequently re-join service. In this event, an employee who re-joins the scheme in the same year of assessment, can pay back all contributions and no tax will be payable. If the employee re-joins and pays back contributions in a subsequent tax year, the gross amount repayable can be set off against the administrator's tax liability.

7.57 Leaving service must be distinguished from leaving active membership of the scheme but remaining in service. For example, employees may, with their employer's agreement, opt out of continued membership of the scheme but remain in the employer's service. In such a case, the leaving service rules do not apply and, subject to the preservation requirements of the Pensions Act,[25] the benefits remain in the scheme until the employee dies, retires or leaves service.

7.58 Where an employee takes a full refund of contributions, no deferred benefits can be granted under the scheme. If, however, a partial refund of contributions is made for pre-1991 contributions, in accordance with the Pensions Act, or if no refund is made, a deferred pension can be granted.

7.59 The simplest case is where no refund of contributions is made. In that case, the maximum deferred pension can either be 1/60th of final remuneration for each year of actual service or a pension calculated on the N/NS x P formula referred to earlier.[26] To provide a measure of protection against inflation, the deferred pension can be increased by the consumer price index up to normal retirement, provided that the benefit remains in the scheme — that is, it is not transferred to a buy-out bond.

Example 7.7

A.N. Other leaves the service of the Widgets Retirement Plan after 10 years of service. Normal retirement date is age 65 and A.N. Other is 35 on leaving having joined the company at age 25. Final remuneration is £21,000 and the scheme promises 1/60th of final remuneration for each year of service. At normal retirement date, A.N. Other would have completed 40 years of service and be entitled to a pen-

---

25 See paras. 12.16, 12.17 and 12.57 et seq.

26 In para. 7.29.

sion of 40/60ths of final remuneration — that is, 2/3rds of final remuneration, which happens to be the overall Revenue maximum pension payable. The maximum deferred pension payable on leaving service calculated on the N/NS x P formula is as follows:

N = 10 (years of actual service from age 25 to 35)
NS = 40 (years of potential service — 25 to 65)
P = 40/60 x £21,000 = £14,000.

$$\frac{10}{40} \times £14{,}000 = £3{,}500$$

Alternatively, the maximum deferred pension could be calculated on the basis of 1/60th of final remuneration for each year of service, or 10/60ths of £21,000 = £3,500, which in this case happens to be the same figure as above. The maximum deferred pension is therefore £3,500 per annum.

7.60 Partial refunds of contributions are treated in a similar manner. The N/NS x P formula is also used, but in this case "N" is actual service completed after the period of service to which the refund relates. For example, where an employee takes a refund of contributions paid prior to 1 January 1991, "N" is actual service completed from 1 January 1991. In a similar way, the maximum lump sum benefit will be calculated either as 3/80ths of final remuneration for each year of service, or on the basis of the formula N/NS x LS. Again, taking the same example, where contributions have been refunded for pre-1991 service, "N" is actual service from 1 January 1991.

RETAINED BENEFITS

7.61 A person who joins the service of a new employer may be entitled to benefits from the scheme of a former employer. Except in limited circumstances, the benefits retained in the former scheme must be taken into account in determining the overall maximum benefit limits. The benefits are referred to in the practice notes as "Retained Benefits". Retained Benefits include the following:

1. Pensions for a member under other schemes
2. Any element of pension already commuted for cash

3. Self-employed-type retirement annuities under section 235 Income Tax Act, 1967
4. The annuity value of any lump sums paid.

Small deferred pensions not exceeding in aggregate £260 and lump sums not exceeding in aggregate £1,000 may be ignored, for this purpose.

7.62 The exception to this rule is that a pension scheme can always provide benefits of not greater than 1/60th of final remuneration for each year of service, irrespective of whether there are retained benefits.[27] Once the 1/60th rule is exceeded, however, either under the uplifted N/60ths scale or the 2/3rds maximum pension rule, retained benefits must be taken into account so that the benefit under the scheme when added to retained benefits will not exceed 2/3rds of final remuneration.

REVALUATION AND PENSION INCREASES

7.63 All the pension benefits considered in this chapter would lose their value in real terms if it were not possible to increase them annually in order to keep pace with inflation. Employees who leave service before retirement and hold deferred pensions are given a measure of inflation protection by the revaluation requirements of the Pensions Act in respect of benefits accrued since 1 January 1991.[28] Revenue limits permit the entire pension to be increased by the consumer price index from the date of leaving service, but schemes are under no obligation to offer anything greater than minimum Pensions Act revaluation.

7.64 Pensions in payment can also be increased, but there is no obligation to do so. Increases can apply to both the employee's pension and spouse's and dependants' pensions. Pensions can be increased to the maximum approvable at retirement. Once that maximum is reached, pensions can be increased by cost-of-living increases measured by reference to the consumer price index (CPI). Alternatively, a flat rate of up to 3 per cent can be guaranteed. This percentage in-

---

[27] Except in the case of a 20% Director where the retained benefit relates to a period of non-pensionable employment under a self-employed arrangement. See para. 7.65.

[28] See para. 12.46 et seq.

crease is applied to the maximum approvable pension, not the pension that the employee actually receives. For example, in the case of an employee whose pension is £30,000 per annum, but whose maximum approvable pension is £50,000, the pension can be increased up to £50,000 and thereafter at the 3 per cent or CPI rate as applicable. In addition to the above methods, the Revenue will normally approve pension increases to put the recipient on a par with current holders of the same employment.[29] Schemes may fund in advance to provide for retirement increases, but the rate of increase assumed in advance must be reasonable. 7.5 per cent is the maximum rate that the Revenue generally regards to be reasonable.

20% DIRECTORS

7.65 Special restrictions apply to 20% Directors who are scheme members. These are persons that control at least 20 per cent of the voting rights of the sponsoring employer or who had more than 20 per cent control within three years of retirement or leaving service.[30] The restrictions are set out in the practice notes and can be summarised as follows:

1. Refunds of member contributions on leaving service are not permitted.
2. Final remuneration must be averaged over three or more consecutive years ending not earlier than 10 years before retirement. The other computation options are not available.[31]
3. For the purpose of calculating final remuneration, previous years of remuneration can only be dynamised (i.e. inflation adjusted) if commutation is restricted: the pension equivalent of the commuted cash cannot exceed one-third of the total pension payable.[32]

---

[29] Pension increases in the public sector are made on this basis — see para. 8.20.

[30] For a definition, see para. 6.79.

[31] On final remuneration see para. 7.5 et seq.

[32] On inflation adjustment, see para. 7.5.

4. On late retirement, the pension and lump sum limits cannot be increased actuarially or by the added-years method except for years of service after age 70, although dynamisation is permitted.[33]
5. The 20% Director cannot at normal retirement take pension or cash by way of commutation without actually ceasing to be an employee and officer of the company at that point.
6. On early retirement, the 20% Director must also cease to be a shareholder. However, the Revenue may waive the shareholder requirement on grounds of hardship to the business.
7. 20% Directors who have paid premiums into a self-employed arrangement in relation to non-pensionable earlier service may be required to take into account the retained benefit under the self-employed arrangement even though the new scheme benefits do not exceed N/60ths for total company service.[34]

---

[33] Late retirement limits are considered at para. 7.23 et seq.

[34] See also para. 7.62.

8

PUBLIC SECTOR SCHEMES

INTRODUCTION

8.1 Public sector pension arrangements have their origins in the eighteenth century. The benefit design of modern pension schemes, both public and private, derives from the Superannuation Act, 1834, which, as we have seen, applied to both Britain and Ireland.[1] Some of the provisions of the 1834 Act still apply to the civil service superannuation scheme. The 1834 Act established the principle of pensions as a reward for service by promising a pension at retirement based on years of service completed to retirement and on retiring salary. Subsequent legislation modified (and added a great degree of complexity to) the civil service scheme but retained the fundamental objective of calculating pensions by reference to service and salary.

8.2 The public sector in its broadest sense comprises the civil service, local administration, the defence forces, Garda Síochána, education, health services and semi-state bodies and companies. The vast majority of pension schemes in the public sector are established by or under statute.

8.3 Public sector schemes can be either funded or unfunded. The local government superannuation schemes and the civil service schemes are unfunded. The cost of paying benefits is financed on a pay-as-you-go basis — there is no advance funding to meet the future liabilities to pay scheme benefits.[2] Many pension schemes of

---

1 See para. 1.11.

2 Although the Brennan Commission recommended in 1936 that they become funded rather than continue to be financed on a pay-as-you-go-basis. The issues regarding funding versus pay-as-you-go in the civil service schemes are examined in Hughes, G. (1988): *The Irish Civil Service Superannuation Scheme*, Dublin: Economic and Social Research Institute; and, more recently, in Joyce, J., Reilly, J. and Smythe, R. (1995):

state-sponsored bodies are also financed on a pay-as-you-go basis, but some (generally the commercial bodies) are funded schemes that are established under irrevocable trusts.[3] These funded schemes have much in common with private occupational pension schemes, but there are certain constraints on the funded schemes of state-sponsored bodies that warrant specific treatment in this chapter.[4]

8.4 Later in this chapter, pension schemes for state-sponsored bodies will be examined, and also the public sector transfer network. But first, there is a review of the statutory basis and benefit design of the civil service and local government schemes. These are the largest public sector schemes established on a statutory basis accounting for approximately 33,000[5] and 70,000 members respectively. There are many other statutory schemes, such as those of the Garda Síochána,[6] the Defence Forces[7] and teachers/education,[8] but it is beyond the

---

"Public Sector Pension Provision", paper delivered to the Society of Actuaries in Ireland, 23 November. A commission has been established by the Minister for Finance to report on occupational pension arrangements for the public service regarding emerging costs, and also regarding existing pension levels and claims for pension improvements. The commission is expected to report in 1998.

3 The objective of being established under irrevocable trusts is that the income and gain earned by such schemes is exempt from income tax and capital gains tax — see para. 6.9.

4 See below at para. 8.40 et seq.

5 Of which, approximately 5,000 are members of the unestablished scheme which currently operates on an administrative basis, but which will be put on a statutory footing when the civil service scheme is consolidated — see para. 8.23.

6 Garda Síochána Pensions Orders, 1925 to 1981.

7 The Defence Forces (Pensions) Acts, 1932 to 1975 and Defence Forces (Pension) Scheme 1937 and subsequent amendments. These are examined to some extent in connection with reductions in benefits — see para. 8.74 below. This and other legislation relating to military service has been the subject of much litigation in the nature of judicial review: *State (O'Shea)* v. *Minister for Defence* [1947] IR 49, *State (Conlan)* v. *Referee Appointed under the Military Service Pensions Act, 1934 and Anor* [1947] IR 264, *State (McCarthy)* v. *O'Donnell and Anor and State (Cuthbert)* v. *Minister for Defence* [1945] IR 126, *O'Doherty* v. *Attorney General and Anor* [1941] IR 569, *White* v. *Minister for Defence* [1936] IR 274, *Conroy* v.

scope of this work to examine these schemes. Suffice it to state that, except for specific conditions arising from the nature of particular employments — for example, defence forces and judiciary — all public sector schemes follow the same broad principles of structure and design.

CIVIL SERVICE SUPERANNUATION SCHEME

8.5 The civil service schemes compare favourably with private occupational pension schemes. The advantages are well summarised as follows:

> The civil service pension scheme has been the envy of the less favoured workers in the private sector because of its high coverage rate and the generosity of the benefits which it provides. Generally these features of the scheme were regarded as goals which employees in the private sector adopted for their own occupational schemes and there was relatively little explicit criticism of the civil service pension scheme in the past. In recent years, however, the emergence of high inflation, following the first oil-crisis in 1973, and of high unemployment, following the second oil-crisis in 1979, have made the benefits of the scheme appear more attractive than ever because they are protected against both inflation and unemployment.[9]

Minister for Defence and Anor [1934] IR 342, *Conway* v. *Minister for Defence* [1930] IR 633.

8 There are many such schemes — for example: National School Teachers' Superannuation Scheme, 1934; Secondary Teachers' Superannuation Scheme, 1929; Contributory Pension Scheme for Non-Teaching Staff of Comprehensive and Community Schools; Contributory Pension Scheme for Clerical Staff serving in National and Secondary Schools; Colleges of Education Pension Scheme, 1954; National University of Ireland General Pension Scheme; University College, Cork Pension Scheme Statute LXXIX; University College, Dublin Pension Scheme Statute XCVI; University College, Galway Pension Scheme Statute XVII Chapter XXV; University of Dublin Trinity College Pension Scheme. There are subsequent amendments to some of these schemes. A substantial number of education schemes are listed as excluded schemes to Parts III or IV or both of the Pensions Act — see the Schedule to the Occupational Pension Schemes (Preservation of Benefits) Regulations, 1992 (SI No 445 of 1992) and Schedule C to the Occupational Pension Schemes (Funding Standard) Regulations, 1993 (SI No 419 of 1993) and para. 8.65 et seq. below.

9 Hughes, G. (1988): *The Irish Civil Service Superannuation Scheme*, Dublin: Economic and Social Research Institute: p. 2.

Statutory Basis

8.6 There are two pension schemes for the civil service — one for established civil servants and the other for unestablished civil servants. Established civil servants are permanent employees and unestablished civil servants are non-permanent or are awaiting permanent status. The civil service superannuation schemes are administered and supervised by the Department of Finance.[10] The scheme for civil service established staff ("the established scheme") is governed exclusively by statute — the Superannuation Acts, 1834 to 1963 and the Superannuation and Pensions Act, 1976 — and by statutory instruments made under that legislation. The non-contributory pension scheme for non-established state employees ("the non-established scheme") is operated on an administrative basis — that is, no regulations have yet been issued. There are 20 individual statutes currently governing civil service pensions but provision was made in the Superannuation and Pensions Act, 1976 to consolidate the legislation in statutory instrument form.[11] It is understood that the consolidation work has commenced but is not far advanced. It is certainly desirable for two reasons that the legislation be consolidated. The first reason is that it will simplify the task of anyone seeking to identify the provisions that are in force and applicable to a given issue. Secondly, it will put on a statutory footing a number of significant administrative changes to the schemes, which are currently governed by internal circulars.[12]

8.7 The Superannuation Act, 1834 was the first legislation that dealt exclusively with pensions. It introduced a cap on pension benefits of 2/3rds of salary after 45 years of service. In no case could benefits exceed this limit.[13] Also, the 1834 Act stipulated that pensions could not,

---

10 Formerly by the Department of the Public Service, the latter department being abolished and its functions transferred to the Department of Finance in 1987.

11 s.2 empowers the Minister for Finance to make new schemes and s.3 to amend existing legislation.

12 s.11 of the 1976 Act repeals the existing legislation from a date to be fixed by the Minister for Finance. This will clearly not occur until the consolidation work is completed.

13 s.10. A form of three year averaging of final salary was also included (s.12). The 2/3rds limit is also one of the main benefit limits imposed by the Revenue as a condition of its approval of pension schemes.

save in exceptional circumstances, be granted to persons over age 65. There was dissatisfaction about various aspects of the pension system for civil servants and, consequently, amending and consolidating legislation was introduced by the Superannuation Act, 1859, which laid down an accrual rate of 1/60th of final averaged salary for each year of service up to a maximum of 2/3rds of final salary.[14] The accrual rate was reduced to 1/80th in the Superannuation Act, 1909,[15] but a tax-free retirement lump sum was introduced to compensate for this reduction[16] and lump sum death benefits were also introduced.[17]

8.8 The transfer of the civil service from British control to that of Saorstát Éireann took place on 1 April 1922. Saorstát Éireann inherited the previous civil service structure and the Superannuation Acts continued to apply as a consequence of Article 73 of the Saorstát Éireann Constitution, which provided that previous legislation would continue in force unless subsequently amended or repealed by the Oireachtas.[18]

Benefit Basis — Established Civil Servants

8.9 The following is a broad summary of the benefit structure of the established scheme.[19]

8.10 ***Eligibility:*** The established scheme is open only to an established civil servant. Broadly, an established civil servant is a person

---

14 s.2.

15 s.1(1).

16 s.1(2).

17 s.2.

18 Art 10 of the Free State treaty specified that benefits for public servants were to be no less favourable than before. This was given force of law by s.2 Irish Free State (Saorstát Éireann) Act, 1922. This gave a legally enforceable right to compensation — *Wigg and Cochrane* v. *Attorney General* [1927] IR 285, and see also *Lonsdale* v. *Attorney General* [1928] IR 35. An excellent summary of the historical development of the civil service scheme is to be found in Hughes, G. (1988): *The Irish Civil Service Superannuation Scheme*, Dublin: Economic and Social Research Institute.

19 The Department of Finance has produced a most helpful superannuation handbook for staff engaged in superannuation work in connection with the civil service superannuation schemes. The authors are indebted to the Department for supplying them with a copy.

holding an established post in the civil service and whose salary is paid out of moneys voted by the Oireachtas. In addition, the person must hold or be deemed to hold a certificate of qualification under section 26 of the Civil Service Commissioners Act, 1956, or must be appointed a principal officer of a department of state.[20] There are also certain minimum service criteria (normally five years) before benefit will be granted.[21]

8.11 ***Contribution:*** The civil service scheme has been non-contributory since the Superannuation Act, 1859, but civil service pay is reduced to take account of the fact that no contribution is deducted from members.[22] However, following the introduction of full (Class A) PRSI for civil servants appointed on or after 6 April 1995, the scheme was made contributory in the case of those paying the full rate of PRSI. The contribution rate is made up of two elements: first, 3.5 per cent of pensionable remuneration less twice the State social welfare contributory old age pension, and second, 1.5 per cent of full pensionable remuneration (i.e. without social welfare offset).[23] In addition, all members of the separate Spouses' and Children's Scheme pay periodic contributions to the scheme of 1.5 per cent of full pensionable remuneration.[24]

8.12 ***Pension:*** A member may retire or be required to retire at any time from age 60 and must retire by age 65.[25] The calculation of pen-

---

20 s.1 of the Superannuation and Pensions Act, 1976.

21 s.2 Superannuation Act, 1859 as amended by Art. 4(a)(i) Civil Service Superannuation Regulations, 1980 (SI No 188 of 1980).

22 A 5 per cent notional contribution can be added for pay comparisons with other employments — Dooney, S (1976): *The Irish Civil Service*, Dublin: Institute of Public Administration: p. 90.

23 Circular LA6/95 of 31 March 1995. See also para. 8.22 below.

24 Contributions due in respect of any service prior to membership of the Spouses' and Children's Scheme or any potential service allowed under that scheme (this arises in the case of death in service or ill-health retirement) are deferred and are deducted from retirement lump sum, preserved lump sum or death gratuity. These deferred contributions are known as non-periodic contributions.

25 ss.2 and 10 Superannuation Act, 1859, except in the case of Prison Officers who must retire by age 60, or at any time after age 55 — Superannuation (Prison Officers) Act, 1919.

sion is 1/80th of pensionable remuneration for each year (or part of year, pro-rata) of reckonable service, subject to a maximum of 40/80ths.[26] In the case of members paying full PRSI, pensionable remuneration for the purposes of this calculation is reduced by twice the State social welfare contributory old age pension.[27] There is provision for ill-health early retirement but early retirement on other grounds is not generally available.[28]

8.13 ***Lump Sum:*** A gross retirement lump sum was introduced by the Superannuation Act, 1909 as compensation for the reduction of the pension accrual from 1/60th to 1/80th. The lump sum is tax free and is calculated as 3/80ths of pensionable remuneration for each year (or part, pro-rata) of reckonable service, subject to a maximum of 120/80ths.[29] The lump sum may have to be reduced to take account of outstanding contributions to the spouses' and children's scheme.

8.14 ***Spouses'/Widows' and Children's Scheme:*** The Civil Service Widows' and Children's scheme was introduced with effect from 23 July 1968.[30] Prior to this there was generally no survivor's benefit payable on the death of a scheme member, other than the death gratuity.[31] The scheme has been compulsory for appointments made since 1 January 1969 but was optional for existing staff.[32] The scheme was

---

26 s.2 Superannuation Act, 1859 as amended by s.1(1) Superannuation Act, 1909 and Art. 4 of the 1980 Regulations.

27 See also para. 8.22 below.

28 Powers of a Minister to grant or refuse early retirement are subject to judicial review — *Egan* v. *Minister for Defence and Ors*, (Unreported, High Court, 24 November 1988, Barr J).

29 s.1(2) Superannuation Act, 1909 as amended by Art. 7(1)(a) of the 1980 Regulations.

30 It operated on an administrative basis until formally regulated by the Civil Service Widows' and Children's Contributory Pension Scheme, 1977 (SI No 132 of 1977).

31 The exceptions were injury warrants and allocation of pensions. Injury warrants are payable in respect of death or serious injury in discharge of duty. Allocation of pension involves the surrender of part of the member's pension in favour of a spouse or dependent relative.

32 Art. 4(1) of the 1977 Regulations.

not opened to female staff until 1 March 1980 and has been compulsory for new female appointees on or after 1 June 1981.[33]

8.15 A pension is paid to the lawful spouse on the death in service, or after retirement, of the member, or on the death of a former member (someone who has left service) entitled to a preserved benefit. Where the member dies after retirement on grounds of ill-health or dies in service, the spouse's pension is half the pension that the member would have received after service to age 65. In all other cases it is half the member's actual pension entitlement.[34] In the case of members paying full PRSI, the benefit is co-ordinated.[35] There are also pensions payable to dependent children, the rates of which depend upon the number of eligible children and whether a spouse's pension is being paid.[36] The spouse's pension ceases on remarriage or cohabitation,[37] but the Minister for Finance has the discretionary power to restore it on compassionate grounds.[38] Children's pensions will not be paid if the spouse's pension ceases, but can be restored at the Minister's discretion.[39]

8.16 A revised scheme, the Spouses' and Children's Scheme, was established in 1984 for new appointments made since 1 September 1984. The revised scheme was optional in the case of staff appointed prior to that date (including pensioners and deceased staff) whether or not they had opted to join the original scheme. The categories of persons entitled to pensions under the revised scheme are wider than under the old scheme and the circumstances in which refunds of contributions are payable are different. The new scheme permits pensions to be paid to non-marital children, children conceived or adopted after retirement/resignation, the spouse or step-children of a marriage occurring after retirement/resignation, and the children of a

---

33 Art. 4, Civil Service Widows' and Children's Contributory Pension (Amendment) Scheme, 1981 (SI No 56 of 1981).

34 Art. 6(4) 1977 Regulations.

35 See para. 8.22 below.

36 Art. 8 1977 Regulations.

37 The meaning of cohabitation is considered in *Foley* v. *Moulton* [1989] ILRM 169 in the context of social welfare benefits.

38 Art. 6(1) & (2) 1977 Regulations.

39 Art. 8(6) 1977 Regulations.

member who was widowed prior to joining the scheme and does not remarry. The old scheme does not permit pensions to be paid to these beneficiaries. In certain circumstances, under both schemes, contributions can be refunded. However, those circumstances are more limited in the new scheme. The revised scheme is currently operating on an administrative basis only — that is, without statutory authority.

8.17 ***Death Gratuity:*** On the death in service of an established civil servant a lump sum benefit is payable, known as a death gratuity. It is payable to the deceased's legal personal representative and is payable in addition to any benefit payable under the Spouses' and Children's Scheme. The benefit is equal to the aggregate of the deceased's total pensionable remuneration on the last day of reckonable service, or, if greater, the gratuity that would have been received on ill-health grounds, had the deceased not died. The latter figure is subject to an overall maximum of 1.5 times pensionable remuneration.[40]

8.18 ***Reckonable Service:*** Benefits under the scheme are computed by reference to service which is reckonable for pension purposes. Reckonable service is computed in years and days — it is not rounded to the nearest month or year.[41] The situations in which reckonable service is or is not counted are quite complex but they include full-time established service, service transferred under the transfer network[42] and certain notional service such as purchased service,[43] ill-health added years and added years for professional and technical qualifications. Overlapping periods of reckonable service are only counted once.

8.19 ***Purchase of Service:*** Established civil servants may purchase additional years of reckonable service by way of periodic contributions or a lump sum. There are two purchase schemes — one introduced with effect from 1 April 1979 and the other with effect from 1 February 1990. Both are established on an administrative basis and are regulated by internal circulars. No statutory instrument has yet

---

40 s.2(1) Superannuation Act, 1909 as amended by s.2 Superannuation Act, 1914 and Art. 7(1)(b) 1980 Regulations.

41 Art. 1 1980 Regulations.

42 On which, see para. 8.48 et seq. below.

43 See next para.

been made. The additional years that can be purchased are calculated under specific actuarial tables.

8.20 ***Pension Increases:*** Civil service pension increases are the envy of private sector schemes. The increases are guaranteed, whereas private sector schemes are often only discretionary. Also, the increases match general pay increases in respect of the pensioner's former grade, whereas private sector increases, if guaranteed at all, are usually set at a fixed rate of interest or capped by reference to consumer price inflation, certainly not by reference to salary increases. Civil service pensions have been indexed since 1950.[44] Increases are now governed by the Pensions (Increase) Act, 1964, which gave the Minister for Finance the power to provide for pension increases.[45] It was not until 1 July 1986, however, that pension increases matched general pay increases.

8.21 ***Preserved Benefits:*** The Pensions Act introduced the requirement for occupational pension schemes to provide certain minimum benefits for early leavers. The civil service schemes were ahead of the Pensions Act in this respect, having introduced the concept of preserved benefits in the Civil Service Superannuation Regulations, 1980.[46] The Pensions Act enables certain schemes that already provide preserved benefits to be exempted from the provisions of the Pensions Act with regard to preservation of benefits, and the civil service schemes have received such exemption.[47] Established civil servants who resign from the civil service on or after 1 June 1973 before attaining age 60, in respect of whom a certificate of diligence and fidelity has been issued and who have completed at least five years of reckonable service, are entitled to a preserved benefit, provided that their service has not been transferred under the transfer network.[48]

---

44 Pensions (Increase) Act, 1950.

45 s.29.

46 SI No 188 of 1980, Art. 7(1)(c)(iii) inserting s.6(b)-(h) into the Superannuation Act, 1909.

47 See later at para. 8.65 et seq.

48 On which, see para. 8.48 et seq.

The preserved benefit is more generous than under the Pensions Act, as will be seen below.[49]

8.22 ***Co-ordination:*** Established civil servants who are full Class A PRSI contributors have their benefits and contributions co-ordinated with the State contributory pension. In the calculation of the member's own pension, pensionable remuneration is reduced by twice the social welfare old age contributory pension. The spouse's and children's pension is calculated on the basis of a reduction of once that rate.[50] Co-ordination is another name for integration that was considered earlier.[51]

Benefit Basis — Unestablished Civil Servants

8.23 The unestablished scheme is governed by a number of departmental circulars[52] but is similar to the established scheme. The principal differences are the following:

1. Normal retirement is at age 66 — there is no facility for voluntary retirement from age 60.
2. The scheme is non-contributory for all members with regard to the member's own pension — that is unestablished civil servants paying full Class A PRSI do not contribute.
3. The contribution to the spouse's and children's scheme is 1.5 per cent of pensionable remuneration less twice the State social welfare contributory old age pension. Under the established scheme, it is based on full pensionable remuneration.
4. The unestablished scheme is co-ordinated with the State social welfare contributory old age pension for all unestablished employees. The established scheme is co-ordinated for full Class A PRSI contributors only.
5. For pension calculation purposes, pensionable remuneration is reduced by twice the annual amount of the social welfare contribu-

---

49 See para. 8.65 et seq.

50 Co-ordination is on an administrative basis — that is, it is administered by departmental circular.

51 See para. 2.16.

52 Circulars of 17 November 1971, 13 July 1976, 31 May 1979 and 29 June 1982.

tory old age pension in all cases. For established civil servants, there is a reduction of only once the old age pension with regard to spouse's and children's scheme benefits.

LOCAL GOVERNMENT SUPERANNUATION SCHEME

Statutory Basis

8.24 There are more than 70,000 members of the local government superannuation schemes. There are two main schemes: one reflects the old scheme basis contained in the Local Government (Superannuation) Act, 1956 and earlier legislation[53] ("the Old Scheme") and the other, known as the "Revision Scheme", incorporates certain changes in scheme basis. The Revision Scheme commenced with effect from 27 May 1977. Only 4–5 per cent approximately of members are still governed by the old scheme and so its significance will be merely historical in time.[54] Bodies included in the local government schemes include local authorities, health boards (including health corporate bodies), vocational education committees, regional technical colleges and other local government committees and bodies[55] (but many local administration bodies are not covered by the local government schemes and have separate schemes).[56] The local government superannuation schemes are administered by the individual

---

[53] Notably the Local Government (Superannuation) Act, 1948.

[54] Many are females who opted to remain in the Old Scheme in order to maintain their right to a marriage gratuity, which either would not have been available to them under the Revision Scheme or would have been subject to stricter conditions.

[55] Such as Joint Drainage Committees, Joint Burial Boards, Library Committees, School Attendance Committees, Fire Services Council, Local Government Staff Negotiations Board, Local Government Computer Services Board.

[56] For example, the regional tourism organisations fall within the terms of the Regional Tourism Organisations Pension and Life Association Scheme. The staff of the central and regional fisheries boards are included in the Central and Regional Fisheries Boards' Staff Superannuation Scheme, 1983. The various harbour commissioners have separate schemes for each harbour.

authorities subject to the overall control and supervision of the Minister for the Environment.[57]

8.25 The Revision Scheme is currently governed by statutory instrument: the Local Government (Superannuation Revision) (Consolidation) Scheme, 1986 ("the 1986 Regulations").[58] The old scheme basis is also contained in statutory instrument form in the Local Government (Superannuation) Act, 1956 (Consolidation) Scheme, 1987.[59] As indicated earlier, benefits were originally contained in primary legislation in the Local Government (Superannuation) Act, 1956. The Local Government Superannuation Act, 1980 repealed the 1956 Act (and the earlier Local Government (Superannuation) Act, 1948) with effect from 10 December 1987[60] and facilitated the consolidation and regulation of the scheme by statutory instrument.[61] In consolidating the original scheme, separate superannuation schemes were established in respect of the old and new basis.[62]

Benefit Basis — Local Government

8.26 The following is a broad summary of the benefit structure of the Local Government Revision Scheme.

8.27 ***Eligibility:*** The Revision Scheme governs eligible officers and employees who become pensionable on or after 1 June 1978, and officers and employees who became pensionable prior to that date and chose the new benefit basis of the Revision Scheme.[63] The Scheme itself revokes earlier schemes.[64] The Old Scheme governs eligible

---

57 Formerly the Minister of Local Government (prior to 1977).

58 SI No 391 of 1986, as amended by the Local Government (Superannuation Revision) (Consolidation) (Amendment) Scheme, 1987 (SI 315 of 1987)

59 SI No 316 of 1987.

60 s.12(2)(c) and SI No 312 of 1987.

61 s.2.

62 s.2. The schemes are made by the Minister for the Environment, with the consent of the Minister for Finance (formerly the Minister for Public Service).

63 Art. 3(1) and 4 of the 1986 Regulations.

64 The Local Government (Superannuation Revision) Scheme, 1984 (SI No 33 of 1984), the Local Government (Superannuation Revision)

employees who became pensionable prior to 1 June 1978 and maintained their existing benefit basis.[65] The Old Scheme as governed by the 1987 Scheme also revoked earlier schemes.[66] The Revision Scheme applies to officers and employees, but there are differences in the benefit basis of each, as will be examined below. Broadly speaking, the term "officer" refers to persons appointed to an office and includes professional, technical, management, office and administration personnel.[67] Employees (non-officers) constitute the balance of the local government workforce.

8.28 ***Contribution:*** The Revision Scheme is a contributory pension scheme.[68] Employees, and officers who pay full Class A PRSI, contribute at the rate of 3.5 per cent of pensionable remuneration less twice the State social welfare contributory old age pension plus 1.5 per cent of full pensionable remuneration.[69] Officers on Class D PRSI pay the higher rate of 5 per cent of pensionable remuneration (with no social welfare co-ordination).[70] Both Class A and Class D PRSI groups pay 1.5 per cent of pensionable remuneration for spouses' and children's

---

(Amendment) Scheme, 1985 (SI No 404 of 1985) and the Local Government (Superannuation Revision) (Job-Sharing) (Amendment) Scheme, 1985 (SI No 406 of 1985). These were transitional provisions.

65 s.5(4) of the 1980 Act prevents the regulations from giving members less favourable benefits unless the member is given an option, except with regard to employees joining on or after 1 June 1978 or 1 January 1970 as regards spouses' and children's benefits.

66 The Local Government (Superannuation) Regulations, 1984 (SI No 32 of 1984), the Local Government (Superannuation) Regulations, 1985 (SI No 407 of 1985) and the Local Government (Superannuation) (Job-Sharing) Regulations, 1985 (SI No 405 of 1985). These were transitional provisions.

67 The meaning of "officer" and "pensionable officer" has been the subject of much litigation: *Hanley* v. *Louth County Council* [1962] IR 204, *O'Cinneide* v. *Kerry County Council* [1954] IR 252, *O'Sullivan* v. *Leitrim County Council* [1953] IR 71, *Flaherty* v. *Minister for Local Government and Public Health and Anor* [1941] IR 587, *R (Dillon)* v. *Minister for Local Government and Public Health* [1927] IR 474.

68 The Old Scheme was originally non-contributory but became contributory on 1 April 1948 — see the High Court case of *Hunt* v. *Clare County Council* [1960] IR 296.

69 Art. 45 of the 1986 Regulations and Circular LA6/95 of 30 March 1995.

70 Art. 23

benefits, where applicable, but in the case of employees pensionable remuneration for this purpose is reduced by twice the State old age pension.[71]

8.29 ***Pension:*** As in the civil service scheme, a member may retire or be required to retire at any time from age 60 and must retire by age 65.[72] The calculation of pension is 1/80th of pensionable remuneration (co-ordinated where applicable)[73] for each year (or part of a year) of reckonable service, subject to a maximum of 40/80ths.[74] There are provisions for early retirement, including ill-health early retirement.

8.30 ***Lump Sum:*** Again, as in the civil service, a gross retirement lump sum (which is tax free) is calculated as 3/80ths of pensionable remuneration for each year (or part) of reckonable service subject to a maximum of 120/80ths.[75] The lump sum may have to be reduced to take account of outstanding contributions to the spouses' and children's scheme.

8.31 ***Spouses' and Children's Scheme:*** Separate widows' and children's schemes were introduced for officers and employees with effect from 23 July 1968 and 27 May 1977 respectively.[76] Prior to this, there was generally no survivor's benefit payable on the death of a scheme member, other than the death gratuity.[77] The scheme has been compulsory for male appointments made since 1 January 1970 (officers)

---

71 Art. 9 of the relevant spouses' and children's scheme and Circular LA6/95.

72 Art. 13(2) (officers), Art. 36(2) (employees).

73 See para. 8.39 below.

74 Art. 15 (officers), Art. 38 (employees).

75 Art. 14 (officers), Art. 37 (employees).

76 They operated on an administrative basis until formally regulated by the Local Government Officers (Widows and Orphans Contributory Pension) Scheme, 1984 (SI No 321 of 1984) and the Local Government Employees (Widows and Orphans Contributory Pension) Scheme, 1984 (SI No 318 of 1984).

77 The exception was allocation of pensions. Allocation of pension involves the surrender of part of the member's pension in favour of a spouse or dependent relative.

and 1 January 1979 (employees) but was optional for existing staff. The scheme has been compulsory for new female appointees since 1 October 1984.

8.32 There are, in fact, four spouses' and children's schemes: the Local Government Officers (Widows and Orphans Contributory Pension) Scheme, 1984[78] (for officers), the Local Government Employees (Widows and Orphans Contributory Pension) Scheme, 1984[79] (for employees), the Local Government (Spouses and Childrens Contributory Pension) Scheme, 1986[80] (for officers), the Local Government Employees (Spouses and Childrens Contributory Pension) Scheme, 1986[81] (for employees).[82]

8.33 The benefit basis of spouses' and children's pensions is similar to that provided under the civil service scheme. In particular, the widows' and orphans' schemes reflect the equivalent civil service widows' and orphans' scheme and the spouses' and children's schemes include the modifications contained in the equivalent civil service spouses' and children's scheme.[83]

---

78 SI No 321 of 1984.

79 SI No 318 of 1984.

80 SI No 364 of 1986 as amended by the Local Government Officers (Spouses and Childrens Contributory Pension) (Amendment) Scheme, 1989 (SI No 240 of 1989).

81 SI No 363 of 1986 as amended by the Local Government Employees (Spouses and Childrens Contributory Pension) (Amendment) Scheme, 1989 (SI No 239 of 1989).

82 There are also ex-gratia pensions which are regulated under the Local Government Officers (Widows and Orphans Ex-Gratia Pension) Scheme, 1984 (SI No 320 of 1984), the Local Government Employees (Widows and Orphans Ex-Gratia Pension) Scheme, 1984 (SI No 319 of 1984), the Local Government Officers (Widows and Orphans Ex-Gratia Pension) (Amendment) Scheme, 1987 (SI No 313 of 1987), the Local Government Employees (Widows and Orphans Ex-Gratia Pension) (Amendment) Scheme, 1987 (SI No 314 of 1987), the Local Government Officers (Widows and Orphans Ex-Gratia Pension) (Amendment) Scheme, 1989 (SI No 242 of 1989), the Local Government Employees (Widows and Orphans Ex-Gratia Pension) (Amendment) Scheme, 1989 (SI No 241 of 1989).

83 See para. 8.14 et seq. above.

8.34 ***Death Gratuity:*** On the death in service of an officer or employee a death gratuity is paid in a similar manner to the civil service scheme.[84]

8.35 ***Reckonable Service:*** Benefits under the scheme are computed by reference to service which is reckonable for pension purposes. As in the civil service scheme, reckonable service is computed in years and days – not rounded to the nearest month or year. Similar principles with respect to what is or is not reckonable service apply to the local government scheme as apply to the civil service scheme.

8.36 ***Purchase of Service:*** Officers and employees may purchase additional years of reckonable service by way of periodic contributions or a lump sum.[85] The additional years that can be purchased are calculated under specific actuarial tables scheduled to the Scheme.

8.37 ***Pension Increases:*** As with the civil service scheme, pensions are increased to keep pace with increases in the salaries of employees of the pensioner's former grade.

8.38 ***Preserved Benefits:*** The interaction of the Pensions Act with preservation of benefits in the civil service was considered earlier.[86] Similar observations apply to the local government scheme. Preservation was introduced with effect from 27 May 1977 and is currently regulated by the 1986 Regulations.[87]

8.39 ***Co-ordination:*** Officers who pay full Class A PRSI, and all employees, have their pension benefits co-ordinated with the State contributory pension. Pensionable remuneration is reduced by twice the social welfare old age contributory pension for the purposes of

---

84 Art. 18 (officers), Art. 41 (employees) 1986 Regulations and see para. 8.17 above.

85 Local Government (Supperannuation) (Purchase) Scheme, 1986 (SI No 421 of 1986) and the Local Government (Superannuation) (Purchase) Scheme, 1992 (SI No 184 of 1992) as amended by the Local Government (Superannuation) (Purchase) (Amendment) Scheme, 1995 (SI No 368 of 1995), which revised the purchase arrangements and closed the 1986 Scheme in respect of new purchases.

86 At para. 8.21. See also para. 8.65 et seq. below.

87 Art. 21 (officers), Art. 44 (employees).

pension calculation. In the case of spouses' and children's pensions for officers, the reduction is once the social welfare pension.[88]

STATE-SPONSORED BODIES

8.40 The previous sections have examined the civil service and local government superannuation schemes which apply to persons directly employed by the State or by local government bodies. In the wider field of the public sector there are state-sponsored bodies which are autonomous public bodies, other than universities, which are neither temporary in character nor purely advisory in function.[89] The statutory and benefit bases of the pension schemes of these bodies are now considered.

Statutory Basis

8.41 These bodies are generally established by statute or under the Companies Acts. A corporation established by statute will usually provide for the establishment of a pension scheme or schemes for its staff. The schemes must comply with any limitations imposed by the statute. The legislation under which the company is incorporated may or may not include requirements regarding pensions. If it does not, the memorandum and articles of association will determine whether or to what extent the company is empowered to establish pension arrangements.

8.42 Examples of bodies established by statute are the Pensions Board and the Electricity Supply Board. Section 17 of the Pensions Act enables the establishment of a scheme or schemes for the Pensions Board. Section 17(1) provides that

> The Board may, with the consent of the Minister [for Social Welfare] and the Minister for Finance, make a scheme or schemes for the granting of superannuation benefits to or in respect of persons appointed to whole-time positions on the staff of the Board.

Note that the scheme requires the consent of the Minister for Finance, in addition to the Minister responsible for the body. This is a typical requirement in the legislation relating to state-sponsored

---

88 Co-ordination is another name for integration which is considered earlier at para. 2.16.

89 Definition adopted from *IPA Yearbook and Diary* (1996): Dublin: Institute of Public Administration: p. 123.

bodies. Any scheme established under section 17 of the Act must be laid before each House of the Oireachtas, and either House can annul the scheme within the next 21 days in which the House has sat.[90] There is power in the legislation to amend or revoke the scheme.[91]

8.43 The Pensions Act, which established the Pensions Board, is a typical example of how modern legislation provides for the establishment of schemes for statutory bodies. In some cases earlier legislation stipulated that schemes be established by statutory instrument or ministerial order.[92]

8.44 In the example of the Pensions Board, there is no reference to the establishment of a fund. Unless the enabling legislation authorises the establishment of a fund, it is arguable that the scheme must be financed on a pay-as-you-go basis.[93] However, it is understood that some semi-state bodies have established funds without it being specifically provided for in the relevant legislation.

8.45 As noted earlier, it is generally the commercial state-sponsored bodies that establish funds. The Electricity Supply Board, for example, has established funded schemes under the Electricity Supply Board (Superannuation) Act, 1942.[94] Detailed requirements for the schemes are set out in the Act,[95] and power was granted to the Minister for Industry and Commerce, in certain circumstances in consultation with the Minister for Finance, to establish a fund.[96]

8.46 Examples of bodies established under the Companies Acts are Bord Telecom Éireann and An Post. These companies are incorpo-

---

90 s.17(6).

91 s.17(3).

92 For example, the ESB schemes established under the Electricity Supply Board (Superannuation) Act, 1942 as confirmed under s.11 of the Electricity (Supply) (Amendment) Act, 1952 and also the Transport Act, 1944, with regard to CIE — see *Fogarty* v. *CIE* 93 ILT 195.

93 The Pensions Board Staff Superannuation Scheme, 1993, established under s.17 of the Pensions Act, is unfunded.

94 s.4.

95 s.7.

96 s.8.

rated under the Companies Acts as a consequence of provisions contained in the Postal and Telecommunications Services Act, 1983.[97] There was included in the 1983 Act a specific requirement for each company to submit a scheme or schemes for approval by the Minister for Communications with the consent of the Minister for Finance.[98] As these companies are incorporated under the Companies Acts, they must also be empowered by their respective Memoranda of Association to establish pension schemes.

Benefit Basis

8.47 Most public sector pension schemes are required to be approved by the Minister for Finance before they can be adopted. A scheme will not be approved unless it embodies certain provisions which are acceptable to the Minister. In practice, the Department of Finance insists upon the adoption of standard rules, known as the "model scheme". There is a model scheme for main pension benefits ("model staff superannuation scheme") and a separate model spouses' and children's contributory scheme. The model scheme is revised from time to time by the pensions section of the Department of Finance, the most recent being dated February, 1993, and it generally corresponds to the benefit basis of the civil service scheme. The introduction to the model staff superannuation scheme states:

> This model scheme and accompanying notes have been prepared for the guidance of public service organisations which propose to introduce a staff superannuation scheme. It embodies all the provisions which are acceptable to the Minister for Finance or which are required by him in a public sector Staff Superannuation Scheme.

The model is more than just a guide. The Department will be slow to approve a scheme which departs from the wording of the model in any material respect.

LEAVING SERVICE — THE TRANSFER NETWORK

8.48 Public sector employees who change employment often remain in the public sector. For example, a person may transfer from a state-

---

97 s.9.

98 s.46.

sponsored body to the civil service or from the civil service to local government. A network is in operation which facilitates the crediting of pension entitlements with the new employer in respect of such employees. This is known as the "transfer network".

8.49 The transfer network enables an employee who transfers from one public sector employer to another to be given a pension credit in the new employer's scheme in lieu of benefits under the previous employer's scheme. This facility was established well in advance of the introduction of transferability of pensions under the Pensions Act, 1990. The Local Government (Superannuation) Act, 1956 and the Superannuation and Pensions Act, 1963 facilitated the crediting of pension benefits for pension scheme members who transferred between branches of the public sector. The public sector in this regard included not just the civil service, but also local authorities, state-sponsored bodies and universities.

8.50 There are two transfer networks, a civil service network and a local government network.[99] Categories of employment covered by the civil service network include the civil service, Garda Síochána, defence forces, national and secondary teachers and non-established State employees employed on or after 1 October 1975. The local government network participators include local authorities, health boards, harbour authorities and vocational education committees. In addition, other bodies can be approved by the Minister for Finance (civil service) or the Minister for the Environment (local government) to participate in the networks. Approved bodies broadly comprise state-sponsored companies and bodies. There are currently over 120 participants in each network.

8.51 One key difference between the two networks is that, in general, the civil service network approves and regulates transfers between participating employers, whereas the local government network approves and regulates *schemes* of participating employers. Consequently, once a participator is approved under the civil service network, all its schemes fall to be regulated by the civil service network. In contrast, a participator approved under the local government network can select which of its schemes are to be regulated by the local government network, and which are not.

---

[99] The local government network was established separately, on legal advice.

8.52 There is clearly an overlap between the two networks, as many of the participating companies and bodies are included in both networks. The civil service network must be used in all cases where the local government superannuation schemes are not involved. Otherwise, the local government network must be utilised.

8.53 The civil service network is governed by section 4 of the Superannuation and Pensions Act, 1963 and a draft transfer scheme issued on 24 April 1979. The local government network was initially governed by the Local Government (Superannuation) Act, 1956,[100] and was later extended by the Local Government (Transfer of Service) Scheme, 1984.[101] The two networks are now broadly similar.

8.54 There are four methods by which a transfer can be made: knock for knock, frozen contribution, uprated contribution and transfer value.[102] The participating employer can choose which method or methods of transfer it wishes to adopt. The method of transfer is subject to bilateral agreement between the employers concerned. A single employer may accept transfers on different bases from different transferring employers. Each of the four methods is now considered in turn.[103]

8.55 ***Knock for Knock:*** This is the common term to describe a transfer method where, in fact, no transfer is ever made. The new employer agrees to credit fully the employee's service that arose in

---

100 s.11(1)(f) and s.34(1)(f).

101 SI No 298 of 1984. This statutory instrument was made pursuant to ss.2 and 5 of the Local Government (Superannuation) Act, 1980. Other statutory instruments relevant to the local government network are the Local Government (Superannuation Revision) (Consolidation) Scheme, 1986 (SI No 391 of 1986), the Local Government (Superannuation) Act, 1956 (Consolidation) Scheme, 1987 (SI No 316 of 1987) and the Local Government (Transfer of Service) (Amendment) Scheme, 1989 (SI No 243 of 1989).

102 In the case of the civil service network, this is regulated by a draft transfer scheme dated 19 April 1979 (paras. 6 and 16). In the case of the local-authority network, the governing legislation is the Local Government (Transfer of Service) Scheme, 1984 (SI No 298 of 1984).

103 There follows a broad summary of the methods. As with the public-service schemes generally, the transfer network is complex. In particular, there are specific circumstances in the governing regulations where pensionable service is or is not recognised in the new employer's scheme.

the old employer's scheme and that was recognised in that scheme for pension purposes. Provided that there is an even flow of employees to and from each of the approved organisations which operate the knock-for-knock method, the effect of recognising service from a former employer should (in theory) be financially neutral. If an employee transfers from one employer to another and then subsequently transfers to a third or subsequent employers in the network, it is the last employer that carries the full cost of the transferred service. However, under the local government network, each previous employer must deal separately with the final employer. This option is the preferred choice of schemes which are unfunded.

8.56 ***Frozen Contribution:***[104] In this method, the old employer agrees that, when the benefit ultimately becomes payable by the new employer, it will make a transfer payment to the new employer. The transfer payment is calculated by reference to the employee's pensionable salary at the date of leaving the service of the old employer rather than by reference to pensionable salary at the date the benefit becomes payable. Similarly, it is only pensionable service up to the date of leaving the old employer that is taken into account. This method is available in the civil service network, but is generally not an option under the local government network.

8.57 ***Uprated Contribution:*** This method is similar to the frozen-contribution method except that the transfer payment is increased (uprated) in line with annual pay increases generally awarded to employees of the old employer of similar grade to the transferring employee. The increase is calculated from the date of leaving the service of the old employer up to the date on which benefits become payable under the new employer's scheme.

8.58 ***Transfer Value:*** This is analogous to a transfer payment between occupational pension schemes that are outside the networks. The old employer pays to the new employer, at the date the employee transfers, a lump sum cash transfer payment calculated by reference to the benefits that the employee has accrued under the scheme of the old employer up to the date of leaving service. There is a table of actuarial factors issued by the Government Actuary that is used to calculate the immediate cash-transfer values.

---

[104] This term and the following transfer terms are not used in the governing regulations. These terms are employed in the text for convenience.

8.59 Transfer contributions under the three transfer methods must be made on a non-coordinated basis. If the old employer's scheme incorporates a social welfare offset (co-ordination), the offset must be ignored for the purposes of calculating the transfer. This has the effect of increasing the transfer payment in such cases.

8.60 The transfer network provisions apply only to situations where both the old employer and the new employer participate in the networks. If the new employer is not a participating employer, then it can join the networks as a participating employer. This requires an application to, and the consent of, the relevant minister (Minister for Finance or the Environment). Otherwise, the member's benefits must be left in the scheme of the old employer.

8.61 Similarly, a person may become a member of a participating employer's pension scheme having formerly been employed by an employer who does not participate in the networks. Again, a transfer can only be made if the old employer agrees to participate in the network.

REGULATORY REQUIREMENTS

8.62 Having considered the statutory basis and regulation of public sector schemes, it is important to review what other statutory regulations do or do not apply to them. The principal regulatory régimes which it is now proposed to examine are the Finance Act, 1972 and the Pensions Act.

Finance Act, 1972

8.63 Schemes which are established by or under any enactment enjoy favourable tax status without the need to seek Revenue approval. The benefit limits imposed by the Revenue on exempt approved pension schemes have their origins in the level of benefits promised by the civil service superannuation scheme. It is not surprising, therefore, that public sector schemes, such as the civil service scheme, are generally exempted from the requirement that the Revenue impose upon occupational pension schemes under the Finance Act, 1972. Employee contributions to the scheme are deductible against income tax in the year in which they are paid, and contributions made by the employer are not treated as a benefit-in-kind liable to income tax.[105] The tax treatment of statutory schemes was considered earlier.[106]

8.64 Statutory schemes are not exempt from tax in respect of the income and gain on investments.[107] This presents no problem for those public sector schemes that are unfunded — for example, the civil service and local government schemes. However, some public sector schemes (notably schemes of commercial state-sponsored bodies) fund for retirement and death benefits in advance. These latter schemes establish a fund which, when invested, will yield income and capital gains. In order for these funds to be exempt from income and capital gains tax, exempt approval must be obtained from the Revenue under Chapter II of Part I of the 1972 Act. They must, therefore, be established under irrevocable trusts.[108] A deed will usually be entered into between the state-sponsored body and the trustees, whereby the scheme is established under irrevocable trusts and the rules, as approved by the Minister for Finance and the minister responsible for the body, will then be appended as a schedule.

Pensions Act

8.65 Public sector schemes promise deferred pensions to members who leave service before retirement which, as has been observed earlier, are potentially more generous than preserved benefits under the Pensions Act.[109] These schemes are also included in the transfer network which achieves portability of pensions within the network of participating employers. Members who move to the employment of an employer outside the network are entitled under the model scheme to have the actuarial value of their benefits transferred to that employer's scheme.

8.66 As will be seen later,[110] Part III of the Pensions Act requires the benefits of a pension scheme member who leaves the scheme early to

---

105 s.17 of the Finance Act, 1972.

106 See para. 6.74 et seq.

107 The reliefs contained in s.17 do not extend to an exemption on investment return.

108 See generally paras. 3.2 and 6.7–6.9.

109 See paras. 8.21 and 8.38.

110 See Chapter 12.

be preserved. Section 37(1) of the Pensions Act empowers the Minister for Social Welfare by regulations made with the consent of the Minister for Finance to exclude schemes or categories of scheme from the preservation requirements of Part III.[111] As the public sector has already introduced preservation of benefits on leaving service, most public sector schemes have been granted exemption from the requirements of Part III of the Act.

8.67 The leaving service provisions in the model scheme had to be revised as a consequence of the enactment of the Pensions Act. It would have been politically unacceptable for the model not to meet the minimum preservation requirements of the Act, even if public sector schemes were exempted from its provisions. Since the Pensions Act requires certain minimum benefits to be preserved, public sector schemes must be seen to match those preservation requirements. The model sets out to do this (except as regards forfeiture)[112] but, in fact, it is somewhat more generous than the Pensions Act in two respects. First, all service is recognised for preservation purposes, whereas the Pensions Act only requires benefits calculated with respect to service completed since 1 January 1991 to be preserved. Secondly, the preserved benefit is uprated in line with salary increases for the former member's grade in accordance with the Pensions (Increase) Act, 1964. The Pensions Act only requires revaluation at the lesser of 4 per cent and increases in the level of consumer prices.[113]

8.68 There is a similar facility under the Pensions Act to exclude schemes or categories of schemes from the funding standard requirements of Part IV of the Pensions Act.[114] Most public sector schemes are unfunded. Accordingly, it would be inappropriate to impose a requirement on such schemes to fund in advance for benefits when there is no fund established in the first place, and so most public sector schemes are exempt from Part IV of the Act.

8.69 It is important to emphasise, however, that public sector schemes are not exempt from the other parts of the Pensions Act. In

---

[111] See para. 12.90 et seq.

[112] See para. 8.71 et seq.

[113] On revaluation, see para. 12.46 et seq.

[114] See para. 9.64 et seq.

particular, these schemes must comply in full with the disclosure of information requirements of Part V, the trustee provisions of Part VI (if there are trustees appointed) and the equality provisions of Part VII.[115] The whistle-blowing requirements of Part VIII[116] and the financial order provisions of Part IX[117] also apply.

OTHER LEGAL ISSUES

Position of the Judiciary

8.70 The State has a constitutional obligation to fix salaries for judges which are not so unreasonable as to prevent a suitable and independent judiciary from being established. As pensions are a form of deferred remuneration, this principle applies to pensions as well. This was decided by Geoghegan J. in *McMenamin* v. *Ireland,*[118] a case in which a district court judge successfully challenged a provision of the Courts of Justice and Court Officers (Superannuation) Act, 1961, which provided for a compulsory reduction in his pension in order to meet the cost of paying him a lump sum at retirement.[119] Geoghegan J. stated.

> I think that it is implicit in the Constitution that judges must receive salaries and pension benefits quite apart from any recruitment considerations. Otherwise, the essential independence of the judges would be undermined. It seems obvious that that constitutional obligation could not be discharged by conferring on judges salaries or pension arrangements which were irrational or wholly inequitable. If, for instance, a salary for a district judge as fixed by statute became so eroded in real terms by reason of inflation that having regard to salary movements in the community generally it was totally out of line and so low as to undermine the secure independence of the judiciary there would be a breach of the constitutional obligation. As pension is nothing more

---

115 See Chapters 13, 4 and 16 respectively.

116 See para. 1.71 et seq.

117 See paras. 1.76, 5.56 and 10.63.

118 [1994] 2 ILRM 368.

119 This is similar to commutation of pension, which is examined at para. 2.24. The compulsory reduction would have put the judge's benefits on a similar footing to the civil service benefit basis. Interestingly, however, the Court considered that any comparison with the civil service was irrelevant to the issues before the Court.

> than deferred remuneration the same principles would apply to pension rights.[120]

However, the Court added that, whilst judges' pension arrangements cannot be irrational or inherently inequitable, the Oireachtas retains the power to determine what is reasonable in the sense of the value or worth of the judge's job.

Forfeiture

8.71 The Pensions Act protects preserved benefits by preventing them from being forfeited or reduced except in limited circumstances. This protection only applies to schemes to which Part III of the Act applies. A substantial number of schemes are, however, not subject to Part III, notably the civil service superannuation scheme. Accordingly, to the extent permitted by legislation or the rules applicable to such a scheme, a member's benefits can be forfeited or reduced. For example, there is provision for forfeiture of pension by persons convicted of treason, felony or criminal offences, whose sentences exceed 12 months, by reason of section 2 of the Forfeiture Act, 1870. Section 34 of the Offences Against the State Act, 1939 used to be an additional ground for refusing benefit but the Supreme Court has held that section 34 is unconstitutional having regard to Art. 40(3) of the Constitution. This issue arose in the case of *Cox* v. *Ireland*[121] in which a community school teacher raised a constitutional challenge to section 34 of the 1939 Act. The Supreme Court held that

> It is clear that the provisions of s.34 of the Act of 1939, when it becomes applicable to any person convicted of a scheduled offence in a Special Criminal Court, potentially constitutes an attack, firstly, on the unenumerated constitutional right of that person to earn a living and, secondly, on certain property rights protected by the Constitution, such as the right to a pension, gratuity or other emolument already earned, or the right to the advantages of a subsisting contract of employment.
>
> It constitutes a major inroad on these rights, for, having regard to the number of activities in which persons employed are funded by State funds or out of local taxation, an inability of a person convicted in this manner, not only to continue in his pre-conviction employment, but to take up employment in any of the other cate-

---

120 *Ibid.*, 378.

121 [1992] 2 IR 503.

> gories of employment coming within the provisions of s.34, is a major curtailment of his earning capacity. Secondly, the unilateral variation and suspension of contractual rights, including rights which may involve the entitlement to a pension to which contribution over a period has been made, constitutes a major invasion of those particular property rights.[122]

The Forfeiture Act was not in issue in that case but since its provisions bear similarity to section 34 of the 1939 Act, it is arguable that section 2 of the Forfeiture Act is invalid having regard to the same constitutional provisions. This view is reinforced by the High Court decision of *Lovett* v. *Minister for Education & Ors*[123] where a forfeiture provision contained in the Secondary Teachers Superannuation Scheme, 1929 was struck down as being ultra vires the enabling statute, the Teachers Superannuation Act, 1928, on the grounds that the Act did not expressly refer to forfeiture of pensions. In following *Cox* v. *Ireland* the Court stated, albeit obiter, that the forfeiture provision also constituted an unjustified interference with the applicant's property rights under the Constitution.

8.72 Article 62 of the local government revised scheme[124] provides for the cancellation of benefit (including preserved benefit) where a person has been convicted on indictment to any term of imprisonment exceeding 12 months. It may be restored subsequently with the consent of the Minister for the Environment. The constitutionality of this provision must be in question as a result of the decision in *Cox* v. *Ireland*.

8.73 It is a condition of receiving benefit under the civil service and local government schemes that the scheme member has served with diligence and fidelity to the satisfaction of the relevant body.[125]

---

[122] *Ibid.*, per Finlay CJ, 522.

[123] (Unreported, High Court, 11 July 1996, Kelly J).

[124] Local Government (Superannuation Revision) (Consolidation) Scheme, 1986.

[125] Superannuation Act, 1859 s.8 (civil service) and Local Government (Superannuation Revision) (Consolidation) Scheme, 1986 Art. 13.1(b) (officers) and Art. 36(1)(b) (employees).

Fair Procedures/Reduction in Pensions

8.74 In a series of cases relating to the Army Pensions Acts, the principle has emerged that, in reviewing pensions, the Minister for Justice has an obligation to adopt fair procedures. It is reasonable to suggest that the same principle would apply to any statutory scheme in which a minister has discretionary powers. In *State (Thornhill)* v. *Minister for Defence*,[126] the Supreme Court stated the position as follows:

> The statutory function of the Minister is to make a *bona fide* individual decision in each such case, having due regard to the terms of the Army Pensions Acts, which, so far as relevant to the instant case, were manifestly intended to grant soldiers receiving a "wound" whilst in service, a special form of pension.[127]

This decision was followed by two further cases on the Army Pensions Acts in 1988, *McKinley* v. *Minister for Defence*[128] and *Breen* v. *Minister for Defence*.[129] Both cases concerned the power of the Minister to abate a "wound" pension, having regard to compensation received in respect of the injury.[130] It should be emphasised that these cases were confined to the issue of fair procedures, not whether the Minister was, in principle, entitled to abate pensions under the legislation.

---

126 [1986] IR 1.

127 Per McCarthy J at 12.

128 [1988] IR 139.

129 [1988] IR 242.

130 The issues are considered further at para. 5.50.

9

ACTUARIAL AND FUNDING MATTERS

INTRODUCTION

9.1 Occupational Pension Schemes promise benefits at a future date. Defined benefit schemes usually calculate pensions by reference to a member's service and salary at or near to retirement. A member's future salary is an unknown quantity. Furthermore, members may die or leave service before retirement, which means that the service they will actually complete in the future is also unknown. It is nevertheless essential for the trustees of a defined benefit scheme to be in a position to estimate the future liabilities of the scheme and to recommend an appropriate funding rate in order to meet those liabilities. This requires the services of an actuary.

9.2 A defined contribution scheme promises a pension based on the value of employer and employee contributions to each member's retirement account. The amount of the employer and employee contributions is known in advance and is normally expressed as a percentage of the member's salary. The trustees of such a scheme do not require actuarial advice to calculate future benefits, and so this chapter will focus primarily on defined benefit schemes. However, there are specific actuarial issues relevant to defined contribution schemes which are considered later.[1]

9.3 The actuary's role in advising the trustees and sponsoring employer of a defined benefit scheme was placed on a statutory footing by Part IV of the Pensions Act. In particular, the Act imposes a minimum solvency test on defined benefit schemes and the scheme actuary is required to certify to the Pensions Board, and the scheme members, the extent to which the scheme is funded, were it to be terminated, and is also required to prepare a valuation report of the assets and liabilities

---

[1] At para. 9.67 et seq.

of the scheme. However, compliance with the minimum-funding standard does not necessarily satisfy the duty of the trustees with regard to the proper funding of a defined benefit scheme. Specific duties imposed upon them by the provisions of the scheme, or (more likely) their general duty to protect the benefit entitlements of the members and other beneficiaries, may require them to observe a higher funding standard.

9.4 The statutory framework is considered later in this chapter, as are the statutory restrictions on investment which must be taken into account in the actuary's valuation. It is first proposed to outline the duties and liabilities of an actuary and the role of actuaries in the pension fund context.

THE ACTUARY

9.5 The role of the actuary originates from the development of insurance markets in the nineteenth century. In particular, life assurance companies needed to calculate mortality rates and life assurance premiums and also to monitor their solvency. It is in this area in particular that actuarial skills developed.

9.6 Actuaries are either members of the Institute of Actuaries or of the Faculty of Actuaries[2] and are either associates or fellows. Both bodies are established by charter in the United Kingdom. Actuaries practising in Ireland must also be members of the Society of Actuaries in Ireland, which was founded in 1972.[3] It is a requirement of the Pensions Act that an actuary must be a Fellow of the Institute of Actuaries (FIA) or a Fellow of the Faculty of Actuaries (FFA) in order to carry out an actuarial valuation and issue an actuarial certificate, although, at the request of the trustees of a scheme, the Minister for Social Welfare may appoint a person with other actuarial qualifications to do so.[4]

---

2 This is the professional body applicable to Scotland.

3 Actuaries in other EU countries can, subject to certain conditions, practise in Ireland under EU reciprocal recognition arrangements, provided that they become members of the Society of Actuaries.

4 Occupational Pension Schemes (Disclosure of Information) Regulations, 1991 (SI No 215 of 1991), Art. 5(8) and see s.51(1) of the Pensions Act.

9.7 The Royal Charter of Incorporation of the Institute of Actuaries[5] provides a useful summary of the requirements of the profession:

> [T]he Profession of Actuary is one requiring a wide and varied training in respect of the frequent employment of its Members in the several capacities of Expert Witnesses, Valuers and Advisers in matters relating to financial questions, particularly in reference to those numerous and important questions involving the scientific application of the doctrine of probabilities and the principles of interest.[6]

In *Irish Pensions Trust* v. *First National Bank of Chicago*,[7] the High Court, in passing, defined "actuary" as follows:

> [T]he word "actuary" connotes, if it does not expressly mean, a person whose business activities include dealing in probabilities based upon assumptions and statistics.

There are three main principles employed by actuaries in the field of pension schemes: discounting, probability and mortality. A brief explanation of these principles can be found in Figure 9.1.

9.8 Actuaries may provide actuarial services as sole traders, in partnership or through a limited liability company. Many actuaries are also employed by insurance companies both in respect of life-insurance business and non-life insurance. In addition actuaries are employed by pensions consultancy firms and professional trustees and, in very large schemes, can be employed in-house by the pension scheme trustees. There are no schemes in Ireland which employ a full-time actuary but there are examples in the United Kingdom, the United States and other countries.

DUTIES AND LIABILITIES OF AN ACTUARY

9.9 The actuary is a professional whose practice is governed by the codes of conduct of the actuarial profession. Even where actuaries are employed by a firm or company, they are personally responsible for

---

5 Recital in Charter of 29 July 1984.

6 Reproduced in Members Handbook of the Institute.

7 (Unreported, High Court, 15 February 1989, Murphy J).

their work and advice.[8] In the context of pension schemes, actuaries are normally retained by either the trustees of the scheme or the employer, or both. They have a contractual obligation to the person who retains them but they have a duty of care in tort to a wider group of people, the beneficiaries of the scheme.

FIGURE 9.1: BASIC ACTUARIAL PRINCIPLES

Discounting: This is the method of calculating the present amount needed to provide a payment at a future date. For example, if £1,000 is needed in five years' time, a sum of money can be invested today in a bank account and earn interest sufficient to yield a total sum of £1,000 in five years' time. Assume for example that the rate of interest on the bank account is 10 per cent per annum. The amount needed to be invested today in order to provide a sum of £1,000 in five years' time is £621. £621 is the discounted value of £1,000 at that particular interest rate of 10 per cent. Pension schemes provide benefits at a future date and so discounting is applied in pension schemes to future transactions relating to pension scheme members, such as future payments of contributions and benefits payable in the future.

Probability: This relates to the mathematical field of statistics. Using data obtained from research in Ireland and the United Kingdom, an actuary can assess the probability of, for example, employees leaving service or taking early retirement. These membership movements are a significant factor to be taken into account by the actuary in valuing the liabilities of a defined benefit scheme.

Mortality: Mortality tables which assess the likelihood of persons dying at specified future ages are available to actuaries. The most obvious instance of mortality tables being employed in pension schemes is in connection with the different actuarial treatment of men and women. Men on average die younger than women. Accordingly, less money is required to buy a particular level of pension for a man than it is for a woman because the pension for the woman will on average be paid for longer. The mortality tables employed by the actuary are usually referred to in the actuary's valuation report.

---

8 Society of Acturies in Ireland Members' Handbook: Memorandum on Professional Conduct and Practice — p. D/2, para. 7.

9.10 It is an implied term of the contract between the employer or trustees and the actuary that the actuary exercise reasonable care and skill. The duty to the employer or trustees in tort is similar: to exercise such skill and competence as an ordinarily competent practitioner would be expected to do. There are no reported cases on the liabilities of an actuary either in Ireland or the United Kingdom but it is reasonable to assume that the normal duties of a professional will apply.[9] It is therefore helpful to look at the case law relating to accountants and solicitors in the context of negligence.

9.11 The courts will have regard to the standards of professional conduct laid down in the relevant codes of conduct. If actuaries follow the requirements of their own professional codes of conduct and the standards of their profession, their duty will normally be discharged.[10] They expose themselves to potential liability if they stray outside those standards. On the other hand, it is not an absolute defence for actuaries to assert that they have followed normal professional procedures. If the procedures are faulty actuaries may not be able to rely on them in their defence to negligence.[11] In a medical negligence case, the Supreme Court expressed the position as follows:

> If there is a common practice which has inherent defects, which ought to be obvious to any person giving the matter due consideration, the fact that it is shown to have been widely and generally adopted over a period of time does not make the practice any less negligent. Neglect of duty does not cease by repetition to be neglect of duty.[12]

9.12 The conclusions of an actuarial valuation are normally expressed as a statement of opinion. The Courts will be slow to interfere with that opinion. The following principle was enunciated in the UK decision in *Re George Newnes Group Pension Fund*:

> In performing this function an actuary must employ an expertise of great refinement which involves the assessing of the weight to be given to many and various contingencies and near imponderables. Some of these, such as mortality tables, may depend on sta-

---

9 See *Bolam* v. *Friern Hospital Management Committee* [1957] 1 WLR 582, 586.

10 *Daniels* v. *Heskin* [1954] IR 73.

11 *Roche* v. *Peilow* [1986] ILRM 189.

12 *O'Donovan* v. *Cork County Council* [1967] IR. 173 per Walsh J.

> tistical data and may be susceptible of more or less demonstrable validation. Others must necessarily be largely a matter of personal judgment. There is considerable scope for justifiable differences of approach and opinion among actuaries, and as the actuary's function is essentially one of estimation, one actuary may very possibly reach a conclusion in a particular case which varies, perhaps widely, from the conclusion of another actuary on the same facts. The court should be very slow to criticise or seek to control the exercise of any discretion or judgment reposed in or required of an expert of this kind in the exercise of a function of this character.[13]

This is reinforced by the decision in *Re Imperial Foods* in which, in the context of a corporate acquisition, the Court reached the decision that it would not interfere with an opinion given by an actuary unless he had used some method or procedure which no other actuary would adopt.[14] There is therefore room for differences of approach and opinion. The professional code of conduct of the Society of Actuaries in Ireland reflects this principle, in the context of criticism by one actuary of another's work:

> A member should recognise that there is room for differences of opinion in relation to actuarial advice and must avoid any action which would unfairly injure the professional reputation of any other member. However, this is not intended to prevent criticism to the client of another member's work for that client where this is properly reasoned and felt to be justified.[15]

9.13 To the extent that the functions of the actuary are not governed precisely by the scheme rules, the actuary must act fairly between the various beneficiaries of the scheme consistent with the rules of the scheme. This duty is summarised (albeit in the context of a scheme wind-up) in *Re George Newnes Group Pension Fund* as follows:

> The function of an actuary in advising how a pension scheme of this kind should be dealt with on the determination of the Scheme is to achieve the greatest practicable degree of fairness between the various persons interested under the scheme consistent with the rules governing that scheme. He cannot ignore or contravene those rules, and in the pursuit of fairness he may also have to pay regard to the spirit of those rules in respects which are not con-

---

[13] (1969) *Journal of the Institute of Actuaries*, Vol. 98, Pt. 3, p. 251.

[14] *Re Imperial Foods Ltd Pension Scheme* [1986] 1 WLR 717.

[15] Society of Acturies in Ireland Members' Handbook: Memorandum on Professional Conduct and Practice — p. D3/4, para. 17

> trolled by their express terms or necessary implication, but, consistently with the rules, he must do his best to achieve as fair a distribution of benefits as the size of the available fund, the character of the Scheme and the circumstances of the contributors make possible.[16]

The interpretation of the rules, however, is a matter of law and an actuary should be cautious about reaching conclusions on the interpretation of the rules without appropriate legal advice. This is supported by another UK decision *Mettoy Pension Trustees Limited*, in which Warner J. reviewed the actuarial evidence tendered and commented:[17]

> [A]ll three actuaries made it clear that in their view the rights of beneficiaries under a pension scheme depended first and foremost on the correct construction of the scheme documents which was a legal matter and not one on which they (the actuaries) were competent to testify. That is manifestly right.

9.14 Actuaries must bear in mind that their advice may be made available to third parties who can reasonably be expected to rely on it.[18] In particular, when advising on the solvency of a pension scheme, it is reasonable for actuaries to expect the members of the pension scheme and other beneficiaries to rely upon their advice. This is even more so where the actuary has prepared an actuarial funding certificate under the requirements of the Pensions Act as the Act imposes statutory duties on actuaries. The Society of Actuaries recognises this statutory dimension in its guidance notes:

> The Actuary is in a special position in that, in addition to the normal responsibilities to his employer or client, when signing a certificate he has statutory obligations laid down on him by the Act.[19]

9.15 The question of whether third parties can rely upon the actuarial valuation and funding certificate must be considered. It is submitted that the members are sufficiently proximate to succeed in a negli-

---

16 (1969) *Journal of the Institute of Actuaries*, Vol. 98, Pt. 3, p. 251. The principle was approved by Walton J. in *Re Imperial Foods Ltd Pension Fund* [1986] 1 WLR 717, 729.

17 *Mettoy Pension Trustees Limited* v. *Evans* [1990] PLR 9, 37.

18 Society of Acturies in Ireland Members' Handbook: Memorandum on Professional Conduct and Practice — p. D/2, para. 9.

19 GN3(ROI) "Actuarial Funding Certificates under the Pensions Act 1990, as amended", para. 2.2.

gence action. Duties of the actuary may extend beyond the members and other beneficiaries of the scheme to a purchasing company in a takeover. The existence and extent of the duty will depend upon the circumstances of each case. Frequently the purchasing company will have retained its own actuary to undertake an actuarial valuation but it may be that the purchasing company relies upon the funding certificate[20] and valuation already prepared by the scheme's actuary.

9.16 It is suggested that the liability of actuaries to a third party should only arise where actuaries are aware, and intend, that a particular third party is to rely upon their advice, report or certificate. This view would be consistent with the duty of an auditor in analogous circumstances which has been considered in the United Kingdom in *Caparo Industries* v. *Dickman.*[21] Lord Bridge, in quoting and approving a statement (which he refers to as a "classic statement") in an earlier dissenting judgment of Lord Denning,[22] stated that the duty of care of an auditor to third parties is confined to circumstances where the auditor shows the accounts to a third party or where the auditor knows that the company will show the accounts to a particular third party so as to induce the third party to invest in the company or take other action. This statement is not just confined to auditors. The duty extends to:

> those persons, such as accountants, surveyors, valuers and analysts, whose profession or occupation is to examine books, accounts and other things, and to make reports on which other people — other than their clients — rely in the ordinary course of business.[23]

This would seem to include the profession of an actuary.[24]

---

20 Although, given the minimum nature of the funding standard, it would be imprudent to do so.

21 [1990] 2 WLR 358 — which case was refered to in the unreported *Primor plc* v. *Stokes Kennedy Crowley and Anor* 1984 No 10038P Supreme Court 19.12.1995.

22 *Candler* v. *Crane Christmas and Co.* [1951] 1 All ER 426 at 433-436.

23 *Ibid.*

24 In a subsequent case of *Galoo Ltd* v. *Bright Grahame Murray* [1995] 1 All ER 16 the UK Court of Appeal permitted a claim to continue against auditors on the ground that the auditors were aware, and intended, that their report was to be relied on by the third party. "Mere forseeability

9.17 Examples of an actuary's potential exposure to liability are the following:

1. Breach of statutory requirements under the Pensions Act
2. An arithmetical error
3. The misinterpretation of the legal documents governing the scheme
4. A misinterpretation of law — for example, a misinterpretation of the provisions of the Pensions Act or of trust law
5. Accepting and using incomplete or inaccurate data.

With regard to data, actuaries have a statutory entitlement to obtain from the employer and the trustees such information as they may reasonably require for the purposes of their functions under the Pensions Act and any regulations made under it.[25]

9.18 Actuaries have a duty to keep confidential any matters relating to the affairs of their clients save where otherwise authorised or required by statute.[26]

FUNDING PENSIONS

9.19 Pension schemes can either set money aside in advance to meet the cost of providing future retirement benefits or can simply wait until the benefit comes into payment and start paying for it at that point. The former option involves advance funding. The latter method is referred to as the "pay-as-you-go" method of funding pension schemes. The remainder of this chapter is primarily devoted to issues arising out of the advance funding of pension schemes. Pay-as-you-go schemes are considered in the context of public sector schemes.[27] Whether or not benefits are funded must be disclosed to the scheme

---

that a potential bidder may rely on the audited accounts does not impose on the auditor a duty of care to the bidder, but if the auditor is expressly made aware that a particular identified bidder will rely on the audited accounts or other statements approved by the auditor, and intends that the bidder should so rely, the auditor will be under a duty of care to the bidder for the breach of which he may be liable." per Glidewell L.J. at p. 37.

25 s.54(4) of the Pensions Act.

26 Society of Acturies in Ireland Members' Handbook: Memorandum on Professional Conduct and Practice — p. D/2, para. 7.

27 See para. 9.64 et seq.

members.[28] Funded defined benefit schemes are usually "balance-of-cost" schemes, which means that the members pay a fixed contribution (for example, 5 per cent of pay) and the employer contributes the balance which the actuary determines to be necessary to fund for the promised benefits. The alternative is for the members and the employer to share the cost of funding for benefits on a pre-determined basis — for example, 50:50. These latter schemes are seldom encountered.

9.20 Before the Pensions Act was introduced, there was no legislation requiring a basic level of funding for pension schemes — a minimum funding standard. In fact, the only regulation was by way of a funding restriction. For schemes approved by the Revenue Commissioners under Chapter II, Part I of the Finance Act, 1972, Revenue restrictions are imposed to ensure that there is no excessive funding of a pension scheme.

9.21 It can be expected that the trustees of a properly run pension scheme understand the need to ensure that the pension scheme is adequately funded to meet the future benefit promise. A minimum funding standard is therefore something of which most pension scheme trustees have little to fear. Serious under-funding of pension schemes can nonetheless arise in five areas:

1. Fraud
2. An error on the part of the actuary in calculating the recommended funding rate
3. Any significant change in circumstances such as a major drop in the value of the fund's assets
4. Failure to fund adequately
5. Benefit improvements.

9.22 We have been fortunate in Ireland to have few examples of fraud on the part of the employer or the trustees. Errors on the part of the actuary in striking the funding rate are also relatively unusual but nonetheless possible. Further, the assumptions adopted by actuaries are generally sufficiently conservative to take account of a significant fall in asset values. By elimination therefore, it can be seen

---

[28] Occupational Pension Schemes (Disclosure of Information) Regulations, 1991 (SI No 215 of 1991), Art. 9 and para. 11 of Schedule C.

that the main causes of concern in funding are the fourth and fifth items: the failure in the past to fund the pension scheme adequately, and benefit improvements.

9.23 There are many reasons why a scheme could be underfunded. The employer may simply have failed to contribute what the actuary has recommended. This is a dangerous situation for the trustees as they have an obligation to ensure that contributions are received.[29] On the other hand, the employer may have contributed in accordance with actuarial recommendations but the actuary's report may be out of date. Again the trustees would be found wanting in a situation like this as they have a duty to commission an actuary's report at regular intervals. Perhaps most concern has arisen in cases where an outdated funding method has been in operation.[30]

9.24 Benefit improvements can have a dramatic effect on the solvency of a pension scheme in that they increase the scheme's liabilities. Improvements may take the form of better retirement benefits for certain members (or perhaps all members) or enhanced benefits on early retirement. No problem arises where the scheme is sufficiently well funded to absorb the additional liability, or where the employer makes an additional contribution in accordance with the actuary's recommendations. Occasionally, however, improvements are made without regard to solvency, and this can result in a significant funding deficit.

9.25 Having identified the various circumstances in which a funding problem can arise in a defined benefit scheme, it is appropriate to examine the statutory funding requirements under the Pensions Act and the role of the actuary in preparing a valuation report and a funding certificate.

---

29 Pensions Act, s.59(a) and *Re Brogden* (1886) 38 ChD 546.

30 Such as the "level annual premium" method which used to be adopted by insurers. In this method, the insurer calculates the cost in a given year of providing benefits for members based on that year's service and based on salary at that date. No account is taken of future salary increases. As the members get older, the period of investment to retirement gets shorter and salary is increased. The funding rate starts as a very modest sum but in time rises rapidly.

FUNDING STANDARD UNDER THE PENSIONS ACT

9.26 As has been indicated above, it is in relation to the funding of defined benefit schemes that most of the actuary's work in the pensions context is carried out. As observed by the High Court in *Irish Pensions Trust* v. *First National Bank of Chicago*:[31]

> There is no doubt that one of the features of schemes of this nature is the expertise of the actuaries who determine or advise the premium or contribution which it is necessary to pay annually to create and maintain a fund out of which benefits of this nature can be met and discharged over a long period of time and in circumstances which may of course vary radically during that period.

Periodically, actuaries are asked to produce a valuation report in which they must

1. Estimate the future liabilities to provide benefits under the pension scheme in order to report on whether there are sufficient assets to meet the accrued liabilities
2. Recommend a contribution rate for the scheme.

In order to estimate future liabilities, the actuary must also estimate what the future value of the assets of the fund will be, by making assumptions on future investment return and future contributions to the scheme and on the movement of members in and out of the scheme — new entrants and withdrawals.

9.27 The assumptions chosen by the actuary, such as the rate of salary increases and the rate of growth in the fund, will have a direct influence on the valuation. The more conservative the assumptions chosen, the higher is the employer's contribution rate likely to be. Employers take a keen interest in actuarial valuations, as they fix the ongoing expense of providing benefits under the pension scheme. If the assumptions prove to be more conservative than actual experience, a surplus is likely to result. This arose in the *First National Bank of Chicago* case where the employer was held by the High Court to have overprovided because of circumstances outside his control as a result of acting on the best advice available (that of the actuary), which subsequent events proved to have been erroneous. The Court held that the failure of the actuary's assumptions to match subse-

---

31 See fn 7.

quent events constituted an erroneous actuarial computation within the meaning of the trust documents.

9.28 Prior to the Pensions Act, there was no legal requirement[32] for an actuarial valuation to be prepared. Schemes funded on a controlled funded basis, which is a modern funding basis designed to ensure a relatively stable employer contribution rate,[33] normally were valued periodically to enable the employer to monitor its funding requirements and either to increase or to decrease its funding rate depending on the actuary's conclusions. The National Pensions Board in its first report[34] recommended that pensions legislation be introduced to require defined benefit schemes to maintain at the very least a specified minimum-funding position, referred to as a minimum-funding standard. This, with preservation of benefits, became one of the main features of the Pensions Act. The funding standard requirements are contained in Part IV of the Pensions Act, in the third Schedule to the Act and in regulations which were subsequently introduced. As a consequence of the introduction of Part IV, the Society of Actuaries in Ireland issued a guidance note for actuaries to comply with the funding standard requirements. This guidance note is binding on actuaries.[35]

9.29 The funding standard under the Pensions Act applies to any occupational pension scheme[36] other than a defined contribution scheme or a scheme which has become frozen before 1 January 1993. A scheme has become frozen on or before that date when service after that date does not entitle the member to any additional retirement benefits (referred to as "long service benefit").[37] The Minister for Social Welfare is empowered by regulations to exempt from the funding

---

32 There was, and still is, a Revenue requirement where the scheme is approved by the Revenue, and, in particular, where the scheme is a small self-administered scheme.

33 As opposed to outdated methods, such as the level annual premium method — see para. 9.23 and fn 30.

34 First Report of the National Pensions Board (Pl 4776) para. 6.34.

35 GN3 (ROI) "Actuarial Funding Certificates under the Pensions Act, 1990 (as amended)".

36 See para. 1.37 for a definition.

37 s.41(1) as amended by s.46 of the Social Welfare Act, 1993.

standard schemes where benefits are paid in whole or in part out of moneys provided from the Central Fund[38] or by the Oireachtas.[39] These are public sector schemes, and regulations have been issued which list the schemes that are so exempted. This list is revised from time to time.[40]

9.30 In order to cope with hardship cases, there is also provision for the Minister for Social Welfare to make regulations which modify the funding standard for specified pension schemes, where it would otherwise be unreasonable or contrary to the interests of members for the standard to apply unmodified.[41]

9.31 There are two documents required of pension schemes to which Part IV applies: an actuarial funding certificate and an actuarial valuation. The former is required to be prepared under Part IV but, oddly, the requirement for an actuarial valuation to be produced is in fact contained in Part V of the Pensions Act — the part dealing with disclosure of information to members.[42]

9.32 The preparation of an actuarial valuation would usually (but by no means always) precede the production of an actuarial funding certificate. The trustees of a scheme to which Part IV applies must cause an actuarial valuation to be prepared by an actuary at least every three and a half years and can choose any date within that period as the effective date of the valuation.[43] There are certain transitional provisions which deal with the production of the first actuarial valuation.[44] For schemes which commenced prior to 1 January 1991 (the date when Part IV came into force), the effective date of the first

---

[38] The Central Fund is the name given to the fund that is required by Article 11 of the Constitution to be formed by the revenues of the State — Constitution (Consequential Provisions) Act, 1937 s.6.

[39] s.52(1).

[40] Occupational Pension Schemes (Funding Standard) Regulations, 1993 (SI No 419 of 1993) Schedule C.

[41] s.52(2) — no such regulations have yet been issued.

[42] s.56(1) as amended by s.22(a) of the Pensions (Amendment) Act, 1996.

[43] s.56(1) and Article 5(7) of the Occupational Pension Schemes (Disclosure of Information) Regulations, 1991.

[44] Article 5(6) of the Disclosure Regulations.

valuation must have been not later than 31 December 1993. For schemes which commenced on or after 1 January 1991, the first valuation had to be prepared with an effective date not later than three and a half years after the commencement of the scheme. External schemes are treated differently.[45]

9.33 Having carried out a valuation, the actuary is then in a position to prepare the actuarial funding certificate which must be in the form specified in the Occupational Pension Schemes (Funding Standard) Regulations, 1993 ("the Funding Standard Regulations").[46] As with the actuarial valuation, schemes must prepare an actuarial funding certificate at an effective date at least every three and a half years and can choose any date within that period as the effective date of the certificate.[47] The Pensions Board can modify the requirement to submit a certificate and other requirments where it would not otherwise be contrary to the interests of members.[48] Similar transitional arrangements apply for the first funding certificate. The funding certificate must be submitted to the Pensions Board by the trustees within nine months of the effective date of the certificate.[49] In preparing the certificate, actuaries must have regard to such financial and other assumptions as they consider to be appropriate on the effective date of the certificate.[50]

9.34 The funding certificate is a "snapshot" of the funding position of the pension scheme at a particular date. There are two main approaches which the legislature could have adopted for a funding standard. The first would be to require the actuary to certify that the assets of the scheme are sufficient to meet the liabilities accrued to date, assuming that the scheme were to continue (that is, taking into

---

45 See para. 9.58 et seq. below.

46 A standard-form funding certificate is contained in Schedule B. The format of the first actuarial funding certificate is set out in schedule A. This is provided for as a consequence of s.42(4) of the Pensions Act, which requires that the actuarial funding certificate shall be in such form as is prescribed.

47 s.42 and s.43(1).

48 s.42(5) as inserted by s.16 Pensions (Amendment) Act, 1996.

49 s.43(2).

50 s.46(1) as substituted by s.56 Social Welfare Act, 1992.

account future salary increases). This is usually referred to as the "past service reserve" approach. The second approach is to assume that the scheme is to be discontinued and wound up at the effective date of the certificate and to require the actuary to certify whether the assets at that date are sufficient to meet the liabilities at the date of the assumed wind up. The former approach is a more onerous standard, as the actuary must take into account that employees will remain in the scheme until retirement, whereas, under the second approach, liabilities are effectively crystallised at the date of assumed wind-up and the actuary need not take into account the potential future salary increases of members. In neither case is future service taken into account.

9.35 It is the second approach which was adopted as the funding standard under Part IV. For schemes which commenced after 1 January 1991 the position is relatively simple. The funding standard is deemed to be met if, in the opinion of the actuary, the resources of the scheme at the effective date of the actuarial funding certificate would be sufficient had the scheme been wound up on that date to provide for:

1. The estimated expenses of administering the wind-up of the scheme[51]
2. Pensions in course of payment
3. Additional benefits secured or granted by way of additional voluntary contributions or transfers from previous schemes
4. Benefits for current active members and deferred pensioners.[52]

For the purposes of this exercise, the actuary may assume that the liabilities of the scheme on that date can be provided by transferring benefits either to another pension scheme or to a buy-out bond.[53]

9.36 It would have been onerous for schemes which commenced prior to 1 January 1991 to have to comply immediately with the funding standard. Accordingly, there are transitional provisions which permit the trustees to meet the funding standard over a tran-

---

51 s.44(b).

52 s.44(a).

53 s.46(1).

sitional period of 10 years.[54] As with schemes which commenced after 1 January 1991, the trustees must meet in full all liabilities in respect of benefits which have accrued on and after 1 January 1991 and all pre-1991 liabilities with regard to items 2 and 3 in the previous paragraph. However, for benefits of current active members and deferred pensioners which have accrued prior to 1 January 1991, the actuary, in the first actuarial funding certificate, must state what is the percentage of coverage for those benefits accrued prior to 1991.[55] This is referred to as the "specified percentage". If the scheme can meet all pre-1991 benefits, then the specified percentage is 100 per cent. However, if there is, for example, a shortfall of 20 per cent for pre-1991 benefits, the specified percentage for that scheme will be 80 per cent — that is, pre-1991 benefits are covered up to 80 per cent only.

9.37 For subsequent actuarial valuations the specified percentage cannot drop below that which has already been certified by the actuary in the first actuarial funding certificate.[56] Using the previous example, if the actuary certifies 80 per cent coverage for pre-1991 benefits at the first valuation date, but can only certify 70 per cent at the second valuation date, the scheme fails to satisfy the funding standard. The first actuarial funding certificate which is due to be prepared after 1 January 2001 (that is, 10 years after the commencement of Part IV) must certify that the specified percentage is 100 per cent — in other words, the shortfall must be eliminated by that date. In this regard, it should be noted that the shortfall need not be eliminated by 1 January 2001 — it must be eliminated by the date of the first actuarial funding certificate that arises after 1 January 2001. If for example a funding certificate has an effective date of 1 January 2000, the next certificate is not required until 30 June 2003. It is only at that point that the funding certificate must show a specified percentage of 100 per cent.

9.38 Section 45 of the Pensions Act gives some assistance in calculating the specified percentage. Broadly, the actuary must work out the cost of securing benefits under headings 1–4 in paragraph 9.35 above. Having subtracted the total cost from the assets of the scheme, the balance is available to discharge pre-1991 benefits. If this balance is

---

54 Although it may be more than 10 years in practice. See next para.

55 s.44(a)(iv).

56 s.45(5)(a).

not sufficient to meet the liabilities for pre-1991 benefits, the shortfall can be identified in order to calculate the specified percentage.[57]

VALUATION REPORTS

9.39 Although requiring that an actuarial valuation be prepared at least every three and a half years, the Pensions Act does not prescribe the content of the valuation report, other than to state that the resources and liabilities of the scheme must be valued by the actuary to the scheme.[58] In reality, however, actuaries do not have a free hand. Valuation reports prepared by actuaries follow a standard format. The format is determined in accordance with Guidance Note 9 (ROI) issued by the Society of Actuaries in Ireland. This guidance note is mandatory on all actuaries who are members of that society practising in Ireland. Since only Fellows of the Institute or Faculty of Actuaries can prepare valuation reports and issue actuarial certificates under the Pensions Act,[59] and those practising in Ireland are members of the Society of Actuaries in Ireland, the guidance note is, in effect, mandatory on all defined benefit schemes in Ireland.

9.40 By seeking an actuarial valuation, the trustees are in effect asking for a solvency valuation. The trustees will want to know whether the fund is adequate to meet their commitments to members under the scheme. The following information is normally regarded as essential under Guidance Note 9 (ROI) to be contained in an actuarial valuation report:

1. Certain basic information about the scheme, such as the effective date on which the valuation is carried out and to whom the valuation report is issued.
2. A summary of the data furnished to the actuary.
3. The reservations of the actuary (if any) concerning the investment policy of the scheme and the scheme data furnished to the actuary for the purpose of the valuation. In addition, the actuary should have access to the audited accounts of the scheme, or, if audited accounts have not been prepared, to the abbreviated annual re-

---

57 See s.45(2).

58 s.56(1).

59 Subject to the exceptions explained at para. 9.6.

port. If this information is not made available to the actuary, a statement to this effect should be made.

4. A statement of the benefits which have been valued (for example, summary of the benefits of the scheme or reference to appropriate documents). It should be stated, if applicable, whether discretionary benefit increases (such as increases in pensions) have been taken into account.
5. A statement of the rates of contribution payable during the inter-valuation period.
6. Whether actual experience since the previous valuation materially differs from the various assumptions that the actuary applied in the last valuation.
7. The assumptions applied by the actuary in this valuation — for example, future price inflation, future salary inflation, likely in come and asset growth in the fund, mortality (death) and morbidity (sickness or ill-health).
8. The valuation method adopted by the actuary.[60]
9. The rate at which the employer should contribute to the fund from the current valuation until the next valuation. This is normally expressed as a percentage of salary or pensionable salary payroll of all the members.[61]
10. Whether the scheme is solvent, and if not, then how much accrued assets fall short of accrued liabilities — referred to as a "shortfall in coverage".

9.41 There are five basic methods of valuation which actuaries can employ in order to determine the value of accrued benefits which have vested. It is not intended to consider the methods in any particular detail, but it is important nevertheless when reviewing an ac-

---

60 There are five such methods and these are explained further at para. 9.42 et seq. below.

61 Pensionable salary is often defined as salary less a deduction to take account of the fact that a State Social Welfare Pension would be payable in addition to the pension under the private pension scheme — see para. 2.16. Also, salary for pension purposes often differs from actual salary paid to an employee. For example, bonuses and fluctuating elements of pay are frequently excluded for pension purposes — see para. 3.38.

tuarial report to have some idea of what each method involves.[62] The basic valuation methods are set out in Figure 9.2. The overall contributions paid under each method will be the same, but the timing of contributions will vary from method to method. In other words, the application of one valuation method may result in the recommendation at any given time of a contribution rate differing from the rate that would result if another valuation method were to be chosen.[63]

9.42 As can be seen from Figure 9.2, there are two basic types of valuation method: accrued benefit valuation and prospective benefit valuation. The accrued methods work out what contribution rate is necessary to meet the liabilities that will arise, or accrue, over the period from this valuation until the next valuation (normally three years). The prospective methods look beyond that three year period and take account of the liabilities that would accrue until the members' normal retirement. The long-term objective of each method is to ensure that the scheme is sufficiently well funded to meet the cost of providing benefits when they fall due.

FIGURE 9.2: VALUATION METHODS

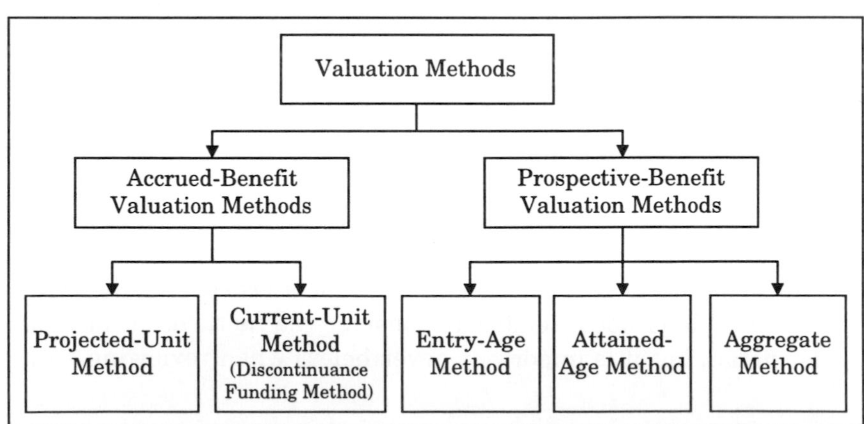

---

[62] The methods are considered in some detail in Lee, E.M. (1986): *An Introduction to Pension Schemes*, Institute of Actuaries and Faculty of Actuaries in Scotland, Chapter 8. For a useful summary, see Escolme, B., Hudson, D. & Greenwood, P. (1991): *Hosking's Pension Schemes and Retirement Benefits* 6th Ed, London: Sweet and Maxwell, Chapter 22.

[63] If a dispute arises, the Courts are unlikely to challenge the method adopted — see para 9.12.

9.43 In assessing the most appropriate method, the actuary will have regard to three principal objectives of a good approach to funding, namely:[64]

1. *Security*: This is considered from the perspective of the members. The scheme should be in a position to secure members' accrued benefits, should the scheme be wound up at any point — in other words, its assets should be sufficient to meet its accrued liabilities.
2. *Stability*: This is an issue for the employer, who will desire a reasonably stable contribution rate in the long term, with little significant fluctuation.
3. *Durability*: This is a concern for both the employer and the members. Pension schemes are normally designed on the assumption that they will continue indefinitely, with older members retiring and new members joining. However, if the flow of new members into the scheme ceases (for example, the scheme is frozen) and the average age of members steadily increases, the existing funding plan may be put under severe pressure. Durability tests the extent to which the funding plan can withstand such changes.

Projected Unit Method: Under this method, the cost of providing benefits over a control period — that is, until the next valuation date (usually three years) — is worked out by calculating the value of benefits which will accrue over that period, taking into account assumed increases in salaries. The resulting cost is expressed as a contribution rate. There is good security for members, as the liability to provide benefits based on expected final pay at retirement is covered in respect of past service. The contribution rate is reasonably stable. There is a gradual rise in the funding rate with age, but not sufficient to cause concerns regarding durability.

Current-Unit Method (Discontinuance Funding Method): This is similar to the projected-unit method. However, the effects of future salaries are not taken into account except where statutory revaluation of deferred pensions is required.[65] This method gives poor security for members in that it only covers past service benefits based on

---

64 See Lee, E.M. (1986): *An Introduction to Pension Schemes*, Institute of Actuaries and Faculty of Actuaries in Scotland, Chapter 8.

65 On revaluation, see para. 12.46 et seq.

current salary, not expected final pay. There is also a lack of stability unless the flow of new entrants keeps the age profile the same. There is a serious problem with durability, as in a frozen scheme, the funding cost would increase dramatically with age.

Entry-Age (or New Entrant) Method: Under this method, the actuary makes an assumption as to the average age of a new member when first included in the scheme. The actuary then calculates the percentage level of pay which, if paid through the working life of this new entrant, would provide the necessary resources at retirement to meet the cost of providing benefits. The security for members is high because, as the average entrant grows older, the contribution rate allows for the increase in the cost of providing benefits — there is allowance for future salary increases. The funding rate is based on an average age and so there is a fair degree of stability. There is also good durability for the same reason as there is security.

Attained-Age Method: The entry age method arrives at a funding rate that meets the future service costs of a typical new entrant. The attained age method seeks to meet the costs of a group. Instead of working out the cost of benefits from an average entry age until normal retirement, as in the entry age method, the attained age method makes the appropriate calculations from the average age of members at that valuation date, not the average entry age. Security, stability and durability are similar to the entry age method. However, the attained age method is a particularly appropriate valuation method for a scheme closed to new members, as it avoids a steady rise in contribution rates with an annual increase in the average age.

Aggregate Method: This is perhaps the easiest valuation method to conceptualise. The contribution rate under this method is calculated by valuing accrued benefits of members to date and future benefits until retirement, taking into account future salary increases. The contribution is the balance needed to meet this liability having subtracted the current value of the fund. This method does not assume that there will be any new entrants, and the target fund to be achieved is therefore quite high. The aggregate method tends to produce surplus, but is not markedly lacking in stability. A high target fund equates with good security for members. The objective of durability is also achieved.

SELF-INVESTMENT/CONCENTRATION OF INVESTMENT

9.44 We have considered the statutory requirements regarding the preparation of an actuarial valuation and funding certificate. There are also regulations which require the actuary to disregard certain scheme investments. It is now proposed to examine these restrictions in the context of the funding certificate and valuation. They are also reviewed in the context of investment elsewhere.[66]

9.45 One of the basic tenets of a prudent investment strategy is to diversify investments. It would obviously be a dangerous course of action to invest the whole of a pension fund in one particular stock. This would be a case of "putting all the eggs in one basket". Excessive investment in a specific asset is referred to as concentration of investment. Similar concerns arise in connection with the investment of part or the whole of the pension fund in the sponsoring employer itself. This is referred to as self-investment and could take the form of (for example) an acquisition by the pension fund of a property with a lease back to the company, a direct equity investment in the employer or a loan (whether secured or unsecured) by the fund to the employer. These terms are defined in regulations under Part IV of the Pensions Act.

9.46 There are certain restrictions placed indirectly upon schemes to which Part IV of the Pensions Act applies. If there is self-investment or concentration of investment above a specified percentage of the resources of the scheme, the actuary must exclude the excess over that specified percentage from assets to be taken into account in preparing the funding certificate.[67] This is illustrated in Example 9.1. It should be noted, however, that the legislation does not prohibit either concentration of investment or self-investment.

Example 9.1

As at 1 January 1998, the Self-Reliant Ltd. Pension Scheme has sufficient resources to meet its liabilities under the funding standard (that is, it is 100 per cent funded) when taking into account all resources of the scheme, including self-investment. However, the actuary warns the trustees that there is significant self-investment in the sponsoring employer and advises that he must exclude 5 per cent of the resources of

---

[66] See para. 10.57 et seq.

[67] Article 5 of the Funding Standard Regulations made pursuant to s.47 of the Pensions Act.

the scheme that are attributable to self-investment. The fund is therefore regarded as being only 95 per cent funded and does not satisfy the funding standard.[68]

9.47 The previous paragraph refers to a specified percentage. The maximum permitted self-investment that can be taken into account by the actuary after 30 June 1997 is 5 per cent of the resources of the scheme. Between 31 December 1993 and 30 June 1997, a transitional percentage of 10 per cent applies. However, the rate remains at 20 per cent at all times for schemes with not more than 12 active members, all of whom are trustees. As for concentration of investment, the maximum percentage that can be taken into account after 31 December 2000 is 10 per cent of the resources of the scheme. The transitional provisions in this case are as follows: for actuarial funding certificates with an effective date after 31 December 1993 but on or before 30 June 1997 the maximum percentage is 20 per cent, and for schemes with an actuarial funding certificate after 30 June 1997 but on or before 31 December 2000 the maximum percentage is 15 per cent. Unlike with self-investment, there is no special treatment for certain small schemes.

Example 9.2

The Self-Reliant Ltd. Pension Scheme is 100 per cent funded when taking into account all resources of the scheme. The actuary prepares a funding certificate with an effective date of 1 April 1997. The fund is valued at £10 million. 30 per cent of the fund (i.e. £3 million) is invested in shares in one of the Irish Banks. As there is concentration of investment in excess of 20 per cent of the resources of the scheme (the specified percentage applying at the time), the regulations limit the amount of the shares that can be included by the actuary for valuation purposes to 20 per cent (i.e. £2 million). £1 million is therefore excluded from the valuation and the fund is deemed to have a value of only £9 million for funding- standard purposes.

9.48 Concentration of investment is defined in the Funding Standard Regulations as being investment exceeding the stated percentage in any one asset other than any of the following:

1. Government Securities
2. Insurance Policies

---

[68] Funding Standard Regulations Article 5.

3. Contracts of Assurance
4. Managed Funds
5. Unit Trusts
6. Cash Deposits with authorised deposit-taking institutions.[69]

9.49 Self-investment is a somewhat more complex definition and it has anti-avoidance provisions to prevent any indirect ways around the self-investment rule. Self-investment means:

> investment of all or part of the resources of the scheme in the business of any one or more of the following persons
>
> (i) the employer of any person employed in the relevant employment,
>
> (ii) an affiliate of the employer of any person employed in the relevant employment,
>
> (iii) any director or shadow director (within the meaning of section 27 of the Companies Act, 1963) of the employer or of an affiliate, or of an associate of any such director or shadow director

An affiliate is defined as being a holding, subsidiary or sister company. An associate of the director or shadow director is defined to comprise the person's spouse, parent, brother, sister or minor child, the trustees of certain trusts, a partner of the person or a body corporate which is controlled by the person.[70] Specific examples which are deemed to be self-investment are also listed in the definition as follows:

1. The occupation, use or letting of land
2. Other property used for the business
3. Loans
4. Moneys due to the scheme from the employer, an affiliate or director/shadow director as in (i), (ii) and (iii) of the definition
5. Shares or other securities of the employer (if it is a company).

9.50 Interestingly, however, investment in land or buildings used for business is not deemed to be self-investment where there is a letting

---

[69] Article 3.

[70] Article 3.

at full market value and there is an independent valuation. The asset must be taken into account on the lower of vacant possession basis and its value subject to the letting.[71] The investment may, however, have to be restricted for valuation purposes, nonetheless, on the grounds of concentration of investment.[72]

FUNDING PROPOSALS

9.51 Although schemes have a 10 year period within which to rectify any funding deficiency in respect of pre-1991 benefits, the liabilities in respect of post-1991 benefits are required to be maintained at 100 per cent. Furthermore, the funding position of schemes with pre-1991 liabilities cannot drop below the percentage certified by the actuary in the first actuarial funding certificate. There will undoubtedly be cases where there is a funding deficiency in respect of post-1991 benefits, or where the specified percentage of pre-1991 liabilities drops below the certified percentage. The Pensions Act anticipates this in section 49. The actuarial funding certificate must state that the scheme either satisfies or does not satisfy the funding standard.[73] If the scheme does not satisfy the funding standard and a certificate has been submitted by the trustees to that effect under section 43, the trustees must submit to the Board a proposal (referred to as a "funding proposal").[74] The funding proposal must be submitted to the Board with the funding certificate.

9.52 The funding proposal must be designed to ensure that, in the opinion of the actuary, the scheme could reasonably be expected to satisfy the funding standard at the effective date of the next actuarial funding certificate.[75] As funding certificates must be prepared not later than at three-and-a-half year intervals, this gives the trustees a maximum of three and a half years to rectify any funding deficiency. Accompanying the funding proposal must be a certificate by the actuary that the proposal can be reasonably expected to satisfy the fund-

---

71 Article 3

72 It may also be forbidden by the Revenue, if it is a small self-administered scheme — see para. 6.81.

73 Funding Standard Regulations Article 4 and Schedules A and B.

74 s.49(1).

75 s.49(1)(a).

ing standard.[76] The proposal must also be signed by or on behalf of the trustees and the employer signifying agreement to the proposal, and must be submitted by the trustees with the actuarial funding certificate.[77] This means that the funding proposal must be furnished to the Board at the same time as the actuarial funding certificate that confirms that the scheme does not satisfy the funding standard. The Board is given discretion to modify any of these requirements where it considers it necessary or appropriate.[78]

9.53 The Board can prosecute the trustees under section 3 of the Pensions Act for failure to submit a funding certificate or, where appropriate, a funding proposal, and it is its policy to do so. In addition, the Board is empowered to direct the trustees to reduce benefits (i.e. liabilities) under the scheme in these circumstances.[79] The objective is to reduce benefits to such an extent that the assets of the scheme are sufficient to meet the reduced liabilities. The mere threat of taking such action may be sufficient to persuade the trustees and the employer to issue a funding certificate or funding proposal as appropriate. The trustees can, however, often be in a difficult position. To prepare a valuation, the actuary needs up-to-date data on the scheme members and usually requires finalised scheme accounts. The employer may not have given this information to the trustees, despite requests to do so.[80]

9.54 The consequences of not complying with these requirements are serious. First, the trustees may be exposed to a claim for breach of trust by the members, on the ground that any reduction in benefits is as a consequence of a failure by the trustees to comply with the requirements of Part IV. Secondly, the employer may have an independent obligation under the employment contract to pay the higher benefits to members, and yet the scheme is now providing reduced

---

76 Guidance Note 3A (ROI) of the Society of Actuaries in Ireland "Funding Proposal under the Pensions Act, 1990 (as amended)" sets out the guidance for any actuary certifying that a funding proposal meets the requirements of the Pensions Act, 1990.

77 s.49(2) as amended by s.18(a) of the Pensions (Amendment) Act, 1996.

78 s.49(3).

79 s.50.

80 And despite s.54(4) which requires the employer to furnish such information as the actuary may reasonably require.

benefits. This could expose the employer to an action for breach of contract although, until such time as the member actually reaches retirement, it is only an anticipated loss.

9.55 A direction by the Board to reduce benefits is by way of a notice in writing to the trustees. Once the notice has issued, there is no provision which allows the Board to withdraw it. Nor does the Act specify under what circumstances the trustees can at a future point increase the benefits again when they have satisfied the funding requirements. In the absence of statutory provision, it would seem that the trustees must look to their powers of amendment under the pension scheme to increase benefits upwards again. Before doing so, the trustees would need to be satisfied that the scheme will be in a position to meet the funding standard at the date of the next actuarial funding certificate.

9.56 The reduction must be such that the funding standard will be satisfied directly after the reduction has taken place.[81] The actuary in this regard would be one retained by the trustees, not by the Pensions Board. The trustees must then take such measures as may be necessary to reduce benefits, and must notify the members of the reduction in benefits within a period of two months, or such longer period as the Board considers appropriate, and then within a further period of one month must submit to the Board details of the reduction, including copies of notifications issued to members and a new actuarial funding certificate which certifies at the date of reduction of benefits that the scheme then satisfies the funding standard.[82]

9.57 The reduction in benefits involves a change in the basis of the pension scheme, which may not be permitted under the rules of the scheme. However, the provisions of Part IV and of any regulations made under that Part override any rule of the scheme to the extent that the rules conflict with those provisions. The direction to reduce benefits also overrides preservation calculations under Part III and the calculation of benefit for priority purposes under Part IV.[83] The requirement of the trustees to reduce benefits would appear to fall within the overriding terms of Part IV. It would nonetheless be of

---

81 s.50(2) as amended by s.19(a) of the Pensions (Amendment) Act, 1996.

82 s.50(3) as amended by s.19(b) of the Pensions (Amendment) Act, 1996.

83 s.50(2) as amended by s.19(a) of the Pensions (Amendment) Act, 1996.

additional comfort to the trustees if the amendment power under the rules of the scheme specifically gave the trustees a unilateral right to amend the rules to effect a reduction in benefits consequent upon a direction under section 50.

OTHER SCHEMES

External Schemes

9.58 The requirements of Part IV of the Pensions Act are modified with respect to external schemes with Irish resident members. An "external scheme" means a scheme established under the law of a country other than the State.[84] Regulations have been made which permit the first funding certificate of an external scheme to have a later effective date than that otherwise permitted under section 43 of the Pensions Act.[85]

9.59 The latest date which may be chosen as the effective date of the first actuarial funding certificate of an external scheme depends upon when the scheme was established.

1. If it commenced prior to 1 July 1991, the effective date should be no later than 31 December 1994.
2. If it commenced on or after 1 July 1991, the effective date should be no later than three and a half years after the commencement of the scheme.

The Pensions Board has power, on application to it, to permit a later effective date to be chosen, where the date is no later than 1 January 1998 and the time extension is reasonable and not contrary to the interests of the members of the scheme.[86]

9.60 Regulations have also been made which modify the funding standard (as well as other parts of the Pensions Act) with respect to

---

[84] s.2(1) of the Pensions Act — definition inserted by s.42(b) of the Social Welfare Act, 1993.

[85] Art. 7(2) of the Funding Standard Regulations as substituted by Art. 3 of the Occupational Pension Schemes (Funding Standard) (Amendment) Regulations, 1995 (SI No 273 of 1995).

[86] *Ibid.*

certain United Kingdom schemes.[87] These regulations, known as the External Scheme Regulations, apply to any external scheme which is governed by the law of England and Wales or of Scotland or Northern Ireland and is managed and controlled in the United Kingdom. In order to confer accountability on a person in the State, the functions of the trustees of a UK scheme are deemed to be conferred also on any employer of the scheme's Irish members.[88]

9.61 Part IV of the Act and the Third Schedule, together with the Funding Standard Regulations, apply to UK schemes with certain modifications.[89] The first funding certificate in respect of an effective date prior to 1 January 1995 is not required to be submitted to the Pensions Board until at the latest nine months after 1 January 1995. The funding standard is also modified so that only benefits in respect of the Irish members need to be taken into account. Irish benefits are benefits which have been accrued by a member in respect of a period of service during which contributions were payable under the Irish Social Welfare Acts or would be payable but for the under-16 or over-66-year age condition relating to contributions under those Acts. Interestingly, although the regulations set out what liabilities must be taken into account, they do not specify what assets are to be included in the valuation — presumably, it should only be assets relating to the Irish members. However, if the Irish part of the scheme is part of a larger UK scheme, it can be expected that the total assets of the scheme will substantially exceed the liabilities with respect to Irish members. The Regulations do not specifically address this point.

9.62 The actuarial funding certificate required under Part IV of the Pensions Act for UK schemes is slightly different from that for Irish schemes, but the differences are not material.[90]

9.63 No regulations have been made modifying the funding standard with respect to any schemes of any other country. If any other foreign scheme providing benefits for members in Ireland has been approved

---

[87] Occupational Pension Schemes (External Schemes) (United Kingdom) Regulations, 1994 (SI No 238 of 1994) as empowered by s.5 and 5(A) of the Pensions Act

[88] Art. 3

[89] Art. 5

[90] See Schedules A and B of the External Scheme Regulations.

by the Revenue Commissioners here, or (where approval is under consideration) otherwise satisfies the definition of "occupational pension scheme", it is subject to the full rigours of the Pensions Act, except with regard to the effective date of the first certificate.

Public Sector Schemes

9.64 The majority of public sector schemes (and many semi-state schemes) are unfunded. This means that the State (or in the case of the semi-state scheme, the semi-state company) pays out benefits as and when they fall due and does not fund in advance to meet pension scheme liabilities. These schemes are therefore operated upon a pay-as-you-go basis. Given that they are unfunded, it makes sense that the funding standard does not apply to them, as those schemes would not be capable of meeting the funding standard.

9.65 The Minister for Social Welfare may make regulations with the consent of the Minister for Finance which exempt such schemes from the requirements of Part IV and the Third Schedule. The condition that must be met before the Minister is empowered to exempt a scheme is that the benefits are paid in whole or in part out of moneys provided from the Central Fund or by the Oireachtas. Schemes which are not financed in this way cannot be exempted.[91] There are currently 78 schemes, together with spouses' and children's schemes relating to those schemes, which have been excluded from the provisions of Part IV.[92]

9.66 Interestingly, the list of 78 schemes is not identical to the equivalent list of schemes excluded from the requirements of Part III of the Pensions Act (i.e. preserved benefits). This means that some schemes are excluded from the requirements of Part III to provide preserved benefits but are not excluded from the funding standard under Part IV, and vice versa.

Defined Contribution Schemes

9.67 The rules of the typical defined contribution scheme contain a promise by the member and the employer to contribute a set amount

---

91 s.52(1).

92 Funding Standard Regulations Article 6 and Schedule C.

to the pension scheme.[93] The member's contribution will be paid into the scheme by the employer at source under the net pay arrangement[94] and the employer will pay its contribution at periodic intervals.

9.68 As the liabilities are known in advance, actuarial valuations are not required for defined contribution schemes. It would be dangerous, however, to assume that the actuary has no role to play in such a scheme. Defined contribution schemes are of recent origin and have become increasingly popular because of their relative simplicity and lower administration costs. However, it can be supposed that members would like to receive a reasonable level of pension at retirement. It is therefore appropriate for an actuary to be retained from time to time to estimate whether the agreed contributions are sufficient to provide reasonable benefits. If not, contribution rates may need to be revised.

9.69 Actuarial calculations may be required in a defined contribution scheme to ensure that members' benefits are unlikely in the future, based on a set contribution rate, to exceed limits imposed by the Revenue Commissioners on benefits.[95] Also, when a member of a defined contribution scheme reaches retirement, the money standing to the member's credit is converted into income (that is, pension) by purchasing an annuity. Annuities are sold by life offices and it is the actuaries of the life offices who determine the annuity rates in the market.

9.70 Actuarial valuations are necessary in target benefit schemes and small self-administered schemes. A target benefit scheme[96] is a defined contribution scheme in which the sponsoring employer indicates, but does not guarantee, that employer contributions will be made to the pension scheme to provide a target benefit based on a proportion of the members' final salary. Here, the role of the actuary is particularly important in calculating a rate at which the employer intends to fund the scheme in order to provide target benefits. Actuarial valuations are required in small self-administered schemes,

---

93 An exception is a stand-alone AVC scheme, which will only involve member contributions.

94 See para. 6.39.

95 See Chapter 7.

96 On which, see para. 2.12.

whether defined benefit or defined contribution, and valuations must be supplied to the Revenue Commissioners every three years.[97]

OTHER ACTUARIAL MATTERS

Winding up

9.71 The actuary has a key role in the winding-up of a defined benefit scheme. The resources of the scheme must be applied in discharging the liabilities of the scheme in a pre-determined order of priority specified by section 48 of the Pensions Act. This requires the actuary to calculate the actuarial value of the liabilities in accordance with the Act, having regard to such financial or other assumptions as the actuary considers appropriate.[98] The actuary will be called upon by the trustees, in particular, to advise them with regard to any surplus or deficit that arises on a winding-up. This matter is examined elsewhere.[99]

Transfer Values

9.72 Part III of the Pensions Act has established a legal framework for the portability of pensions, which enables pension scheme members (in prescribed circumstances) to transfer their benefits to the scheme of a new employer. A member's benefits must be converted into a lump sum in order to effect the transfer. In a defined benefit scheme this requires the actuary to calculate the actuarial value of the member's scheme benefits on leaving the former employer's scheme. The Society of Actuaries in Ireland has issued guidance notes on the basis of calculating individual transfer values, having regard to the requirements of the Pensions Act.[100] This is examined further in a later chapter.[101]

---

97 See para. 6.82.

98 s.46(2).

99 See Chapter 17.

100 GN 11 (ROI) "Retirement Benefit Schemes Transfer Values", September 1993.

101 See Chapter 12.

Corporate Acquisitions

9.73 In the field of corporate acquisitions, the company being acquired (the target) will usually be the subject of a due diligence enquiry by the purchasing company.[102] Often in the past, and unfortunately sometimes in the present also, the liability to provide pensions for employees of the target was frequently ignored by the purchaser. If the liabilities of a pension scheme to provide benefits greatly outweigh the assets, the scheme is regarded as being underfunded. A purchasing company that does not undertake a due diligence enquiry in relation to pension matters runs the risk of becoming liable to meet the deficit of the underfunded scheme. This could make what was considered a highly desirable acquisition, a significant loss-making one. To avoid this, actuaries are employed to assess the current funding position of the target's pension scheme and to consider the adequacy of any warranties provided by the target relating to pension provision.

Insuring Risks

9.74 Schemes which provide a death in service lump sum benefit or a spouse's pension payable on death in service normally insure the risk of providing the benefit with an insurance company. In this way, the cost of providing these risk benefits is reasonably certain, as it is dependent on the premiums charged by the insurance company. The larger the scheme, however, the more cost-effective it may be for the scheme itself to bear the risk of paying a death benefit out of the scheme's resources, rather than paying premiums to an insurance company. Alternatively, the risks may be partly insured with an insurance company and in part carried by the pension scheme. Actuarial advice is essential in determining whether this transfer of risk to the fund is advisable, as the actuary will need to consider the risk of a death benefit claim arising and the ability of the fund to meet the cost of the benefit out of its resources.[103]

9.75 The Pensions Act imposes no regulatory restrictions on insuring benefits. This is an interesting omission. Where the fund bears the risk, rather than it being insured, its solvency could be adversely affected by one or more death claims. However, the actuary is not re-

---

[102] On acquisitions in general, see Chapter 18.

[103] On insuring pension scheme risks, see generally Chapter 11.

quired to take this factor into account in the funding standard, but in practice will have regard to it in striking a funding rate.

Investments

9.76 The actuary will advise on the appropriate mix of investments in the pension scheme. To give a simple example of how this might arise, a scheme with a very young membership can afford to invest a significantly high proportion of the fund in equities. Equities are a relatively volatile form of investment but as the liability to provide benefits for young members will not have to be met for a long time in the future, the scheme can afford to take the risk of short-term fluctuations. On the other hand, pension scheme members who are close to retirement might be adversely affected by a sharp downturn in the market, and so it may not be appropriate to have a high proportion of assets in a volatile investment category such as equities. Accordingly, a lower risk strategy may be appropriate, with greater investment in gilts and index-linked securities. The actuary can advise on the appropriate mix of assets to match the liability profile of a pension scheme.[104]

---

[104] On the actuary's role in investment strategy, see: See Lee, E.M. (1986): *An Introduction to Pension Schemes*, Institute of Actuaries and Faculty of Actuaries in Scotland, Chapter 20. On investment, see Chapter 10.

10

INVESTMENT

INTRODUCTION

10.1 The trustees of a pension scheme, the employer and the members all have an interest in how a pension scheme fund is invested. In defined benefit schemes, the level of benefits is promised in advance. It is not based on the value of the fund. Nonetheless, a poor investment return is of concern to the members as it could affect the funding position of the scheme and, consequently, the security of benefits. As most defined benefit schemes are balance-of-cost schemes,[1] the employer ultimately bears the risk of investment performance, as poor investment return over a protracted period will almost certainly mean a higher cost of funding the scheme for the employer. In contrast, in a defined contribution scheme it is the members who bear the risk of investment performance, as the benefits ultimately payable derive solely from the value of the fund at retirement. In this regard, the value of the fund is influenced by two factors: contributions paid into the scheme and the investment return on the fund.

10.2 This chapter examines the powers and duties of the trustees of occupational pension schemes regarding the investment of pension fund assets. It deals with theories of portfolio management only in passing, as the Courts are not concerned with examining or reviewing such theories.[2] Rather, the Courts and legislation lay down certain fundamental principles which a pension scheme trustee must follow.[3]

---

1 That is, the members pay a fixed contribution and the employer pays the balance sufficient to fund for the benefits under the scheme.

2 On portfolio management and investment generally, see Frost, A.J. and Hager, D.P. (1986): *A General Introduction to Institutional Investment*, London: Heinemann. See also Lawry, R.A.C. (1982): *The Active Role of the Pension Scheme Trustee* Vol. 25 Journal of the Institute of Actuaries Students' Society 113; Escolme, B., Hudson, D. and Greenwood, P. (1991):

10.3 The first part of this chapter focuses on the ways in which the trustees can invest the pension fund. The trustees can either invest directly in assets such as equities and government stock or they can participate with other pension schemes in pooled-investment arrangements such as unitised funds and deferred annuities. The chapter will then examine the principal investment duties of the trustees, particularly having regard to the statutory investment duty imposed by section 59 of the Pensions Act and the statutory restrictions on certain types of investments. Generally, trustees are not experts on pension fund investment and almost always delegate their investment duties to a professional investment manager. The legal issues concerning delegation of investment duties are considered towards the end of the chapter, as are the protections afforded to the trustees in this context. The final section examines buy-out bonds and annuities which are individual policies established to secure a member's benefit entitlements or provide for their investment separately from the pension scheme.

10.4 Before discussing the modes of pension scheme investment, it is appropriate to outline some of the economic factors which influence pension fund investment. There are three factors which particularly influence the investment strategy of Irish pension schemes: the size of pension funds, the overall size of the Irish equity market and foreign exchange risk. Each of these is now considered in turn.

10.5 Irish pension funds are relatively small by the standards of other countries that have substantial private pension provision. Total funds of occupational pension schemes under management in Ireland amount to approximately £16.3 billion.[4] In contrast, total UK funds amount to approximately £522 billion sterling. Accordingly, quite a high proportion of Irish pension schemes are invested in unitised funds or insurance policies, as these are more suitable to smaller-sized pension schemes.

Hosking's Pension Schemes and Retirement Benefits, 6th Ed, London: Sweet & Maxwell.

3 See below, and generally in relation to the UK law of pension fund investment: Quarrell, J.J. (1990): *The Law of Pension Fund Investment*, London: Butterworths; Inglis-Jones, N. (1989): *The Law of Occupational Pension Schemes*, London: Sweet & Maxwell, Chapter 8; Ellison, R. (1987): *Pensions Law and Practice* London: FT Law & Tax, Chapter 9.

4 IAPF Investment Survey, 1995.

10.6 Ireland's domestic equity market is also modest by international standards. There are relatively few quoted Irish companies and this militates against pension funds achieving a diverse spread of Irish equity investments. This was pointed out in a recent IAPF report:

> In the absence of substantial companies becoming quoted on the stock exchange and/or mechanisms being provided for greater participation by pension funds in infrastructural development, it is unlikely, given the need for prudent diversification, that the percentage of domestic assets in Irish pension fund portfolios can be greatly increased.[5]

The main consequence of this is that Irish pension schemes must look abroad to obtain suitable equity investments. In this regard, more than one-third of total pension fund assets are in foreign equities.[6]

FIGURE 10.1: DISTRIBUTION OF IRISH PENSION FUND ASSETS OVER THE VARIOUS INVESTMENT VEHICLES AT END 1995

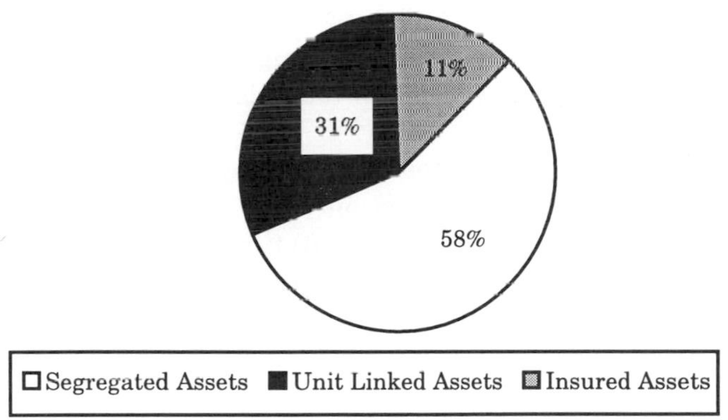

Source: IAPF Investment Survey, 1995.

10.7 The third factor is foreign exchange risk. Foreign investments are denominated in foreign currencies, and yet the benefits under the pension scheme are payable in Irish Pounds. Pension schemes are therefore subject to the fluctuations of exchange rates between Irish

---

5 Walsh, M. and Murray, J. (1993): *Pension Fund Investment*, Dublin: IAPF: p. 5.

6 IAPF Investment Survey, 1995.

Pounds and the foreign currencies concerned.[7] In some instances, the investment manager hedges this risk by engaging in foreign-currency hedging transactions.

MODES OF INVESTMENT

10.8 The purpose of all forms of pension fund investment is to accumulate money in order to pay benefits when they become due. There are two principal approaches to achieving this objective: segregated investment and pooled investment. These approaches can best be distinguished by determining whether the scheme has identifiable assets directly held. If there are identifiable assets, such as stocks, shares or property, investment is described as being on a segregated basis. Otherwise, there is some form of pooling of investments with other pension schemes.

10.9 Segregated investment is undertaken on behalf of pension scheme trustees by professional investment managers, such as banks, stockbrokers or life offices. Pooled-investment facilities are provided primarily by banks and life offices, although there are unit trusts operating independently of the banks which also offer these facilities.[8]

10.10 Smaller pension schemes do not enjoy the economies of scale of larger funds. Accordingly, it is only the larger pension schemes (typically in excess of at least £6 million) that will tend to be invested (either partially or wholly) on a segregated basis.[9] The smaller scheme cannot achieve a sufficiently diverse spread of investments to minimise the risk of poor performance in individual stocks or markets. In addition, the costs of acquisition and disposal of assets in

---

7 Since 1 January 1992, exchange controls have for all practical purposes been removed.

8 An example of this is the Irish Pension Fund Property Unit Trust (IPFPUT) which is a private unit trust that offers units in its fund to pension funds and charities interested solely in investment in property. There are also UCITS. A UCITS is an Undertaking for Collective Investment in Transferable Securities. UCITS are authorised in Ireland under the European Communities (Undertakings for Collective Investment in Transferable Securities) Regulations, 1989 (SI No 78 of 1989) and are regulated by the Central Bank.

9 A notable exception is the small self-administered scheme, where the proprietary member wants to participate in direct investment — see para. 6.77 et seq.

smaller schemes can be prohibitive relative to the size of the fund. Certain investment vehicles seek to overcome these drawbacks by giving pension schemes the opportunity to pool resources in order to enjoy the economies of scale of larger funds. The manager of the pooled fund invests assets from each of the pension schemes that participate in the fund and passes on the investment return (or, in some cases, the loss) to each scheme in the manner prescribed by the particular pooled fund. The two principal types of pooled investment are insurance policies and unit-linked schemes.

Segregated Investment

10.11 As mentioned earlier, in a segregated fund the trustees invest directly in stocks, shares and other assets. It is not just banks and life offices that undertake investment management services of this kind. Stockbrokers also provide this service, as do some other financial institutions.[10]

10.12 With a segregated fund, the trustees typically give the investment manager discretionary control over the investment of the fund. In some cases, investment is fully discretionary; in others, the trustees impose restrictions on the manager. For example, the investment manager may be required to invest no more than a specified percentage of the fund in foreign equities, or may be restricted to holding not more than a specified percentage of the fund in any one asset. The scheme assets will usually be held by a custodian, such as a nominee subsidiary of the manager.[11] The investment manager's legal relationship with the trustees should be set out in a formal investment management agreement.[12]

Pooled Investment — Insurance Policies

10.13 In this century, pension fund investment developed through insurance products such as endowment policies and deferred annuities. Today, there are many different types of insurance product, but what they all have in common is that they offer either an underlying guarantee or the smoothing of investment return, or a combination of

---

[10] An example of other financial institutions would be the ESB, which has its own fund-management subsidiary to undertake investment both for the ESB pension fund and for other funds.

[11] Custodians are considered later — see para. 10.72 et seq.

[12] Investment management agreements are examined at para. 10.69 et seq.

both. This is an attractive option for those trustees (particularly trustees of small schemes) who wish to avoid the volatility of the stock markets. Life offices charge for this stability, and trustees must assess whether it is appropriate in any given case. The unit-linked scheme generally offers no such guarantee or smoothed performance, in that the returns are linked directly to fluctuations in market prices of the underlying assets.[13]

10.14 Deferred annuity and with-profit policies are older types of investment products which have traditionally been offered by life offices. These have largely been superseded by unit-linked policies and deposit administration contracts, but deferred annuities are still purchased to secure the payment of benefits for employees who leave service before retirement.[14]

10.15 In a deferred annuity policy, the insurer guarantees that a set amount of cash or of pension will be available at retirement. The guaranteed cash or pension depends upon the member's age and the premium paid. The guarantee is more modest in a with-profit deferred annuity policy, but is supplemented by an annual bonus declared by the life office out of any surplus disclosed in its actuarial valuations and usually also by a terminal bonus on maturity. Once the annual bonus has been declared, it cannot be taken away from the pension scheme, and each year that an annual bonus is declared, it is added to the previous one. The objective is that the fund should steadily build up over the investment period. However, the terminal bonus may represent a substantial part of the overall return on the policy. This introduces a degree of volatility at maturity. It also results in uncertainty as the terminal bonus is discretionary.[15]

10.16 The premiums paid to the life office by the trustees are invested by the life office in investments such as shares, government stock, foreign securities and property, and the scheme is indirectly (not directly) linked to investment return or loss regarding the underlying investment performance. In good years, where there is a high investment return, the life office declares a bonus in respect of its

---

[13] Unit-linked funds are examined separately at para. 10.20 et seq.

[14] See para. 10.88.

[15] A hybrid with-profit policy, known as a unitised with-profit policy, is considered below, at para. 10.23.

with-profit policies, but the bonus will most likely be less than the investment return that year. The balance will be retained by the life office as reserves for future years. Conversely, in a year of bad investment return, the life office will usually draw on reserves built up in good years to declare a bonus. The objective is to provide a relatively smooth return on investment by eliminating the sharp rises and falls in the investment market. This is a conservative form of investment which has been very popular with pension scheme trustees in the past. However, there are two main drawbacks to with-profit polices:

1. Life offices do not set out the basis upon which they calculate the bonus and there is therefore lack of transparency with regard to investment return and the costs charged by the life office.
2. Bonuses are at the discretion of the life office actuary. The life office is under no obligation to declare a bonus. In times of prolonged poor investment return, the life office may decide to reduce or not to declare annual bonuses.

10.17 Deposit administration contracts operate to some extent on a similar basis to bank or building society accounts. Premiums are paid by the trustees and, after life-office charges and expenses, an investment dividend (interest) is declared. Sometimes a minimum return is guaranteed. For example, if the guaranteed return is 3 per cent and the underlying return on investments is only 2 per cent, the life office will still declare a 3 per cent dividend. If the return is 5 per cent, the life office may (but is not obliged to) declare a dividend of 5 per cent less charges. Like with-profit policies, the life office will seek to smooth the investment return by holding reserves in good years and drawing on reserves in poor investment years.[16]

10.18 A feature contained in almost all policies is the guaranteed annuity rate at retirement. Annuity rates are considered below.[17] Policies guarantee that cash will be exchanged for pension at a guaranteed rate at retirement. Almost invariably, there is also an open-market option which permits the trustees to purchase an annuity from another life office if the latter's rates are more favourable. In the

---

[16] See generally, Iqbal, M. (1979): *Deposit Administration*, Vol. 23 Journal of the Institute of Actuaries Students' Society, 43.

[17] See para. 10.85.

past, many life offices restricted trustees to purchasing an annuity from that life office, effectively preventing access to the open annuity market. This restriction is, generally, not found in modern policies.

10.19 Special conditions apply when there is an early surrender of the policy before benefits have matured. This may arise where investments are being switched to a new investment medium or where the scheme is being wound up and benefits for members are secured by a bond with another life office. There are usually penalties built into life-office policies in these circumstances, which may significantly reduce the expected value of the fund.[18]

Pooled Investment — Unit-Linked Fund

10.20 A unit-linked fund is quite different from a with-profit policy or deposit administration contract. There are no guarantees in a unit-linked fund. Unit-linked funds are established either by life offices or investment banks.[19] Unit-linked funds operated by life offices are regulated under the Insurance Acts 1909–1989. Unit-linked funds established by investment banks are governed by trust law and are regulated by the Revenue Commissioners. The institution (whether life office or investment bank) establishes an investment fund and invests contributions from the trustees of various pension schemes in a pooled investment fund. The institution then calculates the unit price by reference to the value of the underlying investments.

10.21 In a unitised fund established by an investment bank, the investment return on the underlying investments is directly linked to the value of units. In contrast, a unit-linked fund established by a life office involves only a notional linking between the underlying fund and the units. This is generally emphasised in the unit-linked policy. In practice, however, the difference between the two investment media is not one of substance. In each case, the institution receives money from the various pension schemes that participate in the fund and invests the money in a particular fund. No particular asset belongs to any one pension scheme. Instead, the institution sells units to the trustees which represent the extent of the trustees' participa-

---

18 For example, with-profit policies generally incorporate a terminal bonus (which may be substantial). The terminal bonus may be withheld on early termination.

19 Also, unit trusts independent of the banks and life offices can be established — see para. 10.9 and fn 8.

tion in the fund. An illustration of how this operates (in a very simplified format) is set out in Example 10.1. The value of the underlying investments fluctuates and therefore the institution recalculates the unit price on a periodic basis — usually every month, but sometimes daily. It can be seen therefore that the trustees take the full risk of market movements — there is no smoothing of investment return as in the case of a with-profit fund.

Example 10.1

A Life office operates an exempt unit-linked pension fund which currently comprises assets worth £1 million. The unit price, which in this case is calculated monthly, is fixed as follows:

Realisable value of fund assets	*£1,000,000*
Less	
*Monthly Management Charge**	*(£625)*
Adjusted Value	*£999,375*
*Number of Units issued***	*575,238*

The Bid Price of each unit (the price at which the life office buys back units) is calculated by dividing the value of the fund by the number of units i.e.

$$£999{,}375 \div 575{,}238 = £1.74$$

The Offer Price (the price at which the life office sells units) is the Bid Price increased so that the Bid Price is a specified percentage lower than the Offer Price. In this example, the difference is 5 per cent or in other words there is a 5 per cent bid / offer spread calculated as follows:

$$£1.74 \times \frac{100}{100-5} = £1.83$$

Notes:

* *An annual management charge of 0.75 per cent has been assumed.*

** *The number of units has been chosen arbitrarily.*

10.22 Also built into the unit price are the life office's or investment bank's charges for managing the pension fund. There may also be as much as a 5 per cent differential between the price at which the life office sells units to the trustees and the price at which it buys these back. This is referred to as the "bid/offer spread". Also, in the case of life-office funds, the costs of setting up the policy at the outset are often met by issuing what are called "initial units". Initial units have a considerably lower value than ordinary units known as "premium units". If the policy is held to full term, the initial units are converted to premium units, but if the policy is surrendered early, initial units are not converted but are surrendered at the discounted price.

10.23 Another type of investment policy sometimes provided by life offices is a hybrid of the with-profit policy and the unit-linked policy. It is referred to as a unitised with-profit policy. Bonuses are declared with reference to the unit price and, once declared, are guaranteed.

10.24 One key distinguishing factor between unit-linked funds of the banks and life assurance unit-linked funds is that the life office, in addition to managing the investments, often undertakes the administration of the pension scheme, produces pension scheme documentation and undertakes regulatory compliance. The charges for this are usually built into the price of the units. Also, insurance companies generally, if requested, remunerate insurance intermediaries on a commission basis and the commission is part of the costs which the life office seeks to recoup by issuing initial units. In general, with regard to pension funds, banks do not remunerate intermediaries by way of commission and do not issue initial units. They do, however, recoup management costs from the bid-offer spread.

10.25 Many unit-linked funds will typically consist of a balance of Irish equities, foreign equities, property, government stock, index-linked securities and cash. These are often called managed funds. There are also specialised funds which are not balanced in nature. Examples are: equity funds, property funds and cash funds. When a fund reaches a certain size, the trustees can consider (on taking appropriate professional advice) modifying their investment strategy by switching out of a managed fund to a selection of specialised unit-linked funds. This is referred to as sector fund investment. For example, the trustees may decide to allocate 20 per cent of the pension fund to a cash fund, 10 per cent to a property fund, 30 per cent to an Irish equity fund and 40 per cent to a foreign equities fund. The key difference between this sectored approach and that of a managed fund is that, in the former, the trustees can, if they so desire, have control over the allocation of the fund to various sectors. In a managed fund, this is a decision for the investment manager alone.

FIGURE: 10.2: COMPARISON OF UNITISED AND SEGREGATED FUNDS

Unitised Pension Fund	Segregated Portfolio
• Communication tends to be of a general nature with fund manager responsible for a number of schemes. • Meetings are normally half-yearly.	• Individual responsibility by investment manager is assigned to each scheme. • Better and more specific communication with Trustees. • Meetings are usually quarterly.
• Administrative simplicity.	• More complex administration e.g. contract notes have to be maintained and dividends checked.
• A wide spread of investments across companies and territories.	• A narrower spread of investments unless the scheme is very large.
• Trustees have a limited control of investment sector choice and no influence on individual stock selection.	• Trustees'/Actuary's requirements to match liabilities and stock selection can be accommodated.
• The scheme does not own the underlying assets.	• Investments are owned directly by the scheme.
• Unit pricing is determined by investment manager.	• Stock prices are determined solely by market forces.
• Investment holdings may be diluted by cash flow to unit funds from other pension schemes.	• Assets are independent of other pension schemes.
• Unit manager may tend to focus on short-term price performance.	• Longer-term investment objectives may be pursued with less constraint from short-term performance measurement.
• Trustees are not advised of underlying investment transactions.	• All stock transactions are disclosed to the trustees.
• The total size of funds under management presents problems for altering portfolio mix.	• Problems of size much reduced.
• Investment management charges recouped by the bid/offer differential on units.	• There is no bid/offer differential but there are management fees. Potential for lower investment management charges. Possibly higher cost due to monitoring investment and more frequent meetings.
• In the event of a change of fund manager, either units will be sold (with a bid/offer difference) or a transfer could be negotiated of the underlying assets with the agreement of the fund manager.	• Simple transfer of assets in the event of a change of fund manager.

Source: Coyle Hamilton Ltd.

TRUSTEES' INVESTMENT DUTY

10.26 The previous section explored the principal investment choices open to trustees, which can conveniently be divided into pooled or segregated funds. These choices are not unfettered as there are investment duties imposed upon trustees which require them to act prudently. It is now proposed to examine these duties in detail.

10.27 The Trustees of an occupational pension scheme have the duty to ensure that contributions from the employer and (if applicable) the employees are received.[20] But it is not enough to receive contributions. There is a statutory duty imposed by section 59 of the Pensions Act as follows:

> Without prejudice to the duties of trustees generally and in addition to complying with the other requirements of this Act, the duties of trustees of schemes shall include the following:
>
> /. . .
>
> (b) to provide for the proper investment of the resources of the scheme in accordance with the rules of the scheme. . . .

10.28 There are four principles contained in this statutory provision:

1. There must be actual investment.
2. The statutory duty is without prejudice to the general duties of trustees.
3. Investment must be in accordance with the rules of the scheme.
4. Investment must be "proper".

These principles are now considered in turn.

Investment

10.29 At this point it is worth considering what "investment" is. Investment may be defined as the application of money to acquire assets for the purposes of obtaining an income and/or a gain. For example, the purchase of equities will usually yield a dividend (income). In addition, it is hoped that the equities will increase in value over the long term so that when subsequently sold they will realise a gain.

---

20 s.59(a) of the Pensions Act. This is a re-statement of a common law duty — see *Re Brogden* (1886) 38 ChD 546.

Case law suggests that there must always be an income return and that a capital gain is not sufficient to constitute investment.[21] In this context, it has been held that the purchase of property for a purpose other than income is not investment.[22] It is for this reason that investment clauses in trust deeds will usually empower the trustees to invest in assets, "whether or not income producing".

General Duties of Trustees

10.30 The statutory duty under section 59(b) of the Pensions Act is expressed to be without prejudice to the duties of trustees generally. The duties of trustees with regard to investment are to be found primarily in case law. These duties have been touched on earlier.[23] There are also statutory restrictions on investment with regard to self-investment and concentration which have been considered earlier in the context of the funding of defined benefit schemes and are also considered below.[24]

10.31 The overriding duty of a trustee with regard to investment is one of prudence and the avoidance of hazardous investments. Honesty and sincerity are not enough: actual prudence is required.[25] In the context of modern pension schemes this might be considered as the requirement for a reasonable level of investment return within an acceptable degree of risk, or a prudent investment strategy as contrasted with a speculative one. The duty has been considered by Murphy J. in *Stacey* v. *Branch*. This case did not concern a pension scheme, rather it arose out of a will of trust. In summarising the leading authority of *Learoyd* v. *Whiteley*,[26] Murphy J. stated:

---

21 *Re Wragg, Wragg* v. *Palmer* [1919] 2 Ch 58.

22 *Re Power, Public Trustee* v. *Hastings* [1947] Ch 572. But contrast *Re O'Connor* [1913] 1 IR 69 in which the court decided that the acquisition of property in a will trust was an investment.

23 See para. 4.42 et seq.

24 See para. 9.44 et seq. and also para. 10.57 et seq. below.

25 *Cowan* v. *Scargill* [1985] Ch 270, 289 and see Delany, H. (1996): *Equity and the Law of Trusts in Ireland*, Dublin: Round Hall Sweet & Maxwell, p. 329 et seq.

26 *Re Whiteley, Whiteley* v. *Learoyd* (1886) 33 Ch D 347. On appeal to the House of Lords it is *Learoyd* v. *Whiteley* (1887) 12 App Cas 727. Surpris-

> A trustee must, of course, invest trust funds in the securities authorised by the settlement or by statute. To invest in any other securities would be of itself a breach of trust; but, even with regard to those securities which are permissible, the trustee must take such care as a reasonably cautious man would take having regard not only to the interest of those who are entitled to the income but to the interest of those who will take in the future. In exercising his discretion a trustee must act honestly and must use as much diligence as a prudent man of business would exercise in dealing with his own private affairs; in selecting an investment he must take as much care as a prudent man would take in making an investment for the benefit of persons for whom he felt morally bound to provide. Businessmen of ordinary prudence may, and frequently do, select investments which are more or less of a speculative character; but it is the duty of a trustee to confine himself not only to the class of investments which are permitted by the settlement or by statute, but to avoid all such investments of that class as are attended with hazard.[27]

In this extract from the judgment, Murphy J. identifies the exercise of an investment discretion, on the one hand, and the selection of an investment, on the other. It is hard to see any real distinction between the two processes as each involves the exercise of an investment discretion. Yet, the judgment imposes a different duty in each case. Trustees, in exercising their discretion, must use the diligence of a prudent man of business dealing with his *own affairs* but trustees in selecting the investment must take the care of a prudent business man making an investment *for others* for whom he feels morally bound. It is suggested that there is inconsistency in these statements. The judgments in *Learoyd* v. *Whiteley* also contain this inconsistency, Lindley L.J. in the Court of Appeal stating that the trustee must:

> take such care as an ordinary prudent man would take if he were minded to make an investment for the benefit of other people for whom he felt morally bound to provide:[28]

and Lord Watson in the House of Lords expressing the duty thus:

---

ingly, *Stacey* v. *Branch* is the first reported Irish case to approve this decision.

27 *Stacey* v. *Branch* [1995] 2 ILRM 136, 142.

28 (1886) 33 Ch D 347, 355, cited with approval in *Cowan* v. *Scargill* [1985] 1 Ch 270.

> As a general rule the law requires of a trustee no higher degree of diligence in the execution of his office than a man of ordinary prudence would exercise in the management of his own private affairs. Yet he is not allowed the same discretion in investing the moneys of the trust as if he were a person sui juris dealing with his own estate.[29]

Lord Watson then made reference to avoiding hazardous investments and keeping within the investment powers of the trust, as summarised in the above extract from *Stacey* v. *Branch*. Whatever about these inconsistencies, *Stacey* v. *Branch* has, in practice, imposed a surprisingly low standard on a trustee with regard to investment, but there are no Irish decisions on pension fund investment.[30]

Investment in Accordance with the Rules

10.32 The statutory duty imposed upon the trustees is that investment must be in accordance with the rules of the scheme. The investment power may be written widely or narrowly. In a public sector scheme there may be specific limitations imposed by the statute under which the scheme was established. However wide the investment powers of the trustees may be, the Courts still have jurisdiction to review the investment decision. In the words of Meredith M.R. in *Re O'Connor*

> One thing is certain, however unlimited the power of investment may be, the trustee remains subject to the jurisdiction of the Court. The trustee has no power to act dishonestly, negligently, or in breach of trust to invest on insufficient security, but, subject to the power of the Court to compel a dishonest, grossly negligent, or grossly incompetent trustee to account for money he has so invested, it is in the power of a testator or settlor to place in the hands of his trustee money to be invested in the fullest sense of the word. . . .[31]

However, where the investment power is so widely drafted as to amount to an absolute discretion, the trustee may escape liability.[32]

---

29 (1887) 12 App Cas 727, 733.

30 See para. 10.42 et seq. below.

31 *Re O'Connor* [1913] 1 IR 69, 75.

32 *Stacey* v. *Branch* supra.

The investment powers which are typically contained in a pension scheme trust deed are examined below.[33]

10.33 The foregoing comments presuppose that the scheme rules incorporate and circumscribe trustee powers of investment. In the absence of specific investment powers, the investment choices are limited to investments permitted under section 1 of the Trustee Act 1893 as substituted by section 1 of the Trustee (Authorised Investments) Act, 1958.[34] As a consequence, trustees' powers under modern trust documentation are very widely drafted, but it is essential before any investment decision is effected that the trustee powers are considered carefully to ensure that a particular course of action is permitted under the investment clause.

10.34 The consequence of acting outside the trustee powers (acting *ultra vires*) is that the transaction would appear to be void and not be ratifiable subsequently by a later amendment to the investment clause. This means that any arrangements entered into by the trustees as a consequence of acting ultra vires would have to be unwound. This may result in a loss to the fund which leaves the trustees liable in the event of a claim by the members and other beneficiaries of the scheme. When trustees act within their powers, the Courts will be reluctant to impose liability upon them, although trustees should generally take and act upon appropriate professional advice.[35] The Courts will give no such latitude to trustees who act ultra vires. They are under a duty to see for themselves that a proposed investment is authorised and will be liable for any loss resulting from the unauthorised investment.[36]

10.35 Assets may be acquired by the trustees within the powers given to them under the trust deed. If the trust power is subsequently

---

33 At para. 10.37 et seq.

34 This Act empowers the Minister for Finance to make orders listing the investments authorised from time to time. See generally para. 4.43.

35 *Cowan* v. *Scargill* [1985] 1 Ch 270, 289. See also *Martin* v. *The City of Edinburgh District Council* [1989] PLR 9 a Scottish decision, in which the trustees were declared to be in breach of trust (inter alia) for not obtaining professional advice on dis-investing in South African assets; and also *Nestlé* v. *National Westminster Bank plc* [1994] 1 All ER 118.

36 *Rochfort* v. *Seaton* [1896] 1 IR 18.

amended so that the power is restricted, the asset becomes unauthorised, but it does not have to be sold as the trustees can hold assets that cease to be authorised under the trust.[37]

10.36 Problems can arise in practice with certain trust documents produced by life offices. The only investment power may be to invest in policies with the particular life office concerned. It may be possible to amend the trust documents to provide for wider powers if the powers of amendment permit. If not, the only choice may be to establish a new scheme and transfer assets from the old scheme to the new scheme. This may need the consent of members.

10.37 The typical modern pension scheme trust deed usually contains a general statement that the trustees have the same full and unrestricted powers of investment and application of the fund as if they were beneficiaries and absolutely entitled to it. In other words, the trustees can invest in the same way that ordinary individuals can invest their own money.

10.38 The general investment power is often, but not always, followed by a list of specific investment powers. These should be expressed to be without prejudice to the generality of the general investment power so as to avoid limiting the first power by reference to the subsequent specific powers. The list of specific powers would tend to include the following:

1. Investing in stocks, shares, debentures, debenture stock or unit trusts
2. Placing money on deposit or current account
3. Investing in deferred or immediate annuities or endowment policies
4. Participating in a managed fund
5. Investing in land or property
6. Engaging in options and financial futures[38]
7. Effecting insurance.

---

[37] Trustee Act 1893, Amendment Act, 1894, s.4.

[38] It is, however, questionable whether futures and options constitute investments. But they are treated as such by the Revenue with regard to exempt approved schemes — see para. 6.9, fn 11.

Whilst effecting insurance is not strictly an investment, it is still the means by which the trustees can meet the liability to provide certain benefits such as death in service lump sum benefits.[39]

10.39 In addition to these powers of investment, the trustees may have a power to borrow for the purposes of the scheme with a consequent power to charge assets as security. Often, the power to borrow is made subject to consent of the employer.

10.40 The investment clause should specify whether investment decisions are subject to the consent of the sponsoring employer. The employer tends to seek some control over, or input into, the investment decisions of the trustees. Sometimes, the trustees can make investment decisions without employer consent or consultation. It is more common, however, for investment decisions, and decisions to appoint an investment manager, to be subject to the prior consent of the employer, or at least to be subject to prior consultation. In defined benefit schemes the employer has a direct financial interest in securing a good investment return.[40] Although the trustees and the employer have this as a common interest, the employer and the trustees can have different standpoints in practice. For instance, with a defined benefit scheme, a high-risk investment strategy may yield high returns for the employer, and consequently reduce the employer's contribution to the fund. A low-risk strategy may mean a lower return in the future, and consequently a higher contribution rate for the employer. The trustees may see a high-risk investment strategy as being contrary to the interests of the members (because of the risk factor) and may feel that a lower risk strategy is more in keeping with the nature of the liabilities to be funded for under the scheme.

10.41 Yet a third possibility is for investment decisions to be a matter for the employer alone. This may suit the employer but is undesirable from the perspective of the trustees. One of the reasons why occupational pension schemes are usually set up under irrevocable trusts is to pass control of the pension assets from the employer to a third party — the trustees. This objective is considerably undermined where the trustees are excluded from investment decision-making.

---

39 On insuring death in service benefits, see Chapter 11.

40 Because defined benefit schemes are usually balance of cost schemes — see para. 9.19

The problem for trustees is particularly acute with defined benefit schemes, as the trustees of such schemes are required under the Pensions Act to satisfy a minimum funding or solvency standard. For example, investment of the fund in the employer's business could mean that the trustees fail to meet the minimum funding standard, as could a high concentration of investment in one asset such as a property.[41] Also, poor investment decisions by the employer could significantly reduce the value of the scheme's assets. For these reasons, it is prudent for trustees to insist, at the least, upon trustee consent to all investment decisions. Incoming trustees, in particular, need to be wary of an investment clause giving power to the employer alone. It would be advisable for the intended trustee not to become a trustee, if the employer will not agree to change the investment clause.

Proper Investment

10.42 Section 59(b) imposes a duty on the trustees of occupational pension schemes to provide for the "proper investment" of the resources of the scheme, but the Act does not attempt to define what constitutes "proper investment". This will differ from scheme to scheme. Whether investment has been proper or improper in an individual case will ultimately be a matter for the Court but it is likely that the Court will adopt the "prudent man" test, rather than establish a separate duty which might perhaps be more onerous. As already stated, provided that the trustees act within their powers, the Courts are unlikely to review the methods of investment chosen by the trustees. The Courts are not concerned with a failure by one investment fund to outperform another.

10.43 The "prudent man" test on the face of it seems to be a stringent one, but the onus on a beneficiary of proving a breach of trust would appear to be a high one, where trustees have acted within the terms of their investment powers. In *Stacey* v. *Branch*,[42] the trustee of a property took no action to secure a reasonable return on the property. He allowed a caretaker to maintain it rather than let it at a market rent. The High Court acknowledged that this would not have amounted to an adequate discharge by a trustee of his duties in the

---

41 On the regulations concerning self-investment and concentration of investment see para. 10.57 et seq. below.

42 See para. 10.31 above.

absence of specific trust provisions.[43] However, the Court refused to find that there was a breach of trust because the trustee was given absolute discretion with regard to investment, and the trustee had acted in good faith. In effect, the Court construed an investment clause as a provision excluding trustee liability. This is a surprising decision and one that appears to be contrary to the principles enunciated in the early part of this century in *Re O'Connor*.[44]

10.44 A higher duty of care is expected of a professional or paid trustee, but the standard is inconsistently applied. In the UK case of *Bartlett* v. *Barclay's Bank Trust Co. Ltd.*, a case arising out of a speculative investment which resulted in significant losses, the Court held that there had been a breach of trust by the professional trustee.[45] In *Murphy* v. *AIB*, the defendant bank was held to be a trustee in its capacity as mortgagee. It sold the mortgaged property and credited the proceeds to a demand deposit account. The Court found that there was a breach of trust and held that the beneficiaries were entitled to an appropriate return. The Court stated that the appropriate return was not one which a prudent man of business would have obtained but "the yield which would have accrued to the trust fund by investment in the security *least beneficial* to the trust fund",[46] which is clearly a low return.[47] In *Nestlé* v. *National Westminster Bank*,[48] the UK Court of Appeal was of the view that no person making a will would choose the defendant bank for the effective management of their investments, and yet did not find the defendant in breach of trust. The bank thought that it had narrower investment powers than it actually had and yet did not take appropriate advice to determine the extent of its powers. The investment return over the

---

43 [1995] 2 ILRM at 142.

44 On which, see para. 10.32 above. *Re O'Connor* was not mentioned in the decision, nor does it appear from the report to have been cited by counsel. The Court followed *Gisbourne* v. *Gisbourne* (1877) 2 App Cas 300 and *Tabor* v. *Brooks* (1878) 10 Ch 273.

45 [1980] Ch 515. See also *Steel* v. *Wellcome Custodian Trustees Ltd* [1988] 1 WLR 167, *Re Waterman's Will Trusts* [1952] 2 All ER 1054.

46 Emphasis added.

47 [1994] 2 ILRM 220, 225.

48 [1994] 1 ALL ER 118.

period during which the bank managed the investments was lower than could have been obtained through other investment media.[49]

10.45 There are four main headings under which the trustees should evaluate investment strategy in the context of proper investment: investment return, risk, diversity and suitability.

10.46 ***Investment Return:*** The investments of a pension scheme are long-term in nature, as the objective is to provide benefits at retirement. A small difference in investment return over a long period of time will have a significant effect on the value of the pension fund. For example, the difference between an average investment return over 25 years of 8.5 per cent per annum as opposed to 8 per cent on an initial sum of £150,000 is £125,743.

10.47 In evaluating investment return, regard must be had to dealing costs and management fees. The trustees are not expected to obtain the best possible investment return, as return cannot be regarded in isolation of risk, diversity and suitability.[50] With regard to a failure to invest, there is authority that the Court will not assess damages by reference to the best possible return, but possibly by reference to the permitted investment least advantageous to the beneficiaries.[51]

10.48 ***Risk:*** It has already been mentioned that pension scheme investments should be made within an acceptable degree of risk.[52] The trustees' primary duty is to safeguard the trust assets, and any in-

---

49 See Kenny A. (1993): "Are a Bank Trustee's Fees Performance Related?" *The Conveyancer*, Jan-Feb.

50 *Cowan* v. *Scargill*.

51 *Murphy* v. *AIB* [1994] 2 ILRM 220. This decision was made in the context of a private trust where a professional trustee was a trustee by reason of being a mortgagee, but it is questionable whether it would be followed in the case of a pension scheme trust.

52 Para. 10.31 above. However, risk is an imprecise word: "[T]he word 'risk' . . . can mean different things to different people. For example, it can be defined as the chance of a monetary profit or loss, the chance of a higher or lower return than the one expected or the chance of a change of investment values which is not matched by a corresponding change in the liabilities of the fund." Hager, D.P. (1980): "Measurement of Pension Fund Investment Performance", Vol 24, Journal of the Institute of Actuaries Students' Society.

vestment decision must be reviewed in this light.[53] The balance of risk and return was stated in *Cowan* v. *Scargill* as follows:

> ... the power [of investment] must be exercised so as to yield the best return for the beneficiaries, judged in relation to the risks of the investment in question ...[54]

Whether a proper balance between risk and return is achieved in any given case will be a question of fact to be determined by the Court.

10.49 Investment managers differ in the returns they deliver. However, they also differ in the risks they take in achieving that performance. Figure 10.3 compares an ideal, smooth rate of investment growth with the typical variable return of a managed fund.

FIGURE 10.3: IDEAL V. TYPICAL FUND PERFORMANCE

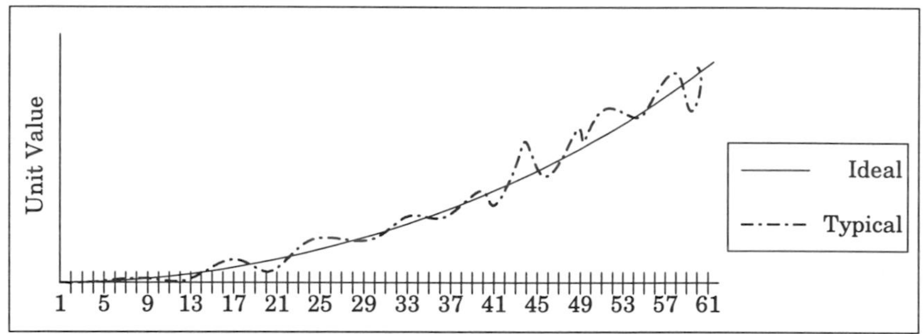

Source: Coyle Hamilton Ltd.

10.50 If return is to be consistent with security, it might be supposed that all investments should be in assets that guarantee a return, such as fixed interest securities (for example, government stock). The returns from fixed interest securities are unlikely to keep pace with salary increases (that is, the member's future spending power). Therefore, schemes tend to invest a proportion of their funds in securities with greater growth potential, such as equities and property.

---

53 *McNamara* v. *Carey* (1867) IR 1 Eq. 9 considered further at para. 10.72 below. See also *Nestlé* v. *National Westminster Bank plc* [1994] 1 All ER 118, where it is stated: "The importance of preservation of a trust fund will always outweigh success in advancement."

54 [1985] Ch 270, 287.

This is attendant with more risk but, over the long term, the return on equities and property should outstrip the return on fixed interest securities.

10.51 ***Diversity:*** Pension schemes tend to invest in a spread of assets, including equities, property, indexed-linked and fixed interest securities. There is no statutory requirement imposed upon trustees to diversify investments,[55] but it is nonetheless a prudent strategy. The objective of such diversification is to ensure that adverse risks in an individual sector or a permanent diminution of the value of a specific stock should not have a significant effect on the overall return on the fund. The trustees must have regard to how the assets are spread — that is, their diversity. Larger funds can afford a wider spread of investments than smaller funds. This principle is put succinctly by Sir Robert Megarry in the *British Museum*[56] case:

> A fund that is very large may well justify a latitude of investment that would be denied to a more modest fund, for the spread of investments possible for a larger fund may justify the greater risks that wider powers will permit to be taken.

10.52 Risk could be stock-specific where there is a substantial holding in one particular stock. Also, risk can be geographically specific. An example of the latter would be a substantial part of the fund invested in a portfolio of Japanese equities. The consequences of overinvestment in one particular stock are obvious. A significant drop in value would result in a diminution in the value of the pension fund. Holding significant investments in a particular geographical area can also present problems. For example, an adverse movement in exchange rates between the Irish pound and the Japanese yen would reduce the value of the Japanese portfolio to an Irish pension scheme.

10.53 A reasonable spread of investments is therefore considered desirable. As mentioned earlier, for smaller pension funds (typically below approximately £6 million) it is generally not cost effective to invest directly in equities, property and other securities as the ad-

---

55 Unlike in the UK which requires diversity under s.6 of the Trustee Investments Act 1961. See also *Cowan* v. *Scargill* supra at 289.

56 *Trustees of the British Museum* v. *Attorney General* [1984] 1 WLR 418, 425

ministration and management costs would be high relative to the value of the fund and there would not be sufficient moneys to provide a reasonable spread of investments. These schemes instead tend to participate in pooled-investment arrangements such as unit-linked funds or insured products. The larger funds can be invested on a segregated basis.

FIGURE 10.4: TOTAL ASSET DISTRIBUTION OF IRISH PENSION FUNDS — END 1995

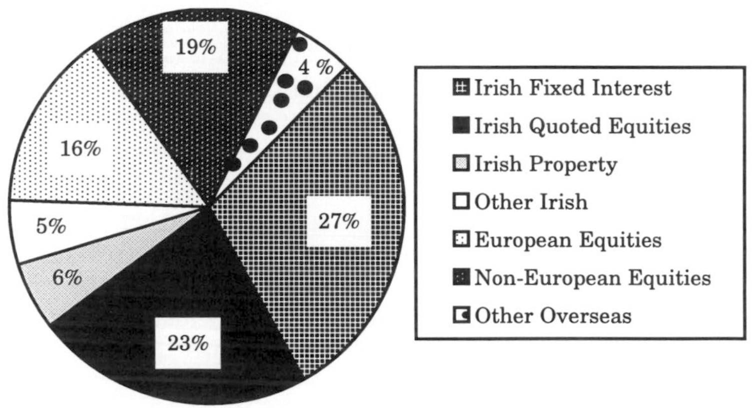

Source: IAPF Investment Survey 1995.

10.54 ***Asset/Liability Matching:*** There is no one recommended mix of investments suitable for every pension scheme. The reason for this is that the liabilities of pension schemes are not the same from scheme to scheme. When a scheme is established, it generally assumes quite long-term liabilities, particularly where the average age of members is young. As the scheme matures, pensions start to be paid. Figure 10.5 illustrates one of the key factors in determining asset mix. It shows the annual return on Irish equity investments over the past 20 years compared with inflation. The graph illustrates the volatility of the investments. At certain points, the equity value drops sharply. Figure 10.6 shows the cumulative equity returns against inflation over the same period and it can be seen that, over the long term, investment returns outstrip inflation.

10.55 In a recently established scheme with a young age profile, pensions will not commence to be paid for many years and so fluctuations in the equity market are not of such concern, provided that the long-term return exceeds salary inflation.[57] The position is different for a mature scheme — that is, a scheme with a high proportion of pensioners.

FIGURE 10.5: ANNUAL RETURNS ON IRISH EQUITIES COMPARED WITH INFLATION, 1966–1995

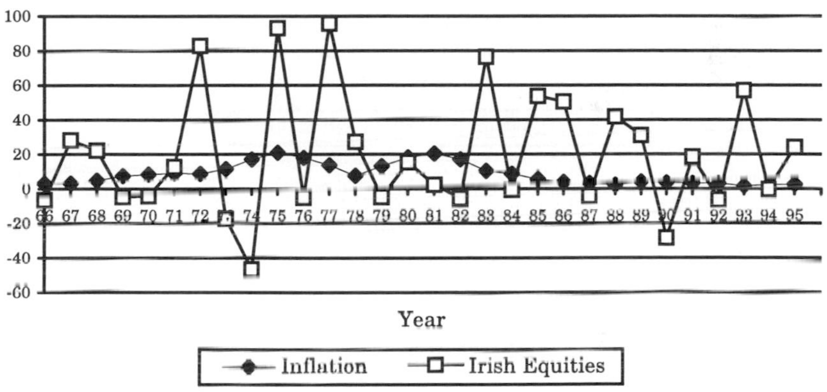

Data derived from: Healy, P. (1996): "Pension Fund Investment: A Liability-Based Approach". Society of Actuaries in Ireland, 20 February.

57 In the funding of a defined benefit scheme, the actuary will normally assume, for valuation purposes, a differential between investment return and salary inflation of about 2 per cent.

FIGURE 10.6: IRISH EQUITY PERFORMANCE VERSUS INFLATION, 1966 TO 1995

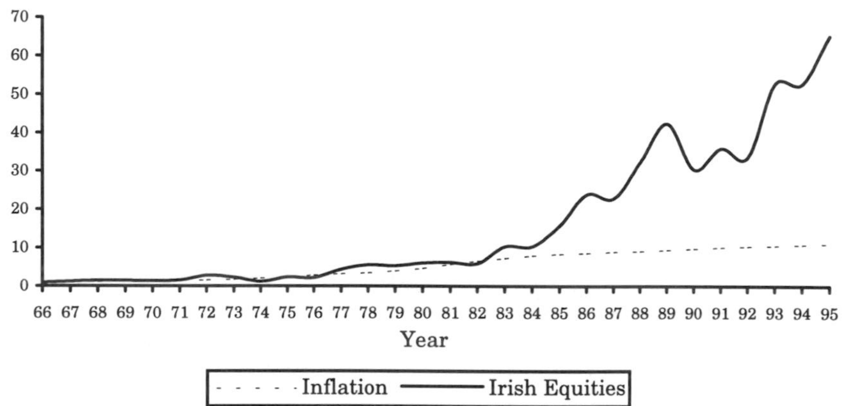

Annualised Rates 1966–1995

Irish Inflation	8.34%
Irish Equity Returns	14.95%
Real Return on Equity	6.10%

Data derived from: Healy, P. (1996): "Pension Fund Investment: A Liability-Based Approach". Society of Actuaries in Ireland, 20 February.

As pensions start to be paid, the scheme will need to realise some of its investments in order to meet its liability to pay pensions. If assets have to be realised but the market has dropped sharply beforehand, a poor return will be obtained from the investments. It makes sense therefore for a mature scheme to reduce its holdings in volatile investments such as equities, and increase the proportion of the fund invested in low-risk investments such as government gilts and cash. Figs. 10.7 and 10.8 illustrate the typical differences in mix of investments between a young scheme and a mature scheme.

FIGURE 10.7: YOUNG SCHEME

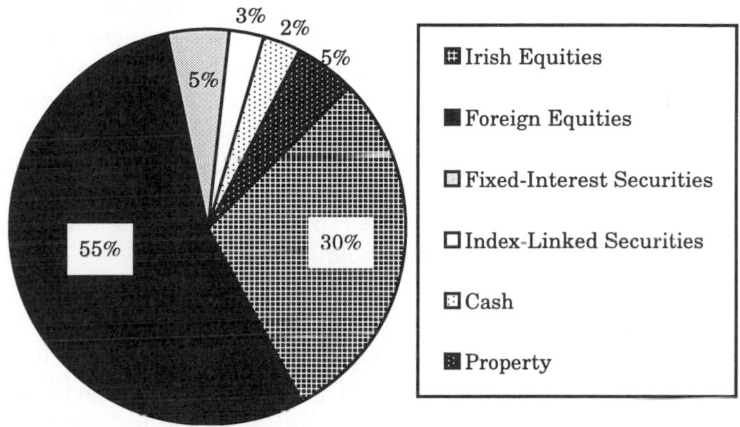

FIGURE 10.8: MATURE SCHEME

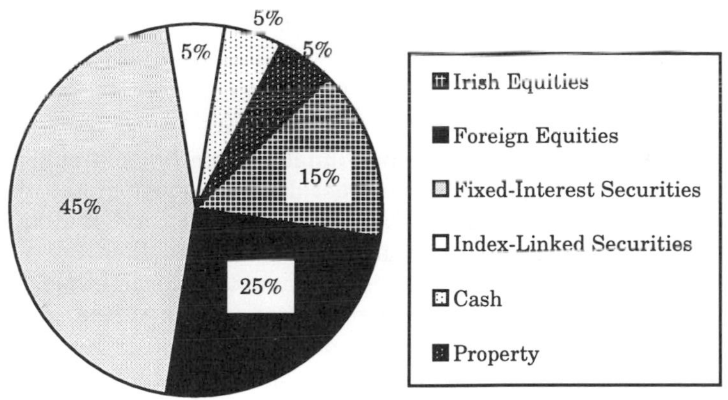

Source: Coyle Hamilton Ltd.

Other Issues

10.56 The extent to which trustees can take into account other issues (for example, moral or political ones) in carrying out their investment duty has been examined in a number of decisions in the UK but does not appear to have received judicial consideration in Ireland. The leading case is *Cowan* v. *Scargill*, in which the Court held that the trustees must refrain from making investments by reason of the personal views that they held:

> In considering what investments to make trustees must put on one side their own personal interests and views. Trustees may have strongly held social or political views. They may be firmly opposed to any investment in South Africa or other countries, or they may object to any form of investment in companies concerned with alcohol, tobacco, armaments or many other things. In the conduct of their own affairs, of course, they are free to abstain from making any such investments. Yet under a trust, if investments of this type would be more beneficial to the beneficiaries than other investments, the trustees must not refrain from making the investments by reason of the views they hold.[58]

The Court went on to state that trustees may even have to act dishonourably (though not illegally) if the interests of their beneficiaries require it. The trustees of pension schemes will have personal preferences and beliefs, particularly where individual trustees also have a management role in the company or are member trustees. Trustees can hold these preferences and beliefs but must act fairly and impartially. This was the conclusion in the Scottish case of *Martin* v. *The City of Edinburgh District Council*, where, in commenting on the principle enunciated in *Cowan*, Lord Murray stated:

> But if it means that each individual trustee in genuinely applying his mind and judgment to a trust decision, must divest himself of all personal preferences, of all political beliefs, and of all moral, religious or other conscientiously held principles, then I do not think that this proposition is either reasonable or practicable. What he must do I think is to recognise that he has those preferences, commitments or principles but nonetheless do his best to exercise fair and impartial judgment on the merits of the issue before him. If he realises that he cannot do that, then he should abstain from participating in deciding the issue (on the analogy of a disqualifying declared interest) or, in the extreme case, resign as a trustee.[59]

---

[58] *Cowan* v. *Scargill* supra 287, 288.

[59] *Martin* v. *The City of Edinburgh District Council* [1989] PLR 9, 16. See also *Bishop of Oxford* v. *The Church Commissioners of England* [1991] PLR 185, a charitable trusts case in which the UK chancery division held that ethical considerations in charitable trusts can be taken into account provided that there is no risk of significant financial detriment.

STATUTORY RESTRICTIONS ON INVESTMENT

10.57 The investment duties so far considered have derived from general trust principles. There are, however, certain (albeit few) statutory restrictions on the trustees' powers of investment, which will now be examined.

10.58 The Pensions Act imposes controls over investments concerning defined benefit schemes. It does so by requiring the actuary to the scheme to disregard certain assets in valuing the scheme's solvency. The indirect consequence is to restrict the amount of investment of a scheme's resources in one particular asset (concentration of investment) or in investment in the sponsoring employer's business (self-investment). The value of assets over a specified percentage must not be taken into account in the actuary's funding certificate. The actuarial funding certificate certifies the scheme's solvency to the Pensions Board.[60]

10.59 Self-investment is the investment by the scheme in its sponsoring employer. Concentration of investment refers to an excessive investment in one particular asset. Neither self-investment nor concentration of investment is illegal. In the case of self-investment, the actuary must currently disregard any self-investment in excess of 10 per cent of the scheme's resources when certifying as to the solvency or otherwise of the scheme in the actuarial funding certificate.[61] In the case of concentration of investment, currently, the actuary must disregard the market value of an investment where in excess of 20 per cent of the scheme's resources. If the trustees have invested in a with-profit policy or unit-linked policy or other unit-linked arrangement, there is only one asset and that is the policy or the units in the unit fund. It would appear at first sight that there is a 100 per cent concentration in one asset, but this is not really the case. The units, or the policy held, are linked to an underlying diversity of investments. It is for this reason that, under the regulations governing concentration of investment, insurance polices, contracts of assurance, managed funds and unit trusts are specifically excluded from the definition.[62] The other investments which are excluded from the defi-

---

60 This topic is considered in greater detail in Chapter 9 — see para 9.44 et seq.

61 There are other transitional percentages — see para. 9.47.

62 Occupational Pension Schemes (Funding Standard) Regulations, 1993 (SI No 419 of 1993) Article 3.

nition are government securities and cash. The reason for their exclusion is that these are extremely low-risk investments and in certain schemes, such as a very mature scheme, it would be desirable to have a high proportion of the fund in government securities or cash.

10.60 Self-investment may involve wider problems than Pensions Act compliance if shares in the sponsoring employer are purchased by the trustees. If the shares are publicly quoted and there are management-appointed trustees, there may be concerns over possible insider dealing.[63] Also, there may be a link between the payment of a contribution into the scheme by the employer and a subsequent purchase by the trustees of shares in the employer. This could amount to financial assistance by the employer to purchase its own shares contrary to the Companies Act, 1963.[64] This is so irrespective of whether the employer is publicly quoted or not. A payment by the employer to the trustees will not amount to "financial assistance" if it amounts to the discharge of a liability lawfully incurred by it, such as normal employer contributions to the scheme. But it may amount to "financial assistance" if the payment is over and above the employer's normal contribution, the purpose of which is to acquire the shares.

10.61 The Revenue impose similar restrictions with regard to small self-administered schemes. Small self-administered schemes are normally established for proprietary directors. One of the attractions of establishing a small self-administered scheme in the past was the facility of purchasing an asset, such as a property, through the pension scheme and leasing it to the employer. Another more overt form of self-investment was an unsecured loan by the pension scheme to the employer. In this example, the employer receives tax relief on the contributions to the pension scheme and then takes the money back by way of a loan (often at less than market rate). This is hardly bona-fide pension provision and the Revenue have countered these abuses by placing restrictions on investment. This topic was considered above.[65] It should be noted that there are no such restrictions with

---

63 Companies Act, 1990, Pt V. Trustees are exempt from the insider dealing requirements if they have acted in good faith — s.110. See generally Keane, R. (1991): *Company Law in the Republic of Ireland* 2nd Ed., Dublin: Butterworths, Chapter 36.

64 s.60.

65 See para. 6.77 et seq.

larger self-administered schemes (generally schemes with 12 or more members). To avoid the small self-administered scheme restrictions, some employers have introduced staff employees. The objective is to increase the numbers up to 12 or more and avoid the Revenue restrictions. The Revenue has recently countered this abuse also.[66]

10.62 There is a clear dividing line between "investment", on the one hand, and "trading", on the other. Occupational pension schemes that are approved by the Revenue under Chapter II of Part I of the Finance Act, 1972 receive their approval on the basis that the trustees will invest the fund but will not undertake trading activities. Trading activities will expose the trustees to tax under Schedule D.[67] Such activities are almost certainly also outside the trust powers generally given to trustees. Trustees are usually only given powers of investment, not powers to carry on a trade. There would not appear to be any reported cases either in Ireland or the United Kingdom in which a determination was made that the trustees were not in fact undertaking genuine investment, but were carrying on a trade.

10.63 The Pensions (Amendment) Act, 1996 introduced a power of the Court on application to it by the Pensions Board to direct the trustees to dispose of any investment held for the purposes of the scheme.[68] The Court may make the order when it is satisfied that the retention of the investment is likely to jeopardise the rights and interests of scheme members and can also direct that the resources of the scheme be restored to the level at which they would have been had the investment not been made. The Court can make the order relating to restoration of resources as against the trustees and any other person who was knowingly concerned in the investment.[69] If the Court is satisfied that there is a reasonable likelihood of an investment of this kind occurring, it may (on application of the Pensions

---

66 See para. 6.78.

67 Whether or not the trustees are trading is a question of fact to be determined having regard to what are referred to as the six "badges of trade". See Thurnham, T. (1987): "UK Pension Fund Trustees, Investment and the Law", *Trust Law & Practice,* July, 9 and Quarrell op. cit. Chapter 2 and also Judge, N. (1995-96): *Irish Income Tax*, Dublin: Butterworths, para. 4.102.

68 s.39 inserting a new s.89 into the Pensions Act.

69 s.89(3).

Board) grant an injunction prohibiting the investment.[70] An example of an investment in relation to which the Board might seek a restoration order would be an unsecured loan by the trustees to the employer or a loan at below market rate. To protect innocent third parties, an order cannot be made against a person unless the Court is satisfied that the investment was not made *bona fide* in the interests of the members and that the person against whom the order is to be made was aware of this or ought reasonably to have been so aware.[71]

DELEGATION

10.64 One of the underlying principles that emerges from a review of trustee investment duties is that trustees should obtain appropriate professional advice on the investment of the fund where they do not themselves possess expertise in investment matters. This section examines the appointment of an investment manager and the legal issues that arise concerning the power of the trustees to delegate their duties and discretions.

Investment Managers

10.65 Pension scheme trustees almost invariably appoint an expert, known as an investment manager, to manage the scheme's investments. There are many reasons why this is desirable but the main ones are that given the huge range of available investments, both domestic and foreign, and the fact that stock markets often fluctuate widely on a given day and timing is therefore of great importance, trustees do not have the expertise or the resources to carry out effective management. The investment process is an uncertain one:

> Investment managers will differ on the distribution of assets to be followed, the way in which new money should be invested, the choice of securities etc. This difference, and indeed disagreement, merely produces the market place as we know it. However, on one thing all investment managers will agree — namely that the whole investment process is uncertain rather than certain — the manager implicitly deals with possibilities. Nobody can say with abso-

---

70 s.90(2) as inserted by s.39 of the Pensions (Amendment) Act, 1996.

71 s.89(4).

> lute assurance what will happen in the markets next week, next year or in five years' time.[72]

In addition, it is inappropriate for smaller schemes to invest directly in assets such as equities or property, and so the trustees of those schemes need an investment manager to gain the advantage of pooled investment.[73]

10.66 The need to delegate to an investment manager was emphasised in the *British Museum* case:

> [T]here are the changed conditions of investment, conditions which require great liberty of choice if, on skilled advice, advantage is to be taken of opportunities which often present themselves on short notice and for short periods; and for this, the provision for delegation is plainly advantageous.[74]

This explains why trustees should delegate. However, they cannot delegate the exercise of their duties and discretions unless there is power to delegate in the trust documents which constitute the scheme.[75] Similar considerations arise with regard to the appointment of a custodian.[76]

10.67 The trustees may delegate on a fully discretionary basis or may place some controls on the investment manager. With life-office policies or unit-linked funds, the institution has full discretion over the investment of the underlying fund assets. The trustees cannot fetter the institution's discretion of investment, as the latter is investing not just on behalf of the trustees of a particular scheme, but on behalf of the trustees of all the schemes that participate in the fund. Restrictions are therefore only feasible in a segregated fund, and are generally not desirable unless the liability profile of the scheme requires special investment treatment.

---

72 Frost, A.J. and Hager, D.P. (1986): *A general introduction to Institutional Investment*, London: Heinemann, pp. 131, 132.

73 See paras. 10.13–10.25.

74 Per Megarry VC, *Trustees of the British Museum* v. *Attorney General* [1984] 1 WLR 418,424.

75 This is summed up in the Latin maxim *delegatus non potest delegare*: a person to whom duties or powers have been delegated cannot delegate those duties or powers to a third party. See *Re O'Flanagan's and Ryan's Contract* [1905] 1 IR 280 and para. 4.64 and 4.65.

76 On custodians see para. 10.72 and 10.73 below.

10.68 There is an emphasis in Ireland on the measurement and monitoring of investment returns of pension funds. Various surveys rank the principal investment managers in order of investment performance, usually on five-year returns.[77] These surveys are a valuable tool in assessing investment management performance but should nonetheless be treated with caution because the extent of the return that would be appropriate in any given scheme depends upon other factors such as risk, diversity and asset/liability matching.[78]

Contractual Terms

10.69 It is prudent for the trustees of a pension scheme to enter into an agreement with the investment manager so that the terms and conditions governing the investment management service are recorded in some detail. The investment agreement is a recent phenomenon. Many schemes still do not have the benefit of written agreements.

10.70 Life offices issue policies, whether they be with-profit policies or unit-linked policies, in order to record the life office's terms and conditions. Sometimes, with larger schemes a separate investment management agreement is also entered into to cover issues which the policy does not address. Unitised funds operated by investment banks are governed by a trust deed, but service agreements are also entered into between the trustees and the investment adviser.

10.71 With segregated funds there is no policy to be issued and, accordingly, an investment management agreement should be negotiated between the trustees and the investment manager. The employer may also be required under the terms of the trust deed to be a party to the agreement. These agreements can be quite sophisticated, which is understandable given that trustees will only make a decision to switch to segregated investment where the fund is sufficiently large to do so.

---

77 For example, Coyle Hamilton Quarterly Investment Manager Survey of managed funds, and CPMS survey.

78 On measuring investment performance, see Hager op. cit., Gardener, T.J.A. (1987): "Pension Fund Performance Measurement — The Way Ahead", Vol. 30 *Journal of the Institute of Actuaries Students' Society* 163; Hymans, C. and Mulligan, J. (1980): *The Measurement of Portfolio Performance*, London: Kluwer; Spain, J. (1986): "Investment Performance: The responsibility borne by the Pension Fund Trustees", *Trust Law and Practice* Sept/Oct, 80.

Some key clauses which should be included in an investment management agreement for a segregated fund are listed in Figure 10.9.[79]

Custodians

10.72 Where funds are invested on a segregated basis, it is essential for a custodian to be appointed. The custodian's responsibility is to hold the assets of the scheme under management as nominee or bare trustee of the pension scheme trustees. A custodian is necessary for the trustees to satisfy their duty to keep the scheme assets secure so that there is no possibility of the assets being regarded as beneficially owned by the investment manager or any third party. The duty to keep trust assets secure is well summarised in the case of *McNamara* v. *Carey*:

> [I]t is not enough for a trustee to keep within the four corners of the deed, and perform literally what is there set down. The very first point to which he must direct his thoughts is the placing of the trust property in security; and, above all, the making it impossible that it shall ever fall under the control of unauthorized persons. If he, even by mere inaction, suffer a state of things to exist or to continue, which, however apparently at the time natural and harmless, results, in the course of future events, in the fund getting under unauthorized control, even though it be that of a co-trustee only — still more that of the settlor himself — and loss follows, the trustee must make it good.[80]

10.73 Where the investment manager is undertaking both investment management and custodial services, the custodian will be appointed by the investment manager and may be a wholly owned subsidiary of the investment manager. A small minority of large schemes will have independent custodians who are appointed directly by the trustees. An advantage of this is that it reduces the control that any one institution has over the assets of the fund and should achieve greater security against fraud and increase the chances of any errors being spotted. The trustees need to weigh these advantages against the additional cost of appointing an independent custodian.[81]

---

79 Guidelines on investment management agreements have been issued by the IAPF: "Guidelines on investment management agreements for pension funds", 1996 May.

80 *McNamara* v. *Carey* (1867) IR 1 Eq. 9, 32 per Christian J.

81 Guidelines on the appointment of custodians have been issued by the IAPF: "Guidelines for trustees regarding pension fund custody agree-

FIGURE 10.9: INVESTMENT MANAGEMENT AGREEMENTS FOR SEGREGATED FUNDS — SOME KEY PROVISIONS

1. The effective date of appointment of the manager.
2. The objective of the manager — usually to provide long-term growth. A performance benchmark may be set.
3. The extent of the discretions given to the investment manager including any restrictions on investment discretion and any guidelines which the trustees may issue with regard to investment. For example, the trustees may wish to control participation in derivatives.
4. A requirement not to increase the market value of any particular asset to greater than a set percentage, without the consent of the trustees. This protects against concentration of investment problems.
5. Provision for the registration of assets, normally in the name of a custodian/nominee as bare trustee of the trustees and provision for the holding of title documents.
6. Establishment and maintenance of bank accounts.
7. The power of the investment manager to appoint agents such as stockbrokers and any restrictions on appointment.
8. An agreed policy on corporate governance e.g. on voting rights attaching to shares.
9. The requirements of the investment manager to supply information to the trustees on a periodic basis and particularly for the purposes of permitting the trustees to comply with disclosure requirements under the annual trustees' report and accounts.[82]
10. Details of the fee structure and in particular a requirement for full disclosure of soft commissions which are benefits received by an investment manager for placing business with a particular stockbroker or other financial institution.
11. Normally the trustees indemnify the manager against actions arising from claims by third parties to entitlement to the assets and the investment manager should indemnify the trustees in respect of negligence, default and fraud of the manager or any employee. This indemnity may also extend to any custodian or other agent. In the absence of a full indemnity a duty should be imposed on the manager with regard to proper selection of custodians and other agents.
12. There should also be provision for the basis upon which the agreement can be terminated.

---

ments". See also a commentary on the guidelines by Seán Hawkshaw: IAPF seminar, 26 October 1995.

82 See generally Chapter 13.

INVESTOR PROTECTION

10.74 In appointing an investment manager, the trustees gain the benefit of professional investment management but they also cede control of the assets of the scheme. This section examines how well protected the pension fund is in the circumstances of life-office investment, unitised funds, segregated investment and bank accounts.

10.75 Pension scheme funds invested with life offices (on a non-segregated basis)[83] are classified as life assurance business and are protected under insurance legislation. Under the Insurance Act, 1989, life offices must maintain a separate account in respect of life assurance business and must maintain such accounting and other records as are necessary to identify the assets and liabilities of that business.[84] The life office can apply its life assurance fund only for the purpose of its life assurance business — that is, the life fund is ring-fenced from the rest of the life office's business. Money from the fund cannot be used for any business of the life office which is not life assurance business.[85] Furthermore, no life office can declare a dividend to its shareholders where the value of the life assurance fund is below the amount of the liabilities of the fund or where the statutory solvency margin has not been maintained.[86] Any surplus can, however, be paid out by way of dividend. It is also prohibited from mortgaging or charging the assets of the life fund, except to the extent required to raise moneys for the life fund.

10.76 It is usual for pension scheme trustees to effect a life-office policy through an insurance broker or, perhaps (but rarely) a tied agent. The Insurance Act, 1989 regulates intermediaries (brokers and agents). A premium paid to an intermediary is deemed to have been paid to the life office, even if the intermediary subsequently defaults in paying the premium over to the life office, provided that the life

---

[83] See para. 10.8 et seq. on the distinction.

[84] s.14.

[85] s.15(6).

[86] s.15(7). The valuation is carried out in accordance with the European Communities (Life Assurance Accounts, Statements and Valuations) Regulations, 1986 (SI No 437 of 1986). In particular, Art. 5 stipulates that, on an annual basis, the life office's actuary must carry out an investigation of its financial condition.

office has accepted a proposal or invited a renewal.[87] Insurance intermediaries must also bond, by way of insurance cover, all premiums received by them from the their clients.[88]

10.77 Pension scheme funds that are invested on a unitised basis with investment managers other than life offices are established under trust deed and are regulated by general trust law.[89] The fund is ring-fenced under general trust law, as the beneficiaries of a trust take priority over creditors in a company liquidation, with regard to trust property, in the sense that the trust assets do not belong to the company. The following statement by Budd J. in *Shanahan's Stamp Auctions* summarises the position:

> Should a person, having trust property in his possession, die or go bankrupt, the beneficiaries under the trust take their property in full in priority to the general body of creditors. The same thing applies in the case of a company in liquidation. . . . [T]he creditors of a company are in general in no better position as against beneficiaries of trust moneys in the company's hands at the time of the liquidation than the company before liquidation. The distinction, as I understand, is based on the fact that the beneficiary seeks his own property, or the proceeds thereof, being aided in equity to obtain restitution. The ordinary creditor, however, can only seek payment of his debt to the extent that there are assets, the property of the deceased debtor, bankrupt or company in liquidation which are available to meet his claim.[90]

10.78 Segregated portfolios are governed by the regulatory framework of the investment manager. Banks undertaking segregated business are subject to regulation by the Central Bank under the Investment Intermediaries Act, 1995. Life-office subsidiaries which undertake investment management services are also regulated under

---

87 s.53.

88 s.47 — provided that the intermediary's turnover is at least £25,000 (s.47(4)).

89 These funds are not permitted to become authorised unit trusts under the Unit Trusts Act, 1990 as the latter Act only applies to unit trusts "providing facilities for the participation by the public" (s.1(1), definition of "unit trust scheme"). The Central Bank is of the view that pension fund unit trusts are not open to participation by the public because participation is confined to trustees of Revenue approved schemes.

90 *Shanahan's Stamp Auctions Ltd.* v. *Farrelly* [1962] IR 386, 444.

this Act, provided that they do not also undertake life assurance business. Furthermore, the Act imposes minimum capital adequacy requirements on investment managers.[91] Stockbrokers are subject to the Stock Exchange Acts. The trust assets are protected by the terms of the investment management agreement (if any) and general trust law as set out in the previous paragraph. The investment agreement will provide for the appointment of a custodian under whose name the scheme assets will be registered as nominee or bare trustee of the pension scheme trustees. This ring-fences the resources of the scheme from the assets of the investment manager.

10.79 Until the Investment Intermediaries Act, 1995, there was no investor protection against fraudulent intermediaries with regard to non-insurance based investments. This was in stark contrast to the regulatory framework introduced by the Insurance Act, in the case of insurance intermediaries. Now, investment intermediaries are required to be authorised under the Investment Intermediaries Act[92] and in certain cases are required to hold a bond in similar terms to insurance intermediaries.[93]

10.80 Pension scheme moneys that are not immediately needed for investment are usually held in a trustee bank account. When assets are realised or units sold, the proceeds will also be paid into a bank account. With regard to trustee bank accounts, the amount deposited with the bank becomes a debt due by the bank to the trustees, and nothing more.[94] Accordingly, in the event of the bank becoming insolvent, the trustees will only rank as an ordinary creditor of the bank. Lest it should be thought that a bank failure is inconceivable,

---

[91] s.19 of the Act enables the supervisory authority to require investment managers to keep a proportion of assets in liquid form. The capital adequacy requirements are set out in EU Council Directive 93/6 of 15 March 1993.

[92] Under Part IV of the Act.

[93] s.51 and the Investment Intermediaries Act, 1995 (Bonding of Intermediaries) Regulations, 1996 (SI No 29 of 1996).

[94] *Foley* v. *Hill* [1848] 2 HLC 28 and *Joachimson* v. *Swiss Bank Corporation* [1921] 3 KB 110; Hapgood, M. (Ed.) (1989): *Paget's Law of Banking*, London & Edinburgh: Butterworths, 10th ed., Chapter 10; Ellinger, E.P. & Lomnicka, E. (1994): *Modern Banking Law*, Oxford: Claredon Press, 2nd ed., Chapter 4.

one need only remember the collapse of Barings Bank. The following conclusion on the Barings' collapse is worthy of note:

> Barings' collapse was due to the unauthorised and ultimately catastrophic activities of, it appears, one individual . . . that went undetected as a consequence of a failure of management and other internal controls of the most basic kind. Management failed at various levels and in a variety of ways . . . to institute a proper system of internal controls, to enforce accountability for all profits, risks and operations, and adequately to follow up on a number of warning signals over a prolonged period. Neither the external auditors nor the regulators discovered [these] unauthorised activities.[95]

The trustees can, of course, minimise the risk of a bank failure, by spreading cash deposits between a number of banks.

10.81 Sometimes moneys are held in an employer bank account rather than in a trustee account. The risks attendant on moneys continuing to be held by the employer are somewhat different. Here, there is also the risk of the sponsoring employer going into insolvent liquidation. The legal status of these moneys from a trust perspective is considered in more detail later.[96]

ANNUITIES AND BUY-OUT BONDS

10.82 The earlier part of this chapter reviewed the investment options open to trustees of an occupational pension scheme, regarding the pension fund. This section will consider the ways in which the trustees can secure payment of a member's pension and the option of transferring benefits to an investment bond known as a buy-out bond.

10.83 When a member of a pension scheme reaches retirement, a pension is immediately payable. Part of the pension may be taken in cash form by the member but, provided that the pension is not eliminated entirely by the exchange of pension for cash, the trustees have an immediate liability to pay a pension income to the member. The trustees must at that point decide whether to pay the pension income out of the fund on a regular (usually monthly) basis until the

---

95 Report of the Board of Banking Supervision Inquiry into the Circumstances of the Collapse of Barings HMSO July 1995.

96 Para. 17.43.

member dies, or to secure the future liability to pay the pension by buying an annuity.

10.84 An annuity is an insurance policy issued by a life office which, in exchange for a cash payment to the life office, guarantees the payment of an income for a set period or for life. An example of how this works is set out in Example 10.2.

Example 10.2

The Superlative Pension Scheme has promised a pension for life to a particular member, Jane Bloggs, of 2/3rds of final salary per annum. Jane's final salary is £30,000, which means that her pension is £20,000 per annum.

The trustees of the Superlative Pension Scheme have decided to secure payment of the pension by buying an annuity from a life office. They shop around in the annuity market and get the best annuity rate available, which is that for every £9.50 of cash, the trustees can buy £1 of pension for Jane for life.

The trustees therefore take out £190,000 from the fund (i.e. £20,000 x £9.50) to buy an annuity of £20,000 payable for Jane's life. This matches the liability of the trustees to pay the pension to Jane. The life office guarantees to pay the pension under the annuity policy.

10.85 With annuities, a set amount of cash buys a particular amount of pension. The rate of exchange between cash and pension is called the annuity rate. Annuity rates are calculated by life offices having regard to actuarial considerations such as mortality[97] and interest rates at the time of purchase. An increase in interest rates will mean that a higher amount of pension can be bought with a given amount of cash, whereas a reduction in interest rates will have the reverse effect. Life offices are effectively betting on the death of the member (the "annuitant"). If the member dies before the date of death estimated by the life office, the life office makes a profit. If the member dies after the estimated date of death, the life office makes a loss.

---

97 See Figure 9.1 in Chapter 9.

10.86 In defined contribution schemes, the trustees will invariably buy an annuity when the member retires. The reason for this is that defined contribution schemes promise a benefit calculated solely by reference to the amount of pension that can be bought from the fund attributable to the member. The Revenue require that the fund attributable to the member is converted to income by purchasing an annuity. With defined benefit schemes, the trustees have more flexibility. If the scheme is not a large one, the trustees will purchase an annuity as the trustees cannot afford to take the risk that the member will live longer than expected. With a large scheme, the trustees may be able to afford to take a risk and pay the pension out of the fund without buying an annuity. Actuarial advice is necessary in this context. By paying the pension out of the fund, the trustees are, in effect, retaining in the fund the profit that would otherwise have been made by the life office.

10.87 Trustees can buy annuities with or without a guarantee. It would be somewhat harsh to pay £190,000 in order to buy a pension of £20,000 (as in Example 10.2) if the member died the next day. Accordingly, life offices usually guarantee that the pension will be payable for a specified period of time even if the member dies within that period. The typical period is five years but a period up to 10 years is available.[98] It is more expensive to buy an annuity with a guarantee than to buy one without. The guarantee may be specified in the rules of the scheme. If, for example, the rules require that the pension be paid for at least five years, the trustees would normally buy an annuity with a five-year guarantee.

10.88 Life offices distinguish between immediate annuities and deferred annuities. An immediate annuity is where an immediate pension income is being secured, such as on retirement. A deferred annuity secures payment of a pension at a future date. Deferred annuities are frequently purchased in circumstances where a member leaves service prior to retirement with a deferred pension.[99] There are two types of deferred annuity: a non-profit deferred annuity and a with-profit deferred annuity. A non-profit deferred annuity guarantees the pension at a future date. A with-profit annuity is a type of investment policy

---

98 The Revenue will not permit a guarantee beyond 10 years. See para 7.46.

99 On deferred pensions see para. 12.3.

which operates in a similar way to a with-profit policy.[100] A cash sum is invested so that with annual bonuses it will increase in value during the deferred period to retirement and its then value will be applied to provide the pension. The with-profit deferred annuity will be sufficient to pay the future pension, provided that bonuses are sufficient.

10.89 Annuities are bought either in the name of the trustees of the pension scheme or in the name of the member. Until recently, annuities were always bought in the name of the trustees. The consequence of this is that the annuity remains an asset of the fund and is simply an investment whereby the liability to pay an income (the pension) is directly matched by a promise by a life office to pay an income to the trustees (the annuity). This means that if the scheme becomes insolvent, the annuities may have to be surrendered in order to meet other liabilities of the scheme.[101] Annuities can, however, be bought in the name of the member or indeed any other beneficiary of the scheme. This can be done regardless of whether there is a power to do so in the rules, provided that the member so directs and the benefit is a preserved benefit under Part III of the Pensions Act.[102] In all other circumstances, however, an annuity can only be bought in the name of the member if there is an express power in the scheme rules permitting it. If the asset (the annuity) ceases to be an asset of the scheme, so too must the liability. Therefore, the asset representing the cash needed to buy the annuity is transferred out of the scheme by purchasing an annuity in the member's name. The rules should stipulate that the trustees are consequently discharged from their liability to provide the benefit to the member.[103]

10.90 A buy-out bond is the generic term for a policy to which an early leaver's benefits can be transferred so that they cease to be subject to the pension scheme. With-profit and non-profit deferred

---

[100] See para. 10.16 above.

[101] *Re H. Williams Pension Fund* (Unreported, High Court, 17 July 1992, Denham J). Part IV of the Pensions Act now gives priority on a winding up to pensions in payment and so the decision in *H. Williams* will have limited application in practice with regard to immediate annuities. See also para. 17.36.

[102] See para. 12.57 et seq.

[103] s. 34(5) of the Pensions Act gives a statutory discharge to the trustees as far as a preserved benefit is concerned.

annuities are examples of buy-out bonds where the annuity is bought in the member's name. The liability to provide benefits under the scheme is bought out, hence the name "buy-out". Buy-out bonds must be approved by the Revenue for the purposes of Chapter II of Part I of the Finance Act, 1972 before they can receive transfers from an approved pension scheme. Approval is not granted on an individual basis. Rather, the Revenue approve the terms of a standard bond issued by the life office. There are other types of buy-out bond aside from conventional annuities. The most common is a unit-linked investment bond. The present value of an early leaver's benefits is invested in the unit-linked bond. The cash paid into the bond increases (or decreases) in value over the investment period in line with the return on the underlying investments of the unit-linked fund. Early leavers hope that the investment return under the bond will provide them with a bigger pension than if they left their benefits in the pension scheme. The risk is that the bond will underperform and they will receive a lower benefit. It is important to note that it is the early leaver's decision to invest in a unit-linked bond. It is not a decision for the trustees. It is advisable that trustees ensure that the early leaver fully understands the nature of the unit-linked investment and that the fund can fall in value as well as rise as life-office explanatory notes may not always spell this out clearly.

VENTURE CAPITAL

10.91 The final aspect of investment which it is proposed to examine in this chapter is venture capital. Venture capital is investment in potentially risky start-up businesses or ventures and is a specialised form of investment undertaken by a small number of venture-capital companies in Ireland.

10.92 In 1993, the Minister for Finance sought to encourage pension schemes to invest to a greater degree in venture capital so as to generate additional jobs. The Minister's concern was that with approximately £14 billion of investments held by Irish pension schemes at the time, a small portion of this money could be diverted to venture-capital investment to the mutual advantage of pension schemes and the economy. There was some suggestion that pension fund income might be taxed. In the light of a new initiative on venture capital, the

Minister indicated that he had no proposal at present to alter the tax-exempt status.[104]

10.93 A report commissioned by the IAPF, the Irish Association of Investment Managers, the Irish Insurance Federation and the Department of Finance subsequently recommended that pension fund moneys should be made available by trustees to venture-type businesses, provided that there is an acceptable rate of return relative to risk.[105] The report also recommended that it would not be unreasonable for pension funds to invest, in aggregate, £10 million per annum, which is the equivalent of 0.08 per cent of total pension fund assets. £49 million has since been committed by pension funds over a five-year period.[106]

10.94 A decision of this kind must be evaluated by trustees on prudential grounds. If pension scheme trustees are requested to consent to a portion of the fund being earmarked for venture-capital investment, they would need to obtain independent advice as to whether it is in fact a prudent investment decision. Job creation may be a desirable social objective but cannot of itself be a sufficient reason to make the investment from a trustee perspective.

---

[104] The statement of the Minister for Finance was made on 24 February 1994.

[105] Walsh, M. and Murray, J. (1993): Pension Fund Investment Report, Dublin: IAPF.

[106] IAPF Venture Capital Initiative Progress Report, November 1994.

11

INSURANCE

INTRODUCTION

11.1 Pension schemes can provide a variety of benefits. There are pensions and cash lump sums at retirement for members, pensions for spouses and dependants and lump sum benefits payable on death. This chapter focuses on whether or to what extent any of these benefits can be insured with a life assurance company ("life office"). It has been seen in the previous chapter that until 25 years or so ago, the liability to pay pensions in retirement tended to be insured with a life office either on a fully guaranteed ("non-profit") or partially guaranteed ("with-profit") basis.[1] In effect, pension schemes were insured against the volatility of investment returns. In more recent times there has been a shift away from traditional insurance products to unitised funds, or in the case of larger schemes, segregated funds. However, insurance still has an important part to play in the context of pension schemes. As well as the risks associated with investment returns, there is what actuaries refer to as mortality risk — that is, the risk of a member dying and a death benefit having to be paid out as a consequence.

11.2 Some schemes do not insure their risks, as they are large enough to bear the risks themselves. Others require insurance cover because they are too small to assume all or part of the risk. The smaller schemes pool their risks with other schemes by obtaining insurance cover from life offices by means of insurance policies. In return for the payment of premiums, the life office undertakes to pay a specified benefit on the happening of a specified event. The event, in almost all cases, will be the death of a member of the pension scheme before retirement.[2] The death benefit will be either a lump sum or a pension payable to the surviving spouse or other dependant of the member.

---

1 See para. 10.13 et seq.

2 It is possible for the trustees to effect disability or critical illness cover (as opposed to death benefit cover) in order to meet the liability (if any) to pay ill-health early retirement pensions.

11.3 Most private occupational pension schemes secure payment of death benefits by way of insurance cover. Some of these occupational schemes promise only insured death benefits. These are usually referred to as "group life only schemes". Unfunded schemes (for example, the non-commercial public sector pension schemes) do not insure death benefits at all, as they are financed on a pay-as-you-go basis.[3] Finally, self-employed persons can obtain insurance to provide death benefits through an arrangement known as a section 235A policy. These latter arrangements are examined elsewhere.[4] Before considering the legal and life-office requirements of insuring death benefits, it is necessary to take a look at the principal features of the various benefits that can be insured.

11.4 Under the Disclosure Regulations, the trustees of an occupational pension scheme must disclose to the members in the explanatory booklet the benefits under the scheme which are guaranteed by an insurance policy. They must also disclose whether payment is subject to any underwriting criteria from the insurer.[5]

INSURED BENEFITS

11.5 Insured benefits under a pension scheme are payable on the death in service of a member of the scheme. They can be in the form of either a lump sum or a pension. There follows a description of the typical benefits that can be insured.

Lump Sum Benefit

11.6 Lump sum benefits are the most common insured death benefit. They are usually expressed as a multiple of the member's salary at or near to death.[6] For example, the life office may insure three times the member's salary. As well as the insured benefit, the scheme may make an additional payment out of the fund of the scheme, such as a payment equalling contributions made during the lifetime of the member.

---

3 On public sector schemes, see Chapter 8.

4 On s.235A policies see para. 6.64 and 6.67.

5 Occupational Pension Schemes (Disclosure of Information) Regulations, 1991 (SI No 215 of 1991) Art. 9 and para. 12 of Schedule C. On disclosure generally — see Chapter 13.

6 Sometimes the benefit is expressed as a multiple of the member's annual pension expectation at retirement assuming no future salary increases.

11.7 Life offices are unconcerned with how the lump sum death benefit is paid. Once the member dies, the life office pays out the benefit to the trustees of the scheme. The trustees must then dispose of the benefit in accordance with the terms of the scheme. The trustees may be required to pay it to a specified individual — for example the spouse or the legal personal representative of the deceased member. It is more likely, however, that the trustees will have a wide power (under a discretionary trust) as to disposal of the lump sum.

11.8 It has been considered earlier, and it is worth noting again, that there are no Revenue restrictions as to the disposal of lump sum death benefits under approved schemes.[7] The benefit can be paid to any person.[8] However, the maximum benefit that can be paid in lump sum form is four times the member's final remuneration, taking into account all lump sums payable on death to the member under any other scheme, together with a refund of member contributions with reasonable interest.[9] This does not prevent the scheme from providing a higher benefit. For example, the scheme may be designed to provide a benefit of six times salary. In this case, four times salary can be paid in lump sum form, but the balance must, in accordance with Revenue requirements, be applied in providing a pension for one or more dependants. Furthermore, the trustees may be empowered under the rules of the scheme to refuse to pay out a lump sum at all and, instead, use the entire lump sum (in the example, six times salary) to provide a pension or pensions. The trustees will do so by purchasing an immediate annuity on the life of the dependant.[10] The trustees may wish to exercise this power of paying a pension rather than a lump sum where, for example, intended beneficiaries are incapable of managing their own affairs.

11.9 Often, different levels of benefit are provided for specific categories of employee. For example, married employees may be covered for four times salary and single employees for twice salary. Great care must be taken by the trustees to make certain that the life office is fully aware of, and has agreed to insure, the different categories of employee at the appropriate levels of benefit.

---

7 Under Chapter II of Part I of the Finance Act, 1972.

8 See para. 7.36.

9 See paras. 7.36 and 7.37 and on the definition of final remuneration see para. 7.5 et seq.

10 On annuities see para. 10.82 et seq.

Spouse's/Dependant's Pension

11.10 Some schemes provide an insured spouse's (or sometimes dependant's) pension. This is to be distinguished from a spouse's death in retirement pension which (unless the scheme is financed on a pay-as-you-go basis) is funded for in advance during the member's service with the employer. Spouses' pensions are payable for life.[11] A few older schemes still provide that spouses' pensions cease on remarriage. Whilst not illegal, such provisions reflect an outdated view of pension provision and should really be removed from the scheme rules.

11.11 This benefit is occasionally referred to as a widow's pension rather than a spouse's pension. Where the pension is restricted to widows, this will amount to sex discrimination.[12] In defined benefit schemes, the benefit is normally insured as a percentage of the member's expected pension at retirement based on all service to the member's normal retirement date, but based on the member's current salary. An example of how the benefit is calculated is set out in Example 11.1. A rare variation on this benefit, which can be found in some old schemes, is to calculate the benefit based on accrued service to date rather than future, or prospective, service. This is undesirable from the point of view of scheme benefit design, as the spouse of a member with short service will receive a much lower pension on death than the spouse of a member with longer service.[13]

11.12 The insurance cover may incorporate pension increases whilst the spouse's pension is in payment, so as to give a measure of protection against inflation. For example, the pension may be expressed to increase at the rate of 3 per cent per annum. The trustees must make certain, in the case of Revenue approved pension schemes, that the rate of increase does not exceed Revenue limits.[14]

---

[11] This is a Revenue requirement for approved schemes — see para. 7.42.

[12] Apart from exceptional circumstances. On sex discrimination see Chapter 16.

[13] Because the pension increases in value, or creeps forward, with each year of service that the member completes, it is sometimes known as the "creeping widow's pension".

[14] See para. 7.64.

Example 11.1

The Beneficent Pension Scheme provides a member's pension at age 65 of 1/60th of salary for each year of company service. It also promises a spouse's pension on the death in service of a member of the pension scheme. The pension is 50 per cent of the member's expected pension. The pension increases at the rate of 3 per cent per annum compound. Ernie Erstwhile dies in service at the age of 45, having been in company service for four years and is survived by his widow, Bertha. Ernie's salary at death for the purpose of calculating pension is £30,000.

"Expected pension" for the purposes of calculating the spouse's pension is the annual pension that the member would have received had he remained in service until normal retirement (65) but with no change in salary.

Ernie's pension at normal retirement would have been 1/60th of salary (£30,000) for each year of company service. His company service completed before he died was four years and, as he was 45 when he died, he would have completed a further 20 years to normal retirement, making a total of 24 years. His pension at normal retirement (based on current salary) would therefore have been:

24/60ths of £30,000 = £12,000

Bertha's pension is 50 per cent of Ernie's expected pension (£12,000) and so her annual pension is £6,000. As the pension increases at the rate of 3 per cent per annum compound, the pension will be worth £6,180 in the second year of payment, £6,365 in the third, etc.

11.13 The calculation of the spouse's pension in a defined contribution scheme is more straightforward. The member's pension expectation is unknown until actual retirement, as the benefit is calculated by reference to contributions paid into the scheme and investment return. Consequently, it is usual for the spouse's pension to be insured on the basis of a percentage of the member's salary rather than pension expectation.

11.14 As with lump sum benefits, spouses' or dependants' pensions payable under exempt approved schemes are subject to Revenue limits. Any one pension (for example, to a spouse) cannot exceed two-thirds of the maximum pension that would be permitted to the member under Revenue rules. The total of all pensions to dependants cannot exceed the member's maximum pension.[15]

11.15 The rules of a scheme may give the trustees discretion to pay the spouse's pension to another dependant in circumstances of separation.[16] The rules may also stipulate that the pension ceases on subsequent remarriage or cohabitation of the spouse. This is now unusual and is likely to be found only in a few older schemes and most public sector schemes. From an insurance perspective, it is important to realise that the insurer may not pay the same amount of pension to the dependant as it did to the spouse. The premium will have been calculated on the basis of a spouse of a particular age. A younger dependant will have a longer life expectancy, which will mean a more costly benefit for the life office to provide. The trustees will therefore need power in the rules of the scheme to adjust the pension, if necessary, to take account of age differences.

Orphans' and Children's Pensions

11.16 If spouses' pensions are payable for life, they must, by implication, cease on death. This will be the case unless an orphan's pension is provided under the rules. The orphan's pension is a continuation of the spouse's pension to the children of the member on the death of the spouse. Not all life offices will insure this benefit and those that do will define precisely what constitutes "children" for the purpose of continuing the spouse's pension. The most common condition of insurance cover is that the life office will continue to pay the spouse's pension provided that, on the death of the spouse, there are children or a child under a specified age (usually aged 18, or 21 if in full-time education or vocational training). The pension ceases when the last child reaches the upper age limit. Some life offices will insure an orphan's pension only where the spouse's pension has commenced to be paid and the spouse subsequently dies. Others will stipulate that an orphan's pension is paid even where the spouse predeceases the member or they both die together.

11.17 Another form of dependant's pension is a children's pension. This is similar to an orphan's pension in that it is payable to children under a specified age limit and ceases to be paid once the last child

[15] See paras. 7.40 and 7.44.

[16] This is becoming more common and is considered in Chapter 15.

reaches that limit. There are, however, two main differences. First, the children's pension is payable immediately on the death of the scheme member, whereas the orphan's pension is usually deferred until the death of the spouse. Secondly, the children's pension is specifically allocated to individual children, whereas in the case of an oprhan's pension the spouse's pension continues to be paid in its entirety to the children, on the death of the spouse, in such proportions as the trustees determine. There are many approaches to apportioning the children's pension, but a typical allocation would be a payment of 10 per cent of the member's expected pension[17] for the eldest child, with 5 per cent for each of the remaining children (in order of seniority), up to a maximum of three such children. The maximum payment would in this example be 25 per cent of the member's expected pension. On the subsequent death of the spouse, children's pensions are sometimes doubled, but if an orphan's pension is payable as well, it is unlikely that children's pensions will be doubled.

Disability Benefits

11.18 The above benefits should be distinguished from employee benefits payable on disability. Disability benefits, also known as Permanent Health Insurance or "PHI" benefits, are insured benefits payable on the disablement of an employee under a policy issued to the employer. Disability benefits are frequently thought of as being part of the overall pension scheme benefit structure, but this is not so. Disability benefits do not form part of the pension scheme benefits and are not subject to the trusts of the scheme.[18]

LEGAL REQUIREMENTS

11.19 The previous section surveyed the benefits that can be insured with a life office. The cover is effected by means of a policy of insurance and is subject to insurance law generally.[19] The Life Assurance

---

17 This would be defined similarly to "expected pension" for the purposes of the spouse's pension — see para. 11.11 above.

18 But see para. 11.40 below.

19 See generally Parkington, M., Leigh Jones, N., Longmore, A. and Birds, J. (Eds.) (1986): *McGillivray and Parkington on Insurance Law*, London: Sweet & Maxwell; and Corrigan, M. and Campbell, J.A. (1995): *A Casebook of Irish Insurance Law*, Dublin: Oak Tree Press.

Act 1774[20] permits a person to effect insurance on their own life or the life of another, provided that in the case of insuring another person, they have an insurable interest in the other. If there is no insurable interest, the policy is deemed to be a gaming contract and is void. The trustees of a pension scheme have an insurable interest in insuring the lives of the pension scheme members because the rules of the scheme promise a benefit in the event of a member's death which the trustees are obliged to pay. With a group pension scheme, the policy will be issued with respect to persons unnamed. There was doubt as to whether such a policy is lawful, as the Life Assurance Act, 1774 does not permit policies to be issued in respect of persons unnamed. This legal uncertainty was removed by section 26 of the Insurance Act, 1989 which states:

> Section 2 of the Life Assurance Act, 1774, as applied by the Life Insurance (Ireland) Act, 1866, shall not invalidate a policy of insurance for the benefit of unnamed persons from time to time falling within a specified class or description if the class or description is stated in the policy with sufficient particularity to make it possible to establish the identity of all persons who, at any given time, are entitled to benefit under the policy.[21]

It should be noted that there must be a sufficiently particular description of the class of persons to be covered so that at any point it is possible to identify all persons who are entitled to benefit. All policies must be reviewed carefully with this in mind. Section 26 applies both prospectively as well as retrospectively.[22]

11.20 As the obligation to provide benefits under the scheme is a matter for the trustees, the policy of insurance must be issued in the name of the trustees, who are usually referred to as "the grantee". It would be incorrect to issue it in the name of the employer as all benefits must be paid through the trust, and consequently the trustees must be the grantee in order to be entitled to receive a payment from the life office. This is of particular concern to the trustees of exempt-approved schemes as the Revenue will require the policy to be issued to the trustees. Otherwise there may be adverse tax consequences for

---

20 As applied in Ireland by the Life Insurance (Ireland) Act, 1866.

21 Sub-section (1).

22 s.26(2).

the members.[23] Also, the employer is not required to provide the benefit independently of the trust.[24] It could possibly be argued that the employer does not have an insurable interest and that the policy is consequently void. Insurers have been known from time to time to issue policies in the name of the employer by mistake.

11.21 Aside from the direct issuing of a policy, trustees of a scheme may become grantee of an already issued policy in one of two ways. First, where there has been a change of trustees, a deed of appointment of new trustees will usually incorporate a clause vesting the assets of the scheme (which would include the policy) in the continuing and new trustees of the scheme.[25] Secondly, the trustees may have a policy issued to them by way of assignment from the trustees of another scheme. This will sometimes arise, for example, in scheme reorganisations where assets and liabilities are transferred from one scheme of the sponsoring employer to another. The assignee trustees can enforce the policy as if they were the original grantee, provided that notice of assignment has been given to the life office, and provided that they have a right in equity to the policy.[26] Assignment may be by endorsement on the policy or by separate instrument,[27] usually an agreement or deed. The life office must acknowledge the notice on request and the acknowledgement constitutes conclusive evidence of the notice having been received.[28]

11.22 In order to effect insurance cover, the trustees of a pension scheme must ensure that there are adequate powers in the documents establishing the trust to enable the trustees to do so. A power to insure

---

23 See para. 6.84 et seq.

24 Although the employee may have an independent contractual right to have a death benefit provided for his or her estate which would give the employer an insurable interest.

25 See para. 4.10.

26 The Policies of Assurance Act 1867 s.1 and s.3 and see *Scottish Amicable Life Assurance Society* v. *Fuller* (1867) IR 2 Eq 53. It was possible to effect an assignment prior to the 1867 Act but there were procedural difficulties associated with it — see generally Hamilton, P. (1995): *Life Assurance Law and Practice*, London: FT Law & Practice, Part A4.

27 s.5 of the 1867 Act. The appropriate wording for the assignment is set out in the schedule to the Act.

28 s.6.

will often be included as one of the powers of investment on the ground that applying part of the resources of the scheme in securing death benefits is akin to investment in its widest sense.[29] Alternatively, the power may be contained in a separate clause. In either event, the appropriate provision will normally state that the trustees have power to effect such insurance, including life assurance, as the trustees consider prudent. In addition, the trustees will be empowered to purchase deferred or immediate annuity contracts and also endowment contracts.

11.23 Trust documents will usually permit the trustees to effect insurance with such life offices as are authorised under the European Communities (Life Assurance) Regulations, 1984.[30] Older trust documents will refer to the Insurance Act, 1936. The Third Life Directive[31] has been implemented in Ireland by the European Communities (Life Assurance) Framework Regulations, 1994.[32] The Framework Regulations restate many of the provisions of the 1984 Regulations including the authorisation procedures for life offices. Unfortunately, the 1984 authorisation procedures have not yet been revoked, and so life offices with existing authorisations continue to be authorised under the 1984 Regulations, whereas newly authorised life offices will be authorised under the 1994 Regulations. If trustees wish to effect insurance with a foreign insurer authorised by its home country, they will need to ensure that the trust documents authorise them to do so.

11.24 An insurance policy is a contract, and the general law of contract applies. However, there are special rules which apply to insurance policies. One of the most important is the obligation of *uberrima fides* or utmost good faith. The trustees of a pension scheme are under the same duty of *uberrima fides* with regard to proposing for insurance cover as any other person seeking insurance. The require-

---

29 See para. 10.38.

30 SI No 57 of 1984.

31 Third Council Directive 92/96/EEC of 10 November 1992 on the co-ordination of laws, regulations and administrative provisions relating to direct life assurance.

32 SI No 360 of 1994.

ments of *uberrima fides* are outside the scope of this work,[33] but can briefly be stated as follows. The person seeking insurance must disclose to the insurer all information (generally referred to as "material facts") which a prudent underwriter would consider relevant in assessing the risk to be insured or fixing the premium. The principle was summarised by the Supreme Court in the *Chariot Inns* case as follows:

> What is to be regarded as material to the risk against which the insurance is sought? It is not what the person seeking insurance regards as material, nor is it what the insurance company regards as material. It is a matter or circumstance which would reasonably influence the judgment of a prudent insurer in deciding whether he would take the risk, and, if so, in determining the premium which he would demand. The standard by which materiality is to be determined is objective and not subjective. In the last resort the matter has to be determined by the court: the parties to the litigation may call experts in insurance matters as witnesses to give evidence of what they would have regarded as material, but the question of materiality is not to be determined by such witnesses.[34]

11.25 Failure to disclose material facts makes the policy voidable at the instance of the life office. The one exception to this is where the insurer applies a free cover (non-medical) limit and waives the requirement for disclosure of medical information concerning employees.[35]

INSURER REQUIREMENTS

11.26 Insurance cover for death benefits is governed by a life assurance policy issued by the life office to the trustees on foot of a proposal form completed by the trustees. For schemes which are approvable under the Finance Act, 1972, the policy is not usually issued until exempt approval is granted. Nonetheless, the life office is usu-

---

33 See Parkington, M., Leigh Jones, N., Longmore, A. and Birds, J. (Eds.) (1986):*McGillivray and Parkington on Insurance Law*, London: Sweet and Maxwell, Chapter 8; and Corrigan, M. and Campbell, J.A. (1995): *A Casebook of Irish Insurance Law*, Dublin: Oak Tree Press, Chapter 17.

34 *Chariot Inns Ltd.* v. *Assicurazioni Generali S.p.a. and Anor.* [1981] IR 199, 226 per Kenny J. See *also Aro Road and Land Vehicles Ltd* v. *The Insurance Corporation of Ireland Ltd* [1986] IR 403, *Keating* v. *New Ireland Assurance Company plc* [1990] 2 IR 383 and *Kelleher* v. *Irish Life Assurance Company Ltd* [1993] ILRM 643.

35 On free cover limits see paras. 11.30 and 11.31 below.

ally "on cover" for the risk from a date agreed with the trustees and confirmed to the trustees' insurance broker. Even where a scheme already has full exempt approval, there are sometimes delays between the date from which cover commences and the date when the policy is issued.[36] The policy contains all material terms of the contract between the trustees and the life office,[37] and yet the cover is in place before the trustees are given these conditions. It is not of particular concern in practice, as the main terms of the cover, including special terms applicable to the particular scheme, are confirmed in writing to the trustees' broker, and the life office's standard policy conditions are known in advance.

11.27 The policy is issued in consideration of the trustees paying an annual premium. The premium is paid to cover the risk of a claim arising in that year. It is calculated by reference to each member's age, sex and any medical or occupational factors that the life office considers relevant.[38] As members get older, the cost of securing insurance cover in respect of them increases. Provided that there are new entrants at a young age to compensate for the older members, the cost of providing benefits as a percentage of total salaries should, however, remain reasonably stable.

11.28 Instead of calculating the individual cost of each member's cover, a scheme can seek a unit rate to apply to all members. This will only be available to larger schemes. The life office calculates the weighted average age of all members and guarantees a rate for a set period of years (usually two) but reserves the right to adjust the rate if there is a major change in the membership (for example a significant reduction in the membership). The weighted average is the average age of members adjusted to take account of the level of benefit when linked with age. For example, if the average age in a scheme is

---

36 Usually by reason of administrative delay on the part of the life office.

37 Except to the extent that the proposal by the trustees is normally deemed by the policy to be incorporated into the policy as a warranty — see for example *Keating* v. *New Ireland Assurance Company*.

38 This is the single premium or "SP" method of costing. Occasionally, cover is effected for the entire period of membership to normal retirement, rather than for one year at a time. This is known as the annual premium or "AP" method.

45, the average age will be adjusted upwards if all the higher earners are over 45 and all the lower earners are younger.

11.29 Life offices will usually require medical evidence before accepting a life assurance risk and may have other underwriting requirements. The life office may decline cover or may grant cover subject to certain conditions. For example, a higher premium may be charged to reflect the additional risk that the life office perceives to exist (a loading), or payment of benefit may be excluded in the case of death arising from a specified cause or medical condition (an exclusion). An employee who is not subject to a loading or restriction is said to be insured at "ordinary rates".

11.30 With schemes above a certain size (typically at least 10 members) the life office will usually waive underwriting requirements up to a specified level: "the free-cover limit" or "non-medical limit". The free-cover limit is expressed as the maximum salary of an employee or sum assured that the life office will insure without imposing underwriting requirements. The terms of the free-cover limit should be specified in the schedule attached to and forming part of the standard policy terms. The life office normally reserves the right to withdraw the free-cover limit.

11.31 The following points must be borne in mind in connection with free-cover limits:

1. The life office will normally only cover (without medical evidence and other underwriting requirements) those employees who are actively at work at the commencement of the cover, or in some cases who are actively at work at the time of any subsequent increase in cover.

2. The life office will require compulsory cover for the class of employees to be covered. The trustees and employer cannot operate the cover on a discretionary basis.

3. As the free-cover limit is a *limit*, higher earners who exceed the limit will be subject to underwriting requirements with regard to that part of the cover which exceeds the free-cover limit.

To the extent that the life office waives its underwriting requirements, the free-cover limit is an exception to the doctrine of *uberrima fides*.[39] But this is still required with respect to all matters other than the specific medical and other evidence regarding the health of employees which is waived. For example, the nature of the employer's business is a relevant matter. If employees were exposed to hazardous materials, such as asbestos, which would be a material fact, and this was not disclosed, the life office could declare the policy void notwithstanding that a free-cover limit was in operation.

11.32 The trustees may be refused cover in respect of an employee on grounds of health or on such other underwriting grounds as the life office considers appropriate. To avoid the trustees being forced to pay out a death benefit when it is not insured, it is important to include a provision in the rules that payment of the benefit is subject to such evidence as to insurability and health as the trustees consider appropriate. A similar statement should be included in the booklet or announcement given to the employee.

PREMIUMS

11.33 Premiums payable to a life office are part of the cost of providing benefits under a pension scheme. In a defined contribution scheme, the employer may, under the rules, be obliged to pay the premium for risk (i.e. death) benefits in addition to its agreed contribution in respect of each member. Alternatively, the trustees may be required under the rules of the scheme to deduct the premium either out of each member's part of the fund or from contributions received. It is desirable from an administration perspective for the insurance premium to be paid separately from the retirement contributions. In extreme cases, where this is not done, the cost of providing insurance cover could exceed contributions paid and thus result in a reduction in pension benefits.

11.34 Insurance premiums paid through defined benefit schemes are also part of the cost of providing benefits under the scheme. This cost will be included in the overall funding rate applicable to the scheme. In a balance-of-cost scheme,[40] the cost will be borne by the employer.

---

39 See para. 11.24.

40 That is, where the members pay a fixed contribution and the employer pays the balance sufficient to fund for the benefits under the scheme.

Otherwise it will be borne in such manner as the trust documents determine.

11.35 The requirement to pay a premium under a policy ceases on termination of the policy. The policy may be for a fixed term or may be of unlimited duration. Some life offices write policies with terms not exceeding two years in order to avoid stamp duty on the policies and in such cases will usually issue a new contract automatically when this period ends. There will be a power to terminate the policy under the policy conditions. The trustees are always given the right unilaterally to terminate the policy subject to a specified notice period. Some life offices reserve the right themselves to terminate the policy unilaterally. This will again require notice except on failure by the trustees to pay the premium. Trustees are given a certain number of days (referred to as "days of grace") before the life office can exercise this right.

11.36 The employees who are covered by the policy (the "insured persons") do not themselves pay the premium, unless indirectly through pension scheme contributions. There is one exception of sorts contained in some policies. It is known as the "continuation option". The continuation option permits an employee who leaves service to continue the insurance cover under an individual policy usually without the need for any further medical or other underwriting requirements. The premium is, however, calculated at a market rate, having regard to the age and sex of the former employee and is usually a "whole-of-life" contract. The policy and cover options are limited and the option is rarely exercised in practice as the individual can usually obtain cheaper cover on the open market.

INSURANCE AND ELIGIBILITY

11.37 The rules of the scheme will usually specify who is eligible to be included in the scheme for death benefits. The first condition is that for Revenue approved schemes the person must be an employee or former employee[41] who is resident for tax purposes in Ireland. There are many possible additional eligibility criteria. For example,

---

41 It would be unusual, in practice, to cover former employees except where the employer wishes to continue cover for a specified period (usually until the next insurance renewal date) in respect of an employee who leaves service or retires early.

inclusion for death benefits may be open to all full-time permanent employees. Another possibility is that it be open to all employees (including temporary and part-time). Alternatively, entry may be at the sole discretion of the sponsoring employer. Where entry is discretionary, it is unlikely that the life office will offer the facility of a free-cover limit.[42]

11.38 Care must be taken to ensure that the rules reflect the employer's intentions and practice (these are sometimes not the same!) Equally, the rules must match the categories of employee whom the life office has agreed to insure — otherwise there will be an uninsured risk. If an employee is included in the scheme for death benefits but is not insured, the trustees (on subsequent death) will have to pay the benefit out of the resources of the scheme, unless the employer agrees to meet the liability immediately. If the employer does not do so, the overall funding position of the scheme may be affected.[43] It could be particularly damaging in a defined contribution scheme[44] as the value of benefits standing to the credit of members might have to be reduced immediately. This could, in either case, constitute a breach of trust and expose the trustees to a claim by other members whose security of benefits may be affected by the reduction in the fund.

UNINSURED RISKS

11.39 Whether or not to insure is one of the more difficult questions facing the pension scheme trustee. As has already been stated,[45] the risk of having to pay out a death claim may be too much for many smaller schemes to bear. Those schemes have little choice but to insure the death benefit.[46] However, larger pension schemes may have sufficient resources to pay out a small number of death claims per year. The rationale of the fund assuming the risk is that the cost of a small number of death claims each year may be cheaper than the in-

---

42 See above, para. 11.30.

43 Funding is considered in Chapter 9.

44 The nature of defined contribution schemes is considered in Chapter 2.

45 See para. 11.2.

46 In particular, small self-administered schemes are required by the Revenue to insure death in service benefits. See para. 6.83.

surance premium being charged by the life office. The cost of meeting a high level of death claims may, however, put a serious strain on the funding position of the scheme[47] and so stop-loss or catastrophe cover would be advisable in most cases.[48] The trustees would require actuarial advice before moving away from a fully insured basis. There are also several intermediate steps before assuming the full risk. The following is a brief outline:

1. Maintain cover but only in relation to the excess over a set amount in each year. This is referred to as "stop-loss" cover. The premium will be lower as less cover is obtained.
2. Insure only part of the benefit and assume the risk in respect of the balance. For example, the death benefit may be four times salary. The trustees may decide to insure only twice salary. This is similar, in effect, to stop-loss cover.
3. Insure only a part of the workforce. For example, staff employees could be insured whereas the fund could bear the risk in respect of works employees.
4. Bear the risk of a set number of employees dying in a year but if that number is exceeded the life office covers the balance. This is known as "catastrophe cover".

11.40 The employer of a defined benefit scheme may wish to carry out a similar exercise with regard to disability insurance. Whilst disability benefits do not form part of a pension scheme, there is an interrelationship between ill-health early retirement and disability benefit. As part of a programme for reducing or eliminating the need for disability insurance, some employers seek to replace disability benefits by enhanced ill-health early-retirement benefits under the pension scheme. This requires actuarial advice and may need additional funding from the employer.

11.41 The trustees of defined contribution schemes usually need to insure their death benefits. The reason for this is that the fund of a defined contribution scheme is divided up between members and there is therefore no common fund out of which a death benefit can be paid.

---

47 Because the death benefits become an immediate liability on the fund, irrespective of the solvency position of the scheme.

48 See points 1. and 4. above.

11.42 As stated earlier,[49] the trustees are obliged to disclose to members the benefits which are insured. However, no obligation is imposed upon them by the Pensions Act to insure benefits. Failure to insure could place the fund in jeopardy. A significant claim could turn a solvent fund into an insolvent one. The purpose of the funding standard under Part IV of the Pensions Act is to ensure pension fund solvency for defined benefit schemes, but Part IV does not require uninsured risks to be taken into account by the actuary in preparing the actuarial valuation and funding certificate. However, in practice, the actuary will take account of uninsured risks in striking a funding rate for the scheme.

MULTINATIONAL POOLING

11.43 Multinational pooling originated in the 1950s but did not gain popularity until the late 1960s.[50] It involves the pooling of risks internationally with the purpose of reducing the overall charges of a multinational company. There are currently at least 11 major international networks of insurers which operate multinational pooling.[51] Separate insurance contracts are placed with local insurers in each country and these contracts are governed by local law and insurance practice. Superimposed on this network of individual insurers is an umbrella contract which attempts to treat each of the local insurance arrangements as a single entity or pool. The pooling of risks internationally follows the traditional principle of spreading risk. In other words, a number of smaller insurance contracts are brought together to form a larger pool. The claims experience in one country may be poor, but this may be outweighed by a favourable experience in another country. The aim overall is that losses will be absorbed and outweighed by gains.

11.44 Overall charges are reduced in the following way. Each year the pooling network prepares an international account based on information supplied to it by each of the local insurers. The account measures the overall claims experience internationally, having regard to factors such as total premiums paid, claims arising and expenses. If income is deemed to exceed expenditure in this account, a dividend is paid to the

---

[49] See para. 11.4.

[50] Multinational pooling is considered generally in Thakkar, Y.M. (1990): *Multinational Pooling*, Zurich: Swiss Reinsurance Company.

[51] *Ibid.* p.5.

multinational company. If there is an overall loss, a payment is required from the company unless the company has obtained participation terms that prevent a company payment from having to be made.[52] Payment of a dividend means, in effect, that the company is receiving a discount on the original premium and is making a cost saving.

11.45 The main qualifying conditions for joining a pool are, first, that local insurance contracts be entered into in at least two countries and, second, that a certain minimum number of lives be covered or a minimum total annual premium be paid, or both. There have, however, been trends in recent years towards offering small group pools where these conditions are not met.[53]

11.46 The parent company enters into a master contract in order to join the network. In the master contract, the insurer which manages the network may undertake to insure employees of the parent company or its subsidiaries, where it is locally authorised to do so. Where it does not so undertake, or in countries where it is not so authorised, it will contract to co-ordinate insurance cover with local insurers, usually referred to as network partners. The typical contract will specify that the network will pay out a dividend if there is a profit in the international account. Conditions for participation are also contained in the contract. Life assurance policies are issued to the pension scheme trustees in accordance with the master contract.

11.47 Many Irish pension schemes have risks placed with network partners in a multinational pooling framework. This is clearly of advantage to the sponsoring employer as its parent company has the potential to receive an international dividend. In this regard, it should be emphasised that the master contract is with the parent company, not with the trustees of the scheme. This is logical as the parent may sponsor separately constituted schemes in different countries, with separate trustees for each. The deed governing the scheme may require the consent of the employer as to the choice of life office, but the trustees may be entitled to select the life office without the need for consent. It would be advisable for a multinational company

---

52 Known as "stop-loss" cover.

53 Thakkar, Y.M. (1990): *Multinational Pooling*, Zurich: Swiss Reinsurance Company, p.7.

participating in a network to incorporate a consent requirement in the deed, when establishing the scheme.

11.48 It is generally desirable for pension scheme trustees to effect insurance with the life office that offers the most competitive rate for satisfactory cover. The network partner may not be competitive and yet the employer will wish to place the insurance business with it so as to receive a benefit by way of dividend under the network. This may be a source of conflict between the employer and the trustees, unless the additional cost is paid by the employer without affecting members' benefits or the value of the pension fund.

12

EARLY LEAVERS

INTRODUCTION

12.1 This chapter examines the entitlements of an occupational pension scheme member on ceasing to be a member before retirement. This usually arises on leaving service. As there is no concept of leaving service in a self-employed arrangement, such arrangements will not be examined here.[1]

12.2 Occupational pension schemes promise pensions at retirement.[2] A member who leaves service prior to retirement has not satisfied the principal condition for receiving pension — to remain in service until retirement. However, as we have seen,[3] the pension is a form of deferred remuneration and so it would seem logical that employees who work for (say) half their potential service with the employer should receive half their pension promise. They may also have contributed to the employer's scheme and should at least expect a pension based on their own contributions.

12.3 Before the introduction of the Pensions Act, most schemes promised benefits for pension scheme members who left service early, although some schemes were far from generous to employees. By way of an immediate benefit, all schemes gave members a refund of their own contributions on leaving service. The refund might be with or without interest on the contributions.[4] As an alternative, many

---

1 Self-employed arrangements are examined in further detail at para. 6.59 et seq.

2 With the exception of schemes which promise death in service benefits solely.

3 See para. 5.2 and *McMenamin* v. *Ireland* [1994] 2 ILRM 368, 378.

4 Refunds were, and still are, subject to tax, currently at the rate of 25 per cent. The tax treatment of refunds is considered at para. 7.52.

schemes gave the option to employees to leave their contributions in the scheme. In that event, there were no immediate benefits[5] — benefits were deferred until later retirement and hence the member's benefit was, and still is, referred to as a *deferred* pension. But member's contributions are only part of the cost of funding the retirement pension. The employer also contributes to the scheme. The more generous schemes provided a pension based on benefits accrued to date of leaving service, typically in circumstances of redundancy or on completing a minimum period of company service — for example, five years' service.

12.4 The statutory protection of early-leaver benefits was considered by the National Pensions Board in its first report. The Board recommended that pension scheme members should be entitled to certain minimum benefits on leaving service and the right to transfer those benefits to another pension scheme:

> A proper system of preservation of pension rights for early leavers should be implemented from which would follow a logical system of transferability reflecting the diversity in occupational pension scheme structures.[6]

It also recommended that the scheme of a new employer should be obliged to accept a transfer from the previous employer's scheme.[7]

12.5 These two principles of preservation and portability were put on a statutory footing in the Pensions Act which, with effect from 1 January 1991, introduced a framework of protection for early leavers from pension schemes. This is contained in Part III of the Act, the Second Schedule and regulations made under Part III.[8] Part III requires schemes to provide a basic minimum level of benefit on leaving service (a "perserved benefit"). This forces schemes with a less generous benefit structure to improve leaving service entitlements up to

---

5 Unless the member was entitled to and took early retirement —that is, an immediate pension. On early retirement, see para. 12.43.

6 First Report of the National Pensions Board (Pl 4776), p.15.

7 *Ibid.* para. 5.12(e) p.56.

8 Two sets of regulations have been made: the Occupational Pension Schemes (Preservation of Benefits) Regulations, 1992 SI No 445 of 1992 and the Occupational Pension Schemes (Preservation of Benefits) (Special Calculations) Regulations, 1993 SI No 217 of 1993.

the minimum.[9] However, schemes which provide better benefits than the Pensions Act minimum can nonetheless continue to provide higher benefits.[10] In certain circumstances, the Act also bars scheme members from taking a refund of their employee contributions. Preservation does not apply retrospectively so that benefits which have accrued prior to 1 January 1991 are not preserved under the Act.

12.6 The conditions for entitlement to preserved benefits under the Act and the calculation of benefit are complex. In particular, improvements or reductions in scheme benefits and transfers of benefits between schemes of the same employer can involve lengthy calculations. In contrast, the transfer provisions, which facilitate pension portability, are straightforward. Each of these issues is examined below, but first it is proposed to consider the circumstances under which employment is treated as terminated for the purposes of establishing a right to preserved benefit.

TERMINATION OF RELEVANT EMPLOYMENT

12.7 The most common instance of employment terminating is on an employee leaving service before retirement. However, the Pensions Act requires the trustees to preserve benefits in other circumstances as well, in that the Act refers to "termination of relevant employment" rather than "termination of employment". Those other events and the meaning of "termination of relevant employment" will now be examined.

12.8 A member's employment is terminated either on retirement or when the member leaves service prior to retirement. Members who reach normal retirement date and draw their pension have satisfied the main object of the pension scheme. They have not left service early and so the preservation requirements of Part III of the Act are not relevant.[11] What Part III of the Act protects is the benefits of a member whose relevant employment is terminated prior to normal retirement. "Relevant employment" is defined as being "any employment (or any period treated as employment) to which a scheme

---

9 As preservation overrides any scheme provisions to the contrary — s.38(1).

10 s.39 as amended by s.15 of the Pensions (Amendment) Act, 1996.

11 But compare the case of early retirement — see para. 12.43.

applies".[12] "Termination of relevant employment" is therefore termination of any employment (or any period treated as employment) to which a scheme applies. This is a confusing phrase and is unsatisfactorily drafted. It is, however, generally considered that a member's relevant employment has terminated when, having been a scheme member, there is no scheme of the employer in which that person is currently an active member — in other words, a member who is actively included in the scheme for retirement benefits and who is not in receipt of pension, or a deferred pensioner.[13]

12.9 The circumstances in which relevant employment is terminated may be summarised as follows (see also the flow chart in Figure 12.1):

1. The member leaves the service of the employer otherwise than in specified circumstances of a company reorganisation or sale.
2. There is an interruption in the member's service (the member leaves and subsequently re-enters service) which is not temporary.
3. The member ceases to be a member of the scheme and is not an active member of any other scheme of the employer.
4. The member ceases to be an active member.
5. The scheme is wound up.

In the first two circumstances, the member has left service. In the remaining three, the member remains in service. Each circumstance is now examined in turn.

Leaving Service

12.10 In general terms, the relevant employment of a member who leaves service is terminated. However, there are two circumstances in which the legislation deems there not to be a termination of relevant employment on a member leaving service. The first is where the employee is a member of a "centralised scheme", and the second is where the employee resumes membership in the same scheme.

---

[12] s.2(1).

[13] This is supported by the Pensions Board's guidance notes on Preservation of Benefits, which, although not binding, are an indication of best practice.

FIGURE 12.1: TERMINATION OF RELEVANT EMPLOYMENT

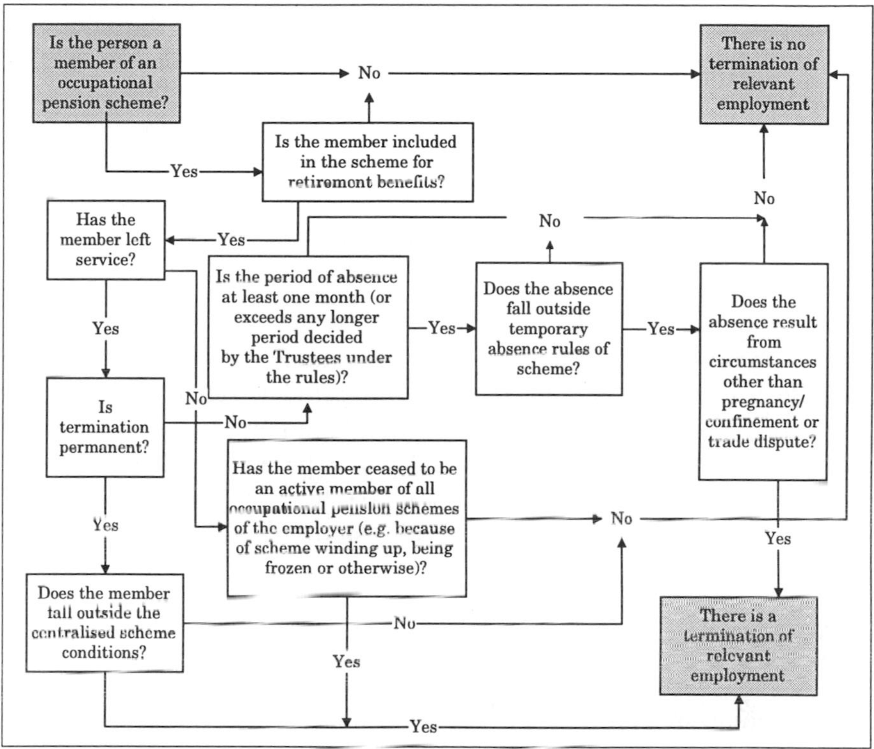

12.11 A centralised scheme is one in which other employers participate.[14] Relevant employment is deemed to continue where, after a period of less than one month of leaving service (or such longer period as the trustees decide in accordance with the rules) an employee enters into relevant employment with another employer who participates in the same centralised scheme.[15]

12.12 A member may leave service because of a change in ownership of the employer or of the business of the employer. Relevant employ-

---

[14] The employers need not be affiliated with each other although the Revenue will require some business connection between them — see para. 6.22 et seq.

[15] Preservation Regulations, Art. 4(a)(i). The Preservation Regulations are made under a power granted to the Minister for Social Welfare under s.37(3) of the Pensions Act as amended by s.54(3) of the Social Welfare Act, 1992 (and also ss.5, 35 and 38).

ment is deemed to continue where, within one month (or any longer period determined by the trustees in accordance with the rules) the employee commences in the relevant employment of the new employer and resumes membership of the same scheme.[16]

12.13 In either circumstance, reckonable service in the first employment is deemed to be reckonable service in the relevant employment of the new employer.[17] If the specific conditions are not satisfied, relevant employment is treated as terminated.[18]

Non-Temporary Absence

12.14 Temporary absence has been examined elsewhere.[19] There is usually a provision in the rules of the pension scheme permitting temporary periods of absence. For example, an employee may be seconded temporarily to another employer. The Preservation Regulations[20] prescribe the periods of temporary absence that do not bring about a termination of relevant employment. These may be summarised as follows:[21]

1. Where the rules of the scheme treat the break as temporary absence
2. Pregnancy or confinement[22] of the member
3. In furtherance of a trade dispute[23]
4. Where the period of absence is less than one month.

---

16 Art. 4(a)(ii).

17 Art. 5. On "reckonable service" see para. 12.24 below.

18 Art. 4(b).

19 para. 6.56 et seq.

20 Occupational Pension Schemes (Preservation of Benefits) Regulations, 1992 — SI No 445 of 1992.

21 See Art. 6 and definition of "temporary absence" in Art. 2.

22 Confinement is defined in s.41 of the Social Welfare (Consolidation) Act, 1993 (formerly s. 28 of the Social Welfare (Consolidation) Act, 1981).

23 As defined in s.8 of the Industrial Relations Act, 1990.

12.15 In each case the member must resume service in the relevant employment of the same employer.[24] For the purpose of subsequently calculating preserved benefits, the period of temporary absence is not included as reckonable service unless the rules otherwise permit, either expressly or under a discretion given to the trustees. In the case of pregnancy or confinement, temporary absence must count as reckonable service where the member is on paid maternity leave.[25]

Ceasing to be a Scheme Member

12.16 Employees can cease to be members of a scheme without leaving the service of their employer. This occurs where their benefits are transferred out of the scheme to a buy-out bond. Their relevant employment is terminated provided that they are not active members of another scheme of the employer.

Ceasing to be an Active Member

12.17 Members cease to be active members where they are no longer accruing retirement benefits. Their benefits become frozen. In these circumstances, if there is no replacement scheme and there is no other scheme of their employer of which they are an active member, their relevant employment is treated as terminated. A member's benefits may become frozen on an individual basis or the scheme itself may become frozen. In the latter situation, benefits for all existing members cease to accrue, and no new members are included in the scheme.[26]

Scheme Wound Up

12.18 Benefits cease to accrue to members when a scheme is wound up. The trustees will secure benefits by purchasing annuities or buy-out bonds or by transferring benefits to another occupational pension scheme. Relevant employment is treated as terminated provided that there is no other scheme of the employer of which the employee is a member.[27]

---

24 Art. 2 (definition of "temporary absence").

25 Art. 6 and Maternity Protection Act, 1994. On "reckonable service", see para. 12.24 below.

26 Any other frozen scheme of which the employee is a member is disregarded and the relevant employment is treated as terminated.

27 See previous footnote.

ACCRUAL OF LONG SERVICE BENEFIT

12.19 As has been seen in the previous section, there are various situations in which relevant employment can be terminated. However, the effect is the same: the member's benefits cease to accrue any further. This concept of accrual of benefit is important in the operation of the preservation requirements of the Pensions Act and is best illustrated by a defined benefit scheme. In such a scheme a specified benefit is promised at retirement and this is usually calculated by reference to salary at or near retirement and service completed to that date. There are other ways of promising defined benefits but this is the most prevalent and illustrates clearly the accrual concept. It is common for private sector defined benefit schemes to promise a pension of 1/60th of final pensionable salary[28] for each year of company service. A member who retires after 40 years of service gets a pension of 40/60ths (2/3rds) of final pensionable salary. Broadly speaking, the member's pension which has accrued at any time before retirement would be 1/60th of final pensionable salary for each year of service completed at that date. For example, the pension accrued after 20 years would be 20/60ths of final pensionable salary based on salary at that point. After 30 years it would be 30/60ths. This principle equally applies to other accrual rates, such as 1/80th or 1/45th.

12.20 Pensions promised under a defined contribution scheme are based solely upon whatever the current value of a member's retirement account (that is, the current value of employer and employee contributions) can secure. The pension accrued at a given time is the value at that time of the member's retirement account.

12.21 The Pensions Act uses the term "long service benefit" to describe the benefits payable on or after normal retirement, as "benefit" under the Act has a wider meaning and includes death benefits payable before retirement. Long service benefit is defined in the Act as

> the benefits which will be payable under a scheme in accordance with an obligation to *or in respect of*[29] a member of a scheme on the

---

[28] Final pensionable salary typically incorporates a deduction to take account of the fact that the State social welfare pension is also payable — see para. 2.16.

[29] Emphasis added.

assumption that he remains in relevant employment until such time as he attains normal pensionable age

This comprises pensions payable to the member and, because of the inclusion of the words "or in respect of", any pension payable to a spouse or dependant on death in retirement.

12.22 It is a fundamental principle of preservation under the Pensions Act that the long service benefit should accrue evenly over the member's service, so that a member who leaves the scheme early should receive the pension that has accrued to date of leaving. Unless the member can take early retirement, the pension will be deferred until retirement.

12.23 Part III of the Act commenced with effect from 1 January 1991.[30] However, it was not made retrospective[31] and so only pensions accrued since 1 January 1991 are preserved under the Act. Any part of a pension that accrued prior to that date is not preserved. Given that, today, most pension scheme members have substantial benefits accrued prior to 1 January 1991, the level of protection under the statutory framework is questionable. In time, however, the benefit accrued since 1991 will form an increasingly greater part of a member's benefits and, of course, members who join a scheme after 1 January 1991 will enjoy full statutory protection. It is also likely that the statutory protection will, in time, be made retrospective.[32]

12.24 The statutory preserved benefit is calculated on service completed by the member as a full member of the scheme since 1 January 1991, or to use Pensions Act terminology, *reckonable service* accrued since that date. Reckonable service means:

---

30 Pensions Act, 1990 (Parts III, IV and V) (Commencement) Order, 1990 SI No 330 of 1990.

31 Because of cost implications — see First Report of the National Pensions Board para. 5.9, p. 55.

32 By 2001, schemes must be in a position on an ongoing basis to cover all liabilities of the scheme, including benefits accrued prior to 1 January 1991 and so there would be no hardship at that point in making preservation retrospective. On funding generally, see Chapter 9.

service in the relevant employment[33] during membership of the scheme but does not include service as a member of the scheme where either —

(a) the only benefit under the scheme in respect of such service is in respect of death prior to normal pensionable age, or

(b) the member has been notified in writing by the trustees that such service does not entitle him to long service benefit;[34]

In short, reckonable service is service as a member of a scheme in which the member is accruing an entitlement to retirement benefits. If the only benefit promised by the scheme is a benefit on death in service, the member's service is not reckonable service. Similarly, if a member is included in a scheme for a death in service benefit but is waiting to be included in the scheme for retirement benefits, the waiting period is not reckonable service. The other circumstance where service is not regarded as reckonable service is where the trustees have so notified the member in writing. The most common example of this is where benefits in a scheme for a member are frozen[35] — the member will receive benefits with respect to service up to a stated date but will not receive benefits relating to future service.

12.25 The Pensions Act requires preservation of benefits in respect of an employee's reckonable service accrued since 1 January 1991, or since becoming a member, if later. The preserved benefit only arises on termination of relevant employment, but not every termination of relevant employment results in a preserved benefit. There are other conditions which an employee must satisfy before gaining entitlement to a preserved benefit.

CONDITIONS FOR ENTITLEMENT TO PRESERVED BENEFIT

12.26 Certain conditions must be satisfied before a member is entitled to preserved benefit under the Act:

---

33 Relevant employment in this context means the employment to which a scheme applies — s.2(1) and see para. 12.7 et seq.

34 s.2(1) as amended by s.53(c) of the Social Welfare Act, 1992, s.42(f) of the Social Welfare Act, 1993 and s.2(d) of the Pensions (Amendment) Act, 1996.

35 It could be an individual member, a class of members or all the scheme members.

1. The member's service in relevant employment terminates otherwise than on death.[36]
2. The member has completed at least five years of qualifying service.
3. Two of those years of qualifying service have been completed after 1 January 1991.[37]

12.27 The first condition that must be satisfied before the benefits of a member are preserved is the requirement that service in relevant employment has terminated. The concepts of relevant employment and termination of relevant employment were considered above.[38]

12.28 The second condition is that the member has completed at least five years of qualifying service. This introduces an important definition under Part III, that of "qualifying service". In relation to a member of a scheme, "qualifying service" means:

> the aggregate of every period of reckonable service,[39] whether or not continuous in each case, under —
>
> 1. the scheme,
> 2. every other scheme relating to the same employment,
> 3. every other scheme relating to any other employment in respect of which rights to long service benefit[40] have been granted under the scheme in substitution for accrued rights under such other scheme:
>
> Provided that no such period, or part thereof, shall be counted more than once.[41]

For the purpose of qualifying for preserved benefits, it is interesting to note that the Pensions Act takes into account all schemes of the same employer. The member may have switched from one scheme of

---

36 s.28(2).

37 That is, the commencement of Part III.

38 At para. 12.7 et seq.

39 Reckonable service is considered above at para. 12.24.

40 Long service benefit is another defined term. See para. 12.21 above.

41 s.27(1).

the employer to another, or may have benefits simultaneously in two (or more) employer schemes. All schemes of the employer of which the member is in reckonable service are counted. However, overlapping periods of reckonable service are counted only once. For example, a member may have five years of reckonable service in one scheme and three in another. If the three years have accrued after the five years, the member has eight years of qualifying service. On the other hand, if the three years have accrued during the five-year period, there is an overlap and the three years are ignored. There is an added complexity in the case of a member who has transferred benefits from the scheme of a former employer to the current employer's scheme. The reckonable service to which the transfer relates is also qualifying service, but, again, overlapping periods are counted only once.[42]

Example 12.1

Helen Troy is employed by Wooden Horses Manufacturing Ltd. on 1 January 1985 and is immediately included in the Wooden Horses Retirement and Death Benefit Scheme for a lump sum payable on death in service. She is included in the scheme for retirement benefits and starts to contribute on 1 January 1989 and then leaves service on 1 September 1993.

She has completed eight years and eight months of service but she has only been in reckonable service since she was included in the scheme for retirement benefits (i.e. since 1 January 1989) and has completed only four years and eight months of reckonable service, which in this case equals four years and eight months of qualifying service.

Helen therefore has no entitlement to preserved benefit under the Pensions Act.

12.29 The third condition is that two years of qualifying service must have accrued after 1 January 1991. This is a transitional provision which delayed the implementation of preservation for a two-year period.

---

42 Proviso to the definition.

FIGURE 12.2: CONDITIONS FOR ENTITLEMENT TO PRESERVED BENEFIT

Has the member's relevant employment terminated?

No → Member is not entitled to preserved benefit

Yes ↓

Has the member's period of inclusion for retirement benefits in (a) the Scheme, and (b) all other schemes of the employer, amounted to at least five years? *(Concurrent periods are only counted once.)*

No → Has a transfer of benefits been received by the Scheme(s) in respect of the member from a former employer's scheme?

No ↑ (Member is not entitled to preserved benefit)

Yes ↓

Does the member's previous service in respect of the transfer plus service in the present Scheme(s) for retirement benefits add up to at least five years?

Yes ↓

Has the member completed at least two years of this combination of service after 1 January 1991?

No → Member is not entitled to preserved benefit

Yes ← (from the previous service question, Yes ↓ from the period of inclusion question)

Has the member been included in the Scheme(s) for retirement benefits for at least two years after 1 January 1991? *Service in respect of any transfer from a former employer's scheme can be included for this calculation.*

No → Member is not entitled to preserved benefit

Yes ↓

Member is entitled to Preserved Benefit (Deferred Benefits in respect of service after 1 January 1991).

Example 12.2

Brian O'Brien is employed by Widget Manufacturing Limited on 1 January 1989 and is immediately included in their pension scheme for a lump sum of 3 times salary payable on death in service. The scheme is non-contributory. He is included in the scheme for retirement benefits on completing one year's service (1 January 1990).

His benefits from his former employer's scheme are transferred into the Widget scheme. He was included in his former employer's scheme for retirement benefits for six years.

He gets dissatisfied with his job and is thinking of leaving service on 1 January 1992 by he wants to ensure that he gets a preserved benefit as

his pension scheme does not give a deferred pension unless the Pensions Act requires it.

He has completed three years of service with Widget Manufacturing but only the second and third years count as qualifying service, and so he has two years of qualifying service under the Widget scheme. However, he can add the qualifying service from his former employer's scheme because his benefits were transferred from the former scheme to the Widget scheme. He therefore has an additional six years of qualifying service, which makes a total of eight.

This is more than the five-year requirement under the Act, but Brian has not completed two years' qualifying service since 1 January 1991, which is the transitional condition that must be satisfied. Accordingly, Brian should wait another year until 1 January 1993 before leaving service. He will then have completed two years since 1 January 1991 and will be entitled to a preserved benefit.

Example 12.3

Peig has two part-time jobs, one with Widget Microprocessors Limited and the other with Floppy Software Limited. She has been included in the Widget Scheme for retirement benefits since 1 January 2002 and in the Floppy Scheme since 1 January 2003. There is also a separate additional voluntary contribution (AVC) scheme with Floppy Software and Peig has been paying AVCs into that scheme since 1 January 2004.

On 1 January 2005, Peig decides to work full-time with Floppy. She leaves the service of Widget Microprocessors and has her benefits transferred to the Floppy scheme.

Peig leaves the service of Floppy Software on 1 October 2005. She has the following periods of reckonable service:

Transfer from Widget Scheme:	*3 years*
Floppy main scheme	*2 years 9 months*
Floppy AVC scheme	*1 year 9 months*
Total	*7 years 6 months*

However, in determining qualifying service, overlapping periods of reckonable service can be counted only once. There is only one year of reckonable service in respect of the transfer from the Widget scheme that does not overlap with the Floppy reckonable service, and so two years must be deducted from the total. All the AVC scheme reckonable service overlaps with the Floppy main-scheme reckonable service, which means that a further one year and nine months must be deducted. This leaves a total of three years and nine months of qualifying service, which means that Peig is not entitled to preserved benefit under the Pensions Act.

PRESERVED BENEFIT COMPUTATION

12.30 Having explored the conditions which must be satisfied in order to become entitled to preserved benefit under the Act, it is appropriate now to consider the basis of calculation of the benefit.

Defined Contribution Schemes

12.31 The computation of preserved benefit for defined contribution schemes is quite simple relative to defined benefit schemes. It will be remembered that the member's pension is determined solely by the value at retirement of the member's retirement account — that is, the value of employer and employee contributions. On termination of relevant employment, the preserved benefit is that part of the retirement account that is attributable to employer and member contributions made after joining service, or 1 January 1991, if later.[43] This is referred to in the Act as "the appropriate contributions".[44] The balance of the retirement account made up of contributions made prior to 1 January 1991 (if any) is not preserved. There are two exceptions, however: additional voluntary contributions (AVCs) and transfer payments received. AVCs made by the member, and transfers of benefits received from a former employer, are preserved in their entirety irrespective of whether contributions were paid before or after 1 January 1991.[45]

---

43 s.30(2).

44 s.30(4).

45 s.30(5) and s.30(6).

Defined Benefit Schemes

12.32 The calculation of preserved benefit under a defined benefit scheme is complex. The Act introduces a formula for calculating preserved benefit:[46]

$$A \times \frac{B}{C}$$

where:

A = The member's pension entitlements on normal retirement and on death in retirement assuming that the member remained in service until then. In the case of a pension calculated by reference to pensionable earnings, it is based on pensionable earnings at date of termination of relevant employment.[47] AVCs and transfers from other schemes are excluded from the formula but are subsequently added back in calculating total preserved benefit.

B = The period of reckonable service completed after 1 January 1991.

C = The period of reckonable service that would have been completed had the member remained in reckonable service until normal pensionable age, and such service had continued to count as reckonable service (in other words, all possible scheme service).

This formula basically preserves the pension accrued since 1 January 1991, or since entering reckonable service, if later. If "A" in the equation was preserved (and nothing more), the entire pension that the member would have received by remaining in service until normal retirement would be preserved. The B/C fraction ensures that only a proportion of the accrued pension is preserved — that is, that portion based on reckonable service completed since 1 January 1991 (or later date of entering reckonable service).

12.33 There is one overriding condition to this formula. The actuarial value of the pension calculated under the formula cannot be less than the amount of contributions (other than AVCs) paid by the member after 1 January 1991, together with any compound interest

---

[46] Contained in the Second Schedule Part A, para. 1(1).

[47] s.29(3) and Second Schedule, Part A, para. 2. It may not be pensionable earnings at retirement — it can be within a "specified period" prior to retirement. If pensionable earnings are averaged at retirement, they must be averaged at date of termination of relevant employment.

on the member contributions that the rules would apply if the member were permitted to take a refund instead.[48] This grants the member, as a minimum, the value of the money paid into the scheme by the member since 1 January 1991.

Example 12.4

*Sinéad commenced employment with the Superlative Superannuation Company at the age of 20. She became eligible to join the pension scheme at age 25 and is entitled to a pension at normal retirement (age 65) of 1/60th of her final year's pensionable salary for each year of company service (with a maximum of 40 years' service taken into account). It is a contributory scheme — members contribute 5 per cent of pensionable salary each year.**

Sinéad: joined the company on 1 June 2004
joined the scheme on 1 June 2009
would have retired on 1 June 2049
left service on 1 June 2029.

Her Pensionable Salary on leaving service was £21,000. In applying the formula

A =	*£21,000 x 40/60*	=	*£14,000*
B =	*1 June 2009 to 1 June 2029*	=	*20*
C =	*1 June 2009 to 1 June 2049*	=	*40.*

*Her preserved benefit is 20/40 x £14,000 = £7,000 per annum.**

* *It is assumed in this example that the actuarial value of the preserved benefit is greater than her member contributions.*

12.34 As with defined contribution schemes, AVCs made by the member are preserved as well. If the AVCs have been made on a defined contribution basis,[49] they are preserved in their entirety irrespective of whether contributions were made before or after 1 January 1991.[50] If the AVCs have been made on a defined benefit basis, the

---

48 Second Schedule, Part A, para. 1(3).

49 For a distinction between defined contribution and defined benefit bases — see para. 2.3 et seq.

50 Note that, for the purposes of Part III only, any part of a defined benefit scheme which is calculated on a defined contribution basis is treated as a

preserved benefit is calculated in accordance with a formula similar to that set out above.[51] The formula is:

$$X \times \frac{Y}{Z}$$

where:

X = the member's additional benefit (or increase in benefit).

Y = the period of reckonable service for which the member has contributed towards such benefit (or increase).[52]

Z = the period of reckonable service for which the member would have contributed towards the benefit (or increase) if remaining in relevant employment until normal retirement.

In summary, the preserved benefit under this formula is the member's increased benefit that has accrued since contribution to the scheme began, not just that part which accrued since 1 January 1991. However, if the member has taken a refund of AVCs paid prior to 1 January 1991, only the increased benefit that has accrued since 1 January 1991 is preserved.[53]

12.35 Benefits transferred from the scheme of a former employer (where there was a termination of relevant employment) are provided as well as the preserved benefit. However, if part or the whole of the benefit which has been transferred from the former employer's scheme relates to service which arose prior to 1 January 1991, and the member takes a refund of contributions paid prior to 1 January 1991, the benefit is restricted. Only that part of the benefit which relates to service arising after 1 January 1991 is to be added to the preserved benefit.[54] A transfer received in circumstances where there has been no termination of relevant employment requires special considerations.[55]

---

defined contribution scheme and vice versa — s.27(2) and (3). The most common instance of where this will happen is with AVCs.

51 s.29(6) and Second Schedule, Part A para. 3.

52 Note that this refers to all reckonable service not just service after 1 January 1991.

53 Proviso to s.29(6).

54 Proviso to s.29(7).

55 See 12.69 et seq. below.

Benefit Improvements and Reductions

12.36 Whilst many pension schemes maintain the same benefit design without any alteration throughout their existence, it is not always possible or desirable to continue the same design, and some schemes may need to improve or reduce benefits. A change in design will normally be instigated by either the employer or the employees. The trustees' consent is usually required but it would be unusual for the trustees themselves to seek a benefit change.[56]

12.37 The main alterations to the benefit design that can arise in a pension scheme are the following:

1. In a defined benefit scheme, the retirement benefit promise is altered.
2. A switch from a defined contribution scheme basis to that of a defined benefit scheme or vice versa.
3. In a defined contribution scheme contribution rates are increased or decreased.
4. Alteration in death in service benefits.
5. Other scheme options, such as early retirement.

The power of the employer and the trustees to change the benefit basis is circumscribed in the case of the employer, by employment law considerations and in the case of the trustees by general trust law.[57] The Pensions Act imposes additional restrictions on the trustees with regard to the first two categories of alteration, which will now be examined. The Act imposes no limitations over the other three categories.[58]

12.38 Changes in the retirement benefits[59] of a defined benefit scheme are regulated by Part A of the Second Schedule to the Act, the

---

56 On the power to alter benefits and the trust implications, see para. 3.10 et seq.

57 See para. 4.26 et seq.

58 Except, to an extent, category 5 — see para. 12.43.

59 "Long service benefit" as defined by the Act.

Preservation Regulations and the Special Calculations Regulations,[60] but only in circumstances of termination of relevant employment — Part III does not seek to protect pensions in payment.[61] The combined effect of the Schedule and the Regulations is that a member whose service in relevant employment terminates before normal retirement is entitled to a preserved benefit which takes into account any benefit improvement which arose beforehand. Conversely, the preserved benefit must also have regard to any benefit reduction. The basic rule is that in calculating the preserved benefit, the effect of the alteration is accrued over reckonable service arising after the alteration, but not before.

12.39 The member's preserved benefit is first calculated as if the benefit alteration did not occur (that is, based on the rules in force prior to the alteration). The preserved benefit is then adjusted by adding a part of the increase in the benefit relating to reckonable service since the alteration (or subtracting in the case of a reduction).[62]

12.40 The preserved benefit entitlements of a member who switches from a defined benefit basis to that of a defined contribution scheme and vice versa are regulated by the Special Calculations Regulations and are considered below.[63]

12.41 Contribution rates in a defined contribution scheme may be altered from time to time. It is unlikely that the employer will force members to increase or decrease their own contributions, as employee contributions have no financial impact on the employer. However, the employer may wish to reduce its own contribution to the scheme or may, indeed, decide to increase it. No recalculation of preserved benefits is, however, required. The preserved benefit is simply the value of employer and member contributions.[64] Any increase or de-

---

60 The Occupational Pension Schemes (Preservation of Benefits) (Special Calculations) Regulations, 1993 which will be referred to as the Special Calculations Regulations — see para. 12.69 et seq. below.

61 See para. 12.8.

62 Second Schedule, Part A, para. 1(2) and the Preservation Regulations Art. 8. The latter regulations specify the basis for calculating a change in normal retirement age.

63 At para. 12.69 et seq.

64 That is, the post-1991 element. Of course, AVCs and transfer payments (if any) need to be added.

crease in contributions will affect the rate of increase of the member's retirement account, but that is all.

12.42 The preservation requirements of the Pensions Act do not impact upon benefits payable on death in service. The death in service benefit may take the form of a lump sum or a pension. Death in service benefits are not long service benefit within the meaning of the Act and do not therefore require to be preserved. However, given that the trustees have a statutory duty to pay benefits in accordance with the rules of the scheme,[65] they clearly cannot ignore the payment of death in service benefits. Nonetheless, there are no statutory restrictions on amending the rules to reduce such benefits.

12.43 There are other scheme options that can affect a member's benefits under a scheme. The obvious example is early retirement. Schemes can be designed to give members the right to retire early as of right. Others may require employer and/or trustee consent. The pension may be reduced to take account of early payment or may be paid without reduction or with only a partial reduction. Part III does not restrict the power of the employer and the trustees from varying a member's early-retirement rights, or indeed preventing a member from taking early retirement. What Part III does require, however, is that the actuarial value of the member's benefits on early retirement must be at least equivalent to the actuarial value of the member's preserved benefit on termination of relevant employment (including revaluation of the preserved benefit).[66] In other words, any option under the scheme cannot result in members receiving less value than their preserved benefit. There is nothing, however, preventing the scheme from providing higher benefits.[67]

Refunds of Employee Contributions

12.44 As mentioned above, the option to take a refund of employee contributions has always been a feature of the vast majority of contributory pension schemes. Having selected this option, the member received a cash refund of contributions paid into the scheme. The contributions were returned either with or without interest, depending

---

65 s.59(c) of the Pensions Act. See para. 4.53.

66 s.39

67 *Ibid.*

upon the design of the scheme. The refund extinguished all further entitlements under the scheme.

12.45 Part III of the Act restricts the circumstances under which a refund can be granted. Where members are not entitled to a preserved benefit, their entitlement to a refund of contributions remains unaffected by the Act and is governed solely by the rules of the scheme. Where, however, members are entitled to a preserved benefit, a refund of contributions cannot (but for one exception) be paid out of the scheme where their relevant employment terminates.[68] The one exception concerns a member who paid member contributions prior to 1 January 1991. Such a member is entitled to a refund of member contributions paid into the scheme prior to 1 January 1991 but not to a refund of member contributions paid after that date.[69] The reason for this is that Part III does not apply retrospectively — that is, prior to 1 January 1991. Any period of service to which a refund of contributions is made cannot be counted as service for the purposes of calculating Revenue-maximum benefit limits.[70]

REVALUATION OF DEFERRED PENSIONS

12.46 Having examined the basis upon which preserved benefits are calculated, it is necessary to consider the effects of inflation on deferred pensions and how the Pensions Act protects preserved benefits against inflation. Inflation has an eroding effect on the value of money. The real value of £100 in 30 years' time, assuming an annual inflation rate of 4 per cent, is only £31 in today's terms. The pension of a pension scheme member who leaves service at age 35 and would normally receive a pension at age 65 will be deferred for 30 years. Unless there is some inflation proofing built into the deferred pension, the pension on retirement will only be worth one-third of its current value (on the 4-per-cent inflation assumption above).

---

68 s.32(1). Members are also restricted in taking a refund where their service in relevant employment has not terminated and they would have been entitled to a preserved benefit had their service in relevant employment terminated — s.32(2) as inserted by s.10 of the Pensions (Amendment) Act, 1996.

69 s.32.

70 See para. 7.60.

12.47 This does not present a problem with defined contribution schemes. The value of the member's retirement account remains invested in the scheme and enjoys the benefit of future investment returns. Assuming that investment returns keep pace with or exceed inflation, the value of the member's pension will not be eroded by inflation.

12.48 This is not the case with defined benefit schemes. They usually promise salary-related benefits. On leaving service, the salary used to calculate the deferred pension will be salary at or near the date of leaving service. Before the commencement of Part III of the Pensions Act, the actuarial value of deferred pensions tended to be fixed at that point in time, with no allowance for the effects of future inflation. Part III now requires that as from 1 January 1996 preserved benefits under defined benefit schemes must be revalued from date of termination of relevant employment to normal retirement by a revaluation percentage prescribed by the Minister for Social Welfare.[71] Unless the Minister varies it,[72] the revaluation percentage must be the lesser of the percentage increase in the general level of consumer prices during the year of revaluation and 4 per cent.[73] This is partial inflation protection not *inflation proofing* because:

1. If inflation exceeds 4 per cent, revaluation will be a maximum of 4 per cent.[74]
2. Only preserved benefits are revalued — that is, benefits calculated by reference to reckonable service completed after 1 January 1991. Deferred pensioners with substantial pre-1991 service are not entitled to revaluation of their pre-1991 benefits. Furthermore, members who do not satisfy the conditions for granting a preserved benefit in the first place are not entitled to any revaluation.
3. Revaluation is only required to be commenced from 1 January 1996.[75] Revaluation was not required for the previous five years during which Part III of the Act was operational.

---

71 s.33(2).

72 By regulations under s.33(6). No regulations have been so made.

73 s.33(5).

74 In this context it is worth remembering that in the mid-1970s, inflation was in double figures. For example, in 1975 it was 20.9 per cent.

The Pensions Act does not prevent schemes from providing more generous benefits. Some schemes promise immediate revaluation (not deferring commencement until 1996). Some also revalue the entire deferred pension, not just the preserved benefit.

12.49 Revaluation is carried out at the end of each calendar year during which the pension is deferred.[76] The first revaluation year will usually be a partial one, from the date of termination of relevant employment to the end of the calendar year calculated in complete months. Each subsequent revaluation year is the next complete calendar year.[77] The last revaluation year is the last complete calendar year ending before the earliest of normal retirement, death or earlier retirement.[78] For revaluation to take place, there must be at least one year between the date of termination of relevant employment (or 1 January 1996, if later) and normal retirement or death (if earlier).

12.50 The method by which revaluation is calculated is set out in Part B of the Second Schedule to the Act. An amount called "the appropriate amount" is added to, and then forms part of, the preserved benefit at the end of each revaluation year.[79] The appropriate amount is the revaluation percentage as explained above, which is applied to the preserved benefit. However, if the first revaluation year was a partial one, the revaluation percentage is reduced to X-twelfths, where "X" is the number of complete months from date of termination of relevant employment to the end of the revaluation year.[80] There are two exceptions to this method of revaluation which arise in the relatively unusual circumstances of career average earnings schemes and defined benefit schemes that are not salary related.[81] It should be emphasised

---

75 s.33(1).

76 s.33(2).

77 Second Schedule, Part B, para. 4(1) as amended by s.41(a) of the Pensions (Amendment) Act, 1996.

78 s.33(2).

79 Second Schedule Part B para. 4(1) as amended by s.41(a) of the Pensions (Amendment) Act, 1996.

80 *Ibid.* para. 4(2).

81 *Ibid.* paras. 5 and 6. Career average earnings schemes are schemes which promise a pension based on the average of a member's earnings over the member's entire career rather than based on salary at or near retirement. The most common example of a non-salary related defined benefit scheme

that for the purposes of revaluation, "preserved benefit" excludes any benefits transferred from the scheme of a former employer.[82]

Example 12.5

John Doe left the Superlative Pension Scheme on 15 June 2001 and he retired on 1 April 2006. The first revaluation year under the Pensions Act is the partial calendar year in 2001 and the last revaluation year is the calendar year 2005. The following revaluation percentages were applied to John's preserved benefit over these revaluation years:

Calendar Year	*Increase in Consumer Price Index*	*Revaluation Percentage*
2001 (6 complete months)	*3.2%*	*1.6%**
2002	*3.0%*	*3.0%*
2003	*2.2%*	*2.2%*
2004	*4.0%*	*4.0%*
2005	*4.9%*	*4.0%***

* *That is, six-twelfths of 3.2 per cent.*

** *Revaluation is capped at 4 per cent even though CPI is greater.*

On applying the statutory revaluation on a compound basis, the cumulative statutory revaluation over the period is 15.7 per cent.

12.51 No part of a member's benefits that have accrued prior to 1 January 1991 can be used to pay for the cost of revaluing the member's preserved benefit. This is stipulated in para. 7 of Part B of the Second Schedule as follows:

> No part of the appropriate amount to be added to preserved benefit under this Part shall be provided by reducing the amount

is one that promised a specific amount of money (e.g. £500) for each year of service. In both cases, the trustees can opt to revalue in the normal way. The alternative methods of revaluation are explored in the Preservation Guidance Notes at paras. 155 to 161.

82 The transfer payment from the former scheme would have already incorporated an element of revaluation if it was a defined benefit scheme and there were preserved benefits. Transfer payments are excluded from revaluation by virtue of s.33(2), which provides for revaluation of preserved benefit calculated under paras. 1 or 3 or both of Part A of the Second Schedule (main pension benefit and AVCs) but not transfer payments.

of any benefit payable under the rules of the scheme concerned in respect of reckonable service completed before the commencement of Part III.

Meeting the scheme's liabilities under the Pensions Act by reducing non-preserved benefits is known as "franking". This is the only anti-franking provision in the Pensions Act. There is no equivalent provision to prevent pre-1991 benefits from being reduced to meet the cost of providing preserved benefits.

DEATH OF A DEFERRED PENSIONER

12.52 If a former member dies before the deferred pension commences to be paid, it is logical that that member's estate, spouse or dependants should receive the value of the deferred pension. Before the commencement of Part III, there was no obligation for a scheme to provide any benefit in respect of the former member. Schemes often paid out only an amount equal to the member's contributions (if any). Part III of the Act now requires, in the case of a member who is entitled to a preserved benefit, that a lump sum must be paid to the former member's personal representative.[83]

12.53 In the case of defined benefit schemes the lump sum is the actuarial value of the preserved benefit immediately prior to death as calculated pursuant to Part III of the Act. This includes the actuarial value of any preserved AVCs or transfer payments received in respect of the former member.[84] For defined contribution schemes it is the accumulated value of the former member's preserved benefit (including AVCs and transfer payments) immediately prior to death, also calculated in accordance with Part III.[85] Pre-1991 benefits (other than transfer values and AVCs) are therefore excluded, but it is open to a scheme to provide more generous benefits and include pre-1991 benefits in the lump sum payment.

12.54 Unlike death in service lump sum benefits, the trustees have no choice in the payment of the preserved lump sum. It must be paid to the personal representative. However, in certain circumstances, in

---

83 s.29(4), for defined benefit schemes, and s.30(3) for defined contribution schemes.

84 s.29(4).

85 s.30(3).

lieu of paying out a lump sum, the scheme can pay out a spouse's or dependant's pension. In other words, a pension income is paid, rather than a lump sum, and the recipient is an individual rather than the estate. There are a number of conditions which must be satisfied for this to happen:

1. The scheme must be a defined benefit scheme.
2. It must provide a pension to a spouse or dependants on death while in relevant employment prior to normal retirement — this is usually referred to as a death in service pension and is typically insured with a life office.
3. The particular member must be within the class of members who are promised this contingent pension.
4. The trustees must have made a decision to provide a pension in respect of the member in lieu of the lump sum

The pension income can then be paid to the deceased former member's spouse or another dependant, as determined by the trustees in accordance with the rules of the scheme. If, however, the former member does not have a spouse or dependant at date of termination of relevant employment, the Act is silent as to whether the trustees can nonetheless provide a dependant's pension in lieu of the lump sum. The guidance notes, which are an indication of best practice, state that the trustees must provide the lump sum in these circumstances, but could subsequently provide a pension instead, should the former member subsequently marry or acquire dependants.[86]

12.55 The spouse's/dependant's pension that can be paid in lieu of a lump sum will normally be expressed as a specified percentage of the member's pension expectation at retirement, based on current salary — for example, 50 per cent of pension expectation. The Act requires only the proportion of the pension relating to service after 1 January 1991 to be provided, and this portion forms part of the member's preserved benefit and must be revalued,[87] but schemes can be more generous and provide the full pension in respect of deferred pensioners.

---

86 Preservation Guidance Notes para. 145.

87 s.29(5)(a) and (b).

OPTIONS FOR DEFERRED PENSIONERS

12.56 On ceasing to be in relevant employment (usually on leaving service) a pension scheme member must be given written notification of the options available to an early leaver. This is a requirement of the Disclosure Regulations.[88] The options may include:

1. A deferred pension payable from normal retirement or, if the rules of the scheme permit, at such earlier date as the member may select. Normally pensions cannot be payable earlier than age 50.[89]
2. An immediate early-retirement pension, which, again, cannot normally be paid earlier than age 50. This option is dependent on the rules of the scheme permitting early retirement.[90]
3. A refund of member contributions, either with or without interest and less tax,[91] in lieu of any pension (if there is no preserved benefit).
4. A refund of member contributions (less tax) made prior to 1 January 1991 with a deferred pension in respect of reckonable service since that date (if there is a preserved benefit).
5. The option to transfer the actuarial value of any deferred pension to the scheme of a new employer or to a buy-out bond.

In many cases the deferred pension will be no more than the preserved benefit under the Act. This will certainly be the case where option 4 has been selected. However, the scheme may provide more generous benefits (i.e. pre-1991 accrued benefits) and so the deferred pension may be greater than the preserved benefit. The preserved benefit is payable in accordance with, and subject to, the rules of the scheme, except where the Pensions Act overrides those rules[92] and if the benefit is not transferred out of the scheme in accordance with

---

88 Article 12 and Schedule E — see Chapter 13 generally regarding disclosure.

89 Unless on grounds of ill-health — see para. 7.27 et seq.

90 The actuarial value of the early-retirement pension cannot be less than the actuarial value of the deferred pension — see para. 12.43.

91 Whether interest on member contributions is payable depends upon the scheme rules.

92 s.31(2).

option 5 above, it is payable out of the resources of the scheme.[93] To the extent that the total deferred pension is greater than the preserved element it will also be payable in accordance with the rules of the scheme and out of the scheme's resources.

TRANSFER PAYMENTS

12.57 When a member leaves relevant employment and is entitled to a deferred pension, that pension is, as the phrase suggests, deferred until retirement. Part or the whole of the deferred pension may be a preserved benefit, and it has been noted that preserved benefits must be paid out of the resources of the scheme and in accordance with the rules. This will occur at normal retirement or perhaps on early retirement, if the rules so permit. However, one of the options open to early leavers is to transfer their benefits to the scheme of a new employer or to a buy-out bond. In these circumstances it is the new scheme or bond that has the responsibility of providing the pension, not the original scheme.

12.58 The Pensions Act promotes the portability of pensions by giving members the right to transfer preserved benefits out of the pension scheme. Before the Act came into force, pension schemes normally facilitated transfers, but sometimes made such transfers subject to employer or trustee consent or both. Clearly, it may be desirable for a member to transfer benefits to the scheme of a new employer and if the member subsequently leaves the new employer's scheme, to transfer the benefits from both schemes to the scheme of yet a further employer. Benefits are consolidated in one scheme (with the final employer), which means that the member need not enquire about pension benefits in the former work places. There may, however, be circumstances where it is not to a member's advantage to transfer benefits, but it is generally considered desirable that members be given the option.[94]

---

93 s.31(1).

94 An example of where it may not be to a member's advantage to transfer is in the case of a defined benefit scheme which does not guarantee pension increases in retirement but which, on a discretionary basis, increases pensions in payment every year. The actuarial value of these pension increases would not be included in the transfer payment because they are

12.59 Part III of the Act entitles members of an occupational pension scheme to have their preserved benefits transferred out of the scheme. They may also be entitled to benefits which are not preserved. In theory, the Act would require the trustees, on the request of the member, to transfer the members' preserved benefits but not their non-preserved benefits (that is, benefits accrued prior to 1 January 1991). In practice, the trustees cannot be selective because the Revenue will not sanction a partial transfer of a member's pension benefits. They require that the entire deferred pension be either transferred out of the scheme or retained in the scheme.[95] As members have a statutory right to transfer their preserved benefit, it would therefore appear that they have a right to transfer their entire benefit. However, the receiving scheme does not appear to have a corresponding duty to receive a transfer of pre-1991 benefits. This conflict between Revenue practice and the Pensions Act will need to be resolved.

12.60 The right to a transfer applies to funded schemes but not unfunded schemes.[96] The most obvious examples of unfunded schemes are public sector schemes financed on a pay-as-you-go basis. The impact of preservation on public sector schemes is considered below.[97]

12.61 In practice, scheme members will be offered a transfer in an options form furnished under the Disclosure Regulations. The options form typically requires the member to select the desired option and return the form to the scheme administrators. The Act formalises this practice by requiring members to notify the trustees in writing of their decision to transfer their benefits, and to furnish the trustees with such information as they may reasonably require.[98] Members must exercise their option within two years of the termination of their relevant employment, or such longer period as the scheme rules

---

discretionary and so the member will effectively miss out on them by transferring.

95 Revenue practice notes.

96 s.34(1).

97 At paras. 12.90 and 12.91.

98 s.34(3).

permit or the trustees determine and cannot exercise the option once payment of their preserved benefit has commenced.[99]

12.62 In order to effect the transfer, the member's deferred pension is converted into a transfer amount, known as a transfer payment.[100] It is the lump sum equivalent of the deferred pension. The Act regulates only the transfer of preserved benefits, and non preserved benefits are therefore transferred in accordance with the scheme rules rather than the Act. In the case of a defined contribution scheme, the calculation of the transfer payment is straightforward. The transfer payment is the accumulated value of the "appropriate contributions" (member and employer contributions paid after 1 January 1991, AVCs and previous transfers (if any)) determined on a date not later than three months following the date of receipt of the member's notification.[101] The value of non-preserved benefits determined by the trustees in accordance with the rules will also be transferred (assuming that the member has not taken a refund of pre-1991 contributions). The non-preserved benefits will be the value of employer and member contributions paid prior to 1 January 1991. In the case of a defined benefit scheme the transfer payment is the actuarial value of the preserved benefit on the date on which the notification is received by the Trustees.[102] The actuarial value of the non-preserved benefit will be determined by the trustees in accordance with the scheme rules and will be transferred in addition to the transfer of the preserved benefit (again assuming that the member did not take a refund of pre-1991 contributions).

12.63 The transfer payment must be applied by the trustees within three months following receipt of the notification.[103] There are two possible ways in which the transfer can be applied: to the scheme of a new employer which is funded and of which the transferring person is a member or prospective member, or to a buy-out bond.[104] The scheme of a new employer is clearly an option only if the former member has

---

[99] s.34(7).

[100] s.34(2).

[101] s.34(2)(b).

[102] s.34(2)(a).

[103] s.34(4).

[104] s.34(3) as amended by s.12(c) of the Pensions (Amendment) Act, 1996.

a new employer and that employer has a funded occupational pension scheme[105] which the former member is eligible to join. The trustees of the new employer's scheme must accept the transfer payment.[106] In this regard, the trustees of the new employer's scheme are required to accept a "transfer payment" only within the meaning of the Act — that is, a transfer of preserved benefits. There is no obligation to accept a non-preserved benefit. However, as noted,[107] the Revenue require that the whole of the actuarial value of the deferred pension be either transferred or retained in the original scheme, and yet the trustees of the new scheme can be forced to accept only a transfer of preserved benefit. Revenue practice may need to be modified in this situation.

12.64 A buy-out bond is a Revenue approved policy or contract of assurance effected with a life office for the purpose of receiving transfer payments from occupational pension schemes. There are various types of bond and these are considered elsewhere.[108] The bond is proposed for by the trustees of the scheme and is written in the name of the former member of the scheme. A transfer payment of preserved benefit can be made only to a bond that is:

1. A policy or contract of assurance
2. Effected with an undertaking, within the meaning of the Insurance Act, 1989[109]
3. Approved of by the Revenue under Chapter II of Part I of the Finance Act, 1972.[110]

12.65 Where the transfer is made to the scheme of a new employer, the trustees of the new scheme must provide benefits of an actuarial

---

105 Within the meaning of the definition in s.2 of the Act — generally a Revenue approved scheme or a public sector scheme, provided that they are funded. See para. 1.37.

106 s.34(6).

107 At para. 12.59.

108 At para. 10.82 et seq.

109 That is, the holder of an authorisation to carry on life-assurance business in Ireland under the European Communities (Life Assurance) Regulations, 1984 (SI No 57 of 1984) or the European Communities (Life Assurance) Framework Regulations, 1994 (SI No 360 of 1994).

110 s.34(3)(b).

value that is equivalent to the amount of the transfer payment in such form as they determine.[111] This means that, provided that the new benefits are actuarially equivalent, the new scheme has complete discretion as to what additional benefits to provide. In practice, there are two methods of providing additional benefits. The first is to grant benefits on a defined contribution basis — that is, the transfer payment will be invested and the additional benefits at retirement will be whatever can be purchased with the transfer payment (together with investment return). The second is to grant added years and months of service in the new scheme. This is feasible only in a defined benefit scheme which promises a pension computed by reference to years and months of service.

12.66 Where the transfer is made to a buy-out bond, the benefits will be calculated on a defined contribution basis, except in the case of a non-profit deferred annuity which promises a specified benefit on retirement.[112] The Act refers to the right of a member to "[direct the trustees] to apply the transfer payment".[113] This effectively means that the trustees have no choice as to the type of buy out bond selected by the member and must do as the member directs — at least in so far as preserved benefits are concerned. The member cannot direct how the non-preserved benefits are to be transferred, unless the scheme rules state otherwise.

12.67 The trustees of the original scheme are given a discharge in respect of any transfer payment which is made to a new scheme or bond pursuant to an application by the former member. The discharge is contained in section 34(5):

> Where —
>
> (a) a person has exercised the entitlement conferred on him under subsection (2),[114] and
>
> (b) the trustees of the scheme from which the transfer payment is being made have complied with the provisions of subsection (4),[115]

---

111 s.34(6). The trustees of the receiving scheme may also have to improve the transfer if it was calculated on an unequal basis — see para. 16.66 et seq.

112 See para. 10.88.

113 s.34(3).

114 That is, the entitlement to apply for a transfer.

then, they shall be discharged from any obligation to provide benefits to which the transfer payment relates.

The effect of the discharge is that the trustees have no further liability to or in respect of the member with regard to the transfer payment. There are, however, two limitations inherent in this discharge. First, the discharge only relates to a transfer payment within the meaning of the Act, which is confined to preserved benefits. Therefore, the statutory discharge does not apply to non-preserved benefits. The rules of the scheme may, however, contain a discharge in these circumstances. Secondly, the trustees must apply the transfer within three months of the member's original application. If the trustees neglect to do so within that time scale or cannot do so because of problems in transferring benefits to the receiving scheme, the trustees do not have the protection of the statutory discharge.

12.68 So far, only transfer payments made with the consent of the member have been examined. If a member refuses to consent to a transfer, the rules of the scheme may prescribe circumstances where the trustees can transfer the benefits without the member's consent. To the extent that the transfer relates to non-preserved benefits, the rules remain unchanged and the Pensions Act has no effect. However, a rule permitting the trustees to effect a transfer of preserved benefit without the member's consent is overridden by the Act.[116] In general, consent of the member is required before a transfer of preserved benefit can be made. Nonetheless, there are two important exceptions to this rule. First, a transfer payment can be made without consent in such circumstances as may be prescribed by regulations made by the Minister for Social Welfare.[117] The circumstances that have been prescribed to date are where the total figure of the transfer payment (of preserved benefit) is less than £3,000,[118] or where the Pensions Board determines that the transfer should be effected on foot of an application to it in writ-

115 That is, they have applied the transfer within three months.

116 Because s.31 states that preserved benefits must be paid out of the resources of the scheme.

117 s.35(1).

118 Occupational Pension Scheme (Preservation of Benefits) Regulations, 1992 (SI No 445 of 1992), Arts. 2 and 3(1) — or such other amount as the Minister may prescribe. To date he has not prescribed any other amount.

ing by the trustees.[119] The trustees must give the member at least 30 days' notice of the transfer, before it can be effected without consent in either circumstance.[120] The trustees are then given an equivalent statutory discharge to that arising on a transfer with consent. The second exception to the rule is on a winding-up of the scheme. The trustees can apply, without the consent of the member, all or part of the resources of the scheme (including non-preserved benefits) in the making of a payment to another funded scheme or a buy-out bond.[121]

SCHEMES OF THE SAME EMPLOYER

12.69 The chapter thus far has examined the issues that arise on a termination of relevant employment and the calculation of preserved benefit in this context. It is now intended to consider two special situations: first, where an employee transfers to another pension scheme of the same employer (or within a group of employers), and secondly, where the employee is simultaneously a member of two or more schemes of the same employer. This is a particularly complex aspect of the preservation requirements of the Pensions Act.

12.70 As stated above,[122] termination of relevant employment occurs where there is no longer a scheme of the employer in respect of which the member is in reckonable service. A member may transfer from one scheme of the employer to another or may simultaneously be a member of two or more schemes of the same employer. For example, the employer may have established separate works and staff category schemes. Members who have been transferred from a works to staff category may have their works-scheme benefits transferred to the staff scheme, or their works-scheme benefits may remain deferred in the works scheme when they join the staff scheme. A third possibility is to remain a member of the works scheme and receive supplementary benefits under the staff scheme. In the first two cases, members cease to be in reckonable service in the works scheme. In the third, they continue to be active members of both schemes.

119 *Ibid.* Art. 3(1).

120 *Ibid.* Art. 3(2).

121 s.48(1)(b) as amended by s.57 of the Social Welfare Act, 1992 and as substituted by s.17 of the Pensions (Amendment) Act, 1996.

122 At para. 12.8.

12.71 In none of the examples in the preceding paragraph has there been a termination of relevant employment, because there continues to be a scheme of the employer to which the member's employment applies. This means that the member is not yet entitled to preserved benefits. However, when members cease to be active members of all schemes of the employer, their relevant employment will have terminated and they will then be entitled to preserved benefit. As there is more than one period of reckonable service involved, there are special regulations which govern the calculation of preserved benefit — the Occupational Pension Schemes (Preservation of Benefits) (Special Calculations) Regulations, 1993[123] which will be referred to here as the Special Calculations Regulations. These regulations were made under section 37(4A) of the Pensions Act,[124] which states that:

> Regulations may specify the method of calculating preserved benefit payable under schemes where on termination of relevant employment a member has periods of reckonable service in more than one scheme relating to the same employment or in a defined benefit scheme and a defined contribution scheme which are both part of the one scheme.

The regulations are extremely complex and, it is suggested, unnecessarily so, which makes it difficult for the trustees to administer situations where there is more than one scheme of the same employer.

12.72 The broad thrust of the Special Calculations Regulations is to calculate a preserved benefit for each period of reckonable service in the employer's scheme and aggregate the preserved benefits, so that the preserved benefit attributable to the member on termination of relevant employment is the sum total of each individual preserved benefit. The Preservation Guidance Notes put it this way:

> In general, the purpose of these regulations is to ensure that such an employee is entitled to an aggregate preserved benefit which is no less than the aggregate preserved benefit to which he/she would have been entitled if his/her periods of reckonable service in the various schemes had each related to different employments.[125]

---

[123] SI No 217 of 1993.

[124] As inserted by s.45 of the Social Welfare Act, 1993 and amended by s.14 of the Pensions (Amendment) Act, 1996.

[125] Para. 115.

The regulations achieve this in a particularly convoluted way. As mentioned earlier,[126] there are three scenarios that can arise:

1. The employee's benefits are deferred in the first scheme until retirement, and the employee becomes entitled to additional benefits in the second scheme.
2. The employee's benefits are transferred from the first scheme to the second scheme and the employee receives benefits solely from the second scheme.
3. The employee remains an active member of the first scheme and receives supplementary benefits under the second scheme.

There follows a brief summary of the various permutations that can arise in each of these scenarios. For the sake of simplicity, it is assumed that there are only two employer schemes. In theory, there could be three or more, but in those circumstances the same principles will apply. Also, the treatment of AVCs and transfers from schemes of a former employer are ignored. AVCs and transfers from former employer schemes are treated in a similar way to normal preserved benefit calculations.[127] The treatment for calculation purposes under the Special Calculations Regulations is different depending upon whether the schemes are defined benefit or defined contribution, or one of each.

Two Defined Benefit Schemes

12.73 ***Deferred benefits remain in first scheme:*** When a member's relevant employment is terminated, there are two deferred pensions, one in each scheme. The preserved benefit for the first scheme will be calculated as if the relevant employment was terminated on the date when the member switched schemes. Under the second scheme, the preserved benefit will be calculated on the basis of the member's reckonable service in the second scheme (ignoring first-scheme reckonable service).[128] However, the member's deferred pen-

---

[126] At para. 12.70.

[127] Art. 6 and Art. 9 deal with AVCs and transfers respectively. See paras. 12.31, 12.34 and 12.35 above in connection with the preservation treatment of these.

[128] Special Calculations Regulations, Art. 4(2) and 5.

sion in the first scheme is enhanced from the switch date until the relevant employment is actually terminated.[129] Enhancement is revaluation by a different name and operates in exactly the same way. The preserved benefit in the first scheme is enhanced (revalued) by the lesser of 4 per cent and the general level of consumer prices during the preceding 12 months.[130] As with revaluation, enhancement commences only from 1 January 1996 onwards. The member's aggregate preserved benefit is paid partly out of the first scheme (to the extent of first-scheme preserved benefit) and partly out of the second scheme (the balance).

12.74 ***Transfer of benefits to the second scheme:*** In the second scenario, there is only one deferred pension, as the first scheme benefits were transferred to the second scheme. Nonetheless, the regulations require the trustees to calculate preserved benefit as if the transfer did not take place (including the requirement to apply the enhancement factor). The two preserved benefits are then aggregated and are payable out of the second scheme only.[131]

12.75 ***Simultaneous membership of both schemes:*** Benefits are calculated in a similar way to para. 12.73, except in this case the member has remained an active member of the first scheme. There is, consequently, no enhancement of benefits in the first scheme, because the member's benefits are not deferred until actual date of termination of relevant employment.

Two Defined Contribution Schemes

12.76 ***All scenarios:*** This is a straightforward situation. In respect of each scheme, the preserved benefit is the accumulated value of contributions paid after 1 January 1991 for the period of reckonable service to which that scheme applies.[132]

---

[129] Art. 5(5)(b), (6) and (7)(b). As with revaluation, there are exceptions where the benefit relates solely to service (not salary) or is of a fixed amount — Art. 5(5)(a).

[130] Art. 5(6).

[131] Art. 4(4).

[132] Art. 4(2) and Art. 7.

First Defined Benefit Scheme, Second Defined Contribution Scheme

12.77 ***Deferred benefits remain in first scheme:*** When the member's relevant employment is terminated, there will be two deferred pensions, one in each scheme. The preserved benefit for the first scheme will be calculated on a defined benefit basis as if the relevant employment was terminated on the date when the member switched schemes. Under the second scheme, the preserved benefit will be calculated on a defined contribution basis in respect of the accumulated value of the appropriate contributions paid in the second scheme (that is, ignoring first-scheme contributions).[133] However, as with the case of a defined benefit scheme followed by another defined benefit scheme, the deferred pension in the first scheme is enhanced from the switch date until the member's relevant employment is actually terminated. The aggregate preserved benefit is paid partly out of the first scheme (to the extent of first scheme preserved benefit) and partly out of the second scheme (the balance).

12.78 ***Transfer of benefits to the second scheme:*** In the second scenario, there is only one deferred pension, as the first-scheme benefits are transferred to the second scheme. If the second scheme continues to give a defined benefit promise, the regulations require the trustees to calculate preserved benefit as if the transfer did not take place (including the requirement to apply the enhancement factor from the transfer date).[134] The two preserved benefits are then aggregated and are payable out of the second scheme only.[135] Instead of continuing the defined benefit promise, the second scheme may convert it to a defined contribution promise.[136] This is done by adding to the member's retirement account the actuarial value of the defined

---

[133] Art. 4(2) and 5.

[134] To the extent that part of a scheme is defined benefit and part defined contribution, each is treated as a separate scheme — Art. 4(5). Hence, in the situation identified in the text, the scheme is treated as two schemes and Art. 4(2) requires that preserved benefit for each period of reckonable service must be calculated separately.

[135] Art. 4(4).

[136] Art. 4(3) and Art. 8.

benefit promise.[137] This actuarial value becomes part of the member's appropriate contributions and is payable from the second scheme.

12.79 ***Simultaneous membership of both schemes:*** Benefits are calculated in a similar way to the first scenario, except in this case the member has remained an active member of the first scheme. There is, consequently, no enhancement of benefits in the first scheme, because the member's benefits are not deferred until actual date of termination of relevant employment.

First Defined Contribution Scheme, Second Defined Benefit Scheme

12.80 ***Deferred benefits remain in first scheme:*** When the member's relevant employment is terminated, there will be two deferred pensions, one in each scheme. The preserved benefit for the first scheme will be calculated on a defined contribution basis up to the date that the member switched schemes. Under the second scheme, the preserved benefit will be calculated on a defined benefit basis in respect of reckonable service under the second scheme.[138] There is no enhancement of benefits in the first scheme, as it remains a defined contribution scheme.[139] The member's aggregate preserved benefit is paid partly out of the first scheme (to the extent of first-scheme preserved benefit) and partly out of the second scheme (the balance).

12.81 ***Transfer of benefits to the second scheme:*** In the second scenario, there is only one deferred pension as the first scheme benefits are transferred to the second scheme. The trustees of the second scheme may continue the defined contribution promise or may agree to provide additional defined benefits in substitution for the defined contribution benefit.[140] In either case, the regulations require the trustees to calculate preserved benefit as if the transfer did not take

---

[137] Art. 8. For the purposes of calculating the actuarial value, the actuary must assume that the member left service on the transfer date with entitlement to statutory revaluation.

[138] Art. 4(2), 5 and 7.

[139] The member continues to enjoy the benefit of any investment return on his retirement account under the defined contribution scheme.

[140] For example, additional years and months of service in the case of a defined benefit scheme that promises a pension related to service and salary.

place.[141] The two preserved benefits are then aggregated and are payable out of the second scheme only.[142] The first-scheme benefit is enhanced as described in the previous paragraph.

12.82 ***Simultaneous membership of both schemes:*** Benefits are calculated in a similar way to the first scenario, except that in this case the member has remained an active member of the first scheme.

One Scheme but a Change in Scheme Basis

12.83 All of the above situations have involved two schemes of the employer. It is possible for a scheme to be switched from a defined benefit basis to a defined contribution basis or vice versa without there being a second scheme.[143] The rules of the scheme are amended but no new scheme is established. The Special Calculations Regulations also apply in this case.

12.84 The change in scheme basis may apply in relation to either future service or both future and past service. If the change applies to future service only, the former basis will continue to apply to a member's service that has accrued up to the change. For example, a defined benefit scheme may switch to a defined contribution basis. The members may remain entitled to a defined benefit promise for past service and only convert to a defined contribution basis for future service. The preserved benefit is calculated as if there are two schemes — one defined benefit and the other defined contribution, and the situations identified above will apply.[144]

12.85 If the change applies to both future service and past service, the Preservation Guidance Notes state that the basis of calculating

---

[141] Art. 4(2) (as interpreted by the Preservation Guidance Notes at paras. 123 and 124), Art. 5 and Art. 7.

[142] Art. 4(4).

[143] These are often referred to as "hybrid schemes" because they are both defined benefit and defined contribution.

[144] Art. 4(5). However, there is still only one scheme and whilst Part III of the Act allows the defined benefit part of the scheme to be treated as a separate scheme from the defined contribution part of the scheme, there is still only one scheme as far as the Pensions Act is concerned. For the purposes of the other Parts of the Act, in particular Parts IV and V, the scheme is treated as a defined benefit scheme, because some of the benefits are calculated on a defined benefit basis.

preserved benefit should be the same as if the member's benefit was transferred from a defined benefit scheme to a defined contribution scheme or vice versa. There is no direct authority for this statement in the Special Calculations Regulations, and so treatment of preserved benefits in this situation is unclear.[145]

FORFEITURE AND LIENS

12.86 It is common for pension schemes to include a rule which provides that a member's benefits will be forfeited in certain stated circumstances, such as fraud or dishonesty or where a member attempts to assign a benefit or becomes bankrupt. In addition, there may be a rule permitting the trustees or employer to reduce benefits by any sum owing by the member to the employer or trustees.[146] These forfeiture and lien rules can continue to be relied upon to the extent that a member's benefits are non-preserved.[147] However, the Pensions Act forbids forfeiture of preserved benefits (except in certain circumstances) and liens on preserved benefits by the employer, by requiring such provisions to be disregarded.[148]

12.87 The only permitted exceptions relate to bankruptcy, assignment or charge or attempted assignment or charge of the preserved benefit payable to or in respect of the member. If the rules so permit, the trustees can, at their discretion, pay the benefit either to the member or to another person as permitted under the rules notwithstanding bankruptcy or assignment. This is provided for in section 36(2) of the Act,[149] which states that:

---

145 The guidance notes assume that the switch from one basis to another automatically creates two schemes for the purposes of preservation calculations. In fact, it does not create two schemes, the reason being that before the switch there is only one scheme and after the switch there is only one scheme. At no point are there two pension schemes.

146 For example, by reason of any moneys or goods misappropriated or damage suffered by the employer or a debt due to the employer.

147 There is some authority under general trust law that forfeiture rules are void on grounds of public policy or, in the case of forfeiture by reason of bankruptcy, on the grounds of a fraud on the bankruptcy laws — see Dierden, K. (1995): "Forfeiture and Employer Liens", Bruges: Association of Pension Lawyers Annual Conference.

148 s.36(1).

149 As inserted by s.13 of the Pensions (Amendment) Act, 1996.

> Notwithstanding paragraph (a) of subsection (1) where a member of a scheme or such other person who is entitled to preserved benefit is or becomes bankrupt (within the meaning of the Bankruptcy Act, 1988), or assigns or charges or attempts to assign or charge the benefit, the trustees of the scheme may, at their discretion, apply any provision of the scheme, under which a benefit may be forfeited and paid, to the member or such other person specified in the provision.

This is a particularly significant protection for a member who becomes a bankrupt. It prevents the pension benefit from forming part of the assets of the bankrupt member to which the assignee in bankruptcy can have recourse. However, it should be emphasised that the protection arises only if the rules so provide and the trustees exercise their discretion.

REVENUE APPROVAL PRACTICE

12.88 Since the introduction of preservation, the Revenue Commissioners have had to revise their practice with regard to deferred pensions. The Pensions Act restricts the entitlement of members to take a refund of their contributions. Where a member has paid contributions both before and after 1 January 1991 and qualifies for a preserved benefit, the Act permits a refund of only pre-1991 contributions. The trustees must secure a deferred pension in respect of post-1991 benefits. However, previous Revenue practice forbade a member to take a partial refund of contributions and a deferred pension.[150] This was referred to as "mixed benefits". In recognition of the fact that the implementation of the Pensions Act would result in many instances of mixed benefits, the Revenue revised their practice and now permit mixed benefits to the extent required by the Pensions Act.

12.89 There are two other issues that have required modification of Revenue practice. The first relates to early retirement. A member who has been granted a preserved benefit may (subject to the rules of the scheme) take early retirement. If the member had completed less than 10 years of service, the preserved benefit could exceed Revenue maximum early-retirement benefits.[151] The second concerns the preserved benefit payable as a lump sum to the estate of a deceased member. This could exceed the maximum lump sum payable on death

---

[150] Subject to certain exceptions.

[151] See para. 7.27 et seq.

in service.[152] In each case, the Revenue have accepted that the Pensions Act requirements must override previous Revenue practice.

PUBLIC SECTOR SCHEMES

12.90 Public sector schemes are examined in Chapter 8. In common with private occupational pension schemes, public sector schemes provide benefits for members who leave service prior to retirement. However, most public sector schemes are financed on a pay-as-you-go (unfunded) basis which could present them with difficulties if they were subject to preservation requirements. Part III gives members who are entitled to preserved benefits the right to transfer their preserved benefit to a buy-out bond or another scheme. Unfunded schemes do not expect to pay out a benefit until retirement, and so the obligation to transfer preserved benefits immediately could place a financial strain on the employer (being the State or semi-state companies). Consequently, the transfer provisions do not apply to unfunded schemes.[153] The operation of the transfer network could be undermined if members of funded public sector schemes were entitled to a transfer payment.[154]

12.91 The preservation requirements of public sector schemes are, in fact, more favourable than under the Pensions Act, in that preservation is based on all pensionable service, not just that which has accrued since 1 January 1991. Accordingly, section 37(1) of the Act empowers the Minister for Social Welfare by regulations made with the consent of the Minister for Finance to exclude schemes or categories of scheme from the preservation requirements of Part III, the Second Schedule and the regulations made under Part III. The Minister must be of opinion that the benefits under the schemes are no less favourable to the members than those required by the Act. There are currently 82 schemes (together with any associated spouses' and children's schemes) which enjoy the benefit of this ministerial exclusion.[155]

---

152 See para. 7.35 et seq.

153 s.34(1) and (3) as amended by s.12(c) of the Pensions (Amendment) Act, 1996. However, they do apply to funded public sector schemes.

154 On the operation of the transfer network, see para. 8.48.

155 Preservation Regulations Art. 11 and Schedule.

13

DISCLOSURE OF INFORMATION

INTRODUCTION

13.1 It is important that members of an occupational pension scheme be entitled to receive basic information about the scheme. A pension is a valuable employment benefit and, furthermore, the members may contribute a part of their salary towards the cost of providing the benefits. However, until the enactment of the Pensions Act, there were no comprehensive statutory provisions imposing obligations on scheme trustees and the employer to furnish meaningful information in relation to a pension scheme to its members. Instead, access to information was to an extent facilitated by a number of different pieces of legislation and, in addition, certain rights to information exist under trust law.

13.2 Chapter II of the Finance Act, 1972, which sets out the procedure for approval of occupational pension schemes, requires that certain information be notified to members. The Terms of Employment (Information) Act, 1994 gives employees the right to obtain certain information in writing concerning their terms of employment. Under trust law, a member of a pension scheme, as a beneficiary of a trust, has a right to obtain from the trustees information regarding the trust and the conduct of the trust.

13.3 In its first report the National Pensions Board recognised that members of occupational pension schemes had these legal rights. However, it advised that the precise nature of the information required to be disclosed was not specified, nor were trustees or employers obliged to advise members of their individual entitlements.[1] The National Pensions Board also noted that whilst there was an obligation on sponsoring employers to furnish information to scheme mem-

---

1 The First Report of the National Pensions Board (Pl. 4776) para. 3.13.

bers (as a requirement of approval under the Finance Act, 1972), the Revenue Commissioners themselves were not normally in a position to monitor or ensure the availability of such information to members of the scheme.[2] The Board also noted that a statutory obligation to disclose information in relation to pension schemes is contained in the Companies (Amendment) Act, 1986. Paragraph 36 of the Schedule to that Act outlines in detail the information to be provided by companies (with the exception of certain types of companies) in their accounts.[3]

13.4 The Family Law Act, 1995 makes provision for disclosure of information to spouses of pension scheme members and this is considered in more detail later.[4]

13.5 Recognising the defects in the then existing body of law relating to disclosure of information the National Pensions Board recommended that statutory provisions be enacted setting out certain basic information which must be furnished to certain categories of persons. The recommendations of the National Pensions Board are given legislative effect by Part V of the Pensions Act and in the Occupational Pension Schemes (Disclosure of Information) Regulations, 1991 made under the Pensions Act (the "Disclosure Regulations").[5] Generally, these impose obligations directly on trustees of pension schemes to cause audited accounts, actuarial valuations and annual reports to be prepared and to make these available to members and other persons on a regular basis. In addition, trustees now have obligations to furnish specific information at certain key times to individual members including when a member joins a scheme, when a member leaves employment, when a member dies or when a scheme is wound up.

13.6 The rest of this chapter contains a detailed consideration of Part V of the Pensions Act and the Disclosure Regulations which ap-

---

2 *Ibid.* at para. 3.14.

3 *Ibid.* At para. 3.16. The accounts disclosure obligations in the Companies (Amendment) Act, 1986 originally applied only to limited companies. The ambit of the legislation has been extended by the European Communities (Branch Disclosures) Regulations, 1993 (SI No 395 of 1993) and the European Communities (Accounts) Regulations, 1993 (SI No 396 of 1993).

4 See para. 15.18 et seq.

5 SI No 215 of 1991.

ply to all occupational pension schemes and also examines the disclosure obligations and the rights to information which existed prior to enactment of the Pensions Act and which continue to exist along side that Act. In addition to private occupational pension schemes, schemes covered by the Disclosure Regulations include public sector schemes. Most of these schemes are not subject to the preservation and funding obligations imposed by Parts III and IV of the Pensions Act but nonetheless must comply with the Pensions Act disclosure requirements.[6]

PERSONS ENTITLED TO INFORMATION

13.7 Part V of the Pensions Act and the Disclosure Regulations made under it impose upon the trustees of pension schemes a duty to disclose financial, legal and benefit information. Certain information must be made available periodically, whereas other information need only be given once. For example, the annual report must be made available annually, whereas a booklet summarising the members' benefits need only be issued on joining the scheme (unless any changes subsequently occur).

13.8 These periodic and specific disclosure obligations will be examined shortly. First, however, it is necessary to identify who is entitled to receive information concerning the scheme. In general, the persons who are entitled to disclosure of information are the following:

1. The members[7] and prospective members[8] of the scheme
2. The spouses of members and prospective members of the scheme
3. Persons within the application of the scheme and qualifying or prospectively qualifying for its benefits
4. An authorised trade union representing the members concerned.[9]

---

6 See Chapter 8 regarding these types of schemes.

7 This term is defined in s.2 of the Pensions Act as meaning any person who, having been admitted to membership of the scheme, remains entitled to any benefit under the scheme — it therefore includes deferred pensioners and pensioners.

8 This term is defined by s.2 of the Pensions Act as meaning any person who is already in relevant employment and is, by virtue of the rules of the scheme or their contract of service, eligible or will be eligible to join the scheme. It would not, for instance, include an employee who may only join the scheme at the invitation of the employer.

13.9 A difficulty in the Pensions Act and Disclosure Regulations generally is the definition of "authorised trade union". The term is defined in section 54(6) of the Pensions Act as a body to whom a negotiation licence (within the meaning of Part II of the Trade Union Act, 1941) was issued. It may be, however, that a group of employees who are members of a pension scheme are represented by more than one trade union. Further, a trade union may have been issued with a negotiation licence which was subsequently revoked under the relevant legislation. On a strict interpretation of section 54(6) such a trade union would nevertheless be an "authorised trade union" for the purposes of the Disclosure Regulations. It is unclear whether disclosure must be made to all trade unions having representation in the work force or only to the trade union representing the majority of the membership. The former interpretation would seem the more correct.

13.10 As noted, the Pensions Act provides that spouses of members and prospective members of schemes have rights to disclosure of information. These rights are to some extent carried forward in the Disclosure Regulations themselves. However, there is not a positive obligation on trustees of schemes to notify spouses that information is available. Such a positive obligation does exist with respect to authorised trade unions and members. Clearly, difficulties may arise in a situation where a member is separated from their spouse. Depending upon the specific terms of the trust documentation, such spouse may have benefit entitlements under the scheme. In practice, however, it may be very difficult for a spouse to obtain information regarding those benefits. It may also be difficult to obtain meaningful information with respect to the value of the member's benefit entitlements under the scheme. Such information would be very important to a spouse seeking judicial separation or some form of order over the member's pension entitlements.[10]

13.11 Under the Disclosure Regulations, certain information must be disclosed to specified persons (members, authorised trade unions) and at specified times, and certain other information need only be disclosed upon request. Further, certain persons (spouses of mem-

---

9 Pursuant to s.54(2).

10 See Chapter 15 for a detailed discussion of pensions in the context of marital breakdown. The Family Law Act, 1995 does make provision for disclosure in relation to pension schemes in the context of marital breakdown.

bers, prospective members) are only entitled to information upon request. The Disclosure Regulations impose obligations directly on the trustees of pension schemes. As noted below,[11] the Pensions Act requires employers to furnish information to trustees on request in order that they may carry out their functions under the Act and the Disclosure Regulations. This is particularly relevant in the context of the trustees' obligations to have accounts and actuarial valuations prepared.

PERIODIC DISCLOSURE REQUIREMENTS

Annual Audited Accounts

13.12 Unless the alternative arrangements set out below[12] apply, the trustees of a scheme must have accounts of the scheme prepared and audited.[13] The Pensions Act further obliges the trustees to have the resources and liabilities of the scheme valued by the scheme actuary at such times as may be prescribed.[14] The trustees must cause to be prepared:

1. The audited accounts of the scheme concerned; and
2. The auditor's report on those accounts.

13.13 The obligation to prepare accounts does not apply to any scheme:

1. That is not a funded scheme, or
2. Under which the only benefit is in respect of death prior to normal pension age, or
3. The members of which have been notified in writing by the trustees that service by a member in relevant employment after 1

---

11 See para. 13.30 below and s.54(4)(a) of the Pensions Act.

12 At para. 13.46 et seq.

13 s.56 of the Pensions Act and Article 4 of the Disclosure Regulations.

14 s.56(1) but subject to s.56(6). See para. 13.19 et seq. below. See also Chapter 9 .

January 1997 does not entitle the member to long service benefit under the scheme.[15]

13.14 A copy of the latest audited accounts and the auditors' report on the accounts must be made available by the trustees to those persons specified in paragraph 13.8 above,[16] not later than nine months after the end of the scheme year to which it relates. In addition, a copy of the latest audited accounts and auditor's report must be furnished free of charge to an authorised trade union representing the members of the relevant scheme not later than nine months after the end of the relevant scheme year and, on request, to any of the persons specified at 1, 2, or 3 of paragraph 13.8 above.[17] The audited accounts required under Article 4 must contain the information specified in Schedule A to the Disclosure Regulations, which may be summarised as follows:

1. An account of the financial additions to and withdrawals from the fund of the scheme during the scheme year to which they relate
2. A statement of the resources of the fund at market value and their distribution including details of self-investment and concentration of investment exceeding 5 per cent of the scheme assets
3. A reconciliation of 1 and 2
4. Comparative figures for the previous scheme year
5. A statement of conformity of the accounts with the Statement of Recommended Practice (SORP) No 1 ("SORP 1") of the Consultative Committee of Accountancy Bodies (CCAB).

13.15 The Disclosure Regulations set out a non-exhaustive list of the matters which must be dealt with in the Auditors' Report.[18] In particular, the auditors must state whether or not they are satisfied that the requirements set out at paragraph 13.14 are satisfied, that in their opinion the accounts give a true and fair view of the financial transactions of the scheme, whether or not in their opinion the contributions payable to the scheme have been received by the trustees, and the reasons for any qualification to those statements.

---

15 s.56(6)(a) as amended by s.63 Social Welfare Act, 1991 and s.22(d) Pensions (Amendment) Act, 1996.

16 Article 4(3).

17 Article 4(4).

18 Article 4(7).

13.16 SORP 1 is not a statutory requirement in Ireland but is a recommendation as to best practice. It has gained general acceptance in practice and the Disclosure Regulations specifically require pension scheme accounts to state whether or not they comply with SORP 1.[19] SORP 1 does not address itself to single-member schemes, free-standing AVC schemes or unfunded schemes. It sets out recommendations for pension scheme accounts as to the basis of accounting (the accruals concept[20]), the content of accounts, the accounting policies, the actuarial position, the valuation of investments, accounting for associated and subsidiary companies, accounting for AVCs, disclosure and the investment report.

13.17 In recognition of developments in relation to accounting practice and pensions in the period since its issue[21] SORP 1 has been revised by the Pensions Research Accountants Group ("PRAG"), a body approved by the Accounting Standards Board for the purpose of issuing SORPs for Pension Schemes.

13.18 Whereas the original SORP 1 focused on the financial statements and did not address the trustees report, the revised SORP 1 places particular emphasis on the importance of the trustees report and sets out detailed recommendations on its contents.[22] The revised SORP 1 was published by PRAG on 6 September 1996 and will apply in respect of accounting periods ending on or after 6 April 1997.

Actuarial Valuations

13.19 The Disclosure Regulations require the trustees of a relevant scheme to cause the resources and liabilities of the scheme to be valued

---

19 Article 4 of and para. 5 of Schedule A to the Disclosure Regulations.

20 See para. 13.64.

21 SORP 1 was issued by the Accounting Standards Board in May 1986.

22 It would appear that at the time of issue of the exposure draft on SORP 1, PRAG was unaware that it applied in Ireland through the Disclosure Regulations. The Pensions Board has subsequently made submissions to PRAG with respect to the Irish aspects of this matter. Following publication of the revised SORP 1 the Pensions Board has announced that it will be reviewing the Disclosure Regulations.

by the actuary of the scheme at certain specified dates.[23] The trustees must also periodically cause a funding certificate to be prepared which certifies the solvency of the scheme. A copy of the funding certificate must be included in the annual report.[24]

13.20 Trustees must also procure that the actuary furnish a report on the valuation. A copy of the latest valuation report must be made available by the trustees of the scheme to those persons specified in paragraph 13.8 above,[25] not later than nine months after the effective date. The report is to be made available for inspection free of charge, on request, to any of the persons specified at paragraph 13.8 above and must be furnished on request on payment of a reasonable charge to any such persons. Any earlier valuation reports prepared under section 56 also have to be made available for inspection upon request.[26]

13.21 A valuation is not required in any of the circumstances set out in paragraph 13.13 or if the scheme is a defined contribution scheme.[27]

13.22 The effective date for the first actuarial valuation to be prepared under the Pensions Act (and the Disclosure Regulations) is:

1. In the case of a relevant scheme which commenced before 1 January 1991, a date not later than 31 December 1993
2. In the case of a relevant scheme which commenced on or after 1 January 1991, a date not later than three and a half years after the commencement of the relevant scheme.

13.23 The effective date of any subsequent actuarial valuation will be a date not later than three and a half years after the effective date of the immediately preceding actuarial valuation.[28]

---

23 s.56(2) and Article 5 of the Regulations. A relevant scheme for the purposes of Article 5 is a scheme to which the Pensions Act applies by virtue of s.56.

24 See para. 13.27 below.

25 Article 5(3).

26 Article 5(5).

27 s.56(6)(b).

28 Article 5(7). See para. 9.33 et seq.

Annual Reports

13.24 The trustees of a pension scheme are obliged to prepare an annual report.[29] The report must contain such information and in relation to such matters as may be prescribed. The annual report must be prepared for whichever of the following periods the trustees may select:

1. Each year beginning on the date specified for the purpose of the scheme in the formal documentation of the scheme
2. Each year beginning on the 1 January
3. Each year beginning on such other day as may be agreed upon with the trustees and the Pensions Board.

13.25 Where the period selected by the trustees changes, a report prepared for a period other than a year, not being more than 23 months, shall, with the approval of the Pensions Board, be regarded as an annual report.[30] It is not uncommon for pension schemes to alter their scheme year — for instance, to coincide with the financial year of the employer where the latter has been changed.

13.26 The obligation to prepare an annual report does not apply to any scheme where:

1. The scheme only provides benefits on death in service
2. The members of the scheme have been notified in writing by the trustees that service by a member in the relevant employment after the 1 January 1997 does not entitle the member to long service benefit.[31]

13.27 Abbreviated annual reports are permitted in certain circumstances[32] by otherwise the Disclosure Regulations set out the detailed

---

29 s.55(1) Pensions Act.

30 s.55(1) as amended by s.21 Pensions (Amendment) Act, 1996.

31 s.55(2) as amended by s.62 Social Welfare Act, 1991 and s.21(b) Pensions (Amendment) Act, 1996. Long-service benefit is defined in s.2 of the Pensions Act. The type of scheme to which s.55(2) refers is a "frozen scheme" — that is, a scheme where no benefits will accrue with respect to future service. The important point is that the members have been notified of the fact that the scheme is frozen.

32 See para. 13.46 et seq.

requirements with respect to a full annual report.[33] The annual report must contain:

1. A copy of the audited accounts (if any) in respect of the relevant scheme year or a summary of the information specified at 1 to 4 in Schedule A to the Disclosure Regulations.[34]
2. A copy of the auditors' report on the accounts.
3. Where appropriate, a copy of the latest actuarial funding certificate.
4. The following information:
   - (i) The names of the trustees (including persons who were trustees at any time during the relevant scheme year)
   - (ii) The name of each actuary, auditor, solicitor, bank and any other person acting for or retained by the trustees during the scheme year
   - (iii) The address for inquiries regarding the scheme
   - (iv) Any change since the previous scheme year in the basic information about the scheme specified in Schedule C to the Disclosure Regulations[35]
   - (v) The number of members in relevant employment and in receipt of benefit under the scheme
   - (vi) A statement of whether or not increases were made during the scheme year to pensions in the course of payment and benefits payable following termination, and by what percentage
   - (vii) A review by the trustees of the financial developments of the scheme during the scheme year

---

33 Article 6.

34 See para. 13.14 above.

35 The information is set out in Figure 13.1. It should be noted that Article 6 does not contain a provision similar to Article 8(5) and Article 9(6) — that is, requiring disclosure only of information "relevant to" a member's rights where there are different rules applicable to different members. This means that if there is an executive benefit structure in place in the scheme and this is improved, then this information should appear in the report.

(viii) The name of each person or organisation concerned in the management of the investments of the scheme

(ix) Whether or not the scheme bears the costs of any investment manager

(x) An investment report containing:

- A statement by the trustees or investment manager of investment policies pursued during the year on behalf of the scheme and any material changes from the previous year
- A review of the investment performance.

It should be noted that items (vii), (viii), (ix) and (x) are not required in the case of unfunded schemes.[36]

13.28 A copy of the latest annual report must be made available by the trustees of the relevant scheme to those persons specified at paragraph 13.8 above,[37] not later than nine months after the end of the scheme year to which it relates. The trustees are obliged to inform the members of the relevant scheme of the availability of the annual report,[38] and a copy of the latest annual report must be furnished free of charge to an authorised trade union representing the members and, on request, to any of the persons specified at 1., 2. and 3. of paragraph 13.8.

13.29 As noted, the annual report must be made available to an authorised trade union without any requirement that a request be received. The other persons entitled to the annual report have no automatic entitlement but must actually request it. The trustees are, however, only under an obligation to notify the availability of the annual report to the members. Those other persons entitled to the annual report (set out at 2. and 3. in paragraph 13.8 above) must therefore rely on someone else to inform them that the annual report is available and that they are entitled to receive a copy. To impose an obligation on the trustees to notify all potential beneficiaries would, it is submitted, be too onerous.

---

36 Article 6(7)(d)(ii).

37 Article 6(3).

38 Article 6(4).

13.30 To carry out valuations or audits, actuaries and auditors need to be able to obtain information on the scheme from the employer. The Pensions Act confers on trustees, the actuary of the scheme and the auditor to the scheme a right to request an employer to furnish information to them in order that they may carry out their functions under the Act.[39] The trustees, the actuary and the auditor are then in turn obliged under Part V of the Act to disclose information in relation to the scheme. The Pensions Act further entitles the actuary or the auditor of the scheme to request the trustees of the scheme to furnish them with such information as they reasonably require for the purposes of carrying out their functions under the Act or regulations made under the Act, and the trustees must comply with any such request.[40] Failure to comply with an obligation to furnish information in accordance with the Pensions Act or under the Disclosure Regulations made under Part V is an offence which is punishable on summary conviction by a fine not exceeding £1,500.[41]

INDIVIDUAL DISCLOSURE REQUIREMENTS

13.31 Under s.54 of the Pensions Act, the trustees of a pension scheme are obliged to disclose:[42]

1. Details about the constitution of the pension scheme
2. Basic information about the pension scheme
3. Information regarding individual benefit entitlements.

The trustees must disclose the information automatically unless regulations prescribe otherwise. The Disclosure Regulations specify that the information may require to be disclosed on request or as a consequence of certain events arising, such as leaving service. The obligations of trustees in relation to each of these areas is now examined.

---

39 See s.54(4)(a).

40 s.54(4)(b).

41 s.54(5) as amended by s.43 Pensions (Amendment) Act, 1996.

42 s.54 also refers to the administration and finances of the scheme. Finances are covered by the requirements concerning accounts and actual valuations. Administration is disclosed through the annual report.

Information about the Constitution of the Scheme

13.32 The trustees of a scheme must make available[43] information relating to the constitution of a pension scheme, being:

1. The contents of the trust deed where the scheme is constituted by a deed
2. The contents of any document establishing the scheme where the scheme is not constituted by a trust deed[44]
3. The contents of the rules
4. The contents of any document amending any of the above
5. The name and address of the employer.

This information must be made available for inspection free of charge upon request. Copies of the documents must be made available on payment of a reasonable charge to the persons listed in paragraph 13.8.

13.33 Where different rules are applicable to different members and prospective members, the trustees are not obliged to disclose any part of a document to a member unless it is relevant to that member's rights under the scheme.[45] The Disclosure Regulations do not provide any guidance as to who is to determine whether or not a document or part of a document "is relevant to" a member's rights under the scheme, nor is there any guidance as to the exact meaning of this expression. The Disclosure Regulations contain similar provisions with respect to explanatory booklets.[46] The general thrust of the Regulations, in this regard, would appear to conform with the common law position as to disclosure. The cases suggest that a beneficiary is entitled to information only regarding that part of the trust property in which the beneficiary has an interest.[47]

---

43 s.54 and Article 8.

44 For instance, a statutory scheme or a letter of exchange.

45 Article 8(5).

46 Article 9(6).

47 See *Low* v. *Bouverie* [1891] 3 Ch. 82, see also the apparently contradictory remarks in *O'Rourke* v. *Darbishire* [1920] AC 581 per Lord Wrenbury at p.626. The remarks of Lord Wrenbury in *O'Rourke* v. *Darbishire* have been cited as authority for the proposition that a beneficiary under a trust is entitled to disclosure of all the trust documents. It is submitted

Disclosure of Basic Information about the Pension Scheme

13.34 The Disclosure Regulations impose on trustees of a pension scheme an obligation to provide certain basic information about the scheme. This information is usually contained in an explanatory booklet, announcement or handbook and must contain the information set out in Schedule C to the Disclosure Regulations.[48] The information required is summarised in Figure 13.1.

FIGURE 13.1: BASIC INFORMATION TO BE DISCLOSED UNDER ARTICLE 9

1	The categories of persons who are eligible to be members
2	The categories of persons who are required as a condition of their employment to be members.
3	The conditions of membership
4	How members' contributions are calculated
5	How employers' contributions are calculated
6	Whether the scheme is approved under the Finance Act, 1972 or such approval is being applied for
7	Whether the scheme is a defined benefit scheme or a defined contribution scheme for the purpose of the Pensions Act
8	The benefits payable under the scheme and the method of calculation
9	The conditions under which benefits are paid and any options relating thereto
10	Which benefits are discretionary
11	Which benefits are funded and which are not
12	Which benefits are insured, and, in such case, whether any underwriting criteria apply
13	The short title of the Act or Acts of the Oireachtas which provides for the setting-up of the scheme and for the determination of the rate or amount of benefits under the scheme
14	Whether and to what extent the employer guarantees payment of the benefits[49]
15	Whether there are discretionary increases of pensions after they become payable[50]
16	The address for inquiries regarding the scheme.

---

that that proposition reads too much into the judgement and that it can in fact be reconciled with *Low* v. *Bouverie*.

48 Article 9.

49 This requirement can pose difficulties in practice. It is unusual for the employer to provide a guarantee as to payment of benefits. To state that none is provided is undesirable for industrial relations reasons. Explanatory booklets are usually silent on the point.

50 Not all schemes provide for discretionary increases. All well drafted schemes will, however, provide a discretionary power for the employer or the trustees (with consent of the employer) to augment benefits.

13.35 The information must be furnished to new members within six months of their becoming members.[51] The specified information must also be made available, on request only, to those persons specified in paragraph 13.8.

13.36 The trustees must notify members of the scheme of any material alteration in the information specified in Figure 13.1 within six months of such alteration.[52] To the extent that any such alteration would constitute a change in the terms of employment, it must be notified by the employer within one month of the date of alteration under the provisions of the Terms of Employment (Information) Act, 1994.[53]

Disclosure of Information Regarding Individual Benefit Entitlements

13.37 There is certain information that is particular to a member, and the Regulations require specific disclosures to individual members regarding their benefits in certain circumstances. The trustees of a scheme must disclose the information specified in Schedule D to the Disclosure Regulations upon request by a member of a pension scheme.[54] Whilst the Regulations only require this disclosure to be made following a request, it is good practice to provide this information on an annual basis to all members. The disclosure usually takes the form of an annual benefit statement. The objective of the requirement is to give members a summary of the benefits by reference to their own personal information. In the case of a member of a defined benefit scheme, the information required to be disclosed is:

1. The amount of the member's benefits and survivor's benefits payable from normal pensionable age or death calculated without regard to salary increases
2. The method of calculation of the amounts specified at 1

---

51 Where the scheme commenced after 1 January 1991 and within four weeks of becoming members where the scheme commenced before 1 January 1991.

52 Article 9(4) of the Regulations.

53 s.5 of the Terms of Employment (Information) Act, 1994.

54 Article 11.

3. The amount of benefits secured by additional voluntary contributions (AVCs)[55] and/or a transfer of rights from another scheme
4. The member's date of entry and the amount of contributions paid and the amount of any transfer payment received
5. The amount of the member's current pensionable salary and the method by which it is calculated
6. The amount of survivor's benefits payable on death of the member prior to normal pensionable age
7. Whether the member or prospective member has an option to purchase additional benefits.[56]

13.38 The following information is required to be furnished to a member of a defined contribution scheme:

1. The date of entry of the member into the scheme and the amount of contributions paid by or on behalf of the member together with any transfer payment
2. The amount of the current salary (if relevant) on which contributions are calculated
3. The accumulated value as at a specified date of the contributions paid by or on behalf of a member
4. The amount of benefit or benefits payable in respect of the death of the member prior to normal pensionable age
5. Whether the member or prospective member may pay AVCs.[57]

13.39 A key difference between the requirements with respect to defined benefit schemes and defined contribution schemes is that trustees are required to state the pension benefit at normal pension date (based on current salary) only in the case of defined benefit schemes. Spouses of members and other beneficiaries are not entitled

---

55 AVCs are defined in s.2 of the Pensions Act as such contributions (if any) as are paid on a voluntary basis by a member to provide additional benefits.

56 Article 11(1) and Schedule D Part 1 of the Disclosure Regulations.

57 Article 11(2) and Schedule D Part II of the Disclosure Regulations.

to this information except in the limited circumstances provided under the Family Law Act, 1995.[58]

Disclosure of Information on Termination of Employment

13.40 The Disclosure Regulations require the trustees of a scheme to furnish certain information to members as soon as practicable upon termination of relevant employment.[59] The information is set out in Schedule E to the Regulations. The type of information which must be disclosed depends upon whether the scheme is a defined benefit scheme or a defined contribution scheme and also whether or not the member has an entitlement to preserved benefit within the meaning of the Pensions Act.[60]

13.41 The information to be made available to a member of a defined benefit scheme on termination of relevant employment is as follows:

Where no preserved benefit entitlement

1. An explanation of any rights and options available to the member on termination of relevant employment.

Where there is a preserved benefit[61]

1. The rights and options available to a member on termination of relevant employment including details of the amount of benefits payable to or in respect of the member both in respect of preserved benefit under the Pensions Act and otherwise
2. Whether any transfer payment is available in respect of the member
3. The procedures for claiming the member's benefits
4. Where a transfer payment has been effected without consent, the name and address of the scheme to which the transfer payment has been made.[62]

---

58 See para. 15.17.

59 Article 12 of the Disclosure Regulations, and see para. 12.8 for the meaning of "termination of relevant employment".

60 As to preservation of benefits, see Chapter 12.

61 See Chapter 12 for a detailed discussion of preserved benefits.

62 Pursuant to Article 12(2)(b) a member not entitled to a preserved benefit is entitled to the information set out at 1. to 4. on request.

13.42 The following information is required to be disclosed in the case of termination of relevant employment of a member of a defined contribution scheme:

Where there is no preserved benefit

1. An explanation of any rights and options available to a member on termination of relevant employment.

Where there is a preserved benefit

1. The rights and options available to the member on termination of relevant employment including details of the accumulated value of the appropriate contributions (within the meaning of Part III of the Pensions Act) and of any other contributions payable to or in respect of the member
2. Whether any transfer payment is available in respect of the member
3. The procedures for claiming the member's benefits
4. Where a transfer payment has been effected without consent, the name and address of the scheme to which the transfer payment has been made.[63]

Disclosure of Information on Retirement or Death

13.43 The trustees of a pension scheme must disclose certain information where a benefit under the scheme becomes payable to a person on retirement or death of a member.[64] The following is the specified information and this must be furnished as soon as practicable after the benefit becomes payable:

1. The amount of the benefit and any options relating thereto and the procedure for exercising them
2. If the amount of the benefit is payable periodically, the conditions subject to which payment will continue

---

[63] Pursuant to Article 12(4)(b) a member not entitled to a preserved benefit is entitled to the information set out at 1. to 4. on request.

[64] Article 13.

3. If the benefit is payable periodically, the provisions under the rules of the scheme whereby the amount payable will be altered.[65]

The regulations require that the specified information is furnished to the member if the benefit is payable on retirement, or to the spouse or other beneficiary if the benefit is payable on death.

Disclosure of Information on Winding-up

13.44 The trustees of a pension scheme, where a decision has been made to wind up the scheme, have to notify that decision to all members of the scheme and authorised trade unions within 12 weeks of the date of the decision.[66] The trustees of a pension scheme are also obliged, as soon as practicable after the proceeds of the realisation of the resources of the scheme are applied in accordance with the rules, to furnish each individual member[67] with:

1. Information relating to the rights and options available to the member regarding benefit entitlements
2. An explanation as to the manner in which any surplus[68] or deficit in the resources of the scheme is being dealt with
3. Information as to who will be liable to pay the benefits after the scheme is wound up and the appropriate address for inquiries.

13.45 The trigger for disclosure under the Regulations is the decision to wind up. However, under most pension scheme trust deeds a number of events can constitute a wind-up event — for instance, the failure of an employer to make contributions in a stated time, or the insolvency of the employer. The language used by the Regulations is not sufficiently precise. It is not clear whether a "decision to wind-up" refers to a formal decision of the trustees, passed at a meeting of the

---

65 Article 13(1) and Schedule F of the Disclosure Regulations.

66 Article 14.

67 Article 14(b). It should be noted that "member" includes deferred pensioners. This obligation may be quire onerous for trustees if a scheme has a significant number of deferred pensioners, some of whom may have left service many years prior to the winding-up.

68 This requirement would, in practice, make it difficult to return a surplus to the employer without any reference to the members. See further Chapter 18.

trustees, or to a decision of the employer. If the trustees are prevented for some reason from making a formal decision (for instance, the unavailability of sufficient trustees to hold a meeting) then it may be argued that there is no obligation to disclose. The guidance notes issued by the Pensions Board provide no assistance as they merely repeat the statutory provisions. It would be a greater protection to members of schemes if there were an obligation to disclose to members the occurrence of a wind-up event. The disclosure requirements of Part V of the Pensions Act are intended as a protection for members of pension schemes. In well-run schemes communications with members will be good. It is with respect to schemes which are not well run that the Disclosure Regulations are principally required. In such schemes if formal decisions are not made or required, the present language in the Regulations concerning disclosure on winding up will not adequately safeguard members' interests.

ALTERNATIVE ARRANGEMENTS

13.46 The Minister for Social Welfare has the power, with the consent of the Minister for Finance, to relieve certain schemes, because of their size or category, from the full disclosure obligations of the Pensions Act.[69] The Minister for Social Welfare has, in the Disclosure Regulations, availed himself of this power. The Disclosure Regulations set out certain alternative arrangements regarding annual reports, annual audited accounts and actuarial valuations with respect to:

1. Defined contribution schemes
2. Small schemes.

A small scheme is any defined benefit scheme where, at the commencement date of the relevant scheme year, there are fewer than 50 active members.[70] For the purposes of this definition, an "active member" means any member who is in reckonable service (that is, currently included in the scheme for retirement benefits) at the commencement date of the relevant scheme year.

13.47 The intention of the exemptions is to reduce the cost to certain schemes of full compliance with the Disclosure Regulations. A small

---

69 s.57.

70 Article 7(2).

defined benefit scheme and defined contribution schemes would, in the absence of the exempting provisions, be obliged to have audited accounts prepared on an annual basis with the attendant cost.

13.48 Where the exemption applies, the trustees of a scheme may, instead of complying with the full disclosure provisions, arrange for an alternative annual report of the scheme to be prepared by a life office or an auditor. The Regulations provide that the report may be prepared: (i) in the case of a scheme where the benefits are secured by one or more policies or contracts of insurance with an authorised insurance undertaking, by a person designated by such undertaking; and (ii) in any other case, by a person who would be regarded as a qualified auditor under the Disclosure Regulations.[71]

13.49 The alternative annual report must contain:[72]

1. A statement of the amount of the contributions paid by the employer and members to the scheme during the scheme year
2. A statement whether or not contributions payable during the scheme year had been received by the scheme within 30 days of the end of the scheme year and paid in accordance with the rules of the scheme and, if appropriate, in accordance with the recommendations of the actuary and, if that statement is qualified a statement of the reasons for that qualification
3. A statement of the manner in which the resources of a scheme are invested including the extent of any self-investment in excess of 5 per cent of the resources of the scheme[73]
4. Except in the case of a defined contribution scheme, a copy of the latest actuarial funding certificate
5. An investment report containing (a) a statement by the investment manager of the investment policies and any changes from the previous year, (b) a review of the investment performance of the scheme's fund

---

71 Article 7(3).

72 Article 7(8).

73 "Self-investment" is defined in Article 3 of the Regulations.

6. The information specified at paragraphs 1 to 4 of Schedule B to the Disclosure Regulations.[74]

13.50 A copy of the latest annual report must be made available by the trustees not later than nine months after the end of the scheme year to which it relates to those persons specified in paragraph 13.8. Under Article 7(5), the trustees must inform the members of the relevant scheme of the availability of the annual report. A copy of the latest annual report must be furnished free of charge to an authorised trade union representing the members of the relevant scheme and, upon request, to the persons specified at 1., 2. and 3. of paragraph 13.8.

BREACHES OF THE DISCLOSURE REGULATIONS

13.51 Section 3(1) of the Pensions Act provides that where a trustee, actuary or auditor of a scheme contravenes a provision of the Pensions Act or regulations they shall be guilty of an offence. Under section 3(3) of the Pensions Act, a person guilty of an offence shall be liable:

1. On summary conviction to a fine not exceeding £1,500 or to imprisonment for a term not exceeding one year, or to both[75]
2. On conviction on indictment to a fine not exceeding £10,000 or to imprisonment for a term not exceeding two years, or to both.

13.52 Section 3(4) provides that where an offence under the Pensions Act is committed by a body corporate, and is proved to have been so committed with the consent or connivance of any person, being a director, manager, secretary or other officer of the body corporate, such person shall, as well as the body corporate, be guilty of an offence.

13.53 Section 3(1)(c) provides that a person prosecuted for an offence under section 3 can, in their defence, seek to prove that the contravention to which the offence relates was attributable to a contravention by one or more other persons and that the accused took reasonable steps in the circumstances that were open to them to

---

[74] See para. 13.27 above at (4)(i) to (iv).

[75] As amended by s.43 Pensions (Amendment) Act, 1996.

secure the compliance of that person or persons with the provision concerned.

13.54 The employer of a pension scheme can be charged with an offence if it fails to comply with its disclosure obligations. As noted above,[76] the employer is obliged under section 54(4)(a) to furnish to the trustees, the actuary or the auditor, information requested by any of them in order that they may comply with their obligations under the Act and the Regulations. Section 54(5) provides that contravention of section 54(4) is an offence punishable on summary conviction to a fine not exceeding £1,500.[77] It would appear that a breach by an employer of its obligations under section 54(4) is not capable of prosecution on indictment and an employer cannot, therefore, be liable to the increased penalties specified in section 3(3)(b).

13.55 Having dealt with the disclosure requirements under the Pensions Act and the Disclosure Regulations the following paragraphs deal with the disclosure obligations imposed by trust law, Revenue requirements for approval of occupational pension schemes, employment law and company law.

TRUST LAW

13.56 Under trust law a trustee has a duty to advise beneficiaries of the manner in which the trust property has been invested and as to the trustees' dealings with the trust property.[78] This duty applies equally to the trustees of a pension scheme. It is clear from general trust law that a beneficiary has a right to see and inspect the trust documents.[79] A beneficiary has a right to require that information with regard to the trust property and the administration of that property be provided by the trustees.[80] If a trustee fails to furnish the information which has been requested, the beneficiary has a right to apply to Court and the trustee will be fixed with the costs of such applica-

---

76 Para. 13.30.

77 As amended by s.43 Pensions (Amendment) Act, 1996.

78 See *Chaine-Nickson* v. *Bank of Ireland* [1976] IR 393.

79 *O'Rourke* v. *Darbishire* [1920] AC 581.

80 *Low* v. *Bouverie* — but only with respect to that part of the property in which he has an interest.

tion.[81] Trustees are obliged under trust law to prepare records and accounts.[82] They are also obliged to allow beneficiaries to inspect and to copy trust documents and accounts and they are obliged to disclose the general nature of the scheme if requested.[83] In the context of a pension scheme, members would be entitled under the above principles, for instance, to information as to their benefit entitlements, the manner in which the assets of the scheme are invested, and the value of those investments. Whilst there is no reported Irish Case on the point, the English High Court in *Hamar* v. *The Pensions Ombudsman*[84] held that there is no general duty imposed by law on trustees of pension schemes to explain to beneficiaries the rights they have under a scheme.

13.57 A shortcoming in the rights conferred by trust law is that the extent of the disclosure obligations is uncertain. Furthermore, there is no positive obligation on trustees or an employer to furnish information to beneficiaries other than on their request. The rights conferred by trust law can only be enforced by a beneficiary through court proceedings which, of their nature, are expensive.

13.58 The Trustee Act, 1893, which is still the principal Irish statute dealing with trusts and trustees, was not enacted with pension schemes in mind and contains no provision obliging trustees to furnish information to beneficiaries or entitling beneficiaries to request it.

REVENUE REQUIREMENTS

13.59 As already noted,[85] it is part of the Revenue approval procedure for occupational pension schemes that certain basic information with respect to the pension scheme must be furnished to members and to those persons entitled to join the pension scheme.[86] In practice, the Revenue Commissioners will accept an announcement letter

---

81 Regarding the trustee's obligations to notify members, see also para. 4.51.

82 *Crawford* v. *Crawford* (1867) LR 1 Eq 436 and *Moore* v. *McGlynn* [1894] 1 IR 74, see also the English case of *Re Tillott* [1892] 1 Ch. 86.

83 Re *David Ireland & Co.* [1905] I IR 133.

84 [1996] PLR I.

85 See para 13.2 above.

86 s.15(2)(b) Finance Act, 1972 and Revenue Practice Notes 26 and 260. See also para. 6.19.

which sets out the principal terms of the scheme. They require confirmation that such announcement letter has in fact been circulated to all employees invited to join the scheme. However, the Revenue Commissioners are not in a position to ensure that these requirements are in fact complied with and that the confirmation is correct. Until recently, the Revenue Commissioners have not attempted to ensure such compliance.[87] Furthermore, the statutory provisions do not confer any direct right on members to such information, nor do they give members any remedy in the event that the requirements for Revenue approval in this regard are breached.

EMPLOYMENT LAW

13.60 Section 3 of the Terms of Employment (Information) Act, 1994[88] requires employers to furnish to employees a written statement containing information in relation to terms of employment including particulars of any arrangements with regard to pension schemes. The written statement has to be furnished within two months of commencement of employment. It may be provided either as a written statement or in another document which is readily available to the employee. In practice, many employers have standard terms and conditions of employment which are furnished to employees on commencement of their employment. The 1994 Act further requires employers to furnish particulars of employment to new employees, within one month after commencement of employment.

13.61 The 1994 Act also obliges employers to notify employees of any changes in the terms and conditions of employment within one month of such changes being effected.[89] This would include the right of an employee to be notified of any changes made to a pension scheme.

---

87 As part of new measures introduced by the Revenue Commissioners to ensure stricter compliance with the Revenue Code, the Revenue now conducts audits on employers. In the course of such audits, occupational pension schemes may be reviewed.

88 This Act replaced those parts of the Minimum Notice and Terms of Employment Act, 1973 dealing with terms of employment.

89 Section 5(1) of the 1994 Act.

Changes effected by statute do not require to be notified to employees under the 1994 Act.[90]

COMPANY LAW

The Companies (Amendment) Act, 1986

13.62 As already noted, the Companies (Amendment) Act, 1986 requires certain companies (other than banks, insurance companies and non-profit- making companies[91]) to disclose in their accounts details of pension arrangements. The obligations relating to disclosure are set out in paragraph 36 of the Schedule to the 1986 Act. Paragraph 36(4) requires that particulars be given of any pension commitments included under any provision shown in the company's balance sheet and any such commitments for which no provision has been made. Paragraph 36(5) requires that the accounts give information as to:

1. The nature of every pension scheme operated by or on behalf of a company including information as to whether or not each scheme is a defined benefit scheme or a defined contribution scheme[92]
2. Whether each such scheme is externally funded or internally financed[93]
3. Whether any pension costs and liabilities are assessed in accordance with the advice of a professionally qualified actuary and, if so, the date of the most recent relevant actuarial valuation
4. Whether, and if so, where, any such actuarial valuation is available for public inspection.

---

90 Section 5(2) of the 1994 Act.

91 These types of companies are required by other legislation (the Central Bank Acts and the European Communities (Credit Institutions: Accounts) Regulations, 1992 (SI No 294 of 1992) with respect to banks, the Insurance Acts with respect to insurance and assurance companies and the Companies Act, 1963 with respect to certain non-profit-making companies) to disclose their accounts and so are excluded from the provisions of the 1986 Act.

92 The differences between defined benefit schemes and defined contribution schemes are considered at para. 2.3. These terms are not defined in the 1986 Act.

93 As regards funding of pension schemes generally, see Chapter 9.

13.63 Parent and subsidiary company accounts must also include a disclosure as to pension commitments undertaken with respect to any parent undertaking or fellow subsidiary undertaking.[94] All company-audited financial statements must also comply with the requirements of SSAP 24.

SSAP 24

13.64 At present, all Irish companies must account for pension costs in accordance with the Statement of Standard Accounting Practice No. 24 entitled "Accounting for Pension Costs" ("SSAP 24").[95] In Ireland, this applied to publicly quoted companies from 1988 and to all companies for accounting periods commencing after 31 December 1992. Prior to SSAP 24, Companies accounted for pension costs on the basis of contributions paid. Clearly this could result in widely different costs from year to year. It also made it difficult to compare the financial results of companies. SSAP 24 requires pension costs to be accounted for on an accruals basis.[96] The objective of SSAP 24 was to introduce a more systematic and rational basis for companies to account for pension costs. This should have enabled greater comparability of pension costs as between companies. However, SSAP 24 has been criticised for failing to achieve this objective. This failure is attributed to the flexibility allowed by SSAP 24 to choose different options in preparing accounts, and by failing to impose disclosure requirements with respect to the options chosen. The Accounting Standards Board has issued a discussion paper on SSAP 24,[97] which proposes changes to SSAP 24.

---

94 Companies (Amendment) Act, 1986, para. 45A of the Schedule as inserted by European Communities (Companies: Group Accounts) Regulations, 1992 (SI No 201 of 1992) at para. 4(3) of the Schedule to those Regulations.

95 Irish subsidiaries of US companies must also comply with US accounting standard FAS 87.

96 This is a basic concept of accounting which requires that revenues and costs are recognised in accounts when they accrue or are incurred (not as money received or paid) and, to the extent that such are notifiably related, that they are connected with one another.

97 "Pension Costs in the Employer's Financial Statements" issued by the ASB on 22 June 1995.

Defects in Company Law

13.65 The disclosure obligations required by company law are imposed directly on the employer company. They relate only to disclosure in that company's accounts and they do not confer any direct right to information on members of pension schemes, unless such members happen to be shareholders of the sponsoring employer. Failing that, the right to information is at best indirect. Members or their representatives can only obtain such information by making a search in the Companies Registration Office. The sponsoring employer may not have filed accounts or, if it has done so, the accounts may be some years out of date.[98] The 1986 Act does not confer any remedy on members of pension schemes if the sponsoring employer fails to comply with its obligations under the Act.

---

[98] In this regard, the Irish Registrar of Companies has in recent years become more vigilant in prosecution of companies which are obliged to and fail to file accounts.

14

MEMBER TRUSTEES

INTRODUCTION

14.1 Prior to the enactment of the Pensions Act a number of Irish pension schemes had member trustees — for instance, those established by some state-sponsored bodies. These were either selected by the employer acting alone or were nominated by employees. Some schemes also had pension committees on which members were represented. However, there did not exist a statutory right of members to participate in the selection of persons for appointment as trustees. The first report of the National Pensions Board recommended that members of funded schemes with more than 50 members should have a legal right to require the sponsoring employer to hold an election for member trustees.[1] This recommendation was carried forward in section 62 of the Pensions Act, which requires the Minister for Social Welfare to make provision by regulation for the selection of trustees by members of pensions schemes. Section 62(1) states:

> The Minister shall provide by regulations, in respect of schemes having not less than a specified number of members, that the members of any such scheme may select, or approve of the selection by the employer concerned, of a person or a specified number of persons who shall be appointed to be a trustee or trustees of the scheme (or who shall be retained as such trustee or trustees, as the case may be).[2]

---

1 First Report of the National Pensions Board (Pl. 4776), Chapter 2, Para. 35.

2 Since the enactment of the Pensions Act, 1990, s.62 has been amended by the Social Welfare Act 1992 and the Social Welfare (No. 2) Act, 1993. s.62(1) was amended in s.15 of the Social Welfare (No. 2) Act, 1993. The amended text, as quoted above, clarifies certain ambiguities in the original text. It makes it clear, firstly, that a scheme may have one trustee only and, secondly, that the selection process may include the retention of an existing trustee or trustees of a pension scheme. s.62(1) as originally

14.2 The Minister made regulations on 21 December 1993, which provide for the selection of trustees by members of pension schemes.[3] These are the Occupational Pension Schemes (Member Participation in the Selection of Persons for Appointment as Trustees)(No. 2) Regulations, 1993 and are referred to in this chapter as "the Regulations". In this chapter the content and application of the Regulations are considered. The Regulations came into force on 1 January 1994. They apply to occupational pension schemes with 50 or more qualified members[4] and to certain smaller schemes.[5] Following implementation of the Regulations, employers and members of pension schemes have four options with respect to the appointment of trustees:

1. To continue the existing trustee arrangements
2. To agree a method of selection of member trustees outside the Regulations
3. To implement an alternative arrangement[6] under the Regulations
4. To implement a standard arrangement[7] under the Regulations.

14.3 The Regulations do not prohibit the maintenance of an existing trustee arrangement. It is quite open to the employer and members to agree that existing arrangements should be maintained or to agree some form of member-trustee representation entirely outside the ambit of the Regulations. The Regulations may be regarded as a last resort in a situation where the employer and the members cannot agree on some form of member-trustee representation. The Regula-

---

enacted was ambiguous and appeared to require that there must be more than one trustee (thereby excluding a sole corporate trustee).

3 The Minister had previously made Regulations for the purposes of compliance with s.62, namely the Occupational Pension Schemes (Member Participation in the Selection of Persons for Appointment as Trustees) Regulations, 1993 made on 27 July 1993. These Regulations were found to be deficient in a number of respects. For example, no provision whatsoever was made for corporate trustees. The Regulations were repealed and replaced by those made on 21 December 1993.

4 See para. 14.6.

5 See para. 14.6.

6 See para. 14.16.

7 See para. 14.12.

tions have a number of shortcomings which make it desirable to avoid resort to them if possible. These shortcomings include:

1. The selection procedure under the Regulations may require that elections be held, which can be both expensive and time-consuming.
2. Once initiated, the selection of trustees by members under the Regulations cannot be terminated. Where a preliminary poll[8] is held and less than 25 per cent of the qualified members vote, the alternative arrangement proposed by the employer is deemed to have been chosen by the members.[9] However, in the circumstances of a low poll, it may be sensible to adopt some other arrangement. It may indicate a lack of interest by the members in the matter of trusteeship of the pension scheme. The Regulations do not provide a mechanism whereby the process may be terminated once it has been commenced.
3. The Regulations operate in a circular manner. Once trustees have been selected pursuant to the Regulations, the employer is obliged to initiate a further selection process upon expiry of the term of office of the member trustees.[10] The Regulations do not contain any power allowing the employer, together with the members, to opt out of the selection process at a future date.
4. The term of office of a member-selected or member-approved trustee is six years.[11] The Regulations do not contain any mechanism whereby a member-selected trustee may be removed from office prior to expiry of the term. This could present serious difficulties. For instance, a trustee may cease to be an employee whether through retirement, change of job or dismissal. Depending on the circumstances of each case, it may not be appropriate for such person to remain as a trustee. However, there is no procedure under the Regulations to facilitate the removal of such trustees.[12]

---

8 See para. 14.17.

9 Article 8(7) — see para. 14.16.

10 Article 18(2) and Article 6(2).

11 Article 12(2).

12 Article 18(1) does provide that a preliminary poll may be requested by at least 50 per cent of the qualified members — this is, however, a very cumbersome method of removing a trustee and also one which cannot be initiated by the Employer.

5. The mandatory requirement that the term of office be six years makes it impossible for the employer to overlap periods of office of trustees. The employer and the members may consider it desirable that the period of office of trustees should overlap so that new trustees can gain experience from existing trustees. It may also be desired to have shorter or longer periods of office for trustees.

6. Where an election is held, an Employer cannot divide the membership into different constituencies for election purposes. This may be desirable where a scheme covers employees situate in different factories or business units in different locations. Different constituencies may also be desirable where a scheme has a large number of pensioners. In such cases, an employer and the members or their representatives must agree a selection procedure outside the Regulations.

14.4 In the light of the above, it may appear obvious that the employer should establish a member-trustee arrangement outside the Regulations. However, if an employer, with a scheme to which the Regulations apply, maintains an existing arrangement or implements an arrangement outside the Regulations, it is in an uncertain position, because at any time an election process may be initiated by the members under the Regulations.[13] It may be argued that to achieve certainty it is preferable that the employer should itself initiate a selection process under the Regulations. However, except in limited cases, the shortcomings of the Regulations themselves and the difficulties that they present outweigh any such uncertainty. The remainder of this chapter will deal with the Regulations and their operation and not arrangements outside the Regulations.

14.5 It should be noted that the Regulations override any provisions in formal pension trust documentation which may conflict with them.[14] Most formal pension scheme documentation would not contain provisions entitling members to appoint trustees. To this extent, the Regulations override such documentation in that they confer a statutory right on members to select or approve of the selection of persons for appointment as trustees. The Regulations do not, however, re-

---

13 Under Article 6(1).

14 s.64(A)(1) Pensions Act (as inserted by s.50 Social Welfare Act, 1993).

move the desirability of a formal deed of appointment of trustee to be entered into by the principal employer.[15]

AFFECTED SCHEMES

14.6 The Regulations apply to the following pension schemes:

1. Schemes with a total of 50 or more qualified members. Qualified members are defined as members in service who are included in the scheme for retirement benefits, and members actively in receipt of benefits.[16]

2. Directly Invested Schemes with 12 or more qualified members. As the name suggests, a directly invested scheme is a scheme that has a direct investment in assets such as stocks, shares or property. The Regulations define a directly invested scheme as one which, at the commencement of a scheme year, is a scheme other than a scheme that has resources composed entirely of one or more of the following:

   (a) Insurance policies

   (b) Contracts of assurance

   (c) Managed funds

   (d) Unit trusts

   (e) Cash deposits with authorised deposit-taking institutions.[17]

SELECTION OF TRUSTEES UNDER THE REGULATIONS

14.7 The process of selecting trustees under the Regulations may be initiated by 15 per cent or more of the qualified members or by an authorised trade union or unions representing at least 50 per cent of active members.[18] An "Active Member" is defined in the Regulations as a member who is in reckonable service.[19] The employer is not

---

15 See para. 14.25.

16 Article 3.

17 Article 3.

18 A "valid request" as defined under Article 3. See also Article 6.

19 Article 3.

obliged to initiate the selection process. The Regulations do, however, provide that the employer may, if it so chooses, notify the trustees to proceed with the selection process.[20] A flow diagram illustrating when a selection process under the Regulations is required is set out in Figure 14.1. To commence the process the members or their authorised trade union must issue a valid request[21] to the scheme trustees, or the employer can initiate the process of its own initiative.

FIGURE 14.1: WHEN SELECTION PROCESS REQUIRED UNDER REGULATIONS

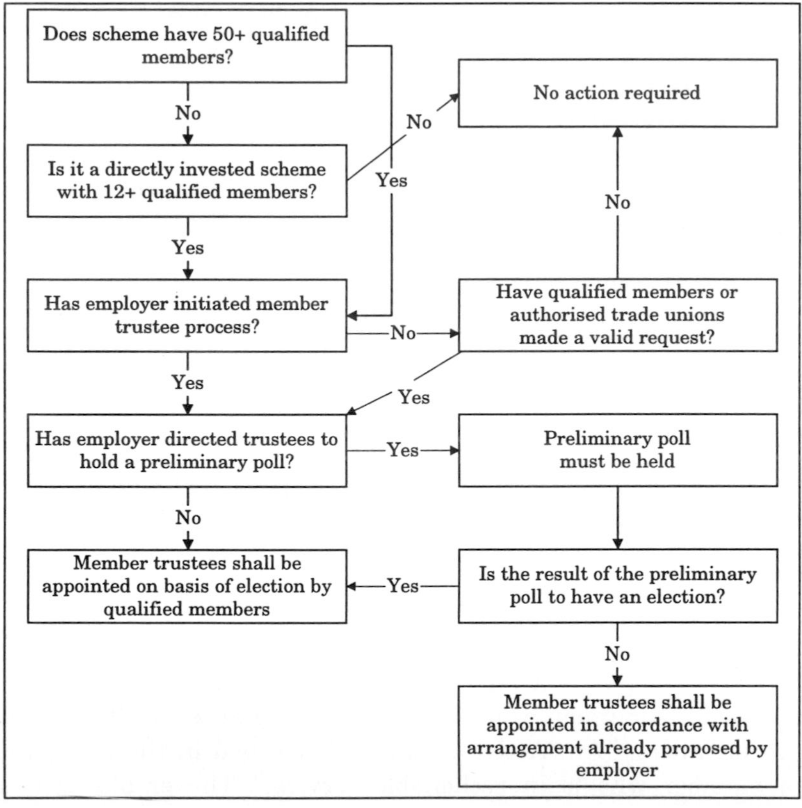

Source: Coyle Hamilton Ltd.

---

20 Article 6(2)(b).

21 Article 3(1) and Article 6(1).

14.8 On receipt of a valid request, the trustees must notify the employer within 14 days of receipt of such request and they must also appoint a returning officer.[22] The trustees must supply the returning officer with a list of qualified members. The employer must, on receipt of a notification from the trustees of a valid request, or may, at any time of its own initiative, direct the trustees either:

1. To hold a preliminary poll in order to offer the members a choice between an election and an alternative arrangement proposed by the employer, or
2. To proceed to the election by qualified members of persons for appointment as trustees.[23]

14.9 The receipt of a valid request by the trustees does not therefore require that a preliminary poll must be held. Equally, it does not mean that an election must take place. The employer may determine that a selection process be initiated (by means of an election), in which case no preliminary poll is required. This is called a standard arrangement in the Regulations. If the employer proposes an alternative arrangement, a preliminary poll is required. If the result of that preliminary poll is the approval of the alternative arrangement, then there is no election.

14.10 If the employer, on receipt of a notification from the trustees under Article 6(1), fails to issue a direction to the trustees within a period of 60 days from the date of receipt, the trustees must instruct the returning officer to proceed with an election to select members for appointment as trustees.

14.11 It should be noted that only qualified members are entitled to take part in the selection process.[24] Persons who may have benefit entitlements under a pension scheme and who are at present excluded under the Regulations would include deferred pensioners, members covered for death benefits only and beneficiaries entitled to survivors' benefits.

---

[22] See para. 14.20 et seq.

[23] Article 6(2).

[24] Article 4.

STANDARD ARRANGEMENT

14.12 In a standard arrangement, the total number of trustees will depend on how many trustees the employer selects to be employer-nominated trustees. The Regulations require that the number of member-elected trustees should be equal to the number of employer-nominated trustees, subject to a minimum of two member-elected trustees.[25] The employer, therefore, at all times, controls the number of member-elected trustees that may be appointed. As will be seen, the employer has some influence on the appointment of the chairperson.[26] Care should be taken to avoid a situation where the election will result in there being such a large number of trustees as to make the conduct of business by the trustees unduly difficult. This may require that some of the existing employer-nominated trustees retire prior to the election process being initiated. If under existing arrangements a sole corporate trustee is used, this cannot be accommodated under a standard arrangement. Under Article 3(1) a sole corporate trustee may be approved only under an alternative arrangement.

The standard arrangement will apply if either:

1. The employer directs the trustees to proceed to the selection by qualified members of persons for appointment as member trustees,[27] or
2. Fifty per cent or more of the qualified members voting in a preliminary poll[28] opt for the standard arrangement.[29]

14.13 Where an election is to be held, the returning officer is directed by the Regulations to make arrangements for the holding of such election and to notify the qualified members of the number of persons to be selected for appointment as member trustees and the arrangements for the holding of the election.[30] Where the number of valid candidates[31] is equal to or less than the number of persons to be selected for appoint-

---

[25] Article 8(2).

[26] See para. 14.23.

[27] Article 6(2)(ii).

[28] See para. 14.17.

[29] Article 8(6)(a).

[30] Article 9(1).

[31] Nominated under Article 10.

ment as member trustees, all the valid candidates, if any, are deemed to be elected.[32] Where the number of valid candidates exceeds the number of persons to be selected for appointment as member trustees, an election to select such persons must be held in accordance with the Regulations.[33] Where an election is required, each qualified member is entitled to one vote, and such election must be taken by secret ballot and according to the principle of proportional representation.[34]

14.14 The Regulations provide that a candidate for appointment as a member trustee must be nominated by either:

1. Not less than 10 qualified members; or
2. Not less than 10 per cent of the qualified members, whichever is the lesser.[35]

14.15 Nominees are not restricted to members of the pension scheme. Article 10 provides that any person shall be eligible to be nominated. "Person" is defined in Article 3(1) as any person over the age of 18 years or a corporate body. A nominee could therefore be a trade union representative or a professional trustee. It is somewhat anomalous that a person who is not eligible to vote in an election may, however, be nominated for election.

ALTERNATIVE ARRANGEMENT

14.16 The election process is a time-consuming and potentially costly exercise. The approach of an alternative arrangement is thus available under the Regulations and will be a desirable option for many employers. For example, if the employer reaches agreement with the members or their representatives as to the persons to be selected as member trustees, this can then be approved by vote of the members under an alternative arrangement. The employer cannot impose an alternative

---

32 Article 11(1).

33 Article 11(2).

34 Article 9(3). The guidance notes with respect to the Regulations issued by the Pensions Board in March 1994 contain considerable detail with respect to the conduct of preliminary polls and elections. They should be of assistance to returning officers faced with what for many will be the unfamiliar task of conducting an election and according to the principle of proportional representation.

35 Article 10(3).

arrangement on the members. On the contrary, the alternative arrangement must be approved by more than half of the qualified members who vote, before it can be implemented under the Regulations.[36]

Under an alternative arrangement there is, however, no election. The employer proposes members to be appointed as trustees and this proposal is then submitted to the members for approval. The total number of trustees is determined at the discretion of the employer.[37]

Preliminary Poll

14.17 If the employer proposes an alternative arrangement, a Preliminary Poll must be held.[38] A preliminary poll consists of a vote by the qualified members to select either:

1. A standard arrangement (an election by secret ballot to select member-nominated trustees); or
2. An alternative arrangement (an arrangement proposed by the employer in which the employer specifies the names of the person or persons or body corporate who, or which, are to be appointed trustees, such selection to be approved by the members).

14.18 If a preliminary poll is required, under Article 6 of the Regulations, the returning officer is directed by the Regulations to make arrangements for the taking of such a poll.[39] The Regulations further provide that, in the taking of the preliminary poll, the returning officer shall arrange for a standard notification to be delivered to each qualified member or sent by post in a registered letter addressed to such qualified member at the member's last known address.[40] The form of the standard notification is specified in detail in Article 8(3).[41] The votes at a preliminary poll taken under Article 8 are given by secret ballot and each qualified member is entitled to one vote.[42]

---

36 Article 8(6)(b).

37 Article 8(2).

38 Article 3, Article 6.

39 Article 8(1).

40 Article 8(3).

41 By reference to Schedule A and B to the Regulations.

42 Article 8(4).

Corporate Trustee

14.19 The Regulations can accommodate the appointment of a corporate trustee.[43] If the existing trustee of a pension scheme is a corporate trustee, it may be maintained. A corporate trustee can be proposed by the principal employer under an alternative arrangement. A sole corporate trustee appointed under an alternative arrangement is not a member trustee for the purposes of the Regulations.[44]

RETURNING OFFICER

14.20 On receipt by the trustees of a valid request,[45] the trustees are required to appoint a returning officer[46] and to supply to that person a list of the qualified members.[47] The person to be appointed as returning officer must be:

1. The secretary of the employer, or, in case there is no such secretary, the officer of the employer who performs the functions of secretary, or
2. In lieu of such secretary or officer, any other person who in the opinion of the trustees of the relevant scheme is competent to perform the functions of returning officer.[48]

---

43 Article 8(2)(II). As to the reasons for using a corporate trustee, see para. 4.6.

44 Article 3(1). The definition of "Member Trustee" in Article 3(1) excludes a sole corporate trustee approved under an alternative arrangement.

45 See 14.7 at footnote 19.

46 Article 6.1.

47 The drafting of Article 6 of the Regulations (dealing with initiation of the process) appears to be defective in that the trustees of a scheme are required to appoint a returning officer upon receipt of a valid request (that is, a request from qualified members or a trade union representative, as specified in Article 6(1)), but are not required to appoint a returning officer upon receipt of a direction from the employer pursuant to Article 6(2).

48 Article 7(1). The language of Article 7(1) is not entirely clear. Article 7(1)(a) and 7(1)(b) appear to offer a choice between the secretary of the employer (or the officer who performs the functions of secretary if there is no secretary) and any other person chosen by the trustees as competent to perform the functions of returning officer. However, because the Regulations do not say that the secretary can refuse to act as Returning Officer, it is unclear whether this is permissible.

14.21 The returning officer is required under the Regulations to arrange for the taking of a preliminary poll[49] if applicable, and, if required, to arrange for an election in accordance with the Regulations. The Regulations prescribe the form of notice and ballot paper to be sent by the returning officer and the time periods within which results should be notified. The returning officer is not entitled to be nominated as, or to nominate, a person for selection as a member trustee.[50]

14.22 Returning officers, in their conduct of the preliminary poll and any election, are required to have regard to such guidance notes (regarding the conduct of preliminary polls and elections) as may be issued by the Pensions Board.[51] In March 1994, the Pensions Board, pursuant to its powers under the Pensions Act, issued detailed guidance notes with respect to the Regulations. It does appear that, at least in part, the Pensions Board has attempted in the guidance notes to "fill in" the gaps in the Regulations or to clarify their meaning. This has not been entirely successful. It is suggested that it is unhelpful to attempt to clarify or add to the Regulations in the guidance notes. They do not have the legal status of a statutory instrument and cannot override the Regulations.

TRUSTEE MATTERS

The Chairperson

14.23 The Regulations provide that there shall be a chairperson of the trustees.[52] Under a standard arrangement, the chairperson is chosen by the employer-nominated trustees and the member-elected trustees at a meeting.[53] The chairperson may be either one of their body or a person selected from outside. If the vote on election of the chairperson is tied, the Regulations provide that the employer shall select the chairperson.[54] Under an alternative arrangement, the chairperson, or the procedure for the selection of a chairperson, is

---

49 Article 8(1).

50 Article 7(3).

51 Article 7(4).

52 Article 5, Article 8.

53 Article 8(2)(iii).

54 Article 13(4).

determined by the principal employer.[55] Whilst not explicit in the Regulations, it would appear that the chairperson when appointed is also a trustee. In the event of a tied vote, the chairperson has a casting vote.[56] Generally, the chairperson has ultimate responsibility to fix the agenda for trustee meetings, and will conduct the business at these meetings and ensure that the matters discussed at meetings are dealt with properly. Minutes of trustee meetings when signed by the chairperson will constitute prima facie evidence of the business actually conducted at the meetings and of any decisions made by the trustees.

Term of Office

14.24 The term of office of a member trustee, whether under an alternative arrangement or a standard arrangement, is six years from the date of appointment.[57] The Regulations provide that the date of appointment of a member trustee is a date 60 days from the date on which the returning officer declares that the member trustees have been elected (under a standard arrangement) or that their selection has been approved (under an alternative arrangement).[58] A sole corporate trustee appointed under an alternative arrangement will remain in office indefinitely subject to the provisions for removal contained in the pension scheme documentation and subject to the result of any subsequent preliminary poll initiated under the Regulations.[59]

14.25 It is unclear from the Regulations how a member-selected or member-approved trustee is actually appointed. Whilst Article 12(1) states that the relevant persons "shall" be appointed as trustees, this is not of itself an appointment. Most trust documents require that trustees must be appointed by deed, and so one is generally required. Article 15(1) requires the returning officer, without delay, to notify in writing to the employer the persons selected or nominated for appointment as trustees and to request the employer to make appropriate arrangements to give full effect to the appointments. The appointment must be effected under the terms of the trust deed. Section

---

55 Article 8(2)(I)(C).

56 Article 14(3).

57 Article 12(2).

58 Article 12(1).

59 Article 12(2).

64A(1) of the Pensions Act states that the Regulations, where necessary, override the provisions set out in the trust deed and rules of the scheme for appointment of trustees. This, however, can only be to the extent of the right to select persons for appointment (usually the formal trust documentation reserves this to the employer). The guidance notes issued by the Pensions Board state that the employer should, as soon as it receives notification from the returning officer, make arrangements to have a deed of appointment or removal of trustees drawn up.[60]

Resignation, Replacement of Elected Trustee

14.26 A member trustee may resign from office by notice in writing to the chairperson.[61] Where a member trustee resigns or dies, a new member trustee is appointed for the unexpired portion of the previous member trustee's term of office.[62] Provided that the unexpired portion of the term of office is less then one year, the office can be left vacant unless the remaining member trustees decide otherwise. Subject to that proviso, if a vacancy occurs and an election had taken place, the chairperson must notify the candidate eliminated with the highest number of votes in such election of the vacancy, and that person must, subject to their agreement, be appointed as the member trustee.[63] If no such election has taken place, or where an election had taken place but there were no further valid candidates available, the existing member trustees must select a person for appointment as member trustee (subject to that person's agreement).[64] Where the existing member trustees fail to select a person to act as member trustee, the chairperson must select a person to be appointed to fill the vacancy.[65]

14.27 When the six-year term of office is completed, the member trustee appointment process will recommence.[66] If a preliminary poll had previously been held, the right to request a preliminary poll can,

---

60 Guidance Notes para. 71 and 75.

61 Article 17(1).

62 Article 17.

63 Article 17(2)(a).

64 Article 17(2)(b).

65 Article 17(3).

66 Article 18(2) and Article 6(2). Article 18(2) states that the trustees must appoint a returning officer in accordance with Article 6(2) and supply to such person a list of the qualified members.

however, be initiated at any time by 50 per cent of the qualified members. To do so, they must submit a request in writing to the trustees of the relevant scheme for such a poll to be held.[67]

67 Article 18(1).

15

MARITAL BREAKDOWN

INTRODUCTION

15.1 The pension is perhaps the second most valuable family asset next to the family home. Sadly, the partners in a marriage may not appreciate its value until the relationship breaks down and the assets of the family are being divided between them. The Family Law Act, 1995 provides that pensions can now be reallocated in favour of a spouse in circumstances of judicial separation or foreign divorce. Furthermore, the Family Law (Divorce) Bill, 1996 which was published on 17 June 1996, will when enacted, include almost identical provisions with regard to Irish divorces.

15.2 In Ireland, the relevance of occupational pension schemes with regard to marital breakdown was raised in a 1992 White Paper.[1] The report stated that:

> A number of solutions have been canvassed in neighbouring jurisdictions to deal with the problem presented by occupational pensions which carry benefits for widows but these have been rejected as being unworkable or inappropriate.[2]

One of those jurisdictions was the United Kingdom. In May 1993 the Pensions Management Institute in the UK commissioned a detailed report on pensions and divorce, which concluded that

---

1 Marital Breakdown a Review and Proposed Changes (Pl. 9104), September 1992.

2 para. 13.7, p.106.

> it would lead to a fairer division of assets on divorce if the courts were given power to reallocate occupational and personal pension rights between the divorcing parties.[3]

The PMI Report went on to consider in depth the various ways in which pensions could be reallocated, and their conclusions were broadly endorsed by the Goode Committee.[4]

15.3 The Family Law Act, 1995 ("the FLA") was initiated in the Dáil in 1994 without the benefit of any detailed Irish report on the allocation of pensions arising from marital breakdown. The intention was to introduce pension adjustment orders in advance of the divorce referendum held on 23 November 1995, to ensure that legislation facilitated the adjustment of all family assets including pensions.[5] When the Bill was initiated, the provisions relating to reallocation of pension rights were not sufficiently comprehensive to meet the requirements of pension schemes. Having taken into account the views of the various representative bodies in the pensions industry and a report issued by the Pensions Board, section 12 was completely revised.[6]

15.4 The FLA allows the Courts to designate a proportion of the pension scheme member's benefits in favour of a spouse or dependent child. This designation of benefit is achieved by a court order referred to in the Act as a pension adjustment order. In general, spouses can leave their benefits in the scheme or can elect to have them split from the member's benefits and transferred out to another scheme or arrangement so as to give the spouse an independent and separate benefit from that of the member. On the happening of certain events, the benefit is automatically split, even if the spouse does not request

---

3 Report of the Independent Working Group on Pensions and Divorce appointed by the Pensions Management Institute in agreement with the Law Society, May 1993 para. 22.1 on p. 52.

4 Report of the Pension Law Review Committee para. 4.16.16.

5 Initially the Bill provided for pension adjustment orders solely in circumstances of nullity, with the intention that divorce could be substituted for nullity in the legislation. Pension adjustment orders were subsequently extended to circumstances of judicial separation as well as nullity, and nullity was later dropped from the Bill so that now, under the FLA, only in circumstances of judicial separation (or foreign divorce/separation) can pension adjustment orders be granted.

6 s.12 now accounts (in terms of text) for over 14 per cent of the FLA as a whole.

it. The Courts are to be assisted by regulations on the designation, splitting and valuation of benefits.[7]

15.5 Only spouses and dependent members of the family can obtain a pension adjustment order. Non-marital partners cannot apply and so, if they separate, no pension adjustments can be made. Usually the man is the principal earner who will be entitled to a pension. For the sake of clarity, therefore, it is assumed in this chapter that it is the man who has the pensionable job. He will be referred to in this chapter as the "member" and the spouse will be referred to as, simply, "the spouse".[8]

15.6 Pension adjustment orders under the FLA are only available in the context of judicial separation or recognised foreign divorces or separations. The Family Law (Divorce) Bill, 1996 contains almost identical provisions to the FLA. When enacted, the comments below will apply equally to situations of Irish divorce.

15.7 The main focus of this chapter is pension adjustment orders as they affect occupational pension schemes. Self-employed arrangements and buy-out bonds are also examined towards the end of the chapter. Other issues that will be considered are the spouse's entitlements to information about the member's pension benefits, the allocation of marital assets without interfering with the member's pension and the effect of a separation agreement on the pension scheme. First, it is proposed to discuss the effects of marital separation on pension entitlements where no pension adjustment order is sought.

PENSION SCHEMES AND MARITAL SEPARATION/DIVORCE

15.8 Separation and divorce have no impact *per se* on the pension scheme member's own pension but they can affect the benefit entitlements (if any) of the spouse, payable on the member's death. In contrast, a pension adjustment order under the FLA can modify the member's pension as well as benefits payable on his death. The order will override the scheme rules to the extent that the latter are inconsistent with the terms of the pension adjustment order. In the absence of an order under the FLA, there are two categories of benefit

---

7 See para. 15.23 below.

8 The FLA uses the term "member spouse" and "spouse" rather than "member" and "spouse" but this, it is suggested, is more confusing than the terminology adopted in the text.

which can be affected by a spouse becoming separated or divorced: pensions payable on the death of a member either before or after retirement, and lump sum benefits payable on the death of the member before retirement.

Pensions Payable on Member's Death

15.9 Many schemes promise a pension to the spouse of a member on his death. These can be pensions payable on death in service or death in retirement, or both. Some also provide children's pensions. Spouse's pensions are, on the face of it, payable to the spouse, in that the spouse continues to be such even though she has become separated from the member. Nonetheless, the rules of the scheme may contain conditions which could prevent the spouse from receiving a pension. Some schemes debar a spouse from receiving any benefit under the scheme if she has ceased to cohabit with the member or is legally or judicially separated. In that event, the pension may not be payable at all, or the trustees may be given a discretion to pay the pension to another dependant.[9]

15.10 Debarring the spouse from receiving benefit is a harsh rule and one that is inconsistent with the concept of pensions forming part of the family assets available for allocation between the spouses. Accordingly, section 13 of the FLA enables the spouse to apply to court for an order negating such a rule.[10] The order directs the trustees not to regard the separation as a ground for disqualifying the spouse from receiving benefit. An order under section 13 can be granted only in the course of judicial separation proceedings or at any time thereafter during the lifetime of the member, or in respect of a judicially recognised foreign legal separation.[11] The judicial separation proceedings must have commenced on or after 1 August 1996, or, in the case of a foreign separation, the legal separation must have occured on or after

---

9 The Revenue Commissioners insist that pensions can be paid only to a dependant which includes the spouse, minor children, children in full-time education and any other person wholly or substantially dependent on the member for the ordinary necessaries of life. See para. 7.38.

10 A similar provision has been inserted into the Family Law (Maintenance of Spouses and Children) Act, 1976 in relation to separation agreements, providing for maintenance or disposition or use of property, being made a rule of court — s.8B as inserted by s.43(c) of the FLA.

11 ss.13(1) and 23.

1 August 1996.[12] Notice of an application must be given to the trustees who are entitled to be represented in court.[13] Any costs incurred by the trustees in complying with the order or in connection with the notice or representations to the court must be borne by the spouses in such proportions as the court determines.[14] In contrast with pension adjustment orders, the trustees have no power to apply to court to recoup undischarged costs out of benefits.[15]

15.11 An order under section 13 is relevant only where it is a condition for receipt of benefit that the spouses are residing together. It has no application where the trustees have discretion on payment. Modern trust documents usually give the trustees a discretion in circumstances where the member and the spouse are living apart (whether judicially separated or not) either to pay the pension to the spouse or to pay it to another dependant. In other words, the spouse's pension then becomes a dependant's pension, with discretion on the part of the trustees as to which dependant will receive it. There may also be power to split the pension between two or more dependants.

15.12 A spouse who is validly divorced from a member ceases to be a spouse and can only be considered for a spouse's or dependant's pension if she is actually dependent on the member.[16] A spouse may be able to establish dependency by reference to continued financial support from the member — for example, maintenance payments.

Lump Sum Payable on Member's Death

15.13 The second class of benefits are lump sum benefits payable on death before retirement. Death in service lump sum benefits are almost always expressed as a multiple of salary (for example, three times basic salary). The benefit is generally paid out under a discretionary trust, although there are schemes where no discretion is

---

12 s.5 and s.23(1) respectively and the Family Law Act, 1995 (Commencement) Order, 1996 (SI No 46 of 1996).

13 s.13(2).

14 s.13(3).

15 Compare s.12(22)(b) and see para. 15.101.

16 See fn 9 above.

given to the trustees.[17] If there is a discretion, this usually empowers the trustees to pay the lump sum in such proportions as they determine to one or more of a wide class of beneficiaries including the spouse but also including any other dependant, child or other relative of the member. The member may also be given the opportunity to complete a nomination form, or letter of wishes, indicating whom he would like to receive the benefit on his death. The nomination form is almost always expressed to be non-binding on the trustees, which means that the trustees can override the member's wishes if they believe that circumstances merit it. A separated spouse will normally be entitled to be considered by the trustees for payment of the death benefit, notwithstanding separation, but will have no guarantee of receiving it. For example, the trustees may be aware of a subsequent relationship formed by the member and may consider that part or all of the benefit should be payable to his partner in the second relationship. A divorced spouse is no longer the spouse of the deceased member and, depending on the wording of the rules, may or may not be entitled to be considered for payment.

15.14 A member may leave service before retirement and be entitled to a deferred pension — that is, a pension deferred until retirement. Benefits payable on the death of a deferred pensioner are generally paid as a lump sum to that person's estate, rather than to the spouse.[18]

15.15 The separated spouse's position is therefore by no means secure where lump sum benefits or spouses' pensions are subject to discretion. A divorced spouse is in a more difficult position as she is no longer the spouse. Indeed, even if the rules of a pension scheme very clearly state that the spouse is entitled to receive all death benefits under any circumstances, those rules could be amended at a future date to the detriment of the spouse.[19]

---

17 Where there is no discretion, lump sum benefits are usually payable solely to the estate of the deceased member or to the spouse.

18 The Pensions Act requires any preserved benefit to be paid to the estate unless, in certain circumstances, a spouse's pension is paid instead — see generally para. 12.54 and 12.55.

19 On powers of amendment, see para. 3.10 et seq.

15.16 To assess the impact of a separation and to determine how significant the pension is in the context of the overall family assets, it is necessary to obtain information about the pension scheme and the member's benefits under it. This is the subject of the following section.

INFORMATION

15.17 The difficulty of obtaining useful information on the pension scheme member's benefits is one of the main problems facing the spouse, and indeed her professional advisers. The spouse may be well informed on this subject, but it is more likely that she may only have a vague idea (if any) as to what pension benefits the member has been promised. In a marital breakdown situation the spouse may have no information to give her advisers. Fortunately, legislation assists the spouse in obtaining details of the pension scheme.

Disclosure Regulations

15.18 The Pensions Act[20] and the Disclosure Regulations made under it[21] give spouses the right to obtain certain information from the trustees of an occupational pension scheme. This right continues to apply in favour of a spouse notwithstanding that proceedings for judicial separation have been instituted or a decree has been granted.[22] Disclosure rights will also continue to apply in the context of Irish Divorces.[23]

15.19 Spouses are entitled to a copy of the latest audited accounts of the scheme and the auditors report,[24] or any earlier accounts or reports, a copy of the latest actuarial valuation in the case of a defined benefit scheme[25] or any earlier valuation and a copy of the annual re-

---

20 s.54.

21 Occupational Pension Schemes (Disclosure of Information) Regulations, 1991 — see generally Chapter 13.

22 s.12(24) FLA.

23 Family Law (Divorce) Bill, 1996.

24 Article 4(3) Disclosure Regulations.

25 Article 5(4).

port on the scheme or any earlier report.[26] This information relates to the pension scheme as a whole. It will assist the spouse in determining how financially secure the overall pension benefits are under the scheme but is of little use in determining the value of the member's specific pension entitlements, unless the member is the sole member of the pension scheme. She is entitled to inspect and obtain copies of the trust documents which govern the scheme, such as the rules of the scheme that set out the details of benefits applicable to the member[27] and certain specified basic information about the scheme such as a summary of benefits (usually in the form of an explanatory booklet) which should be of particular assistance to the spouse.[28] However, none of the foregoing information will actually put a value on the member's pension entitlements or on the benefits payable on his death.

15.20 The member is entitled to obtain specific information on the value of his benefits on request to the trustees.[29] In most well-run occupational pension schemes, members are given an annual benefit statement automatically without having to request it. The spouse has no such entitlement to obtain the benefit statement from the trustees. She can only obtain such information on request to the member.

15.21 The documents required to be disclosed under the Disclosure Regulations are, nonetheless, a useful source of information for a spouse, but they are only available to spouses of actual members or prospective members of the pension scheme. If the member ceases to be a member of the scheme and his benefits are transferred out of the scheme, he is no longer a "member" as far as the Regulations are concerned and his spouse is then not entitled to any information under the Regulations. If the spouse becomes aware that the member is likely to leave service or may be made redundant or dismissed, it may be prudent to make a speedy application for information to the trus-

---

26 Article 6(3) and Article 7(3).

27 Article 8(3).

28 Article 9(3) and Schedule C.

29 Article 11.

tees before she is debarred from doing so.[30] Of course, if the member has transferred his benefits to the scheme of another employer, the spouse is entitled to the above information from the trustees of the new scheme.[31] However, if the member's benefits have been transferred to a life office bond, the spouse is not entitled to the information.[32] Unfortunately, the spouse may not have sufficient information to determine the identity of the life office or new employer, and this information may have to be obtained by discovery in legal proceedings.

Family Law Act

15.22 The FLA has improved the quality of information which a spouse can obtain in connection with the member's pension benefits. The spouse can seek an order from the Court directing the trustees of the pension scheme to furnish her with a calculation of the value and the amount of the member's pension benefits or any benefits payable contingently — that is, on death.[33] The application can be made during the course of judicial separation proceedings or at any time thereafter. Legal separation by way of deed of separation or otherwise is not sufficient to obtain a valuation order under the FLA.

15.23 The valuation is to be determined in accordance with "relevant guidelines" of the Pensions Board. By virtue of section 5(4) of the Pensions Act, the Minister for Social Welfare, with the consent of the Minister for Equality and Law Reform, can make regulations for the purposes of section 12 of the FLA, which will be construed as the "relevant guidelines" specified under the FLA.[34] It is expected that

---

30 Where a pension adjustment order has been made, the spouse must be notified by the trustees of the member leaving service — s.12(12) of the FLA.

31 Provided that the new scheme is an occupational pension scheme to which the Disclosure Regulations apply. See para. 1.37 for a definition of occupational pension scheme.

32 Buy-out bonds are not occupational pension schemes — s.34(3)(b) of the Pensions Act as amended by s.12 of the Pensions (Amendment) Act, 1996.

33 s.12(25).

34 s.5(4) as inserted by s.4 of the Pensions (Amendment) Act, 1996. It was initially intended that only guidance notes would be issued. However, it was subsequently decided to issue formal regulations instead, hence the odd drafting of deeming guidelines to be construed as regulations.

regulations will be issued shortly and section 5(4) of the Pensions Act sets out the matters that may be covered by those regulations.

Discovery/Affidavits of Means

15.24 In both the High Court and the Circuit Court, a spouse can, in the context of judicial separation or divorce proceedings, seek an order for discovery against the member requiring disclosure of all documents and other material relevant to the separation proceedings which are in the possession, power or procurement of the member and which are not privileged. The member's benefit statement could be obtained by this means.

15.25 In Circuit Court proceedings, there is an additional method of obtaining information about the scheme. Under the Circuit Court Rules, wherever financial relief is sought ancillary to the decree of judicial separation, the spouses must exchange affidavits of means.[35] Assets to be disclosed in the affidavit include assets held on trust. In practice, this is regarded as including entitlements under a pension scheme, including death in service entitlements. Pensions in payment received in the previous 12 months are specifically referred to as being required to be disclosed as income.[36] The spouse can require the member to vouch any item referred to in the affidavit.[37]

15.26 The most desirable item of information from the spouse's perspective is the value of the member's entitlements. The information may persuade her that to seek a pension adjustment order under the FLA is the most beneficial course open to her and these orders will be examined shortly. On the other hand, the spouse could use the pension benefit as a bargaining tool to secure an immediate financial settlement without interfering with the pension scheme. This approach is referred to as the adjustment of non-pension assets and is one of the issues considered in the following section.

---

35 Circuit Court Rules (No. 1) of 1994, SI No 225 of 1994, rr. 13 and 14 and Appendix 3. These Rules were made in light of the Judicial Separation and Family Law Reform Act, 1989 and will need to be revised consequent upon the enactment of the FLA.

36 *Ibid.* Appendix 3, Schedule 2, Part 2.

37 r.13(b).

SETTLEMENT WITHOUT A PENSION ADJUSTMENT ORDER

15.27 The pension scheme member and his spouse may seek to settle the issue of the division of their pension entitlements without recourse to a pension adjustment order under the FLA. They may do this by adjusting their non-pension assets and leave the pension benefits intact.

Adjustment of Non-Pension Assets

15.28 The various financial orders available under the FLA give the Courts the flexibility to adjust marital assets without interfering with the pension benefits of the member. Similar options will apply to situations of divorce. The theory is quite simple. The benefit entitlements of the member are taken into account in assessing his financial position *vis-à-vis* his spouse. Non-pension assets are then adjusted by way of (for example) a property adjustment order, and the pension rights of the member are left intact. This approach may work provided that the member has sufficient non-pension assets to compensate the spouse for loss of pension rights, but will be difficult to implement if non-pension assets are of little value. To assess the necessary level of adjustment to non-pension assets, a valuation of the member's benefits will almost certainly be required.[38]

15.29 There is explicit support for the adjustment of non-pension assets in the FLA. Section 12(23) states that:

> The court may make a pension adjustment order in addition to or in substitution in whole or in part for an order or orders under section 8, 9, 10 or 11[39] and, in deciding whether or not to make a pension adjustment order, the court shall have regard to the question whether adequate and reasonable financial provision[40] exists

---

38 Valuation is considered at para. 15.22 above.

39 Periodic payments and lump sum orders, property adjustment orders, miscellaneous ancillary orders and financial compensation orders respectively.

40 Slightly different wording is included in the Family Law (Divorce) Bill, 1996 as Art. 41.3.2 of the Constitution in the context of divorce requires the Court to be satisfied that "*such provision as the court considers proper having regard to the circumstances*" exists or will be made. The Family Law (Divorce) Bill when enacted will also amend s.12(23) of the FLA by substituting the words "proper provision, having regard to the circumstances" for "adequate and reasonable financial provision".

> *or can be made*[41] for the spouse concerned or the dependent member of the family concerned by an order or orders under any of those sections.

Improved maintenance could be given to the spouse in lieu of pension entitlements, or property could be vested by way of a property adjustment order as a substitute for a share of the member's pension benefits. Indeed, the member could be required to effect, assign or continue a policy of life assurance in favour of the spouse or other dependant.[42]

Example 15.1

Jack is a member of the Mutually Satisfactory Pension Scheme. It is a defined contribution scheme and his most recent benefit statement shows that the current value of his benefit is £50,000.

Jack has separated from his wife, Jill, who has commenced judicial separation proceedings. They have no children. Their family assets are as follows:

House (net of mortgage)	*£40,000*
Cash	*£5,000*
Savings Bond	*£10,000*
Car	*£8,000*
Shares	*£3,000*
Pension (current value)	*£50,000*
Total	*£116,000*

On the basis of (for example) a 50:50 split, the family assets could be adjusted whilst keeping the pension intact in the following way:

Jack		***Jill***	
Pension	*£50,000*	*House*	*£40,000*
Car	*£8,000*	*Cash*	*£5,000*
		Bond	*£10,000*
		Shares	*£3,000*

Separation Agreements

15.30 In the context of separation, the adjustment of non-pension assets will arise either under judicial separation proceedings or by

---

41 Emphasis added.

42 This latter power of the Court is provided for in s.11.

way of a separation agreement. Couples who formalise their terms of separation under a separation agreement are able to avoid making an application to court and can decide upon how their assets are to be split between them. Although nothing in the separation agreement can prevent either spouse from applying for maintenance or variation of maintenance, the agreement is final in all other respects.

15.31 The difficulty with separation agreements as far as pensions are concerned is that they can go beyond the adjustment of non-pension assets by attempting to vary pension entitlements payable on the member's death. The trustees are under a legal and equitable obligation, as well as a statutory one,[43] to follow the rules of the scheme, and, in particular, to pay benefits in accordance with those rules. Accordingly, the separation agreement is not binding on them. Many separation agreements nonetheless attempt to vary the member's pension entitlements in one or both of the following ways:

1. By including a clause by which the spouse wholly abandons any entitlements that she may have under the scheme on the member's death
2. By the member undertaking to deliver a nomination form to the trustees of the scheme nominating his spouse as beneficiary of his death in service lump sum benefits (if any).

In a small or individual scheme or a self-employed arrangement, the member may be in a position to rewrite the rules to facilitate the separation agreement,[44] but in group occupational pension schemes there may be difficulties. Each of these instances will now be examined in more detail.

15.32 If the pension scheme rules require the trustees to pay a pension to the spouse, they must do so notwithstanding any agreement between the husband and wife to the contrary. The trustees may, however, have a discretion to pay a spouse's pension to another dependant in cases of separation. The trustees would clearly be influenced by a spouse's abandonment of pension rights in the separation agreement, but whilst they may take this fact into account, they

---

[43] s.59(c) of the Pensions Act.

[44] For example, the member may control the employing company, which may also be the trustee.

might still ultimately decide to pay the spouse's pension to the spouse.

15.33 The trustees are usually required to take the nomination form into account but are almost always entitled to override the member's wishes and pay the death benefit to another beneficiary, under the terms of the trust. Also, the member may breach his separation agreement and fail to send a nomination form to the trustees. Alternatively, he may send the nomination form as agreed but may, at a future date (perhaps years later), furnish a revised nomination form to the trustees, indicating that he wishes his death benefits to be paid to (say) his new partner. In a well-drafted separation agreement, this will amount to a breach of the agreement, but, in reaching their decision, the trustees of the pension scheme must still take into account the revised nomination form.

15.34 The adjustment of non-pension assets has the merit of leaving the pension intact. This is to the advantage of the trustees of the pension scheme and consequently the other members of the scheme who are not involved in the judicial separation proceedings. It should also be cost-effective for the spouses because it avoids or at least limits[45] the need for trustee involvement and, as will be considered,[46] trustee costs must be discharged by the spouses. However, this approach will be inadequate in the following situations:

1. Where, as indicated above, the spouses wish to modify payment of death benefits under a separation agreement and this cannot be facilitated under the scheme rules
2. There are insufficient non-pension assets to compensate the spouse for loss of pension rights.

The alternative option is to apply for a pension adjustment order under the FLA, which is explored in the following sections.

PENSION ADJUSTMENT ORDERS

15.35 The most significant piece of legislation on pensions since the Pensions Act, 1990 is undoubtedly the Family Law Act, 1995. For-

---

45 The trustees may be asked to value the benefit.

46 See para. 15.101 below

merly, there was no power of the Courts to vary pension entitlements in favour of a spouse. The FLA therefore marks a radical departure from the previous legal position. The equivalent section of the Family Law (Divorce) Bill, 1996 when enacted will be almost identical. The main provision of the FLA relating to pensions is section 12 which empowers the Court to award what is referred to as a pension adjustment order. The effect of the pension adjustment order is to grant the spouse, or in certain circumstances a dependent child, a pension entitlement under the scheme in their own right notwithstanding that the rules of the pension scheme may stipulate otherwise. Indeed, the employer that established the scheme[47] will almost certainly not have contemplated that the pension it promised to its employee for services rendered will now be paid, in part, to that employee's spouse or another dependant.

15.36 Pension adjustment orders involve the reallocation of pension rights whereby a specified part of the benefit payable under the pension scheme to or in respect of the member is designated or earmarked for payment directly to his spouse or to a dependont child. As far as retirement pensions are concerned, this means that part or all of the member's pension at retirement is redirected to his spouse (or dependent child) and becomes the income of the spouse (or child).[48] Where the member is already in receipt of pension, the spouse (or child) will receive an immediate pension as a consequence of the order being granted. Where the member is an active scheme member or a deferred pensioner, there is no immediate payment to the spouse (or child) as the pension is not payable until a future date — that is, at retirement, which could be perhaps 20 years or more after the order is made. Pension adjustment orders can also be made in relation to death benefits such as, for example, a death in service lump sum benefit or a spouse's pension payable on death in retirement.[49]

Example 15.2

Mickey joined his company in 1970 and was promised a pension of 1/60th of pensionable salary for each year of company service. He is now retiring in the year 2010 at the age of 65 with a pensionable sal-

---

47 Who will be the settlor of the trust, where the scheme is established under trust.

48 s.12(2).

49 s.12(3).

ary of £60,000 per annum. Ten years earlier, in the year 2000 his wife Minnie obtained a decree of judicial separation. The court awarded 50 per cent of his then pension to Minnie.

At retirement in 2010, part of Mickey's pension is paid to Minnie. Let us assume that Mickey's pension, but for the order, would be £40,000 per annum. Let us also assume that Minnie's designated share is £15,000. At retirement, Minnie receives a pension of £15,000 and Mickey receives the balance — that is, £25,000.

Example 15.3

Mark is a member of the Top-Notch Pension Scheme. The rules of the scheme promise that on Mark's death whilst in the service of his employer, Top-Notch Ltd., a lump sum of three times his salary will be paid either to his estate or to one or more of a wide range of beneficiaries, as the trustees of the scheme decide. The beneficiaries include his wife Mary, his children and any close relatives. He separates from Mary in 1998 and the court designates by way of pension adjustment order half of his death benefit for payment to Mary. One year later, Mark dies in a car accident. His salary at death is £18,000 which means that the death in service benefit is £54,000. The trustees would normally have discretion as to who should receive the death benefit but the court order overrides the discretion of the trustees and requires the trustees to pay half the benefit (£27,000) to Mary. The other half of the benefit remains subject to the discretion of the trustees and they could pay that half to Mary or to any other beneficiary.

15.37 The granting of a pension adjustment order is at the discretion of the Courts. The order is only one of a menu of orders under the FLA and it is open to the Courts to grant one or more of these other orders in substitution for or in addition to a pension adjustment order.[50] It is outside the scope of this work to examine in any detail the other financial orders under the FLA. By way of summary, there are principally eight financial orders in addition to pension adjustment orders. These are:

1. Maintenance orders pending determination of the proceedings (section 7)
2. Periodical payments and lump sum orders (section 8)

---

50 s.12(23).

3. Property adjustment orders (section 9)
4. Miscellaneous ancillary orders such as the conferral of a right to occupy the family home to the exclusion of the other spouse (section 10)
5. Financial compensation orders requiring the effecting, assigning, or continuing to make payments to a policy of life insurance (section 11)
6. An order preserving a spouse's pension entitlements notwithstanding separation (section 13)[51]
7. Extinguishment of succession rights (section 14)
8. Orders for sale of property (section 15).

15.38 The Courts have discretion as to what combination of orders to grant in a given situation but there are certain matters which must be taken into account. These are listed in section 16 of the Act. Section 16(1) sets out the following general principle:

> In deciding whether to make an order under section 7, 8, 9, 10(1)(a), 11, 12, 13, 14, 18 or 25 and in determining the provisions of such an order, the court shall endeavour to ensure that such provision is made for each spouse concerned and for any dependent member of the family concerned as is adequate and reasonable having regard to all the circumstances of the case.[52]

Section 16(2) then lists specific factors to be taken into account, such as the income and earning capacity of each spouse, their property and financial resources and their financial needs.[53] This is certainly wide enough to include benefits under a pension scheme. Indeed, pensions are specifically mentioned in section 16(2)(k) as being required to be taken into account by the Courts in circumstances where the spouse would forfeit benefit by reason of judicial separation. The Court must have regard to:

> the value to each of the spouses of any benefit (for example, a benefit under a pension scheme) which by reason of the decree of

---

51 This is considered at para. 15.10 above.

52 See also fn 40.

53 This list is largely copied from the Judicial Separation and Family Law Reform Act, 1989 s.20(2). s.16(2)(k) is, however, new.

> judicial separation concerned that spouse will forfeit the opportunity or possibility of acquiring...

However, as has already been mentioned,[54] the Courts must have regard to whether adequate and reasonable financial provision exists or can be made by way of any one or more of the first four financial orders listed above before making a pension adjustment order.[55]

CONDITIONS FOR GRANTING A PENSION ADJUSTMENT ORDER

15.39 The conditions for granting a pension adjustment order are contained in sub-section (2) (retirement benefits) and sub-section (3) (contingent benefits) of section 12. A guide to these conditions is contained in the flow chart at Figure 15.1.

Conditions Precedent

15.40 The conditions which must be met before a pension adjustment order will be considered by the Court are the following:

1. Proceedings for the decree have commenced on or after 1 August 1996.
2. The member is still alive.
3. The applicant is the member, the spouse or a person applying on behalf of a dependent member of the family.
4. If the spouse is the applicant, she must not have remarried.
5. The member is a “member” of a “pension scheme”.
6. In the case of death in service benefits, not more than one year has elapsed since the decree.
7. The trustees and the spouse(s) not making the application are on notice of the application.

Each of these conditions is now considered in turn.

---

54 At para. 15.29.

55 s.12(23), but see fn 40 in the context of Irish divorces.

FIGURE 15.1: CONDITIONS FOR GRANTING A PENSION ADJUSTMENT ORDER

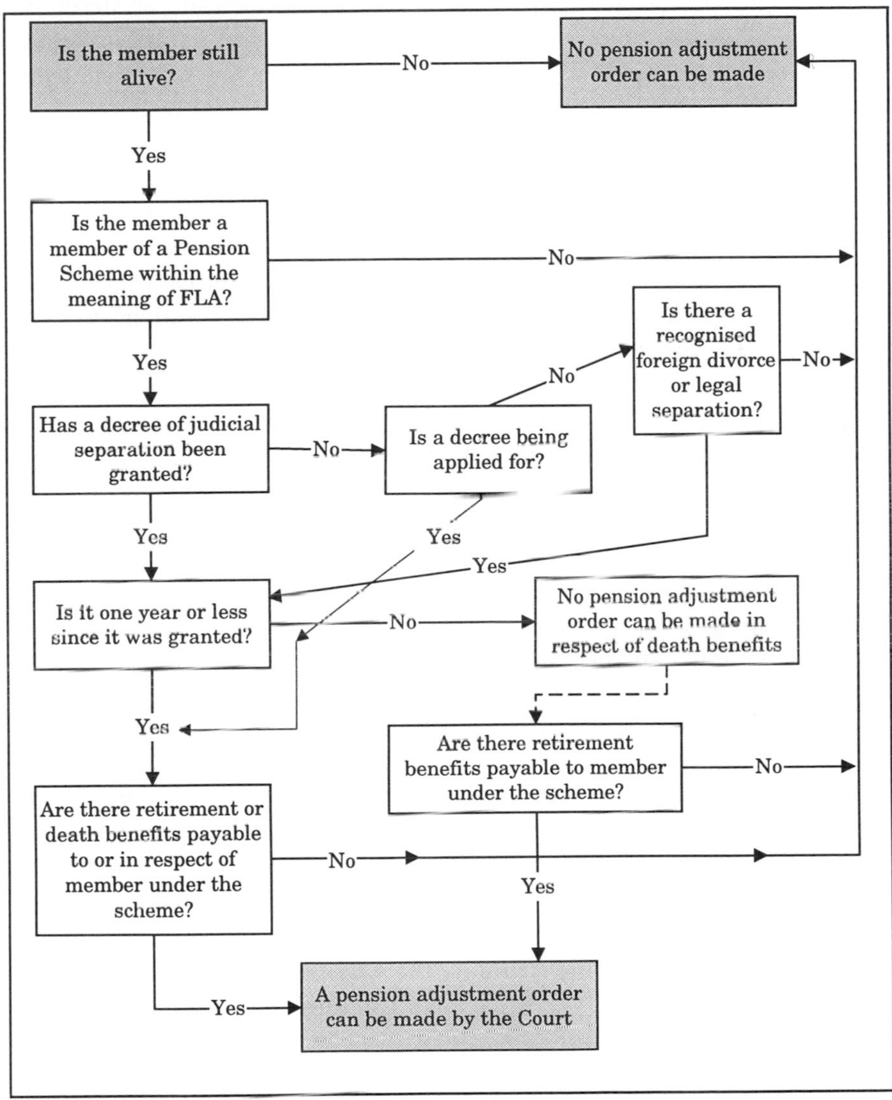

15.41 ***Temporal Effect:*** The FLA does not apply retrospectively. Proceedings for a decree of judicial separation must have commenced on or after 1 August 1996.[56] Orders can be granted in the course of judicial separation proceedings or at any time after an order for judi-

56 s.5 and Family Law Act, 1995 (Commencement) Order, 1996 (SI No 46 of 1996).

cial separation has been granted. Pension adjustment orders can also be granted in respect of judicially recognised foreign divorces or separations, provided that the dissolution or legal separation occurred on or after 1 August 1996.[57] In describing the conditions in detail below, reference will be made only to judicial separation, but the same conditions will apply to foreign divorces and separations as well.

15.42 ***Member's Death:*** An order to adjust retirement benefits (under section 12(2)) can be granted only during the lifetime of the member. If he is dead, no order can be made even though a spouse's pension may then be in the course of payment. Oddly, there is no equivalent reference to "during the lifetime of the member" in connection with the adjustment of contingent benefits under section 12(3). However, section 12(3) refers to the making of an order for payment of benefit "*upon the death of the member*",[58] which may indicate that the member must be alive before an order can be made.

15.43 ***Applicant:*** Application for a pension adjustment order can be made by the spouse or the scheme member. In the case of a recognised foreign divorce, it will be a former spouse that applies. In addition, an application can also be made by a person on behalf of a dependent member of the family, such as a child. Dependent children are considered further below.[59] The Court cannot make an order of its own motion as it requires an application to the Court.[60]

15.44 ***Bar on Remarriage:*** The Court cannot make an order if the spouse who applies for the order has remarried.[61] This is clear when the spouse is applying on her own behalf. It is unclear whether a spouse applying solely on behalf of dependent children is similarly debarred. A person other than the spouse can apply on behalf of a dependent child in these circumstances and so the exclusion of a spouse in these circumstances is unlikely to have been intended. Arguably, the bar on a remarried spouse encourages cohabitation rather than remarriage.

---

57 s.23(1) and the commencement order cited in the previous footnote.

58 s.12(3).

59 At para. 15.49.

60 s.12(2) and (3).

61 s.12(23)(a).

15.45 ***Meaning of "Member":*** The member is a "member" of a pension scheme if he has been admitted to membership of the scheme under its rules and remains entitled to any benefit under it. This definition is equivalent to the same definition under the Pensions Act and would include not only an active member of the pension scheme but also a pensioner and someone who has ceased to be an active member (by reason of leaving service or otherwise) but whose deferred benefits remain in the scheme.

15.46 ***Meaning of "Pension Scheme":*** The member must be a member of a pension scheme within the meaning of the FLA. The term "pension scheme" is defined in section 2 of the FLA to include an occupational pension scheme within the meaning of the Pensions Act. It also includes self-employed arrangements under section 235 of the Income Tax Act, 1967 and buy-out bonds approved by the Revenue Commissioners under Chapter II of Part I of the Finance Act, 1972. Social welfare benefits are, however, specifically excluded. There is a further sweep-up provision that includes within the definition of "pension scheme":

> any other scheme or arrangement (including a personal pension plan and a scheme or arrangement established pursuant to statute or instrument made under statute other than under the Social Welfare Acts) that provides or is intended to provide either or both of the following, that is to say:
>
> (i) benefits for a person who is a member of the scheme or arrangement ("the member") upon retirement at normal pensionable age or upon earlier or later retirement or upon leaving, or upon the ceasing of, the relevant employment,
>
> (ii) benefits for the widow, widower or dependants of the member, or for any other persons, on the death of the member.

This part of the definition would certainly catch unapproved pension arrangements. Foreign schemes or arrangements would also appear to fall within this part of the definition, although in practice it may be difficult to enforce the court order in the jurisdiction in which the foreign scheme is established. Reference to arrangements providing benefits "upon the ceasing of . . . the relevant employment" could be interpreted to include redundancy payments and golden handshakes. Whilst the interpretation of the definition is unclear, it is suggested that the better view would be that redundancy or golden handshake arrangements are excluded on the basis that they do not fall within the general concept of pension arrangements.

15.47 ***Time Limits:*** As far as retirement benefits are concerned, a pension adjustment order can be granted at any time after the decree of judicial separation, provided of course that the member is still alive. The Act is somewhat more restrictive as regards death in service benefits (referred to as "contingent benefits"). In this case, the pension adjustment order can be granted only where not more than one year has elapsed since the date of granting of the decree of judicial separation. With such a tight timescale, it is likely that all applications for decrees of judicial separation in the future will include a request for a pension adjustment order under section 12 (provided of course that the member has benefits under a pension scheme).

15.48 ***Notice:*** An application for an order must be made on notice to the trustees[62] and to the other spouse, or if the application is being made on behalf of a dependent member of the family, to both the spouses.[63] The Court must have regard to any representations made by a notice party.[64] The court order itself must be served on the trustees of the scheme concerned by the court registrar/clerk.[65]

Dependent Member of the Family

15.49 As has been stated, an application for a pension adjustment order can be made on behalf of a "dependent member of the family". A dependent member of the family as defined means a child of both spouses or who is adopted by both spouses under the Adoption Acts or in relation to whom the spouses are *in loco parentis*. The definition also includes a child of only one spouse but where the other spouse has treated the child as a member of the family. In all cases, to fall within the definition, the child must be under age 18 or under age 23 if in receipt of full-time education or instruction at any university, college, school or other educational establishment, or can be of any age if he or she is mentally or physically disabled to such extent that it is not reasonably possible for the child to maintain himself or her-

---

62 s.12(18).

63 s.40.

64 s.12(18).

65 s.12(21).

self fully.[66] The term "dependent child" will be adopted for the balance of this chapter rather than "dependent member of the family".

Persons who can be awarded Benefit

15.50 The Court can make the order in favour of the spouse or a dependent child. Where pension benefits are being adjusted, the order can be in favour of only the spouse or the dependent child, not both. If the spouse should die, the benefit will be in favour of the spouse's personal representative. A benefit to a dependent child can be paid only whilst the person remains a dependent child. For example, if a child is in receipt of full-time education and attains age 23, the benefit must cease.[67]

15.51 In contrast, death in service benefits can be adjusted in favour of the spouse or dependent child or both. However, the order ceases to have effect on the death or remarriage of the person in whose favour the order has been granted.[68] As regards the adjustment of death benefit to dependent children, there is no requirement that the person remain a dependent child. This is understandable as regards a lump sum death benefit which is a once-off payment, but there may be a children's or orphan's death in service pension payable under the scheme and, to be consistent with the adjustment of pension benefits, the order should cease to have effect on the person ceasing to be a dependent child. Indeed, this would be a normal requirement of the Revenue Commissioners with regard to the approval of pension schemes, and so there is an inconsistency between the order as applied to pension benefits and as applied to death benefits.

---

66 s.2(1).

67 This is consistent with the requirements of the Revenue Commissioners in connection with approval of pension schemes. The Revenue will not permit pensions to continue once a child has ceased to be dependent. See para. 7.38. However, the FLA is more restrictive than the Revenue requirements. The Revenue will permit a child to continue to receive pension provided that the child is still in full-time education or vocational training. There is no age limit in this regard unlike the age limit of 23 years in the FLA.

68 s.12(19).

Determining Benefit to be Awarded

15.52 The Court determines the benefit that is to be designated for the spouse or other dependent child by deciding two things: first, the period of scheme membership to be taken into account, referred to as "reckonable service" in the Act, and secondly the percentage of benefit accrued during that period which is to be designated for the spouse. In this regard, there is a distinction to be made between pension benefits and death in service benefits.

15.53 With pension benefits, the Court can adjust only that part of the pension which relates to the member's benefits that have accrued up to the date of the decree of judicial separation (or foreign divorce or separation). The Court cannot take into account pension that may arise from future scheme membership. The Court is empowered to pay the entire benefit accrued to date of the decree to the spouse or dependent child, or such percentage as it determines.

15.54 The position regarding death in service benefits is somewhat simpler. The Court can take the entire benefit into account (that is, including that which derives from future membership) and determine what percentage is payable to the spouse or dependent child. There is no requirement to take account of service accrued to date of the order. There is logic in the difference between the treatment of death in service benefits and pension benefits, in that the former do not accrue with each year of service completed by the member. The death in service benefit is usually the same no matter how many years of service have been completed by the member.[69]

Example 15.4

Let us expand on Example 15.2. Mickey joined his company in 1970 and was promised a pension of 1/60th of pensionable salary for each year of company service. He is now retiring in the year 2010 at the age *of 65 with a pensionable salary of £60,000 per annum. Ten years earlier, in the year 2000, having completed 30 years' service, his wife, Minnie obtained a decree of judicial separation. The Court made a pension adjustment order as follows:*

- *Scheme membership taken into account: 30 years (that is, all scheme membership to date of the decree)*

---

[69] An exception to this statement would be the "creeping widows" pension see para. 11.11.

- *Percentage awarded: 50 per cent of the pension accrued to date of the decree (50 per cent of 30/60ths).*

At retirement in 2010 the Pension Adjustment Order finally comes into operation in the following way:

Mickey would have received the following pension:

1/60 x 40 x £60,000 = £40,000.

However Minnie is entitled to 50 per cent of the pension based on 30 years' service to date of the order:

50% x 1/60 x 30 x £60,000 = ***£15,000***

This means that the pension remaining payable to Mickey is (£40,000 — £15,000) = ***£25,000.***

Example 15.5

In example 15.3, we saw that on Mark's death in service a death benefit of three times salary was payable and the Court designated one-half of his death benefits in favour of his wife, Mary.

Let us assume that, in addition to the lump sum benefit, the scheme provides a spouse's pension on death in service of 50 per cent of the pension that Mark would have received had he survived until his normal retirement, based on salary at date of death. The scheme would have promised Mark a pension of (say) 2/3rds of his final salary at age 65 (normal retirement) — 2/3rds of £18,000. The death in service spouse's pension is therefore one-third of his final salary at death — that is, £6,000 per annum.

The Court awarded one-half of all death in service benefits to Mary, which means that she is entitled to a pension of £3,000 per annum under the order. The trustees, under the rules of the scheme, have a discretion to pay the balance of the spouse's pension to another dependant in circumstances of separation. Mark's subsequent partner, Martha, was dependent on him and the trustees exercise their discretion to pay the remaining £3,000 per annum pension to her, as well as one-half of the lump sum death benefit (£27,000).

Note that the court was not restricted to designating only that part of the spouse's pension accrued up to the date of the decree of judicial separation. It could take the entire death in service pension into account.

15.55 There is a "net-off" provision in section 12 which is intended to avoid an overpayment from the scheme on the death before retirement of the member. The amount of the death in service benefit payable in accordance with the rules of the scheme must be reduced by an amount equal to the death in service benefit designated in favour of the spouse or dependent child.[70]

15.56 By leaving the pension intact, the spouse receives a pension when it comes into payment in accordance with the scheme rules. She does not enjoy the entitlement to an independent and separate benefit from the member. This does not favour a clean break between the member and his spouse, because the spouse has no control over the pension. There follows an examination of the circumstances where the spouse can obtain an independent benefit and also the circumstances where an independent benefit is automatically created.

VOLUNTARY PENSION SPLITTING

15.57 Unless certain events occur, the pension benefit stays intact until it commences to be paid. The member may leave the company, take early retirement, be dismissed or die. The pension benefits payable in each of those circumstances will be different. Therefore, the spouse's benefit depends upon events happening to the member and this may not be satisfactory for the spouse, which is why, in certain circumstances, the spouse can opt for an independent benefit by seeking the splitting of the pension.

15.58 Pension splitting means that the pension benefit is legally split in favour of the spouse. This requires actuarial input in many schemes as the trustees may have to establish a current value regarding a future pension promise. The advantage to the spouse is that the split pension becomes a pension in her own name and is payable to her regardless of what subsequently happens to the member. In other words, the member may subsequently leave service, die, be dismissed

---

70 s.12(16)(a).

or retire early but the pension now payable to the spouse remains intact.

Conditions Precedent

15.59 The following are the conditions that must be satisfied in order to have the pension split:

1. A pension adjustment order has been made in favour of the spouse
2. The order relates to retirement benefits (including death in retirement benefits)
3. The pension has not commenced to be paid
4. The spouse applies to the trustees
5. The spouse furnishes the trustees with such information as they require.

Each of these conditions will now be considered in turn.

15.60 ***Order in favour of Spouse:*** Only the spouse can apply for pension splitting, and only if the original pension adjustment order was made in favour of the spouse.[71] A pension split cannot be sought by or on behalf of a dependent child. The sole purpose is to allow a clean break to occur between the two spouses. A clean break is usually neither desirable nor necessary with dependent children. In fact, there will usually be a continuing relationship between the children and both their parents. However, in certain circumstances, benefits for either the spouse or the dependent child are automatically split. These circumstances are considered below.[72]

15.61 ***Order relates to retirement benefits:*** Only a pension adjustment order which designates part of the retirement benefits in favour of the spouse can be split. Death in service benefits cannot be split. However, retirement benefits include benefits payable on death in retirement. The pension scheme may promise a spouse's or dependant's pension on the death in retirement of the member and part of the death in retirement pension may have been designated under the pension adjustment order in favour of the spouse. On a

---

[71] s.12(4).

[72] See para. 15.74 et seq.

subsequent pension split, the spouse becomes a member in her own right and so the part of the spouse's or dependant's pension that was designated for payment to her will now become a pension payable on her death to her spouse (or another dependant, if permitted under the rules). Ironically, her estranged partner could then become a beneficiary of her pension, if she dies in "retirement" and he survives her!

15.62 ***Pension has not commenced:*** The spouse can apply for a pension split at any time after the pension adjustment order has been made, provided that the benefit has not yet commenced to be paid. The logic of this is that once the pension has commenced to be paid the pension adjustment order immediately comes into operation and part of the pension is at that point paid to the spouse. Any further pension adjustment is unnecessary.

15.63 ***Application to Trustees:*** In contrast to the application for the original pension adjustment order, the pension split does not require the intervention of the Court. The spouse applies to the trustees of the scheme for the pension to be split. There is no court order required other than the original pension adjustment order.[73]

15.64 ***Furnish Information:*** The spouse must furnish the trustees with such information as the trustees may reasonably require. At the very least, the trustees will need evidence of the spouse's age.

Establishing Independent Benefit

15.65 The splitting of the member's benefits results in an independent benefit for the spouse. Its value is to be determined by the trustees in accordance with regulations issued under section 5(4) of the Pensions Act.[74] In the case of occupational pension schemes, the regulations are expected to require the trustees to treat any active member as having left service of his own free will on the date when the trustees receive the application to split. Where, for example, the scheme rules do not grant benefits in respect of service prior to 1 January 1991[75] the spouse's benefits will be similarly restricted.

---

[73] s.12(5).

[74] s.12(4).

[75] The date when the preservation requirements of the Pensions Act came into force.

There are three ways in which this benefit can be established: under the scheme, by transfer to another scheme of which the spouse is a member, or by transfer to a buy-out bond.

15.66 If both the trustees and the spouse so agree, the new benefit which has been split in favour of the spouse can be held in the pension scheme to provide benefits of an actuarially equivalent value based on the fact that the spouse is now a scheme member, and pension must be calculated by reference to her life expectancy and age — not that of her partner.

15.67 If the trustees do not agree to it being held in the scheme, it must be transferred out to another occupational pension scheme of which the spouse is a member, or to a bond. The spouse may determine whether it is to be transferred to the new pension scheme or a buy-out bond. If the spouse does not make that determination, the FLA is silent as to what happens to the benefit. The trustees do not appear to be entitled to leave the benefit in the scheme, as this requires the agreement of the spouse. It is suggested, therefore, that the absence of a determination by the spouse amounts to her agreement to whatever the trustees decide.

Consequences of a Split

15.68 It may seem an obvious choice for the spouse to apply for a pension split given that she can achieve a clean break and enjoy an independent benefit. There are two disadvantages with pension splitting:

1. An active member of an occupational pension scheme will be treated for the purposes of the split as if he left service voluntarily on the date when the trustees received the application to split.[76]
2. Since the member is treated as leaving service, the spouse will not get the benefit of any future salary increases of the member. This has importance for defined benefit schemes but is not relevant to defined contribution schemes, as the latter do not calculate benefits by reference to salary.

15.69 In relation to the first point, many schemes grant restricted benefits on leaving service. In certain circumstances, no benefit at all

---

[76] This will be provided for in the regulations to be issued under s.5(4) — see para. 15.23 above.

could be payable. On a split, the spouse will receive a restricted share or perhaps no share in these circumstances. The leaving service entitlement may be confined to a refund of member contributions, in which case the spouse will only receive her proportionate entitlement to a refund. Benefits on leaving service are considered elsewhere.[77] This requirement does not apply to self-employed arrangements.[78]

15.70 In relation to the second point, the vast majority of defined benefit schemes calculate benefits by reference to service and salary at or near retirement. A spouse who refrains from splitting will receive a designated pension at retirement based on the member's final salary at that point, not salary at the date of the original decree. A spouse who applies for a split will receive a pension based on salary at the date of the split revalued in accordance with the scheme rules.[79] The rate of revaluation will, in most cases, be lower than the rate of future salary increases.

15.71 In calculating the value of a spouse's benefit on a pension split, the scheme rules will normally require the actuary to value the member's benefit based on current salary, but allowing for increases of 4 per cent per annum to normal retirement.[80] A common assumption of salary increases would be in the region of 6 per cent per annum — a full 2 per cent greater. If the spouse does not request the pension to be split she will receive a pension at the member's retirement, based on his actual salary at that point. However, if she seeks a split (say) 20 years previously, her benefit will be based on a rate of salary increase which almost certainly will fall short of true salary increases. Therefore, the pension that she receives on a split, will be lower than the pension that she would receive if she waited for the pension adjustment order to come into operation. However, the spouse's principal advantage in a pension split of achieving a clean break from her partner may be sufficient compensation.

---

77 On leaving service entitlements see generally para. 2.34 et seq. and Chapter 12.

78 All benefits are fully vested in a self-employed arrangement.

79 Revaluation is considered at para. 12.46 et seq.

80 Four per cent (or consumer price increases, if less) is the revaluation rate under the Pensions Act. The Act only requires benefits accrued since 1 January 1991 to be revalued, but scheme rules can be more generous.

15.72 As the pension obtained as a result of a pension split in a defined benefit scheme will almost certainly be lower than if the spouse left her benefits designated in the pension scheme, many spouses may prefer to leave their benefit designated and not seek a pension split, at least initially. It is important to remember that the spouse can apply for a split at any time before the member's benefit commences to be paid. The longer the spouse waits, the better the pension benefit will be, as she will have the benefit of all of the member's salary increases granted prior to the pension split.

15.73 For these spouses, there will be no clean break, and this means that the ultimate benefits which the spouse will receive will depend largely upon circumstances outside her control, such as whether the member leaves service, is made redundant or takes early or late retirement. A number of the sub-sections in section 12 of the FLA seek to redress these problems, and these are now considered.

AUTOMATIC PENSION SPLITTING

15.74 Problems can arise in the future where the spouse relies on receiving a designated benefit under a pension adjustment order. For example, a part of the member's pension may be designated in favour of the spouse. She expects to receive her entitlements when the member retires and begins to receive pension. What if he does not retire? He may leave service early, be made redundant, take early-retirement or late-retirement options or may die. In all these circumstances his benefits will not be the same as they would be if he retired at his normal retirement date. Consequently, his spouse's designated benefits will also vary. The FLA copes with these situations in two ways. First, at any time before the benefit commences to be paid, the spouse can opt for a pension split.[81] This would be the favoured option where the spouse wants to start receiving pension earlier than the member[82] or wants a clean break. Secondly, certain events automatically trigger a pension split without the intervention of the spouse.

---

81 Except in the case of contingent benefits — see para 15.61 above.

82 The earliest age that pension can commence is normally age 50 — on early retirement, see para. 7.27 et seq.

Triggering Events

15.75 The events that automatically trigger a splitting of benefit are the following:

1. Member dies before benefit commences (section 12(7))
2. Spouse dies before benefit commences (section 12(9))
3. Spouse dies after benefit commences (section 12(10)).

In each case it is only retirement benefits that will be split. Death in service benefits cannot be split under the FLA. A cash payment out of the scheme is made and is calculated on the assumption that the spouse's designated benefit was split immediately prior to the event in accordance with regulations issued under section 5(4) of the Pensions Act.[83]

15.76 ***Member dies before benefit commences:*** If a member dies before a pension begins to be paid, there may be a lump sum or a pension payable to a spouse or a dependent child on death, but the member's pension itself does not come into payment because the member has not survived until his retirement. The FLA overrides the pension scheme rules in this regard by requiring the trustees to assume that a pension split occurred immediately before death, and requiring the trustees to calculate the spouse's or other dependant's benefit as if a pension split had occurred. As a consequence, the spouse/dependant receives benefits in her own right.[84]

15.77 There may be a death benefit payable under the rules of the scheme in addition to the benefit required to be paid under the FLA. The death in service benefit must be reduced by an amount equal to the value of that part of the benefit split in favour of the spouse.[85]

15.78 ***Spouse dies before benefit commences:*** This arises where the pension adjustment order was made in favour of the spouse (not a dependent child). The FLA provides that where the spouse dies before payment of benefit commences, the trustees must again assume that a pension split has occurred, and the equivalent benefit will be paid

---

83 See para. 15.23 above.

84 s.12(7).

85 s.12(16)(b).

within three months of the death of the spouse to the spouse's personal representative.[86] This is an odd provision and one that will have actuarial implications for defined benefit schemes, as actuaries would normally assume a gain to the fund in this situation, not a liability for a cash payment to a third party.

15.79 ***Spouse dies after benefit commences:*** Again, this only arises where the order was made in favour of the spouse (not a dependent child). If a spouse dies after payment of the benefit commences and the member is still alive and receiving pension, the trustees must calculate the actuarial value of the future pension payments that the spouse would have received during the member's lifetime if she had remained alive, and the actuarial value must be paid to the personal representative of the spouse within three months of her death.[87]

Non-triggering Events

15.80 There are two key events which do not trigger an automatic split: first, where a dependent child dies and, secondly, where the member ceases to be a member of the scheme (for example, he leaves service).

15.81 If a pension adjustment order has been made in favour of a dependent child and that person dies, the order ceases to have effect in relation to that person.[88] There is no recalculation of benefit as if there was a pension split because, of course, as far as dependent children are concerned, they have no option to have pensions split in their favour.

15.82 Where a member ceases to be a member of the scheme otherwise than on death, the trustees may split the designated benefit but are under no obligation to do so.[89] If they choose not to do so, the spouse can opt for a split at that point. If she does not seek a split, the designated benefit remains attached to the member's benefit and will be subject to the member's normal leaving service options. The bene-

---

86 s.12(9).

87 s.12(10).

88 s.12(11) and s.12(19).

89 s.12(8).

fit may be retained in the scheme as a deferred pension. Alternatively, the whole benefit may be transferred to a bond or scheme of the new employer and the only obligation on the trustees is to notify the spouse and the registrar/clerk of the court.[90] It is then a matter for the spouse to ensure that the trustees of the new scheme or arrangement are made aware of the court order. The trustees' option to split is considered further in the next section.

TRUSTEE INITIATED SPLITTING

15.83 There are two instances where the trustees can initiate the splitting of a designated retirement benefit. Splitting in each case is at the trustees' discretion. First, where a member ceases to be a member, and, secondly, where the scheme is a defined contribution scheme.

15.84 Where a member ceases to be a member otherwise than on death (usually on leaving service), the trustees may calculate the spouse's (or dependent child's) benefit as if a split had occurred and may either retain the spouse's (or dependent child's) benefit in the scheme (provided that the spouse or person on behalf of a dependent child agrees) or transfer the benefit, as determined by the trustees, to another occupational pension scheme or to a buy-out bond.[91] The only circumstances in which the member will cease to be a member is where he leaves service and his benefits are transferred to the scheme of a new employer or a bond, or the scheme is wound up, in which case his benefits must be transferred out in any event, even if he has not left service. The difficulty with the wording of this sub-section is that the only way that a member can cease to be a member of a scheme is if his benefits have already been transferred out of the scheme. Yet, by giving the trustees the option of splitting the spouse's or dependent child's benefit, the sub-section assumes that the benefits have not yet been transferred out of the scheme. This would appear to be a drafting error in the Act.

15.85 A member may cease to be an active member of the scheme either by leaving service or by remaining in service but ceasing to be

---

[90] s.12(12).

[91] s.12(8).

included in the scheme for any benefits.[92] If this situation arises, the trustees must, if no pension split has occurred, notify the registrar or clerk of the court within 12 months of the cessation of active membership and must also notify the other spouse. The trustees are not required to take any further action.

15.86 Special considerations apply to defined contribution schemes. It is usually easy to split defined contribution scheme benefits because there is an account held by the trustees on behalf of the member which has a readily identifiable value.[93] With a defined contribution scheme, the trustees can decide whether to leave the spouse's or dependent child's benefit in the pension scheme or transfer it out into a new pension scheme or buy-out bond. Neither the spouse nor the dependent child can veto the decision. However, if the trustees choose not to transfer a spouse's designated benefit, she can opt for a split in the normal way.

15.87 In each of the above situations the trustees must notify the spouse or dependent child and the registrar/clerk of the court of the split and must give to the spouse or person on behalf of a dependent child particulars of the scheme or undertaking concerned and of the transfer amount.[94]

VARIATION OF ORDERS

15.88 Having examined pension adjustment orders and the splitting of designated benefits, it is appropriate to consider the circumstances in which the original court order can be varied. Most of the orders granted under the FLA, such as periodical payments orders and property adjustment orders, can be varied, discharged or suspended

---

92 A member ceases to be an "active member" on ceasing to be in "reckonable service". Reckonable service is defined in s.12(1) as "service in relevant employment during membership of any scheme". Therefore, although a member may be covered only for death-in- service benefits, he is still regarded as being in reckonable service under the FLA and remains an active member. This contrasts with the definition in the Pensions Act, which specifically excludes any service where the only benefit is on death prior to normal pensionable age. The Pensions Act also ignores any service specifically excluded by the trustees of the scheme.

93 There may, however, be difficulties in obtaining a value in certain insured schemes such as with-profit contracts — see para. 10.13 et seq.

94 s.12(13).

on subsequent application to the Court. Pension adjustment orders, other than orders granted in respect of death in service benefits, can also be varied, discharged or suspended.[95] However, the original order can specifically restrict or exclude the power of the Court to vary the order subsequently.[96]

15.89 Application for a variation order can be made at any time by either spouse or, on the death of a spouse, by any other person whom the Court considers to have a "sufficient interest", or by a person on behalf of a dependent child. The Court may vary the order "if it considers it proper to do so having regard to any change in the circumstances of the case and to any new evidence. . .".[97] The Court may similarly discharge an order, suspend a provision of the order, revive a provision or further vary an order already varied.

15.90 In deciding whether to vary, discharge or suspend an order under section 18, the Court must have regard to the factors which, under section 16, it was required to take into account when it granted the original order.[98]

15.91 There is little difficulty in varying an order provided that the benefit has not yet been split as a result of an application to the trustees by the spouse. The future benefit to be paid to the spouses can be adjusted by a relatively simple change of the trustees' administration records. Even where the pension payments have commenced, a variation in the pensions paid to the member and spouse can be achieved relatively easily. However, a pension that has already been split is more difficult to vary. The trustees will already have incurred time and expense in converting the spouse's designated interest into a pension in her own right. The split pension may even have been transferred into another pension scheme or buy-out bond. Yet the power to vary under section 18 is wide enough to encompass pensions that have already been split. This is supported by the final words of section 18(2):

---

95 s.18(1)(h) and s.18(2).

96 s.12(26). There is an equivalent provision regarding property adjustment orders — s.9(2). s.18(2) which empowers the Court to vary orders is expressly subject to s.9(2).

97 s.18(2).

98 See 15.38 above.

> without prejudice to the generality of the foregoing, an order under this section may require the divesting of any property vested in a person under or by virtue of an order to which this section applies.

and by section 18(6) which states:

> This section shall apply, with any necessary modifications, to instruments executed pursuant to orders to which this section applies as it applies to those orders.

An "instrument executed pursuant to orders" could include, for example, a buy-out bond.

INTERIM RELIEF

15.92 A member may try to defeat a claim for a pension adjustment order by disposing of or transferring his pension benefits before the pension adjustment order is granted by the Court. There are four ways in which this could be done:

1. Transfer his benefits to a buy out bond or the scheme of a new employer. This can happen only if he has left service, or possibly if the scheme is being wound up.
2. Leave service and take a refund of his member contributions. This may eliminate his benefits entirely from the fund. Alternatively, he may only be entitled to a refund of contributions paid prior to 1 January 1991, in which case his benefits will be reduced but not eliminated.[99]
3. Retire and exchange part or the whole of his pension for a cash sum payable directly to him. This is known as commutation.[100] He may be permitted under the scheme to retire at any time after age 50.[101]
4. Transfer his benefits out of the jurisdiction. This can happen only if he has left service and has joined pensionable employment in another country.

The spouse is protected in all of these situations in circumstances where an order has already been granted but is not protected before-

---

[99] On refunds and partial refunds see para. 12.44 and 12.45.

[100] Commutation is considered in detail at paras. 2.24, 2.38 and 7.14 et seq.

[101] See para 7.27 et seq. on early retirement.

hand. Let us assume that no order has been granted. In all four situations, either cash is paid directly to the member or benefits are transferred to another scheme or bond. The first situation is unlikely to be of particular concern, because the spouse can make the trustees of the new scheme a notice party. The practical difficulty is, however, identifying the new trustees. The other circumstances are potentially more serious.

15.93 In the case of refunds of contributions and commutation, the member assumes complete control over cash which he can then dispose of for his own benefit. In the case of transfers to another jurisdiction, his benefits leave the country. There is an added problem with refunds of contributions in that the member may forego a significant part of his pension by taking a refund.

15.94 The FLA addresses this problem by granting the Court two powers: first, the power to restrain the member from taking action, and secondly, power to set aside a disposition. This is provided for in section 35 of the Act and enables the spouse (or person on behalf of a dependent child), who has instituted judicial separation proceedings for relief (a term defined in section 35(1) to include pension adjustment orders), to apply to Court for a restraining order or order setting aside a disposition. An application can be made also by a person divorced or legally separated in another country who has been granted leave to seek a pension adjustment order under section 23(3) of the FLA or intends to apply for leave on completing one year's ordinary residence in the State.

15.95 In order to grant a restraining order, the Court must be satisfied that the member intends to defeat the claim for relief by disposing of or transferring out of the jurisdiction or otherwise dealing with any property.[102] The meaning of "defeating a claim" is defined in section 35(1) in wide terms as meaning (a) preventing relief from being granted, (b) limiting the relief, or (c) frustrating or impeding the enforcement of an order. All of the circumstances set out above[103] could amount to the defeating of a claim as so defined.

---

[102] s.35(2)(a)(I).

[103] At para. 15.92.

15.96 To set aside a disposition that has already been made, the Court must be satisfied that the member intended to defeat the claim for relief by making the disposition — that is, that the disposition was intended to prevent or limit relief or frustrate or impede the enforcement of the order. Dispositions for valuable consideration to a third party who is without notice and acting bona fide are not reviewable.[104]

THE TRUSTEES

15.97 Up to now, pension adjustment orders have, for the most part, been examined from the perspective of the member of the scheme and his spouse. The court order is sought by the member or the spouse or, perhaps, on behalf of a dependent child. The court order is, however, directed at the trustees of the scheme and it is now intended to consider several issues relating to the position of the trustees.

15.98 The starting point is the definition of trustees of a pension scheme which is contained in section 1 of the FLA. The definition is similar but not identical to that contained in the Pensions Act:

> "trustees", in relation to a scheme that is established under a trust means the trustees of the pension scheme and, in relation to a pension scheme not so established, means the persons who administer the scheme.

Where the scheme is established under trust, the identity of the trustees is almost always clear. If it is not established under trust, the person administering the scheme is deemed the trustee for the purposes of the Act. In the case of a self-employed arrangement or a buy-out bond, this will be the life office which issued the bond. The employer may be the administrator of a pension arrangement which has not been established under trust, or there may be an outside administrator.

15.99 The trustees must arrange for the designated or split benefit to be payable out of the resources of the scheme and in accordance with the rules of the scheme or in accordance with regulations issued under section 5(4) of the Pensions Act.[105] Any transfer of benefit must

---

[104] Only "reviewable dispositions" (as defined in s.35(1)) can be set aside. Basically, reviewable dispositions are all dispositions other than those made for valuable consideration without notice where the disponee acted in good faith.

[105] s.12(14) and see para. 15.23 above.

be made from the resources of the scheme. To avoid the double payment of benefits, the benefit payable to, or in respect of, the member must be reduced by the amount of the designated benefit payable pursuant to the order.[106]

15.100 The splitting of the pension in favour of the spouse involves a transfer of benefits. This will be either an internal transfer so that the spouse becomes a beneficiary in her own right, or a transfer to another scheme or buy-out bond. There are several circumstances in which a split can occur. To protect the trustees from having to split the benefit a second time, they are given a discharge from any obligation to make any further payment or transfer pursuant to the order.[107] There is a further protection contained in section 12(20) as follows:

> The court may, in a pension adjustment order or by order made under this subsection after the making of a pension adjustment order, give to the trustees of the scheme concerned such directions as it considers appropriate for the purposes of the pension adjustment order including directions compliance with which occasions non-compliance with the rules of the scheme concerned or the Act of 1990;[108] and a trustee of a scheme shall not be liable in any court or other tribunal for any loss or damage caused by his or her non-compliance with the rules of the scheme or with the Act of 1990 if the non-compliance was occasioned by his or her compliance with a direction of the court under this section.

The trustees are, by virtue of this sub-section, protected from any claim that they have breached the rules of the scheme or the Pensions Act in complying with directions given by the Court. What is odd is that the protection is confined to circumstances where a court direction is given. If the Court grants the pension adjustment order but gives no directions to the trustees, it is arguable that this provision is not a sufficient protection for the trustees. It would therefore be prudent for the trustees to ensure that any order granted by the Court includes specific directions to the trustees.

15.101 Costs incurred by the trustees of a scheme must be borne by either or both of the spouses in such proportions as the Court deter-

---

106 s.12(15).

107 s.12(17).

108 That is, the Pensions Act.

mines. If the Court makes no determination, the costs must be borne equally. The costs that can be recovered by the trustees are:

1. Costs arising with respect to any notice to the trustees and any representations to Court by the trustees under section 12(18)
2. Costs of complying with a pension adjustment order
3. Costs of complying with a direction of the Court either generally under section 12(20) or specifically concerning a benefit calculation under section 12(25).[109]

Where a spouse fails to pay costs, the trustees can apply to court to have costs deducted from the amount of benefit payable to that person.[110]

15.102 In judicial separation proceedings it is likely that the spouses and the Court will need to know the value of the member's benefits under the pension scheme. The need to do so where pension benefits are to be designated is obvious. The spouses may, however, wish to adjust non-pension assets and leave the pension intact, or the Court may take a similar view. In these circumstances, a valuation is likely to be required because the spouse will need family assets equivalent to the pension rights that she might have received if a pension adjustment order had been granted.

15.103 The spouses can commission their own valuation of benefits on the basis of information given to them by the trustees of the scheme, or each spouse can obtain their own report. Alternatively, the trustees can be directed to furnish the Court with a valuation of the retirement benefits that have accrued at the time of making the order and a valuation of the death in service benefits payable under the scheme which, if applicable,[111] have accrued to date of the making of the order.[112] The Court may, of its own motion, direct a valuation and

---

[109] s.12(22)(a).

[110] s.12(22)(b).

[111] In most schemes, the death benefits payable on death in service are the same irrespective of service completed, and so there is usually no concept of accrued contingent benefits. Nonetheless, it is possible for a scheme to provide death in service benefits which increase with service completed. An example would be the "creeping widows" pension — see para. 11.11.

[112] s.12(25).

must do so if either spouse (or a person on behalf of a dependent child) so requests. The direction to the trustees must specify a time period within which the valuation is to be provided to the spouses (and dependent child, if applicable) and the Court.

15.104 In deciding whether to seek a valuation, the spouses should have regard to the fact that the costs of the trustees in complying with the order must be paid by one or both of the spouses. In a defined benefit scheme, the costs could be significant as actuarial advice is necessary. The valuation of defined contribution schemes is usually somewhat easier to achieve (and therefore cheaper), but the member is probably better off seeking a benefit statement under the disclosure regulations (if the member has not already received one), which is free of charge, and which gives a value within the last 12 months of the member's benefit.[113] However, the equivalent benefit statement for a defined benefit scheme will not include a present value of the accrued benefit.[114]

OTHER SCHEMES

15.105 This chapter has focused up to this point on occupational pension schemes. As noted earlier, the FLA applies to other schemes as well as to occupational pension schemes. The main alternatives are self-employed arrangements approved under section 235 of the Income Tax Act, 1967[115] and buy-out bonds.[116]

15.106 Self-employed arrangements are investment policies, issued by a life office, which provide a pension from a specified age based on premiums paid to the life office by the policyholder. These arrangements are approved (subject to certain conditions) by the Revenue Commissioners and, as a consequence, qualifying premiums are tax deductible and the fund is exempt from income and capital gains tax. Policies can be effected either by self-employed persons or by persons in employment who are not included in an occupational pension scheme. The ultimate pension depends on the value of the policy at

---

113 s.11(2) of, and Schedule D Part II to, the Disclosure Regulations.

114 Because it is not a requirement of Schedule D Part I to the Disclosure Regulations.

115 On which, see para. 6.59 et seq.

116 Buy-out bonds are considered at para. 10.82 et seq.

retirement and so, in effect, a self-employed scheme is the equivalent of a defined contribution scheme and should be relatively straightforward to designate or split and also to value. The arrangement is not normally established under trust,[117] and so the trustees are the life office concerned, as the life office administers the scheme and falls within the definition of "trustees" under the FLA.[118]

15.107 One feature that buy-out bonds have in common with self-employed arrangements is that they are also issued and administered by life offices. Buy-out bonds are approved by the Revenue under Chapter II of Part I of the Finance Act, 1972, but are not occupational pension schemes in the normal sense. They are established to receive transfer payments from occupational pension schemes, usually as a consequence of a member leaving service or of the scheme being wound up by the trustees. The bond is applied for by the trustees and is written in the name of the member. It will either guarantee the pension promise that the pension scheme offered, or will provide for the investment of the transfer payment on a unitised or with profit basis.[119] As far as the FLA is concerned, the trustees of the bond are the life office. The designation and splitting should be straightforward in all cases.

REVENUE LIMITS

15.108 All benefits of Revenue approved pension schemes are subject to limits imposed by the Revenue Commissioners.[120] Revenue practice has been modified to cope with the effects of pension adjustment orders. The general principle is that, for the purposes of computing Revenue limits, the designated benefit for the spouse or dependent child is still treated as part of the member's overall benefits. This is so whether or not the designated benefit is subsequently split. Conversely, the designated benefit is not taken into account in computing the spouse's or dependent child's maximum benefits.

---

[117] Unless it is a group scheme — see para. 6.70 et seq.

[118] s.2(1).

[119] For a discussion of unitised and with-profit investment, see para. 10.13 et seq. and 10.20 et seq.

[120] See Chapter 7.

15.109 A pension payable to a spouse or dependent child pursuant to a pension adjustment order is treated as income of the recipient and (subject to allowances) is liable to income tax. If the designated benefit (or any part of it) consists of a proportion of a refund of member contributions, these are liable to income tax under Schedule D Case IV at the same rate as member refunds generally — that is 25 per cent. Any payment to a former spouse consequent upon the recognition of a foreign divorce is exempt from capital acquisitions tax.[121] A similar exemption is contained in the Family Law (Divorce) Bill, 1996 with regard to Irish divorces.

121 FLA s.51.

16

European Equality Law and Pensions

INTRODUCTION

16.1 It is by virtue of Ireland's membership of the European Union that we now have law requiring equal pay for work of equal value.[1] The source of this equal-treatment requirement is Article 119 of the Treaty of Rome which provides:

> Each Member State shall during the first stage ensure and subsequently maintain the application of the principle that men and women shall receive equal pay for equal work.
>
> For the purpose of this Article "pay" means the ordinary basic or minimum wage or salary and any other consideration, whether in cash or in kind, which the worker receives, directly or indirectly, in respect of his employment from his employer.
>
> Equal pay without discrimination based on sex means:
>
> (a) That pay for the same work at piece rates shall be calculated on the basis of the same unit of measurement.
>
> (b) That pay for work at time rates shall be the same for the same job.

16.2 It will be noted that "pay" is defined in a wide fashion which reflects the modern understanding of pay as extending to more than simply wages or salary. Judgments of the European Court of Justice have determined that "pay" under Article 119 encompasses benefits under occupational pension schemes.[2]

---

1 For a thorough examination of the development of Irish Equal Pay Legislation see Curtin, D. (1989): *Irish Employment Equality Law*, Dublin: Round Hall Press.

2 See *Bilka Kaufhaus GmbH* v. *Weber von Hartz* [1986] 2 CMLR 701.

16.3 Irish employees now have rights to equal treatment with respect to occupational pension schemes under the following:

1. The Treaty of Rome, 1957 — Article 119 ("Article 119")
2. The Anti-Discrimination (Pay) Act, 1974 ("the 1974 Act")
3. The Pensions Act, 1990 — Part VII ("Part VII")
4. The European Convention on Human Rights — Article 14 ("the European Convention")[3]

16.4 This chapter examines the rights that arise under Article 119, the 1974 Act and the Pensions Act, 1990, and how those rights have been developed, clarified and at times confused by subsequent amendments of the legislation and judgments of the European Court, the Irish Employment Appeals Tribunal, the Labour Court and the High Court.[4] The extent to which reliance may be placed on the European Convention to found an equality claim will also be considered.

16.5 There are several ways in which discrimination can occur in pension schemes including:

1. Unequal entry requirements
2. Unequal retirement ages
3. Unequal accrual rates for pensions
4. Unequal members' benefits
5. Unequal survivors' benefits

16.6 In addition, the rules of a scheme can be indirectly discriminatory if they have a disproportionate effect on the members of one sex as against the other. This can most commonly occur in a situation where part-time employees are excluded from scheme membership.

---

3 The Convention for the Protection of Human Rights and Fundamental Freedoms, signed on 4 November 1950. Ireland was an original signatory to the Convention.

4 It should be noted that the Equal Pay Act, 1977, one of the other major pieces of Irish equality legislation (and which again implements an EU Council Directive), specifically excludes pensions from its scope. However, s.56(2) of the 1977 Act provides that it and the 1974 Act are to be construed together — see *Bank of Ireland* v. *Kavanagh* [1990] 1CMLR 87 at p.92.

This type of discrimination is at present probably the area of most concern in the context of equality and pensions.

16.7 It may be said at the outset that Ireland has not had the same experience as the UK in relation to sex discrimination and pensions. In the UK there has been a multiplicity of equal-pay claims relating to pensions. The reason for this is undoubtedly that Ireland has historically had equal retirement ages for men and women in the State social security scheme. This was mirrored in private occupational schemes. In the UK, state retirement ages were different for men and women and this practice was followed in private schemes. The issue of equality and pensions was and is therefore far less serious in Ireland than in the UK.[5]

16.8 Under Article 119 of the Treaty, employees have rights directly enforceable against their employers and also against the trustees of the pension scheme[6] subject to the limitations imposed by the various European Court decisions interpreting Article 119. Employees also have rights under the 1974 Act subject to the limitations contained in that Act (limitation of three years' arrears). It is arguable that there is a case for rationalising the position perhaps by taking equal treatment in relation to occupational pension schemes out of the ambit of the 1974 Act and leaving it with Part VII of the Pensions Act.

16.9 On 1 July 1996 the Employment Equality Bill, 1996 was presented by the Minister for Equality and Law Reform. This Bill, when enacted, will repeal the anti-Discrimination Pay Act, 1974 and amend the Equal Pay Act, 1977. Pensions are excluded from the ambit of the proposed Act. The Minister for Social Welfare is to introduce a new Bill to deal with pensions and equality. However, this Bill is not yet drafted.

THE ANTI-DISCRIMINATION (PAY) ACT, 1974

16.10 The Anti-Discrimination (Pay) Act, 1974 came into force on 31 December 1975. Section 2(1) of that Act provides:

---

5 Although some Irish schemes, established by UK employers, have mirrored the discriminatory design in the equivalent UK scheme.

6 *Coloroll Pension Trustees Limited* v. *Russell* [1995] 2 CMLR 357.

> Subject to this Act, it shall be a term of the contract under which a woman is employed in any place that she shall be entitled to the same rate of remuneration as a man who is employed in that place by the same employer (or by an associated employer if the employees, whether generally or of a particular class, of both employers have the same terms and conditions of employment), if both are employed on like work.

16.11 For the purposes of the 1974 Act, "remuneration":

> includes any consideration, whether in cash or in kind, which an employee receives, directly or indirectly, in respect of his employment from his employer.[7]

16.12 It will be noted that the definition of "remuneration" in the 1974 Act is broadly the same as the definition of "pay" in Article 119. The 1974 Act gave effect under Irish law to the provisions of the Council Directive on Equal Pay.[8] The 1974 Act does not expressly state that it applies to occupational pension schemes. It has, however, been held in a number of Labour Court decisions that the 1974 Act covers pensions.[9] Decisions of the Labour Court are not binding on the parties to the proceedings (except in certain circumstances[10]), nor do decisions of the Labour Court constitute binding precedents. Notwithstanding this, its decisions as to the applicability of the 1974 legislation to pension schemes have not been challenged and, in light of the decisions of the European Court with respect to the application of Article 119, those Labour Court decisions appear correct.

16.13 The 1974 Act further provides that if a person is employed otherwise than under a contract, or is employed under a contract which does not include a term satisfying the requirements of section 2 of the Act, the terms and conditions of that person's employment are

---

7 s.1(1) of the 1974 Act.

8 Council Directive 75/117/EEC.

9 *Linson Limited* v. *ASTMS* EP 1/77, *Clery & Co. (1941) Limited* v. *O'Brien* EP17/1984.

10 Including the case of an appeal from a Rights Commissioner under s. 13(9)(a) Industrial Relations Act, 1969, if the parties to the hearing agree that the recommendation of the Court shall be binding under s.20 of the 1969 Act, in the case of a determination of the Court under s.79 of the Pensions Act, and under s.8 and s.10 of the 1974 Act itself.

deemed to include a term satisfying section 2.[11] The effect of this provision is to give persons who are discriminated against under their terms of employment a contractual claim against their employer. Notwithstanding the fact that a claim may be made for breach of contract, the 1974 Act restricts the arrears of remuneration which may be recovered to arrears accumulated in the period of three years before the date on which the relevant dispute is referred to an equality officer.[12]

16.14 It should be noted that the 1974 Act only refers to discrimination on the basis of sex. It does not extend to cover discrimination based on marital or family status. Section 2(3) of the Act states:

> Nothing in this Act shall prevent an employer from paying to his employees who are employed on like work in the same place different rates of remuneration on grounds other than sex.

16.15 It is possible for an employer to discriminate against married persons as regards access to or benefits under a pension scheme. This may not necessarily constitute sex-based discrimination, in which case, no claim lies under the 1974 Act. In *Bank of Ireland* v. *Kavanagh*[13] and *Caminiti and Miley* v. *RTE*,[14] the claimants both lost on this basis. However, Part VII of the Pensions Act specifically covers discrimination with regard to pension schemes based on marital or family status.[15]

EU LAW

Article 119 of the Treaty of Rome

16.16 Article 119 of the Treaty of Rome expressly requires equal treatment of men and women with respect to remuneration and is

---

11 s.4 of the 1974 Act.

12 s.8(5) of the 1974 Act (as amended by the Equal Pay Act, 1977). Under the Statutes of Limitation 1957 to 1991 a claim in simple contract would be statute barred after six years.

13 [1990] 1 CMLR 87.

14 [1994] ELR 1. In *Caminiti* the Pensions Act 1990 was not pleaded as an alternative ground of claim. Reliance might have been placed on Part VII. See para. 16.24 et seq. below.

15 s.67(3)(b); see para. 16.25 below.

directly effective in Ireland. The text of this Article is set out above.[16] A number of Articles of the Treaty have been held by the European Court to be directly effective. This means that they confer rights on individual persons which are sufficiently clear and unconditional as to be enforceable in the national courts of Member States without the requirement for national legislation implementing the relevant EU provision.[17] In a case known as the Second Defrenne case, *Defrenne* v. *Sabena*,[18] the European Court held that Article 119 was directly effective. In that case Ms Defrenne, a former air hostess with Sabena, instituted a number of claims for equal pay. As Belgium had not introduced equal pay legislation it was necessary for Ms Defrenne to rely directly on Article 119 in order to succeed in her claim. The European Court upheld her claim and ruled that Article 119 had direct effect, stating:

> . . . the principle of equal pay contained in Article 119 may be relied upon before the national courts and that these courts have a duty to ensure the protection of the rights which this provision vests in individuals, in particular as regards those types of discrimination arising directly from legislative provisions or collective labour agreements, as well as in cases in which men and women receive unequal pay for equal work which is carried out in the same establishment or service, whether private or public.[19]

16.17 Whilst from 8 April 1976[20] it was clear that Article 119 of the EU Treaty was directly effective, it was to be another nine years before the European Court had the opportunity to rule that "pay" in Article 119 included benefits payable under an occupational pension scheme. This ruling was made by the European Court in the case of

---

16 At para. 16.1.

17 This is in contrast to the position with regard to most Directives of the EU Council, which generally must be implemented into national law before they may be relied on by EU nationals — for example, the Equal Pay Directive 75/117. Whether a provision in the Treaty or in a Directive is directly effective or not is very much a question of fact to be determined in each individual case.

18 [1976] 2 CMLR 98.

19 *Ibid.* at p.125. The response of the EU Council to the *Defrenne* judgment was to introduce a number of equality Directives including those on equal pay (75/117/EEC), equal treatment (76/207/EEC) and equal treatment in matters of social security. (79/7/EEC).

20 The date of the *Defrenne* judgment.

Bilka-Kaufhaus GmbH v. *Weber von Hartz*.[21] In that case, the European Court ruled that a part-time employee could rely on Article 119 in respect of her claim that she was indirectly discriminated against by her employer which, under the rules of its pension scheme, only admitted full-time employees to the pension scheme.

16.18 The situation at this point, therefore, was (and still is) that nationals of Member States could rely directly on Article 119 of the Treaty to found an equal-pay claim with respect to pension entitlements.[22] Article 119 prohibits discrimination on the basis of sex. It does not, however, refer to discrimination which is by reference to marital or family status, but the subsequent EU Equality Directive regulates this issue.

The EU Equality Directive on Pensions

16.19 Subsequent to the *Bilka* decision, the EU Council adopted a Directive on the implementation of the principle of equal treatment for men and women in occupational social security schemes.[23] The Directive had been in preparation for a number of years. Following the *Bilka* ruling, the Directive was, arguably, largely unnecessary but it was nevertheless brought into force. This Directive has as its object to implement, in occupational social security schemes,[24] the principle of equal treatment for men and women.

16.20 The Directive states at Article 5:

> Under the conditions laid down in the following provisions, the principle of equal treatment implies that there shall be no discrimination on the basis of sex, either directly or indirectly, by reference in particular to marital or family status, especially as regards:

---

21 [1986] 2 CMLR 701.

22 For a list of European Court judgments with respect to the application of Article 119 to occupational pension schemes see Appendix 1 of the National Pensions Board Report on Equal Treatment.

23 Council directive 86/378, 24.07.86.

24 This term is defined in the Directive as schemes whose purpose is to provide workers, whether employees or self-employed, in an undertaking or group of undertakings, area of economic activity or occupational sector or group of such sectors with benefits intended to supplement the benefits provided by statutory social security schemes or to replace them, whether membership of such schemes is compulsory or optional.

- the scope of the schemes and the conditions of access to them;
- the obligation to contribute and the calculation of contributions;
- the calculation of benefits, including supplementary benefits due in respect of a spouse or dependants, and the conditions governing the duration and retention of entitlement to benefits.

16.21 The Directive then sets out a list of provisions which would be contrary to the principle of equal treatment.[25] This list also stipulates certain provisions which will not infringe the principle. The Directive refers explicitly to discrimination on the basis of sex and by reference to marital or family status.

16.22 Member States were required to implement the Directive into national law, at the latest, three years after the date of its notification to Member States, being 30 July 1986,[26] and to take all necessary steps to ensure that the provisions of occupational schemes contrary to the principle of equal treatment were revised by 1 January 1993.[27] The Directive states that rights and obligations relating to a period of membership of an occupational benefit scheme prior to revision of that scheme are not affected by the requirements of the Directive.[28]

THE PENSIONS ACT

National Pensions Board Report on Equal Treatment

16.23 On 10 May 1989, the National Pensions Board published its report entitled *Report on Equal Treatment for Men and Women in Occupational Pension Schemes*. The Board noted that, pursuant to the decisions of the European Court, noted above,[29] Article 119 was directly effective. It also observed that Article 119 extended to benefits under pension schemes, and that the Anti-Discrimination (Pay) Act, 1974, also applied to benefits under pension schemes. However,

---

25 See the Directive at Article 6.

26 Article 12 of the Directive.

27 Article 8.1 of the Directive.

28 Article 8.2 of the Directive. The provisions of Article 8 have been overtaken by the decision of the European Court in *Barber* v. *GRE* (see 16.38 et seq. below).

29 See fn 21 above.

the Report concluded, among other things, that the provisions of the 1986 Directive should be implemented into Irish law.[30] In its conclusions, it determined that this was best done in legislation which dealt specifically with pensions and referred to the recommendation contained in its first report that a Pensions Act be brought into force. The recommendation of the National Pensions Board was followed through by the Minister for Social Welfare, and the 1986 Directive was implemented into Irish law as Part VII of the Pensions Act, 1990. Again, following the recommendations of the National Pensions Board, and in order to give employers and trustees time to make the necessary alterations to scheme documentation to meet the equal treatment provisions, implementation of Part VII of the Pensions Act was deferred until 1 January 1993.[31]

Pensions Act — The Principle of Equal Treatment

16.24 Part VII of the Pensions Act implemented into Irish law the 1986 Directive. Part VII requires that occupational benefit schemes comply with the principle of equal treatment.[32] This principle is set out in the Act as follows:

> The principle of equal treatment is that there shall be no discrimination on the basis of sex in respect of any matter relating to an occupational benefit scheme.[33]

Part VII of the Pensions Act applies to what are defined[34] as "occupational benefit schemes". This is wider than the term "occupational pension scheme", which applies in the other parts of the Pensions Act. "Occupational benefit schemes" include, for instance, permanent

30 As a Member State, Ireland was of course obliged to implement the Directive.

31 This deferment was permitted by Article 8 of the Directive (see para. 16.23). The National Pensions Board recognised, at para. 15.13 of their report on equal treatment, that this deferment of implementation of Part VII did lead to the somewhat anomalous position that the equal treatment provisions under the Pensions Act were not in force, but employees already had a right to equal treatment with respect to pension schemes under the provisions of the Anti-Discrimination (Pay) Act, 1974.

32 s.66 and s.67(1).

33 s.67(1).

34 s.65.

health insurance arrangements. It would also include arrangements relating to redundancy.

16.25 The Act sets out an exhaustive list of the matters relating to an occupational benefit scheme which are deemed to constitute sex-based discrimination.[35] These are:

1. Where because of a person's sex, marital or family status, that person is treated less favourably than a person of the other sex
2. Where because of a person's sex, marital or family status, the person is unable to comply with a requirement or condition with which a substantially higher proportion of persons of the other sex or with the other marital or family status can comply and which requirement or condition cannot be objectively justified on grounds other than sex
3. Where a person is penalised for having in good faith referred a dispute to an equality officer or the Labour Court or given evidence in such proceedings.

16.26 In the case of a claim for indirect discrimination, if any question arises as to whether a requirement or condition is justifiable irrespective of the sex of the person to whom it applies, the burden of proof will be on the person asserting that the requirement is justified.[36] This accords with the decision of the European Court in *Bilka-Kaufhaus Gmbh* v *Weber von Hartz.*[37]

16.27 To establish a claim of discrimination it is necessary that there exist a comparator. Claimants must be able to show that they are doing similar work or work of equal value to an employee of the other sex and that the other employee is treated more favourably. This is in common with the requirements of the Anti-Discrimination (Pay) Act, 1974, the Employment Equality Act, 1977 and the terms of the 1986 Directive itself. This condition is one of the sources of criti-

---

35 s.67(3) as amended by s.30 Pensions (Amendment) Act, 1996.

36 s.68.

37 However, see para. 16.54 below with regard to the standard of justification required.

cisms that has been levelled against European equal-pay legislation.[38] Dependent upon the size of the relevant employer, choosing the correct comparator can be difficult and can result in a claim failing.

16.28 Part VII of the Act also stipulates that, if a scheme disallows periods of absence on paid maternity or family leave for the purposes of pension accrual, the principle of equal treatment is infringed.[39]

16.29 Many pension schemes contain powers conferring on the employer discretion in relation to admission to membership or augmentation of benefits. The 1986 Directive specifically requires that where the granting of benefits is left to the discretion of a scheme's management body (which would include trustees or the employer), the latter must take account of the principle of equal treatment.[40] While not explicitly stated in Part VII of the 1990 Act, this requirement would appear to be covered by the general provisions of section 67 of the Act.

16.30 Part VII of the Pensions Act further requires that the principle of equal treatment extend to access to occupational benefit schemes.[41] It is clearly important that the principle of equal treatment apply not only in relation to the rights of existing members of the pension scheme, but also to the right of employees to join a pension scheme in the first place.

Exclusions from the Equal Treatment Principle

16.31 Section 69(1) of the Act lists certain matters which shall not be taken account of in considering whether the principle of equal treatment has been satisfied. These are as follows:

1. Any difference on the basis of the sex of members, in the levels of contributions which the employer makes, to the extent that the difference is for the purposes of removing or limiting differences,

---

38 See Prenderville, O. (1991): "Equality Legislation — A Success or Failure" *Irish Student Law Review*, 1(21).

39 s.72 and s.73.

40 Article 6.2 of the 1986 Directive.

41 s.70. This is also required by Article 119 — as determined by the European Court in *Bilka Kaufhaus* v. *Weber von Hartz*, and affirmed in the *Vroege Case* [1994] PLR 233.

as between men and women in the amount or value of benefits provided under a defined contribution scheme

2. Any difference, on the basis of sex, in the amount or value of benefits provided under a defined contribution scheme to the extent that the difference is justifiable on actuarial grounds

3. Any special treatment for the benefit of women to whom section 72(1) relates[42]

4. Any difference of treatment in relation to any optional provisions available.

16.32 As originally enacted, section 69(1), had taken advantage of one of the optional provisions in the Directive allowing deferment of equality in relation to benefits for a deceased member's spouse or dependants. The European Court subsequently held that the underlying Directive did not comply, in this respect, with the requirements of Article 119,[43] and section 69(1) was amended, prior to its coming into force to remove the exception relating to survivors' benefits.[44]

16.33 The expression "optional provisions available" used in paragraph 4. above is defined in section 69(2) as referring to those provisions of the scheme

1. Which apply only in the case of members who elect for them to do so, and

2. Whose purpose is to secure for those members:

   (i) Benefits in addition to those otherwise provided under the scheme, or

   (ii) A choice with respect to the date on which benefits under the scheme are to commence, or

   (iii) A choice between any two or more benefits.

16.34 Two optional provisions that can result in different treatment for men and women are additional voluntary contributions (AVCs)

---

42 Preservation of differing treatment for the purposes of maternity.

43 *Barber* v. *GRE*. See para. 16.38 below.

44 By the provisions of s.61 of the Social Welfare Act, 1992.

and exchanging pension for cash at retirement (commutation). A woman who pays the same amount of AVCs as a man will usually receive a lower supplementary pension at retirement, because of the application of sex-based actuarial factors. For similar reasons the exchange rate between pension and cash on commutation is often different for men and women. These are examples of optional provisions which are exempted from the principle of equal treatment. Of course, any sex-based discrimination against an employee in being given access to an option of this kind would constitute a breach of the equality principle.

Compulsory Levelling-up

16.35 The Act provides that, where the rules of an occupational benefit scheme do not comply with the principle of equal treatment, there is a compulsory levelling-up[45] — that is, the more favourable treatment accorded by the rules of a pension scheme to persons of one sex is automatically accorded to persons of the other sex. This compulsory levelling-up will apply from 17 May 1990[46] up until the date on which the rules are amended to comply with the principle of equal treatment.

16.36 The Pensions Act contains transitional provisions with respect to inequalities relating to a period of membership in a pension scheme prior to 17 May, 1990. The Act provides that such inequalities may continue for a period, starting on 17 May 1990 and ending on 31 December 1998, or in the case of retirement ages, 31 December 2017.[47] Thus, with respect to inequalities post 17 May 1990, there is a compulsory levelling up, and with respect to inequalities prior to 17 May 1990, there is a deferral for the stated period. The intention of these transitional provisions is to allow a period of time within which

---

45 s.71.

46 This is the date of the European Court judgment in *Barber* v. *GRE*. Note that for self-employed persons the effective commencement date is 1 January 1993.

47 s.71 as amended by s.31 Pensions (Amendment) Act, 1996.

the relevant pension scheme may provide any necessary additional funding to meet the increased obligations.[48]

16.37 The Pensions Act contains specific provisions in relation to pregnancy and childbirth. These provisions effectively exclude the equal treatment principle in relation to pension schemes which provide special treatment for women in connection with pregnancy or childbirth.[49] There are also specific provisions in the Act which protect the entitlements of women while on paid maternity absence.[50] A female member of a pension scheme may also have a claim for breach of statutory rights relating to maternity leave under the provisions of the Maternity Protection Act, 1994. There are also special provisions with respect to family leave.[51]

EQUALITY AFTER BARBER

The Barber Judgment

16.38 Subsequent to enactment of the Pensions Act, but prior to its coming into force, the European Court delivered its judgment in the case of *Barber* v *Guardian Royal Exchange Assurance Group.*[52] This judgment, and the European Court judgments that followed it, completely unsettled the understanding of EU equality requirements as regards pensions. Member States, not unreasonably, understood these requirements to be set out in the Equality Directive (86/378).[53] The European Court in *Barber* found that the Directive did not comply with Article 119 of the Treaty of Rome.

---

48 Following enactment of the Pensions (Amendment) Act, 1996, and pursuant to s.31 of that Act, these transitional provisions have been amended to make it clear that they apply only to current members of a scheme. Members who have ceased to be in employment to which the scheme relates, whether before or during the transitional periods, will continue to have their benefits governed by the provisions in force prior to 17 May 1990

49 s.72.

50 s.72(2) and (3).

51 s.73.

52 [1990] 2 CMLR 513.

53 See para. 16.20 et seq.

16.39 The facts in the *Barber* case are straightforward. Mr Barber was employed by a subsidiary of GRE and he was a member of the Guardian Royal Exchange Pension Fund. In 1980, at the age of 52, Mr Barber was made redundant. He was granted a termination payment and deferred pension under the terms of the pension scheme. If Mr Barber had been a woman aged 52 he would have been regarded as "retired" for the purposes of the scheme and would have been entitled to an immediate pension. Mr Barber instituted sex discrimination proceedings against the GRE, but these were unsuccessful both at an Industrial Tribunal and on appeal to the Employment Appeals Tribunal. He appealed to the Court of Appeal, which stated a case to the European Court for a preliminary ruling as to the applicability of Article 119 of the Treaty. The European Court stated that, as already determined in a previous decision,[54] Article 119 applied to supplementary pension schemes. The Court went on:

> That interpretation of Article 119 is not affected by the fact that the private occupational scheme in question has been set up in the form of a trust and is administered by trustees who are technically independent of the employer, since Article 119 also applies to consideration received indirectly from the employer.

16.40 The European Court decided that Mr Barber had been discriminated against in a manner contrary to Article 119 by reason of the fact that, upon being made compulsorily redundant, he was only entitled to a deferred pension payable at normal pensionable age whereas a woman in the same position would have been entitled to an immediate retirement pension. The Court made it clear that the application of the principle of equal pay must be ensured in respect of each element of remuneration, and not only on the basis of a comprehensive assessment of the total remuneration package.

16.41 The European Court referred to the fact that the 1986 Directive had been issued and that it set out a timetable for implementation of the equal-treatment provision.[55] Member States were entitled to take the view that the 1986 Directive was a correct statement of the law relating to equality. The European Court was also mindful of the possible cost effect on existing occupational pension schemes of its

---

[54] *Bilka-Kaufhaus GmbH* v. *Weber Von Hartz*.

[55] See para. 16.22 above.

decision that Article 119 was of direct effect and rendered unlawful inequalities in pension schemes. In view of this, the European Court imposed a temporal limitation relating to the effect of its judgment. The Court stated:

> . . . overriding considerations of legal certainty preclude legal situations which have exhausted all their effects in the past from being called in question where that might upset retroactively the financial balance of many contracted-out pension schemes. It is appropriate, however, to provide for an exception in favour of individuals who have taken action in good time in order to safeguard their rights. Finally, it must be pointed out that no restriction on the effects of the aforesaid interpretation can be permitted as regards the acquisition of entitlement to a pension as from the date of this judgment.

16.42 The temporal limitation imposed by the European Court was of some comfort. However, the decision and the limitation left quite a number of questions unanswered as to the extent of the application of the equal-treatment principle to pension schemes. The precise meaning of the temporal limitation itself was unclear. It could have been taken to mean that equal treatment applies:

1. To new members joining a pension scheme who begin to pay contributions after 17 May 1990
2. To benefits payable in respect of service performed after 17 May 1990
3. To all pensions which fall to be paid (for the first time) after 17 May 1990
4. To all pension payments made after 17 May 1990.
5. From any of the above dates to schemes other than contracted-out schemes.

16.43 Dependent upon the correct interpretation, the cost implications, particularly for UK pension schemes with a history of sex-based inequality, were enormous. A number of other equal treatment cases were referred to the European Court in the hope of clarifying matters, particularly with respect to the possible retrospective effect of *Barber* v. *GRE*. Those cases are considered below and it will be seen that whilst going a good way to clarifying matters they also brought up further issues.

16.44 In December 1991, the EU Heads of State met at Maastricht and one of the topics discussed was the effect of the European Court judgment in *Barber*. This was of particular concern to the UK Government because of the possible effect on the solvency of UK pension funds. At that meeting, a protocol to the Maastricht Treaty (the "Barber Protocol") was agreed, to the effect that the retrospective effect of the *Barber* judgment be excluded. The matter has been furthered clarified by the European Court judgments referred to below.

Judgment of the European Court Subsequent to Barber

16.45 The judgment of the European Court which have developed the judgment in Barber are principally those given on 6 October 1993 in *Ten Oever*,[56] on 14 December 1993 in *Moroni* v. *Collo GmbH* and on 28 September 1994 in the cases of *Coloroll Pension Trustees Limited* v. *Russell, Fisscher, Smith* v. *Avdel Systems Limited, Van den Akker* v. *Shell, Beaune* and *Vroege*.[57]

16.46 The European Court stated that the effect of the Barber judgment was prospective only — that is, equality could only be claimed in relation to benefits payable in respect of periods of employment subsequent to 17 May 1990, subject to the exception in favour of employees or those claiming through them who had initiated proceedings before that date.[58] The deferment of implementation of equality until 1 January 1993 provided in the 1986 Directive is not consistent with Article 119, and equality must be implemented as from 17 May 1990. Until equality is achieved, the effect of the Barber judgment is that benefits must be equalised upwards.[59] Neither Article 119 nor the Barber judgment requires that benefits be equalised upwards when

---

56 [1993] PLR 317 and [1995] 2 CMLR 357.

57 *Moroni* and the six cases decided on 28 September 1994 are all reported in *the Equality Cases* [1994] PLR. They are also reported in CMLR as follows: *Moroni* and *Coloroll* all at [1995] 2 CMLR 357; *Vroege* and *Fisscher* all at [1995] 1 CMLR 881; *Beaune* [1995] 3 CMLR 30; *Van den Akker* and *Smith* all at [1995] 3 CMLR 543.

58 *Moroni* v. *Collo*.

59 *Avdel*

equalisation is implemented. They may in fact be equalised down. The Pensions Act now reflects this position in Irish law.[60]

16.47 The provisions of Article 119 can be relied on by employees, against both employers and trustees of pension schemes.[61] Further, trustees and employers are obliged to administer pension schemes in accordance with the principle of equal treatment.[62] The European Court left it to national courts to determine how the equality principle should apply where there is a shortfall in the fund. The European Court confirmed its decision in *Neath* v *Hugh Steeper Ltd.*[63] that the use of differing actuarial factors as between male and female members of a defined benefit scheme for the purpose of arriving at equal benefits did not infringe Article 119.[64] Public sector schemes are covered by Article 119 and therefore are required to comply with the equal-treatment principle as from 17 May 1990.[65] The Pensions Act already required this in relation to public sector schemes.[66] The Court has also determined that special arrangements made for a group of members which applied to one sex only would not comply with the equal-treatment principle.[67]

16.48 The temporal limitation in *Barber* and the Maastricht Protocol does not apply to the right to join an occupational pension scheme. This is still governed by the judgment of the European Court in

---

60 s.71(1) as amended by s.31 Pensions (Amendment) Act, 1996.

61 *Coloroll*, also *Barber* v. *GRE*.

62 *Coloroll*.

63 [1994] PLR 1 and [1995] 2 CMLR 357.

64 *Coloroll*.

65 *Beaune*.

66 Note the definition of "employer" and "employee" in s.65 includes "a civil servant of the State or of the Government and an officer or servant of a local authority".

67 *Van der Akker*. This was the practice known as "red circling" whereby a group of employees who had been disadvantaged by an inequality in a scheme were afforded a special treatment which was then not offered to members of the scheme of the other sex. *Van der Akker* determined that this itself amounted to an illegal discrimination.

Bilka-Kaufhaus GmbH v. *Weber von Hartz.*[68] The European Court decisions do not create a right to join a pension scheme. They determined that a restriction on part-time employees joining a scheme could potentially be illegal if it affected a disproportionate number of one sex as against the other.[69] Further, the European Court made it clear that if part-time employees had been excluded from membership of a scheme in contravention of Article 119, the right to join with retrospective effect was subject to the condition that such employees pay the appropriate amount in respect of employee contributions (if the scheme is contributory).[70]

16.49 It is clear from Barber and the subsequent decisions of the European Court that in certain respects the Equal Treatment Directive of 1986 failed to implement properly the requirements of Article 119, and the Directive itself requires amendment. There is at present a proposal by the EU Commission to amend the Equal Treatment Directive.[71] Arising from the European Court judgments referred to above there are a number of areas which deserve particular comment. These are dealt with in the following paragraphs.

PART-TIME EMPLOYEES

16.50 Employers may still discriminate between part-time employees and full-time employees. It is sex-based discrimination that is outlawed by EU law. The European Court confirmed in *Bilka Kaufhaus GmbH* v. *Weber von Hartz* that Article 119 prohibited sex-based discrimination against part-time employees as regards access to pension schemes. In *Bilka*, the European Court referred to its earlier de-

---

68 This was the decision of the European Court in the *Vroege* and *Fisscher* cases.

69 Equality issues with respect to part-time employees are dealt with below at para. 16.50.

70 *Fisscher* and also *Vroege*. Unfortunately, the European Court did not address the question of who should make up the shortfall in capital appreciation on the contributions which have to be put in to the fund.

71 Proposal for a Council Directive Amending Directive 86/378/EEC on the Implementation of the Principle of Equal Treatment for Men and Women in Occupational Social Security Schemes (95/C 218/05). This Proposal was submitted by the Commission on 19 June 1995.

cision in *Jenkins* v. *Kingsgate (Clothing Productions) Limited.*[72] That case did not concern a pension scheme. The plaintiff's claim was that her employer had discriminated against her on the grounds of sex by paying her less (calculated on an hourly basis) than full-time employees. The number of employees involved was important. There were 49 full-time female employees and 34 full-time male employees, five female and one male part-time employee. Jenkins brought her case in the Employment Appeals Tribunal in the UK, which referred a number of questions to the European Court. At the Employment Appeals Tribunal, the employer had argued strongly that the clear discrimination which it operated (the different rates of pay) was not based on sex but on the genuine concern of the employer to prevent absenteeism, and ensure that as many employees as possible worked full-time so that machinery was fully utilised. The European Court in its judgment stated that a policy that affected part-time employees could amount to indirect discrimination on the grounds of sex if it affected a disproportionate number of one sex in comparison with the other and could not be objectively justified by factors not related to sex.[73]

16.51 In *Bilka-Kaufhaus*, the European Court followed the principle in *Jenkins*. In *Bilka*, the Court had to consider indirect discrimination in the context of a dispute related to the right of access to a pension scheme. Rates of pay for full-time and part-time employees were the same, but only full-time employees were eligible for membership of the company pension scheme. Again, the numbers of full and part-time employees concerned were important. Seventy-two per cent of Bilka's employees were female and 28 per cent were male. Ninety per cent of the males worked full-time and 61.5 per cent of females were full-time. This meant that, having regard to the workforce as a whole 2.8 per cent were male part-timers whilst 27.7 per cent were female part-timers — a ratio of one man to ten women. The European Court referred to *Jenkins*, stating that the cases were comparable because whilst wage levels were equal for Bilka's full and part-time employ-

---

72 [1981] 2 CMLR 24.

73 The opinion of Advocate General Warner in *Jenkins* is worth reading as it sets out the reasoning for the approach taken by the European Court. This reasoning has influenced the subsequent decisions on part-timers. It is of academic interest to note that the employer was not represented before the European Court. This was, apparently, for financial reasons. Unfortunately, it meant that the employer's position was not fully argued before the Court.

ees, pensions constituted "pay" for the purposes of Article 119 and as part-time employees did not receive pensions they were being paid less. The Court held:

> . . . Article 119 of the EEC Treaty is infringed by a department store company which excludes part-time employees from its occupational pension scheme where that exclusion affects a much greater number of women than men, unless the enterprise shows that the exclusion is based on objectively justified factors which are unrelated to any discrimination based on sex.[74]

16.52 The European Court followed the approach taken in *Jenkins*, in that it stated the principles involved in determining whether Article 119 was infringed, but left it to the national court to decide whether in fact the apparent discrimination operated by the employer could be objectively justified for economic reasons. The European Court clarified two other points. It stated that it was not enough for the employer to show that it had no positive intention to discriminate against one sex in order to avoid a finding that Article 119 had been infringed. Bilka, in its defence, had argued that it had intended to discriminate against part time workers not against females — the objective was to encourage full-time work by making it comparatively less attractive to work part-time. The European Court also confirmed that Article 119 did not require employers to take positive steps to structure their pension schemes so as to take account of the family commitments of female employees which prevented them from fulfilling the conditions for entitlement to pensions. This was a policy issue for Member States and was outside the ambit of Article 119. Thus, Article 119 does not create a positive obligation to do something, but rather a negative obligation not to discriminate.

16.53 The Equality Directive (86/378/EEC) was subsequently enacted into Irish law in the Pensions Act. Provisions relating to indirect discrimination in relation to pension schemes are set out in section 67. It may be noted that whereas the European Court in interpreting Article 119 stated that what might *prima facie* be sex discrimination would be permitted if it were shown to be based on "objectively justified" factors unrelated to sex, the equivalent provision in the Pensions Act[75] prohibited a condition or requirement "which is not justifiable irrespective of the sex of the persons to whom it applies". These

---

74 [1986] 2 CMLR 701 at 720.

75 s.67(3)(c)(ii).

provisions have now been amended by inclusion of the word "objectively" before "justifiable" by section 30 of the Pensions (Amendment) Act, 1996 to bring them in line with the requirements of Article 119.[76]

16.54 A claim for indirect discrimination in relation to access to a pension scheme for part-time workers would appear to involve a two-stage process. It is necessary for the claimant, both under Article 119 and under the Pensions Act, to establish that the practice or rule of the employer affects a "substantially higher" or "much greater number" of one sex than the other.[77] If the claimant is unable to make this case, it is unnecessary for the employer to justify the practice. Unfortunately, there is no precise meaning to either of the expressions. In some cases the numbers will be straightforward — there will be a limited number of work grades and a large percentage difference between the numbers of one sex and that of the other. However, there will also be cases where there is a multiplicity of grades and types of job, and numbers will be less clear-cut.[78]

16.55 If the claimant is able to establish a case that the employer's practice *prima facie* constitutes discrimination on the grounds of sex, it will be necessary for the employer to attempt to justify the policy. The European Court in *Bilka*, in referring to objective justification of apparent discrimination, stated:

> It falls to the national court, which alone is competent to assess the facts, to decide whether, and if so to what extent, the grounds put

---

76 There is evidence that this is the standard that has been applied by equality officers in cases under the equal pay legislation — see *St Patrick's College Maynooth* v. *Nineteen Female Employees* EP4/1984, DEP 10/1984.

77 The former expression is used in the Pensions Act and the latter in the decisions of the European Court — it is suggested that they can be treated for practical purposes as the same. Neither expression, unfortunately, has a precise meaning.

78 An example of the difficulties presented to a claimant can be seen in *Stafford* v. *FNBS* [EE 04/1995] — a claim under the Employment Equality Act, 1977. The European Commission, in February 1996, submitted proposals to European employer and trades union organisations to change the burden of proof to bring it in line with European Court case law. These proposals will be considered in accordance with the Maastricht Social Protocol to which Ireland is a signatory.

> forward by an employer to explain the adoption of a pay practice which it applies irrespective of the employee's sex, but which in fact affects more women then men, can be considered to be objectively justified for economic reasons. If the national court finds that the means chosen by *Bilka* meet a genuine need of the enterprise, that they are suitable for attaining the objective pursued by the enterprise and are necessary for that purpose, the fact that the measures in question affect a much greater number of women than men is not sufficient to conclude that they involve a breach of Article 119.

16.56 It seems clear that there are therefore three criteria, being:

1. The means chosen should meet a genuine economic need of the employer
2. The means chosen should be suitable for attaining the objective
3. The means chosen should be necessary for that purpose.

16.57 The last criterion is a variation of the familiar "proportionality test" applied in EU law to exceptions to a general principle. If an employer can demonstrate that the policy meets an economic need and is suitable for that purpose but it can be shown that another method could achieve the same economic need but without the discriminatory effect, then the employer will be in breach of the equality principle if it choses a method which is not, strictly, necessary.

16.58 The European Court in the *Fisscher* case[79] confirmed that a right of access to a pension scheme should not mean that those persons previously excluded on sex-discrimination grounds should have any greater rights than those persons already members of the scheme. This means that if the scheme is contributory, part-timers granted access on a retrospective basis will have to pay the back contributions. The European Court did not address the issue of whether or not the new members would also have to pay any additional amount to represent the investment return that would have been achieved by those contributions if they had been invested at the correct time.

---

79 [1994] PLR 243.

Limitations on Actions

16.59 It is not at all certain what, if any, temporal limitations currently exist in relation to potential claims for indirect discrimination in relation to access. A claim could be brought in any of the following circumstances:

1. By a current part-time employee in relation to a scheme that contains provisions excluding part-time employees
2. By a current part-time employee who has been admitted to a scheme that previously excluded part-time employees
3. By a former employee who worked part-time for an employer operating a scheme that excluded part-time employees

In the above situations, different time limits (or even no time limit) may apply, depending on whether the claim is brought under the Pensions Act, Article 119 or the Anti-Discrimination (Pay) Act, 1974.

16.60 On the question of time limits for claims under Article 119, the European Court in *Fisscher*[80] stated:

> . . . in the absence of Community rules on the matter, the national rules relating to time-limits for bringing actions are also applicable to actions based on Community law, provided that they are no less favourable for such actions than for similar actions of a domestic nature and that they do not render the exercise of rights conferred by Community law impossible in practice.

16.61 The comparable time limits under Irish law would appear to be those contained in the Anti-Discrimination (Pay) Act, 1974, if a claim is brought under that Act or under Article 119 by an employee. In the case of former employees, the time limits contained in the Statute of Limitations, 1957 (as amended) would appear to apply if the claim is brought under Article 119. The 1974 Act contemplates only claims by employees, and does not therefore impose a time limit on the commencement of a claim.[81] However, the Act does restrict the

---

80 The Equality Cases [1994] PLR 243 at para. 250.

81 If an employee is being discriminated against in relation to their employment, then logically that discrimination is ongoing during their employment and a time limit for bringing the claim is inappropriate; see

arrears of remuneration which may be awarded to such as accrued in the three years prior to the date on which the dispute was referred to an equality officer.[82] In the case of a claim by a former employee under Article 119 the limitation period under the 1957 Act would be that applicable to a claim in simple contract, being six years.[83]

16.62 The limitations applying to a claim brought under the Pensions Act for indirect discrimination as regards access to a scheme are more problematic. Such a claim would be for failure by the employer to comply with section 70 of the Act.[84] The Act does not set out any time limit. It may be argued that the effect of section 70 is to confer a contractual right on the part-time employee, to which claim the limitation period of six years under the 1957 Act would apply. The matter is by no means certain and it would be appropriate for the Pensions Act to be amended to provide for time limits on the bringing of claims.

16.63 It would appear that the compulsory levelling-up provisions in section 71 of the Pensions Act can apply in the case of part-time employees who are excluded from pension schemes if such exclusion amounts to sex discrimination. If such discriminatory provisions existed in a scheme on 17 May 1990, section 71(1) will operate and the relevant rule will be rendered null and void and the more favourable treatment accorded under the rules of the scheme to persons of the one sex will be applied to those of the other sex. It is not entirely clear whether or not the transitional provisions in section 71(3) will apply.[85] The doubt is caused by reference in sub-section 3 to prior "periods of membership". Part-timers excluded from the scheme will not have any such periods of membership. It is suggested that the deferral was intended to apply and the doubt should be removed by appropriate amendment of the section.

---

also the House of Lords decision in *Barclays Bank plc* v. *Kapur* [1991] PLR 45.

82 s.8(5) of the 1974 Act.

83 s.11 of the 1957 Act. At this stage there have been no Irish reported cases with respect to time limitations. The matter has been considered in the UK, (which saw a very large number of claims filed after the *Fisscher* and *Vroege* decisions), in *Preston* v. *Wolverhampton Healthcare NHS Trust* [1996] PLR 363. It is expected that these cases will be appealed.

84 This section requires an employer to apply the equal-treatment principle as regards access to a pension scheme. See para. 16.30.

85 See para. 16.36 above.

OTHER EQUAL TREATMENT ISSUES

Contributions

16.64 It is settled that ordinary contributions of employees to schemes must be the same for men and women.[86] Additional voluntary contributions of employees are not required to be equal.[87] The right to make additional voluntary contributions, if given by the rules of the scheme, must be given to males and females. Where employers' contributions to a defined benefit scheme differ between males and females, because of the use of actuarial factors, this is permitted by Article 119.[88]

16.65 There is, however, no guidance in the European Court judgments to date with respect to employer contributions to defined contribution schemes. Nor is there guidance regarding contributions by employers to match AVCs paid by employees. The draft directive amending the 1986 Equality Directive proposes that employer contributions to defined contribution schemes must be equal for both sexes, except that different levels of contributions will be permitted where this is necessary to take account of actuarial factors which differ according to sex.[89] The Pensions Act at present makes provision for this.[90]

Transfer Payments

16.66 In *Coloroll*, the European Court ruled that on a transfer of pension rights from one occupational pension scheme to another, the member concerned should not be prejudiced because the first scheme failed to comply with the principle of equal treatment. The European Court stated that:

> . . . in the event of the transfer of pension rights from one occupational scheme to another owing to a worker's change of job, the second scheme is obliged, on the worker reaching retirement age, to increase the benefits it undertook to pay him when accepting the transfer so as to eliminate the effects, contrary to Article 119, suffered by the worker in consequence of the inadequacy of the capital transferred, this being due in turn to the discriminatory treatment suffered under the first scheme, and it must do so in

---

86 *Neath* v. *Hugh Steeper Ltd.*

87 *Coloroll.*

88 *Neath* v. *Hugh Steeper Ltd.*

89 Proposed new Article 6 of Directive 86/378/EEC.

90 s.69(1)(b).

relation to benefits payable in respect of periods of service subsequent to 17 May 1990.

16.67 This requirement places very practical difficulties before trustees of both the transferring scheme and the receiving scheme. It is clear from *Barber* and *Coloroll* that trustees are obliged to administer a pension scheme in accordance with the principle of equal treatment. This is also required by Part VII of the Pensions Act.[91] The trustees of the transferring scheme, if aware of an inequality in the scheme, must administer the scheme in a manner which removes that inequality. However, if there are inadequate funds in the scheme for this purpose, the trustees have no guidance from the European Court as to how to proceed.[92] Pursuant to the preservation requirements of Part III of the Pensions Act, trustees of a receiving scheme are obliged to accept a transfer payment with respect to a member's preserved entitlement. Some trustees may consider refusing to accept a transfer except with respect to that portion which represents the preserved entitlement under the Pensions Act. However, it is understood with regard to exempt approved schemes that the Revenue Commissioners insist that a full transfer be made. This could present problems for an employer hiring a new employee. In the case of individual changes of employment, the trustees of a receiving scheme may find practical difficulties in trying to ascertain whether the transferring scheme has complied with the principle of equal treatment. It is suggested that these difficulties are less likely to arise in the case of bulk transfers in mergers and acquisitions situations, as it is usual in such cases that there will have been an investigation as to the funding and administration of the transferring scheme, and specific queries can be raised both of trustees and the employer as to compliance with the equal treatment provisions.

DETERMINATION OF DISPUTES UNDER THE PENSIONS ACT

Types of Dispute

16.68 Part VII of the Pensions Act contains provisions for determination of disputes which may arise in connection with equality issues. sections 75 and 76 of the Act refer to "dispute", but the word is not defined. The word would therefore appear to have its ordinary

---

91 s.66.

92 This question was raised in *Coloroll* but the European Court left the matter to national courts to determine.

meaning. Broadly, section 75 deals with disputes relating to occupational pension schemes, and these are to be referred to the Pensions Board. Section 76 deals with disputes concerning occupational benefit schemes which are not also occupational pension schemes, and these disputes are to be referred to an equality officer.

16.69 The Act provides that the Pensions Board is to determine any dispute in relation to the following[93]:

1. Whether a scheme is a defined contribution scheme for the purposes of Part VII
2. Whether any rule of an occupational pension scheme complies with the principle of equal treatment
3. Whether and to what extent any such rule is rendered null and void by the compulsory levelling-up provisions of section 71.

Any such matter may be referred to the Board by written application by the trustees of a scheme, an employer, a member or a prospective member, any agent to the scheme and an authorised trade union representing a member or members of the scheme.[94] The Employment Equality Agency may also refer a matter to the Pensions Board for determination. The Act provides that the determination of the Board may be appealed on a point of law to the High Court by the person who made the application to the Board or any other person who was entitled to make such application.[95] A decision of the High Court on appeal would be binding on the parties. It is not clear that a determination of the Board has binding force. The Pensions Act in section 26

---

93 s.75(1).

94 s.75(1) provides that those persons who may make an application under the section are the same as those persons mentioned in s.38(3) of the Act. s.38(3) specifies the trustees, the employer, members and prospective members and such other persons as may be prescribed by Regulation. By Article 10 of Occupational Pension Schemes (Preservation of Benefits) Regulations, 1992 (SI No 445 of 1992) the Minister added to the list in s.38 agents of the scheme and authorised trade unions. An agent of the scheme is defined in Article 2 of those Regulations as including the actuaries, auditors and other accountants and financial and other advisors to the scheme.

95 s.75(3).

contains detailed provisions in relation to the procedures for the making of determinations by the Board.

16.70 Any dispute as to whether:

- a rule of an occupational benefit scheme, other than an occupational pension scheme, complies with the principle of equal treatment
- and to what extent any such rule is rendered null and void by section 71
- any term of an employment regulation, order or collective agreement or contract of employment insofar as it relates to occupational benefits provided under a scheme of the type referred to above complies with the principle of equal treatment
- an employer complies with the provisions of section 70[96]

must be referred by any person concerned to an equality officer for investigation and recommendation.[97] This is in accordance with the recommendation of the National Pensions Board,[98] which concluded that many such disputes would involve issues that would not entirely concern occupational pension schemes, such as questions of equal work, certain forms of indirect discrimination and other conditions of employment. The National Pensions Board considered that the Pensions Board (the statutory body established under the Pensions Act)

---

96 s.70 requires the employer to comply with the principle of equal treatment in relation to the manner in which it affords its employees access to a pension scheme. If a rule of a scheme limits eligibility to full-time employees, this may infringe the equal-treatment principle (see para. 16.50 above with respect to part-timers). In such case, there is a potential infringement of both s.70 and s.67(1). A dispute regarding infringement of s.67(1) must be referred under s.75 to the Pensions Board whereas if the dispute is brought under s.70 it must be referred to an equality officer. The Act would appear to give the employee a choice as to the avenue of redress. This is probably an oversight in the drafting of the Act. Certainly, a dispute as to whether a pension scheme complies with the principle of equal treatment should, it is suggested, be more properly addressed to the Pensions Board.

97 s.76.

98 At para. 15.9 of the Board's Report on "Equal Treatment for Men and Women in Occupational Pension Schemes" .

would not have the necessary competence to deal with cases involving dismissal of employees resulting from such matters.

16.71 Pursuant to section 76, any of the above matters may be referred to an equality officer by any person concerned. A matter may also be referred by the Employment Equality Agency. The equality officer has a duty to investigate the matter referred and to issue a recommendation. The difficulty with the provisions is that the recommendation of the equality officer is not binding. If nothing further is done after the issue of the recommendation the matter could end there and the applicant will be no better off. Section 77 of the Act provides that a person may appeal to the Labour Court:

1. Against the recommendation
2. For a determination that the recommendation has not been complied with.

16.72 An appeal can be made only within 42 days of the date the equality officer issues the recommendation. The appeal procedure is straightforward and merely requires that a letter be addressed to the Chairman of the Labour Court. The Labour Court may hear the appeal in public or private and shall make a determination.[99] The Court has the power to make a number of determinations as set out under the Pensions Act.[100]

16.73 The Pensions Act provides for circumstances in which a determination of the Labour Court under section 78 is not implemented. Any person concerned (or the Employment Equality Agency if it made a referral to the Court) may complain to the Labour Court that its determination has not been implemented. The Court, having investigated the matter, may make such order as it considers necessary directing the person failing to implement its determination to take the action necessary to implement it.[101] Failure to comply with such an order is an offence punishable, on conviction, by fine or imprisonment.[102]

---

[99] s.77(2).

[100] s.78 as amended by s.35 of the Pensions (Amendment) Act, 1996.

[101] s.79(1).

[102] s.79(2).

16.74 The equality provisions in the Pensions Act penalise certain types of dismissals. These are where employees are dismissed solely or mainly because, in good faith, they have made a reference under the Pensions Act relating to equality, or have given evidence in proceedings under the Act, or have notified their employer that they intend to do either of those things. In such cases, the employer shall be guilty of an offence and liable on summary conviction to a fine or to imprisonment.[103] The Pensions Act further provides that, on conviction of an employer for the stated offence, the Court may make such order as it sees fit relating to the dismissed employee including an order for reinstatement or an order for re-engagement, or may impose a fine on the employer, such fine being relative to the remuneration that would have been received by the dismissed person. These powers are similar to the powers of the Employment Appeals Tribunal under the unfair dismissals legislation.[104]

16.75 Apart from the specific matters referred to in the preceding paragraphs, because all occupational benefit schemes must comply with the principle of equal treatment under the Pensions Act,[105] the trustees of those schemes are under an obligation to apply that principle. If they fail to do so, they may be liable to prosecution for breach of the Act.[106] It would be a defence to a prosecution for the trustee to prove that the contravention to which the offence relates was attributable to a contravention by some other person of a provision of the Act and that the trustee took such reasonable steps (if any) in the circumstances as were possible to secure compliance by such other person. Breach of the equality requirements would also expose the employer to the risk of prosecution under the Pensions Act.

THE EUROPEAN CONVENTION ON HUMAN RIGHTS

16.76 Ireland is a signatory of this Convention and has ratified a number of the Protocols[107] to the Convention. The Convention is not

---

103 s.80(1).

104 As to the powers of the Employment Appeals Tribunal and with respect to disputes concerning pension entitlements see para. 5.43 et seq.

105 s.66.

106 s.3(1)(a).

107 The Convention has been amended from time to time by Protocols.

part of Irish law but it confers rights on Ireland as against other Convention signatories and on citizens of Ireland as against Convention signatories including Ireland. It cannot be relied on by an individual against another individual or an employer. The Convention may, however, provide an additional basis for an equality claim. Article 14 of the Convention provides:

> The enjoyment of the rights and freedoms set forth in [the] Convention shall be secured without discrimination on any ground such as sex, race, colour, language, religion, political or other opinion, national or social origin, association with a national minority, property, birth or other status.

16.77 In *Schuler-Zgraggen* v *Switzerland*,[108] a Swiss national succeeded in her claim before the European Court of Human Rights that the decision of the Swiss Federal Insurance Court with respect to her claim for invalidity pension was discriminatory on the basis of sex and therefore infringed her rights under Article 14 and Article 6 (right to a fair hearing). A claimant before the European Court might consider, if appropriate, an additional ground of claim under the Convention. The European Court has indicated in its decisions that it may apply the provisions of the Convention.[109] To date, however, there has not been a reported case in which the Convention has been successfully relied on in relation to pension entitlements before the European Court.

---

108 [1995] PLR 159.

109 See the Second Nold judgment [1974] ECR 491, also Case 36/75 *Rutili* v. *Minister for the Interior* [1975] ECR 1219.

17

WINDING-UP OF PENSION SCHEMES

INTRODUCTION

17.1 This chapter examines the various circumstances in which a pension scheme may be wound up, the provisions usually found in pension scheme documentation dealing with winding up, the issues that may arise on the insolvency of an employer and the possibility of a pension scheme fund being either in surplus or in deficit at that point. There is no legislative obligation to wind up a pension scheme nor is this a requirement of the Revenue Commissioners. It is usual for non-commercial public sector pension schemes not to be established under trust. Being unfunded arrangements, many are also not subject to Part IV of the Pensions Act. For these reasons, many such schemes do not need to make provision for the manner in which the pension scheme will be dealt with on termination. The possibility that such schemes would require to be wound up may be regarded as remote. This chapter will deal with the winding-up of funded pension schemes established under trust.

17.2 Termination of a pension scheme can arise in a variety of situations. It may happen that the employer is quite solvent and continuing in business but has decided to terminate the pension scheme. It should be said that in practice and except in connection with company or pension restructurings,[1] this is an unlikely scenario given the adverse industrial relations consequences on the employer. Alternatively, the employer may be bankrupt or insolvent, but the scheme may be solvent. A further possibility is that both the employer and the scheme are insolvent. These different circumstances will present their own difficulties and are dealt with below. If established under trust, the formal trust documentation should contain detailed provisions dealing with the manner in which the fund of the scheme is to

---

1 See Chapter 18.

be distributed on winding up. The absence of such provisions will present difficulties to the trustees as they will have no guidance as to how the fund of the pension scheme is to be distributed. In such cases it may be necessary for the trustees to make application to the Courts for directions.[2]

TERMINATION OF SCHEME

Reasons for Termination

17.3 There are several reasons why a pension scheme may need to be terminated:

1. A pension scheme is designed to operate over a long period of time and the economic conditions in which the employer conducts business may change. It is usual for the sponsoring employer to reserve to itself the right to amend or terminate the pension scheme, either in defined circumstances or generally.
2. Provision may be made for termination of the scheme in the event of bankruptcy or liquidation of the employer.
3. The trustees of a scheme established under trust will usually have power to terminate the scheme in the event that the employer fails to pay contributions to the scheme or is in breach of its terms in some other way.
4. Termination may be required in the event of insolvency of the fund.[3]
5. The pension scheme may provide for its termination on the expiry of a specified trust period.[4]

17.4 The employer may decide, for its own reasons, that the scheme should be terminated. This is usually provided for in the pension scheme documentation by a clause allowing the employer to give notice to the trustees of its intention to cease to pay contributions. It is

---

2 See para. 3.25 et seq. and paras. 3.43 et seq.

3 In practice, this should apply only in the case of a defined benefit scheme.

4 Such provisions were included to take account of the Rule Against Perpetuities. This rule is now disapplied in the case of pension schemes by s.61A of the Pensions Act as inserted by s.25 of the Pensions (Amendment) Act, 1996. See para. 3.27

important to distinguish between a notice by the employer that it intends to cease to pay contributions to the scheme and a temporary suspension of the employer's liability to contribute — a "contribution holiday". Where a scheme is temporarily overfunded, an employer, usually on the advice of the scheme actuary, may suspend payment of contributions for a temporary period. The formal trust documentation should allow the employer to take such a "contribution holiday" without triggering a winding-up of the pension scheme. Contribution holidays are taken only with respect to defined benefit pension schemes and will usually require trustee consent.

Partial Winding-up

17.5 In the case of a group scheme, provision should be made for what is commonly referred to as a "partial winding-up".[5] This would occur where an individual participating employer (other than the sponsoring employer) notifies the scheme trustees of its intention to cease to contribute to the pension scheme, ceases to carry on business, becomes insolvent or is dissolved, or fails to make payment of contributions to the pension scheme following demand by the trustees. Whether or not a group exists, it is now usual in practice for the formal trust documentation to contain such provisions. Where there are several employers it is usual that participating employers can terminate their liability to contribute, thus triggering a partial windup. Only the principal employer, however, can trigger a full winding-up of the scheme by such notice.

Alternatives to Winding-up

17.6 It may not be necessary to terminate the scheme in certain of the circumstances listed above. An employer may determine to close membership of its pension scheme (that is, not admit new members) but to continue the scheme for existing members. Such a scheme is called a "closed scheme". An employer might do this to reduce its future liabilities for employee benefits. The trust deed should contain a provision allowing closure of the scheme in this manner. Further amendment to the eligibility rules of the scheme may be required.

---

5 It should be noted that "partial winding-ups" are not specifically recognised by the Pensions Act and are not, therefore, the subject of specific provisions of that Act. In the UK, the pensions Act, 1995 has specific regulations governing the conduct of partial winding-ups.

17.7 If the employer has given notice terminating its liability to contribute to the scheme or the employer is insolvent or bankrupt, the trustees of a pension scheme may have the option to defer the termination of the scheme and to continue it as a frozen scheme. Such a scheme is one to which no new members may be admitted and in which the existing members do not accrue any future benefits. Their benefits are, effectively, frozen.

17.8 If required by the trust deed or if the trustees exercise any discretion they have under the deed to wind up the scheme, then the pension scheme must be formally wound up and the fund of the scheme distributed. The trust deed should and usually will contain detailed provisions as to the manner in which the fund is to be dealt with on a winding-up. In addition, there are certain Revenue and Pensions Act requirements. The requirements with which trustees must comply are now considered.

REGULATORY REQUIREMENTS

Requirements of the Revenue Commissioners

17.9 The Revenue Commissioners, whilst requiring that a pension scheme should provide for circumstances in which it may be terminated, do not have any particular requirements as to the priority of payments on winding-up. They stipulate that benefits be secured by transfer payments to other approved schemes or by the purchase of deferred non-assignable annuity contracts or other suitable policies or buy-out bonds. They further require that the scheme should provide for the payment of any ultimate surplus to the employer.[6]

17.10 Any benefit secured on the winding-up of a scheme other than by means of a transfer payment to a new scheme should not exceed the maximum benefit which would be approvable if the employee concerned had withdrawn from service on the date when the benefit was determined.[7]

17.11 Any moneys refunded to the sponsoring employer as surplus on a winding-up are liable to tax under section 23 of the Finance Act, 1972. As the employer will usually be carrying on a business, the re-

---

6 Revenue Practice Notes.

7 Revenue Practice Notes.

fund will be taxed as a receipt of the trade or profession.[8] If the employer is not conducting a business, the refund is chargeable under Case IV of Schedule D. In the case of the wind-up of a group scheme, the Revenue require that any surplus which is ultimately repayable be divided among the participating employers, either in the ratios in which the employers have previously contributed to the fund, or on some other basis agreed with the Revenue.

17.12 Where a scheme is terminated, benefits must be secured either by means of transfer payments to other approved pension schemes or by the purchase as appropriate of immediate or deferred non-assignable annuity contracts or other suitable policies from life offices. Benefits under the scheme will be either immediate benefits (for example, pensions in payment) or deferred (for example, accrued entitlements). Immediate benefits must be secured by immediate annuities, and deferred benefits will be secured under bonds (either deferred annuities or investment policies). Benefits secured should be in annuity form except to the extent that the Revenue allows lump sums to be payable to the former members when the deferred annuity becomes payable at normal retirement age (under the terms of the scheme) or at any earlier date on the grounds of incapacity.

17.13 The Retirement Benefits District of the Revenue permits benefits to be provided either by the assignment to individual employees of paid-up insurance or annuity policies already held for the purposes of the pension scheme, or by purchase of an annuity bond in the employee's own name. On winding-up of a scheme with a single member, it is clearly of benefit that the trustees can assign any existing policy. The winding-up clause in the trust deed must give the trustees power to do this. In the case of schemes with a number of members, the trustees will usually purchase individual buy-out bonds.

17.14 In the case of the winding-up of a small self-administered scheme this may only be effected with the consent of the pensioneer trustee and in accordance with a winding-up rule which has been previously approved by the Revenue.[9]

---

[8] See para. 6.44 et seq.

[9] See para. 6.80.

Pensions Act

17.15 Before the Pensions Act there were no Irish statutory requirements relating to priority of payments on winding-up of a pension scheme. This matter was left entirely to the trust documentation of individual pension schemes. Provided that there are sufficient moneys in the pension scheme fund, the order of priority of payments is not an issue. All the beneficiaries under the scheme, whether pensioners, deferred pensioners or persons in active service, will receive the immediate or deferred benefits to which they are entitled. Priority of payments becomes an issue where there is an insufficiency in the pension scheme fund. This issue should therefore arise only in relation to a defined benefit scheme. In a defined contribution scheme, contributions received and the investment return on such contributions are individually allocated to specific members. In the event of the winding-up of a defined contribution scheme, a member's entitlement is directly linked to the value of the contributions that have been allocated to that member. In the absence of fraud, the fund of a defined contribution scheme should match the liabilities of the scheme. The adequacy of a defined benefit scheme is, however, dependent upon proper funding. Section 48 of the Pensions Act sets out the order of priorities on the winding-up of a defined benefit scheme.[10] As amended by section 17 of the Pensions (Amendment) Act, 1996, section 48 now provides that the resources of a defined benefit scheme which has been wound up after 1 January 1997 must be applied in the following order of priority:

1. Pensions in course of payment or due to or in respect of members who had then reached normal retirement age
2. Additional benefits secured for or granted to or in respect of a member or former member of the scheme as a result of a transfer payment or the payment of additional voluntary contributions and, also, preserved benefits under Part III of the Pensions Act in respect of members and former members.[11]
3. All benefits not preserved under the Pensions Act.

---

10 s.53(1) of the Pensions Act provides that s.48 (and all of Part IV of the Act) overrides any provisions in the rules of a scheme to the contrary.

11 s.48(1)(a).

17.16 The Pensions Act gives the trustees the power, notwithstanding anything contained in the rules of the pension scheme and without the consent of the member concerned, to discharge the liability of the scheme for the benefits payable to or in respect of a member, either by making a transfer to another exempt approved scheme or by purchasing a buy-out bond.[12]

17.17 Section 48(2) provides that nothing in section 48 requires liabilities for benefits to be discharged before liabilities for expenses, fees and costs associated with the winding-up of the scheme. This language differs from section 48 as previously enacted. Prior to the amendment of section 48 there was a mandatory requirement that expenses, costs and fees relating to and associated with the winding-up of the scheme be paid in priority to any other claims on the scheme. The amended section means that the rules of the scheme will apply with respect to payment of the costs and expenses associated with winding up. As a practical matter, it will be appreciated that if provision is not made for payment of fees and expenses related to the winding-up of a scheme, the winding-up itself will in all probability not be properly concluded.[13]

17.18 Under the Disclosure Regulations made under the Pensions Act,[14] trustees of pension schemes now have a statutory obligation to disclose specific information to members of schemes on termination of employment and on winding-up of the scheme. Before the Pensions Act there were no regulations dealing with the obligations of trustees to disclose information on winding-up of a pension scheme. The information that must now be made available on termination of employment is set out in the regulations and differs depending on whether the scheme is a defined benefit scheme or a defined contribution scheme and also on whether or not the member has a pre-

---

[12] s.48(1)(b).

[13] The provisions for priority in respect of payments on the winding-up of a company as set out in s.285 Companies Act, 1963 should be noted. s.285(8) provides that such sums as may be necessary to meet the costs and expenses of the winding-up have priority over those listed in s.285(2) as the preferential debts of a company.

[14] The Occupational Pension Schemes (Disclosure of Information) Regulations, 1991 (SI No 215 of 1991).

served entitlement under the Pensions Act.[15] The details to be furnished on winding-up of a scheme are set out in the Regulations[16] and are briefly:

1. Information relating to the rights and options available to the member regarding benefit entitlements
2. An explanation as to the manner in which any surplus or deficit in the resources of the scheme is being dealt with
3. Information as to who will be liable to pay the benefits after the scheme is wound up and the address for inquiries.

17.19 The Regulations require that the notification to members must be made as soon as possible, and in any event no later than 12 weeks after the decision to wind up has been made.[17] The Regulations are not clear on the point but it is presumed that the decision referred to is a decision of the trustees to wind up. This raises the possibility that if for some reason, such as lack of quorum, no formal trustee resolution is passed, then the disclosure obligation does not appear to arise. However, the winding-up itself does not of necessity depend on a decision of the trustees. It may, under the terms of the trust deed, be triggered by some other event, such as the employer being declared insolvent.

THE TRUST DOCUMENTATION

17.20 It is important that the formal trust documentation should set out clearly how the trustees are to distribute the fund of the pension scheme on winding-up. The winding-up clause should direct the trustees to collect the assets of the fund and then to distribute those assets to the beneficiaries in accordance with their entitlements under the scheme. The beneficiaries will be:

1. Pensioners
2. Active Members who have reached normal retirement date

---

15 *Ibid.* at Article 12 and Schedule E. See also Chapter 13 at paras. 13.40 to 13.42.

16 Article 14 of the Regulations.

17 Article 14(a) of the Regulations.

3. Deferred Pensioners
4. Active Members who have not reached normal retirement date
5. Spouses and other dependent beneficiaries of any of the above

17.21 The winding-up clause should direct the trustees as to how they should deal with any shortfall or surplus in the assets of the fund. The trustees will also be directed to discharge the costs incurred with respect to the winding-up. The winding-up provision should allow the trustees to secure benefits by means of purchasing immediate annuities or buy-out bonds in the names of the members, so that ultimately the pension scheme itself will be left without any liabilities and the winding-up may be concluded. As already noted above,[18] the Pensions Act has imposed specific priorities on winding-up with respect to defined benefit schemes. In the case of such schemes it is now good practice for the formal trust documentation to be amended to incorporate these statutory provisions. In any event, the provisions of the Pensions Act override any contrary terms in the trust deed with respect to winding-up requirements under the Act.[19] The rules of the pension scheme will govern priorities not covered by the Act.

17.22 It is not entirely clear whether a power of amendment in a pension scheme deed may be exercised after the happening of a winding-up event. This will usually depend on the terms of the winding-up clause. If the clause provides that the scheme shall determine and be wound up on the happening of certain events, it is difficult to see how any provisions in the trust deed other then those dealing specifically with winding-up could still be operative. In the English case, *Jones* v. *Williams*,[20] the Court had to consider the validity of a deed of amendment executed after a winding-up event had taken place. The Court stated:

> . . . once [the winding-up clause came into operation] so that the trusts constituted by that Deed determined it ceased to be possible thereafter to operate machinery for varying those trusts. The remainder of the clause contains dispositive directions in mandatory

---

[18] See para. 17.15.

[19] ss.36(1) and 53(1).

[20] [1989] PLR 17.

terms and it would in my view be illogical to treat a power to alter the trusts as surviving the determination of the trusts.[21]

17.23 As with other provisions of a pension trust (including provisions conferring indemnity on trustees) it appears from the decisions that it is possible for a power of amendment to remain operable after a winding-up event has taken place, provided that the power of amendment clause or the winding-up clause expressly allows it. In practice, this is unlikely as the winding-up clause in the trust deed is usually drafted in such manner as to set out precisely how the employer wishes the scheme to be dealt with on a winding-up and such intent would be defeated if a power of amendment could be exercised after the winding-up clause had become operable. If a winding-up is to be effected as part of a reorganisation or for some other such purpose, and not as a result of an insolvency, care should be taken to ensure that the deed and rules of the scheme are in an acceptable form prior to the date of commencement of the winding-up as it may not be possible to alter them after that date.

THE ROLE OF THE TRUSTEES

Securing Benefits

17.24 Aspects of the trustees' role on winding-up of a pension scheme have already been touched on in this chapter. As always, their primary duty is to carry out the terms of the trust. In so doing, the trustees must deal equally with all beneficiaries — not preferring one particular claim to another (unless the trust deed directs otherwise). The trustees will have to distribute the fund in accordance with the winding-up provisions and discharge the liabilities arising on the winding-up. The primary guide to the trustees is the winding-up rule in the Trust Deed. If this is clear, the trustees need only follow those provisions.[22] If it is unclear in some respect, the trustees may require legal advice.

17.25 To determine the liabilities of the scheme and to prioritise the claimants under the scheme, it is important that the trustees can fix the date on which the winding-up actually commences. In *Re H. Wil-*

---

21 Per Knox J. at p.21. See also *Thrells Ltd. (1974) Pension Scheme (In Liquidation)* v. *Lomas* [1992] PLR 233 per Nicholls V-C at p.237.

22 To the extent its provisions are not overridden by terms of the Pensions Act — for example, s.48.

liams and Company Pension Fund,[23] the Court was asked to determine this question. In that case, the employer was ordered to be wound up by the High Court on 9 November 1987. However, the process of realisation of the pension fund only commenced after a substantial lapse of time. The Court ruled that, on the basis of the trust documentation, the date of winding-up of the pension scheme was also 9 November 1987, because under the trust deed the pension scheme was required to be wound up on the happening of the first of certain stated events, in this case being the making of an order to wind up the employer.

17.26 For pensioners, the trustees will wish to secure benefits and to ensure that the scheme has no further liability in respect of those persons. This is always done by purchasing an immediate annuity contract from a life office and is now usually bought in the name of the member.[24] The winding-up clause should permit the trustees to purchase the annuity in the name of the member. In any event, the Pensions Act permits the trustees of a scheme to apply the resources of the scheme in this manner.[25] In the case of deferred pensioners and members who were in service and who are not entitled to immediate pensions, the trustees will purchase buy-out bonds. A buy-out bond is proposed by the trustees but will be a direct contract between the member and the life office and will include a discharge to the scheme and the trustees in respect of any further liability. Because the contract is directly with the life office, the scheme is not required to maintain records in respect of the entitlements of the deferred pensioners. Those entitlements have been "bought out". Deferred pensioners and active members will usually be offered a choice as to the form of buy-out fund from which their entitlements will be paid. The bond may, for example, be a unit-linked policy, a with-profit policy or a non-profit deferred annuity. The beneficiary may also be given a choice of life offices. When the entitlements of all members — whether active, deferred or pensioners — have been dealt with, it then remains for the trustees to complete the wind-up of the scheme. If the fund of the scheme is in deficit or surplus, additional considerations will apply, and these are dealt with below.

---

23 (Unreported, High Court, 31 January 1992, Denham J.)

24 See the decision in *Re H. Williams Pension Fund* (Unreported, High Court, 17 July 1992, Denham J.) and para. 17.36.

25 s.48(b).

17.27 Clearly, it is important that members are given information and appropriate explanations so that correct decisions may be made. The trustees will be concerned to ensure that notifications are made to members and queries answered. In this regard, and dependent on the size of the scheme, it may be useful to have a general meeting with all members to explain how the winding-up will be carried out and the manner in which members will receive their entitlements. This is not in substitution for individual-member notifications, which must, of course, still be made under the terms of the Pensions Act and the Disclosure Regulations.[26]

Trustees Liability Protection

17.28 The issue of trustees' liability and protection has already been looked at in the context of ongoing pension schemes.[27] The trust deed will usually contain both provisions limiting the liability of trustees by excluding certain obligations, and also provisions providing indemnity against liability. In the case of a pension scheme that is being wound up, it will be a matter of construction of the trust deed as to whether these provisions still operate.[28] If the employer itself is insolvent, an indemnity from the employer will be of little value. It may be possible for the trustees to purchase run-off insurance cover on winding-up.

SURPLUS

17.29 Pension documentation will usually give power on a winding-up to augment benefits. This will arise only where the fund of a pension scheme is in surplus.

17.30 It may happen that on wind-up the resources of the scheme exceed the amount necessary to discharge the strict liabilities of the scheme on winding-up, as set out in the winding-up provisions of the scheme documentation. This excess is often referred to as a "surplus". A surplus in this sense will usually not arise in the case of a defined contribution scheme, as the liabilities of such a scheme to the mem-

---

26 See para. 17.18 above.

27 See paras. 3.19 and 4.87 et seq.

28 See para. 3.12.

bers will equate to the total fund of the scheme.[29] As a defined benefit scheme is funded on such basis as will produce a specific benefit at normal retirement date, it is understandable that if the scheme is terminated prematurely, there may be an amount in the fund in excess of that required to meet the strict liabilities.

17.31 In the case of defined benefit schemes, the question of "ownership" of a surplus may arise on winding-up. This question has been considered in *Irish Pensions Trust Limited* v. *First National Bank of Chicago*.[30] In *First National Bank of Chicago*, the principal issue was whether or not a surplus in the pension fund on winding-up was repayable to the employer. The question was determined by interpretation of the trust deed. It has also been the subject of a number of UK and Commonwealth cases. Some of these cases have arisen as a result of purchase and sale transactions — in scheme reorganisations subsequent to sales, a pension scheme has been wound up for the purpose of making a surplus available to the purchaser.[31] Other cases have arisen out of corporate insolvencies.[32] The starting point is always to consider the terms of the formal trust documents. The winding up clause in a defined benefit scheme will direct the trustees as to mandatory payment of benefits, abatement in the case of shortfall and, often, a discretion as to augmentation in the case of surplus. Any ultimate surplus after augmentation of benefits (up to Revenue

---

29 A surplus could arise in a defined contribution scheme if, for example, the scheme had a "vesting period" (that is, a minimum period of time before which all contributions paid by and in respect of the member become allocable for payment of retirement benefit to that member). For example, some defined contribution schemes provide that members who leave within five years of first becoming a member will be entitled to a deferred benefit related to their own contributions only. In such case, the balance remaining in the fund is reallocated immediately or refunded to the employer.

30 (Unreported, High Court, 15 February 1989, Murphy, J.)

31 In *re Imperial Foods Limited Pension Scheme* [1986] 1 WLR 717, *UEB Industries Limited* v. *Brabant* [1991] PLR 109, *Cullen* v. *Pension Holdings Limited* [1992] PLR 135, *Lock* v. *Westpac Banking Corporation* [1991] PLR 167.

32 See *Mettoy Pension Trustees Limited* v. *Evans* [1991] 2 All ER 513, *Thrells Ltd (1974) Pension Scheme (In Liquidation)* v. *Lomas*.

limits) is repayable to the Principal Employer.[33] The power to augment benefits is often left to the discretion of the trustees and may or may not require the approval of the employer. Practice varies in this regard. Some suggest that the better course is that augmentation on a winding-up should not be subject to the consent of the employer if the employer is insolvent. Wind-up of the scheme will often arise in the context of an insolvent wind-up of the employer, and in such a case augmentation of members' benefits should not depend on employer consent. Others would take the view that disposal of surplus is an employer matter in all cases. The matter can be further complicated in insolvency cases if the employer company is the sole trustee of the pension scheme. The discretion to augment benefits then falls to be exercised by the liquidator on behalf of the company. The duty of the liquidator to act in the best interests of the creditors of the company as a whole would require the liquidator to refrain from exercising the augmentation power on grounds of conflict of interest.[34]

17.32 The position, at least in England, is that if the trustees have a discretionary power to augment benefits on a wind-up, the trustees should exercise this power in a just and equitable manner. In *Thrells Limited (1974) Pension Scheme (In Liquidation)* v. *Lomas*, the Court stated:

> When a scheme so provides, members have a reasonable expectation that if the scheme funds permit, namely, if there is a surplus after providing for the estimated liabilities, or a winding up, for the actual liabilities, the trustee will exercise that power to the extent that is fair and equitable in all the circumstances, having particular regard to the purpose for which the power was conferred. The power is an integral part of the scheme. It assumes the existence of a surplus. A trustee should not decline to exercise it solely on the ground that the employer was under no legal obligation to provide the surplus.[35]

---

33 In Ireland, this is a requirement of the Revenue Commissioners for exempt approval. Some of the reported cases deal with schemes approved under the old code which prohibited the return of any part of the fund to the Employer. Therefore, the application of such cases is now limited.

34 See the remarks of Warner J. in *Mettoy Pension Trustees Ltd* v. *Evans* at p.548.

35 Per Nicholls V.C. at p.242. Nicholls V.C. found support in the approach of Warner J. in *Mettoy Pension Trustees Ltd* v. *Evans*. In that case, Warner

17.33 This may also be the case where the discretion to augment benefits on a winding-up is given under the trust deed to the employer. In *British Coal Corporation* v. *British Coal Staff Superannuation Scheme Trustees Ltd*, the Court stated:

> . . . and where the question is as to how far a power to distribute a surplus in the fund should be exercised in favour of the members and pensioners . . . [t]he employer, if he is entitled to so much of the fund as is not distributed amongst members and pensioners cannot properly decide that he will have regard only to his own interest and that he will not distribute any part of the fund to the members or pensioners. He must give full and proper consideration to their claims.[36]

17.34 The view of the English Courts would appear to be that, if there is a discretion given either to the trustees or the employer under the trust deed to augment benefits out of surplus on a wind-up, due regard must be given to that clause. It follows that if the employer does not wish surplus to be applied, at least in part, to augment members' benefits, then it should ensure that no such discretion to augment is included in the deed. An alternative formulation would be for the winding-up clause to provide that the trustees shall not augment benefits unless the employer should decide otherwise. This removes the matter from the discretion of the trustees but does not oblige the employer to make a decision.

Bona Vacantia

17.35 If the employer company is being wound up at the same time as the pension scheme and the scheme is in surplus, it is important that the wind-up of the scheme should be concluded first. Any surplus should be dealt with by augmentation, if appropriate, and then repayment of the remaining surplus to the liquidator for the benefit of the creditors of the company. If the employer company is wound up first, there will then be no person entitled to the surplus and it will

---

J., in considering the question of a discretionary power to augment pensions on winding-up of a pension scheme (the principal employer being in insolvent liquidation), stated: "One cannot in my opinion, in considering a provision in the rules of a 'balance of cost' pension scheme relating to surplus, start from an assumption that any surplus belongs morally to the employer."

36 [1993] PLR 303 per Vinelott J. at p.313.

become payable to the State under the State Property Act, 1954.[37] Whilst payment of funds to the Exchequer may be laudable in other circumstances, it was never intended by the employer company at the time of establishment of the scheme that a surplus would become payable to the State.

DEFICITS ON WINDING-UP OF A SCHEME

17.36 One of the principal benefits of establishment of a pension scheme under trust is that the assets of the scheme are legally separate from those of the sponsoring employer. The pension scheme fund forms no part of the assets of the employer, and in the event of insolvency of the employer the pension scheme fund should be unaffected. In reality, this has not always been the case. The insolvency of a company is often a gradual affair, culminating in a petition to the Court or a creditors' meeting. In the period before that point is reached, an employer in financial difficulty may be tempted to postpone making payment of contributions due to the company pension scheme. Such contributions may be due on its own account or they may have been deducted from employees' salary or wages. In extreme cases, employers have raided the fund of the company pension scheme. If there are insufficient assets in the pension fund to pay all liabilities, it will be necessary for the trustees to reduce the entitlements of the various beneficiaries. This would include pensions. If the trustees had previously purchased annuities in the names of the trustees for the purpose of paying pensions, these annuities, as assets of the fund, must be surrendered.[38] There are statutory provisions which give limited protection to members of pension schemes in the event of insolvency of the employer in a situation where the employer has failed to make contributions to the pension scheme.

Legislative Provisions

17.37 In the case of all employers, the provisions of the Protection of Employees (Employers Insolvency) Act, 1984, state that on application to the Minister for Enterprise and Employment, the Minister

---

37 ss.29 and 30.

38 *Re H. Williams Company Pension Fund* (Unreported, High Court, 17 July 1992, Denham J.).

shall make a payment out of the Social Insurance Fund[39] in respect of unpaid relevant contributions.[40] Relevant contributions are defined as contributions falling to be paid by the employer or by the employees and deducted by the employer under the terms of the pension scheme.[41] The total sum payable with respect to employer contributions is the lesser of:

1. The amounts payable by the employer in the 12 months preceding the insolvency,[42] and
2. The amount certified by an actuary as being necessary to meet the liabilities of the scheme to the employees on the dissolution.[43]

It is arguable that the latter sum could amount to the entire benefit due to the members.

17.38 The amount due with respect to employee contributions is limited to the amount deducted from employees' pay in the 12 months preceding the appointment of a receiver or liquidator. It would appear that the proper claimant under the 1984 Act is the pension scheme and the claim should be made by the trustees. The procedure for making a claim is set out in the Protection of Employees (Employers' Insolvency) (Occupational Pension Scheme) (Forms and Procedure) Regulations, 1990.[44] Statutory Forms IP6 and IP7 must be used. The Form IP6 is used to claim unpaid employee and employer contributions. It must be completed by the trustee or administrator of the scheme and by the representative of the insolvent employer — usually the receiver or liquidator. Where a claim is made in respect of unpaid employer contributions, the Form IP7 must be submitted. This is an actuarial certificate. A copy of the terms of the pension scheme should be submitted with Forms IP6 and IP7.

---

39 As established by s.26 of the Redundancy Payments Act, 1967, see para. 5.52.

40 s.7(1) of the 1984 Act.

41 s.7(2) of the 1984 Act.

42 It should be noted that the term "insolvency" is, for the purposes of the 1984 Act only, defined exhaustively in s.1(3) of that Act.

43 s.7(3) of the 1984 Act.

44 SI No 121 of 1990.

17.39 The term "occupational pension scheme" has a wider meaning in the 1984 Act then in the Pensions Act. Under the 1984 Act, it includes any scheme or arrangement established by an employer to provide benefits in respect of retirement for employees and such an arrangement need not be formally documented or set up under a trust.[45]

17.40 Under the Companies Acts, in the case of corporate employers, unpaid pension contributions are a preferential debt in a liquidation or a receivership.[46] This means that in any liquidation or receivership these amounts, together with any other preferential debts, must be paid in priority to all unsecured debts of the company and also any debts due to holders of floating charges. Unlike the 1984 Act, there is no limit on the amount of the contributions which are preferred. As amongst themselves, the preferential debts abate equally in the case of a shortfall.[47] However, debts secured by a fixed charge have priority over these preferential debts. The fact that the pension contributions rank as preferential debts does not mean that they will, in all insolvencies, be paid. In many insolvencies debts secured by fixed charges will absorb much, if not all, of the funds available on the liquidation. Moreover, much of the debts due to the Revenue Commissioners in insolvencies also rank as preferential and can be substantial, thereby reducing the available funds.

17.41 If the Minister for Enterprise and Employment has made a payment in respect of pension scheme contributions under the 1984 Act, he is subrogated to the rights of the claimant under the Companies Acts as a preferential creditor to the extent of the payment made, and can then prove as such in the liquidation or receivership.[48]

17.42 If the employer is an individual person and is adjudicated bankrupt pursuant to the Bankruptcy Act, 1988, then that Act grants preferential status for any payments due by the bankrupt pursuant to any pension scheme whether in respect of contributions due by the

---

45 *In re Cavan Rubber Limited (In Liquidation)* [1992] ELR 79, see para. 5.54.

46 s.285 (Liquidations) and s.98 (Receiverships) Companies Act, 1963 (both as amended by the Companies (Amendment) Act, 1982.

47 s.285(7)(a) Companies Act, 1963.

48 s.10 of the 1984 Act.

bankrupt or by employees and deducted by the bankrupt from their wages or salaries.[49]

17.43 It may happen that on winding-up of a pension scheme, whether solvent or not, the employer (or its bank) is in possession of contributions (whether employer or employee or both) properly due to the fund. If the employer itself is not insolvent, the provisions of the 1984 act will not apply. The trustees may be able to establish that the employer is a constructive trustee of the moneys in its hands, which it has deducted from employees' pay for the purpose of payment to the fund. Any moneys due to the fund in the hands of the employer's bankers could, arguably, also be fixed with a trust in favour of the fund. The employer's own contributions due to the fund, if still in its hands, would be a debt due to the fund.

17.44 Trustees and beneficiaries of a pension scheme that is owed contributions or is in deficit on winding-up of the employer may have a remedy in the provisions of the Companies Act, 1963, dealing with fraudulent or reckless trading. Section 297A of that Act[50] provides that directors and officers of a company in course of winding-up may be fixed with personal liability by the Court if it appears that they knowingly carried on any business of the company in a reckless manner or were knowingly party to the carrying on of any business of the company with intent to defraud creditors of the company.

17.45 Under the Pensions Act, the Pensions Board has the power to apply to the Court for an order for payment from the employer to a scheme of unpaid member and employee contributions (where the latter have been deducted from pay by the employer).[51]

Receiverships and Liquidations

17.46 ***Receiverships***: The role of a receiver and of a liquidator of a company are quite different. A receiver will usually be appointed by a secured creditor under a power contained in a debenture granted by a company to that creditor. The reason for appointment is usually the failure by the debtor company to make payments due to the secured

---

49 s.81(1)(f) of the Bankruptcy Act, 1988.

50 As inserted by s.138 of the Companies Act, 1990.

51 s.87 of the Pensions Act as inserted by s.39 of the Pensions (Amendment) Act, 1996. See para. 5.56 on this point.

creditor. The receiver will be appointed only over the assets of the company listed in the debenture. In practice, a debenture will usually cover all assets of the company, both present and future. In the case of a company that has established a pension scheme for employees, the "future" assets of the company may include any surplus under that scheme which might ultimately become repayable to the company.[52]

17.47 The appointment of a receiver over the assets of a company does not mean that the directors of that company lose their powers.[53] However, because the receiver is usually appointed over all of the company's assets, the practical effect is that the directors have no powers. If a company in receivership has operated a pension scheme for employees and has acted as trustee of such scheme, the company may continue as trustee. The receiver does not automatically succeed to the role of trustee of the scheme. In theory, the directors of the company can continue to function as directors when the company acts as trustee. In practice, however, this does not usually happen. More often, the receiver as agent of the company will make decisions for the company in the role of trustee.

17.48 The principal duty of the receiver is to manage and deal with the assets of the company over which it is appointed in such manner as to satisfy the claim of the secured creditor and, if appointed under a fixed and floating charge, the preferential creditors.[54] This will require that the receiver keep the company trading and discharge the secured creditor out of the income of the company's trade, sell the company as a going concern or cease trading and dispose of the assets. The receiver will have no legal interest in the company pension scheme as it does not form part of the company's assets. Further, it is not advisable for the receiver to become involved in the administration and trusteeship of the scheme because there is a real possibility that the receiver will end up in a conflict situation.[55] There is, how-

---

52 *NW Robbie & Co. Ltd.* v. *Witney Warehouse Co. Ltd.* [1963] 1 WLR 1324, also *Mettoy Pension Trustees v Evans*.

53 In contrast to a liquidation, see 17.58 below.

54 *In the matter of Eisc Teo (in receivership and liquidation)* [1991] ILRM 760.

55 See the remarks of Warner J. in *Mettoy Pension Trustees Ltd.* v. *Evans* referred to above at fn 34.

ever, the practical difficulty that if the receiver continues the trade of the company in receivership, it will probably be necessary to continue the pension scheme. In many cases, the receiver is the only person in a position to administer the scheme. If the pension scheme trustees are individuals or a professional trustee, the receiver may be able to make arrangements for the trustees to continue.

17.49 The appointment of a receiver need not of necessity lead to the winding-up of a pension scheme. If the receiver is successful in continuing the trade of the company, and satisfies the secured and preferential creditors, the company may ultimately come out of receivership and continue as before. In practice, however, this is not often the case and a receivership often leads to appointment of a liquidator. Where the receiver decides to cease the trade of the company, this will probably constitute a winding-up event under the pension deed. A decision by the receiver to cease trading may also result in the appointment of a liquidator, which would itself usually constitute a winding-up event.

17.50 ***Liquidations***. A liquidator may be appointed either voluntarily or compulsorily. A voluntary liquidation may be either solvent (a members' voluntary liquidation) or insolvent (a creditors' voluntary liquidation). An actively trading company which intends to continue trading would only go into a members' voluntary liquidation for the purpose of a reorganisation. The pension aspects of reorganisations are dealt with in Chapter 18. An insolvent liquidation may also be initiated by a High Court petition. This form of liquidation is referred to as a compulsory or court liquidation.

17.51 In any form of liquidation, the liquidator succeeds to all of the powers of the company. Further, the directors of the company cease to have any power unless, in the case of a members' winding-up, the liquidator or the members in general meeting sanction their continuance,[56] or, in the case of a creditors' winding-up, the committee of inspection appointed on the liquidation or, if there is none, the creditors sanction the continuance of the directors' powers.[57]

---

56 s.258(2) Companies Act, 1963.

57 s.269(3) Companies Act, 1963.

17.52 The company may also have acted as trustee of its own pension scheme. This is quite common in Ireland, particularly in the case of smaller schemes and schemes established through life offices. It is not settled as to whether a liquidator by virtue of his appointment succeeds to the role of trustee. The point is not explicitly included in the powers of a liquidator set out in the Companies Acts.[58] It is arguable that a liquidator should carry out the role of trustee. This will at least ensure that the scheme is properly wound up. However, it is quite possible that acting as trustee may put a liquidator in a conflict situation. As liquidator, he has a duty to carry out the liquidation of the company in the best interests of all the beneficiaries of the company. As trustee, his duty is to act in the best interests of the scheme beneficiaries. In the case where the company is insolvent and the scheme in surplus, there is a clear conflict. For example, the scheme rules may provide on winding-up that benefits in payment and deferred benefits may, at the discretion of the trustee, be augmented out of surplus. A decision by the liquidator, as trustee, to augment benefits would be in the best interests of the scheme members but would not be in the interests of the company creditors to whom the liquidator also owes a duty. This question has been considered in a number of cases in the UK.[59] The correct position would appear to be that liquidators should not act as trustees of a pension scheme if, in so doing, it is probable that they will put themselves in a situation where they will have a conflict of interest. In *Thrells Limited (1974) Pension Scheme (In Liquidation)* v. *Lomas*, the company Thrells Limited went into insolvent liquidation. There was a deficiency in assets of some £2 million. The company was also the sole trustee of the pension scheme, which, on liquidation of the company, also fell to be wound up. The scheme fund was in surplus in the sum of about £505,000 after providing for the strict liabilities of the scheme in accordance with its winding-up provisions. As the Court stated:

> In those circumstances, the liquidator is confronted with an impossible conflict of duties. He is acting as the representative of the unsecured creditors. He also acts for the sole trustee of the Scheme. Accordingly and properly, he has surrendered to the Court

---

[58] At s.231 Companies Act, 1963.

[59] *Mettoy Pension trustees Ltd.* v. *Evans, Thrells Ltd. (1974) Pension Scheme (In Liquidation)* v. *Lomas, Re William Makin & Son Ltd* [1993] OPLR 171.

> the exercise of any discretion vested in the Company as trustee of the Scheme.[60]

In practice, if an independent trustee cannot be found who will act, then the only course is for the liquidator to act and to make application to Court as necessary.

17.53 In both receiverships and liquidations the receiver or liquidator will often attempt to sell the business or assets of the company. Following implementation of the European Communities (Safeguarding of Employees' Rights on Transfer of Undertakings) Regulations, 1980,[61] it was not at first clear whether the Regulations had application in the case of receiverships or liquidations. It is now settled that the Regulations will apply in the case of a receivership,[62] and that they do not apply in the case of a liquidation.[63]

17.54 In an insolvency context, the term "ex-gratia pensioner" will be encountered. This term refers to employees who either are in receipt of or have been promised pensions with respect to which no formal scheme or funding arrangement has been put in place. The pension is not "ex-gratia" in the strict sense, as it is a contractual obligation of the employer.[64] If the employer becomes insolvent, these employees are in the unfortunate position of being unsecured creditors of the company, and they may have little prospect of payment.

Examinership

17.55 In an examinership a company pension scheme should continue without being affected. Under the Companies Acts,[65] a company in financial difficulties can seek the protection of the Courts by applying for appointment of an examiner. If an examiner is appointed, the company is protected from claims of creditors. If the examinership is

---

60 Per Nicholls V.C. at p. 235.

61 SI No 306 of 1980.

62 *Mythen* v. *EAT* [1989] ILRM 844.

63 In Re *Castle Brand Limited (in Liquidation)* (Unreported, High Court, 23 March 1985, Hamilton J.).

64 See *Turner & Ors.* v. *Hospital Trust (1940) Ltd. (In Voluntary Liquidation)* [1994] ELR 35; see also para. 5.7.

65 The Companies (Amendment) Act, 1990 and the Companies Act, 1990.

successful, the company will come out of examinership and continue to trade. If the examinership is unsuccessful, the company will, in all probability, go into liquidation.

17.56 There is no reason why the company should not be made to continue its contributions to the pension scheme on an ongoing basis during the period of the examinership. The trustees of the scheme should insist that this be the case, failing which an application could be made to the Court. If the company has failed to make contributions prior to the examinership, the scheme will then be a creditor of the company for this amount. This historical debt may be the subject of a write-down under the scheme proposed by the examiner. If the company trades on after examinership, the pension scheme should not be affected any further. On the other hand, if the company goes into liquidation or reverts to receivership, the aspects referred to previously will arise.[66]

---

[66] See 17.46 to 17.53.

18

ACQUISITIONS AND RECONSTRUCTIONS

INTRODUCTION

18.1 A pension scheme must be flexible, capable of amendment, alteration, addition and, if necessary, closure. This is so partly because it is designed to operate over a long period of time, during which many things may change, including the overall taxation system in which the employer carries on business. Employees' general expectations with regard to benefits may also change.[1] Pension schemes exist in a commercial environment. Companies that operate pension schemes may themselves be sold, or companies may dispose of business divisions which participate in schemes. Also, such companies may require, for tax or accounting reasons, to reconstruct themselves. Therefore, it is important to consider pension schemes in the context of acquisitions and reconstructions.

18.2 A pension is but one type of employee benefit, although, potentially a very important one. To a purchaser, pensions may rank with other matters such as salaries, life assurance and company cars. They may be considered by the purchaser of a company or business as being of little importance in the context of the transaction. A purchaser entering into an acquisition of a company or business will do so for commercial reasons, which have nothing to do with any pension scheme that may exist for the employees of that company or business.[2] However, the cost of making good a deficit in an underfunded

---

1 The increasing popularity of "flexible" benefit arrangements in recent years is an example.

2 In a number of well-publicised acquisitions in the UK in the 1980s, pension scheme surpluses played a large part in the overall commercial transaction. Certain purchasers were dubbed "corporate raiders" — they were portrayed by some as making purchases in order to acquire pension schemes with surpluses which could be utilised by the purchaser. These cases may well have been overstated. Certainly, the existence of a surplus

pension scheme could exceed the purchase price being paid. It is therefore important that due attention be paid, and in good time, to any pension aspects that may arise on an acquisition. An acquisition may involve a sale and purchase arrangement or a merger. A merger is the combination, in some way, of two separate entities as one new entity, or the absorption of one entity into another.

18.3 Whether one is dealing with an acquisition or a merger, the commercial transaction will usually be effected by one of the following:

1. A sale and purchase of shares
2. A sale and purchase of a business.

From a pensions perspective, it is usual that if a company is sold (a share sale), any pension scheme operated by that company will transfer with the company. The purchaser will, indirectly, acquire the entire scheme. If a business is sold and the employees engaged in that business have pension rights, it is usual that a portion of the company (vendor) pension fund will be transferred to a new or existing scheme of the purchaser. It should be emphasised that this is the usual situation. For simplicity, it will be assumed in this chapter that a share sale will involve acquisition of an entire scheme, and a business sale will involve a transfer of part of a pension fund. In any acquisition, however, it is important to ascertain at an early stage what the existing pension arrangements are, and then to determine how best to deal with pension matters. There is a further type of acquisition transaction which deserves particular mention and this is a management buy-out. Management buy-outs are considered separately below.[3]

SALE AND PURCHASE OF SHARES

18.4 In a sale and purchase of a company the purchaser will acquire all of the issued shares of the target company. As a consequence, the purchaser will acquire all of the assets, creditors, debtors, contracts and employees of the target company. The target company may operate a pension scheme for its employees. Following the acquisition of its shares, the target will continue as employer, and its employees will continue as scheme members. This is illustrated in Figure 18.1.

---

in a pension scheme should be taken into account by both purchasers and vendors (see para. 18.41 et seq.)

3 At para. 18.37 et seq.

The purchaser will be concerned with all aspects of the target company's pension scheme because responsibility for the whole scheme and its members will be assumed on completion of the transaction.

FIGURE 18.1: SALE AND PURCHASE OF SHARES

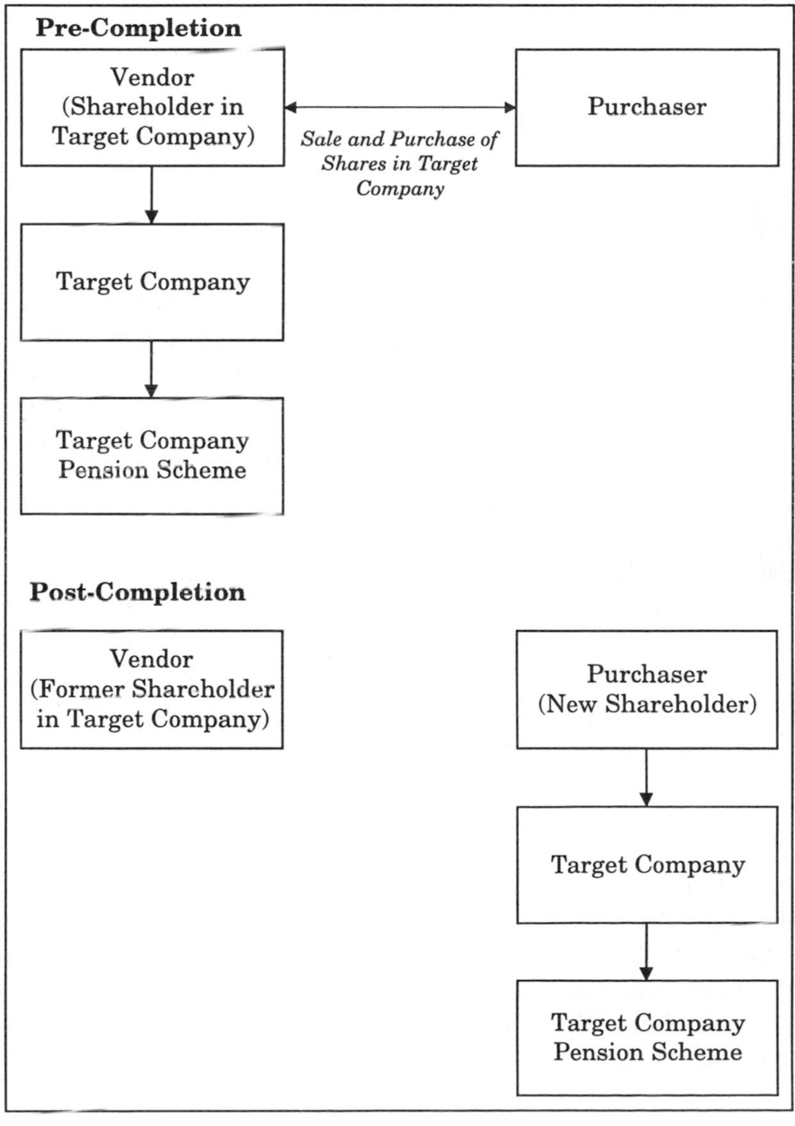

18.5 A purchaser should review any existing pension arrangements that it has. Following completion of the transaction, the purchaser could find itself with a number of schemes to administer. It could also happen, depending on the rules of the relevant schemes, that employees of the target company might be eligible to join the purchaser's existing scheme, or vice versa. If this is a problem, it could be avoided by changing the rules of the purchaser's existing scheme before completion of the transaction. If the purchaser has an existing scheme, it should compare the benefit provisions in the schemes to see if there are any significant differences in the benefit structure. Following completion there may well, at some stage, be pressure from the employees or their representatives to equalise benefits upwards. This is a cost that the purchaser will have to consider.

Funding

18.6 If the pension scheme is a defined benefit scheme, the purchaser should ascertain whether the pension scheme fund is in surplus or deficit. To this end, the purchaser should at an early stage in the transaction engage the services of an actuary. The purchase agreement will need to contain provision for the payment of a balancing sum if the parties' actuaries, on investigation after completion, show the scheme to be in surplus or deficit. Where a deficit is involved, this balancing sum is often referred to as a "short-fall payment". Short-fall payments can also arise where there is a transfer of a portion of a fund to a new scheme — this is considered later.[4] If the pension scheme is in deficit, a common cause is that the target company has not paid sufficient contributions. If this is the case, the company's profits would be overstated and the purchaser must take good account of this if the purchase price is being calculated on the basis of profits, as the purchaser may be paying too much for the target company.

18.7 In a company-sale transaction, a valuation of the pension scheme being acquired is a consideration not just for the purchaser. It is also a matter to be considered by the vendor. If there is a surplus, for instance, the vendor could be selling the company at an undervalue. The vendor should ensure that it is getting value for any surplus in the fund which might allow the target company a "contribution holiday."[5]

---

4 See para. 18.35 et seq.

5 That is, a period during which the target company as sponsoring employer of the pension scheme does not have to make contributions to the scheme.

18.8 Where the pension scheme is a defined contribution scheme, matters are more straightforward. Funding of the pension scheme will not be a concern. The purchaser will need to be satisfied that all contributions due prior to completion have been paid in full. A warranty to this effect must also be contained in the purchase agreement.[6] Warranties should also be obtained on a range of other matters.[7]

18.9 A purchaser acquiring a company with a defined contribution scheme should also investigate whether such scheme replaced a previous defined benefit scheme. If this did happen, the purchaser should be satisfied that employees were made fully aware of the change and of the altered benefits. If the employees are ignorant of changes that have been made, the purchaser might find itself faced with breach-of-contract claims in the future. Prior to and on the coming into force of the Pensions Act, in anticipation of future compliance problems with the funding requirements of the Pensions Act, many defined benefit schemes were changed to defined contribution arrangements.

Equality Issues

18.10 A purchaser should seek confirmation that the rules of the scheme treat males and females equally and that they have always done so. If there is any inequality in the structure or operation of the pension scheme, the purchaser must consider whether this has any cost implications and, if so, how this is to be remedied.[8] Historically, some Irish pension schemes treated males and females differently.[9] The differences often related to the age at which a member might retire on normal pension, or to benefits on death (in particular, survivors' pensions). Inequalities can also exist in the area of access to a pension scheme — for example, if membership is restricted to full-time employees and there are large numbers of female part-time employees, this may amount to an indirect discrimination on the

---

6 Warranties are discussed below at 18.31 et seq.

7 The types of warranties given should, ideally, be the same for a defined benefit and a defined contribution scheme, except as regards funding which is not an issue in a defined contribution scheme. See also para 18.31 et seq. below.

8 See Chapter 16 for a detailed discussion on equality and sex discrimination.

9 Often this was because those companies were subsidiaries of UK companies which had inequalities in their schemes.

basis of sex.[10] Prior to and following the enactment of the Pensions Act, many pension schemes amended their rules to remove inequalities. There are, however, schemes that still have discriminatory features, and care must be taken and proper inquiry made by a purchaser in this regard.

Industrial Relations

18.11 Because the purchaser is acquiring shares in the employer company, there will be no change of employer and the contracts of employment will remain the same. However, for good industrial relations reasons, a vendor may be concerned to ensure that its employees will receive benefits no less favourable than those they enjoyed prior to the purchase. It is in the interests of the vendor to ensure that the employees of the target company are reassured as to their entitlements following the sale as this will assist completion of the transaction. It will also be of comfort to employees in other group companies of the vendor. To this end, the vendor may seek an undertaking in the sale and purchase agreement that pension benefits of employees in respect of past service will be preserved by the purchaser. It is questionable whether a breach of such provision by the purchaser would give the vendor a right of action, as it would not suffer any loss. As with other provisions of the purchase agreement, these matters are for negotiation between the parties. These issues will also arise in a business sale where there is a pension scheme. Whilst provisions of the type referred to in this paragraph may be reasonable with respect to accrued entitlements, as regards the future, it is suggested that it is not reasonable for the vendor to seek to fetter the purchaser's right to reduce or alter benefits.[11]

SALE AND PURCHASE OF A BUSINESS

18.12 In a business-sale transaction, as opposed to a share-sale transaction, the vendor company will usually be disposing of part of its activity. If the vendor has a pension scheme for its employees, those employees involved in the business which is the subject of the transaction will be members of the scheme, but they may not be the

---

10 See *Bilka-Kaufhaus GmbH* v. *Weber von Hartz* [1986] 2 CMLR 701, and see Chapter 16 generally.

11 See para. 18.14 below with respect to the effect of European Communities (Protection of Employees Rights on Transfer of Undertaking) Regulations, 1980.

only members. The vendor will retain the existing pension scheme for the employees remaining in its employment, and the purchaser will wish to take a portion of the fund of that scheme which is referable to the employees of the business being acquired. This is illustrated in Figure 18.2. The transfer of a portion of a fund in these circumstances is often called a "bulk transfer". A purchaser in such a transaction

FIGURE 18.2: SALE AND PURCHASE OF A BUSINESS

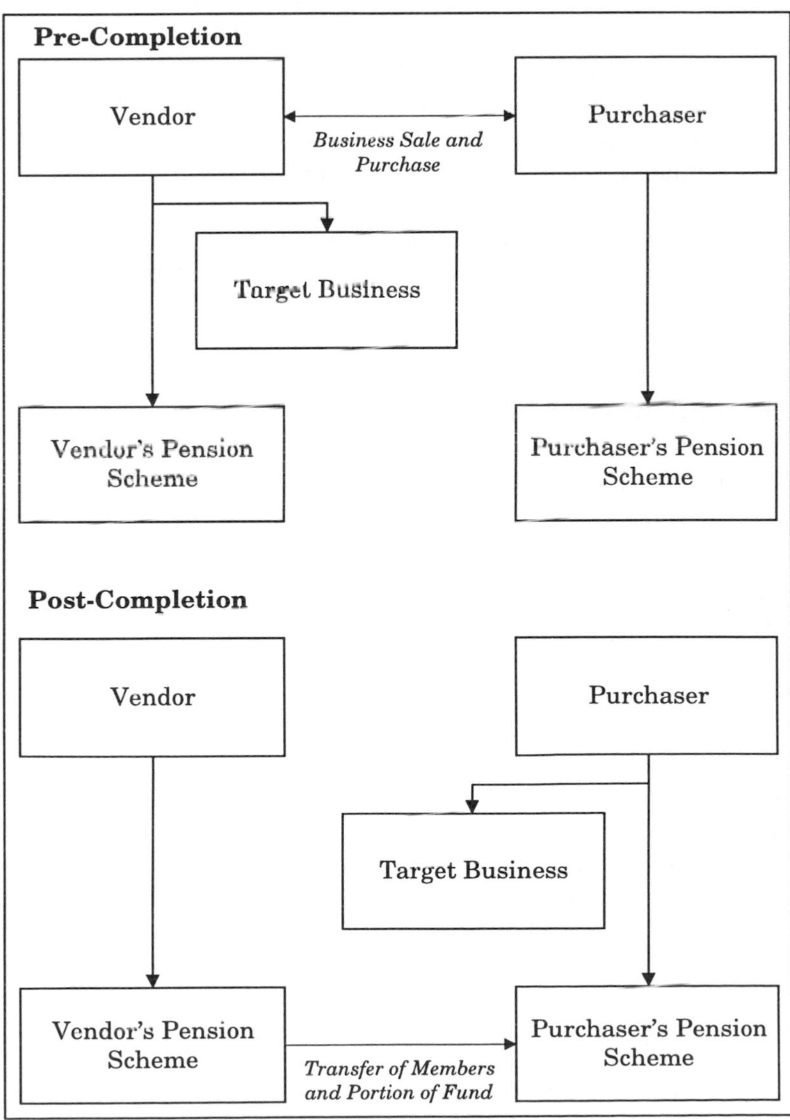

will be concerned with certain aspects of the existing pension scheme and would be particularly concerned as to the amount of the fund to be transferred, the method and timing of transfer and the establishment of the new scheme to receive that transfer. The acquisition agreement between the vendor and the purchaser will need to set out in detail how it is intended to deal with the transfer of a portion of the fund relative to the transferring employees. For ease of drafting, this is now commonly dealt with in a separate schedule to the sale and purchase agreement. If, notwithstanding that the transaction is a business sale, the entire pension scheme is to be acquired, from a pensions perspective this is akin to a share sale. The purchaser will, on completion, replace the vendor as sponsoring employer of the pension scheme. The pensions aspects of the transaction will be the same as those already discussed in relation to a share sale.

18.13 It may happen in a company share-purchase transaction that the target company does not have its own scheme. It may be a member of a group of companies, and participate in a group scheme. In this situation, the purchaser will not acquire the entire pension scheme, but will take a transfer of a part of the fund of the group scheme which will be referable to those employees of the target company who are members of the group scheme. Depending on the precise rules of the scheme, this may entail a "partial winding-up" of the vendor's scheme with respect to those employees of the target company. Alternatively, the rules may provide that a transfer payment be calculated and made. The purchaser will either transfer the employees of the company to its own scheme, or set up a new scheme for those employees. The employees themselves, depending on the trust deed and rules of the pension scheme and the preservation provisions of the Pensions Act,[12] may have other options, such as to take a deferred pension, to leave the scheme, or to have a portion of the fund representing their accrued benefit transferred to a buy-out bond. The purchase agreement will need to contain provisions for the transfer of the relevant employees and a portion of the fund of the group pension scheme to the new or existing scheme of the purchaser. The purchaser would be concerned to ensure that it receives sufficient funds to cover the accrued liabilities in respect of pensions for the employees transferring.

---

12 See para. 18.18 et seq.

Transfer of Undertakings Regulations

18.14 In a business sale it is important to consider the provisions of the European Communities (Protection of Employees Rights on Transfer of Undertakings) Regulations, 1980.[13] These Regulations came into force in 1980[14] and implement into Irish law the EU Acquired Rights Directive.[15] Broadly, in the event of a transfer, the effect of the Regulations is to transfer from the vendor to the purchaser the rights and obligations arising from the contracts of employment, existing at the time of the business sale, between the vendor and its employees. The Regulations go on to provide[16] that the transfer of rights and obligations effected by the Regulations shall not apply to employees' rights to old age, invalidity and survivors' benefits under supplementary company or inter-company pension schemes. The transferee (the purchaser) is obliged to ensure that the pension and survivors' benefits of the employees, and of other persons no longer employed in the transferor's business at the time of the transfer, are protected.[17]

18.15 The precise meaning of the Regulations with respect to pension entitlements has been the subject of some debate. In particular, it has been suggested that the following words in the Regulations contemplate not only rights accrued to the date of the transfer but further require that the transferee must maintain the existing pension arrangements following the transfer:

> . . . the transferee shall ensure that the interests of employees . . . at the time of the transfer in respect of rights conferring on them immediate or prospective entitlement to old age benefits. . . . are protected[18]

It is arguable that this suggestion is incorrect and not consistent with the requirements of the EU Directive. The Directive specifies that the transfer of obligations and rights effected by the Directive shall not apply to pension rights, but requires that Member States adopt meas-

---

13 SI No 306 of 1980.

14 3 November 1980.

15 Directive 77/187/EEC of February 14, 1977.

16 Regulation 4(2).

17 *Ibid.*

18 *Ibid.*

ures to ensure that the rights of employees to pension and survivors' benefits existing at the date of transfer be protected.[19] It is not altogether clear what this means. This question does not appear to have been considered by an Irish tribunal or court. There is also little guidance on the point in the decisions of the European Court.[20]

18.16 The accepted view at present, with respect to application of the Irish Regulations, is that the Regulations require a purchaser to ensure that the accrued pension entitlements of transferring employees are maintained, but no more than that. The purchaser is under no obligation to continue the pension arrangements enjoyed by the transferring employees whilst employed by the vendor. It is submitted that this is quite reasonable. It should be remembered that in all well-drafted pension scheme deeds the sponsoring employer will have reserved the right to discontinue contributions to the scheme. This fact will also be stated prominently in the explanatory booklet issued to members and prospective members. A purchaser succeeding to the rights and obligations of a vendor will have the same right of discontinuance.[21]

---

19 Article 3.3.

20 There appears to be only one decision of the ECJ which considers Article 3.3 of the Directive. This is *The Commission* v. *The Republic of Italy*. (Case 235/84) (Judgement given 10.7.86). In that case, the Commission brought proceedings against the Republic of Italy for alleged failure to implement certain of the provisions of the Directive including Article 3.3. With respect to that part of the claim concerning Article 3.3, the ECJ held that the Commission had failed to bring any evidence to support the case. Nor had it referred to any specific instance in which employee's rights had not been fully safeguarded. The Commission dismissed this part of the claim. The case may be authority for the statement that the Directive does require pension rights to be protected by the transferee (purchaser). However, there is no examination of the precise extent of those rights.

21 The EU Commission has published a proposal for a Directive to replace the 1977 Acquired Rights Directive (OJ No C 274, 1.10.1994, p.10). The proposed directive does not make any amendment to the pension provisions in the 1977 Directive. A very interesting analysis of the requirements of Article 3 of the Acquired Rights Directive, the background to the formulation of the Directive and its implementation into UK law is to be found in the English case *Adams* v. *Lancashire County Council and BET Catering Services Limited* [1996] PLR 49. However, it is important to note that the Irish and English Implementing Regulations differ significantly as regards implementation of Article 3.3.

18.17 In view of the obligation imposed by the Regulations to maintain accrued entitlements, it is clearly of great importance to a purchaser that it ascertain precise details of the accrued pension rights of the transferring employees. It is important that these details be obtained in good time so that the purchaser can decide how it will meet those obligations. The purchaser will need to obtain appropriate professional advice to confirm that the existing arrangements are adequate and properly documented. It will also need to confirm the value of the existing funds (in a defined benefit scheme) and the status of policies in relation to any insured arrangements. A purchaser should verify that the benefit structure which is disclosed by the vendor has been properly communicated to the transferring employees. If a pension benefit promised to an employee is not in fact provided for, or if insufficient funds are transferred, the purchaser will be left to meet the cost of providing those benefits.

Preservation Requirements under the Pensions Act

18.18 The preservation requirements set out in Part III of the Pensions Act have been examined earlier.[22] Briefly, those provisions require that members of occupational pension schemes leaving employment with certain minimum qualifying service be entitled to a preserved benefit calculated in accordance with the Second Schedule to the Pensions Act. The statutory provisions will arise only where a member leaves "relevant employment". This is defined under the Pensions Act as "any employment (or any period treated as employment) to which a scheme applies". This is further qualified by the provisions of the Occupational Pension Schemes (Preservation of Benefits) Regulations, 1992. Generally, the preservation requirements will apply when a member leaves service, and they may also apply when, having been a member of an employer scheme, the member although still an employee is no longer an active member of any scheme of the employer.

18.19 If the preservation requirements apply, the vendor and purchaser will need to ensure that employees are informed of their options in relation to their entitlements. In a business sale where there is to be a transfer to a new employer and a new pension scheme will be established, employees with preserved entitlements may elect to leave their benefits in the old scheme or to have their entitlements transferred to a

---

[22] See para. 12.7 et seq.

buy-out bond rather than the new scheme. In practice, if the benefit structure in the future is to be the same this may make little sense.

DUE DILIGENCE

18.20 A potential purchaser may be allowed the opportunity by the vendor to carry out an investigation or "due diligence" exercise prior to entering into any sale and purchase agreement. This is now quite common in larger transactions. Many of the concerns of the purchaser with respect to a pension scheme can be addressed and dealt with during this investigation process.

Funding

18.21 If a defined benefit scheme is in place and is to be acquired with the purchase, the purchaser should engage an actuary to examine the funding of the scheme — in particular, to assess the liabilities of the scheme and to assess the adequacy of the fund with respect to those liabilities. Where the purchase of a business or a group company is the subject of the transaction and a transfer is proposed, it will be necessary to engage an actuary to advise in relation to the transfer. Copies of the audited accounts of the scheme should be obtained and also, in the case of defined benefit schemes, copies of the most recent actuarial valuations. It is preferable that the last three actuarial valuations be obtained so that the actuary advising the purchaser can compare the basis on which the reports have been prepared.

Membership Data

18.22 It is important that the purchaser obtain as much information as possible in relation to the pension scheme if it is to assess properly the value of that scheme and the potential liabilities. Full membership data should be obtained, including names, addresses, sex, age, date of joining employment, date of joining scheme, salary, pensionable salary, other benefits, and details of any special contractual provisions applying. Membership data should be reviewed and compared with data on employees. It may be relevant whether or not all employees are members of the scheme. If not, there may be employees who are about to become eligible to join the scheme (about to reach qualifying age). There may also be employees who are close to retirement date. The answers to these questions may affect the cost to the employer of maintaining the pension scheme. The investigation of the pension scheme will be part of a wider due diligence exercise being carried out by the purchaser's advisers. The extent to which a purchaser is allowed to investigate prior to entering into a purchase contract will itself be the subject of negotiation and agreement between the purchaser and the vendor. The vendor may well wish to limit the investigation for a number of reasons. It is time-consuming, confidential information about its business will be revealed to a potential competitor,[23] and information may be revealed which will affect the purchase price.

Trust Documentation

18.23 In any acquisition transaction in which a pension scheme is involved, it is very important to consider the actual provisions of the formal trust documentation under which the pension scheme is established. The trust deed and rules may contain provisions requiring action or consent on the part of the trustees of the pension scheme. It is very important to know of the existence of any such provisions. The trustees of the pension scheme will not be parties to the transaction — certainly in their capacity as trustees — and will not therefore be bound by any terms agreed between the vendor and the purchaser. If any problems are revealed on examination of the trust documents, these will either have to be dealt with before completion of the transaction or the documentation relating to the transaction must include specific provisions for adjustment after closing if any adjustment becomes necessary.[24] The purchaser may seek to include in the sale and purchase agreement provisions whereby the vendor is obliged to procure that the trustees of the scheme will take certain action such as to effect transfer of a specific amount. Such provisions will not bind the trustees, but if not complied with by the vendor, the purchaser will have a right of action against the vendor. The vendor would be advised not to give any agreement in such terms. An agreement to "use its reasonable endeavours" would be preferable so far as the vendor is concerned. Clauses which might be contained in the trust deed of a pension scheme and which would be of concern to a purchaser would be provisions in relation to the change of ownership of

---

23 If a due diligence exercise is to be carried out prior to contract, the vendor should require the purchaser to enter into a confidentiality agreement. Under its terms this agreement should bind the potential purchaser, whether or not a purchase agreement is entered into by the parties.

24 See para. 18.35.

the principal employer, possibly triggering a closure of the scheme,[25] or a clause requiring consent of members for transfers, or one requiring consent of trustees for amendment of the trust deed or restricting appointment or removal of trustees. An investigation of the formal trust documents should also confirm that the benefit structure of the scheme set out in those documents concurs with that set out in the latest announcement or booklet issued to members.

18.24 Where a transfer is necessary, the vendor should check the provisions in the trust deed which regulate transfers. These may provide for an apportionment of the fund on a partial winding-up or bulk transfer in a way that might not suit the vendor. For instance, the relevant clause may provide that a proportion of any surplus be included in the transfer amount. If the vendor wishes to retain any surplus that may exist in the fund of the pension scheme, it will be necessary, in such case, to change the provisions of the trust deed. This should be done before negotiations on a transfer amount are commenced with the purchaser. It would in fact be preferable that it be done before any due diligence exercise is undertaken by the purchaser. If the vendor is proposing such action, it may be appropriate for the trustees to obtain advice on the matter. The trustees have a duty to consider the interests of all the scheme members.

18.25 Where a transfer is necessary, the purchaser should also review the provisions of the trust deed which deal with partial winding-up and bulk transfers. Apart from the provisions referred to above, these might provide that the transfer amount is to be decided by the trustees on the advice of the scheme actuary. Whilst this may be an appropriate method of splitting the fund so far as the scheme documentation is concerned, it is not advisable in a sale and purchase transaction. This should not be accepted by a purchaser. Ideally, the transfer amount should be an amount as agreed between the vendor's actuary and the purchaser's actuary, and the sale and purchase agreement should reflect this. It has been held in the UK that a court will not interfere with an opinion given by an actuary unless the ac-

---

25 As to "poison-pill" type clauses in pension scheme documentation, see para. 18.52 et seq.

tuary has used some method or procedure which no other actuary would use.[26]

18.26 The *Imperial Foods* case[27] is illustrative of the points made above with respect to bulk transfers out of a pension scheme and the effect of the formal trust documentation. The case arose out of the sale by Imperial Foods of a number of companies to Hillsdown Holdings plc. Under the terms of the sale and purchase agreement, the purchaser was obliged to set up a new scheme more or less on identical terms, as regards benefits, to the terms of the Imperial Foods Scheme for employees of the companies that Hillsdown had purchased. The trust deed of the Imperial Foods Scheme provided that in a such a situation "The Separated Portion shall be determined by the Actuary and shall be such apportionment of Funds as shall in all the circumstances appear to be appropriate at the time a subsidiary company ceases to be a subsidiary." The Imperial Foods Scheme was substantially in surplus at the time of the disposal and the purchaser maintained that the size of the fund to be transferred should be a pro-rata amount. The actuary for Imperial Foods used the past service reserve method of calculation,[28] which did not include consideration of a substantial amount of the surplus, and the purchaser contended that it should include a proportion of the surplus. Walton J. referring to the *Re George Newnes Pension Fund* case, stated that effectively in this situation it was not for the judge "to make that decision; it was one which is under the terms of the Trust Deed entrusted to the Actuary and he has made his decision." Walton J. went on to state that if it was a method which could be adopted by a competent actuary (and this point was conceded by the purchaser), then the method adopted in that case by the actuary to the scheme was right and proper and could not be overturned. It is clear from the *Imperial Foods* case that where there is to be a transfer of a portion of a fund, determination of the transfer amount cannot be left to operation of the formal trust documentation. It should be agreed as a matter of contract between the vendor and the purchaser. One method is for the actuaries to the parties to agree on the transfer amount. If this

---

26 *Re Imperial Foods Ltd Pension Scheme* [1986] 1 WLR 717; and see also in *Re George Newnes Group Pension Fund* (1969) Journal of the Institute of Actuaries Vol. 98, Part 3, p. 251

27 Op. cit.

28 See para. 9.39 with respect to actuarial valuations.

course is adopted, that part of the purchase agreement dealing with pensions (and this is sometimes set out in a schedule) should set out in detail how the transfer amount will be calculated. Often the pension schedule will itself refer to an annex or letter in which the actuaries (advising the vendor and purchaser respectively) set out their agreement as to the basis of calculation of the transfer amount.

General

18.27 There are other matters which should be investigated as follows:

1. The existence of unfunded pension arrangements or supplementary arrangements for certain employees should be ascertained.
2. The arrangements in respect of insured benefits should be examined. In particular, payment of premiums and level of cover will be relevant.
3. The existence of any actual or potential litigation, disputes or claims relating to the pension scheme should be ascertained.
4. Confirmation should be obtained regarding compliance with the Pensions Act and the requirements of the Revenue Commissioners.

THE ACQUISITION AGREEMENT

18.28 Depending on the timing of the transaction, there may not be a sufficient period of time for investigation before execution of the agreement. It may be that the vendor and the purchaser wish to sign an agreement quickly and to deal with many matters, including pensions aspects, either between signing and completion, or, apart from transfer situations, after completion. If certain matters are to be dealt with between signing and completion, there will be a conditional purchase contract. One of the points upon which completion should be conditional would be matters relating to the pension scheme. The following paragraphs discuss the provisions relating to pensions, which will, typically, be found in the acquisition agreement.

Pension Schedules, Actuaries' Letters

18.29 In the case of a defined benefit scheme and where a transfer payment is to be made, the actuaries advising the parties will usually agree the basis on which the transfer amount will be calculated. This will require agreement as to the assumptions used for valuing the assets and assessing the liabilities and agreement as to the investment return (interest) on the assets between signing of the agreement and transfer of the funds. There will also need to be provision for adjustments. Some members may retire, die or leave service between the date of the agreement and the transfer date. Any such event would reduce the amount to be transferred. Equally, transferring employees may become eligible for membership of the scheme and join, thus increasing the liabilities. Adjustments to the transfer amount would also be required in the case of defined contribution schemes. All of these matters are often dealt with in a separate schedule to the sale agreement. The assumptions agreed by the actuaries may be set out in a letter which is referred to in the pensions schedule. The level of documentation will, of course, depend on the size of the transaction. In complex transactions the method of dealing with matters in separate schedules assists progress of the transaction and the ultimate finalisation of the documentation. It allows particular advisors on each side of a transaction to deal with a particular aspect and to negotiate the documentation for that matter. In simpler transactions this approach may be considered unnecessary.

Participation Periods

18.30 In a business sale, or a share sale where the target participates in a group scheme, it will be necessary for the purchaser to set up a new scheme to provide pension benefits for the transferring members. Usually there is not sufficient time for the scheme to be set up and Revenue approval granted prior to completion of the transaction. The sale and purchase agreement will need to provide that the purchaser can participate in the vendor's scheme for a limited period of time until the new scheme is set up. This will require the consent of the Revenue Commissioners, which should be readily obtainable in such circumstances.[29]

Warranties

18.31 The sale and purchase agreement will usually contain certain warranties in relation to the company or business being purchased. For ease of drafting, these are often set out in a schedule to the main agreement. This schedule should contain specific warranties relative to the pension arrangements for employees. Warranties are contractual statements made by a vendor to a purchaser as to certain matters. They should address all areas of concern. If, subsequent to com-

---

[29] See the Revenue Practice Notes.

pletion, a warranty proves to be untrue, the purchaser will have a right to claim damages from the vendor. Warranties are not a substitute for investigation prior to completion. From the point of view of the purchaser, it is preferable to have both. The actual content of the warranties will vary from transaction to transaction. As with all other parts of the acquisition agreement, they are subject to the normal contractual negotiations between the vendor and the purchaser and their respective advisors. Warranties will usually also be subject to a *de minimis* provision — that is a provision in the part of the agreement dealing with the warranties, to the effect that a claim will not be made by the purchaser against the vendor for a breach of warranty unless the amount of the claim exceeds a specified minimum amount. Often, the purchase contract will specify a maximum amount which may be claimed (typically, a figure equivalent to the total purchase consideration). A further limitation on the ability of the purchaser to claim under the warranties will usually be a time limitation. It is quite usual for the purchase contract to provide that a claim may not be made against the vendor for breach of warranty after a stated period of time has elapsed.[30] In the context of a pension scheme, a time limit on claims may be particularly relevant. If left to their normal course, many potential difficulties regarding pension arrangements would not come to light until employees reach retirement age. This might be many years after the transaction is completed, and outside any temporal limitation on warranty claims. If a purchaser has been unable to undertake a full review of pension and employee benefit arrangements prior to completion, this should be carried out as soon as possible following completion. In the event that there is a difficulty in the pension scheme, a speedy review may prevent the purchaser from being caught by any temporal limitation on action.

18.32 Warranties are usually made subject to matters disclosed by the vendor to the purchaser in a disclosure letter. In fact, it is often said that one of the purposes of warranties is to elicit disclosure from the purchaser. For this reason, warranties are often quite lengthy and may contain statements which the purchaser's advisors believe may be incorrect, or at least not accurate. If the vendor does not qualify the statement, it might subsequently be liable for breach of

---

30 These types of provision are, in practice, referred to as limitations on warranties and are usually found in the section of the sale and purchase agreement dealing with warranties.

warranty. It is therefore obliged to make disclosure against the warranty in order to protect itself. The final form of the warranties and of the disclosure letter will, as with the other transaction documents, be the subject of negotiation between parties. The purchaser's advisors concerned with the drafting of the pension warranties and any actuary engaged by the purchaser must see the draft disclosure letter to be given by the vendor as soon as possible, as this could contain significant qualifications or exclusions in relation to the warranties.

18.33 All those matters discussed in relation to due diligence[31] should also be the subject of appropriate warranties. In a share sale transaction the following matters, in particular, should be covered:

1. If the pension scheme is a defined benefit scheme, there should be a statement that it is properly funded. The warranties should at least say that the scheme is fully funded on a past service reserve basis with allowance for future salary increases.[32] The actuarial assumptions used in making the statement must also be set out in the warranty — these would include assumptions as to leaving service, mortality, salary increases, investment return. Alternatively, reference can be made in the warranty to a side letter setting out these matters as agreed between the actuaries advising the parties. Any funding position lower than this — such as a discontinuance basis — could leave the purchaser with an unfunded liability. A warranty as to a pension scheme being fully funded, which does not set out clearly what is meant by "fully funded", is effectively meaningless. It is important that the actuary advising the purchaser be involved in drafting this warranty.
2. There should be a warranty to the effect that no pension promises have been made to employees, which are not funded. For example, employment contracts may contain provisions in relation to pensions, which are in addition to anything provided in the formal pension scheme and in respect of which no funding arrangements have been made. It is also important in a share sale transaction that the vendor warrant that it has not given any guarantee with respect to payment of pensions in excess of its obligations under the scheme documentation. The warranties should address any practice of the employer in exercising discretions or

---

31 See paras. 18.20 et seq.

32 See Chapter 9.

granting ex-gratia pensions. Such discretionary increases or ex-gratia pensions, if paid or granted on a regular basis, may have achieved the status of a term of employment, and a purchaser may not be able to disregard them.[33] The warranty should state that there are no such practices.

3. There should be a warranty to the effect that there is no other pension scheme or arrangement, funded or unfunded, which the employees of the company participate in or are eligible to join.

4. Payment of contributions and expenses up to the date of completion should be warranted. If the fund of the scheme is managed by a life office or offices, the warranty should confirm that the contributions have been paid over to the relevant office, or if there is no life office involved, that they have been paid to the investment manager.

5. The warranties should state that all death benefits payable under the scheme are fully insured at ordinary rates,[34] that the premia due to the life offices have been paid, and that the policies are in force.

6. The position with respect to the formal documentation of the pension scheme should be warranted. The explanatory booklet to members and any announcements to members should be obtained, and these should be referred to clearly in the warranties. The warranties should state that this documentation is true, complete, accurate and up to date in all respects. The warranty should also provide that all documentation relevant to the pension scheme has been disclosed to the purchaser.

7. There should be a warranty to the effect that the pension scheme is exempt approved by the Revenue Commissioners, and such warranty should further state that no circumstances have arisen which might entitle the Revenue Commissioners to withdraw such approval.

---

33 As to the enforceability of employees' "pension expectations" as opposed to "pension rights", see para. 5.35.

34 If appropriate. As to "ordinary" rates, see para. 11.29. In larger more mature schemes death benefits may be carried by the fund itself and may not be insured. If the warranty is left as suggested, then the position should be revealed in the disclosure letter. See Chapter 11 regarding insurance of benefits generally.

8. There should be a warranty with respect to the absence of any disputes, arbitration, or litigation, whether in process or pending or threatened in relation to the pension scheme.
9. Compliance with the provisions of the Pensions Act should be the subject of a warranty.
10. The latest actuarial report (in the case of a defined benefit scheme), annual audited accounts and annual report for the pension scheme should be warranted.
11. There should be a warranty with respect to the non-existence of arrangements which might be challenged under Article 119 of the Treaty of Rome or the equality provisions of the Pensions Act.[35]
12. All information in relation to employees furnished to the purchaser should be warranted as true, complete and accurate. This warranty may require that the vendor set out in the disclosure letter and warrant as true, complete and accurate, membership data including age, date of commencing employment, date of joining scheme, sex, job description, salary or wage, other benefits. This information is important for the purchaser in assessing the employment obligations to which it will succeed. The information will be important in assessing the status of the pension arrangements. In the case of a defined benefit scheme, in particular, the actuary advising the purchaser will rely on this information being correct. In practice, the purchaser's advisors will seek to obtain this information as early as possible in the transaction.

18.34 In a business sale transaction or where the purchaser acquires a company that participates in a group scheme, it will not be concerned about the funding of the entire pension scheme. A purchaser will not require a warranty with respect to funding. The purchaser will not have any concern, with respect to employees who are not transferring employment, regarding their pension entitlements.[36] The

---

35 Part VII of the Pensions Act. See Chapter 16 for a full discussion of equality issues relating to pensions.

36 The purchaser will wish to ensure that any employee who is not to transfer will not make a claim against the purchaser, or at least that the purchaser will have protection against such a claim. It is usual in practice for the purchaser to seek inclusion in the sale and purchase agreement of an indemnity from the vendor against any such claims.

purchaser will be concerned about the following matters and will require these to be covered by appropriate warranties:

1. Contributions
2. Promises made to employees which are not funded, or ex-gratia pensions
3. Documentation in relation to the scheme
4. Other schemes or arrangements
5. Arrangements with respect to insured benefits
6. Revenue-exempt approval
7. Disputes, arbitration, litigation (in course or threatened)
8. Pension Act requirements
9. Equality issues
10. Accuracy and completeness of employee details.

Post-Completion Adjustments

18.35 If the purchaser's investigations reveal funding difficulties, such that, for instance, an increase in the funding of the scheme may be required, these may necessitate either an adjustment of the purchase price or, if ascertained only after completion, a balancing payment by the vendor to the purchaser. If the cost will not be ascertained before completion, the agreement between the vendor and the purchaser should contain specific provisions to cover any balancing payments that might be necessary. It may happen that post-completion investigation reveals an over-funding. If this is a possibility, the vendor can protect its position by inclusion in the agreement of provision for a balancing payment to it.[37] Such a clause is quite common in sale and purchase contracts. Basically, this is a clause under which the parties agree that certain matters which can only be ascertained after completion will be calculated or vouched in a certain manner by agreed persons, and that a payment will be made from one party to the other. The adjustment clause dealing with pensions will typically provide that the parties, or their actuaries, will agree the amount of any liabilities not ascertained prior to completion, and a payment will be made to one or the other. The intention is that neither party should make a gain or suffer a loss. If completion of the

---

[37] See para. 18.36 below.

sale and purchase contract is going to be delayed and there is to be a transfer out of a pension scheme to a new scheme, it will certainly be necessary to make provision for ascertainment of the transfer amount and for adjustment of that amount. Also, where an agreement specifies that a fixed monetary amount, numbers of units or specified assets will be transferred, then provision should be made for adjustment in the case of gains or losses or for the payment of interest in the event of any delay in effecting the transfer.

18.36 Because the transfer itself will be governed by the provisions of the formal trust documentation rather than the commercial agreement, it can happen that the trustees of the transferring scheme will transfer less (or more) than the amount agreed by the vendor and purchaser, or certified by their actuaries. To take account of this possibility, the purchase agreement should provide that a balancing payment will be made either to the vendor or to the purchaser, as appropriate.

MANAGEMENT BUY OUTS

18.37 A management buy-out ("MBO") can involve either the purchase of a company or the purchase of a business. The usual pension concerns arising from those types of transactions (referred to above) will arise in an MBO as well. There are, however, additional areas to be considered which are peculiar to MBOs. Generally, an MBO is carefully arranged from a financial point of view. The management borrows heavily, usually on the security of the target company's assets, to finance the purchase. The consideration may be paid in stages and there would be interest and principal repayments to be made to the lenders. Management of the company's cash-flow is very important.

18.38 In this context, the cost of funding a company pension must be checked carefully. The company being acquired may have participated in a large group scheme, or the MBO may be of a business, in which case the managers and employees are only some of the members of the scheme. It would be quite dangerous for the purchasers (the management) to assume that they and the employees can continue to enjoy the same pension benefits that they enjoyed as part of a larger organisation. The real cost of these pensions may have been hidden. For instance, the scheme may have been in surplus, and the employer has enjoyed a period where contributions have been reduced. The company or business being acquired might have a disproportionately large number of employees (members) about to join the scheme or near retirement age, when compared with all the members of the scheme as a group. Factors such as these could mean that the real contribution rate, to provide identical benefits to the relevant employees, is significantly higher. The real pension costs need to be checked carefully, and appropriate actuarial advice obtained. On completion of an MBO, the salaries and benefit packages of senior management may increase. If managers are members of a defined benefit scheme, this will put an increased burden on the fund of that scheme. From the point of view of managers, they should consider alternatives to ensure that their pension expectations are maintained.

18.39 Maintenance of good management/employee relations is crucial to a successful MBO, and this consideration must be borne in mind. The employees being transferred will expect to continue to enjoy pension rights similar to those that they previously enjoyed. In the period between the announcement of the MBO and the actual completion of the transaction, there will probably be meetings between management and the employees. Management (the purchasers) may be inclined to make promises to employees which would be costly and difficult to keep. Management's advisers need to ensure that care is taken in this regard.

18.40 In an MBO the pension arrangements may involve a transfer payment to a new scheme. In view of the financial constraints on the new entity, the negotiation of an adequate transfer amount would be very important. An independent actuary should be retained at an early stage to advise the management.

SURPLUS OR DEFICIT — ACQUISITIONS

18.41 The question of "surpluses" is frequently encountered in connection with acquisitions and disposals of companies and businesses.[38] Surpluses can arise in defined benefit schemes through good invest-

---

[38] The question of surpluses and deficits will also arise in the context of the winding-up of a pension scheme — see para. 17.29 et seq. On the winding-up of a defined benefit scheme, all assets of the fund will be realised. If the assets exceed the strict liabilities of the scheme, there is a "surplus". A short-fall in assets will constitute a deficit. See also Chapter 9 in relation to funding and the requirement under the Pensions Act on trustees of a defined benefit scheme to produce a funding certificate at periodic intervals.

ment performance or deliberate or unintentional overfunding.[39] Other factors such as declining membership or redundancy programmes can give rise to a surplus, because defined benefit schemes are funded on such basis that the contributions made to the scheme, together with the investment return on those contributions, will produce sufficient funds to provide the promised benefits at retirement. The question of pension scheme surpluses has been considered in a number of UK and Commonwealth decisions. There has not yet been an Irish case which has addressed the question, although there have been several liquidation cases which have included in their features serious deficits in company pension schemes.[40] These UK and Commonwealth cases are of interest because they considered the meaning of "surplus" in the context of an ongoing scheme, as opposed to one in liquidation.

18.42 In the context of an acquisition, decisions of the Courts demonstrate that the matter of ownership of a pension scheme surplus is not at all straightforward. Certainly a prospective purchaser cannot assume that merely by succeeding to the rights of the principal employer, it will have automatic rights to any surplus. The cases have shown a difference of opinion as to whether there is any such thing as a "surplus" in an ongoing scheme, as opposed to a scheme in the course of winding up, and as to whether any "surplus" belongs to the employer alone, to the employer and the members, or whether in fact it could be stated to belong to any particular group of persons at all. The starting point is the decision of Walton J. in the *Imperial Foods* case[41] and that of Millett J. in the *Courage* case.[42]

18.43 In the *Imperial* case, Walton J. stated:

---

39 There is no statutory definition of surplus in Irish law. Revenue Practice Notes refer to surplus at PN 191 et seq. (In the UK, there is legislation dealing with surplus in pension schemes — s.602 Income and Corporation Taxes Act, 1988).

40 For example, in *Re Castle Brand Limited* (unreported). Also the *H. Williams Company Pension Fund* cases. The Irish case *Irish Pensions Trust Limited* v. *The First National Bank of Chicago* (Unreported, High Court, February 15, 1989, Murphy, J.) did concern a surplus in a pension scheme but on a winding-up. See further para. 17.29.

41 *Re Imperial Foods Ltd. Pension Scheme,* [1986] 1 WLR 717.

42 *Re Courage Group's Pension Schemes, Ryan* v. *Imperial Brewing and Leisure* [1987] 1 WLR 495.

> But what is called, in this connection, a surplus, having no existence in reality, represents, in a case of the present nature, what may be termed temporary surplus funding by the employing company. . . . [P]rovided that the company concerned is financially sound, and there is no question of a discontinuance of the fund, it appears to me that from an economic point of view, the members of the fund . . . are all going to have their expected benefits, as and when they become due to them, paid in due course. . . . [N]ot only is there the possibility that the surplus will be wiped out altogether before the continuing members receive any benefit out of the fund, even if it is not wiped out in this manner, there is no certainty that it will be used for their benefit. Of course, it may be, through the generosity of the company; but it may remain the precise and exact surplus all the remainder of the lives of each and every existing member of the fund continuing in membership. . . . Therefore, the surplus in the continuing fund is not one which can in any way be regarded as applicable to the continuing members alone. If it does produce any benefits they must share those benefits with later entrants to the scheme.[43]

18.44 Millett J., in the *Courage* case, stated:

> . . . any surplus arises from past overfunding, not by the employer and the employees pro rata to their respective contributions, but by the employer alone to the full extent of its past contributions and only subject thereto by the employees. . . . It is, therefore, precisely in relation to a surplus that the relationship between "the company" as the employer and the members as its present or past employees can be seen to be an essential feature of a pension scheme. . . . While they have no legal right to participate in the surpluses in the existing schemes, they are entitled to have them dealt with by consultation and negotiation . . . and not to be irrevocably parted from those surpluses."[44]

18.45 The remarks of both judges were in fact obiter as they reached their decisions on other grounds. Their comments are nevertheless of interest. Both were of the view that a surplus (if such could be identified) could not be said to belong to the members at any particular time. Millett J., however, suggested that employees have some right to be consulted in relation to the matter. The decision of Millett J. has frequently been cited in argument in subsequent cases. In *Imperial*

---

[43] *The Imperial Case* at p.728.

[44] *The Courage Case* at p.515.

Group Pension Trust Limited v. *Imperial Tobacco Limited*,[45] the Court held that a pension scheme operated in the context of the employment relationship. This was a relationship of confidence and there was an implied obligation on the employer, in exercising a power conferred on it by the scheme documentation, not to exercise that power in such a manner as to damage that relationship of confidence.[46]

18.46 In the case *UEB Industries Limited* v. *Brabant*,[47] the New Zealand Court of Appeal held that a surplus which had arisen in a pension scheme fund belonged entirely to the members. The case arose as a result of a share-purchase transaction. The purchaser in acquiring the target company found itself in control of a company whose pension fund had a surplus of some NZ$30 million. The purchaser sought to wind up the scheme and realise the surplus for its benefit. The Court, on interpretation of the scheme deed, held that the scheme was established solely for the benefit of the members. It held that the employer could not amend the deed to allow it to utilise the surplus which had built up in the Fund. The Court was clearly influenced by the various UK decisions which characterised the members of a scheme as not mere "volunteers" but as employees who, as members, had earned their benefits under the scheme by their service to the employer.[48] The Court, however, went on to determine the matter by interpretation of the formal trust documentation. This case was followed by the New Zealand High Court in *Cullen* v. *Pension Holdings Limited*.[49] That Court held that a surplus could, and in that case did, belong to the members, and that a purchaser could not seek to utilise that surplus by amendment of the pension deed.[50]

45 [1991] 1 WLR 589.

46 See further discussion on this point above at para. 5.27.

47 [1991] PLR 109.

48 Reference was made in argument and in the judgment to *Imperial Group Pension Trust Limited* v. *Imperial Tobacco Limited, Mettoy Pension Trustees Limited* v. *Evans* [1991] 2 All ER 513, *Kerr* v. *British Leyland (Staff) Trustees Ltd (1989 CA Transcript 286), Mihlenstedt* v. *Barclays Bank International Ltd* [1989] PLR 91.

49 [1992] PLR 135.

50 A similar approach is to be found in *Sulpetro Ltd.* v. *Sulpetro Ltd. Retirement Benefit Fund* (1990) 73 Alberta LR 44.

18.47 A different approach to the question of employers' and members' rights in relation to pension scheme surpluses is to be seen in the Australian case, *Lock* v. *Westpac Banking Corporation.*[51] Here again, a large surplus had arisen in a pension scheme fund (different estimates put the surplus at around AUS$600 million). The bank sought to obtain a refund of part of this surplus. Actuarial advice demonstrated that it could only utilise a small part of the surplus by a contribution holiday. The Court approved the proposal. The difference in approach of the Courts in *UEB* and *Lock* is in whether, on the one hand, the matter should be determined strictly by applying trust principles (*UEB*) and to view the scheme in isolation as a trust fund for stated beneficiaries or, on the other, to regard the pension scheme as operating squarely in an employment context (*Lock*), the pension scheme trust being a form of guarantee fund put in place by the employer as security for the pension promise which is made to employees. There is a strong argument that the latter approach reflects the reality of the employer/employee relationship more closely.

18.48 The value of thorough investigation of the pension scheme and the formal documentation cannot be overstated. Such a review may reveal problems in the structure of the scheme. The documentation may require that the trustees consent to a contribution holiday, or the documentation may in fact make no provision at all for suspension of contributions.[52] If amendments to the documentation are required, the trustees' consent will probably be required. The trustees will be under a duty to consider the interests of the members if the new employer, for instance, proposes a contribution holiday. The right of an employer to obtain a refund of surplus from an ongoing scheme is not entirely clear.[53] Clearly, payment of a refund to an employer out of an ongoing scheme would require specific provision under the formal trust documentation. It does appear that an excessive surplus in a scheme may cause the Revenue to withdraw approval unless steps are taken to reduce the surplus.[54] A refund can be

---

51 [1991] PLR 167.

52 This would be unusual in a well-documented scheme.

53 Refunds are allowed under UK law and in certain circumstances required. See s.602 ICTA 1988

54 See para. 6.47.

achieved by winding up the scheme, having first transferred the members and a portion of the fund to a new scheme. Such a proposal will almost certainly require trustee consent. The consent of the members being transferred may also be required.[55]

18.49 If a surplus exists in a pension scheme, a vendor may seek to get some value for that surplus. It may argue for the surplus to be reflected in the purchase consideration. For industrial relations reasons it may seek to have the surplus or a portion of it earmarked for the benefit of existing members (its employees). These are issues that will require to be negotiated prior to completion of the sale and purchase.

18.50 A deficit will arise only in the context of a defined benefit scheme. In the context of an ongoing scheme, it is the opposite of a surplus. As far as a vendor and purchaser are concerned, the issues that arise are the reverse of those already noted. If a serious deficit exists, this may present real difficulties. The proposed purchase may be quite unattractive if the purchaser will have to fund the deficit.

THE ROLE OF THE TRUSTEES

18.51 Generally, the sale and purchase transaction would be simple without third parties such as trustees being involved. It would then be a matter for the vendor and purchaser to agree as a matter of contract how issues relating to the pension scheme would be handled. This is not the case, however. The assets of the pension scheme will be vested in the trustees. Further, the trustees will not be party to the transaction documents. As already noted, the vendor and purchaser will make certain contractual agreements with respect to the pension arrangements. The trustees, however, will have an important role. Their consent or action will almost certainly be required for any amendment to the scheme documentation or if a transfer of assets is proposed. The vendor and purchaser are best advised to draft the pension provisions in the transaction documents so that they deal with a situation where the trustees do not agree to transfer the amount agreed by the vendor and purchaser. This can be done by inclusion of a provision for a short-fall or balancing payment to be made to the purchaser or vendor (as appropriate) in the event that the amount transferred by the trustees is less (or more) than that de-

---

55 See para. 18.13 and 18.19.

termined in accordance with the provisions of the sale agreement.[56] The general obligation of the trustees will be to carry out the terms of the trust deed and rules and to act in the best interests of the beneficiaries of the pension scheme. That will include not just current members but also deferred pensioners and pensioners. The trustees must also ensure that they give due regard to the different groups of beneficiaries. As far as the trustees are concerned, it may be necessary for them to be separately advised as to their duties and responsibilities. If the trustees, in following the provisions of the sale and purchase agreement, fail properly to apply the provisions of the scheme trust deed and rules they may be sued by the members of the scheme.[57]

POISON-PILL CLAUSES IN PENSION SCHEME DEEDS

18.52 These types of pension scheme clauses are more usually encountered in the context of contested takeover bids. Such provisions are used by a target company in the hope of making itself less attractive to a predator. Because of their nature, poison-pill clauses are not included in pension trust documentation as a matter of practice. However, if the board of a target company fears that it may be the object of an unwelcome bid, it may consider alteration of the company's pension scheme documentation by inclusion of "poison-pill" type clauses. Such provisions are drafted so that they will come into operation in the event that the takeover offer is successful. These clauses would include:

1. Closure of scheme to new participating companies or new members
2. Restrictions on appointment and removal of trustees or requirement for appointment of an independent trustee
3. Restriction on alteration of contribution rate without consent of trustees
4. Amendment of wind-up rule to provide for mandatory augmentation of benefits
5. Alteration of amendment power in trust deed
6. Increases in early leavers' benefits in redundancy situations
7. Augmentation of benefits in payment.

---

[56] See para. 18.35.

[57] See *Stannard* v. *Fisons Pension Trust Ltd.* [1990] PLR 201.

18.53 The desired intent of these types of provisions is usually to make the pension scheme less attractive by increasing its liabilities, reducing a surplus or reducing the extent to which a successful purchaser can re-organise the pension scheme following completion. It may also be the intent of an employer to safeguard the interests of the employees as members of the scheme. It must be remembered by the advisors to the target company that if the "poison pill" is successful, the target company will be left to deal with its consequences if the bid does not proceed. It will be noted that the thrust of many of the provisions is to alter the balance of power between the employer and the trustees. If the takeover does not succeed, the board of the target will be left in a situation where matters which before would have required their decision, such as contribution rates, augmentation of benefits or reorganisation of the scheme, now require the decision or consent of employees (if the trustees are employees) or of independent trustees. These provisions are something of a "two-edged sword", and the board of the target will need to consider carefully whether such provisions should be adopted. Some of the directors may also be trustees of the scheme. This may place them in a difficult position where their duties owed to the company as directors may conflict with their duties owed to the beneficiaries of the pension scheme. In this case they will need to check the terms of the trust deed to ensure that they can act while having a conflict of interest.[58]

18.54 If the target is a quoted company, then its freedom to adopt "poison-pill" provisions may be restricted by the City Code on Take-Overs and Mergers. The Code regulates a takeover bid for a company which is publicly quoted on the Irish or UK Stock Exchange.[59] It restricts the actions that a target can take at a time when a bid has been received or is expected. Rule 21 of the Code specifies that a board of a target company cannot without shareholder approval and during the course of an offer, or before that date if the board has reason to believe that a bona fide offer might be imminent ". . . (d) enter

---

[58] See para. 4.29 et seq. with regard to trustees' conflicts of duty and interest.

[59] The Irish Stock Exchange has been established as an independent Stock Exchange in accordance with EU requirements. At present, the ISE operates the existing City Code pending adoption of a similar code. The necessary legislation, the Irish Takeover Panel Bill, 1996, was published during the Summer Recess.

into contracts otherwise than in the ordinary course of business." Note 8 to Rule 21 states:

> This Rule may apply to proposals affecting the offeree company's pension scheme arrangements, such as proposals involving the application of a pension fund surplus, a material increase in the financial commitment of the offeree company in respect of its pension scheme or a change to the constitution of the pension scheme. The Panel must be consulted in advance in relation to such proposals.

The effect of Rule 21 is that if a company board wishes to put "poison-pill" clauses into the company's pension scheme documentation, it should do so well in advance of a bid. As with other aspects of a defence to a hostile takeover bid, the directors of the target in considering adoption of "poison-pill" provisions must consider whether their actions are in the best interests of the company and the shareholders. If they are not, the directors will, under company law, be in breach of their fiduciary duties, and this would undermine the validity of the proposals.

18.55 It should be noted that in the case of a hostile takeover bid there will be no negotiated sale agreement between the parties. The acquisition is effected by the bidder issuing a public offer document and pursuant to such offer purchasing sufficient shares from shareholders of the target to give effective control. The purchaser does not get any opportunity to carry out detailed due diligence on the target, except with respect to matters which are in the public domain. The purchaser will not be given warranties with respect to the target.

18.56 In an agreed takeover situation, a vendor may seek to include in the sale agreement the very types of provision which in hostile takeovers are characterised as "poison-pill" clauses. In such cases, the vendor is usually attempting for industrial relations reasons to safeguard the interests of the employees.[60]

RECONSTRUCTIONS

18.57 A company may wish to restructure its employee benefit arrangements, or a group of companies may need to restructure themselves at a corporate level. These reconstructions may impact on existing pension arrangements. They do not present the same range of concerns and potential problems as an acquisition because they are es-

---

[60] See para. 18.11.

sentially "internal" to the company or group. Two types of reconstructions in which pension schemes may be involved are now considered.

Reconstruction of Pension Arrangements in a Group of Companies

18.58 It may happen over time that a company will acquire a number of businesses or subsidiaries, each operating its own pension scheme. To maintain different pension schemes in a group of companies can be administratively difficult and expensive. It is therefore attractive to a group to reorganise their pension arrangements in a centralised scheme. This will allow membership details to be centrally maintained, notifications to members will often be dealt with at the one location and there can be one fund for the entire membership. Having one fund should produce savings in respect of audits and actuarial valuations (in the case of defined benefit schemes). If the funds are managed, their consolidation in one fund will produce savings in management charges. An example of this type of restructuring is illustrated in Figure 18.3.

18.59 To effect the reorganisation will require, first, a close examination of the benefit structures in the various schemes. A decision must be made by the board of the group company, together with those of the subsidiaries, as to whether the benefits provided by the schemes, if different (and there will inevitably be differences), will be equalised or maintained. It may be decided to maintain the differences in the case of existing members so that none are prejudiced, and to equalise benefits for new members.

18.60 The next step will be to examine the trust deeds of the various schemes to determine how transfers may be effected and what consents are required. Transfers are usually effected by the trustees and may require member consent. No consent will be required under the Pensions Act if the transfer is between schemes of the same employer. The trust deed may provide that member consent is not required in the case of a transfer to another scheme of the same employer or of the parent company. This is also provided by the Pensions Act in the case of winding-up of a defined benefit scheme.[61] For good industrial relations reasons it may, however, be wise to consider notifying employees and requesting consent to any transfer. Provided

---

[61] s.48.

FIGURE 18.3: RECONSTRUCTION OF PENSION ARRANGEMENTS IN A GROUP OF COMPANIES

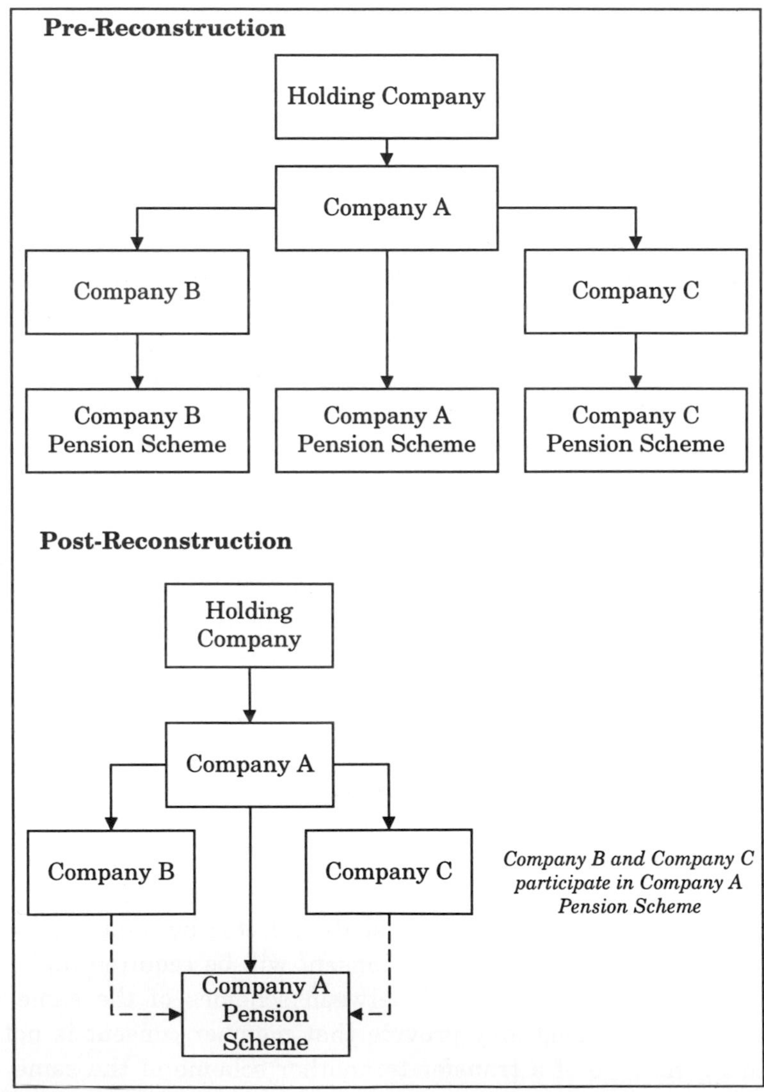

that the new scheme is well funded and offers identical or improved benefits and that accrued entitlements are preserved in the new scheme, there would be no good grounds to refuse consent. Trustees should also be satisfied in such circumstances that the transfers are in the best interests of the members. It may then be decided to prepare the announcements to employees. Meetings should be held with the workforce or their representatives to explain the proposals and to deal with queries. Consent forms (if required) may conveniently be issued to members with the announcements.

18.61 Following this stage, transfers can then be effected to the new centralised scheme. This may be either an entirely new scheme established for the purpose, or an existing scheme, suitably modified. The companies employing the transferring members will need to become participating companies in the new centralised scheme. The trust deed will therefore need to contain provisions allowing such participation. The usual provision is that a company associated with the sponsoring employer may participate by entering into a deed of adherence, to which deed the sponsoring employer and the trustees will also be parties. Under this deed, the participating company undertakes to observe those terms of the trust documentation as apply to it. Any such adherence will require the consent of the Revenue Commissioners, but approval will be readily obtainable in the case of group companies.[62] After the transfers have been effected, new explanatory booklets should be issued to the members. The rules of the new or modified scheme will require redrafting to take account of the differing benefit provisions if these are not equalised. For ease of drafting, it is convenient to schedule separately the rules applying to different classes of members. This will also facilitate the trustees in complying with the requirements of the Disclosure Regulations.[63]

18.62 In this type of reconstruction, there will be no change of employer for any of the members of the various schemes. The reconstruction does not trigger the preservation requirements of the Pensions Act as there is no termination of relevant employment.[64]

---

62 See Revenue Practice Notes at paras. 236 and 238 and also paras. 3.24 and 6.22.

63 SI No 215 of 1991. Article 8 requires the trustees of a scheme to make disclosure of the constitutional documents of the scheme, and Article 8(5) provides that where different rules apply to different members, the trustees are required to disclose to a member only that part of a document which relates to the member's rights under the scheme.

64 s.28(2) Pensions Act.

Reconstruction of a Group of Companies with a Centralised Pension Scheme.

18.63 A group of companies with a centralised pension scheme may decide for corporate reasons to reorganise itself. This may be done for taxation or accounting reasons. In such cases, it may be necessary to transfer employees from one group company to another. An example of this type of reconstruction is set out in Figure 18.4.

18.64 This type of reconstruction will not involve a transfer of scheme membership or a transfer of funds. The relevant employees will remain members of the same pension scheme, and their entitlements will remain the same. If their employment is to be transferred to a new company which does not already participate in the scheme, it will be necessary to check the provisions of the trust deed to ensure that it allows associated companies to participate in the scheme. If the existing trust deed does not allow participation, it will be necessary to amend the deed.[65] Provided that the transfer of employment is effected within the period of one month (or such longer period as the trustees of the scheme decide in accordance with the rules of the scheme), the preservation requirements of the Pensions Act will not apply.[66]In practice, the transfer from employment of one group company to the other will take place immediately. If such a transfer is effected in connection with the transfer of a business, the Transfer of Undertakings Regulations will apply.[67]

---

65 See para. 18.61.

66 By virtue of Article 4(a)(i) of the Occupational Pension Schemes (Preservation of Benefits) Regulations, 1992 (SI No 445 of 1992).

67 SI No 306 of 1980. See above at para. 18.14 et seq.

FIGURE 18.4: RECONSTRUCTION OF A GROUP OF COMPANIES WITH A CENTRALISED PENSION SCHEME

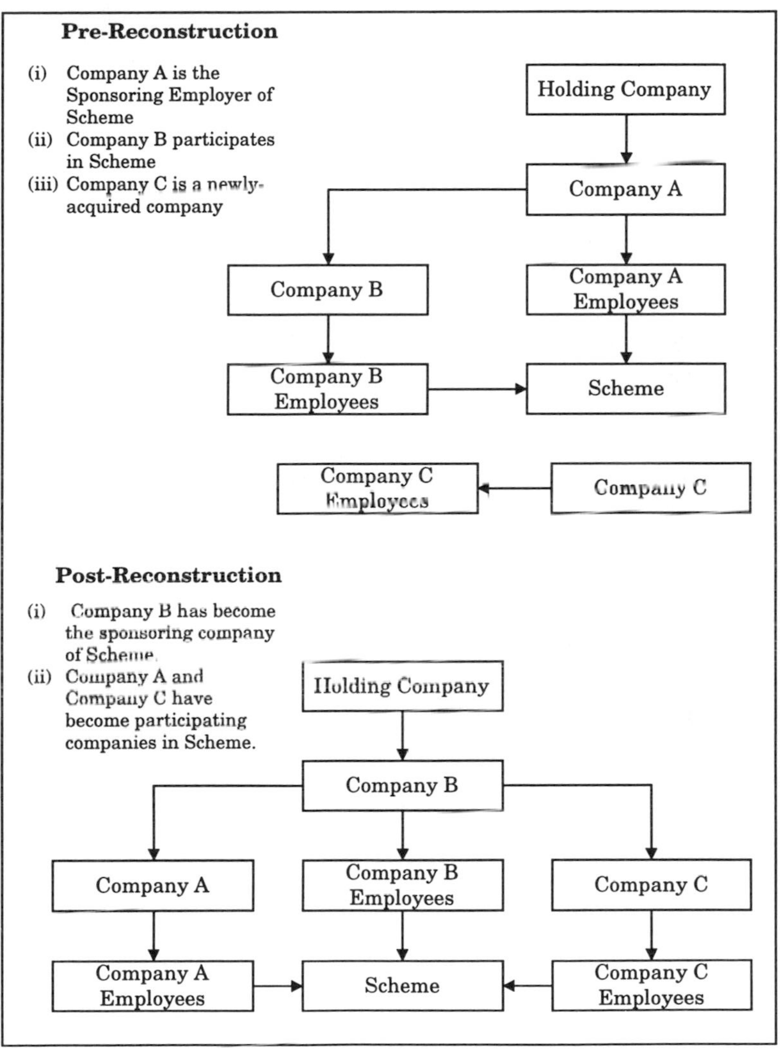

APPENDIX I

GLOSSARY OF PENSION TERMS COMMONLY ENCOUNTERED

Accrued Benefits
The benefits of a pension scheme member for service up to a given date.

Active Member
A member of a scheme who is included in the scheme for retirement benefits and is continuing to accrue retirement benefit — usually a member who is in service.

Actuary
A professional adviser whose business activities include dealing in probabilities based upon assumptions and statistics and principles of interest. Actuaries practising in Ireland are Fellows or Associates of the Society of Actuaries in Ireland.

Actuarial Assumptions
In a *defined benefit scheme*, assumptions such as those relating to investment return, price inflation, salary increases, mortality and morbidity, which the actuary employs in carrying out an actuarial valuation or other actuarial calculation.

Actuarial Funding Certificate
A certificate prepared and signed by an *actuary*, which confirms the solvency or otherwise of a *defined benefit scheme* on a prescribed basis under the *Pensions Act* and which must be submitted by the trustees to the *Pensions Board* at least every three and a half years.

Actuarial Valuation
An investigation of a *defined benefit scheme* by an actuary to determine whether the scheme is in a position to meet its liabilities — that is, the benefits promised under the scheme — and also to determine the future *funding rate*.

Additional Voluntary Contributions ("AVCs")
Contributions to a scheme, which a member is not obliged to make and which are paid in addition to the member's normal contribution (if any). These payments are made in order to secure additional benefits for the member, which can be calculated either on a *defined benefit scheme* basis (by purchasing additional years and months of *pensionable service*) or on a *defined contribution scheme* basis.

Annuity
A series of payments made at specified intervals for life, for a stated period or until a specified event occurs. It is usually secured by purchasing an annuity policy from an insurance company.

Associated Employer
An employer which is sufficiently closely connected with the *Principal Employer*, whether by shareholding or through common business interest, as to be permitted by the *Retirement Benefits District* to participate in the *Principal Employer's* scheme and which so participates.

Augmentation
The improvement in the benefits payable to or in respect of a scheme member over and above the member's normal entitlements under the scheme.

Buy-Out Bond
An *annuity* or investment policy purchased by the trustees of a scheme in the name of a member or other beneficiary in substitution for benefits otherwise payable under the provisions of the scheme. This commonly occurs on the member leaving service, on retirement and also on the winding up of the scheme.

Closed Scheme
A scheme which has ceased to be open to new members.

Commutation
An option given to a member at retirement to exchange pension for a cash sum.

Concentration of Investment
The holding of a significant proportion of a scheme's resources in one asset.

Contributory Scheme
A scheme under which members are required to contribute.

Co-ordination
See *integration*.

Deferred Annuity
An *annuity*, payment of which is deferred to a future date.

Deferred Pension
A pension that is deferred until retirement. This usually arises on a member leaving service without taking immediate early retirement.

Defined Benefit Scheme
An *occupational pension scheme*, under which the benefits provided are specified (defined) in the provisions of the scheme and which is not a *defined contribution scheme*.

Defined Contribution Scheme
An *occupational pension scheme*, under which the benefits at retirement for each member are determined solely by reference to the contributions paid by and in respect of the member and the investment return on those contributions.

Escalation
The annual increase in pensions in payment or *deferred pensions* by reference to a specified percentage, salary increases or price inflation. Increases may be promised in advance or may be discretionary.

Exempt Approved Scheme
A scheme that is established under irrevocable trusts (or is otherwise acceptable to the Revenue Commissioners) and is approved by the *Retirement Benefits District* for the purposes of section 16(1) of the Finance Act, 1972. These schemes enjoy certain tax reliefs.

Final Pensionable Salary/Earnings/Pay
In a *defined benefit scheme*, the member's pay at or near retirement or leaving service, which is used for the purposes of calculating retirement benefits. This may be pay at a fixed date or averaged over a number of years (usually three).

Final Remuneration
The maximum remuneration which the *Retirement Benefits District* will permit to be used for the purposes of calculating the maximum benefits that can be paid to or in respect of a member.

Final Salary Scheme
A *defined benefit scheme*.

Frozen Scheme
A *closed scheme* under which all members have ceased to accrue retirement benefits in respect of future service.

Funding Rate
In a *defined benefit scheme*, the rate (usually expressed as a percentage of total pensionable payroll) which the *actuary* advises is required to be paid into the scheme to meet the liabilities of the scheme to provide benefits.

Hybrid Scheme
A scheme in which some benefits are calculated on a *defined benefit scheme* basis and other benefits are calculated on a *defined contribution scheme* basis.

Integration
The design of a pension scheme whereby State social welfare benefits are taken into account in the calculation of benefits under the scheme.

Immediate Annuity
An *annuity* which commences to be paid immediately or very close to the time when it is purchased.

Money Purchase Scheme
A *defined contribution scheme*.

Non-Contributory Scheme
A scheme under which members are not required to contribute.

Normal Retirement Date ("NRD")/Normal Retirement Age ("NRA")/Normal Pension Date ("NPD")
The date fixed in the provisions of a scheme at which the member can receive an immediate retirement benefit without the requirement of employer consent and without any actuarial reduction in benefits.

Occupational Pension Scheme
Any scheme comprised in one or more instruments or agreements that is capable of providing retirement or death benefits or both, and which is approved by the Revenue Commissioners under Chapter II of Part I of the Finance Act, 1972 (or the approval of which is being considered) or which is a public-sector scheme.

Paid-Up Pension ("PUP")
See *deferred pension*.

Past Service Reserve
The *accrued benefits* of a *defined benefit scheme* as valued by an *actuary* at a given date. The value is calculated by reference to the *pensionable salaries* of *active members* projected to *normal retirement date*, as opposed to current pensionable salaries, but by reference to *pensionable service* completed to the date of calculation only.

Pay as You Go
The method of financing the cost of scheme benefits out of the employer's cash flow, where no advance funding of benefits is made.

Pensionable Salary/Pensionable Remuneration
The term usually adopted in *defined benefit scheme* rules and booklets to describe that part of the member's remuneration which is used in order to calculate benefit and/or contributions. The term may also be used in *defined contribution schemes* for contribution purposes.

Pensionable Service
The period of a member's service which is taken into account for the purpose of calculating pension under a *defined benefit scheme*.

Pensioneer Trustee
In relation to a *small self-administered scheme*, a body or individual widely involved with pension schemes and their approval, which is prepared to give an undertaking to the Revenue Commissioners that

it will not consent to any termination of a scheme of which it is trustee, otherwise than in accordance with the terms of the winding-up rule approved by the *Retirement Benefits District*, and will ensure compliance with other Revenue requirements.

Pensions Act
The Pensions Act, 1990 as amended by the Social Welfare Act, 1991, the Social Welfare Act, 1992, the Social Welfare Act, 1993, the Social Welfare (No 2) Act, 1993 and the Pensions (Amendment) Act, 1996.

Pensions Board
A body established under the *Pensions Act*, the principal objects of which are to monitor and supervise the operation of the Act and pensions developments and to regulate *occupational pension schemes*.

Practice Notes
Notes issued by the *Retirement Benefits District* of the Revenue Commissioners with regard to the approval requirements for becoming *exempt approved schemes* and to the requirements for continued approval.

Preserved Benefit
That part of the benefits that arise out of termination of employment or ceasing to be an *active member*, which is payable at a later date — that is, retirement — and which will be either protected by the preservation requirements of the *Pensions Act* or under public-sector legislation or regulations.

Principal Employer
In a scheme in which more than one employer can participate, the participating employer which is vested with special powers regarding the operation and termination of the scheme and the appointment of trustees and which is the employer that usually establishes the scheme.

Qualifying Service
The term used in the *Pensions Act* to describe the period of service as an *active member* of an *occupational pension scheme* which the member must complete in order to be entitled to a *preserved benefit*. Service as an *active member* of all *occupational pension schemes* of the employer is aggregated, as is similar service which relates to any

transfer payment received by the scheme. However, overlapping periods are only counted once.

Reckonable Service

In public-sector schemes this term has the same meaning as *Pensionable Service*. Under the *Pensions Act* it is the period of service with an employer during which the employee is an *active member*.

Retirement Annuity Contract

A policy issued under section 235 or 235A of the Income Tax Act, 1967. See *self-employed arrangement*.

Retirement Benefits District

The branch of the Revenue Commissioners which is responsible for the monitoring and approval of *exempt approved schemes*.

Revaluation

A term used in the *Pensions Act* to describe the increases required to be made to a *preserved benefit* from the termination of employment or scheme membership until *normal retirement date*.

Self-Employed Arrangement

A policy (or possibly a trust scheme) approved by the Revenue Commissioners under section 235 or 235A of the Income Tax Act, 1967 in respect of a person who is self-employed or is not in employment that is pensionable under an exempt approved scheme or a scheme established under statute.

Self-Investment

The investment of part or all of the resources of an *occupational pension scheme* in, or any loan to, the employer or any associated entity. Such investment is regulated under the funding and disclosure requirements of the *Pensions Act*.

Small Self-Administered Scheme

An *exempt approved scheme* with few members (generally under 12), established for the purpose of providing benefits for employees or directors who have significant shareholdings (at least 20 per cent) in the employer, and which is not administered under an insurance policy. The scheme is subject to special approval restrictions and the appointment of a *pensioneer trustee*.

Target Benefit Scheme
A *defined contribution scheme* under which the members are notified that specified retirement benefits are being funded for by the employer but are not guaranteed, in that each member's benefits are at all times subject to the value of contributions paid by and in respect of the member. If the specified benefits were to be guaranteed, the scheme would be a *defined benefit scheme*.

Transfer Network
The systems operated in the public sector to enable employees in pensionable employment in the public sector to receive a full credit for pension purposes on transferring to another part of the public sector.

Transfer Payment
A payment made from one scheme to another or to a *buy-out bond* in substitution for benefits otherwise payable under the first scheme.

Transfer Value
The amount of any *transfer payment* — in the case of a *defined benefit scheme* usually calculated on the advice of an *actuary*.

Uprating
In public-sector schemes, the increase of *preserved benefits* and pensions in line with the salary grade of the former member or pensioner.

Vested Benefit
The benefit to which a member is entitled as of right. In the case of pensioners, it is the pension of which they are currently in receipt. In the case of former members entitled to *deferred pensions*, it is their *deferred pension*, which may comprise or include a *preserved benefit*. For *active members* it is the *deferred pension* to which they will become unconditionally entitled should they leave service.

APPENDIX II

PENSIONS ACT, 1990 (CONSOLIDATION)

INTRODUCTION

In this appendix is set out, with kind permission of the Government Supplies Agency, the Pensions Act, 1990, as subsequently amended by the Social Welfare Act, 1991, the Social Welfare Act, 1992, the Social Welfare Act, 1993, the Social Welfare (No. 2) Act, 1993 and the Pensions (Amendment) Act, 1996.

The amendments effected consist of additions to, substitutions for and repeals of the original (or previously amended) provisions of the legislation. The nature of the amendments together with a note of the effecting legislation is indicated by notes in the margin.

Generally, the following words are used to indicate different types of amendment:

"as amended by"	means that some words in the original (or previously amended) provision have been changed.
"as substituted by"	means that an entirely new section, subsection, paragraph or subparagraph has been enacted in place of the original (or previously amended) provision.
"as inserted by"	means that an entirely new section, subsection, paragraph or subparagraph has been inserted.
"repealed by"	means that a section, subsection, paragraph or subparagraph of the original (or previously amended) provision has been repealed and deleted.

If the margin note commences with a specific reference to a subsection, paragraph or subparagraph in the Act, the amendment affects only that part to which reference is made.

If the margin note appears at the commencement of a section without any specific reference, it refers to the entire section.

If the margin note appears opposite a subsection, paragraph or subparagraph but without any specific reference, it refers to the entire subsection, paragraph or subparagraph as appropriate.

The following abbreviations are used in the margin notes:

"SW Act 1991"	The Social Welfare Act, 1991 (No. 7 of 1991)
"SW Act 1992"	The Social Welfare Act, 1992 (No. 5 of 1992)
"SW Act 1993"	The Social Welfare Act, 1993 (No. 5 of 1993)
"SW (No. 2) Act 1993"	The Social Welfare (No. 2) Act, 1993 (No. 32 of 1993)
"P(A) Act 1996"	The Pensions (Amendment) Act, 1996 (No. 18 of 1996)

Number 25 of 1990

PENSIONS ACT, 1990

[As amended by the Social Welfare Act, 1991, the Social Welfare Act, 1992, the Social Welfare Act, 1993, the Social Welfare (No. 2) Act, 1993 and the Pensions (Amendment) Act, 1996]

ARRANGEMENT OF SECTIONS

PART I
PRELIMINARY AND GENERAL

PART II
ESTABLISHMENT OF PENSIONS BOARD

PART III
PRESERVATION OF BENEFITS

PART IV
FUNDING STANDARD

PART V
DISCLOSURE OF INFORMATION IN RELATION TO SCHEMES

PART VI
TRUSTEES OF SCHEMES

PART VII
EQUAL TREATMENT FOR MEN AND WOMEN IN OCCUPATIONAL BENEFIT SCHEMES

PART VIII
COMPULSORY AND VOLUNTARY REPORTING TO THE BOARD

PART IX
MISCELLANEOUS APPLICATIONS TO THE HIGH COURT

FIRST SCHEDULE
AN BORD PINSEAN - THE PENSIONS BOARD

SECOND SCHEDULE
PRESERVATION AND REVALUATION OF BENEFITS

PART A
PRESERVATION OF BENEFITS

PART B
REVALUATION OF PRESERVED BENEFITS

THIRD SCHEDULE
FUNDING STANDARD - BENEFITS

Number 25 of 1990

PENSIONS ACT, 1990

AN ACT TO REGULATE OCCUPATIONAL PENSION SCHEMES AND TO PROVIDE FOR EQUAL TREATMENT OF MEN AND WOMEN UNDER OCCUPATIONAL BENEFIT SCHEMES, FOR THOSE PURPOSES TO PROVIDE FOR THE ESTABLISHMENT OF A BODY (TO BE KNOWN AS AN BORD PINSEAN - THE PENSIONS BOARD) TO SUPERVISE SUCH SCHEMES AND THEIR OPERATION, TO DEFINE THE FUNCTIONS OF THAT BODY AND TO PROVIDE FOR CONNECTED MATTERS. [24th July, 1990]

BE IT ENACTED BY THE OIREACHTAS AS FOLLOWS:

PART I
Preliminary and General

1. - (1) This Act may be cited as the Pensions Act, 1990. Short title and commencement.

(2) This Act shall come into operation on such day or days as may be appointed by order or orders of the Minister, either generally or with reference to a particular purpose or provision, and different days may be so appointed for different purposes and different provisions of this Act.

2. - (1) In this Act, unless the context otherwise requires - Interpretation.

"actuarial value" means the equivalent cash value of a benefit (including, where appropriate, provision for any re-valuation of such benefit) calculated by reference to appropriate financial assumptions and making due allowance for the probability of survival to normal pensionable age and thereafter in accordance with normal life expectancy on the assumption that the member of a scheme, at the effective date of calculation, is in a normal state of health having regard to his age;

"actuary", in relation to a scheme, means a person appointed in pursuance of this Act to act as actuary, for the purposes of this Act, of the scheme, and "actuarial" shall be construed accordingly;

"additional voluntary contributions" means such contributions (if any) as are paid on a voluntary basis by a member of a scheme and are designed to fully provide additional benefits;

"administrator" has the meaning assigned to it by section 13(1) of the Finance Act, 1972;

as substituted by s.42(a) SW Act 1993

"auditor", in relation to a scheme, means a person appointed in pursuance of this Act to act as auditor, for the purposes of this Act, of the scheme;

inserted by s.2(a) P(A) Act 1996

"authorised person" means a person authorised as an authorised person under *section 18*;

"benefits", in relation to a scheme, means, other than in *Part VII*, either or both of the following, that is to say -

(a) benefit for the member of a scheme at normal pensionable age or in respect of earlier or later retirement, or on leaving the relevant employment, and

(b) benefit for the member's widow, widower, or dependants or others, on the death of the member;

"the Board" means the body established by *section 9*;

"chairman of the Board" shall be construed in accordance with *paragraph 3* of the *First Schedule*;

"the chief executive" means the chief officer of the Board appointed under *section 15*;

"defined benefit scheme" means, subject to *section 27*, a scheme which is not a defined contribution scheme;

"defined contribution scheme" means, subject to *section 27*, a scheme which, under its rules, provides long service benefit, the rate or amount of which is in total directly determined by the amount of the contributions paid by or in respect of the member and includes a scheme the contributions under which are used, directly or indirectly, to provide -

(a) benefits, other than long service benefit, and

(b) long service benefit the rate or amount of which is in total directly determined by the part of the contributions aforesaid that is used for the provision of the long service benefit;

"early retirement rule" means a provision of a scheme under which a member may retire with entitlement to an immediate benefit where either - *inserted by s.42(b) SW Act 1993*

(i) the member's right is subject to the consent of some person or the satisfaction of some condition not relating only to age or period of service in relevant employment or both, or

(ii) the calculation of the member's immediate retirement benefit involves or may involve an actuarial reduction which exceeds 0.25 per cent., or such other percentage as may be prescribed, multiplied by the number of completed months by which the member's age at retirement is less than a stated age; *Paragraph (ii) as substituted by s.2(b) P (A) Act 1996*

"external member" in relation to a scheme, means any person who, having been admitted to membership under the rules of the scheme, remains entitled to any benefit under the scheme in respect of a period of service whilst employed outside the State; *as inserted by s.42(b) SW Act 1993*

"external scheme" means a scheme established under the law of a country other than the State; *as inserted by s.42(b) SW Act 1993*

"the establishment day" means the day appointed by the Minister under *section 8*;

"functions" includes powers and duties;

"funded scheme" means a scheme under which some or all of its resources are set aside in advance to provide benefits in a manner which is independent of the employer's business activities;

"immediate retirement benefit" means a benefit payable to a member under the rules of a scheme immediately on retirement from relevant employment but does not include a refund of the member's contributions with or without interest or a transfer of an amount of money from the scheme - *as inserted by s.42(c) SW Act 1993*

(i) to another scheme, or

(ii) for application under a policy or contract of insurance approved by the Revenue Commissioners under Chapter II of Part I of the Finance Act, 1972;

"long service benefit" means the benefits which will be payable under a scheme in accordance with an obligation to or in respect of a member of a scheme on the assumption that he remains in relevant employment until such time as he attains normal pensionable age;

as substituted by s.53(a) SW Act 1992

"member", in relation to a scheme, means, subject to *section 62*, any person who, having been admitted to membership under the rules of the scheme, remains entitled to any benefit under the scheme in respect of a period of service whilst employed within the State;

"the Minister" means the Minister for Social Welfare;

as substituted by s.42(d) SW Act 1993

paragraph (a) substituted by s.2(c) P(A) Act 1996

"normal pensionable age" means the later of -

(a) the earliest age at which a member of a scheme is entitled under the rules of the scheme (other than under any early retirement rule) to receive an immediate retirement benefit, or

(b) the age of 60 years:

Provided that if a member of a scheme is required to retire from relevant employment at an age below 60 years with entitlement under the rules of the scheme to receive an immediate retirement benefit, normal pensionable age means the age at which the member is required to retire from relevant employment;

as substituted by s.53(b) SW Act 1992

"occupational pension scheme" means any scheme or arrangement -

(a) which is comprised in one or more instruments or agreements, and

(b) which provides or is capable of providing in relation to employees in any description of employment within the State, benefits, and

(c) (i) which has been approved of by the Revenue Commissioners for the purpose of Chapter II of Part I of the Finance Act, 1972, or

(ii) the application for approval of which under Chapter II of Part I of the Finance Act, 1972, is being considered, or

(iii) which is a statutory scheme to which *section 17* of the Finance Act, 1972, applies, or

(iv) which is a scheme other than a scheme specified in *subparagraph (i), (ii)* or *(iii)* and where the benefits are paid in whole or in part out of moneys provided from the Central Fund or moneys provided by the Oireachtas, or

(v) which has been approved by the Revenue Commissioners for the purpose of one or more of the following, that is to say, section 32 of the Finance Act, 1921, or section 34 of the Finance Act, 1958, or sections 222 or 229 of the Income Tax Act, 1967;

paragraph (v) as inserted by s.42(e) SW Act 1993

"prescribed" means prescribed by regulations made by the Minister under this Act;

"preserved benefit" has the meaning assigned to it by *section 28*(2);

"prospective member" means any person who is already in relevant employment and who, by virtue of his contract of service or the rules of the scheme is or will be eligible to join the scheme or will in any event join the scheme if his service in relevant employment continues and the relevant terms of his contract of employment or, as the case may be, the relevant terms of the rules of the scheme remain unaltered during that time;

Definition substituted by s.42(f) SW Act 1993 (previously substituted by s.53(c) SW Act 1992)

"reckonable service" means service in the relevant employment during membership of the scheme but does not include service as a member of the scheme where either -

(a) the only benefit under the scheme in respect of such service is in respect of death prior to normal pensionable age, or

Paragraph (a) as substituted by s.2(d) P(A) Act 1996

(b) the member has been notified in writing by the trustees that such service does not entitle him to long service benefit;

"regulations" means regulations made by the Minister under this Act;

"relevant employment" means any employment (or any period treated as employment) to which a scheme applies;

"resources", in relation to a scheme, means the funds out of which the benefits provided by the scheme are payable from time to time, including the proceeds of any policy of insurance taken out, or annuity contract entered into, for the purposes of the scheme;

"revaluation percentage" has the meaning assigned to it by *section 33*;

"rules", in relation to a scheme, means the provisions of a scheme, by whatever name they are called;

"scheme" means an occupational pension scheme;

"trustees", in relation to a scheme, which is established under a trust, means the trustees of the scheme and, in relation to a scheme not so established, means the administrator of the scheme and, accordingly, references to trustees shall, except in *sections 59, 62, 63* and *64*, be construed as including references to administrators.

(2) In this Act -

(a) a reference to a Part is to a Part of this Act unless it is indicated that a reference to a Part of a Schedule to this Act or of some other enactment is intended,

(b) a reference to a section or a Schedule is a reference to a section of, or a Schedule to, this Act unless it is indicated that reference to some other enactment is intended,

(c) a reference to a subsection, paragraph or subparagraph is a reference to the subsection, paragraph or subparagraph of the provision in which the reference occurs unless it is indicated that reference to some other provision is intended.

(3) In this Act a reference to an enactment shall be construed as a reference to that enactment as amended or extended by any other enactment including this Act.

Offences.

3. - (1)(a)Where a trustee contravenes, in his capacity as trustee, a provision of this Act or a regulation thereunder, he shall be guilty of an offence.

(b) Where an actuary or auditor of a scheme contravenes, in his capacity as such actuary or auditor, a provision of this Act or a regulation thereunder, he shall be guilty of an offence.

as inserted by s.43(1) SW Act 1993

(bb) Where a person who is required under regulations made under *section 5A*, to carry out any of the duties imposed upon trustees by this Act or by any regulations thereunder contravenes, in his capacity as such a person, a provision of this Act or any regulations thereunder, he shall be guilty of an offence.

as substituted by s.3(a) P(A) Act 1996 (previously amended by s.43(2) SW Act 1993)

(c) In a prosecution for an offence under *paragraph (a)*, *(b)* or *(bb)* it shall be a defence for the accused person to prove that the contravention to which the offence relates was attributable to:

(i) a contravention by one or more other persons of a provision of this Act or a regulation thereunder and that he took such reasonable steps (if any) in the circumstances as were open to him to secure the compliance of the person or persons aforesaid with the provision concerned, or

(ii) a failure by an actuary, auditor or other person to prepare a document which the accused person had instructed the actuary, auditor or other person to prepare and that the accused person took such reasonable steps (if any) in the circumstances as were open to him to secure the preparation of the said document by the actuary, auditor or other person aforesaid.

(2) Where in any report, certificate or other document required for the purposes of any provision of this Act or regulations thereunder, a person makes a statement which is, to his knowledge, false or misleading in any material particular, he shall be guilty of an offence.

Subsection 3(a) as amended by s.43 P(A) Act 1996

(3) A person guilty of an offence under *subsection (1)* or *(2)* shall be liable -

(a) on summary conviction to a fine not exceeding £1,500 or to imprisonment for a term not exceeding one year, or to both,

(b) on conviction on indictment to a fine not exceeding £10,000 or to imprisonment for a term not exceeding 2 years, or to both.

(4) Where an offence under this Act is committed by a body corporate and is proved to have been so committed with the consent or connivance of or to be attributable to any neglect on the part of any person, being a director, manager, secretary or other officer of the body corporate, or a person who was purporting to act in such capacity, that person shall, as well as the body corporate, be guilty of an offence and shall be liable to be proceeded against and punished as if he were guilty of the first-mentioned offence.

(5) Proceedings for a summary offence under this Act may be brought and prosecuted by the Board.

as inserted by s.3(b) P(A) Act 1996

(6) Notwithstanding the provisions of section 10(4) of the Petty Sessions (Ireland) Act, 1851, summary proceedings for an offence under this Act may be commenced -

(a) at any time within 2 years from the date on which the offence was committed, or

(b) at any time within 6 months from the date on which evidence sufficient in the opinion of the Board to justify initiating the proceedings, comes to the Board's knowledge, not being later than 5 years from the date on which the offence concerned was committed.

Continuing offences.
as inserted by s.44 P(A) Act 1996

3A. - Where a person, after conviction for an offence under this Act, continues to contravene the provision concerned, he shall be guilty of an offence on every day on which the contravention continues and for each such offence he shall be liable to a fine -

(a) on summary conviction, not exceeding £250, or

(b) on conviction on indictment, not exceeding £5,000.

4. - Notwithstanding anything contained in any enactment, information held by the Board for the purposes of this Act may be transferred by the Board to the Revenue Commissioners and information held by the Revenue Commissioners for the purposes of Chapter II of Part I of the Finance Act, 1972 relating to occupational pension schemes may be transferred by the Revenue Commissioners to the Board.

Exchange of information.

5. - (1) The Minister may make regulations -

Regulations generally.

(a) for any purpose in relation to which regulations are provided for by any of the provisions of this Act, and

(b) for prescribing any matter or thing referred to in this Act as prescribed or to be prescribed.

(2) Except in so far as this Act otherwise provides, any power conferred thereby to make regulations may be exercised -

(a) either in relation to all cases to which the power extends, or in relation to all those cases subject to specified exceptions, or in relation to any specified cases or classes of case, and

(b) so as to make, as respects the cases in relation to which it is exercised -

(i) the full provision to which the power extends or any lesser provision (whether by way of exception or otherwise),

(ii) the same provision for all cases in relation to which the power is exercised or different provision for different cases or classes of case, or different provision as respects the same case or class of case for different purposes of this Act,

(iii) any such provision either unconditionally or subject to any specified condition.

(3) Without prejudice to any specific provision of this Act, any regulations may contain such incidental or supplementary provisions as may appear to the Minister to be expedient for the purpose of the regulations.

as inserted by s.4 P(A) Act 1996

(4)(a) The Minister may, with the consent of the Minister for Equality and Law Reform, make regulations specifying guidelines for the purposes of section 12 and the reference in subsection (1) of the said section 12 to any relevant guidelines for the time being in force under section 10(1)(c) shall be construed as a reference to any relevant guidelines specified as aforesaid and for the time being in force.

(b) Without prejudice to the generality of paragraph (a), guidelines specified by regulations under that paragraph may -

(i) make provision in relation to the manner in which a contingent benefit, a designated benefit, a residual benefit or a transfer amount payable under a scheme, the actuarial value referred to in subsection (10) of section 12 or the value and the amounts referred to in subsection (25) of section 12 should be calculated and, in particular, but without prejudice to the generality of the foregoing, provide that, in making such a calculation, regard should be had to one or more of the following:

(I) whether the scheme concerned is a defined contribution scheme or not,

(II) the amount of retirement benefit payable (or which, but for the making of the relevant order for the decree of judicial separation, would have been payable) under the scheme concerned to or in respect of the member spouse concerned,

(III) the period of reckonable service of the member spouse for the purposes of such retirement benefit,

(IV) the period concerned and the percentage concerned specified in the order concerned under subsection (2) of section 12 pursuant to paragraphs (i) and (ii) respectively, of that subsection,

(V) the value, the actuarial value or the accumulated value, as may be appropriate, of the whole or the appropriate part of such retirement benefit as aforesaid,

(VI) whether, at the date of the making of the relevant order under subsection (2) of section 12, the member spouse was an active member of the scheme concerned or was being paid retirement benefit, or was entitled to any other benefit payment of which is deferred, under the scheme concerned,

(VII) the amount of contingent benefit payable (or which, but for the making of the relevant order for the decree of judicial separation, would have been payable) under the scheme concerned on the death of the member spouse concerned,

(VIII) the percentage concerned specified in the order concerned under subsection (3) of section 12,

(ii) specify the manner in which a transfer amount should be applied under section 12,

(iii)specify the manner and the circumstances in which a contingent benefit, a designated benefit, a residual benefit or a transfer amount should be paid or applied pursuant to section 12 (including the period, and the manner of its ascertainment, during which such a payment should be made) and, in particular, but without prejudice to the generality of the foregoing, where -

(I) the member spouse concerned retires upon or before or after attaining normal pensionable age,

(II) the member spouse dies before payment of the designated benefit has commenced,

(III) the member spouse dies after payment of the designated benefit has commenced,

(IV) the member spouse ceases to be an active member of the scheme concerned,

(V) the person in whose favour the relevant order under subsection (2) of section 12 is made dies before payment of the designated benefit has commenced,

(VI) the person in whose favour the order aforesaid is made dies after payment of the designated benefit has commenced,

(VII) the person in whose favour the said order is made ceases to be a dependent member of the family as defined in section 2 of the Family Law Act, 1995,

(VIII) in the circumstances specified in subsection (5) of section 12, a spouse makes an application under that subsection,

(IX) the trustees of the scheme concerned apply the transfer amount concerned under or in accordance with subsection (6) or (8) of section 12,

and

(iv) make such other provision as may be necessary or expedient for the purposes of section 12 and for enabling it to have full effect.

(c) In making regulations under paragraph (a), regard shall be had to any relevant principles, purposes or policies of this Act, the Income Tax Acts, the Family Law Act, 1995, any relevant current practices of the Revenue Commissioners in approving schemes, any relevant guidelines, guidance notes or codes of practice of the Board and any relevant guidelines of the Society of Actuaries in Ireland for the time being in force and the desirability of promoting equity and consistency in the treatment of individual cases, minimising any costs incurred under section 12 and conforming with good pensions practice.

(d) In this subsection -

"accumulated value" means-

(i) the realisable value of the units, shares or securities at a particular date, or averaged over a particular period before that date in which, pursuant to the rules of the scheme, the contributions for retirement benefit paid by or in respect of a member spouse under the scheme are invested, or

(ii) the realisable value of the contributions for retirement benefit paid by or in respect of a member spouse under a defined contribution scheme, together with the notional rate of interest or other investment return prescribed under the rules of the scheme, or

(iii) the amount of the proceeds of any insurance policies in which, pursuant to the rules of the scheme, the contributions for retirement benefit paid by or in respect of a member spouse under the scheme are invested,

less, in each case, the amount of any of the expenses of the scheme that, pursuant to the rules thereof, fall to be discharged out of the said realisable value or proceeds;

"active member", "actuarial value", "contingent benefit", "defined contribution scheme", "designated benefit", "retirement benefit", "scheme" and "transfer amount" have the meanings assigned to them by section 12;

"residual benefit" means the amount of retirement benefit remaining in respect of the member spouse concerned after deduction therefrom of the relevant designated benefit or the amount of contingent benefit in respect of the member spouse concerned remaining after deduction therefrom of the amount of contingent benefit payable pursuant to an order under subsection (3) of section 12 or the amount of payment made under subsection (7) of section 12;

"section 12" means section 12 of the Family Law Act, 1995.

Regulations.

as inserted by s.44 SW Act 1993

5A. - Regulations may provide that the provisions of this Act and of regulations thereunder shall apply to-

(a) schemes with external members, or

(b) external schemes, or

(c) schemes where the majority of the trustees are not resident within the State,

with and subject to such modifications as may be prescribed and such regulations may require persons other than the trustees of such schemes to carry out in relation to those schemes any of the duties imposed upon trustees by this Act or by regulations thereunder.

Laying of regulations before Houses of Oireachtas.

6. - Every regulation made by the Minister under this Act shall be laid before each House of the Oireachtas as soon as may be after it is made and, if a resolution annulling the regulation is passed by either such House within the next 21 days on which that House has sat after the regulation is laid before it, the regulation shall be annulled accordingly, but without prejudice to the validity of anything done thereunder.

Expenses.

7. - The expenses incurred by the Minister in the administration of this Act shall, to such extent as may be sanctioned by the Minister for Finance, be paid out of moneys provided by the Oireachtas.

PART II
Establishment of Pensions Board

8. - The Minister may by order appoint a day to be the establishment day for the purposes of this Part.

Establishment day.

9. - (1) On the establishment day there shall stand established a body to be known as An Bord Pinsean - The Pensions Board, and in this Act referred to as "the Board", to perform the functions conferred on it by this Act.

Establishment of Board.

(2) The provisions of the *First Schedule* shall have effect with respect to the Board.

10. - (1) The functions of the Board shall be -

Functions of Board.

(a) to monitor and supervise the operation of this Act and pensions developments generally;

(b) to advise the Minister either at his request or on its own initiative on all matters relating to the functions assigned to the Board under this Act and on matters relating to pensions generally;

(c) to issue guidelines or guidance notes on the duties and responsibilities of trustees of schemes and codes of practice on specific aspects of their responsibilities;

as substituted by s.5 P(A) Act 1996

(cc) to issue guidelines or guidance notes generally on the operation of this Act and on the provisions of the Family Law Act, 1995, relating to pension schemes (within the meaning of section 2 of the Family Law Act, 1995);

as inserted by s.5 P(A) Act 1996

(d) to encourage the provision of appropriate training facilities for trustees of schemes;

(e) to advise the Minister on standards for trustees of schemes and on their implementation;

(f) to publish an annual report and such other reports as it may from time to time consider necessary;

(g) to perform such tasks as the Minister may from time to time request.

(2) The Board shall have such powers as are necessary for or incidental to the performance of its functions.

Conferral of additional functions on Board.

11. - (1) The Minister may, with the consent of the Minister for Finance, by order -

(a) confer on the Board such additional functions connected with the functions for the time being of the Board as he considers appropriate, and

(b) make such provision as he considers necessary or expedient in relation to matters ancillary to or arising out of the conferral on the Board of functions so conferred.

(2) The Minister may by order amend or revoke an order under this section (including an order under this subsection).

(3) Every order made by the Minister under this section shall be laid before each House of the Oireachtas as soon as may be after it is made and, if a resolution annulling the order is passed by either such House within the next 21 days on which the House has sat after the order is laid before it, the order shall be annulled accordingly, but without prejudice to the validity of anything previously done thereunder.

Consultants and advisers.

12. - Subject to the prior approval of the Minister, the Board may from time to time engage such consultants or advisers as it may consider necessary for the performance of its functions, and any fees due to a consultant or adviser engaged under this section shall be paid by the Board out of moneys at its disposal.

Gifts.

13. - (1) The Board may accept gifts of money, land or other property upon such trusts or conditions (if any) as may be specified by the donor.

(2) The Board shall not accept a gift if the trusts or conditions attached to it would be inconsistent with its functions.

Committees of Board.

14. - (1) The Board may establish committees to assist and advise it in relation to the performance of any of its functions.

(2) The members of a committee established under this section shall be appointed by the Board.

(3) A committee established under this section may include persons who are not members of the Board.

(4) A member of a committee established under this section may be removed from office at any time by the Board.

(5) The Board may at any time dissolve a committee established under this section.

(6) The Board may appoint a person to be chairman of a committee established under this section.

(7) There may be paid out of the income of the Board to members of a committee established under this section such allowances for expenses incurred by them as the Board may, with the consent of the Minister and the Minister fo Finance, determine.

15. - (1) There shall be a chief officer of the Board who shall be known, and is referred to in this Act, as the chief executive. Chief executive.

(2) The chief executive shall be appointed, and may be removed from office at any time, by the Board with the consent of the Minister.

(3) The chief executive shall not be a member of the Board.

(4) The chief executive shall carry on and manage and control generally the administration and business of the Board and perform such other functions as may be determined by the Board.

(5) The chief executive shall devote the whole of his time to his duties as chief executive and shall not hold any other office or position without the consent of the Board.

(6) The chief executive shall hold office on and subject to such terms and conditions (including terms and conditions relating to remuneration) as may be approved of by the Minister with the consent of the Minister for Finance.

(7) The chief executive shall be paid, out of moneys at the disposal of the Board, such allowances for expenses incurred by him in the performance of his functions as may be determined by the Minister with the consent of the Minister for Finance.

(8) The chief executive may make proposals to the Board on any matter relating to its activities.

Staff of Board.

16. - (1) The Board may appoint such, and such number of, persons to be members of the staff of the Board as it may determine with the consent of the Minister and the Minister for Finance.

(2)(a) A member of the staff of the Board shall hold his office or employment on such terms and conditions (including terms and conditions relating to remuneration and superannuation) as the Board may, with the consent of the Minister and the Minister for Finance, determine.

(b) A member of the staff of the Board referred to in *paragraph (a)* shall be paid, out of the moneys at the disposal of the Board, such remuneration and allowances for expenses incurred by him as the Board may, with the consent of the Minister and the Minister for Finance, determine.

(c) The Board may, with the consent of the Minister, at any time remove any officer or servant of the Board from being its officer or servant.

(3) The grades of the staff of the Board, and the number of staff in each grade, shall be determined by the Board with the consent of the Minister and the Minister for Finance.

(4) The Board may perform any of its functions through or by the chief executive or any other member of its staff duly authorised by the Board in that behalf.

Superannuation of staff of Board.

17. - (1) The Board may, with the consent of the Minister and the Minister for Finance, make a scheme or schemes for the granting of superannuation benefits to or in respect of persons appointed to whole-time positions on the staff of the Board.

(2) A scheme under *subsection (1)* shall fix the time and conditions of retirement for all persons (including the chief executive) to or in respect of whom superannuation benefits are payable under the scheme or schemes and different times and conditions may be fixed in respect of different classes of persons.

(3) The Board may, with the consent of the Minister and the Minister for Finance, make a scheme amending or revoking a scheme under this section including a scheme under this subsection.

(4) If any dispute arises as to the claim of any person to, or the amount of, any superannuation benefit payable in pursuance of a scheme or schemes under this section such dispute shall be submitted to the Minister who shall refer it to the Minister for Finance, whose decision shall be final.

(5) No superannuation benefits shall be granted by the Board on the resignation, retirement or death of a member of the staff of the Board (including the chief executive) otherwise than in accordance with a scheme or schemes under this section.

(6) A scheme under this section shall be laid before each House of the Oireachtas as soon as may be after it is made and, if a resolution annulling the scheme is passed by either such House within the next 21 days on which that House has sat after the scheme is laid before it, the scheme shall be annulled accordingly, but without prejudice to the validity of anything previously done thereunder.

Authorised persons.

18. - (1) The Board may authorise in writing such and so many persons as it considers necessary to be authorised persons to inspect or investigate on its behalf the state and conduct of a scheme.

Subsection (1) as substituted by s.6(1)(a) P(A) Act, 1996

(2) The Board or an authorised person may, in relation to a scheme, require the employer concerned or the trustees of the scheme to furnish it within such reasonable period as may be specified with such information and explanations and such books of account and other documents in relation to the scheme as may be specified.

as substituted by s.6(1)(b) P(A) Act 1996

(3) An authorised person shall be furnished with a certificate of his appointment as an authorised person and when exercising any power conferred on him by this section asan authorised person shall, if requested by a person affected, produce the certificate or a copy thereof to the person.

as inserted by s.6(1)(b) P(A) Act 1996

(3A) An authorised person, for the purpose of obtaining any information which may be required by the Board in relation to a scheme, may -

(a) at all reasonable times enter the premises of any employer, trustee or agent, as the case may be,

(b) make such examination or inquiry as may be necessary to determine whether the provisions of this Act are being or have been complied with,

(c) inspect and take copies of or extracts from any records (including in the case of information in a non-legible form a copy of an extract from such information in permanent legible form) relating to the scheme,

(d) remove and retain any books of account and other documents and other records in relation to the scheme for a reasonable period for their further examination or for the purpose of any legal proceedings, and

(e) require any person by or on whose behalf data equipment is or has been used or any person having charge of, or otherwise concerned with the operation of, the data equipment or any associated apparatus or material, to afford him all reasonable assistance in relation thereto.

(4) The duty to produce or provide any information, document, material or explanation shall extend to any person being an officer or employee of the employer or a trustee or agent, as the case may be, or appears to the Board or the authorised person to have that information, document, material or explanation in his possession or under his control.

as inserted by s.6(1)(c) P(A) Act 1996

(4A) An authorised person shall not, other than with the consent of the occupier, enter a private dwelling unless he has obtained a warrant from the District Court under subsection (4D) authorising such entry.

(4B) Where an authorised person in the exercise of his powers under this section is prevented from entering any premises an application may be made under *subsection (4D)* authorising such entry.

as inserted by s.6(1)(c) P(A) Act 1996

(4C) An authorised person, where he considers it necessary, may be accompanied by a member of the Garda Síochána when performing any powers conferred on an authorised person by this Act.

as inserted by s.6(1)(c) P(A) Act 1996

(4D) If a judge of the District Court is satisfied on the sworn information of an authorised person that there are reasonable grounds for suspecting that there is information required by an authorised person under this section held on any premises or any part of any premises, the judge may issue a warrant authorising an authorised person, accompanied by other authorised persons, at any time or times within one month from the date of issue of the warrant, on production if so requested of the warrant, to enter the premises and exercise all or any of the powers conferred on an authorised person under this section.

as inserted by s.6(1)(c) P(A) Act 1996

(5) If any employer, officer or employee of the employer, trustee of a scheme or agent to the scheme -

(a) wilfully obstructs an authorised person in the exercise of his powers under this section, or

(b) refuses without reasonable excuse to produce to such person any information, document, material or explanation when required to do so under this section, or

(c) refuses without reasonable excuse to answer any questions put to him by the authorised person with respect to the affairs of the scheme,

he shall be guilty of an offence under this section and shall be liable -

(i) on summary conviction to a fine not exceeding £1,500 or to imprisonment for a term not exceeding one year, or to both,

as amended by s.43 P(A) Act 1996

(ii) on conviction on indictment to a fine not exceeding £10,000 or to imprisonment for a term not exceeding 2 years, or to both.

(6) In this section "agent", in relation to a scheme, includes the actuaries, auditors and other accountants and the financial and other advisers to the scheme.

(7) Any reference in this section to an officer, employee or agent of a scheme includes a reference to a person who has been, but no longer is, an officer, employee or agent (as the case may be) of the scheme.

as inserted by s.6(1)(d) P(A) Act 1996

(8) The Board may prepare or cause to have prepared one or more reports on any investigation carried out under this section and may make a copy of any such report available to any person whom the Board considers appropriate.

as inserted by s.6(1)(d) P(A) Act 1996

(9) For the purposes of the law of defamation, the publication by the Board of any report prepared under this section shall be absolutely privileged.

[Note: *s.6(2) of the Pensions (Amendment) Act, 1996 provides as follows:*

An authorised person authorised under Section 18(1) of the Principal Act and holding office immediately before the passing of this Act shall continue in office as if authorised under the said subsection(1) inserted by this section]

Membership of either House of Oireachtas or of European Parliament by members or staff of Board.

19. - (1) Where a member of the Board is -

(a) nominated as a member of Seanad Éireann, or

(b) elected as a member of either House of the Oireachtas or as a representative in the European Parliament, or

(c) regarded pursuant to section 15 (inserted by the European Assembly Elections Act, 1984) of the European Assembly Elections Act, 1977, as having been elected to the European Parliament to fill a vacancy,

he shall thereupon cease to be a member of the Board.

(2) Where a person who is a member of the staff of the Board is -

(a) nominated as a member of Seanad Éireann, or

(b) elected as a member of either House of the Oireachtas or as a representative in the European Parliament, or

(c) regarded pursuant to section 15 (inserted by the European Assembly Elections Act, 1984) of the European Assembly Elections Act, 1977 as having been elected to the European Parliament to fill a vacancy,

he shall thereupon stand seconded from employment by the Board and shall not be paid by, or be entitled to receive from, the Board any remuneration or allowances in respect of the period commencing on such nomination or election or when he is so regarded as having been elected, as the case may be, and ending when he ceases to be a member of either such House or a representative in such Parliament.

(3) A person who is for the time being entitled under the Standing Orders of either House of the Oireachtas to sit therein or is a representative in the European Parliament shall, while he is so entitled or is such a representative, be disqualified from becoming a member of the Board or the staff of the Board.

(4) Without prejudice to the generality of *subsection (2)*, that subsection shall be construed as prohibiting, *inter alia*, the reckoning of a period mentioned in that subsection as service with the Board for the purposes of any superannuation benefits.

Advances by Minister to Board.

20. - The Minister may from time to time with the consent of the Minister for Finance, advance to the Board out of moneys provided by the Oireachtas, such sums as the Minister may determine for the purposes of expenditure by the Board in the performance of its functions.

Borrowing by Board.

as inserted by s.60 SW Act 1991

20A. - The Board may, for the purpose of providing for current or capital expenditure, from time to time, borrow money (whether on the security of the assets of the Board or otherwise), including money in a currency other than the currency of the State, subject to the consent of the Minister and the Minister for Finance and to such conditions as they may determine.

Disclosure by member of Board of interest in proposed contract.

21. - A member of the Board who has -

(a) any material or financial interest in any body corporate with which the Board proposes to make any contract, or

(b) any material or financial interest in any contract which the Board proposes to make,

shall disclose to the Board the fact of that interest and the nature thereof, and shall take no part in any deliberation or decision of the Board relating to the contract, and the disclosure shall be recorded in the minutes of the Board.

Accounts and audits of Board.

22. - (1) The Board shall keep in such form as may be approved of by the Minister with the concurrence of the Minister for Finance all proper and usual accounts of all moneys received or expended by the Board including an income and expenditure account and balance sheet and, in particular, shall keep all such special accounts as the Minister may from time to time direct.

(2) Accounts kept in pursuance of this section shall be submitted as soon as may be after the end of the financial year of the Board to which they relate to the Comptroller and Auditor General for audit and a copy of the income and expenditure account and of the balance sheet and of such other (if any) of its accounts as the Minister may direct and a copy of the Comptroller and Auditor General's report on the account shall be presented to the Minister as soon as may be and the Minister shall cause copies of each of the documents aforesaid to be laid before each House of the Oireachtas.

Reports and information to Minister.

23. - (1) The Board shall furnish to the Minister such information regarding its income and expenditure as he may from time to time require.

(2) As soon as may be after the end of each financial year of the Board, but not later than 6 months thereafter, the Board shall make a report to the Minister of its activities during that year and the Minister shall cause copies of the report to be laid before each House of the Oireachtas.

(3) Each report under *subsection (2)* shall include information in such form and regarding such matters as the Minister may direct.

(4) The Board shall, whenever so requested by the Minister, furnish to him information in relation to such matters as he may specify concerning or relating to the scope of its activities generally, or in respect of any account prepared by the Board or any report specified in *subsection (2)* or *(4)* or *section 22(2)* or the policy and activities, other than day to day activities, of the Board.

Disclosure of information.

Subsection (1) as amended by s.7 P(A) Act 1996

24. - (1) A person shall not, without the consent of the Board, disclose any information obtained by him while performing (or as a result of having performed) duties as a member, or member of the staff of, or member of a committee of, or an adviser or consultant to, the Board.

as amended by s.43 P(A) Act 1996

(2) A person who contravenes *subsection (1)* shall be guilty of an offence and shall be liable on summary conviction to a fine not exceeding £1,500.

(3) Nothing in *subsection (1)* shall prevent the disclosure of information in a report made to the Board or by or on behalf of the Board to the Minister.

Fees payable to Board.

25. - The trustees of a scheme shall pay annually to the Board out of the resources of the scheme fees of such amount as may be prescribed with the consent of the Minister for Finance and different fees may be prescribed under this section in respect of different classes of schemes.

Provision in relation to determinations by Board under *sections 38, 53, 58, 64A* and *75.*

26.-(1)(a)A question falling to be determined by the Board under *section 38, 53, 58, 64A or 75* shall be determined by it either, in its absolute discretion, without or after an oral hearing by the Board (or such member or members of the Board or other person or persons as the Board may authorise for that purpose).

Subsection (1)(a) as amended by s.50(b) SW Act 1993

(b) Any person concerned may make representations to the Board in relation to such a question as aforesaid and in reaching its determination the Board shall take account of any such representations.

(2) Representations under *subsection (1)* shall be made in writing or, if an oral hearing is being held under *subsection (1)* in relation to the question concerned, at the hearing.

Proviso as inserted by s.8(a) P(A) Act 1996

Provided that representations at an oral hearing shall be made in accordance with any procedure prescribed under *subsection (6)*.

(3) The person or persons holding an oral hearing under this section shall have power to take evidence on oath and for that purpose any of the persons aforesaid may administer oaths to persons attending as witnesses at the hearing.

Subsection 4(a) as amended by s.8(b) P(A) Act 1996

(4)(a) The person or any of the persons holding an oral hearing under this section may, by giving notice in that behalf in writing to a person, require the person to attend on such day and at such time and place as is specified in the notice to give evidence at the hearing in relation to the question to be determined by the Board or to produce at the hearing any documents in his possession, custody or control relating to any such question or to do both.

(b) A notice under *paragraph (a)* may be given either by delivering it to the person to whom it relates or by sending it by post in a prepaid registered letter addressed to the person at the address at which he ordinarily resides.

(c) A person to whom a notice under *paragraph (a)* has been given and who refuses to give evidence or gives false evidence at an oral hearing under this section or refuses or willfully fails to produce any document to which the notice relates at such a hearing shall be guilty of an offence and shall be liable -

Subsection 4(c)(i) as amended by s.43 P(A) Act 1996

(i) on summary conviction, to a fine not exceeding £1,500 or to imprisonment for a term not exceeding one year, or to both,

(ii) on conviction on indictment, to a fine not exceeding £10,000 or to imprisonment for a term not exceeding 2 years, or to both.

(5) The person or persons holding an oral hearing under this section may order a person concerned to pay to any other person concerned a reasonable sum in respect of expenses occasioned by the person in relation to the hearing and any such sum may be recovered by the person concerned from the other person concerned, as a simple contract debt in any court of competent jurisdiction.

(6) Subject to the provisions of this Act, the procedure at oral hearings under this section shall be such as may be prescribed and regulations for the purposes of this subsection may, without prejudice to the generality of the foregoing, make provision for the notification of persons concerned of the making of representations under this section, of the date, time and place of such hearings and of determinations of the Board under *section 38, 53, 58, 64A* or *75*, for the circumstances (if any) in which persons concerned may present their cases at such hearing through representatives (including legal representatives), for the making of a sufficient record of the proceedings at such hearings and for such other matters as the Minister considers necessary or expedient for the purposes of this section and for giving full effect to it.

Subsection (6) as amended by s.8(c) P(A) Act 1996

PART III
Preservation of Benefits

Interpretation *(Part III).*

27. - (1) In this Part and the *Second Schedule*, except where the context otherwise requires -

"qualifying service", in relation to a member of a scheme, means the aggregate of every period of reckonable service, whether or not continuous in each case, under -

(a) the scheme,

(b) every other scheme relating to the same employment,

(c) every other scheme relating to any other employment in respect of which rights to long service benefit have been granted under the scheme in substitution for accrued rights under such other scheme:

Provided that no such period, or part thereof, shall be counted more than once;

"transfer payment" has the meaning assigned to it by *section 34(2)*.

(2) Where the rate or amount of part of the long service benefit payable under a defined benefit scheme is directly determined by an amount of contribution paid by or in respect of the member, then, for the purposes of this Part and the *Second Schedule*, the scheme in so far as it relates to such part of the long service benefit shall be treated as a defined contribution scheme and, in so far as it relates to other benefits (including the remaining part of the long service benefit) shall be treated as a defined benefit scheme.

(3) References in this Part and the *Second Schedule* to a defined contribution scheme or a defined benefit scheme shall be construed as including references to a part of such scheme.

Entitlement to preserved benefit.

28. - (1) Subject to *section 37*, this Part and the *Second Schedule* shall apply to any member of a scheme who has service in relevant employment after the commencement of this Part.

(2) A member of a scheme whose service in relevant employment terminates otherwise than on death after the commencement of this Part but before normal pensionable age and who has completed at least 5 years' qualifying service of which at least 2 such years fall after the commencement of this Part, shall be entitled to a benefit (in this Act referred to as a "preserved benefit").

Preserved benefit - defined benefit scheme.

29. - (1) In this section -

"contingent pension" has the meaning assigned to it by *subsection (5)*;

"scheme" means a defined benefit scheme.

(2) A preserved benefit shall be provided under a scheme only in respect of -

(a) a long service benefit, or

(b) where, by the exercise of an option under *subsection (5),* the trustees so determine, a contingent pension.

(3) A preserved benefit shall be calculated in accordance with *Part A* of the *Second Schedule*.

(4) Subject to *subsection (5)*, on the death of a member of a scheme who is entitled to a preserved benefit under the scheme before such benefit commences to be payable, an amount shall be payable under the scheme to his personal representative in respect thereof equal to the actuarial value of the preserved benefit (including any preserved benefit under *subsections (6)* and *(7)*) immediately before the death of the member concerned.

(5)(a) Where a scheme provides for a pension payable to, or for, either or both the widowed spouse or any dependants of the member concerned in the event of that member's death while in relevant employment prior to his attaining normal pensionable age (in this section referred to as "a contingent pension") the trustees of the scheme may, in lieu of the benefit specified in *subsection (4)*, provide under the scheme a contingent pension calculated in accordance with *paragraph 1* of *Part A* of the *Second Schedule* and such benefits shall be deemed to form part of that member's preserved benefit.

(b) For the purposes of *paragraph (a)*, references in paragraph *1* of *Part A* of the *Second Schedule* to long service benefit shall be construed as references to a contingent pension within the meaning of this section.

(6) Where a member of a scheme is entitled to additional long service benefit under the scheme by virtue of the payment of additional voluntary contributions, a preserved benefit in respect of such benefit shall be calculated in accordance with *paragraph 3* of *Part A* of the *Second Schedule* and shall be provided in addition to the preserved benefit under *subsection (2)*:

Provided that if the member has received a refund of any such contributions paid by him during any period of reckonable service prior to the commencement of this Part, then, in calculating the amount of any preserved benefit under this subsection, any period of reckonable service prior to the commencement of this Part shall be disregarded.

as amended by s.54 (1) SW Act 1992

(7) Where additional long service benefit has been granted under a scheme to a member in respect of a transfer of accrued rights from another scheme, where such accrued rights result from the termination of the employment to which that scheme applies, that benefit shall be provided in addition to the preserved benefit under *subsection (2)*:

Provided that if the member has received a refund of the contributions paid by him to the other scheme prior to the commencement of this Part which were included in the rights transferred from the other scheme then, in calculating the amount of any preserved benefit under this subsection, any additional long service benefit accrued under that other scheme prior to the commencement of this Part, shall be disregarded.

Preserved benefit - defined contribution scheme.

30. - (1) In this section -

Definition as inserted by s.9(a) P(A) Act 1996

"accumulated value" of any appropriate contributions means the amount which the trustees determine to be equal to-

(a) the realisable value of the resources of the scheme, in accordance with the rules of the scheme, which represent those contributions, less

(b) the amount of any of the expenses of the scheme which, under the rules of the scheme, are to be discharged out of those resources;

"appropriate contributions" shall be construed in accordance with *subsections (4), (5)* and *(6)*;

"scheme" means a defined contribution scheme.

(2) A preserved benefit shall be provided under a scheme and it shall be such that its actuarial value at the date on which payment of it commences is equal to the accumulated value on that date of the appropriate contributions in respect of the member concerned under the scheme.

(3) On the death of a member of a scheme who is entitled to a preserved benefit before such benefit commences to be payable, an amount shall be payable under the scheme to his personal representative in respect thereof equal to the accumulated value of the appropriate contributions under the scheme in respect of the member immediately before his death.

(4) Subject to *subsections (5)* and *(6)*, the appropriate contributions shall be the contributions paid by or in respect of the member concerned for the purposes of long service benefit from the commencement of this Part, or, if later, the date of the commencement of the relevant employment, but excluding additional voluntary contributions and any payment representing a transfer of accrued rights from another scheme.

(5) Where a member of a scheme is entitled to additional long service benefit under the scheme by virtue of the payment of additional voluntary contributions, the appropriate contributions shall be all such contributions:

Provided that if the member has received a refund of any such contributions paid by him prior to the commencement of this Part, the appropriate contributions shall be the contributions paid by him from the commencement of this Part.

(6) Where additional long service benefit has been granted under a scheme to a member in respect of a transfer of accrued rights from another scheme, where such accrued rights result from the termination of the employment to which that scheme applies, the appropriate contributions shall be the amount of the payment received by the trustees of the scheme in respect of such accrued rights:

as amended by s.54 (2) SW Act 1992

Provided that if the member has received a refund of contributions paid by him, prior to the commencement of this Part, under that scheme which were included in the rights transferred, the appropriate contributions shall be the portion of the payment received by the trustees which represented rights accrued after such commencement.

as substituted by s.9(b) P(A) Act 1996

(7) Where benefits under a scheme are secured under one or more policies of assurance, the realisable value, on the date on which payment of preserved benefit commences, of the resources of the scheme which represent the appropriate contributions paid by or on behalf of a member shall, for the purposes of this Part, be the proportion of the proceeds of every such policy applicable to those contributions.

Payment of preserved benefit.

31. - (1) A preserved benefit shall be payable out of the resources of the scheme.

(2) Except as provided for in this Part, a preserved benefit shall be payable in accordance with, and subject to, the rules of the scheme being the rules as at the date of the termination of the relevant employment.

Non-entitlement to refund of contributions.

32. - (1) A member of a scheme who is entitled to preserved benefit under the scheme in accordance with the provisions of this Part shall not be entitled to receive a refund of any contributions paid to that scheme after the commencement of this Part.

as inserted by s.10 P(A) Act 1996

(2) A member of a scheme, who would be entitled to preserved benefit under the scheme in accordance with the provisions of this Part if his service in relevant employment were to terminate, shall not be entitled to receive a refund of any contributions paid to that scheme after the 1st day of January, 1991.

Revaluation of preserved benefit.

33. - (1) In this section and *Part B* of the *Second Schedule* "revaluation year" means a year beginning not less than 5 years after the commencement of this Part.

(2) Where in respect of any preserved benefit payable under a defined benefit scheme to or in respect of a member and calculated in accordance with *paragraph 1* or *3* or both of *Part A* of the *Second Schedule*, there is a period of at least one year between -

(a) the commencement of the first revaluation year or the date of the termination of the member's relevant employment, whichever is the later, and

(b) the date on which he attains or would attain normal pensionable age or the date of his death, whichever is the earlier,

then, the preserved benefit shall be revalued annually as soon as may be after the end of each revaluation year in accordance with the provisions of *Part B* of that Schedule.

(3) A revaluation shall not be made under this section in respect of a member of a scheme after -

(a) the date of payment of preserved benefit to or in respect of him, or

(b) the date of his attainment of normal pensionable age, or

(c) the date of his death,

whichever is the earliest.

(4) The Minister, after consultation with the Minister for Finance, shall, in respect of each revaluation year, prescribe the percentage (in this Act referred to as "the revaluation percentage") which shall determine the amount by which the preserved benefit is to be increased by the revaluation thereof under this section for that year. *as amended by s.11 P(A) Act 1996*

(5) The percentage prescribed under *subsection (4)* in respect of a revaluation year shall be -

(a) the percentage that equals the increase in the general level of consumer prices during that year calculated by the Minister in such manner as he thinks appropriate, or

(b) 4 per cent,

whichever is the lesser.

(6) The Minister may by regulations vary the percentage specified in *subsection (5)(b)*, but any such variation shall not apply in the case of preserved benefit the entitlement to which arises before the date of the making of the regulations concerned.

(7) Where, in the opinion of the Minister, no increase in the general level of consumer prices occurred during a revaluation year, he shall not prescribe a percentage under *subsection (4)* in relation to that year and the revaluation of any preserved benefit that, but for this subsection, would fall to be made as soon as may be after the end of that year shall not be made.

Entitlement to transfer payment.

34. - (1) This section shall apply to a member of a funded scheme who is entitled to a preserved benefit under this part.

(2) A member of a scheme to whom this section applies shall be entitled to the transfer of an amount of money from the scheme (in this Part referred to as a "transfer payment") in accordance with *subsection (3)* equal -

as amended by s.12(a) P(A) Act 1996

(a) in the case of a defined benefit scheme, to the actuarial value of the preserved benefit, and of any amount payable under *section 29(4)*, on the date on which the relevant application under *subsection (3)* is received by the trustees, and

as substituted by s.55 SW Act 1992

(b) in the case of a defined contribution scheme, to the accumulated value of the appropriate contributions under the scheme in respect of the member, such value to be determined on a date not later than 3 months following the date of the receipt of the application.

Repealed by s.12(b) P(A) Act 1996

....

as substituted by s.12(c) P(A) Act 1996

(3) A member of a scheme who is entitled to a transfer payment under *subsection (2)* may exercise such right by making an application in writing to the trustees of the scheme providing them with such information as they may reasonably require and directing them to apply the transfer payment -

(a) in the making of a payment to another funded scheme which provides or is capable of providing long service benefit and of which he is a member or a prospective member, or

(b) in the making of one or more payments falling to be made under policies or contracts of assurance that are effected on behalf of the member with one or more undertakings (within the meaning of the Insurance Act, 1989) and that are approved of by the Revenue Commissioners under Chapter II of Part I of the Finance Act, 1972, which policies or contracts of assurance shall not be deemed to be an occupational pension scheme for the purposes of this Act.

(4) Where the trustees of a scheme receive an application under *subsection (3)*, they shall apply the transfer payment concerned, within the period of 3 months following the date of the receipt of the application, in the manner directed by the application under *subsection (3)*.

(5) Where -

(a) a person has exercised the entitlement conferred on him under *subsection (2)*, and

(b) the trustees of the scheme from which the transfer payment is being made have complied with the provisions of *subsection (4)*,

then, they shall be discharged from any obligation to provide benefits to which the transfer payment relates.

(6) Where a member of a scheme directs the application of a transfer payment in accordance with *subsection (3)(a)*, the trustees of the scheme to which the transfer payment is being made shall accept such payment and shall provide benefits of an actuarial value that is equivalent to the amount of the transfer payment in such form as they may determine.

(7) A member of a scheme shall not be entitled to a transfer payment under this section if -

(a) payment of his preserved benefit has commenced, or

(b) he fails to exercise the entitlement within a period of 2 years (or such longer period as may be provided for by the scheme or determined by the trustees of the scheme) after the date of the termination of the relevant employment concerned.

Power of trustees to effect transfer payment.

35. - (1) Notwithstanding anything contained in *section 34*, the trustees of a scheme may, in such circumstances as may be prescribed, instead of providing a preserved benefit out of the resources of the scheme, effect, without the consent of the member concerned, a transfer payment from the scheme by making one or more payments referred to in *section 34(3)(b)*.

(2) Where the trustees of a scheme have effected a transfer payment in accordance with *subsection (1)* they shall be discharged from any obligation to provide benefits to which the transfer payment relates.

Provision of schemes relating to forfeiture and lien to be disregarded.

36. - (1) Any provision of a scheme -

(a) providing for the forfeiture of a preserved benefit, or

(b) enabling the employer of a member to exercise a lien on the member's preserved benefit,

shall be disregarded for the purpose of this Part.

as inserted by s.13 P(A) Act 1996

(2) Notwithstanding *paragraph (a)* of *subsection (1)* where a member of a scheme or such other person who is entitled to preserved benefit is or becomes bankrupt (within the meaning of the Bankruptcy Act, 1988), or assigns or charges or attempts to assign or charge the benefit, the trustees of the scheme may, at their discretion, apply any provision of the scheme, under which a benefit may be forfeited and paid, to the member or such other person specified in the provision.

Exclusion from and modification of *Part III* and *Second Schedule.*

37. - (1) Where the Minister is of the opinion that the benefits provided under schemes or categories of schemes during a period that the Minister considers to be of reasonable length for the purposes of this subsection are no less favourable to the members concerned than those required by this Act to be provided under the schemes or categories of schemes, he may by regulations made with the consent of the Minister for Finance exclude those schemes or categories of schemes from the application of this Part and the *Second Schedule*.

(2) Where the Minister considers that it would be unreasonable, having regard to their nature and character, and would be contrary to the interests of their members, to require specified schemes or categories of schemes to comply fully with specified provisions of this Part and the *Second Schedule*, he may by regulations made with the consent of the Minister for Finance provide that those provisions shall apply in relation to those schemes or categories of schemes with specified modifications, being modifications that in the opinion of the Minister are reasonable and do not materially alter those provisions.

(3) Where the Minister so provides by regulations, then notwithstanding anything in this Part, in the cases specified in the regulations -

(a) a period of a person's reckonable service under a scheme in different employments may be treated for the purposes of this Part as a period of reckonable service under the scheme in such one or more of those employments as may be specified;

(b) a person's reckonable service in any employment may be treated in the case of interruption of such employment as terminated or not terminated;

(c) a member's service in relevant employment may be treated as terminated or not terminated.

as inserted by s.54(3) SW Act 1992

(4) The Minister may by regulations specify the method of calculating preserved benefit payable under schemes and for such adjustments of the amounts of such benefit as may be necessary to facilitate its computation.

(4A) Regulations may specify the method of calculating preserved benefit payable under schemes where on termination of relevant employment a member has periods of reckonable service in more than one scheme relating to the same employment or in a defined benefit scheme and a defined contribution scheme which are both part of the one scheme.

as amended by s.14 P(A) Act 1996 (previously inserted by s.45 SW Act 1993)

(5) This Part shall not apply to a scheme established under the Defence Forces (Pensions) Acts, 1932 to 1975.

as inserted by s.61 SW Act 1991

Conflict between *Part III* and schemes.

38. - (1) The provisions of this Part, of any regulations made thereunder and of the *Second Schedule* shall override any rule of a scheme to the extent that that rule conflicts with those provisions.

(2) Any question as to -

(a) whether any provision of this Part (including the application of any provision as modified by regulations), any regulations made thereunder or the Second Schedule conflicts with any rule of a scheme, or

(b) whether a scheme is a defined benefit scheme or a defined contribution scheme for the purposes of this Part, or

as inserted by s.54 (4) SW Act 1996

(c) whether a member's service in relevant employment may be treated as terminated for the purposes of this Part,

shall be determined by the Board on application to it in writing in that behalf by a person specified in *subsection (3)*.

(3) The following persons shall be entitled to make an application under *subsection (2)* in respect of a scheme:

(a) the trustees of the scheme;

(b) any person who is an employer of persons in relevant employment to which the scheme applies;

(c) any member or prospective member of the scheme;

(d) such other persons (if any) as may be prescribed, being persons who, in the opinion of the Minister, ought to be entitled to make such an application.

(4) An appeal to the High Court on a point of law from a determination of the Board under *subsection (2)* in relation to a scheme, may be brought by the person who made or a person who was entitled to make the application concerned under *subsection (2)*.

Schemes may provide higher benefits.

as amended by s.15 P(A) Act 1996

39. - Nothing in the other provisions of this Part or in the *Second Schedule* shall be construed as precluding a scheme from providing benefits, in lieu of preserved benefit, on a higher scale, or payable at any earlier, or, at the request of the member of the scheme at any later, time or otherwise more favourably than is provided for under this Part:

Provided that -

(a) such benefits are of an actuarial value that is equivalent to or greater than that of preserved benefit,

(b) on the death of a member before any such benefit commences to be payable the amount thereof shall not be less than the amount that would, but for this section, have been payable by virtue of *section 29(4)* or *30(3)*, as appropriate,

(c) a member who is entitled to preserved benefit under this Part shall not be entitled to receive a refund of any contributions paid to the scheme after the commencement of this Part.

PART IV
Funding Standard

Interpretation *(Part IV).*

40. - In this Part and the *Third Schedule*, except where the context otherwise requires -

"an actuarial funding certificate" has the meaning assigned to it in *section 42*;

"the effective date" has the meaning assigned to it in *section 42*;

"funding proposal" has the meaning assigned to it in *section 49*;

"funding standard" shall be construed in accordance with *section 44*;

"relevant scheme" means a scheme to which this Part applies by virtue of *section 41*;

"certified percentage" means a percentage specified for the purposes of *section 45(4)*;

"specified percentage" has the meaning assigned to it by *section 44*.

Application *(Part IV).*

41. - (1) Subject to *section 52*, this Part shall apply to any scheme other than -

as substituted by s.46 SW Act 1993

(a) a defined contribution scheme, or

(b) a scheme under which service in the relevant employment after the 1st day of January, 1993, does not entitle the members to long service benefit and, where any long service benefit is determined by reference to a member's earnings, such earnings in the case of all members relate to a date or a period prior to the 1st day of January, 1993.

(2) Notwithstanding *subsection (1), section 48* shall apply to any scheme other than a defined contribution scheme.

Actuarial funding certificate.

42. - (1) The trustees of a relevant scheme shall, from time to time in accordance with *section 43*, submit to the Board a certificate, in this part and the *Third Schedule* referred to as "an actuarial funding certificate".

(2) The trustees of a relevant scheme shall cause actuarial funding certificates to be prepared by an actuary who shall certify therein that as at the date, in this Part referred to as "the effective date", on which the liabilities and resources of the scheme are calculated for the purposes of *section 44* either -

(a) the scheme satisfies the funding standard provided for in *section 44*, or

(b) the scheme does not satisfy the funding standard.

(3) In the case of a relevant scheme which commenced before the commencement of this Part, the first actuarial funding certificate submitted in accordance with *section 43* shall also state the certified percentage in relation to the scheme.

(4) An actuarial funding certificate shall be in such form as may be prescribed.

as inserted by s.16 P(A) Act 1996

(5) The Board, where it considers that it is necessary or appropriate and would not be contrary to the interests of the members of a scheme, may modify the requirements of *subsections (1)* and *(2)* in respect of such scheme in such circumstances and on such terms as it considers appropriate.

Effective dates for actuarial funding certificates.

43. - (1) The first actuarial funding certificate shall have an effective date -

(a) in the case of a relevant scheme which commenced before the commencement of this Part, not later than 3 years after such commencement, and

(b) in the case of a relevant scheme which commenced on or after such commencement, not later than 3 1/2 years after the commencement of the scheme,

and a subsequent actuarial funding certificate shall have an effective date not later than 3 1/2 years after the effective date of the immediately preceding certificate.

(2) Unless otherwise prescribed, an actuarial funding certificate shall be submitted to the Board by the trustees of the scheme within 9 months of the effective date of the certificate.

Provisions relating to funding standard.

44. - Subject to the subsequent provisions of this Part, a relevant scheme shall be deemed to have satisfied the funding standard if, in the opinion of the actuary, the resources of the scheme at the effective date of the actuarial funding certificate would have been sufficient, if the scheme had been wound up on that date, to provide for -

(a) the liabilities of the scheme consisting of -

(i) benefits in the course of payment to which *paragraph 1* of the *Third Schedule* relates,

(ii) benefits, other than those referred to in *subparagraph (i),* which consist of additional benefits secured or granted under the scheme on behalf of the member concerned by way of additional voluntary contributions or a transfer of rights from another scheme to which *paragraph 2* of the *Third Schedule* relates,

(iii)benefits, other than those referred to in *subparagraphs (i)* and *(ii)*, payable in respect of reckonable service completed after the commencement of this Part to which *paragraph 3* of the *Third Schedule* relates, and

(iv)the percentage (in this Part referred to as the "specified percentage") of any benefits, other than those referred to in *subparagraphs (i)* and *(ii)*, payable in respect of reckonable service completed prior to such commencement to which *paragraph 4* of the *Third Schedule* relates, and

(b) the estimated expenses of administering the winding up of the scheme.

Provisions relating to schemes commencing before commencement of this Part.

45. - (1) This section applies to relevant schemes that came into operation before the commencement of this Part.

(2) The actuary shall determine the percentage, if any, of the benefits under a scheme to which *paragraph 4* of the *Third Schedule* relates that, in his opinion, could have been provided at the effective date of the first actuarial funding certificate in relation to the scheme from the resources of the scheme if -

(a) the scheme had been wound up on that date, and

(b) (i) the liabilities of the scheme for benefits under the scheme specified in *subparagraphs (i), (ii)* and *(iii),* of *subsection (a)* of *section 44*, and

(ii) the estimated expenses of administering a winding up,

had already been discharged from resources of the scheme.

(3) In determining the percentage referred to in *subsection (2)*, the actuary shall have regard to the order of priority accorded to each category of membership in the rules of the scheme concerned respecting a winding up thereof but only in so far as they apply to the benefits to which the said *paragraph 4* relates and the actuary may determine a different percentage for each such category of membership.

(4) The first actuarial funding certificate in relation to a scheme shall state a percentage for each category of membership to which, pursuant to *subsection (3)*, a different percentage applies (in this Part referred to as "the certified percentage"), being the lesser of -

(a) the percentage determined by the actuary pursuant to *subsections (2)* and *(3)*, and

(b) 100 per cent.

(5) For the purposes of this Part -

(a) where an actuarial funding certificate relates to an effective date not more than 10 years after the commencement of this Part, the specified percentage shall be the certified percentage,

(b) where an actuarial funding certificate relates to an effective date more than 10 years after such commencement and on such commencement the scheme concerned was a funded scheme, the specified percentage shall be 100 per cent.

Matters to which actuary is to have regard.

Subsection (1) as substituted by s.56 SW Act 1992

46. - (1) In completing an actuarial funding certificate, the actuary-

(a) in addition to complying with the other provisions of this Part, shall have regard to such financial or other assumptions as he considers to be appropriate on the effective date of the certificate, and

(b) notwithstanding anything contained in the rules of a relevant scheme, may assume that the liabilities of the scheme on winding up could have been provided by applying all or part of the resources of the scheme in the making of -

(i) a payment to another scheme, or

(ii) one or more payments falling to be made under policies or contracts of assurance that are effected on behalf of the member with one or more undertakings (within the meaning of the Insurance Act, 1989) and that are approved of by the Revenue Commissioners under Chapter II of Part I of the Finance Act, 1972,

such payment or payments to be equal to the actuarial value of the benefits specified in *subparagraphs (i), (ii)* and *(iii)* of *section 44(a)*, and the percentage of the benefits specified in *section 44(a)(iv)*.

(2) In determining the benefits to be paid on the winding up of a relevant scheme, the actuary shall, in addition to complying with *section 48*, have regard to such financial or other assumptions as he considers to be appropriate.

Limitations on calculation of resources of relevant scheme.

47. - In respect of any calculation made for the purposes of this Part, the resources of a relevant scheme on any date to which such calculation relates shall exclude investments in excess of a prescribed percentage within a prescribed class or description of investments.

Priorities on winding up of relevant scheme.

48. - (1) In applying the resources of a relevant scheme which has been wound up after the 1st day of January, 1997 -

(a) the trustees shall discharge the liabilities of the scheme for the following benefits in the following order -

as substituted by s.17 P(A) Act 1996 (previously substituted by s.57 SW Act 1992)

(i) firstly, the benefits specified in *paragraph 1* of the *Third Schedule* to or in respect of those persons, who, at the date of the winding up, were within the categories referred to in that paragraph, to the extent that they are not already discharged, and

(ii) secondly, the benefits specified in *paragraphs 2* and *3* of the *Third Schedule* to or in respect of those members of the scheme who, at the date of the winding up, were within the categories referred to in those paragraphs, to the extent that they are not already discharged,

before discharging the liabilities of the scheme for other benefits, and

(b) the trustees may discharge, notwithstanding anything contained in the rules of the scheme and without the consent of the member concerned, the liability of the scheme for benefits payable to or in respect of any member by -

(i) making a payment to another funded scheme which provides or is capable of providing long service benefit and of which he is a member or a prospective member, or

(ii) making one or more payments under policies or contracts of assurance that are effected on behalf of the member with one or more undertakings (within the meaning of the Insurance Act, 1989), and that are approved of by the Revenue Commissioners under Chapter II of Part I of the Finance Act, 1972, which policies or contracts of assurance shall not be deemed to be an occupational pension scheme for the purposes of this Act,

of an aggregate amount not less than the actuarial value of the benefits payable on the winding up under the rules of the scheme, subject always to *paragraph (a)*.

(2) Nothing in this section requires liabilities for benefits to be discharged before liabilities for expenses, fees and costs associated with the winding up of the scheme.

Funding proposal.

49. - (1) Where, in accordance with the provisions of *section 43*, the trustees of a scheme submit an actuarial funding certificate which certifies that at the effective date of the certificate the scheme does not satisfy the funding standard, they shall submit to the Board a proposal (in this Part referred to as a "funding proposal") in accordance with the provisions of this section.

(2) A funding proposal shall -

(a) contain a proposal designed to ensure that, in the opinion of the actuary, the scheme could reasonably be expected to satisfy the funding standard at the effective date of the next actuarial funding certificate,

(b) be certified by the actuary as meeting the requirements of *paragraph (a)*,

Paragraphs (c) and (d) as substituted by s.18(a) P(A) Act 1996

(c) be signed by or on behalf of the employer and by or on behalf of the trustees of the scheme, in each case signifying agreement to the proposal, and

(d) be submitted by the trustees of the scheme with the actuarial funding certificate to which it relates.

(3) The Board may, where it considers it necessary or appropriate in any individual case, modify the requirements of *subsection (2)* in respect of the scheme or schemes to which that case relates in such circumstances and on such terms as it considers appropriate.

as inserted by s.18(b) P(A) Act 1996

(4) In this section 'employer' means the employer who undertakes the role of principal employer for the purposes of such scheme's approval by the Revenue Commissioners under Chapter II of Part I of the Finance Act, 1972.

Direction by Board to trustees.

50. - (1) The Board may, by notice in writing, direct the trustees of a scheme to take such measures as may be necessary to reduce, in respect of members of the scheme then in relevant employment, the benefits which would be payable to or in respect of them from the scheme where -

(a) the trustees of the scheme fail to submit an actuarial funding certificate within the period specified in *section 43*, or

(b) the actuarial funding certificate certifies that the scheme does not satisfy the funding standard and the trustees of the scheme have not submitted a funding proposal in accordance with *section 49*.

(2) The reduction in benefits under *subsection (1)* shall- *as substituted by s.19 (a) P(A) Act 1996*

(a) to the extent specified, override the provisions of *subparagraph 1(2)* of the *Second Schedule* and *subparagraph 4(b)(i)(1)* of the *Third Schedule*, and

(b) be such that the scheme would in the opinion of the actuary concerned satisfy the funding standard in accordance with *section 44* immediately following the reduction.

(3) Where the Board gives a direction under *subsection (1)*, the trustees of the scheme shall -

(a) (i) take such measures as may be necessary to reduce, in respect of members of the scheme then in relevant employment, the benefits which would be payable to or in respect of them from the scheme such that the scheme would, in the opinion of the actuary concerned, satisfy the funding standard in accordance with *section 44* immediately following the reduction, and *as substituted by s.19(b) P(A) Act 1996*

(ii) notify the members of the scheme of the reduction in benefits within a period of 2 months, or such longer period as the Board considers appropriate.

(b) within a further period of one month, submit to the Board -

(i) details of the reduction in benefits including copies of the notifications issued to members of the scheme, and

(ii) an actuarial funding certificate certifying that at the effective date, being the date of the reduction in benefits, the scheme satisfies the funding standard.

Qualification for appointment as actuary of scheme.

51. - (1) A person shall not be qualified for appointment as actuary for the purposes of this Act to a scheme -

(a) unless he possesses the prescribed qualifications, or

(b) if he is a member of a class of persons standing prescribed for the time being for the purposes of this section.

(2) A person shall not act as actuary to a particular scheme at a time when he is disqualified under this Act for appointment to that office and, if an actuary of a scheme becomes so disqualified during his term of office as such actuary, he shall thereupon vacate his office and give notice in writing to the trustees of the scheme that he has vacated his office by reason of such disqualification.

Exclusion from modification of *Part IV* and *Third Schedule*.

52. - (1) Where the Minister considers that some or all of the benefits under specified schemes or categories of schemes are, or may be, paid in whole or in part out of moneys provided from the Central Fund or moneys provided by the Oireachtas, he may by regulations made with the consent of the Minister for Finance exclude those schemes or categories of schemes from the application of this Part and the *Third Schedule.*

(2) Where the Minister considers that -

(a) it would be unreasonable, having regard to their nature, character and resources and the methods by which benefits payable under them are funded, and

(b) it would be contrary to the interests of their members,

to require specified schemes or categories of schemes to comply fully with specified provisions of this Part and the *Third Schedule*, he may by regulations made with the consent of the Minister for Finance provide that those provisions shall apply in relation to those schemes or categories of schemes with specified modifications, being modifications that, in the opinion of the Minister, are reasonable and do not materially alter those provisions.

53. - (1) The provisions of this Part and of any regulations made thereunder shall override any rule of a scheme to the extent that that rule conflicts with those provisions.

Conflict between *Part IV* and schemes.

(2) Any question as to -

(a) whether any provision of this Part (including any such provision as modified by regulations), any regulation made thereunder or the Third Schedule conflicts with any rule of a scheme, or

(b) whether a scheme is a defined benefit scheme or a defined contribution scheme for the purposes of this Part,

shall be determined by the Board on application to it in writing in that behalf by a person who, in relation to the scheme, corresponds to a person mentioned in *section 38(3)* in relation to a scheme mentioned therein.

(3) An appeal to the High Court on a point of law from a determination of the Board, under *subsection (2)* in relation to a scheme, may be brought by the person who made, or a person who was entitled to make, the application concerned under *subsection (2)*.

PART V
Disclosure of Information in Relation to Schemes

Disclosure of information in relation to schemes.

54. - (1) It shall be the duty of the trustees of a scheme to furnish information to the persons specified in *subsection (2)* on the following, that is to say -

(a) the constitution of the scheme,

(b) the administration and finances of the scheme,

(c) the rights and obligations that arise or may arise under the scheme, and

(d) such other matters as appear to the Minister to be relevant to schemes in general or to schemes of a particular description to which the scheme belongs and are prescribed.

(2) The persons to whom *subsection (1)* relates are -

(a) the members and prospective members of the scheme,

(b) the spouses of members and prospective members of the scheme,

(c) persons within the application of the scheme and qualifying or prospectively qualifying for its benefits,

(d) an authorised trade union representing the members concerned,

as inserted by s.20 P(A) Act 1996

(e) the Board in any case in which the Board so requests the trustees by notice in writing.

(3) Notwithstanding *subsection (1)*, the Minister may by regulations provide that information in relation to such of the matters aforesaid as may be specified shall be furnished by the trustees of the scheme to such of the persons specified in *subsection (2)* as may be specified in the regulations only if so requested by those persons.

(4)(a) The trustees, the actuary or the auditor of a scheme may request an employer to whom the scheme relates to furnish them or him with such information as they or he may reasonably require for the purposes of their or his functions under this Act or regulations thereunder and the employer shall comply with any such request.

(b) The actuary or the auditor of a scheme may request the trustees of the scheme to furnish him with such information as he may reasonably require for the purposes of his functions under this Act or regulations thereunder and the trustees shall comply with any such request.

(5) A person who contravenes *subsection (1)* or *(4)* or regulations under *subsection (3)* shall be guilty of an offence and shall be liable on summary conviction to a fine not exceeding £1,500. *as amended by s 43 P(A) Act 1996*

(6) In this section "authorised trade union" means a body to whom a negotiation licence (within the meaning of Part II of the Trade Union Act, 1941) was issued under the said Part II.

55. - (1) The trustees of a scheme shall prepare an annual report containing information in relation to such matters as may be prescribed with the consent of the Minister for Finance concerning the operation of the scheme during whichever of the following periods the trustees may select, that is to say: Annual reports.

(a) each year beginning on the date specified for the purpose of the scheme -

(i) in any document comprising the scheme or which is included among the documents comprising it, or

(ii) in the rules of the scheme,

(b) each year beginning on the 1st day of January, or

(c) each year beginning on such other day as may be agreed upon by the trustees and the Board:

Priviso as substituted by s.21(a) P(A) Act 1996 (Proviso previously inserted by s.58 SW Act 1992)

Provided that-

(i) where the period selected by the trustees is altered, a report prepared for a period other than a year, such period not to exceed 23 months, shall, with the approval of the Board, be regarded as an annual report for the purposes of this section, and

(ii) where the scheme is in operation for part only of the year selected, a report prepared for a period including that part of the year and not exceeding 23 months shall be regarded as an annual report for the purposes of this section.

as substituted by s.62 SW Act 1991

(2) S*ubsection (1)* of this section shall not apply to -

(a) a scheme, the only benefit under which is in respect of death prior to normal pensionable age, or

Paragraph (b) as substituted by s.21(b) P(A) Act 1996

(b) a scheme under which service in the relevant employment after the 1st day of January, 1997, does not entitle the members of the scheme to long service benefit and, where any long service benefit is determined by reference to a member's earnings, such earnings in the case of all members relate to a date or a period before the 1st day of January, 1997.

Audited accounts and actuarial valuations.

Subsection (1) as substituted by s.22(a) P(A) Act 1996

56. - (1) The trustees of a scheme shall -

(a) cause the accounts of the scheme in respect of such periods as may be prescribed to be audited by the auditor of the scheme,

(b) cause the resources and liabilities of the scheme to be valued by the actuary of the scheme at such times as may be prescribed, and

(c) in respect of each such audit and valuation, cause to be prepared the documents to which this section applies.

(2) The documents to which this section applies are -

(a) the accounts of the scheme concerned,

(b) the auditor's report on the accounts specified in *paragraph (a)*, and

(c) the actuary's report on his valuation of the assets and liabilities of the scheme.

(3) For the purposes of this Act a person shall not be qualified for appointment as auditor of a scheme -

as substituted by s.47(1) SW Act 1993

(a) unless he is qualified to be appointed as an auditor of a company in accordance with the Companies Acts, 1963 to 1990, or

(b) if he is a member of a class of persons standing prescribed for the time being for the purposes of this section.

(4) A person shall not act as auditor of a particular scheme at a time when he is disqualified under this section, for appointment to that office and, if an auditor of the scheme becomes so disqualified during his term of office as such auditor, he shall thereupon vacate his office and give notice in writing to the trustees of the scheme that he has vacated his office by reason of such disqualification.

Subsection 4(A) repealed by s.47(2) SW Act 1993 (previously inserted by s.59 SW Act 1992)

(4A) ....

(5) The form and content of any document to which this section applies may be prescribed with the consent of the Minister for Finance and those documents shall comply with any regulation under this subsection.

(6)(a) Subsection (1) and paragraphs (a) and (b) of subsection (2) shall not apply to -

as substituted by s.63 SW Act 1991

(i) a scheme that is not a funded scheme, or

(ii) a scheme, the only benefit under which is in respect of death prior to normal pensionable age, or

(iii) a scheme under which service in the relevant employment after the 1st day of January, 1997, does not entitle the members to long service benefit and, where any long service benefit is determined by reference to a member's earnings, such earnings in the case of all members relate to a date or a period before the 1st day of January, 1997.

Paragraph (iii) as substituted by s.22(d) P(A) Act 1996

Paragraph (b) as amended by s.22(c) P(A) Act 1996

(b) *Paragraph (b)* of *subsection (1)* and *paragraph (c)* of *subsection (2)* shall not apply to -

(i) a scheme that is a defined contribution scheme, or

(ii) a scheme that is not a funded scheme, or

(iii)a scheme the only benefit under which is in respect of death prior to normal pensionable age, or

Paragraph (iv) as substituted by s.22(e) P(A) Act 1996

(iv)a scheme under which service in the relevant employment after the 1st day of January, 1997, does not entitle the members to long service benefit and, where any long service benefit is determined by reference to a member's earnings, such earnings in the case of all members relate to a date or a period before the 1st day of January, 1997.

Modification of *Part V.*

57. - Where the Minister considers that it would be unreasonable, having regard to their nature and character and the size of their membership, to require specified schemes or categories of schemes to comply fully with *sections 54, 55* and *56,* he may by regulations made with the consent of the Minister for Finance provide that those sections shall apply in relation to those schemes or categories of schemes with specified modifications, being modifications that, in the opinion of the Minister, are reasonable and are not such to relieve the trustees of the obligation to furnish such information under those sections as is appropriate in all the circumstances.

Conflict between *Part V* and schemes.

58. - (1) The provisions of this Part and of any regulations made thereunder shall override any rule of a scheme to the extent that that rule conflicts with those provisions.

(2) Any question as to -

(a) whether any provision of this Part (including the application of any provision as modified by regulations) or any regulation made thereunder conflicts with any rule of a scheme, or

(b) whether a scheme is a defined benefit scheme or a defined contribution scheme for the purposes of this Part,

shall be determined by the Board on application to it in writing in that behalf by a person who, in relation to the scheme, corresponds to a person mentioned in *section 38(3)* in relation to the scheme mentioned therein.

(3) An appeal to the High Court on a point of law from a determination of the Board under *subsection (2)* in relation to a scheme, may be brought by the person who made, or a person who was entitled to make, the application concerned under *subsection (2)*.

PART VI
Trustees of Schemes

General duties of trustees of scheme.

59. - Without prejudice to the duties of trustees generally and in addition to complying with the other requirements of this Act, the duties of trustees of schemes shall include the following:

(a) to ensure, in so far as is reasonable, that the contributions payable by the employer and the members of the scheme, where appropriate, are received;

(b) to provide for the proper investment of the resources of the scheme in accordance with the rules of the scheme;

(c) where appropriate, to make arrangements for the payment of the benefits as provided for under the rules of the scheme as they become due;

(d) to ensure that proper membership and financial records are kept;

as inserted by s.48 SW Act 1993

(e) if the scheme is wound up, to apply the resources of the scheme in discharging its liabilities without undue delay in accordance with the rules of the scheme and where applicable, with *section 48.*

Cost of trustee training. *as inserted by s.23 P(A) Act 1996*

59A. - Notwithstanding anything in the rules of a scheme, the trustees of a scheme may meet reasonable costs and expenses incurred in receiving appropriate training on their duties and responsibilities as such trustees from the resources of the scheme.

Duty to register scheme.

60. - (1) Subject to the following subsections, it shall be the duty of trustees of a scheme to ensure that the scheme is registered with the Board.

(2) A scheme shall be registered not later than -

(a) in case the scheme commenced before the commencement of this section, one year after such commencement,

(b) in any other case, one year after the commencement of the scheme.

(3) It shall be the duty of the trustees of a scheme to provide the Board, in such a manner as may be prescribed, with such information as may be prescribed for the purposes of this section.

Restriction of Perpetual Funds (Registration) Act 1933.

61. - (1) Sections 7, 8, 10, 12(2), and, in so far as it relates to those sections, section 14 of the Perpetual Funds (Registration) Act, 1933 shall not apply in the case of a scheme.

as inserted by s.24 P(A) Act 1996

(2) The validity or effect of any alteration in the rules of a scheme shall not be affected by the failure to register such alteration in the Register of Perpetual Funds notwithstanding any provision in the rules of the scheme requiring such registration.

Rule against perpetuities

as inserted by s.25 P(A) Act 1996

61A. - (1) The rules of law and equity relating to perpetuities, inalienability and accumulations and the provisions of the Accumulations Act, 1892, shall not apply and shall be deemed never to have applied to any trust to which this section applies.

(2) Subject to *subsection (3),* this section shall apply to -

(a) any trust which as created had or subsequently has as its main purpose the provision of relevant benefits within the meaning of section 13(1) of the Finance Act, 1972, and which is capable of receiving approval under Chapter II of Part I of that Act, and

(b) any trust which is also an occupational pension scheme notwithstanding that it may cease to be an occupational pension scheme.

(3) This section shall not apply to any trust the resources of which have, whether in whole or in part, been returned before the passing of the *Pensions (Amendment) Act, 1996*, by reason of the rules or provisions referred to in *subsection (1).*

(4) The persons (if any) having the power to amend a trust to which this section applies may amend the said trust so as to dispense with any limitations on the duration of the said trust the purpose of which is to ensure compliance with the rules or provisions referred to in *subsection (1),* notwithstanding any provision of the said trust to the contrary.

Selection by members of funded schemes of persons for appointment as trustees.

s.62 as substituted by s.15 SW Act (No.2) 1993 (subsection (2) previously substituted by s.60 SW Act 1992)

62. - (1) The Minister shall provide by regulations, in respect of schemes having not less than a specified number of members, that the members of any such scheme may select, or approve of the selection by the employer concerned, of a person or a specified number of persons who shall be appointed to be a trustee or trustees of the scheme (or who shall be retained as such trustee or trustees, as the case may be).

(2) Regulations under this section -

(a) shall determine the circumstances in which a person, or category of persons, who, having been admitted to membership of the scheme and remaining entitled to any benefit under the scheme, is or are to be regarded for the purpose of this section as being a member or members of the scheme,

(b) may specify the manner in which the selection, or the approval of the selection by the employer concerned, of a person or persons for appointment or retention as a trustee or trustees by members of schemes, for the purpose of *subsection (1)*, shall be made, and

(c) may make such other provision as the Minister considers necessary or expedient for the purpose of this section and for enabling it to have full effect.

Appointment and removal of trustees by High Court.

Subsection (1) as substituted by s.49 SW Act 1993

63. - (1) The High Court (in this Part referred to as "the Court") may, on application to it by the Board by petition, make an order -

(a) for the removal of a trustee of a scheme and the appointment of a new trustee, and

(b) that a trustee so removed shall not act as a trustee of a scheme for such period as the Court may order.

as substituted by s.26(a) P(A) Act 1996

(2) The Court may make an order under *subsection (1)* in relation to the trustees of a scheme, if it considers -

(a) that any of the trustees have failed to carry out any of the duties imposed on them by law (including this Act), or

(b) that the scheme is being or has been administered in such a manner as to jeopardise the rights and interests thereunder of the members of the scheme.

(3)(a) A petition under this section shall be served only on the existing trustees unless the Court directs otherwise.

(b) Upon the hearing of a petition under this section, the Board, the existing trustees of the scheme concerned, the employer concerned and the members of the scheme shall be entitled to be heard unless the Court directs otherwise.

(4) A trustee of a scheme appointed under this section shall, as well before as after the resources of the scheme become by law vested in him have the same powers, authorities and discretions and may in all respects act as if he had been originally appointed a trustee by the rules of the scheme.

(5) An order under this section may make provision for such ancillary and consequential matters (including the vesting of the property of the scheme concerned in the trustees appointed by the order and (notwithstanding anything contained in the rules of the scheme) the making of payments from the resources of the scheme or from the employer to the trustees appointed by the order in respect of fees, expenses or other matters relating to their duties as such trustees) as the Court considers necessary or expedient. *as amended by s.26(b) P(A) Act 1996*

(6) An order under this section shall not operate further or otherwise as a discharge to any former trustee of the scheme concerned than an appointment of new trustees under any power for that purpose contained in any instrument would have operated.

(7) Where any land of which the ownership is registered under the Registration of Title Act, 1964, becomes vested, by order under this section, in any person or persons, the registering authority under that Act shall, upon production of the relevant order under this section, and upon payment of the appropriate fee, register that person or those persons in the appropriate register maintained under that Act as owner (within the meaning of that Act) of the land.

(8) Where an order is made under this section, any assets vested by the order that immediately before the commencement of the order were standing registered in the books of any bank, corporation or company or were entered in any register kept in pursuance of any enactment in the names of the former trustees of the scheme concerned shall, upon such commencement, be transferred into the names of the new trustees of the scheme.

Suspension of trustees.

as inserted by s.27 P(A) Act 1996

63A. - (1) The Court may, on application to it by the Board, make an order on such terms and subject to such directions as to notification of relevant parties as it may think suspending a trustee of a scheme from being a trustee of the scheme to which the application relates -

(a) pending completion of an investigation by or on behalf of the Board into the state and conduct of the scheme,

(b) where proceedings have been instituted against him for an offence involving dishonesty or deception and have not been concluded,

(c) where a petition has been presented to the Court for an order adjudging him bankrupt and proceedings on the petition have not been concluded,

(d) where the trustee is a company, if a petition for the winding up of the company has been presented to the Court and proceedings on the petition have not been concluded,

(e) where an application has been made to the Court for a disqualification order against him under Part VII of the Companies Act, 1990, and proceedings on the application have not been concluded, or

(f) where the trustee is a company and, if any director were a trustee, the Court would have power to suspend him under *paragraph (b), (c)* or *(e).*

(2) An order under *subsection (1)* may apply to a particular scheme, a particular class of schemes or schemes in general.

(3) An order under *subsection (1)(a)* shall be in force for a period not exceeding 12 months: However, on application to it by the Board, the Court may by order extend that period for a further period not exceeding 12 months.

(4) An order made under *subsection (1)* (other than under *paragraph (a)*) shall be in force until the proceedings to which the order relates are determined.

(5) Where an order is made under *subsection (1)* the person suspended by the order from acting as a trustee shall not, while the order is in force, exercise any functions as a trustee of a scheme to which the order applies.

(6) An order under *subsection (1)* may be made on any of the grounds in *paragraphs (b)* to *(e)* of that subsection whether or not the proceedings were instituted, petition presented or application made (as the case may be) before or after the passing of the *Pensions (Amendment) Act, 1996.*

(7) The Court may, on the application of any person suspended under *subsection (1)*, by order revoke the order, either generally or in relation to a particular scheme or a particular class of schemes, but a revocation made at any time cannot affect anything done before that time.

(8) An order under this section may make provision as respects the period of the trustee's suspension for matters arising out of it and in particular for enabling any person to execute any instrument in his name or otherwise act for him and for adjusting any provisions of the scheme governing the proceedings of the trustees to take account of the reduction in the number capable of acting.

(9) Where the Court makes an order under *subsection (1)* it may by that order or by a further order appoint any person to be a trustee in place of, and for such period as the Court may direct not exceeding the period of suspension of, the person suspended from acting as a trustee.

(10) An order referred to in *subsection (9)* may make provision for such ancillary and consequential matters (including the vesting of the property of the scheme concerned in the trustees appointed by the order and (notwithstanding anything contained in the rules of the scheme) the making of payments from the resources of the scheme or from the employer to the trustees appointed by the order in respect of fees, expenses or other matters relating to their duties as such trustees) as the Court considers necessary or expedient.

(11) Where an order referred to in *subsection (9)* ceases to have an effect, the Court may by a further order make provision for the vesting of the property of the scheme concerned in the persons who are the trustees of the said scheme.

(12) Where any land of which the ownership is registered under the Registration of Title Act, 1964, becomes vested, by order under this section in any person or persons, the registering authority under that Act shall, upon production of the relevant order under this section, and upon payment of the appropriate fee, register that person or those persons in the appropriate register maintained under that Act as owner (within the meaning of that Act) of the land.

(13)Where an order is made under this section, any assets vested by the order that immediately before the commencement of the order were standing registered in the books of any bank, corporation or company or were entered in any register kept in pursuance of any enactment in the names of the former trustees of the scheme concerned shall, upon such commencement, be transferred into the names of the new trustees of the scheme.

Offence.
as inserted by s.27 P(A) Act 1996

63B. - A person who purports to act as trustee of a scheme while removed from being a trustee of a scheme under *section 63* or suspended from being a trustee of a scheme under *section 63A* shall be guilty of an offence and shall be liable -

(a) on summary conviction to a fine not exceeding £1,500 or to imprisonment for a term not exceeding one year, or to both,

(b) on conviction on indictment to a fine not exceeding £10,000 or to imprisonment for a term not exceeding two years, or to both.

Appointment and removal of trustees by Board.

as substituted by s.28 P(A) Act 1996

64. - (1) Where in relation to a scheme, there are no trustees or the trustees cannot be found, the Board may, if it considers it desirable to do so, by order under its seal -

(a) appoint a new trustee or new trustees of the scheme in substitution, where appropriate, for any existing trustee or trustees; and

(b) vest, subject where necessary to transfer in the books of any bank, corporation or company, the assets of the scheme in the persons appointed trustees of the scheme by the order.

(2) The Board shall, not later than 21 days after the date of an order under this section, publish a notice in a daily newspaper published in and circulating throughout the State giving particulars of the order.

as substituted by s.28(a) P(A) Act 1996

(3) Every trustee of a scheme appointed under this section shall, as well before as after the resources of the scheme become by law vested in him, have the same powers, authorities and discretions and may in all respects act as if he had been originally appointed a trustee by the rules of the scheme.

(4)(a) A person having an interest may, within 21 days after the publication of a notice under *subsection (2)* (or such longer period as the Court may fix, being a period that, having regard to the circumstances of any particular case, the Court considers to be reasonable), appeal to the Court against the making of the order to which the notice relates.

Subsection (4)(a) as amended by s.28(b) P(A) Act 1996

(b) On an appeal under this subsection the Court may make such order confirming, annulling or varying the order concerned and such order as to costs as it thinks fit, but if the Court annuls or varies an order under this section that has come into operation, the annulment or variation shall be without prejudice to the validity of anything previously done thereunder.

(c) The Board, the trustees, the employer and the members of the scheme concerned shall be entitled to be represented and heard on any appeal under this subsection.

(d) An order under this section shall not come into operation -

(i) during the period of 21 days from the date of the publication of the notice under *subsection (2)* in relation to the order, or

Subparagraph (i) as amended by s.28(c) P(A) Act 1996

Subparagraph (ii) as amended by s.28(d) P(A) Act 1996

(ii) if an appeal against the order is brought during the period aforesaid, before the final determination of the appeal or any appeal from such determination or the withdrawal of either such appeal.

as amended by s.28(e) P(A) Act 1996

(5) An order under this section may make provision for such ancillary and consequential matters (including the vesting of the property of the scheme concerned in the trustees appointed by the order and (notwithstanding anything contained in the rules of the scheme) the making of payments from the resources of the scheme or from the employer to the trustees appointed by the order in respect of fees, expenses or other matters relating to their duties as such trustees) as the Board considers necessary or expedient.

(6) An order under this section shall not operate as a discharge of any liabilities of a former trustee of the scheme concerned to any greater or different extent than the appointment of new trustees under any power for that purpose contained in any instrument would have operated.

(7) Where a body corporate is appointed under this section to be, or a body corporate appointed under this section becomes, sole trustee of a scheme the terms of which provide for or require the appointment of more than one trustee, then, during such time as the body corporate holds the office of trustee of the scheme and is the only such trustee -

(a) the rules of the scheme shall be deemed to provide for or require the appointment of one trustee only, and

(b) one trustee only shall be deemed to have been originally appointed under the terms of the scheme.

(8) Where any land of which the ownership is registered under the Registration of Title Act, 1964, becomes vested, by an order under this section, in any person or persons, the registering authority under that Act shall, upon production of a copy of the order sealed with the seal of the Board, and upon payment of the appropriate fee, register that person or those persons in the appropriate register maintained under that Act as owner (within the meaning of that Act) of the land.

(9) Where an order is made under this section, any assets vested by the order that immediately before the commencement of the order were standing registered in the books of any bank, corporation or company or were entered in any register kept in pursuance of any enactment in the names of the former trustees of the scheme concerned shall, upon production after such commencement of a copy of the order sealed with the seal of the Board, be transferred into the names of the new trustees of the scheme.

Conflict between *Part VI* and schemes.

as inserted by s.50 SW Act 1993

64A. (1) The provisions of this Part and of any regulations made thereunder shall override any rule of a scheme to the extent that that rule conflicts with those provisions.

(2) Any question as to -

(a) whether any provision of this Part (including the application of any provision as modified by regulations) or any regulations made thereunder conflicts with any rule of a scheme, or

(b) whether a scheme is a defined benefit scheme or a defined contribution scheme for the purposes of this Part,

shall be determined by the Board on application to it in writing in that behalf by a person who, in relation to the scheme, corresponds to a person mentioned in *section 38(3)* in relation to the scheme mentioned therein.

(3) An appeal to the High Court on a point of law from a determination of the Board under *subsection (2)* in relation to a scheme, may be brought by the person who made, or a person who was entitled to make, the application concerned under *subsection (2)*.

PART VII
Equal Treatment for Men and Women in Occupational Benefit Schemes

Interpretation *(Part VII).*

65. - In this Part, unless the context otherwise requires -

"the Act of 1946" means the Industrial Relations Act, 1946;

"the Agency" means the Employment Equality Agency;

"the Court" means the Labour Court;

"employee" means a person who has entered into or works under (or, in the case of a contract which has been terminated, worked under) a contract of employment with an employer, whether the contract is (or was) for manual labour, clerical work or otherwise, is (or was) expressed or implied, oral or in writing, and whether it is (or was) a contract of service or apprenticeship or otherwise, and includes a civil servant of the State or of the Government and an officer or servant of a local authority within the meaning of the Local Government Act, 1941, an officer or servant of a harbour authority, health board or vocational education committee and any reference to employment shall be construed accordingly;

"employer", in relation to an employee, means the person by whom the employee is (or, in the case where the employment has ceased, was) employed under a contract of employment, and for the purposes of this definition a civil servant of the State or of the Government shall be deemed to be employed by the State or the Government (as the case may be) and an officer or servant of a local authority within the meaning of the Local Government Act, 1941, or of a harbour authority, health board or vocational education committee shall be deemed to be employed by the local authority, harbour authority, health board or vocational educational committee (as the case may be);

as inserted by s.51 SW Act 1993

"equality officer", means an equality officer of the Labour Relations Commission appointed under section 37 of the Industrial Relations Act, 1990.

as substituted by s.29(a) P(A) Act 1996

"member" means any person who, having been admitted to membership under the rules of an occupational benefit scheme, remains entitled to any benefit under such scheme in respect of a period of membership whilst employed or self-employed within the State;

"occupational benefit scheme" means any scheme or arrangement which is comprised in one or more instruments or agreements and which provides, or is capable of providing, occupational benefits in relation to employed or self-employed persons in any description of employment or self-employment within the State, but does not include - *as substituted by s.29(b) P(A) Act 1996*

(a) any individual contract made by or on behalf of an employed or a self-employed person, or

(b) any scheme which has only one member, or

(c) any scheme for the benefit of employees under which the benefits are provided in full by contributions paid by the employees;

"occupational benefits" means benefits, in the form of pensions or otherwise, payable in cash or in kind in respect of -

(a) termination of service,

(b) retirement, old age or death,

(c) interruptions of service by reason of sickness or invalidity,

(d) accidents, injuries or diseases arising out of or in the course of a person's employment,

(e) unemployment, or

(f) expenses incurred in connection with children or other dependants;

and, in the case of a member who is an employee, includes any other benefit corresponding to a benefit provided by virtue of the Social Welfare Acts, the Maternity (Protection of Employees) Act, 1981, or the Health Acts, 1970 to 1987, which is payable to or in respect of the member as a consequence of his employment;

["the Social Welfare Acts" ....] *Repealed by s.29(c) P(A) Act 1996*

66. - Subject to *sections 69* and *72*, every occupational benefit scheme shall comply with the principle of equal treatment. Schemes to comply with principle of equal treatment.

Principle of equal treatment.

67. - (1) The principle of equal treatment is that there shall be no discrimination on the basis of sex in respect of any matter relating to an occupational benefit scheme.

(2) The principle of equal treatment shall apply in relation to members' dependants as it applies in relation to members.

(3) For the purposes of this section, discrimination on the basis of sex shall be deemed to occur in respect of a matter relating to an occupational benefit scheme in but only in the following cases -

(a) where because of a person's sex the person is treated less favourably than a person of the other sex,

(b) where a person is treated, by reference to his marital or family status, less favourably than a person of the other sex with the same status,

(c) Where because of a person's sex the person is unable to comply with a requirement or condition -

(i) in respect of which the proportion of persons of the other sex able to comply with such requirement or condition is substantially higher than the proportion of persons of the first mentioned sex so able, and

as amended by s.30(a) P(A) Act 1996

(ii) which is not objectively justifiable irrespective of the sex of the persons to whom it applies,

(d) where because of a person's marital or family status the person is unable to comply with a requirement or condition -

(i) in respect of which the proportion of persons of the other sex with the same status able to comply with such requirement or condition is substantially higher than the proportion of persons of the first mentioned sex so able, and

as amended by s.30(b) P(A) Act 1996

(ii) which is not objectively justifiable irrespective of the sex of the persons to whom it applies,

(e) where a person is penalised for having in good faith -

(i) made a reference under *section 75, 76* or *77*,

(ii) given evidence in any proceedings under this Part, or

(iii) given notice of an intention to do anything referred to in *subparagraphs (i)* and *(ii)*.

68. - If any question arises as to whether a requirement or condition, falling within *paragraphs (c)* and *(d)* of *subsection (3)* of *section 67* is justifiable irrespective of the sex of the persons to whom it applies, it shall be for those who assert such justification to prove it.

Onus of proof in certain cases.

69. - (1) In determining whether a scheme complies with the principle of equal treatment under *section 66*, account shall not be taken of -

Supplementary provisions to *section 66*.

(a) any difference, on the basis of the sex of members, in the levels of contributions which the employer makes, to the extent that the difference is for the purposes of removing or limiting differences, as between men and women in the amount or value of benefits provided under a defined contribution scheme,

(b) any difference, on the basis of sex, in the amount or value of benefits provided under a defined contribution scheme to the extent that the difference is justifiable on actuarial grounds,

(c) any special treatment for the benefit of women to whom *section 72(1)* relates,

(d) ....

Repealed by s.61(a) SW Act 1992

(e) any difference of treatment in relation to any optional provisions available.

(2) In this section -

"defined contribution scheme" has the meaning assigned to it under *section 2* but as if the reference therein to "benefits" were a reference to "occupational benefits";

"optional provisions available" means those provisions of a scheme -

(a) which apply only in the case of members who elect for them to do so, and

(b) whose purpose is to secure for those members -

(i) benefits in addition to those otherwise provided under the scheme, or

(ii) a choice with respect to the date on which benefits under the scheme are to commence, or

(iii)a choice between any two or more benefits.

Repealed by s.61(b) SW Act 1992

(3) ....

Equal treatment and access to schemes.

70. - An employer shall comply with the principle of equal treatment in relation to the manner in which he affords his employees access to an occupational benefit scheme.

Non-compliance, compulsory levelling up.

Subsection (1) as substituted by s.31(a) P(A) 1996

71. - (1) Where a rule of an occupational benefit scheme does not comply with the principle of equal treatment it shall, to the extent that it does not so comply, be rendered null and void by the provisions of this Part with effect from the 17th day of May, 1990, in the case of a rule relating to employed persons and with effect from the 1st day of January, 1993, in the case of a rule relating to self-employed persons and the more favourable treatment accorded to it by persons of the one sex shall be accorded by it to members of the other sex in respect of periods of membership in that scheme up to the date on which the rule is amended to comply with the principle of equal treatment.

(2) Where more favourable treatment is accorded to any persons under a scheme by virtue of *subsection (1)*, the trustees of the scheme or (where appropriate) the employer shall take such measures as are necessary to give effect to that subsection.

as substituted by s.31(b) P(A) Act 1996 (previously substituted by s.62 SW Act 1992)

(3) Where any rule of an occupational benefit scheme relating to employed persons is rendered null and void by *subsection (1)*, nothing in this Part shall preclude any rights or obligations, relating to a period of membership in that scheme before the 17th day of May, 1990, from remaining subject to the provisions of the scheme in force during that period of membership -

(a) during the period beginning on the 17th day of May, 1990, and ending on the 31st day of December, 1998, or, in the case of retirement ages, the 31st day of December, 2017, or

(b) in respect of members who cease to be in relevant employment to which that scheme applies before or during the period referred to in *paragraph (a)*.

(4) Where any rule of an occupational benefit scheme relating to self-employed persons is rendered null and void by *subsection (1)*, nothing in this Part shall preclude any rights or obligations, relating to a period of membership in that scheme before the 1st day of January, 1993, from remaining subject to the provisions of the scheme in force during that period of membership. *as inserted by s.31(b) P(A) Act 1996.*

72. - (1) Subject to the provisions of this section, nothing in this Part shall prevent a scheme from providing special treatment for women in connection with pregnancy or childbirth. Maternity provisions.

(2) Where an occupational benefit scheme contains a rule -

(a) which relates to continuing membership of, or the accrual of rights under, the scheme during any period of paid maternity absence in the case of a woman who -

(i) is, or

(ii) immediately before the commencement of such period, was,

an employee and which treats that woman in a manner other than that in which she would be treated under the scheme if she was not absent from work and was in receipt of remuneration from her employer during that period, or

(b) which requires the amount of any benefit payable under the scheme to or in respect of any such woman, to the extent that it falls to be determined by reference to her earnings during a period which includes a period of paid maternity absence, to be determined other than it would so be determined if she was not absent from work, and was in receipt of remuneration from her employer during that period, it shall be regarded to that extent as not complying with the principle of equal treatment.

(3) Where a scheme is regarded as not complying with the principle of equal treatment by virtue of *subsection (2)*, the trustees of the scheme or (where appropriate) the employer concerned shall take such measures as are necessary to ensure that the treatment accorded to the woman concerned under the scheme is no less favourable than that which would be accorded to her thereunder throughout the period of maternity absence concerned if she were not absent from work and was in receipt of remuneration from her employer during that period.

(4) In this section "period of paid maternity absence" means any period -

(a) throughout which a woman is absent from work due to pregnancy or childbirth, and

(b) for which her employer, or (if she is no longer in his employment) her former employer, pays her any contractual remuneration.

Family leave provisions.

73. - (1) Where an occupational benefit scheme contains a rule -

(a) which relates to continuing membership of, or the accrual of rights under, the scheme during any period of paid family leave in the case of a member who is an employee and which treats the member in a manner other than that in which he would be treated under the scheme if he were not absent from work, and was in receipt of remuneration from his employer, during that period, or

(b) which requires the amount of any benefit payable under the scheme to or in respect of any such member, to the extent that it falls to be determined by reference to his earnings during a period which includes a period of paid family leave, to be determined other than it would so be determined if he was not absent from work and was in receipt of remuneration from his employer during that period,

it shall be regarded to that extent as not complying with the principle of equal treatment.

(2) Where a scheme is regarded as not complying with the principle of equal treatment by virtue of *subsection (1)*, the trustees of a scheme or (where appropriate) the employer concerned shall take such measures as are necessary to ensure that the treatment accorded to the member concerned under the scheme is no less favourable than that which would be accorded to him thereunder throughout the period of family leave concerned if he was not absent from work and was in receipt of remuneration from his employer during that period.

(3) In this section "period of paid family leave" means any period -

(a) throughout which a member is absent from work for family reasons, and

(b) during which the employer pays him any contractual remuneration.

Principle of equal treatment and collective agreements, etc.

as substituted by s.32 P(A) Act 1996

74. - (1)(a) Where a rule or term of an agreement or order to which this section applies does not comply with the principle of equal treatment, it shall, to the extent that it does not so comply, be rendered null and void with effect from the 17th day of May, 1990, and the more favourable treatment accorded by it to persons of the one sex shall be accorded by it to persons of the other sex in respect of periods of employment to which that rule or term applies up to the date on which the rule or term is amended to comply with the principle of equal treatment.

(b) This section applies to -

(i) a collective agreement,

(ii) an employment regulation order within the meaning of Part IV of the Act of 1946, and

(iii) a registered employment agreement within the meaning of Part III of the Act of 1946 registered in the Register of Employment Agreements.

(2) Where more favourable treatment is accorded to any persons under an agreement or order by virtue of *subsection (1)* the employer shall take such measures as are necessary to give effect to that subsection.

(3) Where any rule or term of an agreement or order is rendered null and void by *subsection (1)*, nothing in this Part shall affect any rights accrued or obligations incurred under that rule or term relating to a period before the 17th day of May, 1990 -

(a) during the period beginning on the 17th day of May, 1990, and ending on the 31st day of December, 1998, or, in the case of retirement ages, the 31st day of December, 2017, or

(b) in respect of members who cease to be in employment to which that rule or term applies before or during the period referred to in *paragraph (a)*.

Equal treatment: contract of employment.

as inserted by s.33 P(A) Act 1996

74A. - (1) Where a contract of employment contains a term (whether expressed or implied) which does not comply with the principle of equal treatment, the term shall, to the extent that it does not so comply, be rendered null and void with effect from the 17th day of May, 1990, and the more favourable treatment accorded by it to persons of the one sex shall be accorded by it to persons of the other sex in respect of periods of employment to which that term applies up to the date on which the term is amended to comply with the principle of equal treatment.

(2) Where more favourable treatment is accorded to any persons under a term (whether expressed or implied) of a contract of employment by virtue of *subsection (1)*, the employer shall take such measures as are necessary to give effect to that subsection.

(3) Where any term (whether expressed or implied) of a contract of employment is rendered null and void by *subsection (1)*, nothing in this Part shall affect any rights accrued or obligations incurred under that term relating to a period before the 17th day of May, 1990 -

(a) during the period beginning on the 17th day of May, 1990, and ending on the 31st day of December, 1998, or, in the case of retirement ages, the 31st day of December, 2017, or

(b) in respect of members who cease to be in employment to which that term applies before or during the period referred to in *paragraph (a)*.

75. - (1) Any dispute as to -

Determination of disputes.

(a) whether a scheme is a defined contribution scheme for the purposes of this Part,

(b) whether any rule of a scheme, which is also an occupational benefit scheme for the purposes of this Part, complies with the principle of equal treatment, or

(c) whether and to what extent any such rule is rendered null and void by *section 71*,

shall be determined by the Board on application to it in writing in that behalf by a person who, in relation to the scheme, corresponds to a person mentioned in *section 38(3)* in relation to the scheme mentioned therein.

(2) Where it appears to the Agency that the rules of a scheme referred to in *subsection (1)* fail to comply with the principle of equal treatment, the matter may be referred to the Board by the Agency and the reference shall be treated for the purpose of this Act as an application under *subsection (1)*.

(3) An appeal to the High Court on a point of law from a determination of the Board under *subsection (1)*, in relation to a scheme, may be brought by the person who made, or a person who was entitled to make, the application concerned under *subsection (1)*.

76. - (1) Any dispute as to -

Equality officers.

Subsection (1) as substituted by s.34 P(A) Act 1996

(a) whether any rule of an occupational benefit scheme, other than an occupational pension scheme, complies with the principle of equal treatment,

(b) whether and to what extent any such rule is rendered null and void by *section 71*,

(c) whether any term of a collective agreement or employment regulation order specified in *section 74*, insofar as it relates to occupational benefits provided under a scheme referred to in *paragraph (a)*, complies with the principle of equal treatment,

(d) whether and to what extent any such rule or term is rendered null and void by *section 74*,

(e) whether any term of a contract of employment (whether expressed or implied), insofar as it relates to occupational benefits provided under a scheme referred to in *paragraph (a)*, complies with the principle of equal treatment,

(f) whether and to what extent any such term is rendered null and void by *section 74A*, or

(g) whether an employer complies with the provisions of *section 70*,

shall be referred by any person concerned to an equality officer for investigation and recommendation.

as substituted by s.34 P(A) Act 1996

(2) Where it appears to the Agency that -

(a) a rule of an occupational benefit scheme referred to in subsection (1),

(b) a rule or term of a collective agreement or employment regulation order referred to in subsection (1)(c), or

(c) a term of a contract of employment referred to in *subsection 1(e),*

does not comply with the principle of equal treatment or an employer fails to comply with the provisions of *section 70*, the matter may be referred to an equality officer by the Agency and the reference shall be treated for the purpose of this Act as a reference under *subsection (1).*

(3) Where a dispute is referred under this section to an equality officer, he shall investigate the dispute and issue a recommendation thereon.

(4) Any information obtained by an equality officer in the course of an investigation or appeal under this Part as to any trade union or person or as to the business carried on by any person which is not available otherwise shall not be included in any recommendation or determination without the consent of the trade union or person concerned, nor shall any person concerned in proceedings before an equality officer or the Court disclose any such information without such consent.

(5) A recommendation under this section shall be conveyed -

(a) to the Court and to the parties to the dispute, or

(b) in the case of a reference under *subsection (2)* to the Court, the Agency and to such person or persons as appear to the equality officer to be concerned.

(6) An equality officer may provide for the regulation of proceedings before him in relation to an investigation before him under this Act.

(7)(a) An equality officer may, for the purpose of obtaining any information which he may require for enabling him to exercise his functions under this Act, do any one or more of the following things:

(i) at all reasonable times enter premises,

(ii) require an employer or his representative to produce to him any records, books or documents that are in the employer's power or control and as respects which the officer has reasonable grounds for believing that they contain information of the kind so required and to give him such information as he may reasonably require in regard to any entries in any such records, books or documents,

(iii) inspect and take copies, or copies of extracts from, any such records, books or documents.

(b) Any person who obstructs or impedes an equality officer in the exercise of his powers under this subsection or does not comply with a requirement of an equality officer under this subsection shall be guilty of an offence and shall be liable -

(i) on summary conviction to a fine not exceeding £1,500 or imprisonment for a term not exceeding one year, or to both, *as amended by s.43 P(A) Act 1996*

(ii) on conviction on indictment to a fine not exceeding £10,000 or imprisonment for a term not exceeding 2 years, or to both.

(8) An investigation by an equality officer under this Act shall be conducted in private.

Investigation of disputes by Court.

77. - (1) A person concerned or (in the case of a reference under *section 76(2)*) the Agency may appeal to the Court -

(a) against a recommendation under section 76, or

(b) for a determination that such a recommendation has not been complied with.

(2) The Court shall hear and determine an appeal under this section and shall convey its determination -

(a) in the case of a reference under section 76(1) to the parties to the dispute,

(b) in the case of a reference under *section 76(2)* to the Agency and such person or persons as appear to the Court to be concerned.

(3)(a) A hearing under this section shall be held in private, but the Court may, if requested to do so by a party to the dispute or a person referred to in *section 76(2)*, hold the hearing in public.

(b) Where a hearing under this section is being held in public the Court may, if it is satisfied that any part of the hearing concerns a matter that should, in the interests of any party to the dispute, or of a person referred to in *section 76(2)* be treated as confidential, hold that part of the hearing in private.

(c) Sections 14 and 21 of the Act of 1946 shall apply to an appeal under this section.

(d) An appeal under this section shall be lodged in the Court not later than 42 days after the date of the equality officer's recommendation and the notice shall specify the grounds of the appeal.

(4) Any information obtained by the Court in the course of an investigation or appeal under this Part as to any trade union or person or as to the business carried on by any person which is not available otherwise shall not be included in any recommendation or determination without the consent of the trade union or person concerned, nor shall any person concerned in proceedings before an equality officer or the Court disclose any such information without such consent.

(5) A party to a dispute determined by the Court under *subsection (1)* or, in the case of a determination in a matter referred to under *section 76(2)*, the Agency or any other person concerned may appeal to the High Court on a point of law.

Powers of Court under *section 77.*

as substituted by s.35 P(A) Act 1996

78. - The Court may, in pursuance of a determination of the Court, under *section 77* as may be appropriate -

(a) determine whether a rule of a scheme referred to in *section 76(1)(a)* complies with the principle of equal treatment,

(b) determine whether and to what extent any such rule is rendered null and void by *section 71*,

(c) determine whether any term of a collective agreement or employment regulation order specified in *section 74*, insofar as it relates to occupational benefits provided under a scheme referred to in *section 76(1)(a)*, complies with the principle of equal treatment,

(d) determine whether and to what extent any such rule or term is rendered null and void by *section 74*,

(e) determine whether any term of a contract of employment (whether expressed or implied), insofar as it relates to occupational benefits provided under a scheme referred to in *section 76(1)(a)*, complies with the principle of equal treatment,

(f) determine whether and to what extent any such term is rendered null and void by *section 74A*,

(g) determine whether the employer concerned has complied with the provisions of *section 70*,

(h) recommend to a person or persons concerned a specific course of action.

Failure to implement determination of Court.

Subsection (1) as amended by s.36 P(A) Act 1996

79. - (1) Where a person concerned or (in a case which relates to a reference under *section 76(2)*) the Agency complains to the Court that a determination under *section 78* has not been implemented, the following provisions shall have effect:

(a) the Court shall consider the complaint and shall hear all persons appearing to the Court to be interested and desiring to be heard,

(b) if after such consideration the Court is satisfied that the complaint is well founded, the Court may by order direct the person failing to implement the determination to do such things as will, in the opinion of the Court, result in the determination being implemented by that person.

(2) If, where an order is made by the Court under *subsection (1)*, the direction contained in the order is not carried out within 2 months from the date of the making of the order (or, where there is an appeal under *section 77(5)*, within 2 months of the date of the order of the High Court on the appeal) the person to whom the direction is given shall be guilty of an offence and shall be liable -

as amended by s.43 P(A) Act 1996

(a) on summary conviction, to a fine not exceeding £1,500 or to imprisonment for a term not exceeding one year, or to both,

(b) on conviction on indictment, to a fine not exceeding £10,000 or to imprisonment for a term not exceeding 2 years, or to both.

Offences relating to certain dismissals and effect, etc.

Subsection (1) as substituted by s.37 P(A) Act 1996

80. - (1) Where an employee is dismissed from an employment solely or mainly because, in good faith, the employee -

(a) notified the Board of an alleged breach of this Act,

(b) made to the Board a report under *section 83* or a voluntary report of any matter concerning the state and conduct of a scheme,

(c) made a reference under *section 38, 53, 58, 64A, 75, 76* or *77*,

(d) gave evidence in any proceedings under this Act, or

(e) gave notice to his employer of his intention to do anything referred to in *subparagraph (a), (b), (c)* or *(d)*,

the employer shall be guilty of an offence and shall be liable -

(i) on summary conviction, to a fine not exceeding £1,500 or to imprisonment for a term not exceeding one year, or to both,

(ii) on conviction on indictment, to a fine not exceeding £10,000 or to imprisonment for a term not exceeding two years, or to both.

(2)In a prosecution for an offence under this section the onus shall be on the employer to satisfy the Court that the doing of anything referred to in *subsection (1)* was not the sole or principal reason for the dismissal.

(3)(a) On conviction of an employer for an offence under this section, the Court may, if it thinks fit and the dismissed employee is present or represented in court and consents -

(i) order the re-instatement by the employer of the dismissed person in the position which that person held immediately before the dismissal on the terms and conditions on which that person was employed immediately before that dismissal, together with a term that the re-instatement shall be deemed to have commenced on the day of the dismissal,

(ii) order the re-engagement by the employer of the dismissed person either in the position which that person held immediately before the dismissal or in a different position which would be reasonably suitable for that person on such terms and conditions as are reasonable having regard to all the circumstances, or

(iii)impose on the employer, in addition to any fine imposed under subsection (1*)*, a fine not exceeding the amount which, in the opinion of the Court, the dismissed person would have received from the employer concerned by way of remuneration if the dismissal had not occurred:

Provided that that amount shall not exceed -

as amended by s.43 P(A) Act 1996

(I) if the conviction was a summary conviction, an amount which together with the fine imposed under *subsection (1)* does not exceed £1,500,

(II)if the conviction was on indictment, an amount equal to 104 weeks' remuneration of the dismissed person.

(b) The amount of a fine imposed under paragraph (a) shall be paid to the employee concerned.

(c) Without prejudice to any right of appeal by any other person, the employee concerned may appeal against the amount of the fine under this subsection, either (as the case may be) to the High Court or to the judge of the Circuit Court in whose circuit the district (or any part thereof) of the justice of the District Court by whom the fine was imposed is situated, and the decision on such an appeal shall be final.

(d) Proof of the payment by an employer of a fine imposed under *paragraph (a)* shall be a defence to any civil action brought against him by the employee concerned in respect of the remuneration referred to in *subparagraph (iii)* of that paragraph.

Provisions supplemental to *section 80.*

81. - (1) Where a person, in respect of whose dismissal from employment a prosecution for an offence under *section 80* has not been brought, complains to the Court that that dismissal was solely or mainly because the person did in good faith a thing specified in *section 80(1)* the following provisions shall apply:

(a) the Court shall investigate the complaint, and shall hear all persons appearing to the Court to be interested and desiring to be heard;

(b) an investigation under this subsection shall be held in private, but the Court shall, if requested to do so by a party to the dispute, hold the investigation in public;

(c) where an investigation under this subsection is being held in public the Court may, if it is satisfied that any part of the investigation concerns a matter that should, in the interests of any party to the dispute, be treated as confidential, hold that part of the investigation in private;

(d) if after such investigation the Court is satisfied that the complaint is well founded, the Court may -

(i) order the re-instatement by the employer of the dismissed person in the position which that person held immediately before the dismissal on the terms and conditions on which that person was then employed and that the re-instatement shall be deemed to have commenced on the day of the dismissal,

(ii) order the re-engagement by the employer of the dismissed person either in the position which that person held immediately before the dismissal or in a different position which would be reasonably suitable for that person on such terms and conditions as are reasonable having regard to all the circumstances, or

(iii)order the payment by the employer to the dismissed person of such compensation as the Court considers reasonable in the circumstances not exceeding an amount equal to 104 weeks' remuneration of that person.

(2) Subject to *subsection (5)*, if the employer concerned does not comply with an order under *subsection (1)* within 2 months of the date of its making, he shall be guilty of an offence and shall be liable -

(a) on summary conviction, to a fine not exceeding £1,500 or to imprisonment for a term not exceeding one year, or to both, *as amended by s.43 P(A) Act 1996*

(b) on conviction on indictment, to a fine not exceeding £10,000 or to imprisonment for a term not exceeding 2 years, or to both.

(3)(a) On conviction of a person for an offence under this section, the Court may, if it thinks fit and the dismissed person concerned is present or represented in court and consents -

(i) order the re-instatement by the employer of the dismissed person concerned in the position which that person held immediately before that dismissal on the terms and conditions on which that person was then employed and that the reinstatement shall be deemed to have commenced on the day of the dismissal,

(ii) order the re-engagement by the employer of the dismissed person either in the position which that person held immediately before the dismissal or in a different position which would be reasonably suitable for that person on such terms and conditions as are reasonable having regard to all the circumstances, or

(iii) impose on the employer, in addition to any fine imposed under *subsection (2)*, a fine not exceeding the amount which, in the opinion of the Court, the dismissed person would have received from the employer concerned by way of remuneration if the dismissal had not occurred:

Provided that that amount shall not exceed -

as amended by s.43 P(A) Act 1996

(I) if the conviction was a summary conviction, an amount which together with the fine imposed under subsection (2) does not exceed £1,500,

(II) if the conviction was on indictment, an amount equal to 104 weeks' remuneration of the dismissed person.

(b) The amount of a fine imposed under *paragraph (a)* shall be paid to the employee concerned.

(c) Without prejudice to any right of appeal by any other person, the employee concerned may appeal against the amount of a fine imposed under this subsection, either (as the case may be) to the High Court or to the judge of the Circuit Court in whose circuit the district (or any part thereof) of the justice of the District Court by whom the fine was imposed is situated, and the decision on such an appeal shall be final.

(d) Proof of the payment by a convicted person of a fine imposed under *paragraph (a)* shall be a defence to any civil action brought against him by the employee concerned in respect of the remuneration referred to in *subparagraph (iii)* of that paragraph.

(4) A complaint under this section shall be made to the Court not later than 6 months from the date of the dismissal concerned or such longer period as the Court considers reasonable having regard to the circumstances.

(5) The employer concerned may, notwithstanding section 17 of the Act of 1946, appeal against an order under *subsection (1)* to the judge of the Circuit Court in whose circuit the person carries on business.

Part VIII as inserted by s.38 P(A) Act 1996

PART VIII
Compulsory and Voluntary Reporting to the Board

Definition (*Part VII*).

82. - In this Part "relevant person" means, in relation to a scheme, a person who -

(a) is an auditor of the scheme, or

(b) is an actuary of the scheme, or

(c) is a trustee of the scheme, or

(d) is an insurance intermediary (within the meaning of section 2 of the Insurance Act, 1989), in relation to the scheme, or

(e) is an investment business firm (within the meaning of section 2 of the Investment Intermediaries Act, 1995), and -

(i) has advised on the scheme, or

(ii) has received any payment in relation to the investment of any of the resources of the scheme, or

(f) has been instructed to prepare, or who has prepared, an annual report of the scheme in accordance with *section 55*, or

(g) has been appointed by the trustees of the scheme to carry out, or who is carrying out, any of the duties of the trustees of the scheme under *section 59*.

Obligation to disclose misappropriation, etc., of resources of schemes to Board.

83. - (1) Subject to *subsection (2)*, where a relevant person has reasonable cause to believe that a material misappropriation or a fraudulent conversion of the resources of a scheme to which he is a relevant person has occurred, is occurring or is to be attempted, that person shall, as soon as practicable, give to the Board a report in writing of the particulars of the misappropriation or conversion, as the case may be.

(2) *Subsection (1)* does not apply to any belief formed as a result of information obtained before the passing of the *Pensions (Amendment) Act, 1996*.

(3) A relevant person shall be guilty of an offence if the person -

(a) fails to comply with *subsection (1)*, or

(b) knowingly or wilfully makes a report under *subsection (1)* which is incorrect.

(4) Where a relevant person is found guilty of an offence under this section the person shall be liable -

(a) on summary conviction to a fine not exceeding £1,500 or to imprisonment for a term not exceeding one year, or to both,

(b) on conviction on indictment to a fine not exceeding £10,000 or to imprisonment for a term not exceeding two years, or to both.

(5) In a prosecution for an offence under *subsection (3)* it shall be a defence for the accused to show that the contravention to which the offence relates was attributable to another person failing to comply with *subsection (1)* and that the accused took such reasonable steps in the circumstances as were open to him to secure the compliance of that other person with that subsection.

(6) In a prosecution for an offence under *subsection (3)* in relation to a failure to comply with *subsection (1)* it shall be a defence for the accused to show that he was, in the ordinary scope of professional engagement as a barrister or solicitor, assisting or advising in the preparation of legal proceedings and would not have had reasonable cause to believe that a material misappropriation or a fraudulent conversion of the resources of the scheme had taken place if he had not been so assisting or advising.

Protection of person making report to Board.

84. - Where a person makes a report, whether in writing or otherwise, in good faith to the Board of any matter concerning the state and conduct of a scheme, whether or not that person is a relevant person and whether or not the report is required to be made under *section 83(1)*, no duty to which the person may be subject shall be regarded as contravened and no liability or action shall lie against the person in any Court for so doing.

Privilege for Board publishing reports made to it under *section 83* etc.

85. - For the purposes of the law of defamation, the publication by the Board of any report made to it-

(a) under *section 83(1)*, or

(b) otherwise of any matter concerning the state and conduct of a scheme, shall be absolutely privileged.

shall be absolutely privileged.

Part IX as inserted by s.39 P(A) Act 1996

PART IX
Miscellaneous Applications to the High Court

Definition (*Part IX*).

86. - In this Part "the Court" means the High Court.

Court may order employer to pay arrears of contribution.

87. - (1) Subject to *subsection (2)*, the Court may, on application to it by the Board, make an order directing an employer to pay arrears of contributions to a scheme.

(2) The Court may make an order under *subsection (1)* if it is satisfied -

(a) that any contributions payable to the scheme by that employer on his own account have become due and remain unpaid, or

(b) that any contributions payable to the scheme by a member of the scheme have been deducted by that employer from the pay of the member but have not been paid to the scheme.

Court may order restoration of resources of scheme.

88. - If, on application to it by the Board, the Court is satisfied that any of the resources of a scheme have been wrongfully paid or transferred to any person, and that such payment or transfer is likely to jeopardise the rights and interests of the members under the scheme, the Court may order such person, and any other person who the Court is satisfied was knowingly concerned in the wrongful payment or transfer, to take such steps as the Court may direct for restoring the resources of the scheme to the level at which they would have been if such wrongful payment or transfer had not been made.

Court may order disposal of investment.

89. - (1) Subject to this section, the Court may, on application to it by the Board, make an order directing the trustees of a scheme to dispose of any investment held for the purposes of the scheme.

(2) The Court may make an order under *subsection (1)* when it is satisfied that the retention of the investment is likely to jeopardise the rights and interests under the scheme of the members of the scheme.

(3) Subject to *subsection (4)*, where the Court makes an order under *subsection (1)* it may by that order, or by a further order, direct the trustees, and any other person who the Court is satisfied was knowingly concerned in the investment, to take such steps as the Court may direct for restoring the resources of the scheme to the level at which they would have been if the investment had not been made.

(4) An order under *subsection (3)* shall not be made unless the Court is satisfied that the investment was not made *bona fide* in the interests of the members of the scheme and that the person against whom the order is to be made was aware of this or ought reasonably to have been aware of this.

Injunctions.

90. - (1) If, on application to it by the Board, the Court is satisfied that there is a reasonable likelihood that a particular person will do any act which constitutes a misuse or misappropriation of any of the resources of a scheme and that such misuse or misappropriation is likely to jeopardise the rights and interests under the scheme, of the members of the scheme, the Court may grant an injunction restraining him from doing so.

(2) If, on application to it by the Board, the Court is satisfied that there is a reasonable likelihood that any of the resources of the scheme will be invested in a manner which is likely to jeopardise the rights and interests under the scheme, of the members of the scheme, the Court may grant an injunction prohibiting such investment.

(3) If, on application to it by the Board, the Court is satisfied that the state and conduct of a scheme are being investigated by or on behalf of the Board and that the order hereinafter mentioned is desirable to ensure that the rights and interests under the scheme, of the members of the scheme, are not jeopardised pending the outcome of such investigation, the Court may grant an injunction prohibiting any person from disposing of, selling, pledging, charging or otherwise dealing with any of the resources of the scheme.

FIRST SCHEDULE
AN BORD PINSEAN - THE PENSIONS BOARD

Section 9(2).

1. The Board shall be a body corporate with perpetual succession and an official seal and power to sue and be sued in its corporate name and, with the consent of the Minister, to acquire, hold and dispose of land or an interest in land or to acquire, hold and dispose of any other property.

2. The Board shall consist of a chairman, and 14 ordinary members, who shall be appointed to the Board by the Minister.

as amended by s.40(a) P(A) Act 1996

3. A person appointed to be the chairman of the Board may be referred to (including in any document relating to appointment) by that designation or by such other designation as the Board considers with the concurrence of the Minister appropriate.

4. The chairman of the Board may at any time resign his office by letter addressed to the Minister.

5. Notwithstanding *paragraph 10(1)* the Minister may at any time remove the chairman of the Board from office.

5A. If the chairman of the Board dies, resigns, becomes disqualified or is removed from office the Minister shall appoint a person to be chairman of the Board and the person so appointed shall hold office for the remainder of the term of office of the chairman occasioning the vacancy and shall be eligible for reappointment as chairman of the Board.

as inserted by s.40(b) P(A) Act 1996

6. Subject to the provisions of this Schedule, the chairman of the Board shall hold office on such terms and conditions as the Minister may determine.

7. The chairman of the Board shall be paid, out of moneys at the disposal of the Board, such remuneration (if any) and allowances for expenses incurred by him (if any) as the Minister, with the consent of the Minister for Finance, may determine.

8.(1)Of the ordinary members of the Board -

(a) two shall be representative of trade union members of whom one shall be a trustee of an occupational pension scheme,

as substituted by s.40(c) P(A) Act 1996

as substituted by s.40(c) P(A) Act 1996

(b) two shall be representative of employers' members of whom one shall be a trustee of an occupational pension scheme,

(c) two shall be representative of occupational pension schemes,

(d) one shall be a representative of the actuarial profession,

(e) one shall be a representative of the accounting profession,

(f) one shall be a representative of the legal profession,

(g) one shall be a representative of the Minister for Finance, and

(h) one shall be a representative of the Minister.

as substituted by s.40(d) P(A) Act 1996

(2) The members of the Board representing trade union members shall be persons nominated for appointment thereto by such organisation as the Minister considers to be representative of trade unions of workers as the Minister may determine.

as substituted by s.40(d) P(A) Act 1996

(3) The members of the Board representing employers' members shall be persons nominated for appointment thereto by such organisation as the Minister considers to be representative of employers as the Minister may determine.

(4) The members of the Board representing occupational pension schemes shall be persons nominated for appointment thereto by such organisation or organisations as the Minister considers to be representative of occupational pension schemes.

(5) The member of the Board representing the actuarial profession shall be a person nominated for appointment thereto by such organisation or organisations as the Minister considers to be representative of the actuarial profession.

(6) The member of the Board representing the accounting profession shall be a person nominated for appointment thereto by such organisation or organisations as the Minister considers to be representative of the accounting profession.

(7) The member of the Board representing the legal profession shall be a person nominated for appointment thereto by such organisation as the Minister considers to be representative of the legal profession.

(8) The member of the Board representing the Minister for Finance shall be such officer of the Minister for Finance as the Minister for Finance may determine.

(9) The member of the Board representing the Minister shall be such officer of the Minister as the Minister may determine.

9. Each ordinary member of the Board shall be a part-time member of the Board and, subject to the provisions of this Schedule, shall hold office on such terms and conditions as the Minister may determine.

10. (1) The term of office of the chairman shall be 5 years.

(2) The term of office of an ordinary member of the Board shall be such period not exceeding 5 years as the Minister may, with the consent of the Minister for Finance, determine when appointing him and, subject to the provisions of this Schedule, shall be eligible for re-appointment as such member.

11. (1) If an ordinary member of the Board dies, resigns, becomes disqualified or is removed from office, or is appointed chairman of the Board under *paragraph 5A*, the Minister may appoint a person to be a member of the Board to fill the casual vacancy so occasioned and the person so appointed shall be appointed in the same manner as the member of the Board who occasioned the casual vacancy.

as amended by s.40(e) P(A) Act 1996

(2) A person appointed to be a member of the Board by virtue of this subparagraph shall hold office for the remainder of the term of office of the member occasioning the vacancy he is appointed to fill and shall be eligible for reappointment as a member of the Board.

12. A member of the Board whose term of office expires by effluxion of time shall be eligible for re-appointment as a member of the Board.

13. Notwithstanding *paragraph 10(2)* the Minister may at any time remove an ordinary member of the Board from office.

as amended by s.40(f) P(A) Act 1996

14. An ordinary member of the Board may at any time resign his office as a member by letter addressed to the Minister.

15. A member of the Board shall be disqualified from holding and shall cease to hold office if he is adjudged bankrupt or makes a composition or arrangement with creditors or is sentenced by a court of competent jurisdiction to a term of imprisonment or penal servitude.

16. Each ordinary member of the Board shall be paid, out of moneys at the disposal of the Board, such remuneration (if any) and allowances for expenses incurred by him (if any) as the Minister may, with the consent of the Minister for Finance, sanction.

17. The Board shall hold such and so many meetings as it considers appropriate for the performance of its functions.

18. The Minister may fix the date, time and place of the first meeting of the Board.

19. The quorum for a meeting of the Board shall be 5.

20. At a meeting of the Board -

(a) the chairman of the Board shall, if present, be the chairman of the meeting.

(b) if and so long as the chairman of the Board is not present or if the office of chairman is vacant, the members of the Board who are present shall choose one of their number to be chairman of the meeting.

21. The chairman of the Board, and each ordinary member of the Board, present at a meeting thereof shall have a vote.

22. Every question at a meeting of the Board shall be determined by a majority of the votes of the members present and voting on the question and, in the case of an equal division of votes, the chairman of the meeting shall have a second or casting vote.

23. The Board may act notwithstanding one or more than one vacancy among its members.

24. Subject to the provisions of this Schedule, the Board shall regulate, by standing orders or otherwise, the procedure and business of the Board.

25. The Board shall, as soon as may be after its establishment, provide itself with a seal.

26. The seal of the Board shall be authenticated by the signature of the chairman of the Board or some other member thereof authorised by the Board to act in that behalf and by the signature of an officer of the Board authorised by the Board to act in that behalf.

27. Judicial notice shall be taken of the seal of the Board and every document purporting to be an instrument made by the Board and to be sealed with the seal (purporting to be authenticated in accordance with *paragraph 26)* of the Board shall be received in evidence and be deemed to be such instrument without proof unless the contrary is shown.

28. Any contract or instrument which, if entered into or executed by a person not being a body corporate, would not require to be under seal may be entered into or executed on behalf of the Board by any person generally or specially authorised by the Board in that behalf.

SECOND SCHEDULE
PRESERVATION AND REVALUATION OF BENEFITS

Section 29.

PART A
PRESERVATION OF BENEFITS

Calculation of preserved benefit - defined benefit scheme

1. (1) In the case of a defined benefit scheme, where the basis of calculating long service benefit does not alter between the commencement of *Part III* or, if later, the date of commencement of the member's relevant employment and the date of termination of relevant employment the amount of preserved benefit shall be calculated in accordance with the formula -

$$A \times \frac{B}{C}$$

where -

A is the amount of long service benefit (excluding any such benefit which is being secured by way of additional voluntary contributions or which represents a transfer of accrued rights from another scheme) calculated at the date of termination of the member's relevant employment,

B is the period of reckonable service completed after the commencement of *Part III*, and

C is the period of reckonable service that would have been completed if the member had remained in relevant employment until normal pensionable age and such service had continued to qualify for long service benefit.

(2) Where the basis of calculating long service benefit is altered between the commencement of *Part III* or, if later, the date of commencement of the member's relevant employment and the date of termination of the member's relevant employment the amount of preserved benefit shall be the sum of -

(a) the amount calculated in accordance with the formula set out in *subparagraph (1)* where A is calculated on the basis of the rules of the scheme in force at the commencement of *Part III* or, if later, the date of commencement of the member's relevant employment, and

(b) an amount calculated in accordance with the formula -

$$D \times \frac{E}{F}$$

where -

D is the amount of the difference in long service benefit calculated at the date of termination of relevant employment applicable to the alteration,

E is the period of reckonable service completed after the date on which the basis of calculation was altered, and

F is the period of reckonable service that would have been completed from the date of such alteration if the member had remained in relevant employment until normal pensionable age and such service had continued to qualify for long service benefit:

Provided that where there is more than one such alteration each alteration shall be separately calculated in accordance with this formula and they shall be aggregated for the purposes of the calculation of the amount.

(3) Any preserved benefit calculated under this paragraph shall be subject to a minimum of such amount as will ensure that the actuarial value of such benefit is equal to the amount of any contributions (excluding additional voluntary contributions) paid by the member in respect of the period of reckonable service completed after the commencement of *Part III* together with compound interest thereon at the rate, if any, applicable under the rules of the scheme to refunds of members' contributions on leaving service.

2. Where a scheme provides for benefits to be calculated in relation to a member's pensionable earnings at, or in a specified period, prior to his attaining normal pensionable age or on earlier death, or in some other way relative to such earnings, preserved benefit shall be calculated, in a corresponding manner, by reference to his earnings at, or in the same period before, the date of termination of his relevant employment.

Benefit provided by additional voluntary contributions

3. (1) In the case of an additional long service benefit referred to in *section 29(6)* preserved benefit in respect of such additional benefit, shall include an amount calculated in accordance with the formula -

$$X \times \frac{Y}{Z}$$

where -

X is the amount of such additional benefit (or increase in benefit),

Y is the period of reckonable service for which the member of the scheme has contributed towards such benefit (or increase in benefit), and

Z is the period of reckonable service for which such member would have contributed towards such benefit (or increase in benefit) if he had remained in relevant employment until normal pensionable age.

(2) For the purposes of *subparagraph (1)*, "increase in benefit" means a benefit secured by an increase in the rate of contribution previously contracted and each such increase in benefit shall for the purposes of this paragraph be treated separately.

PART B
REVALUATION OF PRESERVED BENEFITS

Paragraph 4.(1) as amended by s.41(a) P(A) Act 1996

4. (1) Any preserved benefit payable under a defined benefit scheme shall be revalued annually at the end of each revaluation year, by adding the appropriate amount to the amount of preserved benefit as at the last day of the previous calendar year (or as at the date of termination of relevant employment in any case where a member's relevant employment has terminated since the last day of the previous calendar year), such preserved benefit to include any previous revaluation.

(2) Except as provided for in *paragraphs 5* and *6* below the appropriate amount shall be calculated in accordance with the formula -

$$\frac{P \times R}{100}$$

where -

P is the amount of preserved benefit as at the last day of the previous calendar year (or as at the date of termination of relevant employment in any case where a member's relevant employment has terminated since the last day of the previous calendar year), and

as amended by s.41(b) P(A) Act 1996

R is the revaluation percentage.

Provided that in any case where a member's relevant employment has terminated since the last day of the previous calendar year R is X/twelfths of the revaluation percentage where X is the number of complete months from the date on which the member's relevant employment terminated to the end of the revaluation year.

Proviso as inserted by s.41(c) P(A) Act 1996

5. (1) This paragraph applies to a scheme which provides long service benefit the rate or amount of which is calculated by reference to -

(a) the member's average pensionable earnings over the period of service on which such benefit is based, or

(b) the member's total pensionable earnings over the period of service on which such benefit is based.

(2) Any preserved benefit provided under a scheme to which *subparagraph (1)* applies shall be revalued -

(a) by revaluing the pensionable earnings of the member concerned during each revaluation year in any manner in which they could have been revalued during that year if the member had remained in the same reckonable service, or

(b) in accordance with *paragraph 4*,

whichever the trustees of the scheme consider appropriate.

6. (1) This paragraph applies to a scheme which provides long service benefit -

(a) the rate or amount of which is calculated by reference solely to the member's length of service, or

(b) which is of a fixed amount.

as substituted by s.41(d) P(A) Act 1996

(2) Any preserved benefit provided under a scheme to which *subparagraph (1)* applies shall be revalued in accordance with paragraph 4 provided that, where the trustees of the scheme consider that by revaluing a preserved benefit in such a manner a member whose service in relevant employment has terminated would be treated more favourably than a member who remains in reckonable service in relation to the period of reckonable service to which the preserved benefit applies, they may revalue the preserved benefit on such other basis and such other dates as they consider just and equitable.

7. No part of the appropriate amount to be added to preserved benefit under this Part shall be provided by reducing the amount of any benefit payable under the rules of the scheme concerned in respect of reckonable service completed before the commencement of *Part III.*

THIRD SCHEDULE
FUNDING STANDARD - BENEFITS

Section 44.

1. The benefits for the purposes of this paragraph shall be all future benefits payable under the rules of the scheme to or in respect of a person who at the effective date of the certificate is receiving benefits or has reached normal pensionable age, excluding future increases in such benefits which are, at the effective date of the certificate, contingent upon the exercise of some person's discretion.

as substituted by s.52 (1) SW Act 1993 (previously substituted by s.63(a) SW Act 1992)

2. The benefits for the purposes of this paragraph shall be any additional benefits secured for or granted to or in respect of a member of a scheme under the scheme by way of additional voluntary contributions or a transfer of rights from another scheme. Such benefits shall be calculated as at the effective date of the certificate and shall be -

as substituted by s.52 (2) SW Act 1993

(a) where, at the effective date of the certificate, the member's service in relevant employment has terminated and a transfer payment has not been applied in accordance with *section 34* or *35*, preserved benefit payable in respect of such additional benefits calculated in accordance with *Part III* or, if no such preserved benefit is payable, the benefits payable under the rules of the scheme in respect of the additional voluntary contributions or the transfer of rights, and

(b) where, at the effective date of the certificate, the member is in relevant employment, preserved benefit in respect of such additional benefits calculated in accordance with *Part III*, as if the member's service in relevant employment had terminated on such date but, other than for the purposes of *section 48*, disregarding any provision requiring the completion of a minimum period of qualifying service.

Paragraph (b) as amended by s.42(a) P(A) Act 1996

3. The benefits for the purposes of this paragraph shall be calculated as at the effective date of the certificate and shall be -

(a) in the case of a member of that scheme whose service in relevant employment terminated after the commencement of *Part IV* but prior to the effective date of the certificate and in respect of whom a transfer payment has not been applied in accordance with *section 34* or *35* the greater of -

(i) all preserved benefits (including future revaluations thereof and those benefits payable on the death of the member entitled to preserved benefit) calculated in accordance with *Part III*, and

(ii) the benefits payable under the rules of the scheme in respect of reckonable service completed after the commencement of *Part IV*, and

Paragraph (b) as substituted by s.63(b) SW Act 1992

(b) in the case of a member of that scheme then in relevant employment, the greater of -

(i) preserved benefits (including future revaluations thereof and those benefits payable on the death of the member entitled to preserved benefit) calculated in accordance with the provisions of *Part III*, and

Paragraph (ii) as amended by s.42(b) P(A) Act 1996

(ii) the long service benefits payable under the rules of the scheme in respect of reckonable service completed after the commencement of *Part IV* but prior to the effective date of the certificate together with any other benefits payable on the death of the member entitled to long service benefit in respect of such period of reckonable service,

as amended by s.42(c) P(A) Act 1996

calculated as if the member's service in relevant employment has terminated on the effective date of the certificate but, other than for the purposes of *section 48*, disregarding any provision requiring the completion of a minimum period of qualifying service which may prevent the member concerned from acquiring an entitlement to benefit on termination of such employment.

4. The benefits for the purposes of this paragraph shall be calculated as at the effective date of the certificate and shall be -

(a) any benefit payable under the rules of the scheme in respect of reckonable service completed prior to the commencement of *Part IV* to or in respect of a member of that scheme -

(i) whose service in relevant employment terminated prior to the effective date of the certificate, and

(ii) who has not exercised any right to a transfer payment to another scheme,

and

(b) a benefit payable to or in respect of a member then in relevant employment whose reckonable service commenced before the commencement of *Part IV* being -

(i) subject to *clause (ii)*, in the case of a defined benefit scheme, the greater of - *as amended by s.64(a) SW Act 1991*

(I) the amount determined by the formula -

$$L \times \frac{M}{N}$$

where -

L is the amount of long service benefit calculated as at the effective date of the certificate on the basis of the rules of the scheme in force on the commencement of *Part IV*,

M is the period of reckonable service completed prior to the commencement of *Part IV*, and

N is the period of reckonable service that would have been completed if the member had remained in relevant employment until normal pensionable age and such service had continued to qualify for long service benefit:

Provided that, where the rules of the scheme in force at the commencement of *Part IV* provided for benefits to be calculated in relation to a member's pensionable earnings at, or in a specified period prior to, his attaining normal pensionable age or in some other way relative to such earnings, the benefit under this clause may be calculated in a corresponding manner by reference to his earnings at, or in the same period before the effective date of the certificate, and

Paragraph (ii) as substituted by s.42(d) P(A) Act 1996 (previously amended by s.63(c) SW Act 1992)

(II) the long service benefits payable under the rules of the scheme in respect of reckonable service completed before the 1st day of January, 1991, together with any other benefits payable on the death of the member entitled to long service benefit in respect of such period of reckonable service calculated as if the member's service in relevant employment had terminated on the effective date of the certificate but disregarding any provision which may prevent the member concerned from acquiring an entitlement to benefit on termination of relevant employment, less, where under *paragraph 3* the amount of benefits calculated in accordance with *subparagraph (b)(i)* of that paragraph exceeds the amount calculated in accordance with *subparagraph (b)(ii)* of that paragraph, the difference between these two amounts.

as substituted by s.64(b) SW Act 1991

(ii) in the case of a defined benefit scheme where the rate or amount of part of the long service benefit payable thereunder is directly determined by an amount of contribution paid by or in respect of the member of the scheme -

(I) in so far as it relates to such part of the long service benefit, a benefit whose actuarial value is equal to the then accumulated value of the contributions paid by or in respect of the member of the scheme for the purpose of long service benefit prior to the commencement of *Part IV*, and

(II) in so far as it relates to the remaining part of long service benefit, a benefit calculated in accordance with *clause (i)*.

Repealed by s.64(b) SW Act 1991

(iii)..........

APPENDIX III

STATUTORY INSTRUMENTS AND ORDERS MADE UNDER THE PENSIONS ACT, 1990

Statutory Instrument	SI No	Effective from	Enabling Section(s) of Pensions Act
Pensions Act, 1990 (Sections 60 and 61) (Commencement) Order, 1990	329 of 1990	1.1.91	1(2)
Pensions Act, 1990 (Parts III, IV and V) (Commencement) Order, 1990	330 of 1990	1.1.91	1(2)
Pensions Act, 1990 (Parts I and II) (Commencement) Order, 1990	331 of 1990	21.12.90	1(2)
Occupational Pension Schemes (Disclosure of Information) Regulations, 1990[1]	*332 of 1990*	1.1.91	5, 51, 54, 55, 56 & 57
Pensions Act, 1990 (Part II) (Establishment Day) Order, 1990	343 of 1990	21.12.90	8
Occupational Pension Schemes (Disclosure of Information) Regulations, 1991	215 of 1991	1.8.91	5, 51, 54, 55, 56 & 57
Pensions Act, 1990 (Sections 59, 63 and 64) (Commencement) Order, 1991	259 of 1991	1.11.91	1(2)
Occupational Pension Schemes (Registration) Regulations, 1991	325 of 1991	10.12.91	5 & 60
Occupational Pension Schemes (Funding Standard) Regulations, 1991[2]	*371 of 1991*	30.12.91	5, 42, 43, 47 & 52
Occupational Pension Schemes (Fees) Regulations, 1991	372 of 1991	30.12.91	5 & 25

---

1 Revoked with effect from 1 August 1991

2 Revoked with effect from 31 December 1993

Statutory Instrument	SI No	Effective from	Enabling Section(s) of Pensions Act
Occupational Benefit Schemes (Equal Treatment) Regulations, 1992[3]	*365 of 1992*	1.1.93	5 & 71(3)
Pensions Act, 1990 (Part VII) (Commencement) Order, 1992	366 of 1992	1.1.93	1(2)
Occupational Pension Schemes (Fees) (Amendment) Regulations, 1992	367 of 1992	1.1.93	5 & 25
Occupational Pension Schemes (Preservation of Benefits) Regulations, 1992	445 of 1992	1.1.93	5, 35, 37 & 38
Occupational Pension Schemes (Member Participation in the Selection of Persons for Appointment as Trustees) Regulations, 1993[4]	*216 of 1993*	1.1.94	5 & 62
Occupational Pension Schemes (Preservation of Benefits) (Special Calculations) Regulations, 1993	217 of 1993	1.8.93	5 & 37
Occupational Pension Schemes (Member Participation in the Selection of Persons for Appointment as Trustees) (No. 2) Regulations, 1993	399 of 1993	1.1.94	5 & 62
Occupational Pension Schemes (Funding Standard) Regulations, 1993	419 of 1993	31.12.93	5, 42, 43, 47 & 52
Occupational Pension Schemes (External Schemes) (United Kingdom) Regulations, 1994	238 of 1994	31.7.94	5 & 5A

3 Revoked with effect from 2 July 1996

4 Revoked with effect from 21 December 1993

INDEX